# RETAIL

# MARKETING

# MANAGEMENT

## Text and Cases

# RETAIL

# MARKETING

# MANAGEMENT

# Text and Cases

**MICHAEL R. PEARCE**
The University of Western Ontario

**Nelson Canada**

**Canadian Cataloguing in Publication Data**

Pearce, Michael R., 1946–
    Retail marketing management

Includes bibliographical references and index.
ISBN 0-17-603438-2

1. Marketing — Canada — Management.   2. Marketing —
Canada — Management — Case studies.   I. Title.

HF5415.13.P43 1992        658.8'00971        C91-094862-3

**Acquisitions Editor**   Peter Jackson
**Supervising Editors**   Jane Hammond & Nicole Gnutzman
**Art Director**   Bruce Bond
**Indexer**   Riça Night
**Cover Photo**   Yorkdale Shopping Centre, Toronto —
                        Owned and Operated by Trilea Centres Inc.
**Photographer**   Steven Evans

Printed and bound in Canada by Tri-Graphic Printing
1 2 3 4   TRI   95 94 93 92

*This book is dedicated to my family*
*Kathy, Roger, Michelle, David, and Sarah*
*who were understanding, supportive, and patient*
*as I worked on this book*
*instead of spending that time with them.*

# ▪ Preface

Over the past five years as this book was being written, retail marketers have experienced tumultuous changes in their markets. Only retailers with many years of experience can recall a time of greater difficulty and uncertainty. And, at no time has retailing been more complex than it is today. Plain and simple, retail marketing is a tough business, getting tougher. This book was undertaken at the request of my students and my clients: "Provide us with something more practical, less theoretical, more interesting, and better written than the other books we've seen" was the call I have attempted to satisfy. My hope is that both students of retail marketing and retail marketing managers will find this book helpful.

This is neither a textbook nor a casebook, but rather both at the same time. Those people who are accustomed to conventional textbooks will wonder why there aren't even more examples in the chapters. The cases are intended to meet this request, in fact, to exceed it; they provide a window on what it is like to be a retail marketing manager. Those readers accustomed to casebooks will be surprised (and hopefully pleased) at the amount of textual material. The chapters are intended to help problem solvers be more effective and efficient by providing some structure and background material. This book mirrors my experience and observation that retail marketing management is a professional discipline that is best mastered through a combination of examining what successful practitioners do and then trying to build skills through actual problem solving.

The cases in this book were written with the gracious co-operation of many, many retail marketing managers. It takes both time and courage to have a case written about one's organization, yet the benefits to all of us are tremendous. Over the years, I have written nearly 150 cases on organizations around the world. I never cease to be delighted at the willingness of managers to share their experiences. To them I offer a heartfelt thank you.

Many, many people have contributed to this book and to the ongoing body of work it represents here at the Western Business School. I have been encouraged by my colleagues in the Marketing Area Group, supported by the administration, and helped by many staff members. I particularly wish to single out Professor John Kennedy as my greatest supporter and greatest constructive critic. His insights have improved this book significantly. Katherine Vyse and Ed Bennett both contributed much to this through their diligence when they were research assistants to me. Greg Dalzell of Apple Canada supported me with computer equipment that greatly increased my productivity. There are many more individuals who have contributed as well; I hope you will forgive me for not listing your names here. To all of you, thanks.

I am indebted to my students who encouraged me to learn a great deal about retail marketing and, above all, I am indebted to my friends and colleagues in retail marketing management around the world who honoured me with their confidence and trust. I have attempted to share here much of what you have so graciously shared with me.

Dr. Michael R. Pearce
LONDON, CANADA

# CONTENTS

## PART

## INTRODUCTION TO RETAIL MARKETING MANAGEMENT

PART

THE RETAIL MARKETPLACE

PART

# THE ELEMENTS OF THE RETAIL MARKETING PROGRAM

P A R T

# RETAIL MARKETING PLANNING AND IMPLEMENTATION

# I

**P A R T**

## Introduction to Retail Marketing Management

CHAPTER

# A DECISION-MAKING APPROACH TO RETAIL MARKETING

## INTRODUCTION

The sole intent of this book is to improve the practice of retail marketing, including the making of better retail marketing decisions and the effective implementation of those decisions in a competitive marketplace. Currently, three very effective and complementary ways to improve the practice of retail marketing management exist. These are (a) observation and analysis of what other managers do, (b) simulation of practice through case method discussions, and (c) learning through actual experience. This last "trial-and-error" way has been the most common approach in the retailing profession, but it has often been accompanied by considerable risk, time, and cost.

This book was written with a focus on the first two ways and *describes* how retailers manage marketing as well as *provides practice* through the use of cases describing actual situations retail marketers have faced.

## WHAT IS RETAIL MARKETING MANAGEMENT?

**SECTION**
**ONE**

Retailing is a fascinating field encompassing a major component of the economy in every country of the world. Retailers are a varied lot, operating outlets that range from the proverbial, single-unit "Mom & Pop" store to multidivisional, multinational companies. In fact, there are so many types of retailers that one might think it would be impossible to discuss more than a subset of them in any single book. It

3

could be argued that store-based retailing is entirely different from non-store-based retailing, that product retailing is different from service retailing, and that small-scale retailing is different from large-scale retailing. The basic premise of this book, however, is that these diverse forms of retail marketing have more in common than most of us realize.

This book is not so much about retailers as it is about the retail marketing *function*. When retail marketing is looked at in this way, there are important shared characteristics among seemingly different ways of performing retail marketing tasks. From this viewpoint, one would not worry so much about classifying a firm as a retailer or a manufacturer, but would focus on management of the particular marketing tasks the firm chooses to undertake. The distinction is very important because firms are increasingly crossing "traditional" boundaries of business. Re-tailers, for example, are integrating backward to engage in manufacturing, whereas manufacturers are integrating forward to operate their own retail outlets, and wholesalers are integrating in both directions.

**Retail marketing management** concerns the formulation, implementation, and evaluation of marketing programs intended to result in exchange of goods and services with the ultimate customer to the profitable benefit of the retailer and the satisfaction of the customer. It is about being chosen as the source from whom to buy. This definition will be elaborated upon throughout this book, but it is impor-tant to point out here that it embraces much of what some people call "consumer marketing" and some of what some people call "industrial marketing." The focal point is the direct interaction of buyer and seller, perhaps best captured by the metaphor of "the last metre of the distribution system," where customer and vendor make the final exchange. This definition is not an attempt to widen the traditional scope of retailing, but rather to state that the decision-making approaches examined in this book apply to a wide variety of firms engaging in the retail function, some of whom may not have thought of themselves as retailers; in addition to department stores and supermarkets, this would include banks, theatres, restaurants, resorts, museums, schools, and a host of others. Henceforth in this book, the word **retailer** refers to a person or organization engaging in the retail marketing function.

Despite their many differences, all retailers share some common charac-teristics. First, they occupy a unique position in the business system by directly linking production with consumption. This was succinctly described more than four decades ago by Boris Emmet:

> Thus, it is clear that the retailer is at once in the position of acting as purchasing agent for the consumer and as selling agent for the manufacturer. Closer to the ultimate consumer than any other agency, the retailer wields peculiar influence.[1]

Second, all retailers face common decisions. Typically, any retailer produces or buys products in advance of customer order, arranges to have these goods and associated services available and attractively presented to customers in desirable places, such as stores and catalogues, at desirable times. Yet, while these tasks can be described rather briefly, the actual range of choices available to retailers to accomplish them is staggering. Retailing is a tough business that is getting even tougher. In many countries, markets are saturated, economic growth has decelerated, economic conditions are uncertain, and major components of costs have risen more dramatically than price increases can absorb. Competitors have crossed traditional boundaries scrambling retail strategies; new technologies have eroded old power bases and created new ones (although often to the benefit of retailers); and, perhaps most importantly, customers have not only continued to change but have also become much more demanding in all respects. In this increasingly challenging environment, all retailers are looking for new answers to old questions: Where should I locate? What products should I carry? How much should I spend on advertising? What exactly is good customer service and does it pay? And so on.

How does one succeed in retailing? Talk to retail practitioners and observers and they are quick to share conventional wisdoms, such as "The most important three things are location, location, and location," or "Goods well-bought are already half-sold," or "If it doesn't sell right away, mark it down." Such rules-of-thumb reflect the pragmatic, learn-by-experience nature of many retail managers. However, the world of retailing has become so complex that such simple prescriptions for action are often insufficient and sometimes even dysfunctional. Retailers need more sophisticated approaches to management decisions for all aspects of the retailing task. To that end, this book is about retail marketing management, not all of retailing. It is about a systematic, professional, and very pragmatic approach to making better retail marketing decisions.

Marketing management itself is not a new professional discipline, but retail marketing management is. Consider the following statement by Alasdair McKichan, president of the Retail Council of Canada:

> Twenty years ago, marketing was a function of large consumer goods manufacturers. It was not a word in the retail vocabulary. Ten years ago, Canadian retailers spoke about marketing, but they used the word inaccurately as a synonym for merchandising and sales promotion. What a change a decade has wrought. In the more advanced cases, retailers market their stores as though they were branded goods and their suppliers almost tag along in the bit parts. The development should not be a surprise. Today's regional shopping centres became the crucibles in which individual companies were subjected to the full heat of each other's competition. . . . The components of marketing each achieved a new maturity and required enhanced skills.

These comments constitute a clear call for a greater understanding and greater application of marketing management methods in the retailing field. It seems paradoxical that the discipline of marketing began with the study of retail distribution methods at the turn of the 20th century, yet now near the turn of the 21st century, we see much of retailing practice lagging behind other aspects of business in the use of professional marketing.

## THE FUNDAMENTAL NEED FOR A MARKETING ORIENTATION

There are many definitions of marketing but some of them may strike the retail practitioner as too abstract or too tedious to be helpful in decision-making; however, the essence of marketing is anything but abstract, tedious, or useless. The essence of retail marketing is the **orientation** the retail marketer takes toward his or her *relationship* with the marketplace. The most straightforward way to think about this is to contrast marketing orientation with buying orientation and selling orientation.

**Buying orientation** refers to the placement of retail management's greatest attention on sourcing the products and services offered for resale. Managers who adopt this orientation follow vendor developments carefully, develop elaborate buying programs, like to get involved in inventory-level issues, and so on. The basic belief underlying this approach is that if the retailer's assortment of goods and services is "right," then customers will come and success will be assured.

**Selling orientation** refers to the placement of retail management's greatest attention on communicating incentives to buy. Managers who adopt this orientation spend disproportionate time on advertising, sales-incentives schemes, mark-down programs, sales-techniques training, and visual merchandising. The basic belief underlying this approach is that assortment, facilities, location, and so on, don't have to be first-rate, but that the communications effort does.

**Marketing orientation** refers to the placement of retail management's greatest attention on understanding customer needs, wants, and habits in the competitive context *before* undertaking assortment and communication activities. Managers pursuing this approach demonstrate continuous sensitivity to, and curiosity about, the marketplace, believing that by understanding customers better than the competition does, they can also satisfy them better. Similarly, these managers believe that a good understanding of suppliers and their circumstances enables a more effective relationship with vendors. Such managers are somewhat humble; they realize that it is a great mistake to assume that their customers share their own tastes, ways of shopping, reactions to advertising, and so on. In short, *the marketing orientation is based on the idea that marketing is about people, not just about products and services.*

There are, of course, examples of retailers who have succeeded by following largely a buying or selling orientation as opposed to a marketing orientation. It is not that that those approaches don't work, but rather that the marketing orientation has proven to be more successful, more often.

Another way to examine what retail marketing means is to compare it with merchandising. **Merchandising** refers to the activity of acting as the supplier's selling agent in moving goods through retail outlets. Merchants work hard at display techniques, personal selling, pricing, and so on. **Marketing** refers to the activity of acting as the manufacturer's selling agent and the customer's purchasing agent at the same time.

Dan Sweeney, a principal at Management Horizons, a major retail consulting firm in the United States, recently summed up the difference between merchandising and marketing by saying that "marketers are oriented to the front door of the store (customers coming in); merchandisers are oriented toward the back door (merchandise coming in)."[2] Sweeney's comments about marketing and merchandising are summarized in Exhibit 1.1.

---

EXHIBIT 1.1
Marketing versus
Merchandising

## 1. Target Customer

*Marketing*—pre-selected consumer segment market opportunity

*Merchandising*—people who typically buy our kind of merchandise

## 2. Competition

*Marketing*—pre-selected consumer shopping alternatives

*Merchandising*—all other stores selling our kind of merchandise

## 3. Strategic Objective

*Marketing*—to drive long-term profit growth and have an insulated competitive position through market penetration

*Merchandising*—to sell more goods than last year

## 4. Competitive Advantage

*Marketing*—more compelling offer of core merchandise to core customers than that of the core competition

*Merchandising*—beat all competition on all factors in all merchandise categories

## 5. Planning Horizon

*Marketing*—time required for phased market development and penetration

*Merchandising*—next merchandising season against same season last year

## 6. Principal Planning Vehicle

*Marketing*—annual update of long-term marketing plan

*Merchandising*—representing current resources, brands, styles, colours, etc.

## 7. Pricing

*Marketing*—price points established to optimize demand by target customers

*Merchandising*—maximize gross margin while seeking competitive parity

## 8. Advertising

*Marketing*—communicate and reinforce the market position to target customers

*Merchandising*—show product and price, drive traffic, meet last year's sales

## 9. Store Design, Presentation

*Marketing*—reinforce market position, encourage and facilitate shopping

*Merchandising*—maintain the store, supervise the people, sell the merchandise

**10. Store Management**

*Marketing*—manager in a position to penetrate trade area market

*Merchandising*—maintain the store, supervise the people, sell the merchandise

**11. Merchandise**

*Marketing*—purchasing agent for customers

*Merchandising*—selling agent for suppliers

---

In conclusion, excellent retail marketers examine retail marketing decision alternatives with a thorough knowledge of marketplace circumstances and make decisions that best fit those circumstances—they look at the whole picture from the vantage points of both seller and buyer.

## How Retail Marketing Differs from Manufacturer Marketing

Marketing applies to retailing both conceptually and practically. Whereas consumer goods manufacturers think of marketing as an effort to motivate customers to buy their products (what may be called **product motivation**), retailers have an even more complex task. For a retailer, marketing means motivating customers *not only* to buy products and associated services (product motivation) *but also* to buy them from him or her, rather than from a competitor (what may be called **patronage motivation**). Yet, despite this higher level of complexity, virtually all the basic marketing principles and methods that have been have developed in manufacturer marketing apply to retail marketing. There are, however, *typical differences* between manufacturer marketing and retail marketing:

1. Retailers carry a larger assortment of more diverse merchandise, much of which changes more rapidly than it does for a manufacturer. Retailers are less committed to any particular product or product line. In addition, retailers offer a broader range of services to their customers.

2. Retailers have more complicated accounting and performance evaluation tasks due to the greater diversity of assortment, as well as to highly variable pricing practices.

3. Retailers have many more transactions with customers than do manufacturers, but each is of lower value.

4. Manufacturers have a few highly trained and well-paid sellers dealing with their customers, whereas retailers have a much higher number of customer contact people, each of whom is generally less well trained and rewarded.

5. Retailers make greater use of part-time employees, particularly in customer contact positions.

6. Retailers typically have greater difficulty controlling merchandise investment because of greater variety, shrinkage, obsolescence, and fashion risk.

7. Retailers have had greater difficulty applying productivity measures and improvements due to the high, but varied, personal-service intensity of their operations.

8. Retailers often operate from relatively more and smaller locations that deal with diverse markets (trading areas), which creates greater pressures for decentralization of management decision-making and creates a lack of standardization in marketing programs and activities.

These differences, taken as a whole, mean that retailers face different and often greater marketing challenges than do conventional manufacturers.

## RETAIL MARKETING PROGRAM ELEMENTS

Retail marketing management is the integration of many decisions that may be summarized as follows: (a) the selection of a **target market** (those customers who will be the focus of efforts), (b) the **design of an offer** (the products, services, promises, and experience the customer will receive), and (c) the **delivery of that offer** (the extent to which the intended and promised offer actually happens in terms of in-store service, stocking levels, post-sale help, etc.).

The marketing decisions concerning the target, offer design, and offer delivery can be called collectively the **retail marketing program**. This program encapsulates all the activities the retail marketer is undertaking to create and nurture a relationship with his or her customers. Some call these program elements "the controllables" as a way to indicate that these are activities and initiatives over which the retailer has some control or discretion. Others call these elements the **retail marketing mix** as a way to indicate that the retail marketer must blend these ingredients into a successful recipe.[3] The following list is a brief outline of the major retail marketing program elements for most retailers:

1. Target market selection: How is the trading area defined? Who are the primary customers the retailer is seeking to attract and satisfy? The secondary target? What methods of understanding the customers will be used? What methods of staying close to customers will be used?

2. Assortment: What goods and services will be offered to customers? Variety? Depth and breadth? Branding? Ancillary services?

3. Location: Which region, city, area, site? Terms of tenancy?

4. Physical facilities: What format, physical environment, layout, etc.?

5. Hours: What seasons, days, times of day will the retailer be available to customers?

6. Pricing: What price levels or changes to them (markdowns, price promotions, etc.)?

7. Display: What techniques of visual merchandising? Fixtures?

8. Advertising: What mix of store advertising versus item advertising, budget, media, message, scheduling, etc.? Direct mail? Catalogues?

9. Promotion: What methods, budget, message, timing, etc.?

10. Publicity and public relations: What activities in order to be perceived as good and valued in the community?

11. Atmospherics: What use of colour, aroma, sound, etc.?

12. Personal selling and customer care: What mix of personal and impersonal selling and service? What training and incentives for salespeople? In-store versus out-of-store?

13. Organization for marketing: What organizational design and operating methods are most appropriate to ensure marketing decisions are well formulated?

Clearly, each of these program elements represents a variety of decision choices facing a retailer. Exactly what the options are for a particular retailer depends on the individual circumstances of that retailer. And, often, various elements in the program can be substituted for one another. For example, a retailer may wish to offer lower prices instead of personalized point-of-sale service. (These program elements will be discussed in subsequent chapters.)

## ■ RETAIL MARKETING STRATEGY

The retail marketing program concept allows one to describe any retailer's marketing activities and to examine how each element of the program relates to the intended market, to the other elements of the program, to the retailer's organizational circumstances, and to the performance achieved in the marketplace.

The overall concept used to describe this formulation and implementation of a marketing program in its totality is retail marketing strategy. **Retail marketing strategy** refers to the overall thrust of the retail marketing program as well as its individual components. It describes the retailer's concept and positioning in the marketplace as well as how that positioning is being sought. It is greater than the sum of the parts.

### IKEA'S MARKETING PROGRAM

As an example of how one might use the retail marketing program concept to describe a retailer's approach, here is a brief description of the retail marketing program of IKEA, reportedly the world's largest furniture retailer with sales of more than $3 billion and serving more than sixty million customers in roughly two dozen countries. As of 1990, there were seven Canadian stores and four U.S. stores, with three more under construction. Note that IKEA does depart from the following strategy somewhat in some markets and that this is just a summary:

### Target Market

IKEA focuses on the segment of the market that wants lightweight, movable, modern furniture of reasonable quality and doesn't view the purchase as being for a lifetime. The market served spans a wide age spectrum, but the majority of customers are "baby boomers" in the household- and family-formation stage. This market approaches furniture-buying with high involvement, low emotion, and relatively low self-confidence. It is not the market that wants exclusives and a high degree of decorating advice. It is a market that wants "instant gratification," which is addressed through immediate "take-home" and assembly of the products.

## Location

Most stores are free-standing in "potato field" locations, meaning that they are built on inexpensive land at some distance for most of the shoppers in a store's trading area. The idea is that the stores are "destination stores" to which shoppers will drive on a special trip. IKEA considers its prime trading area to be within a one-hour drive of a store. There are some shopping centre locations as well. Stores are generally some distance away from any furniture competitors.

## Layout

Most stores are in the 4500–6300 m² (50 000–70 000 square foot) range, although store sizes vary greatly, with recent North American stores roughly 18 000–27 000 m² (200 000–300 000 square feet). The flagship store in Stockholm is about 36 000 m² (400 000 square feet). The layout is warehouse showroom style, with space divided between displays of room settings and stock available to customers on warehouse shelving. Traffic is routed through the entire assortment then through the warehouse area and the housewares and furnishings area prior to checkouts.

## Assortment

IKEA offers a wide range of machine-made kit furniture (known as *knock-down* furniture) as well as furnishings and housewares. Using simple Scandinavian designs and natural materials, IKEA offers about 15 000 SKUs (stock-keeping units). Products are about 95 percent designed by IKEA and produced to specifications by contractors throughout the world. Value for money is emphasized with highest quality standards for the parts of products most important and most visible to customers. The focus is on presenting the merchandise assortment in natural roomlike settings that allow customers to see how the furniture goes together and to self-select what they need.

## Price

IKEA offers moderate price points relative to most competitors, and attempts to position itself as "best value for the money" in its markets. Prices are generally set for one year at a time, by virtue of the catalogue that is published in early fall. There is usually only one sale per year, just prior to publication of the next catalogue. Prices are "everyday-low-prices."

## Atmosphere and Display

The room settings are more exciting and more tasteful than those of discounters and junior department stores, but less so than those of specialty chains and some department stores. The whole atmosphere is upbeat, "Swedish-modern," and family oriented.

### Customer Care

The customer is asked to do many of the tasks most furniture retailers perform, such as item selection, order writing, item picking from the warehouse shelves, home delivery, and assembly. The operation is almost entirely self-service with great reliance placed on floor samples, the catalogue, tags, and displays. There are no salespeople on the floor, but there are customer service desks for questions and orders. Customers are provided with tape measures, catalogues, pencils, and paper to make shopping easier.

There are baby-care rooms with free diapers, a supervised "ballroom" for young children, strollers, and assorted other amenities to make the shopping visit pleasant and to encourage people to take their time. An in-store restaurant (typically serving Swedish food) fulfils the purpose of allowing people to take a break and make shopping decisions.

### Communications

The bulk of the communications effort is focused on the catalogue, which costs IKEA more than $2 each. This catalogue displays about three-quarters of the items available in the store and is full of information to allow customers to measure spaces, figure out furniture combinations, and so on before coming to the store. Advertising (primarily in newspapers), with an upbeat, humorous and self-effacing style, is also used.

Although more dimensions of the IKEA program could be described, the preceding illustrate several important points about retail marketing management that will now be discussed.

## FORMULATING AND EVALUATING RETAIL MARKETING PROGRAMS

Retail marketing programs are formulated and implemented to achieve performance. They are designed and adjusted in the light of marketplace circumstances and organizational realities. Figure 1.1 shows the major building blocks of retail marketing management that will be discussed in this book.

---

### FIGURE 1.1
### The Basic Retail Marketing Management Model

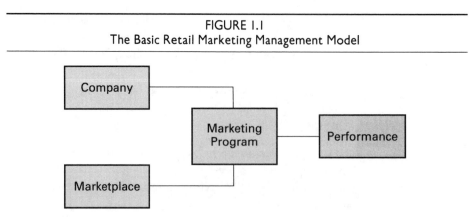

Success stories such as IKEA abound in retail marketing. These stories are more than inspirational. They can be studied for insights into what successful retail marketers do and why such actions work. Alert retail marketers constantly study the experience of other retailers for ideas as to what might be adapted to their own organization and, of course, what should not be tried. IKEA's retail marketing program is a consistent, integrated blend of choices that has resulted in an attractive and differentiated presence in the marketplace. It has also given competitive leverage to IKEA, and superior performance results.

IKEA's retail marketing approach demonstrates four tests of any proposed or existing retail marketing program. The first test is whether the program works, as measured by marketplace position, space productivity, personnel productivity, merchandise and merchandising efforts, and overall financial performance. This is called the **program-performance fit**. The IKEA retail marketing program is working well, as demonstrated by its consistently high-level performance in markets around the world.

The second major test of any retail marketing program is how well it fits with the marketplace. This notion is called the **program-marketplace fit**. IKEA's program seems well suited to its customers, competitors, suppliers, and general conditions.

The third test asks how well the elements of the program fit together. This is called the **program-elements fit**. In IKEA's marketing program, the various elements integrate well with one another to make a coherent, harmonious whole; they reinforce, rather than detract from, one another.

Finally, the fourth test is how well the program suits the company's objectives, management style, and basic strengths. This is called the **program-company fit**. IKEA's marketing program is consistent with the values and culture of the management (especially of the company's founder, Ingamar Kampraad); it serves corporate mission and objectives; fits with the company's management style and systems; and is consistent with the core strengths and capabilities of the company.

In short, one formulates and evaluates retail marketing programs with consideration for these four criteria:

1. Program-performance fit
2. Program-marketplace fit
3. Program-elements fit
4. Program-company fit

As the retail marketer constructs and/or evaluates a marketing program, she or he should constantly refer to these four criteria of fit. The ensuing questioning, analyzing, and evaluating of options is a central part of the discipline of retail marketing management decision-making. The merits of particular ideas can be compared with one another using this approach. Each of these notions of *fit* will be illustrated more fully in later chapters, but a brief introduction follows here.

### Program–Performance Fit

FIGURE 1.2

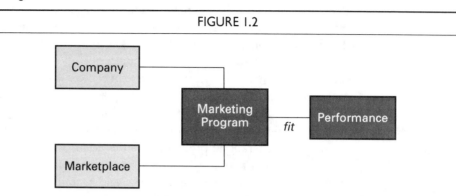

The ultimate test of any retail marketing program is its performance in the marketplace. This can be speculated upon before the program is implemented and examined during and after its implementation. For example, prior to implementation, one might ask:

a.   What revenues are expected?

b.   What margins?

c.   What are the implications for expenses and expenditures?

d.   What are the implications for asset management?

e.   What level of performance must be delivered for the proposed program to be worth implementing?

f.   How will performance be monitored?

Similarly, after implementation, one might ask:

a.   What profits were realized and what was the return on assets employed?

b.   What level of customer traffic, yield, and average transaction size were achieved?

(Performance goals, profit dynamic, and ways to assess retail marketing performance are the subject of Chapter 3.)

### Program–Marketplace Fit

FIGURE 1.3

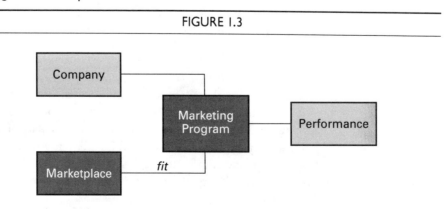

Every retailer operates in a marketplace that typically can be divided into five components: customers, competitors, suppliers, cohabitors, and the general forces of the environment. With the help of one's suppliers and sometimes one's co-habitors (such as neighbours in a shopping area, members of a co-operative group, and so on), a retailer tailors his or her offerings to customer wants, needs, habits, and expectations. Excellent retailers offer something different and better than other competing retailers. Another way to think about this is that excellent retail marketers develop retail marketing programs that add more value to their customers' lives than do the programs of their competitors.

**Customer understanding**    The starting place is customer analysis. One examines both existing and potential customers, and often contrasts them for insights. The idea is that the retail marketer wants to know who customers are (in demographic, psychographic, and other terms); what they want and when and where they want it; and how and why they make buying and usage decisions. Retail marketers need to know what expectations customers have of them in areas such as assortment, convenience, value, information and interaction, services, atmosphere, experience, and integrity. Each retailer needs to know how these expectations apply to his or her particular organization. Similarly, retailers know customers are complex in their motivations, search and processing of information, habits, and circumstances; retailers need to know how that understanding can apply in any particular situation.

As one learns more about customers, it becomes apparent that they fall into groups, and these groups are called **market segments**. Segments are groups of customers who are alike within the group but differ across groups. (There are many ways to segment retail markets and this will be discussed later.) Retail marketers segment markets because it is rarely possible to be all things to all people; it is better to be special to a subset of the total market than not special to anyone. This approach leads one to the selection of particular segments as target markets and to tailoring program aspects to them by knowing their special characteristics.

In short, high-performance retail marketers are constantly trying to get closer to their customers, to understand their perceptions of the world better, and to predict their response to their marketing initiatives and to those of their competitors. (The field of customer product and patronage motivation is a complicated, fascinating, and rewarding one, and it is the subject of Chapter 4.)

**Competitor understanding**    A retailer also needs to examine existing and potential competitors. (This will be discussed further in Chapter 5.) It is very important that all the relevant competitors are identified as the customers would define them. For example, department stores such as The Bay or Macy's do not compete simply with other department stores, but also with specialty stores, mass merchandisers, mail order firms, and so on. Retailers have learned that they need to understand competitive strengths and weaknesses as perceived by the marketplace in order to understand their own marketing performance and to make sure that their own marketing decisions are as competitively powerful as possible. What makes one retailer's offer any different and any more appealing to customers than the programs of its competitors? Is there some salient added value that will influence customers to choose one retailer over another? Is that competitive advantage sustainable or is it temporary and fragile? This notion of competitive differentiation is central to retail marketing. It is very difficult to find a unique and viable position in today's overcrowded retail marketplace.

**Cohabitor understanding**    Most retailers operate in a context that includes other organizations that are involved with the retailer's relationships with customers. These organizations may be neighbouring retailers in a shopping centre, other stores on a streetfront in the downtown area, or landlords and developers. These cohabitors may of course include competitors, as discussed above, but may also include organizations that are either unrelated or highly complementary. Retailers offering "shopping goods" (goods that customers wish to compare from retailer to retailer) often group together. Examples would include automobile dealerships, furniture and furnishings stores, and fast food outlets. These groupings often create a "draw" for customers that individual retailers could not match on their own. Similarly, shopping centres and business areas often form associations and other groupings to advertise and promote the interests of their members, thus giving each retailer additional marketing leverage. Alert retailers are always seeking partnerships with complementary cohabitors to extend their customer attraction through association. Affinity marketing, cross-promotional efforts, and other partnership arrangements have increased and will continue to increase dramatically.

**Environmental understanding**    Environmental analysis refers to examination of the relevant political/legal, economic, social, and technological aspects of the broader marketplace. One may chart social changes (such as two-income families or environmentalism) that in time will impact on customer values and behaviours, or technological changes (such as item scanning at point-of-sale) that in time will impact on one's ability to compete. This "big picture" sensitivity is how retail marketers stay prepared for the inevitable shifts in the market. For example, alert hospitality retailers, particularly in fast food, know now that the pool of teenage labour is about to shrink remarkably and that they must rethink their hiring, training, and other personnel practices and then proact in order to have the people they need to provide personal customer service in the near future. Similarly, aware retailers are constantly monitoring real estate and advertising developments. (These issues will be discussed further in Chapter 13.)

**Supplier understanding**    The final dimension of program–marketplace fit analysis involves assessment of supplier availability, terms and conditions, physical distribution activities, and the overall nature of retailer–vendor relationships. Excellent retail marketers apply the same kind of thinking to their suppliers as they do to their customers, competitors, and cohabitors; in brief, they attempt to answer the question, What does it take to have good relationships with valued suppliers? Such thinking often results in new and creative approaches to retail marketing. (Supplier understanding will be discussed further in Chapter 7.)

## Program–Elements Fit

---
### FIGURE 1.4
---

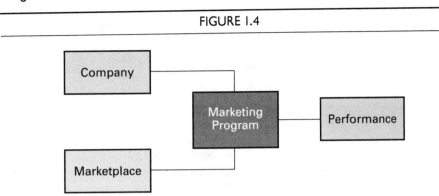

As one prepares, evaluates, and considers changes to a retail marketing program, there is a need to challenge oneself constantly with questions about how the various elements of the program fit together: Does the pricing approach support the assortment mix or does it send contradictory signals to the customer? Does the level of customer service and care accord with the prices? Are consistent messages being sent to the customers about who the retailer is and what he or she stands for, or are the customers somewhat confused? The best marketers promise what they can deliver and deliver what they promise; the program elements are supportive of one another. A sure way to disappoint, even alienate, a market is to promise more than can be delivered, yet many would-be marketers do just that in an attempt to win customers. If a retailer promises lowest prices and most knowledgeable salespeople, he or she had better ensure that that is what is available. The only way to ensure that each element of the retail marketing program is consistent with the other elements is to have someone periodically examine how each element contributes to the total retail marketing strategy and not allow one retail marketing decision to be made independent of the rest of the elements. For example, a decision to change assortment should not be made without consideration of the impact on service quality. (The many issues of program design and elements fit are discussed especially in Chapters 7–13.)

## Program–Company Fit

---
### FIGURE 1.5
---

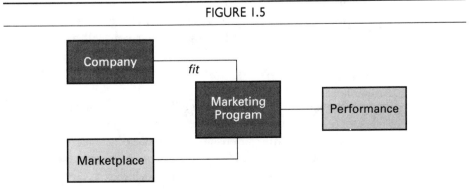

Much has been written by academics, consultants, and other management gurus about missions, goals and objectives, and other dimensions of strategic planning. Much of what they say about assessing corporate internal strengths and weaknesses can be simplified with the following questions:

a.  What is the retail marketer trying to accomplish and when?

b.  Is there reason to believe that he or she can accomplish that purpose in that time period?

c.  Does the marketing program make sense for the particular retailer's values and culture, resources and managerial and systems capabilities? If not, which should change, the program or the organization? For example, marketing programs require financial resources to implement. What working capital requirements will planned increases in inventory require? What increases in accounts receivable are foreseen?

d.  If there is more than one organizational unit (for example, more than one store or more than one merchandise grouping), do the marketing programs of the units reinforce one another or do they hurt one another?

e.  Is there evidence that the program is on track in terms of the retailer's mission and objectives, aspirations, values, and capabilities?

By systematically and periodically examining these and similar questions, one often finds the need to modify the retail marketing program design. (Such questions are addressed further, especially in Chapters 2, 3, and 13.)

## Practising Decision-Making: The Use of Cases

**SECTION**

**TWO**

In this book, the term **case** refers to a written description of a situation that a retail decision-maker has actually faced. Sometimes, names, places, and other facts have been disguised at the request of the individuals and organizations involved because in each instance those individuals provided permission to use their stories. The objective of each case is to leave you at a decision point much like the one faced by the decision-maker in the case. There are also some *exercises*, presented to enable you to practise techniques of decision-making in a more concise context.

In each case, you will be expected to analyze the situation, determine what problems and opportunities exist, generate and evaluate alternative courses of action, and recommend a plan of action. In short, you are to deal with the case as if you were in it, with the exception that you will not be able to implement your recommendations and see the results.

You will face several common frustrations with the case method—most notably, a shortage of information and time, uncertainty as to how results will work out, and a wish to dissociate yourself from the mistakes of the decision-maker in the case. These frustrations are normal and crucial to having you simulate the actual pressures and frustrations faced by real decision-makers.

Cases can be used in a variety of ways. In a course of study, you will probably be asked to do some or all of the following:

1. Individual preparation for a class discussion
2. Small group discussion in preparation for a class discussion
3. Class discussion
4. Written report or in-class presentation of a case
5. Written examination of your ability to handle a case

Each of these situations is somewhat different and will require a variation in your approach. While your instructor may have specific instructions, here are a few general guidelines for you.

## INDIVIDUAL PREPARATION

Cases can be complicated and controversial. You may or may not have specific assignment questions to help you as you prepare a case. Such assignment questions should always be regarded as only a guide to the *main task* each time — namely, you must be ready in class to recommend what you would do as the main decision-maker and then to explain why. Each case should be regarded as a challenge to your ability to *sort* information into relevant versus irrelevant, to *interpret* information, to *decide* on a course of action, and to *argue* your viewpoint persuasively with others who may have different recommendations.

Cases can take more time than you have available to prepare. Remember at all times that your purpose is to make *decisions*; the earlier you identify the decision choices that face you, the sooner you can begin to focus your efforts on the information and analysis that is actually relevant to those choices. Cases include both information required to make decisions and information that gives you background to the decision situation; the former you must become very familiar with, the latter you speed through. Here are some steps you might follow:

1. Read the case once quickly to get an overview.
2. Skim the case exhibits, if there are any, to see what data are available.
3. Note who the decision-maker is, the timing of the decision, what the apparent concerns of the decision-maker are, and why these concerns have arisen. This information is usually in the first couple of paragraphs and/or the last couple of paragraphs of the text.
4. Read the case more carefully with a pen or marker in hand. Highlight or indicate key information. In the margins, write notes of thoughts that occur to you as you read. In fact, write all over the case; this helps you get going and also gets you much more familiar with the case facts. Don't make separate notes on other paper until later.
5. Keep in mind the retail marketing decision-making framework as a way to sort information and get ready to make decisions. If this framework doesn't work well for you, develop your own.
6. Evaluate the performance of the current marketing program. How does this compare with the aspirations of management? With your assessment of potential performance? With the performance of similar competitors?

7. Identify the current, if any, retail marketing program of the organization. Describe it in your own words using the headings of the retail marketing decision-making model.

8. Identify the apparent decision choices to be made in terms of problems to solve and opportunities to seek. These include issues raised explicitly in the case and those issues that have occurred to you. Remember you may add or subtract from this list later.

9. Working your way through the four types of fit (program–performance, program–marketplace, program–company, and program–elements), does the current or proposed retail marketing program make sense? If this is a start-up, what program would make the most sense? One way to do this is to ask, under each analytical heading (such as customer analysis), Why is the current marketing program working as well as it is or not as well as it could? Beware of trying to use all the information in the case. Each time you examine a fact or opinion, ask yourself, How does this help me make a decision? This "so what" test will help you sort useful from interesting, but useless, information.

10. Generate some alternative approaches. What might be alternative ways to realize opportunities or solve problems? You should always be able to generate two or three alternatives, even if some appear more promising to you from the outset.

11. Evaluate the alternatives by working through the marketing decision-making model. You want the alternatives that make the most logical sense and that promise the highest likelihood of realizing the performance objectives you believe appropriate for the organization. The best test is to compare your projection of future performance without changes in strategy with the performance you believe your recommended strategy will achieve.

12. Prepare detailed action recommendations. These should be as specific and practical as possible and as actionable as possible (that is, could you pass them on to another in the organization with the result that this person would know exactly how to proceed?).

Do not call individuals and organizations in the cases for more information. They have given much time already and have requested that they not be bothered. However, supplementing your case preparation with visits to stores and shopping centres as well as keeping informed about retail industry developments through reading will aid you immensely.

Preparing a case takes time and practice. Some students deceive themselves, thinking, "I could do one if I had the time" or some such excuse. Waiting until an exam or report to do a thorough case preparation is much like preparing for a track meet by watching others practise.

## SMALL GROUP PREPARATION FOR CLASS

Ideally, you will have an opportunity to discuss informally your preparation of a case with some of your classmates prior to the class. Many students find such study group sessions the most rewarding part of the case method experience. A good group session is a sharing situation in which you discover ideas you may have overlooked or not weighed. Your colleagues will also benefit from your input.

The effectiveness of a small group case discussion can be increased substantially if you adhere to the following guidelines:

1. Each individual should come to the group meeting with a thorough analysis of the case and an understanding of any associated readings. The small group session is not the place to start preparing the case.

2. Each individual is expected to participate actively in the discussion. The small group discussion is an excellent place to check out your analysis before going into class.

3. It is not necessary to have a group leader in the sense of a decision-maker. Every individual is responsible for making decisions based on what is said plus his or her own case analysis. A group discussion facilitator, on the other hand, can help keep the discussion on track and ensure everyone has an opportunity to speak, thus making your meeting more productive and satisfying.

4. It is not necessary to have a recording secretary. Each individual is responsible for his or her own notes. It is important to be able to recognize a good idea when you hear one.

5. Consensus is normally not necessary. Everyone does not have to agree with everyone else. The exception, of course, is for group reports and presentations.

6. Iron out any individual disagreements after the regular small group discussion, especially if only one or two people are involved.

7. Set a time limit for discussion and stick to it. Effective small group case discussions can sometimes take less than thirty minutes.

Remember, two people can be a group. Spend some time with a friend over the phone or face to face sharing your respective case analyses. You will feel better about your own preparation and be more confident about contributing to the class discussion.

## CLASS DISCUSSION

In actual situations when managers address the issues represented in these cases, there are nearly always different views on interpretation of data and on what could and should be done. Therefore, you should expect that during a case discussion your classmates will also express several different views. The essence of the case method is the process of stating points of view, defending positions, and listening actively so as to understand and constructively criticize the positions of others. Rarely will you leave the classroom unchanged in your position or perspective after discussing a case. However, in spite of the common interest of all class members in resolving the case issues and in spite of the guidance of the instructor, class discussions will sometimes seem repetitious and disorganized. This is unavoidable and natural, especially during the early stages of a course. Over time, as a group develops its group decision-making ability, case discussions will be more orderly, efficient, and satisfying to all.

The need to be a skilful communicator arises repeatedly in management, and the case method presents an ideal opportunity to practise talking and listening skills. For some, *talking* in a group situation is difficult and threatening. Such individuals might avoid talking in class even though they realize they are not getting full value out of the experience. If you are one of these individuals, the only way to overcome this problem is to jump in and begin. Make a habit of participating regularly in class. Do not wait until you have a major presentation to make where you will hold the floor for a lengthy period. Adding a key piece of information or questioning something can be done in a few sentences and may be the best way for you to begin active involvement. Your instructor and your classmates will be supportive of your efforts. Remember, the classroom is a place where we can learn from one another's mistakes as much as, or more than, from one another's "correct" solutions. The cost of making a mistake in class is minimal relative to making a mistake in the marketplace.

For others, *listening* is a poorly developed skill. Some individuals, in fact, have a tendency not to listen, but rather simply to wait for their turn to speak. The case method helps all of us to learn to listen more carefully. You should be able to contribute to the overall flow of the discussion by referencing what others have said and relating your ideas to their ideas.

The case method depends on everyone's willing interaction. Without that essential ingredient, cases become interesting stories rather than opportunities to develop the ability to make and argue for management decisions. Most students, not surprisingly, are interested in learning "what actually happened" or what the instructor would do. This information will not always be forthcoming. However, learning is inherent in the process and habit of making decisions, more than in reviewing what others decided to do.

## AFTER CLASS

After class, take a few minutes to analyze your preparation in comparison with what happened in class. Was your preparation "in the ball park" or inadequate? Did you spend enough time preparing? Was your small group session effective? What can you do better next time? What general lessons were learned? For example, you may not need to remember how the market for a particular convenience store is segmented, but you should be interested in remembering approaches on how to segment a retail market.

## REPORTS, PRESENTATIONS, AND EXAMINATIONS

In a typical class discussion of a case, exactly what gets done is a function of (*a*) the students—what preparation was done, who actively participated in the discussion, how one person related to the previous comments of another, and so on; and (*b*) the instructor—his or her pedagogical objectives and performance as a moderator and a discussion traffic cop. Instructors view a case course as a sequence of problems that gradually foster the development of decision-making skills. With this longer time horizon, instructors often find it advisable to emphasize a specific analytical technique on one occasion, problem identification on another occasion, and so on. Thus, it is possible that many class sessions are not complete, balanced developments of a case analysis and plan of action.

Sometimes, instructors wish to provide students with opportunities for a more complete, balanced treatment of cases. In these situations, they often allow extra preparation time and may even ask for an oral presentation of a case (individually or in a group) or a written report to management on how you would handle a particular situation and why. Frequently, case method courses use cases for examinations: you may be given a case and asked to do whatever analysis and make whatever recommendations you deem appropriate.

In reports, presentations, and examinations, instructors generally expect more complete, balanced arguments for a particular course of action. Such exercises are not intended to result in a diary of how you or your group looked at a case, nor does you instructor want a rewritten version of the case. A report, presentation, or examination is supposed to be a concise, coherent exposition of what to do and why. In fact, a good report, presentation, or exam usually starts where many students leave off in their regular individual preparation for a case class. In short, think of a report, presentation, or examination as an organized, more fully developed (and perhaps rewritten) version of your regular class preparation notes.

You will find that your audience—instructor, business executive, or whoever—has particular ideas about how a report, presentation, or examination should be organized. Find out as much as you can about format and other expectations before embarking on your task.

## CONCLUSION

Retail marketing management involves making a host of decisions about the retail marketing program. Following a marketing orientation means making those decisions with full understanding of the nature of the marketplace in which the retailer operates and full consideration of the retailer's particular circumstances, values, and aspirations. Retail marketing management means systematic analysis, decision-making, and implementation of activities designed to improve the retailer's relationship with customers and other partners in the marketplace. The composite of all these decisions is called the retail marketing program, which, added to the other dimensions of the retailer's approach to the market, constitutes the retailer's strategy. The four basic tests of the appropriateness of any proposed or in-place retail marketing program are as follows: program–performance fit, program–marketplace fit, program–elements fit, and program–company fit. Cases provide an exciting, effective way to experience retail marketing and build managerial skills.

### REVIEW QUESTIONS

1. Select a retailer who operates in your area. Based on your observations, describe that retailer's marketing strategy using the conceptual model presented in this chapter and the IKEA example.

**2.** Make an appointment to interview a retail marketing manager. This person may be a store manager, a bank manager, a restaurant manager, a museum administrator — in short, someone whom you consider to be a retail marketer. Ask that person the following questions:

   a. How did you come to be in this job?

   b. What do you do on a typical day?

   c. What do you like most and least about retail marketing?

   d. What is your retail marketing program? (Tip: Many students have found that this question has to be explained in parts to managers.)

**3.** Who is the most interesting retail marketer you have encountered? Why?

**4.** If you were "president for a week" of your regular grocery store, what would you change to make the store a better retail operation?

**5.** When evaluating your recommended strategy for a retail marketer, why compare "projected performance with changes to the strategy" with "projected performance without changes to the strategy" instead of with "performance last year"?

## KEY TERMS

- retail marketing management
- retailer
- orientation
- buying orientation
- selling orientation
- merchandising
- marketing
- product motivation
- patronage motivation
- target market

- design of an offer
- delivery of an offer
- retail marketing program
- retail marketing mix
- retail marketing strategy
- program–performance fit
- program–marketplace fit
- program–elements fit
- program–company fit

## NOTES

1. Boris Emmet, *Catalogues and Counters* (Chicago: University of Chicago Press, 1950), p.1.

2. Dan Sweeney, as quoted in "Marketing versus Merchandising in Retailing," *Canadian Retailer*, November 1984, p.1.

3. For a different treatment of this concept, see William Lazer and Eugene J. Kelley, "The Retailing Mix: Planning and Management," *Journal of Retailing*, vol. 37 (Spring 1961), pp. 34–41.

CHAPTER

# RETAIL MARKETING STRATEGY

## INTRODUCTION

Chapter 1 examined the basic dimensions of retail marketing using the concept of the "retail marketing program." This chapter looks at the way overall marketing programs are formulated. The basic notion discussed is retail strategy—the meaning of the term and the major strategic alternatives available to a retail marketer.

All retailers are interested in achieving performance goals. The formulation and implementation of retail marketing strategies are simply intended to achieve these goals. Chapter 3 examines the various performance measures used in retailing, while the discussion in this chapter is concerned with formulating the strategy to achieve high performance.

It isn't easy to be a high-performance retailer. An article in *Time* magazine entitled "No Holds Barred" described retailing in the United States as follows: "This is a dangerous and potentially deadly time to be a retailer in America. The number of stores has grown at a rate faster than the U.S. population, setting off a competitive battle as wild and unpredictable as a Wrestlemania spectacular."[1] The article went on to discuss how some experts believe the United States has 40 percent more retail capacity than it needs. This same situation exists increasingly in all developed countries today.

The reality of retail marketing is its competitive intensity, complexity, and ever-changing nature. Marvin Traub, chairman of Bloomingdale's and winner of the National Retail Federation's 1991 gold medal for Retailer of the Year, put it simply:

> The basic tenet I have always held about retailing at Bloomingdale's is that you have to change—and that is the one thing that doesn't change. Any store that doesn't recognize that consumer tastes and demographics are changing is going to lose out.[2]

No one firm can do everything right, but analysis of the high performers indicates that they simply perform some important marketing activities better than do their competitors (and that they perform the rest of those activities at least as well). In other words, these high performers become remarkable for their ability to excel at something important to their customers. They are outstanding in the sense of being distinctly different from other retailers in the same market. Consider the performance of Toys 'R' Us. In 1982, Toys 'R' Us sales were $783 million from 120 stores. By 1989, this toy retailer had become the top-ranked specialty chain in the United States, operating 615 stores (404 toy supermarkets in the United States, 74 toy supermarkets in other countries, and 137 apparel stores called Kids 'R' Us). Their sales had risen 20 percent over the previous year to a total of $4.8 billion, with earnings also up 20 percent, for a total of $321 million.

High-performance retail marketers are outstanding in terms of both their strategic approaches and their ability to execute them. Their managements understand how to market better than do those of their competitors. Jim Williams, president of the National Retail Merchants Association (now called the National Retail Federation) in the United States, expressed this idea as follows:

> Seat of the pants merchandising ended with the end of the Second World War, only too many people haven't noticed it yet . . . the number of people who start up in business and go out of it in a short time prove without a doubt that you don't just have to be an artist to be a retailer; you also have to be a scientist, an economist, a technician, a professional businessman.

Yet retail success doesn't come with one or two "big" ideas, as Wilfred Posluns, co-founder of Canada's Dylex Corporation, a very successful group of nearly two dozen apparel chains, explained:

> There's no simple answer to success. It consists of a hundred different things— getting the right margins, having the right merchandise, cost controls, watching every item of expense. It's never one thing but a hundred things; it's a tenth of a point here, a hundredth of a point there, and management has to continually work on those areas. Our own experience has shown that every time operational people get involved in other divisions than those for which they are responsible, they take their eye off the ball and they do not have the right perspective and grasp of the problem.[3]

Figure 2.1 summarizes the major concepts examined in this chapter.

## FIGURE 2.1

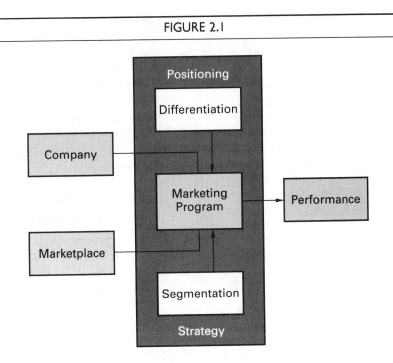

### THE NATURE OF STRATEGY

### THE NEED FOR STRATEGIC RETAIL MARKETING

It may seem surprising to suggest that there is a greater need for retail marketing strategy. Such a suggestion is not intended to mean that some retailers are not already active adherents and proponents of strategic planning, but rather that there is great potential for wider-spread adoption of this systematic approach. Retail practitioners constantly make innumerable decisions about what products to offer, how to communicate with customers, and so on. The basic notion, then, is to facilitate such decisions and to make them more effective by placing them in a coordinated, more systematic framework. Many retailers have resisted such approaches claiming either that they haven't time or that the approaches are unduly formalized. Such resistance forgoes opportunities for significant improvement in management decision-making and is often based on an over-estimation of the requirements of the strategic planning discipline. Increasingly, the choice for a retailer is not whether to engage in strategic planning but what strategy to have, as the following statements point out:

> Retailers are entering a new strategic era, in which customer research, store positioning, and power marketing have become the prerequisites to profitable survival.[4]

> Strategic planning, which came late to retailing, has been clasped to its breast like a long lost cousin. Desire, perspiration, and tears, along with a varying degree of wisdom, are being applied to it. Nearly every company today, regardless of its size or industry segment, has a strategic plan or a strategic planner or an on-going plan in its divisions, not all good or effective, perhaps, but in place for better or worse.[5]

Smart strategic retail marketers exhibit the following characteristics:

1. They understand the economics of their business, past and future.
2. They segment the market and use that segmentation to design marketing programs.
3. They examine customers and competitors by market segment.
4. They seek new competitively advantageous ways to conduct business based on an understanding of key success factors by market segment.
5. They are selective as to the segments, products, stores, and other marketing activities to which they will devote time and money.

## THE CONCEPT OF STRATEGY

There has been a great deal written and discussed about corporate strategy in the last few years. Consultants and academics in particular have promulgated innumerable conceptions and prescriptions of strategic planning. Practitioners have experimented with many of these approaches, finding some enormously useful and others of limited value. However, less of this effort and experimentation has occurred within the retail marketing field.

The whole idea behind strategy is to develop a sense of overall direction for an organization, a conceptual framework, and an overarching set of guidelines that will help all members of the organization coordinate their efforts and resources by focusing on that directed thrust. Note M.E. Porter's comments on strategy:

> Competitive strategy concerns how to create competitive advantage in each of the businesses in which a company competes. Corporate strategy concerns two different questions: what businesses the corporation should be in and how the corporate office should manage the array of business units. Corporate strategy is what makes the corporate whole add up to more than the sum of its business unit parts.[6]

In other words, the strategy puts boundaries around what the organization will do and how it will be done. F.D. Wiersema defined strategic marketing as follows:

> Strategic marketing is defined as having the dual task of providing (1) a marketplace perspective to the process of determining corporate direction, and (2) guidelines for the development and execution of marketing programs that assist in attaining corporate objectives. The definition implies that a marketplace perspective is an important, yet not the only, ingredient in setting a firm's

objectives, and further, that objectives place certain constraints on the firm's marketplace activities.[7]

Certainly every retail marketer does have a strategy implicit in his or her countless decisions. Such a strategy may never be discussed or even written down. However, as that retailer's marketplace becomes more complex and competitive and as size of the operation increases, there is increasing value to being more formalized, to making explicit written statements of strategy both for review and for execution.

Retail success is not simply the product of a few grand strategic decisions, but rather the sum of innumerable little decisions and actions. The action in retailing takes place in individual buyer's offices, on the floor in the stores, in the distribution centres, and so on. The task of the retail executive is to make sure all of this activity is coordinated and supported so that it all adds up to the sum total desired. This is the particular role of retail strategic marketing.

It is important to realize that retail marketing can be planned at several different levels of aggregation. For example, one might prepare a marketing plan for *different levels of merchandise,* such as a merchandise line (e.g., one brand of men's shirts), a classification (e.g., all men's dress shirts), or a merchandise group (e.g., men's furnishings); or one might prepare a marketing plan for *different organizational units,* such as a store, a region, or a division. These many different possibilities mean that retail marketing planning must and does occur simultaneously in many places in a large organization, resulting in a cascade of strategic plans, much like a set of wooden boxes, each successively smaller so as to fit inside one another. All the concepts discussed in this chapter apply to all these levels of aggregation.[8]

Not all retail marketing decisions are "strategic." William King offered the following method of distinguishing strategic from other decisions:

> A strategic issue is a condition or pressure on the business, created by internal or external developments, that involves:
> 1. possible outcomes that will have a high impact on future performance;
> 2. controversy, in that reasonable people can take and defend different positions on how to deal with the issue; and
> 3. strategic consequences, since the resolution may mean implementing a change in strategy.[9]

## TRADITIONAL WAYS TO CLASSIFY RETAIL MARKETING STRATEGIES

Traditional discussions of retailing typically begin with classification schemes and definitions. Retail operations in such discussions are classified by the **types of merchandise carried** (e.g., general merchandise versus grocery, limited line versus broad line); by **ownership** (e.g., independent versus chain, owned versus franchise); by **location** (e.g., free-standing versus shopping centre); by **method** (e.g., store versus non-store); and by **type of store** (e.g., department store, discount store, supermarket, catalogue showroom, drug store, hardware store, specialty store, etc.).

However, these classifications are becoming less and less relevant as retailers cross traditional boundaries; for example, what exactly does one call a scaled-down Sears store in a strip mall location—a department store? a mass merchandiser? a limited line store? a variety store? Unless one is preparing a statistical review, it probably doesn't really matter; more importantly, one needs to know whether to examine the store as a competitor or as a source of potential ideas for one's own operation.

Thus, there is some merit in trying to cluster retail operations according to shared characteristics, because these clusters provide insights into viable retail marketing strategies. Michael Porter expressed this notion in general as follows:

> An industry can thus be viewed as composed of clusters or groups of firms, where each group consists of firms following similar strategies in terms of the key decision variables. . . . I define such groups as strategic groups. Firms within a strategic group resemble one another closely. . . . Between strategic groups, however, the situation is different.[10]

The key decision variables used to cluster retail operations into strategic groups include the effort customers will expend, functions performed by the retailer, extent of ego-involvement, and strategic approach used.

### Customer Effort

One of the earliest attempts to classify customer effort was in 1923 by Melvin Copeland.[11] He distinguished among **convenience**, **shopping**, and **specialty goods** on the basis of customer shopping behaviour. Briefly, Copeland asserted that customers would exert different amounts of effort depending on the kind of good being sought. Convenience items were expected to be readily available with limited effort required. These items differed from shopping goods in that customers typically had pre-established brand preferences (or had no preference at all) for convenience items, whereas they wished to compare attributes, prices, and so on, for shopping goods at several retailers before making purchase decisions. Thus, milk and cigarettes were regarded as convenience items requiring wide distribution, but appliances and cars were regarded as shopping items requiring selective distribution. Specialty items were regarded as items for which the customer would expend extra effort, typically because of pre-established preference and loyalty. Such items, such as high-priced imported cars, would typically be distributed exclusively. This simple but appealing classification scheme has endured remarkably.

Forty years later, L.P. Bucklin extended Copeland's classification scheme by suggesting that stores could be similarly labelled: for example, a convenience store was one that customers expected to find close at hand and to exert a minimum amount of effort within. Bucklin created a 3 × 3 matrix by combining products and stores. He maintained that one might find a convenience store carrying a specialty item, and so on.[12]

## Functions

Another way to classify retailers is on the basis of what **functions** they perform. One may distinguish full-service retailers from self-service, factory outlets from co-operative societies, and so on. Stanley Hollander describes this idea as follows:

> Retailers have four major alternatives with regard to any conceivable activity:
> 1. They may perform the work; that is, they or their employees may actually do it.
> 2. They may contract out the work to specialized functionaries such as contract-delivery companies, building maintenance organizations, management consultants, and sales finance companies.
> 3. They may, and in a limited number of instances do, share the work with other competitive or non-competitive retailers. [This could be extended to franchising arrangements which are so common today.]
> 4. They may shift the work either back to the wholesaling and manufacturing suppliers or forward to consumers.[13]

## Ego-Involvement

Walter Salmon distinguished goods and, hence, stores on the basis of **ego-involvement**. High ego-involvement items, such as apparel, automobiles, cosmetics, and so on, differ from low ego-involvement items, such as routine groceries and household cleaning supplies. Where low ego-involvement applies, the customer does not regard the purchase as a reflection on him- or herself. Low ego-involving goods and stores must compete on the basis of functionality, convenience, and price; whereas high ego-involving goods and stores compete on the basis of image, association, and psycho-social gratification.

## Strategic Approach

There are other classification approaches such as **size, merchandise line breadth and depth**, and **extent of value-added**. For example, a discount department store such as Zellers may be regarded as a low value-added and low merchandise specialization operation as compared to an apparel specialty boutique such as the Harry Rosen operation, which is high value-added and high merchandise specialization. Such attempts at classification generally boil down to descriptions of retail formats, which are in reality shorthand descriptions of strategic clusters.

Consider the supermarket. Should we classify the supermarket as one of several types of stores carrying primarily grocery products—that is, convenience stores, food terminals, warehouse outlets, box stores, superstores, combination stores, hypermarchés, or food emporiums, to name a few? Or should we classify the supermarket more generically as a strategic type that can be applied to toys (e.g., Toys 'R' Us), drugs (e.g., Shoppers Drug Mart), and many other merchandise categories? W.R. Davidson and A.L. Rogers propose the following:

The concept of the supermarket is historically associated with grocery products. In reality, it is a certain method of operation—that is, stores with facilities to expedite customer self-service (generally providing a shopping cart) and designed to facilitate multiple item shopping using a central checkout for processing customer transactions and collecting merchandise data. Rapid continuing growth of this method of operation in practically all lines of retail trade has occurred and is accelerating.[14]

## SECTION TWO

### DECISION-MAKING APPROACHES

As discussed in Chapter 1, every retail marketer has to decide what market to compete in, whom to target, and what to offer relative to the competition. These strategic decisions are called **market choice, target market selection**, and **competitive differentiation**. Taken together, they may be expressed as the retail marketer's **positioning strategy**. Each of these topics is addressed in this section.

### RETAIL MARKET CHOICE

What are the boundaries of the market that a retailer will serve? This question is the starting point for retail marketing strategy, and it is a question all retailers should periodically return to as their market circumstances change. Take, for example, a retailer of women's apparel; considering the growing market of career women, should the retailer define the market as "working clothes for career women" or "all-occasion clothes for career women"? This choice will have profound implications for assortment, store location and size, display techniques, and so on.

Usually, there are a variety of ways to define any particular retail market. Different definitions could lead to significant differences in strategy because of variations in size of market estimates, relevant competitors, and market segments, to name a few. Generally speaking, retail markets may be defined on several dimensions, including **geography** (local, regional, national, international), **types of customers** (a discussion of target market choice follows), and **value-added** (such as added product features and/or convenience). The best way to define markets is from the perspective of targeted customers, because customers may not perceive or experience product differentiation or substitution in the same way as retailers do. For example, traditionally, apparel retailers have organized themselves around merchandise classifications, presenting departments of apparel such as evening wear, sportswear, and so on. Over the past decade, many apparel retailers have attempted to reorganize around customer types and lifestyles. Helen Galland, president of Bonwit Teller, put it this way:

> I believe the customer—and her way of life—is fast becoming the classification, rather than the merchandise . . . age group over 30, under 30, over 50 . . . sophisticated . . . affluent . . . and don't underestimate the conservative. I can see whole stores designed with selling areas by customer classifications in settings to attract that segment of the market to whom their message is directed. I am

convinced that we are about to witness a great change in merchandising practices and that there will be new and exciting ways of presentation. I see the future customer of varying ages and tastes heading for the little shops or corners of the store to find the total look presentation of compatible merchandise, rather than shopping for individual items.[15]

There is no single always-best approach to defining a retail market. However, a necessary starting point in any retail marketing strategy discussion is reaching some agreement on the scope of the market to be served by the strategy. A good definition of the market will include a general description of which kinds of customers will be served, in which geographic area, competing with which other retailers, offering which general products and services with which general value-added. All of these descriptors of the market will be greatly refined as the strategy itself is prepared so one need not agonize over this first step; the retail market choice specification simply helps frame the rest of the strategic effort.

Notice that the level of specificity of these descriptions of the market to be served is totally at the discretion of the retail marketer. Too narrow a definition may limit opportunities and neglect relevant competitors; too broad a definition may not provide sufficient focus to guide strategic choices and implementation.

## RETAIL TARGET MARKET SELECTION

A close look at customers usually reveals that they differ in many ways. This often means that one marketing approach will be regarded as appropriate by some retailers and inappropriate by others. However, despite many differences, customers often can be grouped according to some shared characteristics. **Retail market segmentation** is an appropriate and useful effort if these characteristics are helpful in understanding differences in (*a*) what customers want, (*b*) how customers perceive the retailer and the program offering, and/or (*c*) how customers react to various aspects of the marketing program. Once segments have been identified and examined, the retail marketer can select segments to be addressed, which are called **target markets**, and segments to be ignored.

It is important to note that it is not always appropriate to segment retail markets narrowly. In fact, there are sometimes instances where retail marketers find new growth opportunities through **market segment aggregation**, which is combining segments to expand a served market.

There are many ways to describe customers that enable formation of customer segments. These descriptors can be broadly classified as describing either the customers or the customers' reactions to the retailer's offer before, during, or after the purchase. In most retail markets, the broad **customer descriptors** are as follows:

- demographic (age, sex, income, etc.)
- geographic (place of residence, of work, etc.)
- psychographic (lifestyle, interests, activities, opinions, media habits, general shopping habits, etc.)

In most retail markets, **descriptors of customer responses** to marketing efforts are as follows:

- benefits sought (functions desired, features, service required, value added sought, etc.)
- cognitive factors (knowledge of stores and products, awareness of competitive programs, perceptions of purchasing risk, etc.)
- affective factors (attitudes toward brands, opinions of stores, etc.)
- sensitivity (to price, to place of purchase, etc.)
- purchasing behaviour (extent of pre-planning, deliberation periods, amount purchased at a time, purchasing occasions, loyalty patterns, etc.)
- usage behaviour (how used, amount used per use, frequency of use, recency of use, etc.).

These and other approaches to segmenting a retail market are undertaken to gain greater insight into serving a market and, in particular, to discern whether particular segments merit separate marketing approaches. The more one studies customers, the more apparent it is that retail segmentation is both fascinating and demanding. Alasdair McKichan provides an example:

> The demographic changes accentuating the older, rather than the younger parts of the population, the new prudence in spending, the further fragmenting of the market into highly individualistic segments, the diminishing significance of the family as a living and economic unit, the sharpening of the consumer decision-making process induced by the recession, all required the retailer to develop a whole new set of skills towards his customer.[16]

Any retail market segmentation effort can be assessed in terms of whether it provides clear answers to the following questions:

1. Is the segment large enough to justify any differential efforts in serving it?
2. Is the segment different enough to merit a differential approach?
3. Are the differences likely to endure over time long enough to merit a differential approach?
4. Can the segment be reached with the marketing tools available (e.g., is there an appropriate advertising vehicle)?
5. Are the segments compatible with one another or do they indicate the need for clear choices of which to serve?
6. What are the incremental costs and payoffs of serving one segment differentially from other segments?

In short, segmentation analysis allows the retail marketer to assess the relative attractiveness of various portions of the defined retail market. In this way, marketers can determine retail market target(s) to provide a clear focus for marketing program formulation. Thus, market segmentation allows a refinement of the served market definition as discussed previously. Wilfrid Posluns of Dylex, a firm that has used market segmentation as its key strategy for growth, stated the importance of segmentation as follows:

> Market segmentation strategies will continue to dominate the growth area of retailing. Intense competition and rising costs associated with marketing to customers who are on the fringes of a segment are increasing the importance of a well-defined strategy even if the result is to turn away that business which does not match it. Specialist merchants who direct their marketing towards specific rationalized customer segments will continue to be more effective, productive, and efficient and to appeal to the customers who most value the attributes which they represent.[17]

Exhibit 2.1 provides a summary of this discussion of retail market segmentation. (Chapter 4 will examine retail segmentation in greater depth.)

---

*EXHIBIT 2.1*
*Retail Market*
*Segmentation*
*Summary*

**Segmentation by customer characteristics:**

**1.** Demographic

**2.** Geographic

**3.** Psychographic

**Segmentation by customer interaction with marketing efforts:**

**1.** Benefits sought

**2.** Cognitive factors

**3.** Affective factors

**4.** Sensitivity

**5.** Purchasing behaviour

**6.** Usage behaviour

---

## RETAIL COMPETITIVE DIFFERENTIATION

The basic notion underlying retail competitive differentiation is that variation of the total package of benefits offered to the customer can result in competitive advantage, hopefully even sustained competitive advantage. Any retailer is differentiated *relative* to competitors so this concept can be used only in conjunction with an understanding of competitive circumstances. Most retail offerings, because of their multifaceted nature, are differentiated to some extent from one another. Thus, the question becomes, what are the salient points of differentiation?

It is important to remember that retailers can differentiate on a product motivation basis and on a patronage motivation basis. For example, A.I. Cohen and A.L. Jones note that, as competition increased in American retailing, with the familiar avenues closed, retailers were left with two means of increasing their selling power and market share. First, they could develop their own products and labels, which many have done by using foreign sources to get better value or exclusivity or both. Second, they could sell more than mere merchandise: they could differentiate themselves by carefully selecting their market segments and projecting merchandise images designed to attract specific and well-differentiated audiences.[18]

Similarly, Stanton Cort concluded that the tremendous increase in specialty retailing in the United States was a consequence of efforts to differentiate:

> The rush to specialty operations is in part an attempt to avoid some of the non-discretionary merchandise distributors' problems. The theory is that, if anything substantial about the operation (merchandise assortment, sales people, store, total presentation, etc.) can be differentiated from other stores in the minds of some groups of consumers, hopefully those consumers will think less about price and/or convenience when deciding whether to shop the store.[19]

Sharp retail marketers seek *meaningful* points of difference that will make customers choose them again and again over competition. Being different is not sufficient; being meaningfully better is a major step toward marketing success. Notice that "better" may mean offering "more" (such as more service, more selection) or "less" (such as less waiting, less inconvenience). The differences must be salient; retail marketing history is replete with examples of firms that offered marginally different products or services and met with market indifference at best. Too few retailers focus on enhancement of a competitive edge. Instead, there is rampant copying. This suggests there is enormous potential for improved retail performance.

Ideally, a differentiator seeks differences that customers value highly but that other competitors find hard to match. These differences may be in the nature of the **product–service offering** itself, in the **cost–price ratio** of providing that offering, or in **related marketing efforts**, such as the method of communicating about the store and its products and services. The possibilities for differentiation are usually extensive unless constrained by governmental regulation.

It is important to distinguish between *attempts* at retail differentiation (what the retail marketer is trying to accomplish) and *achieved* retail differentiation (how the customers actually perceive competitive offerings). Clearly, the latter is the more important concept of differentiation.

Each retailer's program offering can be conceived as a "package of benefits" as perceived and experienced by the customer. Customers have needs, wants, and expectations of retailers. This means there are usually a variety of ways to vary the retail offering compared with the offerings of retail competitors. The major dimensions around which much of this book is organized are six customer expectations: assortment, convenience, customer care, information, value, and experience. These expectations provide a simple but powerful way to summarize competitive retail marketing differentiation.

## Assortment

Most retailers are differentiated from one another by their **assortment** of both products and services offered to customers. Assortment is a tough but powerful way to gain a differential competitive edge in retailing. Most retailers have found it is now harder than ever to have exclusive merchandise, unique services, more merchandise, or to consistently buy better than their competitors. Jim Nordstrom of Nordstrom put assortment in perspective in an article by Joan Bergman: "The retail business is becoming more sophisticated, but the issues have not changed much since 1901 (when Nordstrom was founded). You still need the right stuff, in the right quantities."[20]

As will be discussed in Chapter 7, assortments of products and services may be classified according to their variety, breadth, depth, and branding. Variations on these dimensions enable many different assortment strategies. For example, three basic assortment strategies for differentiation are uniqueness, dominance, and opportunism. **Uniqueness** means offering—and being perceived to be offering— something other retailers in that trading area do not. Often this comes by virtue of sourcing of the product. In the extreme, one designs and has manufactured an exclusive line and puts one's label on it. Marks and Spencer, Sainsbury, Sears, Radio Shack, and Canadian Tire are examples of leading retailers who have significant commitments to private label programs. Some retailers, such as Loblaws, have made product assortment the major point of difference with their competitors. Loblaws has had enormous success with its generic and President's Choice programs and recently launched its Green line of environmental- and body-friendly grocery and household products. It is not necessary, however, to have a private label program or to be large to be unique in assortment; a specialty confectionery store, for example, may be the only place in town that carries Belgian chocolates. Some retailers retain the uniqueness of their assortment by having a limited number of outlets. For example, L.L. Bean maintains only one store in Freeport, Maine, which makes the store itself unique. Sporting Life has done the same in Toronto.

Sometimes, small differences are enough to be important to customers. This idea is summed up by the notion of "adding extra value" to the product and service. Retail marketers with savvy look for ways—big and small—to add a little something to the product. For example, a men's apparel retailer offers to sew buttons on the inside pockets of a suitcoat to deter pickpockets; a gift store offers to gift-wrap items free of charge; a jewelery store not only repairs the ring but gives it a thorough cleaning; and a department store (in Japan) offers to bolt a locked box on its customers' homes so that deliveries can be left safely when customers are at work.

Another assortment strategy is **dominance**. This approach need not mean enormous stores, but rather a wider and deeper selection of merchandise in the chosen categories relative to the selection offered by other retailers in that trading area. Hence, a store offering "everything for the kite lover" may be only 800 square feet (72 m²) while a store offering "all your routine shopping needs" may be 100 000 square feet (9000 m²). The basic appeal of each is offering customers assurance that a trip to that one store is probably enough to examine all relevant product offerings in a product category.

**Power assortments** refer to exceptionally large assortments by any standards, the retailers carrying them often now being labelled as "category killers." For example, Toys 'R' Us has been growing at 23 percent compounded per year for several years, with its toy supermarket format in stores averaging more than 45 000 square feet (4050 m²). By combining grocery and warehouse operations with general merchandise margins and state-of-the-art systems, Toys 'R' Us has double the productivity per square foot of its nearest competitor, Child World. Toys 'R' Us gives the impression not only in reality, but is, both uncharacteristically broad and deep in assortment. Management has committed the organization to be "never out of stock" on an assortment of more than 18 000 SKU's. While Toys 'R' Us offers everyday low prices, their prices are by no means the lowest in the toy marketplace.

Another assortment strategy is **opportunistic buying**, which focuses on buying whatever is on-deal. While at first glance this might appear to be simply a price-oriented strategy, it is also an assortment strategy. It usually results in lack of merchandise continuity, frequent changes in selection, and an offer that some customers regard as more interesting, if not less expensive. This approach is typical of the "off-price" outlets, outlets that offer everything from end-of-runs to closeouts and liquidations.

### Convenience

A second way to gain a differential competitive edge is through **convenience**. Convenience is another of those marketing words that is too often bandied about without clarification. Convenience is multifaceted, just like service, care, and value. The term includes access, shopping ease, transaction speed, and so on. From the customer's viewpoint, convenience means *saving time and/or effort in shopping*. Retailers may respond to convenience expectations with location, layout, item placement, transaction ease, hours, and other initiatives (as will be discussed more fully in Chapter 8).

Some retailers are in danger of losing their traditional convenience edge. For example, North American department stores once were the convenient "one-stop" shopping places. But as shopping centres and malls grew—becoming, as someone said, giant department stores put on their sides—North American department stores were caught between trying to be part of the movement by joining as anchor stores and trying to stay separate by maintaining downtown and other free-standing locations. Most North American department stores are no longer "full-line, everything for everybody stores." They no longer can be counted on "to have it if anybody has it in the marketplace." Today this convenience position is held by the regional mall, except perhaps for groceries and some hard goods stores. In Japan, by way of contrast, the Japanese department store seems still to be the centre of the Japanese retail community.

There are many retailers attempting to offer extra convenience in terms of **access, transaction processing speed**, or **shopping ease**. While general merchants often seem to have lost the convenience edge, grocery retailers are working hard at achieving or maintaining it with superstores and other formats. This makes a lot of sense because of customer expectations. In the grocery trade, for example, recent analysis of A.C. Nielsen data suggests the growing importance of convenience in North American society today. A study in the United States found that Americans spend 15 percent of their food money on takeout foods from all sources—a much increased percentage showing interest in convenience. In Canada, convenience stores are growing rapidly and now account for roughly 5 percent of the Canadian total of grocery sales. The top selling items in grocery stores today are all convenience-oriented items, such as tetrapak fruit drinks, frozen breakfasts, and microwavable meat pies. Another example of the convenience-seeking nature of the customer today in the grocery trade is a 1988 finding by POPAI (Point of Purchase Advertising Institute) that 69 percent of American shoppers do not make shopping lists before going grocery shopping, but prefer instead to make their decisions in-store, likely because that is more convenient for them.

All retailers do not need to be the "most convenient" to customers. Some retailers have achieved the coveted **destination store** status, which means that customers plan trips to them and will overlook a certain measure of inconvenience to get there or to shop there. However, most aspects of convenience are important parts of all retailers' offers. Convenience holds great potential for the creative marketer simply because all its dimensions have yet to be exploited.

## Customer Care

A third way to get a differential competitive edge is through customer care, which is the term that is used throughout this book to include and go beyond what many people call customer service. **Customer care** is more than providing services such as alterations, gift wrapping, or credit; it refers to the total way in which a retailer manages relationships with his or her customers. It is not just what is done for customers, but also how it is done. All retailers are in the customer care business, even those who profess they are self-service, because all retailers must manage relationships with customers.

Retail marketers must make choices about how to manage encounters with customers, what standards to have, and what overall systems to put in place to ensure appropriate relationships with customers. (This is discussed in more detail in Chapter 9.) Care strategies may be considered in terms of relative level, extent of personal interaction, and extent of customization.

A large variety of customer care levels is possible. Exceptionally high customer care, for example, is a point of strong competitive advantage for L. L. Bean and Nordstrom. In 1989, Nordstrom's sales increased to $2.8 billion in 59 apparel and shoe specialty department stores that were founded on superior customer care. With a sales average of more than $400 per square foot, Nordstrom's performance gets attention from other retailers, but their management has been reluctant to talk about efforts in customer care, as evidenced by this remark by Bruce Nordstrom, one of the three co-chairpersons: "We don't want to talk about our service. We are not as good as our reputation. It is a very fragile thing. You just have to do it every time, every day."[21] In Canada, a retailer becoming known for exceptional customer care and service is Brettons, a large-scale fashion apparel specialty store.

By the same token, a retailer may seek competitive advantage by *reducing* customer care levels. Some retailers have dramatically reduced customer care and service by either eliminating amenities and benefits for customers or transferring tasks such as delivery and assembly to the customer. Twenty years ago, for example, when retailers were busy adding services, Spagg's, a retailer in the Boston area was subtracting them. Spagg's told its customers that only cash would be accepted, that items would not be price-marked, and that items left in cut-open cases would have to be selected by customers and taken home in their own (or purchased) shopping bags. Many discounters have followed this lead.

Providing the highest possible level of customer care is not always appropriate. Instead (as will be discussed in Chapter 9), a retailer should seek to meet, even exceed customer expectations for customer care for a particular type of store and particular category of merchandise and services. These expectations vary greatly according to a variety of circumstances.

Another dimension of customer care is the combination of **personal and impersonal delivery of services** to the customer. Service need not be entirely personal; but some customers highly value personal interaction with salespeople who help make selections, provide product information, and generally make them feel good about their selection or decision to buy. Such customers view the shopping trip as more than just obtaining products to take home. Many of the elderly members of the population, in particular, value such personal interactions with salespeople and are upset if this is no longer available. Other customers seem to prefer avoiding personal interaction with salespeople, claiming that they would rather encounter a good informative display than wait interminably for a woefully uninformed and surly salesclerk. Caring for customers' needs can happen in a variety of ways. This is the reasoning behind point-of-order terminals in the catalogue showroom stores of Best Products. These terminals tell the customer what is in-stock, increase the transaction speed, alert the warehouse to pick stock for delivery before the customer has even paid for it, and increase sales of related items. Similarly, retailers such as Florsheim Shoes are experimenting with interactive videos in place of on-floor salespeople.

A third dimension of customer care is the **extent of relationship customization** that occurs. This describes the extent to which customers' needs are treated individually rather than in a programmed, "one-set-of-rules-for-all" way. For instance, many apparel stores now offer personal shopping services for their "better" customers. Personal shoppers pre-select wardrobes, sometimes special-order garments and accessories, and then may even present these to the customer during off-hours or in the customer's home or place of work. This approach differs from an approach that offers everyone free gift wrapping in its obvious degree of customization.

Customer care is a topic of great interest throughout retailing today and will undoubtedly continue to intrigue and puzzle retailers in the years ahead as customers become more demanding. Major challenges on this topic include finding and keeping enough suitable, on-floor salespeople and finding ways to offer increased customer care with fewer people. Demographics and the traditional low pay, low status, and low job satisfaction of such jobs are combining to bedevil retail marketers.

## Information

All customers need and expect **information** about assortment, price, the retail marketer's practices, and so on. There are a great variety of ways to provide this information, ranging from mass media advertising, promotion, in-store signs and displays, personal selling, and direct marketing (as will be discussed in more detail in Chapter 10). Information strategies may be considered on two major dimensions: amount of information provided and delivery.

Some retailers have sought competitive advantage by being superior in the *amount* of information they provide. For example, as discussed in Chapter 1, IKEA is now the world's largest furniture store chain. While its merchandising approach is distinctive in many ways, a key method used is to provide a lot of information about its products. Its yearly catalogue minutely details much of the 15 000 SKU assortment and allows individuals to prepare for a shopping trip; customers can measure space in rooms against dimensions given in the catalogue, can see which pieces fit with which, can read about the construction of articles and the quality levels determined by use-tests, and so on. In short, as shown in this example, a lot of the risks inherent in furniture buying are eliminated, or at least reduced, by providing information.

Another similar and related dimension of providing information is the *way* in which it is provided. This may include such aspects as "media vehicles," scheduling, the amount of effort customers must expend to get information, and the extent to which the information is provided personally (such as by salespeople) or impersonally (such as by in-store displays). An English firm established in 1976, The Body Shop, is committed to a comprehensive program of provision of information. Now in thirty-three countries, The Body Shop was created, according to Mary Krierke, on the notion that "The others are all talking about 'beauty'. We've eliminated the word. We want to align ourselves with the health industry. For the cosmetic industry to survive into the next century, it has to go the route of health."[22] The Body Shop focuses on wellness and health as beauty; it does not use media advertising, but rather carefully orchestrated publicity and lots of in-store informational campaigns to stress its integrity in assortment decisions, its product ingredients and use, its basic values and concern about cruelty to animals, and so on. Every salesperson is trained and tested on human anatomy knowledge relevant to the 350 SKU assortment. All products are offered with information sheets describing suitable users and uses. Further information is available on request from the store product file on such issues as exact product ingredients. The last tier of information available to customers, if necessary, is the U.K. chemist who created the product.

There are a great variety of direct marketers. Cataloguers, for instance, are tapping into the tremendous desire in the marketplace for information about products and services. Catalogues are not merely for the time-poor and the shut-in markets; they are a source of market information that a growing proportion of the population seems to like. Some cataloguers are superb in blending theatre, art, and information into an entertaining, enticing whole.

## Value

A fifth way to get a differential competitive edge is through the **price/value** relationship, which is not necessarily "discount retailing." The basic idea behind "value" is to give more benefits per dollar spent and/or shopping effort expended than do competitors. Retail marketers must make strategic choices about the price–benefit relationship, whether to offer everyday-low-pricing (EDLP) or regular-special pricing, and, of course, many choices about price points and price changes. (These decisions will be discussed in more detail in Chapter 11.)

One strategic approach to value retailing is to **add value** through enhanced products and services. There are many possibilities, including product modification, rebates for parking costs, personal shopping counselling, and post-purchase use instruction. Nissan recently offered purchasers of its 300ZX sportscar a two-day "high-performance driving" course as part of the purchase price. Retailers following this approach look for ways to add benefits that customers value highly but that cost the retailer relatively less than the perceived value to the customer. In other words, the idea is to add something the customer values at, say, $1.00, but that costs the retailer, say, $0.50.

Another approach is to **reduce prices** for the assortment offered by reducing overhead and/or buying costs. Any lower price strategy must be founded on (a) better buying and/or (b) higher volume and/or (c) reduced overhead via lower service levels and reduced amenities and/or (d) increased operating efficiencies. The discounters, such as Kmart; the off-pricers, such as TJMaxx; the warehouse clubs, such as Price Club; and the catalogue showrooms, such as Consumers Distributing, to name but a few, have all attempted to gain a competitive edge through sharp pricing, either "special limited time prices," "everyday-low-prices," or declining prices determined through an "automatic" markdown scheme such as that made famous by Filene's basement years ago.

There is a large segment of the population, not necessarily those with lower incomes, that will trade ambiance, convenience, and effort in exchange for lower prices. Increasingly, the market is fragmenting so much that the value offer will inevitably be redefined and segmented again and again. Particularly as the population ages, many people now will make a different trade-off of effort versus money than they did in the past. These people are older, wealthier, and busier, so where once they gladly traded time and effort to save money (travelled to out-of-the-way locations, accepted self-serve formats, coped with unassembled products, bagged their own groceries, and carried cash instead of credit cards), they will now happily pay extra to save time and effort. (Note, however, that such things as an economic recession will cause most customers to re-examine their notions of value.)

Value/price is a difficult way to achieve a competitive edge. Retail history is full of stories of the rise and fall of firms that based their strategy solely on price. Value must be conceived of as more than price. Reducing prices alone appears to be a vulnerable strategy over time because someone always finds a way to undercut the price leader eventually.

## Experience

The sixth way of achieving a differential competitive edge is through providing an exciting, even novel, shopping **experience**. Retail marketers do this by manipulating sensory stimulation (all senses are possible), particularly in-store (as will be discussed in detail in Chapter 12). Experience strategies may be considered on three dimensions: retail format novelty, atmospherics, and extent of surprise.

**Retail format novelty** means appealing to customers' desires for something new and different. For example, current experiments with non-store electronic retailing such as Comp-U-Card and The Home Shopping Network are more than just new technologies from the customers' viewpoint. They are different ways to do the familiar task of shopping and hence are often initially tried "just to see what it is like."

Creating differentiation through **atmospherics** is a much-used approach to retail differentiation. However, this is getting harder and harder to do—and much more expensive. Essentially, atmospherics involves the use of exciting, unusual store design, dramatic visual merchandising, and a host of sensory stimuli. For example, Banana Republic, a division of The Gap, has been known for its delightful fantasy interiors, as has The Limited's femininely seductive Victoria's Secret. Fast food operators seek to vent their cooking odours into the corridors of malls to entice consumption while other retailers use perfumes and lighting and music to win customers.

Another way to differentiate the shopping experience is on the basis of **surprise**. For example, some stores are renowned for being unpredictable in the merchandise they carry, the promotions they run, their in-store events, and so on. Military surplus stores have long realized the draw of strange merchandise. Some discounters, such as Toronto's Honest Ed's, have managed to surprise and delight customers with outrageous decor and promotion. Many shopping malls regularly schedule unannounced "happenings" to add spice to the shopping experience. All of these approaches are intended to add excitement to shopping, a task that many customers view as simply tedious. There is a danger, of course, in constant change. Many retailers have learned, to their dismay, that many of their customers resist change and would prefer long-term consistency rather than change that is seemingly for change's sake.

Despite all these attempts to add to the shopping experience, unfortunately, customers often seem to get bored and jaded quickly. Hungry for new experiences, they constantly seek them out, which means the life cycles of most forms of shopping experience are very short. Still, there is constant experimentation with the experience dimensions of retailing. There is a danger that experience may be elevated to first place in management's concerns, to the point that they forget they are retailers of goods and services. A dramatic illustration of this elevation of the shopping experience is Canada's West Edmonton Mall, the much-publicized prototype of the mega-entertainment mall. This 710-store behemoth is an experience, with its amusement park, submarine rides, and so on, and tourists flock to it. But there are rumblings that it is not a proportionately strong retail sales machine—and it needs to be to support the incredible investment that has been made.

In conclusion, there are six basic dimensions for retail differentiation and several alternatives for each. Exhibit 2.2 provides a summary of retail differentiation.

*Exhibit 2.2*
*Retail*
*Competitive*
*Differentiation*
*Summary*

---

**1. Assortment**

    **a.** Uniqueness

    **b.** Dominance

    **c.** Opportunism

**2. Convenience**

    **a.** Save time

    **b.** Save effort

**3. Customer Care**

    **a.** Level

    **b.** Personal/Impersonal

    **c.** Extent of customization

**4. Information**

    **a.** Amount

    **b.** Delivery

**5. Value**

    **a.** Add value

    **b.** Reduce price

**6. Experience**

    **a.** Novelty

    **b.** Atmospherics

    **c.** Surprise

---

## Positioning

We have briefly examined the major dimensions of a retail marketing strategy: market choice, target market selection, and competitive differentiation method. A way to combine these dimensions into a statement of strategy is called **retail competitive positioning**, meaning the way in which specific customer segments are targeted with differentiated offers. Any retail marketer should be able to enunciate his or her positioning strategy in a paragraph. Positioning can refer to both the *efforts of the marketer,* such as choice of target segment and package of benefits to offer to that segment, and the *perceptions of the customer(s)* as to the way competitive offerings relate one to another. This latter conception of positioning is often used in advertising situations as a way to understand the mental maps of stores and brands that customers use to distinguish one from another. As shown in Figure 2.2, retail competitive positioning achieved is a result of how the strategic choices made interact with the marketplace.

---

### FIGURE 2.2

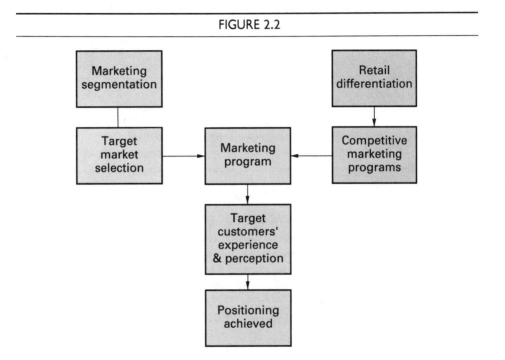

Customers make choices among the competitive retailers they encounter on the basis of dimensions they themselves feel are important. No retail marketer can be superior on all possible positioning dimensions; not only do these positioning dimensions change over time, but so do the ways customers value performance along them. Thus, positioning is not a static concept.

**Repositioning** is a term that suggests either the marketer or the customer or both have shifted the relative position of a particular store, product, or service. Generally speaking, this is more difficult to do than initial positioning. It is important to recognize that all stores, products, and services tend to be positioned in the minds of customers or potential customers, regardless of any explicit effort by a retail marketer to position them. Some firms attempt to position their offering (a *proactive stance*), while other retailers let their customers position it for them (a *reactive stance*); and then they may attempt to reinforce this achieved position.

Sherwin Williams, for example, repositioned their paint and wallcoverings stores on the basis of "something for all six walls in a room," which led them to add carpets and other products and services. Similarly, Beaver Lumber, Canada's leading retailer of lumber and building materials to the contractor and do-it-yourself market, with 158 outlets, responded to the 1990–91 recession by repositioning toward the front-end retail business as opposed to the back-end contractor business. The former offered higher margins and more growth as new home construction dropped and renovations increased. President Murray Bozniak explained:

> Beaver is approaching the recession differently than most companies. In general, there are two strategies: defensive and offensive. Defensive is fire-fighting. We're taking the aggressive approach because we're actively gaining market share. We hope to come out of this downturn of 18 or 24 months in a solid position.[23]

Retail positioning and repositioning requires careful retail customer analysis and segmentation analysis to choose target markets; it requires careful competitive analysis and self-analysis to choose a differentiation strategy. In other words, retail market positioning is the underlying core of a retail marketing strategy. Stanton Cort summed up the sentiment from a conference of retailers on this topic as follows:

> Though their wording differed, both the retailers and the shopping center developers emphasized two common strategies for successful operation in the future market. First, the retailer must develop a clearly focussed concept of the operations to attract some specific target customer group. Then the retailer must implement that concept better than existing or potential competitors.[24]

Robert Gill, vice-chairperson and chief operating officer for J.C. Penney, when interviewed by *Stores* about the retail outlook for 1991, was quoted about J.C. Penney's positioning plans as follows:

> The 1991 consumer will be thinking thrifty, meaning looking for value and avoiding waste. Impulsive, indulgent shopping will be left behind. Designer labels, upscaling and higher prices will be far less important. In a broad shift to the thrifty '90's from the greedy '80's Americans will want their own personal style, reflecting substance, authenticity, and the real thing.
>
> At Penney's, next year's strategy will center around an intensified private label effort, backed by 100 quality control inspectors; lifestyle marketing to link Penney merchandising, visual presentation, customer service and advertising, and incremental use of a $1 billion, five year expansion and renovation program.
>
> The theme of the national television commercials is "J.C. Penney—Where Fashion Comes to Life". The messages depict the store and our merchandise as being part of real people's everyday lifestyle.

Our goal is to create a distinct position for Penney that reasserts our traditional reputation for value and authenticity. We want to set ourselves apart from other department stores and provide consumers a reason to shop, buy, and stay with us.[25]

## RETAIL MARKETING STRATEGY DECISION-MAKING

Two important points remain in this discussion of retail marketing strategy. First, this chapter may give the impression that retail marketing is a mechanistic, orderly field amenable to formularized thinking. Nothing could be further from the reality of retail marketing. In fact, perhaps the concept of planning itself is somewhat misleading. Henry Mintzberg distinguished "crafting strategy" from "planning strategy." His concept applies well to retail marketing strategy:

Imagine someone planning strategy. What likely springs to mind is an image of orderly thinking. . . . Now imagine someone crafting strategy. A wholly different image likely results, as different from planning as craft is from mechanization. Craft involves traditional skill, dedication, perfection through the mastery of detail. What springs to mind is not so much thinking and reason as involvement, a feeling of intimacy and harmony with the materials at hand, developed through long experience and commitment. Formulation and implementation merge into a fluid process of learning through which creative strategies evolve . . . the crafting image better captures the process by which effective strategies come to be. . . . Strategies can form as well as be formulated. . . . Sometimes they [people] can be smarter by allowing their strategies to develop gradually through the organization's actions and experiences . . . an additional view of the strategist as a pattern recognizer, a learner if you will who manages a process in which strategies (and visions) can emerge as well as be deliberately conceived. . . . To manage strategy then at least in the first instance is not so much to promote change as to know when to do so.[26]

The final point about achieving excellent marketing performance has to do with how a marketing strategy is integrated into all other activities of the company, as is exemplified in the following discussion of Benetton, the casual-clothing company.

## BENETTON'S INTEGRATED APPROACH

Benetton is a high-profile manufacturer and retailer of casual clothing, particularly woollen sweaters and cotton knitwear. Its growth has been startling. That growth, and the firm's four rags-to-riches Italian founders and their two-decade-plus corporate history, make fascinating material for the press. But there is much behind the success of this organization of more than a dozen chains and four thousand stores worldwide that isn't often discussed in the newspaper articles. The single most important reason for the firm's success appears to be the way it has integrated marketing into its overall corporate strategy and activities.

Benetton's concept of retailing is to make space, money, inventory, and people more productive. Its owners have done this with a highly interrelated strategy for dealing with the great uncertainties of a fashion-oriented business. Benetton uses small stores (the great majority are franchised) that impose a kind of discipline on everyone. There is little room for storage of inventory. The stock has to be replenished flexibly and fast, yet at a reasonable cost. There is really no place for the sales employees to hide in a store. This store size and format is entirely controlled by Benetton. They approve the site, offer three interior design options, provide the fixtures, and decide on the merchandise mix. In short, they operate a highly controlled franchise system run by Benetton agents working on commission. The method of operations is not dissimilar from that of some of our best fast food operations.

There's even more to their marketing approach. They offer a fashion basic item with appeal across national boundaries. Their designs are simple and the colours vivid. Their stores are colour-blocked, presenting a palette of basic and in-vogue fashion colours to the customer. While the emphasis is on self-service, staff are active on the floor. Much of their time, by the way, is spent refolding and replacing merchandise on the shelves—each garment must be folded and displayed in a certain way. Most Benetton stores have excellent housekeeping. Again, because the store size is small this is easier. Promotion and advertising aim to reach fashion-conscious "actives," 18 to 40 year olds interested in casual wear, and focus on the store itself rather than on individual items. The company concentrates on a few very basic items such as pullovers and sweatshirts, injecting a small (but significant to the customer) flourish of colour or print. In this way, Benetton adds high value to the customer but at low cost. Items are sold essentially on a low-margin, high-volume basis.

This marketing strategy would not be sufficient if it were not supported by a strong operations and logistics strategy. Benetton is the world's leading consumer of wool, which it can source as economically as anyone. Benetton's production process is a dual one. First, it involves speculation about quantity and style of order by retailers far in advance of sale to allow Benetton to produce at low cost. Second, it involves postponement of orders (at additional cost) to allow the retailers to respond as market circumstances change. Basic stock orders (about 80 percent of orders) are placed seven months ahead. Benetton produces these *in greggio* (undyed form) then dyes the whole garment (rather than the yarn) closer to the actual selling season. Benetton also prepares the "flash collection" (about 10 percent of orders)— about fifty fabric-style-colour items allowed to be added to the line very close to the season based on early sales results; and allows a "reassortment" order (about 10 percent of orders) during the season, which are fill-in orders with a five-week turnaround from order to factory to store. To be both a low-cost producer and a highly responsive producer is accomplished through extensive mechanization, a total reformulation of the garment fabrication and dyeing process, and extensive subcontracting. This results in economies of production, very flexible capacity, and relatively low capital investment. Quality is centrally controlled.

Benetton replaces inventory with information by linking its agents electronically with the factory, developing a process for rapid replenishment of the most popular items with premium transport (up to 20 percent of the items), and having an economic system for handling conventional in-quantity orders. All merchandise is preticketed in the currency of the country of destination with electronically processable codes. Physical distribution is further supported by state-of-the-art warehousing.

The company's financial strategy is also interesting. Basically, it has passed much of the risk on to its retailers and contractors for capital investments in store fixtures, manufacturing facilities, and equipment. This has freed Benetton to use its resources to greatest effect and to grow remarkably fast. Although Benetton does finance nearly all retail inventories, such inventories are easy to finance because they are guaranteed sales under Benetton's no-return policy.

All of these elements of strategy combine to give Benetton an advantage over its competitors in most markets; but even Benetton is vulnerable. Its strategy was far more competitively advantageous in Europe than in the United States, which it entered in 1983, and where it appears to have expanded too fast and somewhat carelessly—U.S. licensees complained about too many Benetton stores being placed too close together.

## CONCLUSION

Retailers formulate retail programs with regard for market definition and choice, market segmentation, differentiation, and positioning. There are many ways to approach each of these strategic dimensions of retail marketing, which will be elaborated in the remaining chapters, especially Chapter 13. Formulating retail marketing strategy requires both creativity and hard work. The process may be summarized as follows:

1. Identify the current strategy in terms of target segment(s) and the six dimensions of retail strategy (assortment, convenience, information, care, value, experience).
2. Evaluate the performance of the current strategy (what is working well and what is not and why).
3. Compare the performance achieved with the desired performance.
4. Examine marketplace circumstances and trends for opportunities and threats.
5. Examine corporate strengths and weaknesses.
6. Identify what decision alternatives can be considered.
7. Evaluate the merits and implications of these alternatives.
8. Decide what to do.
9. Decide how to implement the decisions.
10. Decide how to prepare for the next round of decisions.

## REVIEW QUESTIONS

Suppose you wished to open a store catering to big and tall men's apparel needs. You would know that all large men differ in their body proportions too. For example, some large men may be considered "athletic," which means they have different body proportions than other large men. The "drop" (difference between upper body and waist) is more extreme for athletic men, averaging 8–10 inches as opposed to a more normal six inches (for example, a size 40 jacket with a size 32 pants is an 8 inch drop). Suppose you have discovered that the big and tall merchandise available to you comes in sizes of 46 to 60 regular and long, 42 to 70 portly short, regular, and long in a variety of basics and fashion apparel, including outerwear. You could carry both sportswear and working clothes. To the extent that you can, with such limited information, speculatively address the following questions:

1. How would you segment the market?
2. What assortment strategy would make sense?
3. What convenience strategy would make sense?
4. What information strategy would make sense?
5. What customer care strategy would make sense?
6. What value strategy would make sense?
7. What experience strategy would make sense?
8. What would you name your store?

## KEY TERMS

- types of merchandise carried
- ownership
- location
- type of store
- convenience goods
- shopping goods
- specialty goods
- functions
- ego-involvement
- size
- merchandise line breadth
- merchandise line depth
- extent of value-added
- market choice
- target market selection
- competitive differentiation
- geography
- type of customers
- retail market segmentation
- market segment aggregation
- customer descriptors
- descriptors of customer responses
- product–service offering
- cost–price ratio
- related marketing efforts
- assortment
- dominance
- power assortments
- opportunistic buying
- convenience
- access
- transaction processing speed
- shopping ease
- destination store
- customer care
- personal and impersonal delivery of services
- extent of relationship customization
- information
- value
- experience
- retail competitive positioning
- repositioning

## NOTES

1. Janice Castro, "No Holds Barred," *Time*, April 11, 1988, pp. 40–42.

2. As quoted in *Stores*, January 1991.

3. Wilfred Posluns, "Three Ways to Profit in Today's Environment: Segmentation of the Market," Retail Council of Canada Annual Convention, 1983.

4. Bert C. McCammon, Jr., "The New Strategic Era in Retailing," Annual Convention of the National Retail Merchants Association, 1984.

5. Isadore Barmash, "How They Plan," *Stores*, September 1983, pp. 7–15.

6. M.E. Porter, "From Competitive Advantage to Corporate Strategy," *Harvard Business Review*, May–June 1987, pp.43–59.

7. F.D. Wiersema, "Strategic Marketing: Linking Marketing and Corporate Planning," *European Journal of Marketing* 17 (June 1983), pp. 46–56.

8. For example, see J. Barry Mason and M.L. Mayer, "Strategic Planning: The Search for Differential Advantage," in *Modern Retailing*, (Plano, Texas: Business Publications Inc., 1987), chapter 4.

9. William R. King, "Using Strategic Issues Analysis," in *Long Range Planning*, 1982, pp. 45–49.

10. M.E. Porter, "The Structure Within Industries and Companies' Performance," *The Review of Economics and Statistics*, May 1979, pp. 214–227.

11. Melvin T. Copeland, "Relation of Consumers' Buying Habits to Marketing Methods," *Harvard Business Review*, April 1923, pp. 282–89.

12. L.P. Bucklin, "Retail Strategy and the Classification of Consumer Goods," *Journal of Marketing*, January 1963, pp. 50–55.

13. S.C. Hollander, "Who Does the Work of Retailing?" *Journal of Marketing*, July 1964, pp. 18–22.

14. W.R. Davidson and A.L. Rogers, "Changes and Challenges in Retailing," *Business Horizons*, January–February 1981. See also: J.M. Hawes and W.F. Crittenden, "A Taxonomy of Competitive Retailing Strategies," *Strategic Management Journal* 5 (1984), pp. 275–87, and W.R. Davidson, A.D. Bates, and S.J. Bass, "The Retail Life Cycle," *Harvard Business Review*, November–December 1976, pp. 89–96.

15. Helen Galland, "Specialty Store Retailing," Retail Council of Canada Annual Convention, April 1981.

16. Alasdair McKichan, "Management Skills in Retailing—1985," *Business Quarterly*, Spring 1986, pp. 105–9.

17. Wilfred Posluns, "Three Ways To Profit in Today's Environment: Segmentation of the Market," Retail Council of Canada Annual Convention, 1983.

18. A.I. Cohen and A.L. Jones, "Brand Marketing in the New Retail Environment," *Harvard Business Review*, November–December 1978, pp. 141–48.

19. S.G. Cort, "Focussed Retailing" from the seminar New Thrusts in Retailing, Harvard Business School, June 1973.

20. Joan Bergman, "Nordstrom Gets the Gold," *Stores*, January 1990, pp. 44–76.

21. Ibid.

22. Mary Krierke, "The Body Shop: Natural Beauty," *Stores*, September 1987, pp. 92–97.

23. "Beaver Lumber: Hamering Out New Possibilities," *Canadian Retailer*, December–January 1990–91, p. 23.

24. S.G. Cort, "Focussed Retailing" from the seminar New Thrusts in Retailing, Harvard Business School, June 1973.

25. Isadore Barmash, "Disquieting Times in 1991," *Stores*, December 1990, pp. 13–19.

26. Henry Mintzberg, "Crafting Strategy," *Harvard Business Review*, July–August 1987, pp. 66–75.

CHAPTER

# RETAIL MARKETING PERFORMANCE

## ■ INTRODUCTION

**Retail performance assessment** means determining how well or how poorly a retail operation is doing or might do in the future relative to some standard of comparison, either internally or externally derived. It is the very important step decision-makers must go through before formulating and implementing managerial changes. Retail marketers assess retail performance to determine whether changes are required, to assist in selecting the most promising actions for management, and to help predict the likely outcomes of changes if they are implemented.

While a bottom line measure, such as net profit, reveals overall performance, it does not advise management on how to improve the bottom line. Managers need to know how well various parts of the operation are performing and why. The sorts of decisions retail marketers face include: (a) Should the merchandise mix be changed? (b) Should existing selling space be reduced? and (c) Should the store be redesigned? Such questions cannot be answered solely with overall bottom line measures, which means retail marketers need a variety of ways to decompose performance.

Much attention has been focused lately on "excellence" in management. Excellence is a judgment based on various performance measures across companies and industries. One of the findings in these studies of excellence is that excellent managements understand the critical performance dimensions of their business and constantly strive to improve upon them. Retail performance is assessed both to set managerial goals and to measure progress against those goals. Performance assessment helps focus efforts on the most important parts of a retail business by dramatizing the key dimensions of success. Performance assessment is necessary for all retailers: it doesn't matter how big the organization is, whether it is publicly or privately owned, whether it has a broad or limited assortment, or whether it is a single- or multi-unit operation.

It is important to recognize that retail performance assessment occurs at several different levels in a firm. The measures used and the use to which they are put vary greatly by level. At the **firm level**, overall measures of both financial performance (such as return on common equity) and marketing performance (such as image positioning in the competitive marketplace) are used. At the various **operations levels** (divisions, regions, stores, departments), performance measures relating to the use of assets by these units, such as dollar contribution per square metre or square foot of selling space, are used. Similarly, at the many **merchandising levels** (groups, classifications, categories, lines, items), performance measures related to buying and selling, such as gross margin return on investment in inventory and direct product profitability, are used.

The intent of this chapter is to illustrate the most common and most important performance measures, used primarily at the firm, store, and merchandise levels. Most of the measures listed can be adapted to other levels. Performance assessment in retail marketing is an ongoing effort. Some measures are taken continuously, others annually; and some occur at intervals in-between. While most of the measures discussed in this chapter appear to be annual, they can all be adapted to a shorter or longer time period.

There are many more possible measures of performance than are described in this chapter. For example, a retail marketer may wish to monitor the firm's performance with regard to environmental behaviour, treatment of minorities, or any other area of concern. Despite the apparent focus on financial performance in this discussion, the approaches outlined in this chapter can be broadened to address these sorts of situations as well.

## MODELS OF PERFORMANCE

■
SECTION
■
ONE
■

## THE RETAIL PROFIT DYNAMIC

Retail marketers are usually interested in making money, in achieving an acceptable return on investment in inventory, space, people, and other assets. It is important, therefore, to understand how retailers do make money. This understanding provides the basis for making appropriate marketing decisions and evaluating their likely or actual impact on retail profitability. A starting place is to address some simple but powerful questions as shown in Figure 3.1.

FIGURE 3.1

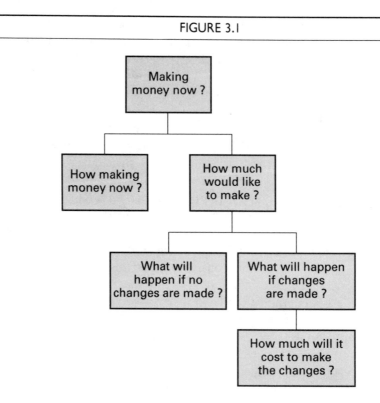

This chart also demonstrates that the appropriate focus of attention is future performance, with or without changes in marketing method. This is more relevant than comparing last period's results with next period's results.

Figure 3.2 shows the profit dynamic for most retailers. Each component is explained in detail in this chapter, for each component can affect and be affected by the marketing and financial strategy of the retailer. This schematic allows one to isolate the major contributors to retail profitability and then in turn to focus on the major marketing approaches to affecting these components. Changes in marketing strategy can be and should be related directly to this profit dynamic to ascertain which of the myriad things that a retailer could do are most worth doing. In short, the profit dynamic is a way to diagnose performance and predict future performance.

Table 3.1 shows some sample numbers to indicate different paths to profitability. Each of the columns shows a different scenario increasing the return on investment from 9 percent to 12 percent. To realize each scenario would require a different marketing emphasis; for example, increasing the yield may involve more aggressive sales efforts in the store. Obviously, these numbers are merely for illustration—and indicate the need for careful analysis in each specific situation.

As various numbers are calculated, retail marketers can gain insights into the *sensitivity* of the ultimate performance measure of the changes, enabling them to determine which activities or changes are most important to success. The chart is

## FIGURE 3.2

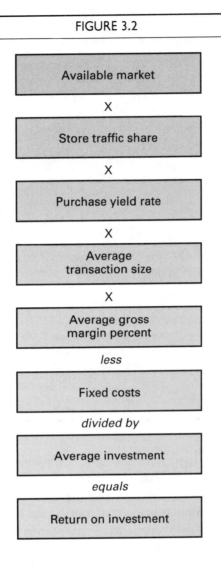

illustrative of only *some* of the approaches that could be taken. For example, the possibility of reducing fixed costs is not depicted in the chart.

The **available market** refers to the market size (expressed as the number of potential customers) to which a retailer has access. The size is based on nature of the assortment, store location(s), reach of advertising and promotion, and the saturation level of other trade area competition. Retailers may decide to seek ways to increase their "natural" market size. A car dealer in a small town, for example, may decide to discount dramatically and advertise this in a nearby major city in hopes of attracting nonresidents of the town to the dealership. In other words, the retailer must balance the costs of seeking a wider market with the returns likely from that broader market. Should a retailer locate in a high-traffic but high-rent store or in a lower-traffic, lower-rent store? Often, retailers find it more profitable to focus on

TABLE 3.1
The Retail Profit Model and Various Ways to Achieve 12% ROI

| | Base | Market up 10% | Traffic up 10% | Yield up 10% | Trans. Size up 10% | GM up 10% |
|---|---|---|---|---|---|---|
| 1. Available Mkt | 10 000 | 11 000 | 10 000 | 10 000 | 10 000 | 10 000 |
| × | | | | | | |
| 2. Traffic Share | 25% | 25% | 28% | 25% | 25% | 25% |
| = | | | | | | |
| Store Traffic | 2500 | 2750 | 2750 | 2500 | 2500 | 2500 |
| × | | | | | | |
| 3. Yield Rate | 50% | 50% | 50% | 55% | 50% | 50% |
| = | | | | | | |
| No. of Purchases | 1250 | 1375 | 1375 | 1375 | 1250 | 1250 |
| × | | | | | | |
| 4. Transaction Size | $25 | $25 | $25 | $25 | $28 | $25 |
| = | | | | | | |
| Revenue | $31 250 | $34 375 | $34 375 | $34 375 | $34 375 | $31 250 |
| × | | | | | | |
| 5. Average GM | 40% | 40% | 40% | 40% | 40% | 44% |
| = | | | | | | |
| Contribution | $12 500 | $13 750 | $13 750 | $13 750 | $13 750 | $13 750 |
| − | | | | | | |
| 6. Fixed Costs | $8 000 | $8 000 | $8 000 | $8 000 | $8 000 | $8 000 |
| Profit | $4 500 | $5 750 | $5 750 | $5 750 | $5 750 | $5 750 |
| ÷ | | | | | | |
| Avg Invmt (cost) | $50 000 | $50 000 | $50 000 | $50 000 | $50 000 | $50 000 |
| = | | | | | | |
| ROI | 9% | 12% | 12% | 12% | 12% | 12% |

increasing yield rates from their current traffic than on increasing market size or store traffic share. When considering available market, one might think of the basic marketing task as market expansion.

**Store traffic share** refers to the number of customers (expressed as a percentage of the available market) that enter the store or otherwise initiate contact with the retailer. This percentage is affected by the effectiveness of the advertising and promotion and other forms of communication, the draw of store facilities design and exterior signage, shopping frequency of customers, hours, and referrals. Retailers may decide to focus efforts on improving traffic share by means of vigorous promotions, continuity programs, aggressive pricing on draw items, and so on. From this vantage point, the marketing task is to improve penetration of the available market.

**Purchase yield rate** refers to the number of potential customers who become actual purchasers (expressed as a percentage of store traffic). This is the task of converting browsers to buyers. Purchase yield is based on layout, in-stock assortment, display and atmospherics to encourage purchasing, personal selling, and overall customer service and care. Above all, it is based on attracting appropriate people into the store in the first place; that is, targeting and attracting the right potential customers so that, in-store, they are more easily converted into buyers.

High traffic and low yield may indicate poor in-store efforts or that inappropriate people are being drawn into the store. A century ago, specialty retailers positioned "floorwalkers" at the doors to screen customers before admitting them to the store. Once admitted, customers were expected (and expected themselves) to buy before leaving. The basic marketing task in this respect is sales and service. The concepts of available market, store traffic share, and yield relate to one another as shown in Figure 3.3.

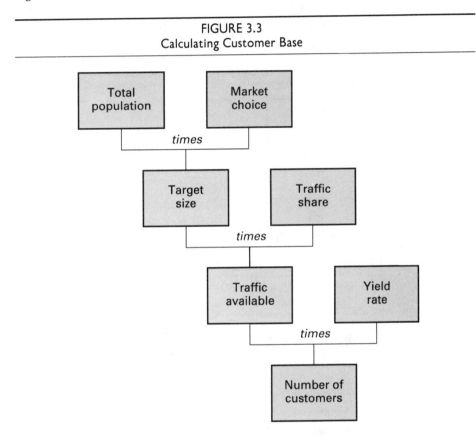

**FIGURE 3.3**
**Calculating Customer Base**

**Average transaction size** refers to the dollar amount of the average transaction. It is based upon the assortment, item pricing levels, and all the factors that affect purchase yield. For example, if the assortment strategy includes related items, then salespeople have the opportunity to offer add-on purchases, such as accessories for clothing. Average transaction size focuses attention on the frequent trade-off between "high volume – low prices" and "low volume – high prices." For example, high-service specialty apparel stores offset low traffic flow by relying on cross-selling to increase average transaction size. Again, the basic marketing task is sales and service.

**Average gross margin percentage** refers to the average maintained markup percentage realized on all transactions. This is basically sales revenue less cost of goods sold, with appropriate adjustments to each set of factors. The average gross margin is affected by initial pricing decisions and subsequent markups and mark-downs. It is also crucially affected by the mix of goods and services sold. This is why most retailers find analysis of sales, margins, and costs by category more informative than overall store analysis. A car dealer should analyze each aspect of the operation separately: new cars, leased sales, used car sales, and service, as examples. Gross margin represents contribution to fixed costs and profit and thus is a very important number to understand, track, and manage. The basic marketing task is maintaining margin. Figure 3.4 illustrates how revenues and costs relate to generate contribution to fixed costs and profit.

## FIGURE 3.4
### Calculating Contribution

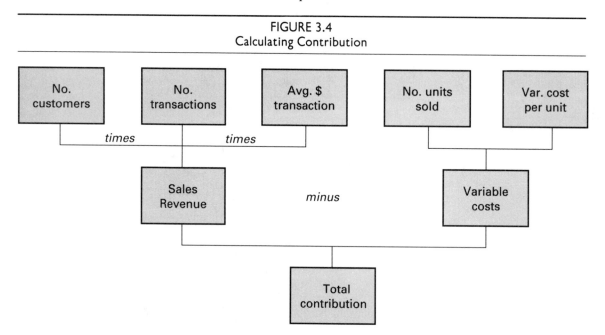

**Fixed costs** refer to all the period operating costs for space, people, inventory, marketing (such as advertising), and other overhead that does not vary according to volume sold or cannot be treated as direct cost of goods sold figures. In other words, these costs are largely independent of the overall quantity of goods sold and of the specific items sold. Retail marketers must control these costs closely. For example, investments in inventory and commitments to occupancy costs are two major fixed cost commitments retailers typically make. Further, many marketing decisions have a direct bearing on fixed costs. A decision, for instance, to increase the number of personal selling staff will impact on the payroll fixed costs. This suggests that one way to think about the basic marketing task is getting sufficient sales and margin impact from the fixed costs expended.

Retail marketers often assess how much business is required to cover their fixed costs (called **breakeven analysis**) or to cover their fixed costs plus a profit target (called **required volume analysis**). Required business may be calculated in unit volumes or dollar volumes. These forms of analysis do not show what volumes will be realized, but rather what must be realized to meet the specified targets under the specific price–cost relationships. Breakeven volume may be calculated using the following formulas:

> $ Fixed costs divided by $ average unit contribution = Breakeven unit volume

> $ Fixed costs divided by average % contribution = Breakeven dollar volume

Required volumes are calculated the same way but dollar target profits are added to the dollar fixed-cost figures. Figure 3.5 summarizes required volume analysis.

FIGURE 3.5
Calculating Required Volumes

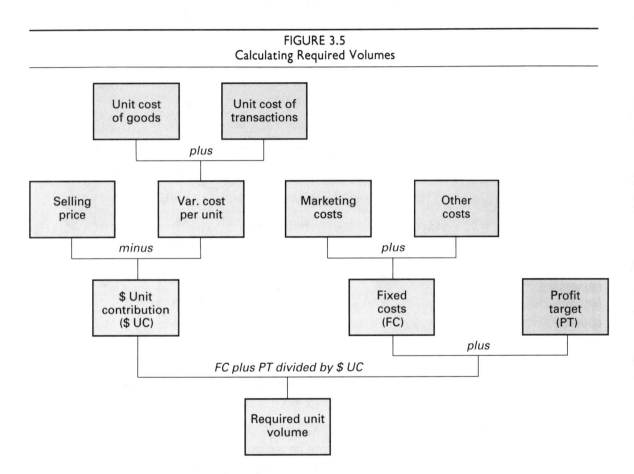

**Average investment** refers to the amount committed to assets such as inventory and real estate. These investments usually transcend any particular annual accounting period and are indications of the basic type of business. A large full-line department store retailer faces very different investment implications than a small convenience store retailer does. Retail marketers frequently make decisions that have not only revenue and cost implications but also investment implications. These investments in turn drive the need to achieve acceptable returns. All retailers of goods must manage inventory turnover carefully, balancing the need to be in-stock with the costs and risks of carrying inventory over time. This suggests another way to think about the basic marketing task—Return on Investment (ROI) management. Figure 3.6 summarizes the ROI approach for retail marketers.

FIGURE 3.6
Calculating ROI

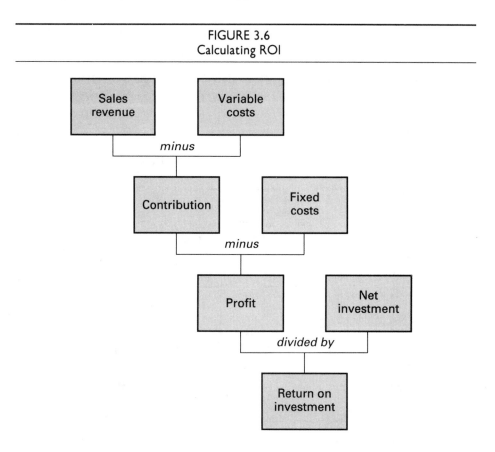

The retail profit dynamic provides a simple but powerful dynamic for understanding the way in which any particular retailer is, or is not, doing well. The profit dynamic model has the following advantages:

1. It focuses attention on the principal financial objectives of the retailer—namely, achieving an adequate return on equity.
2. It identifies the major pathways a retailer can follow to improving return on investment.
3. Finally, it dramatizes the major areas of retail management decision-making—namely, market size choice, market penetration, sales and service, gross margin management, fixed cost management, and ROI management.

The calculations are straightforward, although, as explained elsewhere in this chapter and other parts of the book, the calculations can be made more sophisticated than those presented above. One begins by decomposing a retailer's operations into this profit dynamic to see how the performance actually works. Then, each element of the performance can be examined as to its level relative to goals, history, or the levels achieved by other comparable retailers to determine whether improvement is reasonable and necessary.

## OTHER MODELS OF PERFORMANCE

There are other models of retail performance that provide comparable insights into management. Most notable of these is the Strategic Profit Model (SPM) advanced by Robert Lusch and others.[1]

$$\text{Return on net worth} = \frac{\text{Net profit}}{\text{Net sales}} \times \frac{\text{Net sales}}{\text{Total assets}} \times \frac{\text{Total assets}}{\text{Net Worth}}$$

This model, elegant in its simplicity, is exceedingly powerful because it isolates the three major components of financial success—namely, margin management, asset management, and debt management. These indicate the major marketing and financial pathways to improving Return on Net Worth (RONW).

A related model for assortment planning was proposed by Robert Lusch, and is shown in Figure 3.7.[2]

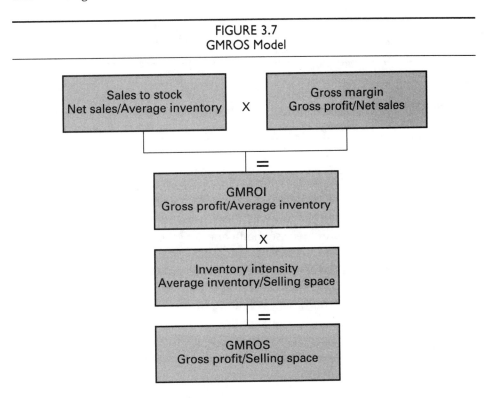

FIGURE 3.7
GMROS Model

The remainder of this chapter deals with various ways to measure and evaluate retail marketing performance—it is an elaboration of the retail profit dynamic and the SPM.

## PERFORMANCE DIMENSIONS AND MEASURES

### PERFORMANCE MEASURES

There are so many individual measures of retail performance that a complete cataloguing of them is not attempted in this chapter. As an illustration, it is interesting to note that Professor Jack Gifford of the University of Miami did a survey of performance indicator usage with a list of 136 different measures.[3] However, it is possible to group performance indicators under five headings, as follows: general financial results, merchandise and merchandising productivity, space productivity, personnel performance, and marketplace performance. These categories are shown in Figure 3.8.

---

**FIGURE 3.8**
**Performance Indicators**

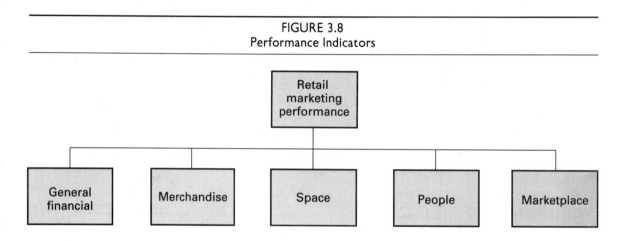

### General Financial Results

The measures used to assess overall financial performance of retail firms are basically the same as those used by the great majority of business firms. These measures are essentially ones of (*a*) **operating performance for a period of time** (typically summarized in an income statement, which can then be transformed into a variety of ratios, such as sales growth percentages); (*b*) **financial position at a point in time** (typically summarized in a balance sheet, which can also be transformed into a series of ratios, such as the current ratio); and (*c*) **changes in financial position** (typically summarized in a cash flow or funds flow statement).[4] Most practitioners agree that the single most important summary measure of a retailer's performance is net profit to net worth (shareholder's equity) (RONW). Exhibit 3.1 shows some of the more common measures used.

### Merchandise and Merchandising Productivity

Merchandise inventory typically represents 40 to 60 percent of a retailer's total assets; and cost of goods sold ranges between 50 to 80 percent of net sales. Accordingly, it is a critical dimension of the retail marketing task to manage well.

EXHIBIT 3.1
General Financial
Performance and
Position
Assessment

## 1. Sales Growth Rate

Change in net sales of one period relative to another period, usually expressed as a percentage. This, and other growth ratios can be adjusted to "real growth" by using an inflation "deflator factor." Measures trends in volume and revenue performance. Can do similar "growth" measures for all indicators over time.

## 2. Profit Margin: Net Profit to Net Sales

Net profit, after tax but before extraordinary items, expressed as a percentage of net sales. Measures amount of net profit produced by each dollar of sales.

## 3. Net Profit to Total Assets

Net profit after tax but before extraordinary items expressed as a percentage of year-end total assets (average total assets could be used). Total assets may or may not include capitalized leases. Measures return on all invested funds by both creditors and equity holders.

## 4. Return on Net Worth: Net Profit to Net Worth

Net profit after tax but before extraordinary items expressed as a percentage of year-end net worth (equity). Measures return on net equity invested.

## 5. Working Capital

Current assets minus current liabilities. Easy measure of liquidity, but can be misleading, depending particularly on salability of inventory.

## 6. Days Receivable

Accounts receivable divided by average daily sales. Measures quality of credit management.

## 7. Days Payable

Accounts payable divided by average daily purchases. Measures quality of account payable and working capital management.

## 8. Current Ratio

Current assets divided by current liabilities. Very common but crude indicator of liquidity.

## 9. Quick (Acid Test) Ratio

Current assets less inventory and prepaid items divided by current liabilities. A tougher test of liquidity.

## 10. Debt Coverage

Net profit before interest and taxes divided by period interest costs. (Can be expanded to be "fixed charges coverage.") A measure of capacity to handle debt and other fixed commitments.

## 11. Earnings Per Common Share

Net profit after tax less preferred dividends divided by number of issued common shares. Used commonly as an indicator of value of shares issued.

Merchandise and merchandising productivity measures help assess all those activities related to selecting and obtaining, storing, pricing, and advertising and promoting the assortment of goods and services offered for sale. On-the-floor selling efforts are included under the Personnel heading because of the personal service dimension of that activity.

Assessing **inventory management performance** is one of the more complex aspects of retail performance assessment. Inventory value is the amount at which the inventory is assessed. Investment in inventory is the value of the inventory less accounts payable for inventory purchases. For example, there are questions of inventory valuation such as the cost method versus the retail method, and book versus physical count (all of which are addressed in Chapter 7). These are issues for the accounting specialists. The important point here is that depending on the method of valuation used—and whether that method is changed—different ratios may result when using the basic formulas shown in Exhibit 3.2. The ratios shown use the term "**average inventory**," which should be the sum of at least two different estimations of inventory value over time (such as opening and ending inventory) divided by the total number of estimations.

*Exhibit 3.2*
*Performance of*
*Merchandise and*
*Merchandising*
*Units*
*Assessment*

1. **Gross Margin Percentage**
   Dollar gross margin divided by dollar net sales expressed as a percentage. An indication of gross profit level, but often not a good indication of contribution level.

2. **Inventory Turnover (also known as Stock Turn)**
   Net sales divided by average inventory at retail (sales to stock ratio) or cost of goods sold divided by average inventory at cost. May also be done on the basis of physical units, which is number of units sold divided by average number of units stocked. Turn is an important way to determine the level and trends in the level of investment in inventory relative to sales generated.

3. **Markdown Percentage**
   Dollar markdowns divided by dollar retail sales expressed as a percentage. An indication of pricing skill and/or salability of merchandise.

4. **Gross Margin Return on Inventory Investment (GMROI)**
   Gross margin divided by average investment in inventory. Investment inventory is best done using a cost method of inventory valuation, but the retail method can be used. Shows the relationship between investment in inventory and gross margin generated by that investment. Points out that the ratio may be improved by increasing turnover and/or by increasing margin and allows analysis of the relative merits of both courses of action.

5. **Direct Product Profit (DPP)**
   Gross margin + payment discounts + merchandising allowances + forward buy profits = adjusted gross margin. Adjusted gross margin − warehouse costs (labour, inventory, space) − transportation costs − store costs (stocking labour, checkout labour, space, inventory) = direct product profit.

   This method is used at an item, category, or department level to refine gross margin to "contribution to profit." Gross margin is adjusted upward, then "direct product costs" are subtracted. The calculation of direct product costs is often difficult and/or the result of arbitrary allocation methods.

### 6. Accounts Payable/Inventory Dollars
Accounts payable (best if averaged) divided by average inventory investment. Provides an indication of the amount of inventory investment financed via vendor credit.

---

The two most powerful measures of merchandise and merchandising performance, Gross Margin Return on Investment in Inventory (GMROI) and Direct Product Profit (DPP), deserve elaboration beyond Exhibit 3.2.

**Gross Margin Return on Investment in Inventory (GMROI)**    Gross margin has traditionally been a very important measure of performance for retailers and is central to most retail pricing decisions. The actual calculation of gross margin can be complicated (see the discussion in Chapter 11). The important point here is that this figure is typically used to summarize the performance of merchandise lines, groups, and departments, and indeed stores and chains. Usually, gross margin is calculated as a percentage of net sales.

A relatively recent elaboration of the gross margin performance approach has been the ratio of gross margin to inventory investment (at cost), which is known as GMROI. GMROI inventory at cost may be calculated by dividing total dollar gross margin by dollar cost of average inventory then multiplying by 100:

$$\text{GMROI at cost} \quad = \quad \frac{\text{Total dollar gross margin}}{\text{Total dollar cost of inventory}} \times 100$$

$$\text{GMROI at cost} \quad = \quad \text{Turnover rate} \times \% \text{ gross margin}$$

$$\text{GMROI at retail} \quad = \quad \frac{\text{Net dollar sales}}{\text{Average inventory at retail}} \times \frac{\text{Total dollar gross margin}}{\text{Net dollar sales}} \times 100$$

**GMROI inventory at retail** can be calculated very easily by multiplying an adjusted turnover rate times gross margin percentage, times 100 to convert to a percentage.

Although inventory can be valued at retail or at cost, using inventory valued at retail is not really an accurate indication of investment cost; but in many organizations it is more readily available than inventory at cost.

To illustrate the difference between using inventory at cost and at retail, consider this example: sales $200, gross margin 40%, and average inventory at cost $40.

$$\text{GMROI at cost} \quad = \quad \frac{(200 \times 0.40)}{40} \times 100 = 200\%$$

$$\text{GMROI at retail} \quad = \quad \frac{200}{40/0.6} \times 0.40 \times 100 = 120\%$$

In this example, inventory at cost had to be recalculated at retail to obtain a stock turn rate of 3. This was done by dividing the value of inventory at cost by the cost of goods sold percentage, which was 60%. Alternatively, one could calculate cost of goods sold (0.6 x 200) and divide that by average inventory at cost to get a turn rate of 3. The resultant GMROI at retail is the same (allowing for rounding differences).

GMROI inventory at cost is 200%, whereas GMROI inventory at retail is 120%. GMROI may be expressed in dollars or as a percentage. It shows what return is being achieved on the investment in merchandise inventory. For example, if the calculation reveals $2.00, then each dollar invested in inventory valued at cost is returning $2.00 in gross margin for the year period. This ratio has only recently been used by more than a limited number of retailers. The impetus for its use has been the very high inventory carrying costs retailers have faced, which have prompted wide-ranging efforts to reduce investment and increase returns.

Obviously, GMROI can be dramatically altered by changes in inventory turnover and/or by changes in gross margin. For example, GMROI inventory at retail of 200% can be achieved with a gross margin of 25% and 8 turns or a gross margin of 50% and 4 turns. Recently, there have been efforts to drive the entire merchandising budgeting process on the basis of target GMROIs.

There are many arguments for using GMROI compared to earlier methods of merchandise performance assessment. For example, George Waybright, director of Management Information Systems of Pic'N'Pay Stores Inc., wrote:

> Should the financial personnel ever be concerned about the rate of sale of an item? In retailing there always appears to have been the dichotomy between reporting on unit and dollar sales, dollars for the financial personnel and units for the merchandising personnel. GMROI is a blend of the two views, but it is a financial measure of the performance of investments made by the merchandisers. This gives the financial side of the house the ability to analyze, report, and make recommendations on merchandise items, classes, or vendors.[5]

However, there are major shortcomings to focusing on gross margin as opposed to more sophisticated measures of profitability. Professor Walter Salmon of the Harvard Business School, a long-time advocate of contribution analysis in retailing, argued as follows:

> The use of gross margin percentages has misled many general merchandise retailers in merchandising emphasis. It has stimulated the overemphasis of fashion merchandise and the underemphasis of some other products on which new competitors have made fortunes.[6]

Professor Salmon went on to argue that he believes dollar contribution per unit of space is the superior standard by which to judge a merchant. This leads us to the concept of direct product profit.

**Direct Product Profit (DPP)**    The basic idea behind **direct product profit** (the term used in the grocery and drug field)—and its variant, **Profit Contribution**

**Reporting** (PCR) (the term used in the general merchandise field)—is that retail managers should be focusing on contribution to fixed costs and profit, not simply on gross margin. Three retail consultants from Touche Ross explained DPP as follows:

> DPP focuses on contribution margin. That is, it measures the profit of individual retail items in individual stores. DPP equals an item's gross margin dollars, plus discounts and allowances, less direct handling, selling, and inventory holding costs. It may be aggregated to develop results for brands, categories, departments, stores, etc., thus forming the basis for merchandising decisions. . . .
>
> . . . DPP's increased accuracy is illustrated as follows where the gross margin overstates the realized profit by 86 percent.[7]

They went on to provide the following example to show that, whereas gross margin appears to be $6.45, the DPP is only $3.46. If this were compared to another item, there may be dramatic differences "below the gross margin line" that would impact on marketing decisions.

| | |
|---|---:|
| Retail price | $18.95 |
| Cost | 12.50 |
| *Equals* GM dollars | 6.45 |
| *Plus* discounts and allowances obtained: | |
| Payment discount | 0.30 |
| Merch. allowances | 0.50 |
| *Equals* adjusted GM | $7.25 |
| *Less* direct handling costs: | |
| Distcentre dir. labor | 0.41 |
| Distcentre inv. exp | 0.18 |
| Distcentre oper. exp. | 0.12 |
| Transport to stores | 0.14 |
| Promotion costs | 0.20 |
| Retail direct labor | 1.78 |
| Retail invent. exp. | 0.15 |
| Retail oper. exp. | 0.81 |
| *Equals* direct prod. costs | $3.79 |
| Direct product profit equals | $3.46 |
| *Times* no. of units sold/week | 28 |
| *Equals* DPP/week | $96.88 |
| *Divided by* sq. ft. of space | 2.8 |
| *Equals* DPP per sq. ft. per week | $34.60 |

Such an example is not contrived. *Drug Store News* reported a McKinsey study of 54 dry grocery categories for a major U.S. retailer where GM was compared with DPP: "There simply wasn't any correlation between the two columns."[8]

DPP and PCR offer many important benefits to retailers who have had to cope with "averages" of incomplete performance numbers for far too long. Two consultants from Arthur Andersen working with Neiman Marcus to implement PCR summarized the major benefits as follows:

1. Remove conflicts that often confuse managers.
2. Heighten management awareness of the profit implications of actions and decisions, improving communication inside and outside the company.
3. Help management in strategy development.
4. Provide a workable company-wide standard that helps management evaluate, reward, and motivate personnel in an objective manner and corresponds to the standard that stockholders apply to operations, namely profitability.[9]

## Space Productivity

Space accounts for 20 to 30 percent of a retailer's total assets and 5 to 15 percent of total expenses. The major activities involved are management of real estate and physical facilities, as shown in Exhibit 3.3.

---

*EXHIBIT 3.3*
*Space*
*Productivity*
*Assessment*
*(Space may be in*
*square feet or*
*square metres)*

### 1. Sales/Foot²
Net sales divided by square feet (usually selling space). Quick index of sales generated throughout a store or in different parts of a store. Often used to suggest re-examination of space usage.

### 2. Transactions/Foot²
Number of transactions divided by square feet (usually selling space). A variation on sales/foot² that gives some idea of store traffic. Could also look at average transaction size per square foot.

### 3. Gross Margin/Foot²
Gross margin divided by square feet (usually selling space). Shows how many gross margin dollars generated by use of space.

### 4. Gross Margin Return on Inventory Investment/Foot²
GMROI divided by square feet (often selling space combined with storage space). Shows the return on investment in inventory as placed in various parts of total store space; i.e., combines space and inventory productivity assessment.

### 5. Direct Product Profit/Foot²
DPP divided by square feet (typically selling space). Shows the contribution to net profit before fixed costs of total store space or part of that space for comparison purposes. A refinement of GM/foot².

### 6. Net Profit/Foot²
Net profit (usually after tax but before extraordinary items) divided by square feet (usually selling space). Shows how much net profit generated by use of space. Could be misleading if many arbitrary overhead charges.

---

As an example of the space measures listed in Exhibit 3.3, consider net dollar sales per square foot of selling space. **Sales per square foot** (or per square metre) is a very commonly used measure expressed in dollars of sales generated in part or all of a store or group of stores. While gross space can be used, it is usually more appropriate to use selling space only. This measure can be used to compare alternate uses of space, such as for one merchandise line versus another. It can also be used to compare departments or stores of different size by reducing the difference to a common base.

Although this measure is widely used, there are several problems with it. First, it does not take into account vertical differences in merchandise presentation or use of walls. If there are dramatic differences within an organization, one may wish to use a cubic measure, although this is rarely done because of the work involved. If displays are of standard height and/or depth, the calculation is usually simplified by using linear metres or feet, a common approach in the grocery business where standard size display gondolas are often used. (Obviously, Imperial or metric measures of space may be used.)

Second, selling space frequently changes within a store on a merchandise category basis although less often on a total store basis. When there are dramatic changes or seasonal differences in selling space, calculations of sales per square foot should be done more frequently than the usual annual calculation.

Third, and most important, this performance indicator is too often used by management without consideration for the different costs of space within and across stores, the differing market potentials of these units, and the differing costs and margins on various merchandise categories. In other words, it should not be used as a critical performance indicator unless operations are relatively simple and homogeneous (for example, only a very limited line is sold).

Notice that merchandise performance and space productivity can and should be combined. For example, many consider GMROI and DPP per square foot of selling space the most powerful approaches to managing retail operations.

## Personnel Performance

People typically represent 15 to 25 percent of a retail marketer's net sales and 40 to 70 percent of total operating costs. It is a difficult task to assess retail personnel performance especially when staff are engaged in a variety of tasks that cannot be specifically tied to certain "outputs" such as sales. The major reasons for assessing personnel performance (other than for individual career decisions) are to manage the difficult trade-off of labour costs and service quality. Decisions such as how many staff to have on the sales floor, how to schedule them, and so on are facilitated by tracking performance of staff on a variety of measures, as shown in Exhibit 3.4. Many retailers today track these sorts of measures continuously. (Service quality and other such issues are addressed further in Chapter 9.)

---

*EXHIBIT 3.4*
*Personnel*
*Performance*
*Assessment*

**1. Sales/Employees**
Net sales divided by number of employees (all employees or sales employees only) A quick indication of staffing level relative to sales volume.

**2. Transactions/Employees**
Number of transactions divided by number of employees. Indication of how many

purchasing customers being handled per employee. Useful to compare with store or department traffic level.

**3. Foot²/Employees**

Square footage (usually selling area) divided by number of employees (usually sales employees). Indication of sales staff coverage in the store or department. Obviously, this will vary greatly by merchandise categories and by formats of the store.

**4. Gross Margin/Employees**

Gross margin divided by number of employees. An indication of gross profit generated per employee.

**5. Net Profit/Employees**

Net profit divided by number of employees. An indication of net profit generated per employee.

---

As shown in Exhibit 3.4, the issue of part-time and full-time staff can complicate calculations. The best solution to this problem is to convert figures for part-time employees to their full-time "equivalents."

## Marketplace Performance

Assessing marketplace performance involves assessment of relative competitive position in the marketplace and consumer patronage patterns. These measures require information gathering outside the boundaries of the retail firm. Some retailers routinely collect information about customers and competitors to calculate awareness levels or share of market or other such performance indicators. Too many retailers, however, collect such external information sporadically, if at all. Some marketplace intelligence is vital to guide retail management decisions. There are three basic categories of information relevant to the assessment of marketplace performance for any retailer: customer analysis, non-customer analysis, and competitor analysis, as shown in Exhibit 3.5.

It is usually not necessary to hire outside researchers or consultants or to spend lots of money to gather useful information about a marketplace. In fact, any good merchant is doing this all the time and has his or her employees doing it as well. Retailers who shop the competition and who regularly get on the floor are gathering this kind of information. The important point is to do this information gathering and analysis in sufficient detail to detect marketplace changes *before* those changes are fully reflected in financial and operating results. Marketplace performance assessment helps a retailer to understand why financial and operating results are as they are and to prepare more thoughtfully for changes in business approach.

There are countless ways to examine a retailer's market. For example, one might profile all the demographic characteristics of current versus potential customers or one might profile the marketing programs of key competitors. A retailer might track customer satisfaction levels via returns records or subscribe to research services to monitor product or competitor performance. (Chapters 4, 5, and 6 will

EXHIBIT 3.5
Marketplace
Performance
Assessment

## 1. Market Share Position

Net sales divided by total sales of relevant competitors, expressed as a percentage. An indication of what share of total available market is being captured by the retailer. Caution: there is a danger of believing market share increases will bring proportionate profit increases. This is not always the case.

## 2. Awareness Level

The percentage of a defined population that are aware (aided or unaided) of the store (or something specific about the store) at a given point in time. An often-used measure of communication effectiveness (i.e., did people see the advertising?). Can be combined with measures of knowledge, recall, performance, attitudes, etc., to track where in the "purchasing process" the retailer needs to improve his or her marketing efforts.

## 3. Image Held by Customers

There are a wide variety of measures intended to compare customer perceptions of the retailer with their perceptions of other retailers. The measures are derived from asking questions such as, "On a scale of 1 to 6 rank the following five stores on overall price level. . . . " Researchers use semantic scales, cluster analysis, perceptual mapping, etc., to make this appear quite complicated, but the basic principle is straightforward.

As discussed in Chapter 2, central to retail strategic planning is the concept of "positioning." This means focusing one's efforts on specific target segments with a store "offer" that is perceived by those customers to be more attractive than the offers of relevant competing retailers. This image measure is a way to see how well one is doing in this regard.

## 4. Image Held by Noncustomers

See above discussion—the difference, of course, is focusing on noncustomers. This is less easy to do (i.e., one can't administer surveys in-store or send to the store's mailing list), but it is often very useful to find out why some people are not customers. Frequently, it is based on perceptions of the retailer that are fundamentally different from the perceptions held by customers. This information then provides insights into what action, if any, might be taken to attract these potential customers.

## 5. Patronage Loyalty

There are a variety of ways to measure this, such as asking Where would you go first to buy (product or service)? The intent is to measure loyalty to the *store* as opposed to specific products. A good way to assess competitive strength. When loyalty is low, it takes very little to switch the customer from one retailer to another.

---

elaborate on many of these approaches to understanding one's position and performance in a marketplace.)

## CHOOSING, GATHERING, AND USING PERFORMANCE MEASURES

If performance measures are viewed as diagnostic and predictive tools, then, depending on the decision situation, some of these will be found to be very general and not too informative while others will be very specific and very helpful. A retailer must pick the correct tool for the job at hand because no one performance measure provides all the diagnostic capability she or he needs. A doctor does not attempt a complete physical with just a blood sample; instead, he or she uses many tests. Similarly, professional retail marketers use a variety of diagnostic techniques to assess the health of a retail business. Discussed below are seven suggestions for selecting and using performance measures.

**Select the most important measures for the firm**   The individual manager or analyst is in the best position to determine which measures will provide the information and insight most needed to manage a particular operation. It is best to select the most important measures first; one can add to the list later if one so desires. For example, one may be particularly concerned with pricing decisions and may therefore focus closely on the markdown measures, sales levels during promotional periods, and so on. The objective is to improve decision-making, not to compile an encyclopedia of useless facts and figures. Don't calculate ratios for periods of time that are not relevant. In short, design an approach that works, and don't let the accountants reign supreme. Dominic Mangone, vice-president and controller of Montgomery Ward & Co., wrote about this problem as follows:

> We often found ourselves arguing over the measurement of accounting instead of the measurement of merchandise and the measurement of results. What we have done is switch to measuring only the incremental, marginal, and controllable aspects of our various business segments. We've switched all of our reports to a contribution basis of accounting. We've done this for several reasons. The first reason is that we felt that incremental accounting or contribution accounting better focuses management's attention on the aspects of the business that can be currently impacted and controlled. What we are doing now is only charging our departments and stores for those costs and expenses that they can control; have authority over; or responsibility for. This keeps their attention on those things they can take action on.[10]

**Use multiple measures**   Don't rely on one or two key figures to understand performance. If you wish to keep the list short, use those measures that reflect critical issues, such as the use of inventory investment. Obviously, one does not want to fall into such traps as believing that if sales go up, all is well.

Retail marketers wish to see the situation from several points of view to be in a position to interpret what it all means. For example, if sales per square foot have declined, is this a bad sign? Perhaps the gross margin per square foot has increased due to changes in merchandise assortment or pricing procedures; or perhaps sales have not declined as much as they would have if there had not been "that big promotion last fall," and so on. Without thoughtful interpretation of multiple measures, performance assessment is not just a waste of time—it can be misleading and dangerous.

**Gather and select information**   Each performance indicator requires specific information in order to be calculated and interpreted. One should establish what information is already available and assemble it in a form that allows performance assessment. Information may be needed that is not readily available. In such situations, a retailer must decide on a way to get that information in as accurate and timely a fashion as possible but at a cost that doesn't exceed the value of that information. One may wish, for example, to gather data on where the customers live. One may change the point-of-sale procedures to gather such information for later analysis or may commission a special study. (Chapter 6 discusses retail research methods further.)

Nearly all of the performance indicators described here can be readily implemented by most retail firms. Much of the data can be extracted from financial and sales information already being collected although not always being used effectively. Other data sources such as inventory records, personnel and supplier records, and published information can provide the information for many of the remaining indicators. Cash register tapes can provide number of transactions, payroll records can provide number of hours worked by sales employees, and a simple tape measurement can provide selling space area, to give a few examples.

Major changes have been occurring in the amount and quality of information available to retail marketers. No longer must retailers wait for physical inventory counts, vendor invoices, and reports from store managers eye-balling store shelves. Technology has changed all that incredibly, as Chuck Harrison wrote in 1991:

> Today's in-store systems are technological nerve centers on which retailers rely to integrate point-of-sale activities, back-office functions, customer service and marketing programs. Clearly the industry leaders have been able to achieve a competitive advantage through the application of technology at the store level. One only has to look at the success of retailers like Mrs. Fields', The Limited, Kmart, Target, Toys 'R' Us and Wal-Mart to confirm that the application of technology to processes in the store can help a retailer to achieve market share.[11]

Decision support systems and their supporting technologies (such as scanning) are the current preoccupation of most corporate retail marketing executives and their Management Information Systems (MIS) staffs.[12] Such systems, in addition to their cost and complexity, have had a major impact on decision-making processes and on the role of retail marketers such as store managers. Moses Cheung, a partner with Deloitte and Touche in its Retail and Distribution Services Group, expressed these impacts as follows:

> In the past, retailers did not have any corporate system that was able to keep track of detail store-by-store or zone-by-zone. Because of the lack of corporate information systems, the only way to react to local market demand and therefore use the "pull" concept instead of "push" to get the right product to the right place

was to have the store manager understand what is selling. Headquarters was relying on the store manager to understand that the store manager was the missing link in providing merchandise information.

With the technology we have today, you still can execute a "pull" concept because of the POS capability and the telecommunication capability of corporate to get detail transactions from POS. So somebody sitting in the home office can have lots of data to analyze; they do not need the store manager to provide that information.

The trend I foresee is for retailers to keep the managers busy doing the job they are there for—servicing the customer, running the operations to make sure it is a well-run and cost-efficient operation—not loading them down with merchandising information and merchandising decisions.[13]

On the whole, little additional data gathering is required for most smaller retail marketers to implement the performance assessment approach outlined in this chapter. And any additional data gathering can be done by the individual retailer at low cost. For example, a study of traffic patterns by the front door is an ideal project for a small group of volunteer students seeking some exposure to retailing as part of their education. In such a case, the retailer should ensure that the study meets his or her needs as well as those of the students.

**Calculate performance measures consistently**   Because performance measures can be individually defined, it is important to define them in a consistent way for a business. For example, one may define occupancy cost as rent only—that definition should be followed each time that term is used in a performance measure calculation so that one is "comparing apples to apples," as the expression goes.

**Understand the composition of the measures**   Performance measures are signals that operations are proceeding well or that more attention needs to be paid to a particular aspect of the business. A retailer using performance measures in this signalling fashion must know what factors were used to calculate any particular ratio or percentage. This is particularly true if someone else in the firm does the calculations or if an outside accountant does them.

As mentioned previously, most of the measures listed are ratios, or fractions. The ratio number is the result of a particular numerator divided by a denominator. To improve the ratio, one can affect the numerator, or the denominator, or both. For example, to improve GMROI, one might change markup strategies to affect margin and/or one might change inventory investment via changes in ordering procedures. This point seems very obvious, but its power is sometimes missed by those retailers who concentrate on only one or a few of several ways to improve performance.

**Be careful in comparisons with other measures**   If a retailer calculates GMROI using inventory valued at retail and he or she is comparing it with "industry" data using inventory valued at cost, then he or she is not making a meaningful comparison. Always seek definitions of performance measures to avoid this problem.

Measures of performance are meaningful only when viewed against some point of comparison. An inventory turnover of 3.7 means little unless it is known, for example, that the firm previously had a turnover of 6.2 or that similar competitors had a turnover of 5.3 or that management had set a goal of 6.4. In short, there are four usual comparison methods:

1. History: One may compare this period's performance with last period's, and so on, to examine favourable and unfavourable trends. Notice that a key problem in this respect is that dollar trends are affected by inflation. Ideally, one should correct for inflationary effects on costs and prices by using deflator factors. Some retailers use the Consumer Price Index, others use Gross National Expenditure or specific retail sector indices with which they have become familiar. No one indicator is perfect; however, if one deflator index is used, it should be used consistently to ensure the comparability of results. Thus, while sales may have grown by 5 percent in current dollars, a decline may have been suffered in "constant dollars." Some retailers use unit volume trends to avoid the problems associated with year-to-year comparisons involving dollar measures alone.

2. Other units of the organization: If there are relatively similar categories or departments or stores, one can compare the results of one unit with those of another for the same time period. Thus, the women's clothing department may be performing better in terms of gross margin per square foot than the children's wear department.

3. Industry data: Although not always available, information about how competitors or other comparable stores are performing can be a useful method of putting performance in perspective. Such information appears in the trade press or is periodically made available by industry groups. Again, care must be taken to ensure results are not misinterpreted. For example, one would obviously not compare the number of sales employees per square foot of selling space in high-service stores with that in self-serve stores.

4. Management objectives: Many retailers set explicit goals that not only provide targets for achievement but also constitute benchmarks for performance assessment. This approach is fine provided the goals are well defined and realistic. If management sets unrealistic targets, the staff has not necessarily performed poorly in not achieving those goals. Ideally, management objectives should be set with careful attention to a firm's history and circumstances.

**Set performance objectives**   After analyzing past performance and considering future circumstances, one can begin setting performance goals for the future. These goals should not be rigidly maintained if circumstances change, but they do serve a useful purpose. They help decide what actions are most likely to achieve the results desired and they help assess performance in the future by providing a frame of reference. All action ideas should be assessed in relation to the question, What impact will this action have on performance? The question can never be answered completely or with certainty, but it helps managers focus on key issues such as what changes in customer behaviour are anticipated and what investments are required to implement that merchandising idea.

In the final analysis, success depends on judgment and decision-making skills, not on any formulaic approach to retailing. For example, knowing precisely last year's sales per square foot does not tell one what overall strategy to adopt in response to the new competitor who opened across the street yesterday.

Over time, retailers tend to make their performance assessment approach increasingly comprehensive by broadening the scope of data collection and analysis. In larger retail organizations, responsibility for each performance measure is typically assigned to individual managers. Caution must be exercised in this delegation because of the highly interrelated nature of many of the aspects of retailing covered by these performance indicators. Responsibility for performance should whenever possible be assigned only to those who can influence the results achieved. The development of item coding (UPC and the like), the growing use of scanning and other item-movement-tracking methods, and the increasing use of the computer by retail managers have all led to a tremendous surge in the amount of data that are available for performance assessment. The emerging task is to find a way to cope with all of these data to improve the quality of retail performance assessment efforts.[14]

## CONCLUSION

Retail marketing decision-makers are interested in improving performance, so it is essential to understand retail marketing performance, how it may be affected, and how it is measured. The retail profit dynamic and the five categories of performance measures—general financial results, merchandise and merchandising results, space productivity, personnel productivity, and marketplace performance—all aid in these deliberations. Without an understanding of performance, a retail marketer is literally "flying without instruments in a crowded sky on a dark night."

### REVIEW QUESTIONS

1. What is the difference between GMROI and DPP? Does a retail marketer need to use both?

2. How does stock turnover affect GMROI?

3. Do you have any concerns about taking the responsibility for gathering information and making decisions on merchandising away from the store manager in a multi-unit operation?

4. *Stores* reported in December 1990 the following results for U.S. department stores and specialty stores. What do you observe from the data?

| | 1989 | 1988 | 1987 |
|---|---|---|---|
| **Department Stores** | | | |
| Average gross sale | $38.95 | $36.39 | $26.69 |
| Gross margins (%) | 40.00 | 40.38 | 40.33 |
| GMROI ($) | $2.09 | $2.50 | $2.45 |
| Sales per square foot | $169.12 | $151.85 | $141.26 |
| Annual stock turn (x) | 2.55 | 2.87 | 3.00 |
| **Specialty Stores** | | | |
| Average gross sale | $39.82 | $31.32 | n/a |
| Gross margins (%) | 43.22 | 42.81 | 40.83 |
| GMROI ($) | $2.22 | $2.03 | $2.14 |
| Sales per square foot | $248.28 | $193.70 | $218.75 |
| Annual stock turns (x) | 2.47 | 2.62 | 2.16 |

David P. Schulz, "NRF's New FOR: Profits Dip," *Stores*, December 1990, pp. 26–28. Reprinted by permission.

## KEY TERMS

- retail performance assessment
- firm level
- operations levels
- merchandising levels
- available market
- store traffic share
- purchase yield rate
- average transaction size
- average gross margin percentage
- fixed costs
- breakeven analysis
- required volume analysis
- average investment
- performance over a period of time
- financial position at a point in time
- changes in financial position

## NOTES

1. For further background on ROI and Strategic Profit Models in retailing, see Robert F. Lusch, "The New Algebra of High Performance Retail Management," *Retail Control*, September 1986, and his book, *Retail Management* (Cincinnati: Southwestern Publishing, 1990); Daniel J. Sweeney "Improving the Profitability of Retail Merchandising Decisions," *Journal of Marketing*, January 1973, pp. 60–68.

2. Robert F. Lusch, "Two Critical Determinants of Retail Profitability and Productivity," in *Retailing Issues Letter* (Zale Corporation and Texas A&M University, April 1986).

3. Jack Gifford, "Teaching Retail Financial Management to Marketing Majors." A presentation to American Collegiate Retailing Association Annual Meeting, New York, 1985.

4. For more background on general financial analysis techniques, see Erich A. Helfert, *Techniques of Financial Analysis* (Homewood, Illinois: Irwin, 1982); or James C. Van Horne, *Fundamentals of Financial Management* (Englewood Cliffs, N.J.: Prentice-Hall, 1980).

5. George Waybright, "GMROI: Get More Return on Investments," *Retail Control*, October 1984, pp. 2–10.

6. W.J. Salmon, "Farewell to Gross Margin." A speech delivered to Top Management Symposium, National Retail Merchants Association, New York, February 1984.

7. Harris Gordon, Daniel O'Connor, and John Phipps, "Direct Product Profit: Introducing A Comprehensive Measurement of Retail Performance," *Retail Control*, September 1986.

8. See, for example, Alan L. Gilman, "The Benefits of Looking below Gross Margin" *Retailing Issues Letter*, Arthur Andersen & Co., November 1988, for a discussion of the importance of contribution analysis in retail marketing.

9. David Y. Schwartz, and Larry R. Katzen, "Profit Contribution Reporting: A New System for Measuring Retail Performance," *International Journal of Retailing*, Arthur Andersen & Co., Spring 1985, pp. 43–53.

10. Dominic M. Mangone, "How to Measure Merchandise Profitability," *Retail Control*, October 1984, pp. 11–20.

11. Chuck Harrison, "Using In-Store Systems to Achieve a Competitive Advantage," *Retail Control*, January 1991, pp. 3–7.

12. For a good overview of these issues, see "What the Non-MIS Manager Needs to Know," *Chain Store Age Executive*, October 1990, pp. 2B–20B; and "Note on the Use of Information Technology in Retailing" Harvard Business School, 9-189-024, 1988.

13. Gary Robins, "In-Store Support Systems," *Stores*, August 1990, pp. 43–51.

14. For example, see Jeffrey Rothfeder and Jim Bartimo, "How Software Is Making Food Sales a Piece of Cake" *Business Week*, 2 July 1990, pp. 54–55.

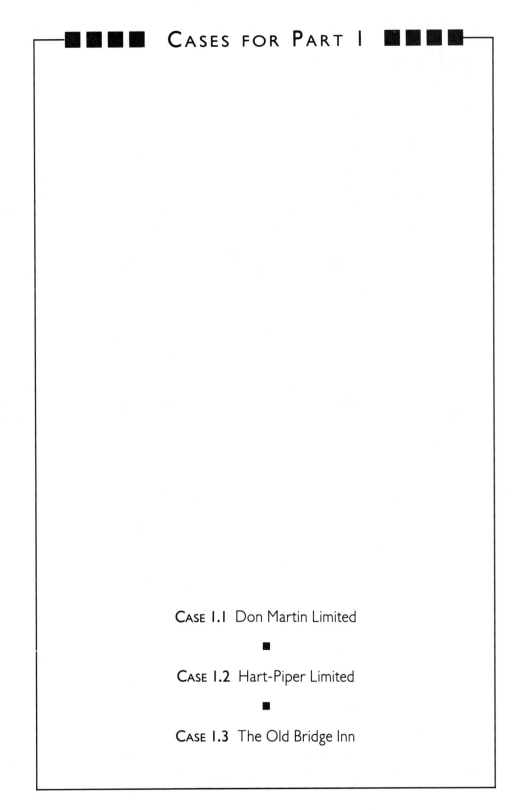

# CASE 1.1    Don Martin Limited

Don Martin leaned far back in his chair and said: "The thing that is killing us is service". Martin surveyed his ten-thousand-square-foot downtown store and continued to discuss his business.

In 1964, I started with auto supplies. I had five hundred square feet and all the business I could handle. In 1969, I expanded to three-thousand feet, and in 1974 I enlarged the store to five-thousand square feet and broadened my line of products. In 1975, I moved to a new location a few blocks from the old store. At that point, I was selling auto supplies, sporting goods, housewares, bicycles, photographic equipment, motorcycles, TVs, appliances, and radios. I was doing a total volume of $2,500,000.

I continued to do well in the new location. This street is a main thoroughfare and it is right in the heart of the city's blue-collar district. People come here because they can get everything they want on this block. I carry a selection of name brands in most of my product lines, and I augment some lines with non-name brands.

I've checked the other stores in this area. There are a lot of different brands offered for the comparison shopper. There's a big furniture store across the street and several hardware stores, and two or three drugstores in this area. There are several stores that sell audio equipment, TVs, and appliances. The store across the street offers a wide variety of branded big-ticket items. With all that selection, customers come down here, wander from store to store, and often buy on impulse. Although parking on the street is difficult, there is a large metered parking lot right behind my store. However, some people don't seem to know the parking lot is there.

I've always wanted a really big place. In 1984, the store next to mine became available and I bought it. I took out the wall between the two stores and made one ten-thousand-square-foot store. With each previous expansion, I had achieved an immediate increase in sales volume. This time it didn't happen. For a couple of years, I was just breaking even, and last week, when we finalized the figures for 1986, I realized that I was losing money (Exhibit 1).

*EXHIBIT 1*

|  | 1984 | 1985 | 1986 |
|---|---|---|---|
| **Don Martin Limited** Percent Income Statements, 1984–86 |  |  |  |
| Revenues | 100.0 | 100.0 | 100.0 |
| Gross Profit | 32.5 | 30.5 | 35.6 |
| EXPENSES: |  |  |  |
| Selling |  |  |  |
| Sales wages | 12.3 | 11.6 | 13.8 |
| Advertising, excluding co-op advertising[a] | 2.9 | 2.7 | 4.0 |
| Balance of selling and delivery | 1.8 | 1.7 | 1.6 |
| Occupancy | 5.8 | 3.8 | 6.0 |
| General and administration | 4.9 | 4.7 | 3.8 |
| Accounts receivable and credit[b] | 4.8 | 5.1 | 8.3 |
| Total expenses | 32.5 | 29.6 | 37.5 |
| Profit (loss) | 0 | .9 | (1.9) |

[a] Co-op about 2 percent of total advertising.
[b] Includes wages, interest, bad debts, collection less service charges earned.

I'm sure there are enough people in town to make this business a success, and I think people know about my business. I advertise frequently in all the newspapers and on radio. I spend about $100,000 a year on newspaper advertising alone. Generally, my ads have my store name at the top and show all the best buys at my store. I write my own ads. I usually feature one or two loss leaders, but the rest of the items in the ad are listed at their regular price. My ads let people know what I'm offering, and that's the important thing.

I have several problems, but the service I offer to my customers seems to be the main one. When a guy comes to my store for a baseball glove, I have a salesman on the spot to help him. My customers used to expect this kind of service, but now I don't know. Money is tight these days, and people seem willing to do without service if they can save a few cents. Just look at the business that big discount store several blocks east of here is doing. Most of my customers are people who live in this area. They're hard workers without a lot of money to spend on extras.

However, I still think my services attract customers and keep them coming back. I have offered credit for the last few years, which has definitely increased sales — people want credit on the big-

ticket items. I also have offered delivery service. But all these things cost money. I pay $1000 a month just for gas. I have to pay six men to staff my warehouse and run my truck, four women to keep track of credit, three general office women, and two cashiers.

Of course, buying and renovating the new store was expensive. I had to add more salespeople too. I now have a total staff of twenty-six as opposed to sixteen last year. The store is open six days a week, twelve hours per day. My ten salespeople work a twelve-hour day, four days a week. They seem to like this setup. I give them good benefits and a fair commission plus a guarantee, but it's hard to supervise so many salespeople in a store this large. I've been having a big problem with theft. I really have no way of knowing how much I'm losing, but I'm afraid that even my own staff may be stealing from me. I just can't be everywhere at once. I have about five hundred different suppliers, and I spend three-quarters of my time with them. There are just not enough hours in the day.

In order to give people their merchandise right away, I have always carried a good-sized inventory. You can see what we have on the floor here, and there is twice as much upstairs in the warehouse. That ties up a lot of money (Exhibit 2). I buy

EXHIBIT 2

| Product Line | Average Mark Up As A Percent Of Sales[a] | Sales Volume ($000) | | | | Ending Inventory At Retail ($000) | |
|---|---|---|---|---|---|---|---|
| | | 1983 | 1984 | 1985 | 1986 | 1985 | 1986 |
| Automotive | 31 | 32 | 32 | 26 | 24 | 30 | 28 |
| Sporting goods | 34 | 230 | 266 | 246 | 250 | 94 | 126 |
| Houseware/ hardware | 38 | 76 | 84 | 102 | 100 | 74 | 84 |
| Car radio | 26 | 56 | 60 | 56 | 50 | 24 | 30 |
| Tires | 30 | 42 | 26 | 20 | 24 | 32 | 28 |
| Cameras | 30 | 314 | 308 | 330 | 304 | 124 | 138 |
| Tools | 32 | 184 | 200 | 208 | 220 | 100 | 102 |
| Motorcycles | 26 | 202 | 266 | 266 | 326 | 34 | 40 |
| Appliances | 25 | 246 | 310 | 340 | 360 | 146 | 160 |
| TV/stereo | 26 | 462 | 500 | 560 | 500 | 156 | 274 |
| Miscellaneous | 33 | 376 | 354 | 376 | 350 | 140 | 174 |
| | | 2,200 | 2,406 | 2,530 | 2,508 | 954 | 1,184 |

Don Martin Limited Product Performance

[a] On net sales which are 4 percent less than gross sales because of returns and allowances. Four-year average.

EXHIBIT 3
Store Layout,
1986

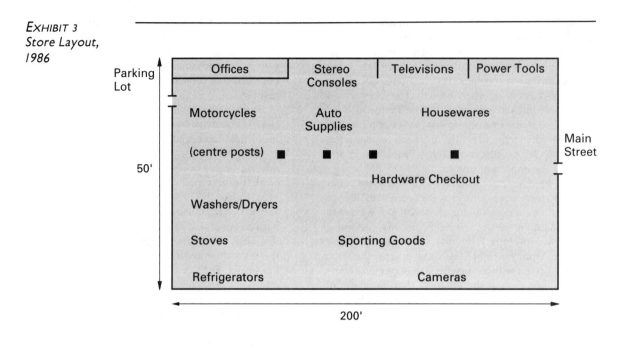

direct from manufacturers but in small quantities and, therefore, can't take advantage of any volume rebates, offered by the salespeople I see.

I've been wondering whether some of my product lines fit together. I have so many things to sell to so many people, but if I cut any lines, I'm going to lose the sure profit that I am already making on those lines. (See Exhibit 3 for the store layout.)

I wondered whether everybody on the street was going through the same thing, but most of the guys tell me they are having about the same year as last year. It wasn't great, but they're surviving.

I'm going to have to do something soon. Canadian Tire and others like them carry products similar to mine, and their net income before tax in 1986 was a lot more than mine.

I think there are a variety of options. One thing I could do is close up the business and rent out the space. As a matter of fact, I've already been offered rent of $130,000 a year for it.

Another alternative is to sell the business outright, but with the profit picture the way it is, I'm afraid I wouldn't get much for it. Besides, I like working for myself. I've been in business 23 years and can't imagine either retiring or taking orders from someone else.

Raise my prices? I did last year. Business is slow enough as it is without scaring them away. We stay competitive in price with the stores in this area and it's tough to sell anything now.

I could go to a self-serve type outlet in order to cut costs or perhaps cut down my product lines. The problem is deciding which items to cut and how to get rid of the stock I already have. The manager of the photography department would like to operate on his own, and I've been getting a lot of pressure from my store manager to set up a separate motorcycle business. The store manager has a lot of experience in motorcycles and he is sure that he could run it and make it work. Two of my other employees would go into it with him if I went that route. It would cost some money to do it, but it might be profitable in the long run.

I realize that I could possibly combine some of these ideas. I have been told that I could partition off part of the store. If I did that, I could either rent out some of the space or use it for the motorcycle shop the boys have been talking about. Maybe I could even do both. This is the most difficult decision I ever had to make."

# C A S E  1.2   Hart-Piper Limited

In early 1987, Mr. R.A.H. Pottlewaite, controller of Hart-Piper Limited, a family-owned, medium-sized department store in Edmonton, Alberta, completed a summary of operating data for the record and tape department. His study had been requested by store management, who were debating the future of the department and, indeed, the possibility of replacing it with a leased beauty salon. The study had been prompted by the heavy competitive pressure being experienced by the record and tape department and a general desire of store management to trade away from direct competition and into areas of higher quality and fashion.

The president of Hart-Piper was Mr. Stuart Piper, who represented the third generation of Pipers to run Hart-Piper. In the mid 1980's, Hart-Piper operated five stores: the original Edmonton store and outlets in Fox Creek, Camrose, Kimberly, and Wetaskiwin. General administration and most buying was handled by a staff located at the Edmonton store.

The Hart-Piper Edmonton store was located conveniently in central Edmonton. The city had become known recently for the huge West Edmonton Mall, but Hart-Piper had preferred to remain freestanding in the central core rather than locate in the suburbs of this roughly 750,000 population city. Hart-Piper had grown steadily over the years building on both the urban and surrounding regional trade. By 1987, the Edmonton store was approximately 55,000 square feet consisting of a basement and two upper floors.

The Edmonton store had experienced reasonably good sales levels and due to its location, steady customer traffic especially during the midday. The main merchandising thrust was in soft goods with extensive apparel and accessory lines for the whole family. Piece goods and household textiles were well represented. The store was reasonably strong in such lines as small appliances, home entertainment, cameras and accessories, china and jewelry. Major appliances and hardware had been largely discontinued and home furnishings lines downplayed considerably in recent years.

Profit growth had not paralleled sales performance, however, as prices had come under pressure from the dramatic increase in retail stores in Edmonton. Reacting to this, Hart-Piper had started to upgrade the lines carried in an attempt to recapture good margins. These steps were so recent that it was not clear what the effect on sales and dollar margins would be.

## The Record and Tape Department

Until 1985, sales of records and tapes had been solid contributors to Hart-Piper and excellent traffic builders. Recently, several general merchandise competitors had started to discount records and many specialty acoustics stores had opened in the market. Margins started to deteriorate as Hart-Piper attempted to remain competitive and, by 1987, the company was "only about breaking even on record and tape sales". Hence, management had requested a full study on the department, which was only located in the main store.

The record and tape department occupied about 850 square feet adjacent to the Home Entertainment (TV, stereo, radio, video) department on the second floor of the store. The mix of records stocked was broad, attempting to encompass the preferences of the student market (high school and university) and the general population to whom Hart-Piper targeted the store. Records and tapes were purchased solely through distributors although increasingly competitors were dealing directly with record and tape suppliers. This latter development "probably gives them three or four more percentage points than us to work with," according to the Hart-Piper buyer whose responsibilities included the record and tape department. "On the other hand, we get excellent service from the distributor, we can keep our inventories down, and we have some leverage for returns,'' she said.

A comparison of Hart-Piper's record and tape department with selected local competitors is given in Exhibit 1. Mr. Pottlewaite's operating performance summary is given in Exhibit 2.

## A Beauty Salon

By coincidence, Mr. Piper had recently been approached by the general manager of Edmunds, a quality image franchised salon chain, with a proposal to locate a unit in at least the Edmonton Hart-Piper store. Mr. Piper had subsequently checked out Edmunds including visiting several locations. He was favorably impressed by everything he read and saw. He also found out that the host stores were favorably impressed with their experience with Edmunds as a tenant.

While detailed negotiations had not been entered into, a rough outline of the potential arrangements had been discussed. Hart-Piper would be responsible for all renovations and improvements, to be done according to a general plan provided by Edmunds. It was anticipated that the necessary plumbing, wiring, fixtures, etc. would amount to about $45,000. Hart-Piper would receive 18 percent of Edmunds sales volume as rent for the space; Edmunds personnel estimated that first year sales would be about $180,000 with an average transaction value of

EXHIBIT 1

| | Hart-Piper | Discount Disc | Cam Music | Mr. Scholar | Bwana Junction |
|---|---|---|---|---|---|
| Location: | Central City | Central City | Central City | Central City | Periphery of Core |
| Hours of Operation: | 9:30–5; 6 days a week | 9:30–5; 6 days a week | 12:00–7; M–F 9:00–5 Sat. | 12:00–7; M–F 9:00–5 Sat. | Irregular |
| Store Atmosphere: | Department store image | Five and Dime | Promotional, discount | Upscale | Bazaar |
| Price Policy: | Aggressive to meet competition | Deep discount on selected items | Price leader, many specials | Competitive | Very low, irregular |
| Service Offered: | On-the-floor sales help | Self-serve | Mostly self-serve | Sales help | Self-serve |
| Assortment Description: | Very broad | Largely popular | Very broad | Classical, rare albums | Pop, special discount albums |
| Delivery: | Free on purchases over $15.00 | None | None | None | None |
| Credit: | Store charge card | None | All credit cards | Store charge accounts All credit cards | Visa, M/C |

Hart-Piper Ltd.<br>Comparison of Record and Tape Department With Selected Competitors

$18.75. Edmunds would be responsible for its own personnel, their benefits, all materials and promotional expenses, operating insurance, etc., and measurable utility costs. Hart-Piper was responsible as landlord for general costs such as heat, building insurance, security, and so on.

## One Reaction

Charles Piper, Stuart Piper's son and currently in charge of the home entertainment department, was quite against a change. "Records and tapes are an integral part of our whole scope of home entertainment merchandising," he noted "and we can't just set them aside for some nebulous promises from a hairdresser. We should keep them, build the department by adding newer products such as video camcorders and compact disc players. We need this base for our future. Why can't we get space somewhere else?"

EXHIBIT 2

| Hart-Piper Ltd. Operating Data for Record and Tape Department | | | |
|---|---|---|---|
| | 1985 | 1986 | 1987 |
| Net Sales | $332,910 | $291,630 | $247,020 |
| Average Sale | 8.70 | 8.43 | 8.10 |
| Cost of Goods Sold | 239,694 | 209,976 | 186,501 |
| Average Inventory at Cost | 32,832 | 32,304 | 28,257 |
| Gross Margin | 93,216 | 81,654 | 60,519 |
| Expenses | | | |
|   Sales Promotion* | 1,332 | 876 | 1,728 |
|   Total Department Management** | 7,656 | 7,290 | 4,692 |
|   Selling*** | 26,634 | 27,123 | 26,430 |
|   Cost of Carrying Inventory | 2,664 | 3,207 | 3,951 |
|   Logistics # | 666 | 1,167 | 1,728 |
|   Total | $ 38,952 | $ 39,663 | $ 38,529 |
| Contribution to Overhead | $ 54,264 | $ 41,991 | $ 21,990 |

  \* Sales promotion expense comprises: net newspaper outlay, preparation expense, direct mail and other advertising expense, and display costs.

 \*\* Total department management expense comprises: department management payroll, payroll taxes and fringe benefits, department travel and miscellaneous department management outlays.

\*\*\* Total selling expense comprises: net salespeople's salaries, payroll taxes, register shortages, departmental supplies and other direct charges.

  # Logistics consists of receiving and marking merchandise, wrapping and packing and delivery.

# **C A S E** 1.3    The Old Bridge Inn

One day in October 1981, Tim Agnew, fourth-year business student at the University of Western Ontario, approached his friend and fellow classmate Tom Bauer with a problem. The Inn which Tim's mother owned and operated in Young's Point, Ontario, had encountered financial difficulties. Cash reserves had dwindled to zero. Mrs Agnew had no more personal resources to invest in the Inn. Creditors, including the federal government, had threatened to place a lien on the premises if payments were not met. At the same time Mrs. Agnew had just taken ill, and was unable to properly deal with the situation. As a result, Tim decided to leave school in order to run the business. He wondered if Tom might have any suggestions as to how the Inn's operations should be managed.

On the first weekend in November, Tom set out from London for Young's Point, which is located 20 km northeast of the city of Peterborough (see Exhibit 1). While the initial drive along Highway 401 was rather uninteresting, the

scenery soon improved as Tom turned north onto Highway 115 outside Port Hope. After a 45-minute drive Tom saw a weather-beaten sign indicating that his destination was near. Almost before he realized it, Tom drove through Young's Point and found himself in the country again. There was no sign of the Inn. Remembering Tim's description of the Inn as lying beside the Trent-Severn canal system, Tom retraced his route. Near the point where the highway crossed the Otonabee River he saw, buried among a myriad of nameplates, a tiny sign for the Old Bridge Inn. Following the sign to the end of a short dead-end road Tom found himself in front of a large two-storey red-brick building. On the rood of the building stood a relatively small, simple sign stating: Old Bridge Inn.

Tom pulled his car into the empty parking lot adjacent to the building, got out, and approached the front door. The curtains were drawn and inside there appeared to be no sign of life. Tom pulled on the door and found, much to

*EXHIBIT I*

| | |
|---|---|
| Rock Cross Ⓐ | Potash Kettles Ⓝ |
| Indian Head Ⓑ | Academy Theatre Ⓞ |
| The Dam Bobcaygeon Ⓒ | County of Victoria Museum Ⓟ |
| The Beehive Ⓓ | |
| Waterfalls & Rapids Ⓔ | Kirkfield Lift Lock Ⓠ |
| Church on the Rock Ⓕ | Upper Mill Pond Ⓡ |
| Balancing Rock Ⓖ | Hydraulic Lift Lock Ⓢ |
| Buckhorn Wilderness Centre Ⓗ | Filter Plant Park & Zoo Ⓣ |
| The Serpent Mounds Ⓘ | Trent University Ⓤ |
| Lang Country Village Ⓙ | Peterborough Centennial Fountain Ⓥ |
| Curve Lake Indian Reserve Ⓚ | Scenic Drive Ⓦ |
| Peterborough Petroglyphs Ⓛ | Museum Ⓧ |
| | Peterborough Airport Ⓨ |
| The Gorge Ⓜ | Lindsay Airport Ⓩ |

his surprise, that it was open. He walked in, his eyes trying to accustom themselves to the darkness. "Good afternoon, can I help you?" a voice asked from the back. It belonged to Mary, the 21-year-old cook. After explaining the purposed of his visit, Tom was shown upstairs where he found Tim.

## HISTORY OF THE INN

Tim provided Tom with a brief background of the Inn. The main support beam dated back to 1887. The Inn had originally been built as a general store/roadhouse at the junction of the Otonabee River and the old Highway 28. Its clientele was then composed mainly of loggers and raftsmen. Initially business flourished; however, as Highway 28 was expanded and moved 50 metres to the west in 1940, business dropped off. The original bridge beside which the Inn stands is now closed to vehicular traffic and open only to pedestrians.

With the decline in business the Inn fell into a state of disrepair. It changed ownership several times, being used exclusively as a private resi-

dence. In 1955 the Inn was bought by Mr. Russ Brooks. He obtained a liquor licence, hired a honky-tonk piano player, and turned the Inn into a local drinking establishment. Tim summed up the Inn's previous reputation as being a "booze-it-up joint." Although ownership of the Inn changed hands four times within the Brooks family, its operations remained essentially unchanged. Throughout this period the Inn had a record of consistent, though minimal, earnings losses.

## AGNEW FAMILY INVOLVEMENT

In August of 1980 the Old Bridge Inn was purchased by Mrs. Annabelle Agnew. Mrs Agnew, a widow of 10 years, had been left an inheritance by her late husband. With her sons no longer living at home, Mrs. Agnew decided that she wished to try her hand at running a business. While visiting a real estate agent one day in her hometown of Toronto she saw a picture of the Inn, and immediately fell in love with it. Although she had no previous experience in the restaurant business, Mrs. Agnew had taken sev-

EXHIBIT 2

### The Old Bridge Inn
### Income Statement
### for the year ended October 15, 1981

| Revenues | | | |
|---|---|---|---|
| Food sales | $62 995 | | |
| Cost of food | 19 821 | (31%) | $43 174 |
| Beverage sales | 29 665 | | |
| Cost of beverages | 10 369 | (35%) | 19 296 |
| Other revenue | | | 2 108 |
| Gross margin | | | $64 578 |
| Expenses | | | |
| Telephone | $    695 | | |
| Utilities | 5 512 | | |
| Services | 3 396 | (3.5%) | |
| Advertising | 4 272 | | |
| Office supplies | 592 | | |
| Kitchen/Bar supplies | 1 588 | (1.6%) | |
| Entertainment | 5 497 | | |
| Wages | 41 763 | (44%) | |
| Insurance | 1 273 | | |
| Depreciation | 4 220 | | |
| Taxes | 789 | | |
| Interest | 8 343 | | $77 940 |
| Profit/(Loss) | | | ($13 362) |

eral Cordon Bleu cooking courses. She decided that the Inn presented a perfect opportunity to combine business with her love of cooking. As a result, a purchase agreement was drawn up in which ownership was transferred to Mrs. Agnew at a "distress price" of $75 000. A further $15 000 was invested to restore the Inn to its current condition.

## DIFFICULTIES FACING THE INN

Although Mrs. Agnew had been able to increase gross sales from $ 10 000 to over $90 000, the Inn was still faced with financial difficulties (see Exhibit 2). The Inn had narrowly succeeded in paying off its overdue accounts, and its cash reserves were now non-existent (see Exhibit 3). Mrs. Agnew was hoping to find a new buyer for the Inn, but sale of the Inn before the turn of the new year seemed highly unlikely. In order for the Inn to survive that long a positive cash flow was badly needed. The cash flow problem was aggravated by the fact that most of the Inn's revenues were generated by tourists during the summer season (see Exhibits 4 and 5).

While cash flow was the Inn's most pressing concern, profitability in the past had been hurt by a high level of operating expenses. Tim had taken several steps to reduce these expenses. Cost of food sold had been reduced drastically by arranging for a weekly delivery from a large Ontario meat processing firm rather than buying at retail from a local supermarket. Renegotiation of the Inn's first mortgage at 14% through a Small Business Development Bond from a chartered bank would save an additional $2450 annually. Tim also felt sure that the Inn's wage expenses were too high, although he was unsure how they might be reduced.

## THE INN'S UPSTAIRS

Having explained the history of the Inn and the current difficulties facing it, Tim decided to give Tom a tour of the premises. They started off by viewing the second floor. This level consisted of two unattached sections, each accessible via its own staircase (see Exhibit 6). The larger section consisted of eight single rooms and two bathrooms. Five of the eight rooms were cur-

EXHIBIT 3

### The Old Bridge Inn
### Balance Sheet
### (October 15, 1981)

| | | |
|---|---:|---:|
| *Assets* | | |
| Cash | | $    — |
| Inventory: Food | | 1 900 |
| Beverage | | 2 000 |
| Bar/Dining supplies | | 400 |
| Office supplies | | 500 |
| Building — | $44 459 | |
| less depreciation | 2 046 | 42 413 |
| Equipment — | 12 353 | |
| less depreciation | 2 174 | 10 179 |
| Land | | 35 000 |
| Total | | $92 392 |
| *Liabilities* | | |
| A/P | | $ 9 912 |
| First mortgage | | 42 000 |
| Second mortgage | | 8 000 |
| | | $59 912 |
| *Equity* | | |
| Agnew | | $32 480 |
| | | $92 392 |

rently inhabited by Mrs. Agnew, Tim, and their Great Dane, Abraham. The remaining three rooms were used to store various articles.

The smaller upstairs section, consisting of four rooms and a bathroom, was available for rent on a nightly basis. Each room was simply furnished, and contained a mirror and wash-basin. Three of the four rooms held double beds, while the fourth held two single beds. The nightly charge per room was $18. Income derived from the rental of rooms accounted for almost all that listed under "Other Revenue" in the operating statements.

## KITCHEN OPERATIONS

The next stop on the tour was the kitchen (see Exhibit 7). The kitchen area had been built onto the Inn in 1955. A long wood-topped counter ran down the middle of the kitchen, making man-oeuvering rather cumbersome. One side of the kitchen was lined with a counter containing a household dishwasher; three sinks; two ovens, one with six ranges, the other with a heating plate; a microwave oven; and a deep freezer. The other wall of the kitchen was occupied by three large old refrigerators, and shelves containing numerous articles/memorabilia from the Agnew family past.

An outline of typical operations was obtained through discussion with Mary, the cook. The initial part of the day was spent on the preparation of food items prior to cooking. Such preparation was carried out on an ongoing basis from 10:00 a.m. until early evening. It was interrupted frequently as customer orders for meals were received.

Further discussion revealed the existence of several recurring problems. A major concern was the limited cooking capacity. The two stove/ovens combined were only able to heat a maximum 12 plates at any given time. The microwave oven presented an even greater bottleneck. It was only able to accommodate five individual servings of vegetables. Cycle time for the microwave was approximately three minutes, compared to five minutes for the oven.

EXHIBIT 4

### The Old Bridge Inn
### Income Statement
### for the six months ended April 15, 1981

| Revenues | | |
|---|---:|---:|
| Food sales | $11 869 | |
|     Cost of food | 5 478 | $ 6 391 |
| Beverage sales | 6 723 | |
|     Cost of beverages | 2 484 | 4 239 |
| *Gross margin* | | $10 630 |
| *Expenses* | | |
|     Telephone | $   484 | |
|     Utilities | 3 227 | |
|     Services | 1 616 | |
|     Advertising | 1 602 | |
|     Office supplies | 342 | |
|     Kitchen/Bar supplies | 1 382 | |
|     Entertainment | 1 630 | |
|     Wages | 12 656 | |
|     Depreciation | 4 220 | |
|     Interest | 2 181 | $29 340 |
| *Profit/(Loss)* | | ($18 710) |

During banquets or the peak summer period, when up to 70 people might be eating dinner at the same time, this lack of capacity became a definite problem. Maintaining enough clean dishes and glasses to serve customers also became a problem during busy periods, since the household dishwasher had a cycle time of 45 minutes. To help alleviate this problem, a student was sometimes hired to wash dishes by hand.

Another problem mentioned was the lack of space in the kitchen. In the summer the kitchen was often staffed by five people: Mrs. Agnew acting as head cook, Mary as assistant cook, two kitchen helpers, and a dishwasher. In addition, waitresses would constantly walk in and out of the kitchen to place pick-up orders. As a result it was "near impossible to make it from one end of the kitchen to the other without knocking someone or something over."

## THE DINING AREA

The scene which he just heard described contrasted sharply with the calm Tom found as he entered the dining area. Although it was 6:00 p.m. on a Saturday evening, there were only four couples in both dining rooms. Tom sat down at the polished wood bar and ordered a drink from the bartender, Karen. He chuckled to himself as he tried to picture what a group of fishermen in hip-waders would look like amidst the dark oak beams, Tiffany lamps, and spotless silverware. Apparently, hobby fishermen frequently walked over to the Inn from the nearby locks during the summer months, but few actually stayed for a drink or a meal after looking in the door.

A piano standing in one corner of the front dining room caught Tom's attention and he enquired if it was ever used. Karen replied that during the summer the Inn had a policy of providing live entertainment every Friday and Saturday evening. A singer/songwriter from the Peterborough musicians' union was usually hired at a cost of $150 per weekend. Most of the performers played middle-of-the-road pop, although the Inn's most popular performers had

EXHIBIT 5

The Old Bridge Inn
Income Statement
for the six months ended October 15, 1981

| | | | |
|---|---|---|---|
| Revenues | | | |
| Food sales | $51 126 | | |
|   Cost of food | 14 343 | | $36 783 |
| Beverage sales | 22 942 | | |
|   Cost of beverages | 7 885 | | 15 057 |
| Other revenue | | | 2 108 |
| Gross margin | | | $53 948 |
| | | | |
| Expenses | | | |
| Telephone | $   211 | | |
| Utilities | 2 285 | | |
| Services | 1 780 | | |
| Advertising | 2 670 | | |
| Office supplies | 250 | | |
| Kitchen/Bar supplies | 206 | | |
| Entertainment | 3 867 | | |
| Wages | 29 107 | | |
| Insurance | 1 273 | | |
| Taxes | 789 | | |
| Interest | 6 162 | | $48 600 |
| Profit/(Loss) | | | $ 5 348 |

EXHIBIT 6

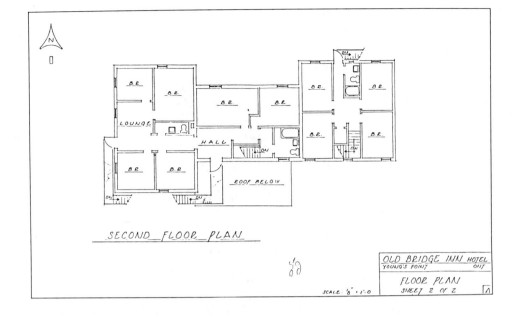

been a country and western duet. Advertisements in the local newspapers and radio were used to notify the public of upcoming entertainers.

Through further discussion with Karen, Tom discovered that the low turnout was a common occurrence in the off-season. In fact the Inn often closed its doors early due to a lack of customers. The Inn's mainstay patrons during the winter season fell into three groups: young couples, families, and senior citizens. Of these, the last group seemed to represent the only steady repeat customers. Most customers lived outside a 10 km radius from the Inn. When asked why this was so, Karen conceded that the Inn had earned a bad reputation among the local populace. Most disliked the high class image which the Inn conveyed. Comments such as "The

EXHIBIT 7

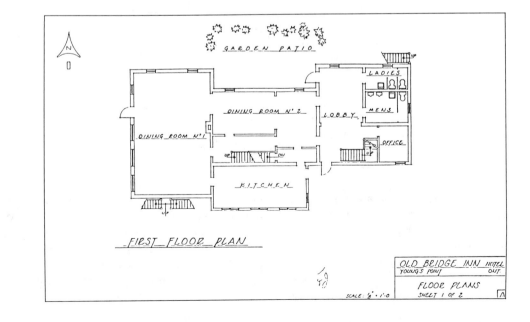

EXHIBIT 8

**THE OLD BRIDGE INN**

Young's Point, Ontario
(705) 652-3661

## Menu

| | |
|---|---|
| Roast Beef. | $ 10.50 |
| Peter's Seafood Pot. | $ 9.25 |
| Lobster, Shrimp & Crab in a creamy Sherry sauce. | |
| Barbecued Ribs | $ 8.95 |
| Sirloin Steak | $ 9.50 |

above served with Homemade Vegetable soup or tossed salad & Parsley Potato.

choice of creamed carrots, onions, Ratatouille or cauliflower & broccoli in a cheese/wine sauce.

## Desserts

| | |
|---|---|
| Pumpkin Pie | $ 1.50 |
| Raisin Pie | $ 1.50 |
| Tipsy Trifle | $ 1.75 |
| Coffee, Tea or Milk | .40 |

prices are too high," "I can't relax there," "Why don't you get rid of this silver and get some brighter tablecloths!" were typical of the local sentiments.

In addition, there were unflattering comments about the level of service, especially during the summer. One local banquet group was so upset by the slow service that its members had vowed never to return to the Inn. Word of such incidents spread quickly throughout the community, and as a result Karen felt that the Inn would have to work hard in order to regain the confidence and business of the local population.

By this time Tom was getting rather hungry,

and as a result, Tim's offer of a complimentary meal was gratefully accepted. While glimpsing over the handwritten menu (see Exhibit 8) and wine list, Tom mentioned several points which Karen had raised previously. Tim agreed that the Inn did not have a strong local draw. He felt that its current operations were targeted at the middle and upper income groups living in the Peterborough area (see Exhibit 9). The problem of poor service was probably the combined result of limited cooking capacity and inexperienced waitresses. Hiring waitresses with the desired level of experience from the local pool had proven to be difficult in the past.

With the arrival of the meal, the conversation broke off. Tom had ordered the soup of the day to start off his meal. The first spoonful of piping hot broth convinced him that the soup was definitely homemade. The main course turned out to be as pleasant a surprise as the appetizer. The seafood creole was warm, the vegetables crisp, and the potatoes plentiful. With the mention of dessert Tom started to eye his waistline. However, within no time at all he found himself ordering a second serving of a freshly baked pumpkin pie.

As Tim and Tom contemplated the day's progress over a second complimentary bottle of wine, their thoughts were interrupted by a vocal uprising from the side dining room. A table of four middle-aged customers was demanding that the waitress bring over Mrs. Agnew and the dog, Abraham. Tim walked over to the table and explained that Mrs. Agnew was sick and lying upstairs in bed. However the group persisted with their demand until Tim grudgingly went upstairs to call his mother and the dog. Upon Tim's return Tom eagerly inquired as to the nature of the problem. "No problem at all," replied Tim, "It's just a bunch of my mother's friends who get upset if they don't see her and the dog whenever they come here."

## THE PATIO

With the completion of the bottle of wine, Tim and Tom got up to finish their tour of the Inn. All that remained was the patio. Although it was dark outside, floodlights helped to illuminate the patio area. The patio was a recent addition to the Inn, having been set up by Tim the previous summer. Cedar tables and benches had been hand built by a local artisan. The maximum number of customers allowed on the patio under the liquor licence was 66 people.

During the summer the patio had been open every day from noon until 11:00 p.m. A portable bar had been set up outside. An additional bartender had been hired to take orders and serve both food and drinks. Four large vats filled with ice served to keep the drinks cold. A self-serve barbeque was set up for customers wishing to grill hamburgers, etc. Other items could be ordered via the bartender from the kitchen. These items were typically similar to those offered on the luncheon menu. No full-course meals were offered outside. A small speaker system hooked into the main system indoors broadcast music or live performances from insides when they occurred.

Although the patio was moderately successful, Tim felt that the Inn had not taken full advantage of the potential which it offered. Tim thought that most of the people using the patio were customers who were waiting for an empty table inside so they could eat a full dinner. Tim also thought that the live entertainment offered on weekends in the front dining room served to draw customers from the patio inside. As a result, the level of patio sales usually dropped abruptly after 9:00 p.m.

Having completed the rather lengthy tour of the Inn, Tim suggested that Tom might want to take a look at the operations of the Chemong Lodge. The Lodge was an operation similar to the Inn located 14 km away in Bridgenorth. En route to Bridgenorth, the two decided to stop off at the Commercial Hotel, the local watering hole. The Commercial was typical of most small town bars — loud, crowded, and unpretentious, with entertainment provided by a guitar player dressed in cowboy attire. After a lively discussion with Fred, an elderly regular who also frequented the Inn, Tom and Tim continued on their way.

The Chemong Lodge was an interconnected network of log cabins built by its owner, with

*EXHIBIT 9*

# Census Agglomeration of Peterborough*

*Market*: 34% above national average

| | |
|---|---|
| Retail sales, 1979 | $280 000 000 |
| % Canadian total | 0.37 |

*Per capita*     $4 265

*Income 7% above national average*

| | |
|---|---|
| Personal disposable income, 1979 | $505 800 000 |
| % Canadian total | 0.30 |

*Per capita*     $7 706

*Current Growth Rate 2% per decade*

| | |
|---|---|
| Population, June 1, 1979 | 65 600 |
| % Canadian total | 0.28 |
| % Change 1976–79 | +0.47 |

## Population
### 1976 Census

| | | |
|---|---|---|
| Total | | 65 290 |
| Male | | 31 450 |
| Female | | 33 840 |
| Age groups: | Male | Female |
| 0–4 | 2 250 | 2 120 |
| 5–9 | 2 410 | 2 400 |
| 10–14 | 3 050 | 2 910 |
| 15–19 | 3 310 | 3 355 |
| 20–24 | 3 185 | 3 095 |
| 25–34 | 4 620 | 4 565 |
| 35–44 | 3 320 | 3 410 |
| 45–54 | 3 485 | 4 005 |
| 55–64 | 3 025 | 3 565 |
| 65–69 | 1 135 | 1 425 |
| 70 + | 1 670 | 3 000 |

*Families*

| | 1976 |
|---|---|
| No. | 16 965 |
| Avg. no. per family | 3.3 |

*Level of Schooling*

| | 1976 Census | % Total |
|---|---|---|
| Population 15 yrs. + | 50 210 | 100 |
| Less than gr. 5 | 880 | 2 |
| Grades 5–8 | 9 010 | 18 |
| Grades 9–10 | 10 845 | 22 |
| Grades 11–13 | 14 340 | 29 |
| Post-secondary, non-university | 7 740 | 15 |
| University only | 4 390 | 9 |
| University & post-secondary, non-university | 30 015 | 6 |

*Note*: Level of Schooling refers to the highest grade or year completed by the person. Those currently enrolled reported their present grade or year.

*Households*

| | 1976 |
|---|---|
| No. | 21 620 |
| Avg. no. per household | 2.9 |

## Housing

| | 1976 Census | % Total |
|---|---|---|
| Occupied dwellings | | |
| No. | 21 620 | 100 |
| Owned | 14 320 | 66 |
| Rented | 7 300 | 34 |
| Type of dwelling | | |
| Single detached | 14 385 | 67 |
| Double | 665 | 3 |
| Row | 750 | 3 |
| Apartment | 4 335 | 20 |
| Duplex | 1 395 | 6 |
| Mobile | 10 | |

*Mother Tongue*

| | 1976 Census | % Total |
|---|---|---|
| English | 61 755 | 94.6 |
| French | 530 | 0.8 |

*Racial Origin*

| | 1971 Census | % Total |
|---|---|---|
| British | 53 545 | 84.2 |
| French | 2 635 | 4.2 |
| German | 1 905 | 3.0 |
| Italian | 1 180 | 1.9 |
| Netherlands | 1 420 | 2.2 |
| Polish | 470 | 0.7 |
| Scandinavian | 385 | 0.6 |
| Ukranian | 200 | 0.3 |
| Other | 1 835 | 2.9 |

*Employment*

| (1961 = 100) | Peter-borough | Canada |
|---|---|---|
| 1974 | 140.8 | 142.8 |
| 1975 | 147.6 | 141.1 |
| 1976 | 140.6 | 144.1 |
| 1977 | 132.5 | 144.3 |
| 1978 | 136.0 | 146.5 |

*Homes Built*

| | 1978 | 1977 | 1976 |
|---|---|---|---|
| No. | 605 | 781 | *883 |

*For 1971 area

## Labour Force

| 1976 Census | Male | Female |
|---|---|---|
| In labour force | 18 025 | 11 845 |
| Participation rate | 75.8 | 44.8 |
| 15–24 yrs. | 4 525 | 3 830 |
| 25–44 | 7 390 | 4 510 |
| 45–64 | 5 670 | 3 230 |
| 65 + | 445 | 270 |
| Employed | 16 860 | 10 485 |
| Unemployed | 1 165 | 1 355 |
| Unemployment rate | 6.5 | 11.4 |
| Married females in labour force | | 7 305 |
| Participation rate | | 45.3 |

*Religion*

| | 1971 Census | % Total |
|---|---|---|
| Protestant | 36 055 | 62.0 |
| Roman Catholic | 15 300 | 26.3 |

*Note*: For the city of Peterborough only

*Retail Trade*
### 1971 Census

| | | |
|---|---|---|
| Total sales $000 | | 133 569 |
| Stores, no. | | 457 |
| Year-end inventory, $000 | | 15 481 |
| Employees, no. | | 2 614 |
| Payroll, total, $000 | | 14 045 |

| By kind of business group | Stores No. | Sales $000 |
|---|---|---|
| Food | 74 | 33 934 |
| Groceries, confectionery & sundries | 14 | 1 105 |
| Grocery | 17 | 2 186 |
| Combination* | 22 | 28 955 |
| Meat markets | 5 | 702 |
| General merchandise | 18 | 21 352 |
| Department | 3 | 14 364 |
| General merchandise | 4 | 3 526 |
| Variety | 9 | + |
| Automotive | 125 | 37 212 |
| New motor vehicle dealers | 15 | 22 317 |
| Tire, battery, etc. | 5 | + |
| Home & auto supply | 2 | + |
| Service stations | 55 | 6 831 |

| | | |
|---|---|---|
| Garages | 10 | 730 |
| Paint & body shops | 16 | 1 280 |
| Apparel & accessories | 59 | 9 112 |
| Men's & boys' clothing | 15 | 1 790 |
| Women's & misses | 15 | 1 446 |
| Family clothing | 4 | 3 029 |
| Family shoe | 14 | + |
| Hardware & home furnishings | 55 | 10 211 |
| Hardware | 7 | 977 |
| Furniture | 5 | 758 |
| Furniture, TV, radio, appliance, etc. | 13 | 6 374 |
| Other stores | 126 | 21 746 |
| Pharmacies | 12 | 2 738 |
| Liquor | 4 | 5 331 |
| Jewellery | 12 | 1 314 |
| Sporting goods | 13 | 1 157 |

+ Confidential
* Grocery stores with fresh meat.

### Household Facilities

| | 1971 Census No. | % Total |
|---|---|---|
| Occupied dwellings | 18 770 | 100.0 |
| Dwellings with: | | |
| Refrigerator | 18 730 | 99.8 |
| Home freezer | 5 920 | 31.5 |
| Television | 18 290 | 97.4 |
| Automobile | 15 345 | 81.7 |
| Furnace heating | 15 720 | 83.7 |
| Fuel: | | |
| Oil | 13 270 | 70.7 |
| Electricity | 1 655 | 8.8 |
| Coal | 60 | 0.3 |
| Gas | 3 650 | 19.4 |

### Taxation Statistics

| Income class: | 1977 | % of Total |
|---|---|---|
| Under $2 500 | 6 893 | 16.0 |
| $2 500–5 000 | 7 229 | 16.8 |
| 5 000–7 500 | 6 220 | 14.5 |
| 7 500–10 000 | 4 327 | 10.1 |
| 10 000–12 500 | 4 105 | 9.5 |
| 12 500–15 000 | 4 274 | 9.9 |
| 15 000–20 000 | 6 292 | 14.6 |
| 20 000–25 000 | 1 620 | 3.8 |
| 25 000–30 000 | 1 109 | 2.6 |
| 30 000 & over | 952 | 2.2 |
| Total returns, no. | 43 021 | 100.0 |
| Total Inc., $000 | 434 460 | |
| Average income, $ | 10 099 | |
| Total tax, $000 | 60 997 | |
| Average tax, $ | 2 276 | |

### Building Permits

| | 1978 | 1977 | 1976 |
|---|---|---|---|
| | (-$000-) | | |
| Value | 15 001 | 22 225 | 32 742 |

*Note:* For city of Peterborough only.

### Earnings

| | Average weekly earnings $ | |
|---|---|---|
| | Peter- borough | Canada |
| 1974 | 183.61 | 178.09 |
| 1975 | 205.08 | 203.34 |
| 1976 | 225.25 | 228.03 |
| 1977 | 239.18 | 249.95 |
| 1978 | 250.22 | 265.37 |

### Manufacturing Industries

| | 1976 |
|---|---|
| Plants | 70 |
| Employees | 9 825 |
| | ($000) |
| Salaries, wages | 136 187 |
| Mfg. materials cost | 173 163 |
| Mfg. shipments, value | 374 768 |
| Total value added | 219 227 |

### Banking

| | |
|---|---|
| Branches, no. (1979) | 19* |
| Cheques cashed: | ($000) |
| 1978 | 3 395 659 |
| 1974 | 2 072 940 |

* For city of Peterborough only.

### Newspapers

| | |
|---|---|
| Newspaper, daily: | 1979 |
| *Examiner* (Thomson) | |
| Circulation, total | 23 712 |
| city | 15 388 |
| outside | 8 324 |
| Newspaper, weekly: | |
| Review | 29 700 |

### Radio Stations

CHEX, 10 000 watts.
CKPT, 10 000 watts.
CFMP-FM, 31 400 watts.
CKQM-FM, 50 000 watts.

### Television Station

CHEX-TV, Video, 163 000 watts ERP.

### Population

| 1976 Census: | | |
|---|---|---|
| Total | | 9 785 |
| Male | | 4 720 |
| Female | | 5 065 |
| Age groups: | Male | Female |
| 0–4 | 425 | 380 |
| 5–9 | 400 | 360 |
| 10–14 | 425 | 435 |
| 15–19 | 415 | 420 |
| 20–24 | 420 | 415 |
| 25–34 | 745 | 720 |
| 35–44 | 475 | 460 |
| 45–54 | 500 | 555 |
| 55–64 | 450 | 540 |
| 65–69 | 180 | 235 |
| 70 + | 285 | 555 |

### Families

| | 1976 |
|---|---|
| No. | 2 590 |
| Avg. no. per family | 3.2 |

### Mother Tongue

| | 1976 Census | % Total |
|---|---|---|
| English | 9 265 | 94.7 |
| French | 100 | 1.0 |
| Netherlandic & Flemish | 110 | 11.1 |

### Port Hope

#### Households

| | 1976 |
|---|---|
| No. | 3 317 |
| Avg. no. per household | 2.9 |

#### Housing

| | 1976 Census | % Total |
|---|---|---|
| Occupied dwellings, no. | 3 320 | 100 |
| Owned | 2 245 | 68 |
| Rented | 1 075 | 32 |
| Type of dwelling: | | |
| Single detached | 2 110 | 64 |
| Double | 230 | 7 |
| Row | 135 | 4 |
| Apartment | 715 | 22 |
| Duplex | 110 | 3 |
| Mobile | — | — |

#### Earnings

| | Average weekly earnings $ | |
|---|---|---|
| | Port Hope | Canada |
| 1974 | 172.54 | 178.09 |
| 1975 | 199.22 | 203.34 |
| 1976 | 222.99 | 228.03 |
| 1977 | 245.28 | 249.95 |
| 1978 | 263.32 | 265.37 |

#### Building Permits

| | 1978 | 1977 | 1976 |
|---|---|---|---|
| | ($000) | | |
| Value | 10 963 | 2 174 | 1 706 |

#### Employment

| (1961 = 100) | Port Hope | Canada |
|---|---|---|
| 1974 | 189.3 | 142.8 |
| 1975 | 180.5 | 141.1 |
| 1976 | 183.5 | 144.4 |
| 1977 | 189.1 | 144.3 |
| 1978 | 188.7 | 146.5 |

#### Level of Schooling

| | 1976 Census | % Total |
|---|---|---|
| Population 15 yrs. + | 7 370 | 100 |
| Less than gr. 5 | 190 | 3 |
| Grades 5–8 | 1 305 | 18 |
| Grades 9–10 | 1 780 | 24 |
| Grades 11–13 | 2 165 | 29 |
| Post-secondary, non-university | 1 025 | 14 |
| University only | 545 | 7 |
| University & post-secondary, non-university | 360 | 5 |

*Note:* Level of Schooling refers to the highest grade or year completed by the person. Those currently enrolled reported their present grade or year.

---

Source: Statistics Canada
* Reproduced by permission of the Minister of Supply and Service Canada.

approximately twice the seating capacity of the Old Bridge Inn. Items offered on the menu were typically of the surf-'n-turf variety, with entrées priced about $2.00 higher than the Inn's. At the time of the visit the Lodge was slightly over one-quarter full. Most of the customers were well-dressed couples in their late twenties or early thirties. By eavesdropping on various conversations Tim and Tom established that most of the customers were from Peterborough.

The next day Tom inquired about the Inn's advertising policy. Tim retrieved copies of newspaper advertisements which had been placed in the *Peterborough Examiner* and the local *Kawartha Sun* (see Exhibit 10 for examples). Tom was unable to determine the exact frequency with which advertisements were placed as the Inn did not have a formal expenditure control system. He estimated that a daily listing in the *Peterborough Examiner* at a cost of $42 and a weekly listing in the *Kawartha Sun* at a cost of $35 were representative of the Inn's summer advertising expenditures. During the off-season advertising dropped off substantially.

The Inn also placed occasional 30-second spots on the local AM and FM radio stations (see Exhibit 11). Mrs. Agnew would phone the radio station to inform them of various events she wanted publicized. The announcer would then write a commercial and read it on the air without further consultation. Due to the ad hoc nature of the Inn's radio advertising, Tim felt it was largely unsuccessful in delivering an accurate picture of the Inn to potential customers. In addition to its local radio advertisements, the Inn had also received free publicity through a highly complimentary review broadcast throughout Ontario on CBC Radio (see Exhibit 12).

Tim was concerned that the Inn was not getting the maximum return from its advertising expenditures. He was unsure whether the frequency of advertising was optimal, especially the heavy weighting in the summer. On the whole, he suspected that the Inn advertised with about the same frequency as its competitors. Tim also wondered if the ads were conveying the right message to his customers and potential customers. He believed the Inn had a fairly widespread reputation for the quality of its food. However, he worried that many people who had heard of the Inn did not know where it was located. In order to help Tom formulate an advertising strategy, Tim had collected some information about the local media as shown in Exhibit 13.

*EXHIBIT 10*

Summer 1991                    Summer 1981

EXHIBIT 10 (cont'd)

Kawartha Sun
September 3, 1981

Peterborough Examiner
October 1981

*Note*: Telephone number has changed since these advertisements.

EXHIBIT 11

---

**Sample Radio Commercial for the Inn**

---

Media Music 908/2/3.

Where Katchewanooka and Clear Lake Waters join, under the settler-trodden wooden bridge, stands the OLD BRIDGE INN. This Hallowe'en, enjoy the fun of an old-fashioned Box Lunch Social — just a dollar and a half per couple, with proceeds going to UNICEF. The ladies will prepare an attractive Box Lunch to be auctioned to the eager beaux at 6:30 p.m. Book now for your Christmas or New Year's party — and remember the Hallowe'en Box Lunch Social — at the OLD BRIDGE INN, just off Highway 28 at Young's Point.

---

EXHIBIT 12

---

**CBC Commentary**
**Young's Point — The Old Bridge Inn**

For Ontario Morning — CBC

I think we have here at Young's Point what is probably the finest Inn in the province. I know there are others at Caledon East, Huntsville, Elora, Acton, Bayfield, Niagara-on-the-Lake, Jackson's Point, and possibly Deep River which, according to the Ontario Morning correspondent seems to have everything — but the *Old Bridge Inn* is surely the most beautifully situated. A two-storey turn-of-the-century house of warm and solid red brick, it stands guard over the Old Wooden Bridge which fords the Otonabee River and gives access to the locks of the Trent Canal and keeps a constant eye on the thundering waters of the Dam. The old bridge is closed to cars and so it is a walker's dream and an Oasis to those seeking peace, away from the world of the traffic that passes out of hearing on to the Kawarthas and Buckhorn Lakes. The Village of Young's Point cleverly hides under the new bridge, comfortably

*EXHIBIT 12 (cont'd)*    enfolding its 300 or so regular residents. Not everybody here sounds like me but their ancestors all came from where this voice first sounded in Ireland in a house between the River Barrow and the Royal Canal in County Kildare. This Meeting of the Waters is Canada's version of that famous Vale of Avoca, not far from Dublin, that inspired Thomas Moore to write his immortal song *The Meeting of the Waters*!

> *There is not in this wide world a valley so sweet*
> *As that vale in whose bosom the bright waters meet*
>     the poem ends:
> *Sweet vale of Avoca, how calm could I rest*
> *In thy bosom of shade, with the friends I love best*
> *Where the storms that we feel in this cold world should cease*
> *And our hearts, like thy waters, be mingled in peace.*

So it is at Young's Point as I say to myself with Shakespeare's Falstaff: "Shall I not take mine ease in mine Inn?" If *location* is an essential of the good Inn so indeed is the Innkeeper, and let me tell you our Innkeeper Annabelle is as refreshing as the sight and sound of the waters alongside her Inn. She inherits a fine tradition following on the genial original Russ Brooks, now in retirement and on guard over the other end of that wooden bridge in the original family residence and the original post office, which in turn faces today's post office where despite the charm of Mrs. Jack Young, Winnie and Dorothy, the world intrudes in the mail as we all pick up there with the inevitable bill from Sears, Simpsons or Eaton's. After location and an Innkeeper, I suppose the atmosphere of an Inn is the third element of the trinity of graces an Inn should possess. What I call Annabelle soup is always homemade although called by more accurate names from day to day or Jour to Jour. The food is always homely but imaginative and lends to your whiskey or wine a distinction it might not otherwise have. There are some rooms, should you require to take your ease overnight.

An Inn is a serious matter and I wish there were more to act as an oasis and haven as we travel our long lonely roads.

As Dr. Johnson said in March of 1776, "There is nothing which has yet been contrived by man by which so much happiness is produced as by a good tavern or Inn." Anyway, I wonder, does your community boast an Inn that has that Trinity of Graces, each separate, none greater than the other, of LOCATION, INNKEEPER, BILL OF FARE? If you'll excuse me, I'll get up from my chair and go down to the Inn and test out what G.K. Chesterton said in his *Song Against the Grocers*:

> *God made the wicked grocer*
> *For a mystery and a sign*
> *That men might shun the awful shop*
> *And go to Inns to dine*
> *The righteous minds of Innkeepers*
> *Induce them now and then*
> *To crack a bottle with a friend*
> *Or treat unmoneyed men.*

This is Tony Ross, your intrepid reporter from far Young's Point. Cheers, and Slainthe.

---

\* Reprinted with permission of CBC Ontario Morning.

EXHIBIT 13

# Local Media Information
## for Peterborough area, 1981

**Radio**[1]

I. CHEX-AM

| 60 second spots | 1x | 156x | 312x |
|---|---|---|---|
| Class "AAA" | 29.20 | 21.80 | 18.75 |
| Class "AA" | 19.95 | 18.15 | 14.50 |
| Class "A" | 17.20 | 14.50 | 12.10 |
| Class "B" | 14.60 | 12.10 | 9.70 |

30 seconds — 75% of 60 second rate

---

CHEX-AM TIME CLASSIFICATIONS

| Class "AAA" | (Rotation) | 6:00 a.m.–10:00 a.m. Monday to Saturday |
|---|---|---|
| Class "AA" | (Rotation) | 10:00 a.m.–3:00 p.m. Monday to Saturday Select hours Sunday |
| Class "A" | (Rotation) | 3:00 p.m.–6:30 p.m. Monday to Saturday |
| Class "B" | (Rotation) | 6:30 p.m.–Midnight 5:00 a.m.–6:00 a.m. Monday to Saturday |
| Remote Broadcast | | $95.00 per hour plus lines and location costs |

Tags on National Announcements                                    $5.75
All Night Radio                          Midnight to 6:00 a.m.
                                         Rates on request

---

SATURATION CONTRACTS

| 150 × 60 seconds .. 15.95 | 30 seconds .. 13.45 |
|---|---|
| 300 × 60 seconds .. 13.95 | 30 seconds .. 11.45 |
| 500 × 60 seconds .. 13.30 | 30 seconds .. 10.90 |
| 750 × 60 seconds .. 12.70 | 30 seconds .. 10.35 |
| 1000 × 60 seconds .. 12.10 | 30 seconds .. 9.70 |

25% of spots in total to be aired each 3 months

| News & Sports — 5 minutes | 1x | 156x | 312x |
|---|---|---|---|
| Class "AAA" | 37.50 | 24.20 | 20.60 |
| Class "AA" | 35.10 | 20.60 | 18.15 |
| Class "A" | 32.60 | 18.15 | 16.00 |
| Class "B" | 30.25 | 15.70 | 13.30 |

10 minutes — 40% additional

[1] Data reprinted with permission of Kawartha Broadcasting Co. Ltd.

*EXHIBIT 13 (cont'd)*

TOTAL AUDIENCE PLAN

| 10% — AAA | 40% — AA | 30% — A | 20% — B |
|---|---|---|---|

| | 10x | 20x | 30x |
|---|---|---|---|
| 60 seconds | | | |
| | 193.05 | 358.60 | 499.95 |
| | 19.30 | 17.93 | 16.66 |
| 30 seconds | 166.65 | 292.82 | 399.30 |
| | 16.66 | 14.64 | 13.31 |

## GENERAL INFORMATION

Contracts are subject to cancellation by either party by a 30-day advance written notice. Cancelled or interrupted contracts are subject to short rate. Advertisers who reduce or interrupt their schedule must begin a new contract for discount purposes. Accounts are due and payable in Canadian funds when rendered.

**2.** CFMP-FM

## CFMP-STEREO-FM-101.5

| Announcements | | One | 104 | 156 | 312 |
|---|---|---|---|---|---|
| *Class AAA* | | | | | |
| | 60 seconds | 18.00 | 13.00 | 12.00 | 11.00 |
| 6:00 a.m.–12:00 noon | | | | | |
| | 30 seconds | 15.00 | 10.00 | 9.00 | 8.00 |
| Monday–Friday | | | | | |
| *Class AA* | | | | | |
| 12:00 noon–6:00 p.m. | 60 seconds | 16.00 | 11.00 | 10.00 | 9.00 |
| Monday–Friday | | | | | |
| | 30 seconds | 13.00 | 8.00 | 7.00 | 6.00 |
| Saturday & Sunday | | | | | |
| *Class A* | | | | | |
| | 60 seconds | 14.00 | 9.00 | 8.00 | 7.00 |
| 6:00 p.m.–sign-off | | | | | |
| | 30 seconds | 11.00 | 6.00 | 5.00 | 4.00 |
| Monday–Friday | | | | | |

| Announcements | | One | 104 | 156 | 312 |
|---|---|---|---|---|---|
| *News & Sports* | | | AAA | AA | A |
| (5 minutes) | | | | | |
| | 3x weekly | | 16.00 | 14.00 | 12.00 |
| (10 minutes 40% additional) | 6x weekly | | 12.00 | 10.00 | 8.00 |

EXHIBIT 13 (cont'd)

| Saturation Packages | | | 10x | 20x | 30x | 50x |
|---|---|---|---|---|---|---|
| Best available times | 60 seconds | | 13.50 | 13.00 | 12.50 | 12.00 |
| to be used within 2 weeks | 30 seconds | | 10.50 | 10.00 | 9.50 | 9.00 |

| Saturation Contracts | | | 300x | 500x | 750x | 1000x |
|---|---|---|---|---|---|---|
| | 60 seconds | | 10.50 | 10.00 | 9.50 | 9.00 |
| (to be used in 12 months) | 30 seconds | | 7.50 | 7.00 | 6.50 | 6.00 |

SPECIAL FEATURE & PROGRAM RATES ON REQUEST

Card No. 5 Effective September 1, 1981

## Newspaper[2]

**1.** *Kawartha Sun*

Circulation: 20 000 in the Kawarthas and Lakeshore Districts

| Full page: (tabloid size) 31¢/line | | ($416.64) |
|---|---|---|
| 1/2 page & up: 32¢/line | OR | $4.48/column inch |
| 1/4 page — 1/2 page: 33¢/line | OR | $4.62/column inch |
| 1/8 page — 1/4 page: 34¢/line | OR | $4.76/column inch |
| 1/16 page — 1/8 page: 35¢/line | OR | $4.90/column inch |
| Transient rate: 37¢/line | OR | $5.18/column inch |
| Feature rate: 37¢/line | OR | $5.18/column inch |

**2.** *Peterborough Examiner*

Circulation: 23 391[3]

Full page (highest non-volume rate): 46¢/line ($1 275.00)

All sizes at flat rate of 46¢/line

Format: 9 columns × 308 lines each

Position charge: 15% extra

Colour (min. size 600 lines):   1 colour × $165

2 colour + $245

[2] Data reproduced with permission of *Peterborough Examiner*.
[3] Circulation in 1979.

Before Tom left, Tim reiterated what he felt to be the Inn's most pressing problems. First among these was cash flow. Tim had initially thought that closing the Inn's doors during the winter would be a possible solution. However, in order to sell the Inn he felt the onus would be on him to prove to a potential buyer that it was a viable ongoing business concern. Short-term funds of up to $5000 could likely be obtained from a local bank to implement operational changes, provided that all expenditures were accounted for in advance. A plan to improve the long-term profitability of the Inn was also important, since Tim figured that there was only a 50% chance that the Inn would be sold before the following summer.

As Tom was about to leave, Tim gave him a letter he had received on Friday by registered mail, reproduced here as Exhibit 14. Tim felt that the tone of the second paragraph served to bring into focus the urgency of the situation currently facing the Inn and its operations. "Let me know very soon what you think I should do," continued Tim, "because time is running out."

*Exhibit 14*

Ontario
Ministry    Retail
of          Sales Tax
Revenue     Branch

208 Dundas St. East
Belleville, Ontario
K8N 1E3

(613) 962-9108
Zenith 71820

**REGISTERED MAIL**

November 4, 1981

Refer to: D.E. Graham
V.P. #47289651

The Old Bridge Inn
Young's Point, Ontario
K0L 3G0

Attention: *Mr. Agnew*

Dear Sir:

We would like to thank you for the two cheques in the amount of $2,500.00 and $2,875.80 to clear your outstanding tax liability of $5,375.80. Your proposal to pay your outstanding tax liability is accepted on the conditions that your current return is filed on or before the due date and your cheques are honoured when presented for payment.

If the above conditions are not kept we will have no alternative but to take whatever legal action that we deem necessary to collect without further notification to you.

Interest will continue to accrue at 12 percent per annum on the unpaid balance.

Yours very truly,

*T. O'Sullivan*

Acting District
Compliance Supervisor

TOS:jb

* Letter reprinted with permission.

# 2

## PART

# THE RETAIL
# MARKETPLACE

CHAPTER

# RETAIL CUSTOMERS

## ■ INTRODUCTION

Retail marketers succeed by serving and satisfying customers. Accordingly, every retailer should be vitally concerned with identifying and understanding both current and potential customers. While some retailers seem able to prosper without any apparent attempt to get close to their customers, with increasing competition this is a dangerous stance to take. It is only through sensitivity to customer needs, wants, expectations, aspirations, and habits that a retail marketer is able to design and deliver competitively powerful marketing offers. Figure 4.1 is a summary of the major concepts in this chapter.

This notion of sensitivity to customers is not a new idea. In 1726, for example, Daniel Defoe captured the need for the retailer to understand the customer:

> Trade must not be entered into as a thing of light concern. It is called business very properly, for it is a business of life and ought to be followed as one of the great businesses of life. Trade must, I say, be worked at, not played with. He that trades in jest will certainly break in earnest, and this is one reason indeed why so many tradesmen come to so hasty a conclusion of their affairs.
>
> The sum of the matter is this. It is necessary for a tradesman to be subject, by all ways possible, to his business; his customers are to be his idols; so far as he may worship idols by allowance, he is to bow down to them and worship them; at least, he is not in any way to displease them or show any disgust or distaste at anything they say or do. The bottom of it all is, that he is intending to get money by them, and it is not for him that gets money by them to offer the least inconvenience to them by whom he gets it, but he is to consider that, as Solomon says, "The borrower is the servant to the lender," so the seller is servant to the buyer.[1]

FIGURE 4.1

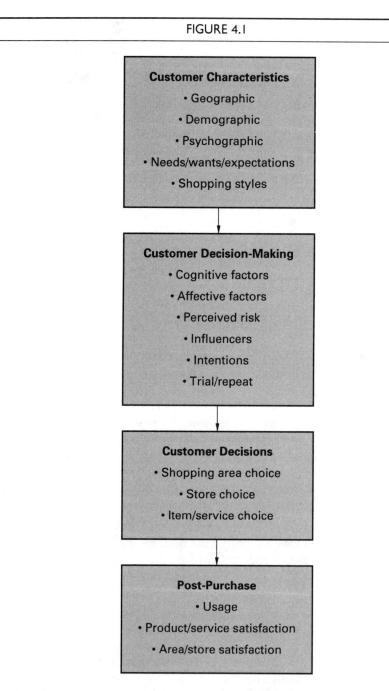

Retail marketers attempt to identify and understand current and potential retail customers for four basic reasons:

1. To assist in target market selection. Retailers select target markets because it is not possible to be all things to all people. Customer understanding provides the facts upon which to base this target selection.

2. To determine market potential. Once a target area and customer group have been selected, the retailer will want to estimate the number of customers, their ability and willingness to buy products and services in his or her assortment, their possible frequency and amount of buying, and their likelihood of buying from him or her.

3. To design the appropriate marketing offer and ensure its delivery. Retailers make a wide variety of detailed decisions on where to locate, what assortment to carry, how to display their merchandise, and so on. Having some indications of which choices are more likely to win customer approval and patronage aids immensely in making these choices.

4. To assess the reasons for retail performance. Every retailer is interested in maintaining or improving performance; however, he or she needs to know both what happened and why it happened in order to make appropriate decisions. A retailer may know that customer traffic has fallen, but not know what to do about it. Understanding why traffic is down can help provide the answers to this problem (it may be necessary, for example, to change signage, alter advertising media, and so on).

It is critical that retail marketers view themselves as purchasing agents for their customers, not just selling agents for their suppliers. The former is a market-driven approach and the latter a corporate-driven approach. A market-driven retailer will invest effort, money, and time in anticipating and reacting to customer needs and trends. He or she will set high standards for customer responsiveness, even create expectations among customers for this, then set out to satisfy those expectations.

There are a host of questions a retail marketer may have about his or her current and potential customers, including:

a. How many current and potential customers are there in this (however defined) trading area?

b. Which customers are most promising?

c. What do those customers particularly want from a store (or catalogue or whatever retail form) like this?

d. What do they think and feel about competitors?

e. Can customers be lured away from competitors? Which ones? How?

f. What do these customers think and feel about this store? Are they likely to leave for a competitor?

g. How can these customers be reached most efficiently and effectively to tell them about this retail marketer's offering?

h. Where is a particularly good place to locate?

i. What price levels are best?

j. What other services should be offered?

The list can be a much longer one. While insights about customers do not dictate which decisions a retail marketer must take, they can help a retailer decide the merits of alternatives.

Ultimately, a retail marketer wants as many of the people as possible in his or her trading area to purchase those goods and services he or she offers. This means that the retailer wants to favourably influence customer decisions as to where to shop and what to buy. To obtain these favourable outcomes, it is necessary to understand how customers make patronage and buying decisions. This inquiry leads to an examination of customer characteristics and customer decision-making processes. For the retailer who deals personally with a few customers, this discussion may seem redundant, but increasingly retailers are not able to get to know their customers personally. (In Chapter 6, some ways to get information about customers will be examined). The focus in this chapter is on the kind of information that would be useful to have.

■
SECTION
■
ONE
■

## RETAIL CUSTOMER CHARACTERISTICS

Some major ways of segmenting retail markets (introduced earlier, in Chapter 2) are by customer descriptors and by descriptors of customer responses to marketing efforts. This section discusses the range of descriptors.

An enormous amount of information has been gathered about, and a great deal of speculation devoted to, understanding customers—past, present, and future. For example, Ken Dychtwald and Greg Gable of Age Wave Inc. summarized their recent book *The Shifting American Marketplace* as follows:

> The marketplace is changing. People are living longer, healthier, and more productive lives, and we are likely to see further expansions of life expectancy. At the same time, fewer babies are being born, causing a shrinkage in the number and relative proportion of the young in our society. The baby boomers are leaving youth and migrating into middle age. By the year 2000, they will have filled the 35–54-year-old age bracket. As a result, spending power is becoming increasingly concentrated in the hands of a more mature consumer base. The clear and unmistakable implication is that business is about to face a larger, more powerful mass of mature consumers as we enter the 1990's and beyond.[2]

Dychtwald and Gable went on to outline ten predictions about how the American marketplace will develop, as shown in Exhibit 4.1.

*EXHIBIT 4.1*
*Dychtwald*
*and Gable's*
*Predictions*

1. The concerns and perspectives of middle age and maturity will become dominant.
2. In middle age, the baby boomers will retain many of their cohort characteristics, including their tendency to delay traditional markers of maturity, their diversity, their distrust of authority, their educational attainment, and their entanglement with the media and marketing arms of business.
3. Middle-aged and maturing consumers will be embarking upon "cyclic life styles" and will defy the age markets traditionally associated with maturity.
4. The new middle-aged will seek ways to balance work, family, and recreation.
5. People in middle age will become increasingly concerned with health and wellness.

6. Men and women are becoming increasingly similar in the marketplace.

7. Seasoned consumers evaluate their choices based on years of consumer experience and product trials. They will seek and recognize quality above all else.

8. Convenience and comfort will become increasingly important consumer issues.

9. Middle-aged consumers will be looking for ways to increase their sense of control.

10. Middle-aged and maturing consumers will be increasingly interested in purchasing "experiences" rather than "things."

---

Not surprisingly, there are disagreements among the experts on trends and rationales. Nonetheless, most experts look at the same **basic dimensions of customers**. These are the major subject of this chapter.

The ways customers think, feel, and behave are in large part affected by their own characteristics and circumstances, independent of marketing activities intended to influence them. Accordingly, a good starting place for customer understanding is with the customer. There are five major sets of characteristics typically used to describe retail customers:

1. geographic
2. demographic
3. psychographic
4. needs/wants/expectations
5. shopping style or orientation

## GEOGRAPHIC CHARACTERISTICS

The first level of customer analysis is usually geographic because this puts some boundaries around the population of interest to the retailer. The geographic area served by a retailer is called the **trading area**. Most retailers operate in geographically constrained markets, such as a city or a neighbourhood, although some retailers have very broad trading areas. For example, the trading area of a residential convenience store is very small, especially compared to the trading area of U.S. mail order giant L.L. Bean.

The geographic area served can be considered at the national, regional, metropolitan, city, and neighbourhood levels. The retailer is interested in the population that lives, works, and shops in that geographic area, as well as the climate, the transportation infrastructure, the topological features (rivers, mountains, etc.), and any other feature of the trading area that determines how many customers there are, the way in which customers shop, and the way in which retailers compete for their patronage. Retailing, for example, is very different in a rural area than in a highly developed major urban centre; mobility patterns are different, the time and effort it takes to go the same distance varies greatly, and so on. Geography has taken on new meaning with the advent of **census tract** and **postal code analysis**. In each instance, data are collected and analyzed at a micromarket level. A retail marketer may map his or her customers on a local postal code map (as will be described further in Chapter 8); then, using other studies of household characteristics in those postal codes (usually developed from government census data by such commercial services as CompUSearch, ACORN, Cluster-Plus, PRIZM, and VISION), ascertain an approximate profile of the customers based on where they live.[3]

The sales or **buying power** represented in a trading area is of great interest to a retailer. Retailers frequently attempt to calculate buying power indices, particularly before making a site selection decision and when assessing the impact of major changes in a market, such as development of a new shopping centre. Most buying power indices involve calculation of the number of households in an area times average discretionary household income in the area times the percentage of disposable income typically spent on a particular product or service category. Most of the information needed for buying power calculations can be obtained from census tract reports, published surveys of local markets, and buying pattern studies. The most difficult part is obtaining good expenditure data.[4] These are often much more general than an individual retailer would like. Nonetheless, this approach does provide a rough indication of market potential in the trading area.

The **index of retail saturation** is a measure of the extent of over-storing or under-storing in a trading area relative to market demand. This measure is calculated by multiplying the number of prospective customers in the area (or households) by the average expenditure per person (or household) for a particular product or service category. This number is then divided by the total square footage of relevant competing retailers (planned competition could also be added in) in the area. The higher the resultant index, expressed in dollars per square foot (or square metre), the better the potential for adding retail space in that trading area. (Trade area analysis will be discussed further in Chapter 8.)

## DEMOGRAPHICS

**Demographics** refer to the basic characteristics of a population. These characteristics, such as number of people, age distribution, educational levels, and so on, tend to change relatively slowly and, for the most part, in a relatively predictable fashion. All types of marketers have long focused on the demographics of their customers for two basic reasons: first, this information is relatively easy to obtain from government and other secondary sources and, second, most marketers have believed that buying behaviour is related to these demographic factors. Demographic analysis is a usual second step in the description and analysis of any retailer's marketplace. A retailer typically begins by creating a profile of current customers based on the major demographic dimensions shown in Exhibit 4.2.

Seldom is any one of these characteristics adequate to select a target market or prepare a marketing program. A 1990 report on American grocery shoppers confirms this point:

> Certain supermarket characteristics, such as cleanliness and clearly labelled prices, have universal appeal. But beyond these basic store traits, customers

differ widely in what they want in their supermarkets. The key for a retailer is to have a handle on local demographics and adjust the store's makeup accordingly.

Older shoppers look for a good meat department and helpful managers. Younger customers, who are likely to be employed full time, are generally more interested in one-stop shopping features, a good deli, hot takeout foods, and late hours.[5]

---

*EXHIBIT 4.2*
*Major Demographic Dimensions*

1. population size
2. population growth trend
3. age distribution
4. gender
5. occupation
6. income (personal and household: total, disposable, discretionary)
7. education
8. ethnic and cultural background
9. language
10. religion
11. marital and family status
12. household number and size
13. mobility (number moving per year)

---

One might think that focusing on one **age group**, such as the elderly market, would be a relatively easy task. However, research has shown that generalizations about age simply do not hold true. In her article, "Over 49: The Invisible Consumer Market," Rena Bartos describes the many segments in the "over 49" market, dispelling any myths about older customers.[6] By the same token, most marketers still talk in terms of generations to describe their markets—for example, the baby boomers, the "twentysomething,"[7] and the Nintendo generation.[8]

Similarly, there are many changes in **occupation** that are impacting on retailing. For example, consider the increasing proportion of women who have jobs outside the home (nearly 60 percent of all Canadian women age 18 or older versus 24 percent in 1950) and the increasing number of people who are working less with their hands (an indicator of the evolution to a "service society"). And, it is not just what people do for a living that is changing, but also where it is being done. For example, after doing research in 1988 on the American home office market, The Workbench, a New York–based furniture retailer offered several observations, including:

1. 25 million Americans work from home today. Full-time homeworkers have increased by 20% in the past year.
2. Homeworkers typically have an average of eight or nine years' professional

work experience. Roughly 75% are white collar—or what is becoming known as plaid collar.

3. Computers are in 35% of American households in 1988, up 25% from 1987.

4. The computer and the fax are cited as essential tools for the successful homeworker.

5. Design experts agree that the home office will require the same design considerations as the conventional office, including lighting, productivity, comfort, and safety.[9]

**Gender** is not always a very reliable characteristic for customer understanding. For example, contrary to a long-held stereotype, not all women love to shop: a 1983 survey of Canadian female shoppers by the Retail Merchants Association indicated that approximately 40 percent of women interviewed found shopping a nuisance. Judith Langer, president of Langer Associates in New York, recently advised marketers to rethink how genders were used as customer descriptors: "become aware of the sexes on three levels: gender role (the reality of how each sex is living today), gender ego (what each sex prides itself on), and gender fantasy (the images each sex responds to emotionally)."[10]

The changing **age distribution** of the population is of great concern to retail marketers. In the next two decades, the proportion of the Canadian and U.S. population over 50 years old will increase from about 24–25 percent to more than 33 percent. This "greying of North America" is highly significant since wealth is concentrated in the hands of the "mature" segment of the population. There will be not only requirements to change for retailers, but also remarkable opportunities. Retailers in the food sector, for example, need to know that as a population ages, people tend to eat less red meat, more fish, more chicken, and a lot more vegetables, and they want much smaller serving sizes.[11]

Another concept of value for retail marketers is **family life stage**. Typically, a population can be divided into groups showing that as people age, their other demographic characteristics change as well. Exhibit 4.3 shows one schema for life stage analysis in the United States.

---

*EXHIBIT 4.3*
*Life Stage*
*Analysis[1]*

1. **Bachelor**—Independent, young, early stage of career, low discretionary income

2. **Newly married**—two incomes, relative independence, present and future oriented

3. **Full Nest 1**—youngest child under 6, one income, limited independence, future oriented

4. **Full Nest 2**—youngest child over 6 but dependent, one and a half incomes, husband established in career, limited independence, future oriented

5. **Full Nest 3**—youngest child living at home but independent, highest income level, independent, thoughts of retirement

6. **Empty Nest 1**—no children at home, independent, good income, thoughts of self and retirement

7. **Empty Nest 2**—retirement, limited income and expenses, present oriented

8. **Sole Survivor I**—only one spouse alive, actively employed, present oriented, good income

9. **Sole Survivor 2**—only one spouse alive, retired, feeling of futility, poor income.

---

[1] Barry Berman and Joel R. Evans, *Retail Management: A Strategic Approach* (New York: Macmillan, 1989), p. 149. Reprinted by permission.

Each of these life stage segments has different needs and habits, different levels of discretionary income, and different shopping behaviour, all of which require differing approaches by the retail marketer.

**Household characteristics** are another way to examine and categorize customers. Households may be categorized by type: some households are family (related individuals living together) while others are nonfamily; some are several people while some are a single person. Or households may be categorized by size: in most countries, the trend is toward smaller numbers of people per household on average. Another dimension is the rate of household formation, a statistic of particular interest to retailers offering furniture and furnishings or other products and services for the home.

One of the most notable trends has been the dramatic increase in the proportion of single households. Leonard Berry identified the significance of the "buy-for-one" customer:

> The rapid growth of households headed by individuals not living with family members holds important implications for executives used to thinking largely in the context of husband, wife and two to four children. The implications arise from the not surprising conclusion that singles tend to spend their money differently than do couples with children at home. And in no way is this difference in consumption behavior better revealed than in the fact that singles buy for one instead of for four or five. Singles buy about one-fourth of all passenger cars, but about one-half of all smaller cars. . . . Singles are more inclined to smaller food packages and indeed represent the market for the "one-serving" package sizes that are appearing on the market. . . . Singles are a source of concern for the life insurance industry, which sells a service designed to protect family members.[12]

Retailers must be concerned with both their customers' willingness to buy and their **ability to buy**. In 1989, for example, 65 percent of Canadian households with annual incomes over $55 000 had a microwave oven while in households with incomes under $10 000 only 18 percent had microwaves.[13] Retailers, for the most part, are appealing to customers for their discretionary income—the money that is available to spend after paying for basic commitments, such as shelter. (Disposable income, on the other hand, refers to the amount of money left after paying taxes.) The amount of discretionary income depends on many factors, including the savings rate and amount of consumer debt. Lately, North American customers have been spending more and more of their income, compared to past levels and compared to patterns in other countries. The U.S. savings rate in the third quarter of 1987, for instance, was 2.8 percent compared to the 9 percent level in the 1970s, and compared to 15 percent in Japan and 13 percent in West Germany.[14]

Yet another way to categorize customers is on the basis of **physical traits**, such as size (weight and height), right- or left-handedness, acuity of the senses, and physical disabilities, to name a few. For example, as people age, their vision, hearing, flexibility, strength, and endurance decline. Such physical changes (and the emotional changes that go with them) are too often not recognized by retailers serving a maturing market. There are other cases, however, where many retailers have focused on the special physical needs of some market segments. For instance, The Westminster Lady is a retail operation in the United States offering sleepwear, lingerie, and exercise dancewear to women sizes 14 to 72. Diane Wildowsky, size 24, began this operation after becoming discouraged while trying to find such items for herself through other retailers. The National Association for the Advancement of Fat Americans and other such organizations provided encouragement because they believed an important segment of the market was being ignored by retailers.[15] Similarly, there are stores that carry left-handed items, stores that are designed to be especially accessible to people with disabilities, and so on.

## Psychographics

Demographics sometimes fail to help the retail marketer sufficiently in understanding and predicting customer wants, expectations, and behaviour; hence the introduction of a third level of customer analysis — psychographics. **Psychographics** is the study of characteristics of the population that relate to its activities, interests, opinions, and values.

Emanuel Demby, sometimes referred to as one of the "fathers" of psychographic analysis, defined psychographics as follows:

> The use of psychological, sociological, and anthropological factors, such as benefits desired (from the behaviour being studied), self-concept, and lifestyle (or serving style), to determine how the market is segmented by the propensity of groups within the market — and their reasons — to make a particular decision about a product, person, ideology, or otherwise hold an attitude or use a medium. Demographics and socioeconomics are also used as a constant check to see if psychographic market segmentation improves on other forms of segmentation, including user/nonuser groupings.[16]

The most important concept in psychographics is lifestyle. **Lifestyle** refers to the way individuals spend not just their money, but also their time and energies. While some people prefer to spend their leisure time watching television, others prefer to engage in sports, and so on. Canadian leisure time declined from 26.2 hours per week in 1972 to 16.2 hours in 1990.[17]

**Values** are constantly changing deep-seated convictions that shape every individual's behaviour, offering retail marketers a smorgasbord of opportunities to tailor their offerings to various segments. Experts have suggested that some of the major values on the increase in North America today are quality, environmental consciousness, naturalness, spirituality, conservativeness, healthiness, experience, and moral stability.[18]

One recent term used to describe lifestyle behavioural change is cocooning, a term attributed to Faith Popcorn. **Cocooning** refers to the tendency to stay home and enjoy being there. Cocooners watch more television, look upon their homes as places to decorate and express themselves, and places in which to entertain. Cocooners are obvious targets for home entertainment retailers, home furnishing retailers, home security retailers, and others.[19]

Retail marketers study lifestyles because of their link to shopping behaviour. According to Ernest Risch, "consumption activity is a manifestation of psychic inclinations—mind and body are one—consumption behavior is an external expression of an internal feeling."[20]

There are many dimensions to psychographic analysis, such as:

1. alienation
2. conservatism
3. innovativeness
4. self-confidence
5. activities
6. interests
7. opinions
8. values
9. me-consciousness
10. fashion consciousness

One well-known example of psychographic segmentation is "values and lifestyles" (**VALS**). This approach was originated in 1978 by SRI International. In 1989, VALS2 was introduced by SRI; this divides customers into eight groups according to their psychological characteristics and their "resources" (education, income, self-confidence, health, and eagerness to buy). Exhibit 4.4 shows a brief outline of these eight segments.

*EXHIBIT 4.4*
*VALS2*
*Segments[1]*

1. Actualizers are successful, sophisticated, active, "take-charge" people with high self-esteem and abundant resources. Their possessions and recreation reflect a cultivated taste for the finer things in life.

2. Fulfilleds are mature, satisfied, comfortable, reflective people who value order, knowledge, and responsibility. Most are well-educated, and in, or recently retired from, professional occupations. Although their incomes allow them many choices, they are conservative, practical consumers.

3. Believers are conservative, conventional people with concrete beliefs and strong attachments to traditional institutions. As consumers, they are conservative and predictable, favoring American products and established brands.

4.  **Achievers** are successful career and work-oriented people who like to, and generally do, feel in control of their lives. They are deeply committed to their work and their families. As consumers they favor established products that demonstrate their success to their peers.

5.  **Strivers** seek motivation, self-definition and approval from the world around them. Unsure of themselves and low on economic, social and psychological resources, they are deeply concerned about the opinions and approval of others. They emulate those who own more impressive possessions, but what they wish to obtain is generally beyond their reach.

6.  **Experiencers** are young, vital, enthusiastic, impulsive, and rebellious. They seek variety and excitement. They are avid consumers and spend much of their income on clothing, fast food, music, movies, and video.

7.  **Makers** are practical people who have constructive skills and value self-sufficiency. They experience the world by working on it. They are unimpressed by material possessions other than those with a practical or functional purpose.

8.  **Strugglers'** lives are constricted. Chronically poor, ill-educated, low-skilled, without social bonds, aging and concerned about their health, they are often despairing and passive. They are cautious consumers; and while they represent a very modest market for most products and services, they are loyal to favorite brands.

---

[1] Excerpted from Penny Gill, "Know your customer?" *Stores*, November 1989, pp. 31–43. Reprinted by permission.

For sheer volume of attention, none of the lifestyle classifications has yet matched that of the **Baby Boomers**. Extensively researched and incessantly wooed, the baby boomers are those people born between 1946 and 1964. This means that the leading edge of the baby boom are now in their forties, and that the peak of the baby boom are in their early thirties. Baby boomers are better educated and earn higher incomes, in real terms, than their parents did at a comparable age. Compared to their parents, boomers waited longer to marry and had smaller families. They represent about one-third of the North American population and its discretionary income. Not only are boomers an immensely important segment of the population in terms of numbers, they are also significantly different on a variety of levels from other customers.[21] However, beware: boomers are as changing a customer group as any other in the market. This group once ate junk foods, but now frequents nutrition centres; they once protested, but now are highly conservative, and so on. Stephani Cook of TvB (Television Bureau) characterized these people as striving together to be different and in this way saw them as similar to adolescents.

One distinguishing factor about the baby boom generation is that it is visually oriented, more interested and accustomed to pictures and images than to words. Their parents are the opposite. This is the generation that grew up with television and is most comfortable with television.[22]

One way to reach a lifestyle group is through music. Each generation and indeed each segment of each generation has its own special music—music that will remain special to them for their entire lives. When used, this particular music signals "this message is for you."

Another example of an important "lifestyle" segment is working women. Actually, this group is now so large in Canada and the United States that it needs to be segmented into smaller groups (such as career women) to be manageable for retailers. The proportion of women in a population who are working varies by age and educational background segments. Higher percentages of university trained women work, and are more likely working in professional occupations. These women in particular are time-poor, need professional wardrobes, and have the money to pay for them; so it is no surprise that many retailers are hastening to woo them. However, many retailers are finding this is not an easy-to-understand or easy-to-please group.[23]

While much of psychographic analysis focuses on how customers live their lives now, it is useful to remember that customers' current behaviour is partly determined by their expectations for the future, or what some call "customer outlook." Customers hold opinions regarding the outlook for their economy, their personal finances, employment prospects, and so on. These opinions create a mood of optimism or pessimism, lead to personal satisfaction or dissatisfaction, and so on, and thus are indicators of what retailers can expect customers will spend and on what kinds of items. Some organizations, such as The Conference Board, regularly track these overall levels of customer confidence.

While some retailers may focus on distinct lifestyle categories within any particular trading area, others may be interested in larger groups of people in larger geographic areas. This kind of customer analysis focuses on ethnic and cultural characteristics. These are the deep-rooted values, habits, and ways of living that are shared across peoples of a shared region or language and religious origin. Canada's ethnic mix has undergone dramatic change:

> Canada's most recent demographic statistics show unprecedented numbers of third language ethnic consumers in major urban centres across the country. The ethnic population of Toronto now stands at 58%, with Vancouver, Edmonton, Calgary, Winnipeg, Ottawa and Montreal all showing huge increases, some verging on the majority.
>
> Millions of immigrants to Canada work, shop, bank, entertain and worship in as many as 93 different languages. Canada is indeed a cosmopolitan country and the strength of this growing third language market force is creating major changes in the retail sector.[24]

Sometimes a society has widely diverse characteristics, such as various different lifestyles, and sometimes there is more homogeneity. Japan has a very homogeneous culture, which means that Westerners are prone to misunderstand that market.[25] George Fields, one of Japan's premier market researchers, wrote: "Americans are optimists while the Japanese are pessimists. As a result, Americans borrow and spend, trusting in the future, while the Japanese, distrustful of the future, save and lend."[26]

## Needs, Wants, and Expectations

All retailers, whether they are offering apparel or meals, appliances or overnight accommodation, need to realize that they are offering a "package of benefits" to their customers that is much more than the basic product or service. A restaurant meal, for instance, is more than just the food and drink on the table. It may also be a night out, a reflection of ability to pay, an indication of social standing, a place to be seen, a social gathering, a special occasion, and so on. This kind of thinking about the wants, needs, and expectations that the customer brings to the buying situation offers retailers valuable insights into the design and execution of marketing programs. Kodak advertises "memories," Hallmark "sentiments," and the Bell Telephone system "that long-distance feeling." Such marketing approaches originate in understanding that the product is what the product does for the customer. The fourth level of customer analysis is identification of the specific needs, wants, and expectations of customers.

As discussed in Chapters 1 and 2, retail customers want and expect *assortment, convenience, information, care and service, value,* and *experience*. The difficult question is which of these wants and expectations are most important for which customers in what circumstances. The same person may shop carefully for the lowest price generic toilet paper and for the highest price designer jeans. Analysis of customer **needs** (what they feel they must have), **wants** (what they feel they would like, if possible), and **expectations** (what they think should and/or will happen) can be done on a general or a very specific basis, such as for a particular store or product.

Needs, wants, and expectations can be studied in terms of their *dimensions* (for example, value for money) and their *importance* (for example, more important than just a matter of convenience). Grocers, for instance, track the changing values and interests among their customers regarding food and food shopping. According to an article in *Progressive Grocer*, what the average shopper wants in a supermarket has stayed relatively stable; however, different segments have differing wants. For example, younger shoppers are more reluctant to speak with supermarket employees, express more dissatisfaction with their shopping experience, and spend less time in-store; yet, these same shoppers exhibit greater store loyalty and more likelihood to impulse shop. Table 4.1 shows the top-rated "wants" the average U.S. shopper had for supermarkets in 1990. These ratings changed relatively little from a survey two years earlier.

Along with the changing pattern of work and leisure, changing patterns of food preparation, and changing patterns of appliance ownership (microwaves are now in 60–70 percent of North American homes), it is no surprise to see a shift in grocery stores to a greater concern for meal occasions as opposed to just ingredient occasions.

Customers have needs and wants regarding products and services, stores, shopping centres, and, in fact, every aspect of the retail marketing system. For example, a U.S. survey regarding what shoppers wanted in shopping malls discovered that the most-wanted services, in order of importance, were as follows: daycare/drop-in/babysitting services; more restrooms; package/coat check or

TABLE 4.1
What the Average U.S. Supermarket Shopper Wants[1]

| Rank | Characteristic | Score |
|------|----------------|-------|
| 1 | Cleanliness | 93.6 |
| 2 | All prices labelled | 91.5 |
| 3 | Freshness date marked | 91.0 |
| 4 | Accurate, pleasant checkout clerks | 90.3 |
| 5 | Low prices | 89.2 |
| 6 | Good produce department | 88.3 |
| 7 | Good meat department | 86.9 |
| 8 | Convenient store location | 85.0 |
| 9 | Good dairy department | 84.7 |
| 10 | Good parking facilities | 84.7 |
| 11 | Shelves usually well stocked | 84.7 |
| 12 | Short wait for checkout | 84.1 |
| 13 | Unit pricing signs on shelves | 83.6 |
| 14 | Good layout for fast, easy shopping | 83.1 |
| 15 | Frequent sales or specials | 81.6 |
| 16 | Good selection of nationally advertised brands | 80.7 |
| 17 | Helpful personnel in service departments | 80.6 |
| 18 | Does not run short of items on special | 79.6 |
| 19 | Aisles clear of boxes | 78.9 |
| 20 | Good frozen food department | 78.4 |

[1] "57th Annual Report," *Progressive Grocer*, April 1990.

lockers; package wrapping/shipping; and improved physical amenities, such as seating areas and automatic doors.[27]

Retail marketers are also discovering changing customer wants and expectations about service while the customer is selecting/obtaining products and services and about post-sale support. For example, M. Lele and U. Karmarkar wrote:

> When making purchases, customers often believe they are buying more than the physical item: they also have expectations about the level of post-purchase support the product carries with it. This support can range from simple replacement of a faulty item to complex arrangements designed to meet customer needs over the product's entire useful life. Our investigations show that defining these expectations of support and meeting them effectively can be critical to a successful marketing effort.[28]

(This topic of customer care and service will be discussed further in Chapter 9.)

## Shopping Style or Orientation

While lifestyle captures the idea that customers have distinctive patterns in how they live their lives, **shopping style** or orientation is a concept used to characterize distinctive modes of shopping that transcend the product or service category and thus become characteristics of the customers themselves. The fifth level of customer analysis involves identification of specific shopping styles (or orientations). Several researchers and authors have advanced the idea that customers have varying ways of shopping; that is, have differing shopping orientations or styles. For example, Gregory Stone classified shoppers in four groups:

1. The economic shopper who views shopping solely as an economic activity that is to be performed as efficiently as possible.
2. The personalizing shopper who individualizes the experience by shopping at stores where personal relationships with store personnel can be developed and maintained.
3. The ethical shopper who feels a moral obligation to patronize specific stores.
4. The apathetic shopper who has little interest in shopping and tries to minimize involvement and effort.[29]

Some researchers have largely replicated Stone's propositions, while others have developed additional typologies. As discussed in Chapter 2, merchandise products can be classified according to the extent to which the shopper's own self-image is involved in the purchasing, owning, and using of the item. Professor Walter Salmon of the Harvard Business School distinguished between high ego-involving items such as apparel and home furnishings and low ego-involving items such as cleaning products and children's underwear. This concept helps explain why customers often do not act as "rational economic beings" when making store and product choices. Price appeals are more appropriate on low ego-involving items because price will be traded off for the extra psychic benefits high ego-involving items provide. Typically, retailers offering high ego-involving items must compete in narrower market segments than those offering low ego-involving items. This is because customers' self-images vary so much more than their ability to pay. Self-images are based on taste, lifestyle, and so on, as discussed previously. Arthur Cohen and Ana Jones described this phenomenon as follows:

> Anyone, regardless of income, might shop for the lowest price or best value when buying an electric can opener. But it would seem that in categories involving ego, affordability is the chief measure of value; people shop for things like outer clothing at the store whose market image coincides most closely with the self-image they aspire to project, and thus they are likely to pay the most they can afford.[30]

Another variation on shopping style and orientation is the occasion or type of trip. In the grocery trade, for example, some retailers believe that customers differ markedly in their choice of stores and in their needs, wants, and expectations according to the **type of trip**. Several observers of customer behaviour in the grocery field have characterized five basic types of trips:

1. routine grocery shopping (regular periodic trip to meet routine grocery needs)
2. stock-up trips (less-frequent trips to buy some items in greater quantities to carry in inventory)
3. fill-in trips (trips in-between routine trips to get items that are needed)
4. emergency trips (trips to get special items urgently needed such as diapers and formula)
5. adventure trips ("let's see what's available")

Another approach might involve distinguishing between routine re-buys, modified re-buys, and new buys as a way to indicate the extent of **deliberation** the customer may go through in making patronage and product–service purchase decisions.

For some time, many market observers have commented on the growing proportion of purchases that are made based on an in-store decision rather than a pre-store planned decision. This distinction between **planned purchasing** and **impulse purchasing** has been vague and subject to varying operational definitions by researchers; thus, for the most part, it is important to be very careful about drawing any conclusions from extant research. There are frequent articles about this in the popular trade press. For example, a 1982 Point-of-Purchase Advertising Institute study in U.S. drugstores found that 60 percent of shoppers made their final buy decisions while in the store.[31] Other research has shown that there are more likely three types of shoppers, based on when they make decisions relative to the visit to the store:

1. Planners—View product usage and performance as key factors in purchase decisions and are able to make decisions prior to entering the store. Simplifier cognitive style.
2. Partial planners—Engage in careful in-store shopping behavior involving more search and greater price sensitivity than impulse buyers or planners. Clarifying cognitive style.
3. Impulse buyers—Engage in very little in-store information processing. Simplifier cognitive style.[32]

Another dimension of shopping style is characterized by the extent of home versus **outshopping behaviour**. Outshopping refers to shopping and purchasing outside one's hometown. This concept is not very precise, but the idea is obvious: some people who live and/or work in one particular trading area do a substantial amount of their shopping in other towns and cities. Researchers have made some interesting findings about outshoppers relative to those who do not outshop:

- Frequent outshoppers have more unfavourable attitudes toward local shopping conditions and more favourable attitudes toward shopping in other (usually larger urban) areas.
- Outshoppers tend to be less price conscious.
- Outshoppers tend to expose themselves to more sources of information.[33]

Outshopping has taken on a new urgent meaning for Canadian retailers. A growing number of Canadians began to cross the Canada–U.S. border with the passage of the Free Trade Agreement in the late 1980s. While statistics are arguable, the overall impact has been clearly negative on Canadian retailers, particularly those located near border crossings and those offering items, such as clothing and appliances, that are readily available at attractively lower prices at "off-price" and "factory outlet malls" in the United States. There appears to be considerable confusion among the Canadian public about what "free trade" really means; some seem to think it means no limit on shopping in the United States and others seem to think that duties are much lower. In any event, U.S. retailers built new stores and malls, advertised aggressively in Canada, and apparently profited from this out-shopping. Canadian retailers had difficulty responding, faced with higher costs and a government unwilling to fully enforce customs regulations. Then, in 1991, the imposition of a Canadian federal general sales tax—the goods and services tax (GST)—of 7 percent (basically a value-added tax such as in Europe), combined in many instances with existing provincial sales taxes, resulted in further impetus to cross the border to shop: the currency exchange difference has essentially been nullified by the sales tax rate.

A final dimension of shopping style and orientation is **loyalty.** Some customers return again and again to the same store and/or buy again the same product or service. Loyalty refers to repeat purchase behaviour. It is important to realize that loyalty may be to the product or service ("brand loyalty") or to the store, salesperson, or even shopping area ("retailer loyalty"). Obviously, a retailer would prefer to have the latter type of loyalty, which, aside from adding comfort and security to the retailer's business, also adds power to the retailer's bargaining position with vendors. Loyalty is not always the result of carefully considered preference based on the relative merits of alternatives. Sometimes loyalty is based on habit and inertia, which might be captured by the thought "it's easier to keep doing the same thing than to think about changing it." Retailers strive to move people up the retail loyalty ladder as shown in Exhibit 4.5.

*EXHIBIT 4.5*
*The Retail*
*Loyalty Ladder*

---

5. **Advocate**—a client who actually promotes the retailer to friends and acquaintances
4. **Client**—someone with whom there is a relationship beyond an exchange of money for goods or services
3. **Customer**—someone who has purchased
2. **Prospect**—a potential customer with demonstrated ability and interest in buying
1. **Suspect**—a potential customer, a maybe

---

This section of the chapter focused on customer characteristics: geographic, demographic, psychographic, needs/wants/expectations, and shopping styles.[34] The next step is to understand how customers make choices: how they choose or reject a retail marketer's offer.

## RETAIL CUSTOMER DECISION-MAKING

Identifying customer characteristics, as discussed in Section One, is one way of segmenting a market and formulating an appropriate marketing program. An alternative approach involves more attention to the process by which customers make shopping area, store, and product choices. Understanding this process enables a retail marketer to find ways to help customers move to purchase decisions (rather than "get stuck" part way through the process) and to influence the nature of those decisions.

The **decision process model** conceptualizes customers going through several stages from awareness of a need or want to repeat purchasing and post-purchase feelings. The basic stages are as shown in Exhibit 4.6.

*EXHIBIT 4.6*
*Decision Process*
*Model*

1. **Awareness**—of a need or want, of some products or services that may satisfy that demand, and of some retailers who may provide those products or services
2. **Knowledge**—of the characteristics of candidate products or services and of retailers
3. **Attitudes and preferences**—associated feelings and beliefs about alternative products or services and about alternative retailers, leading to some preferences
4. **Intentions**—inclinations to patronize certain retailers and to purchase certain products or services
5. **Purchase**—the actual transaction
6. **Post-purchase**—usage behaviour, post-purchase experiences and feelings, repeat or nonrepeat purchase behaviour

Not all customers go through this process consciously, nor do they go through these stages at any standard pace. Rather, the value of this concept is to indicate three major points.

1. Customers approach buying as a problem with a **problem-solving approach**, which includes gathering information, weighing alternatives, making decisions, and evaluating decisions after they are made. A retailer should be looking for ways to help customers solve "buying problems" such as providing the right information at the right time in the places customers go looking for that information.
2. There are **decision stages**, which suggests that different marketing stimuli are appropriate for customers at different stages. At the early stages, more advertising and mass communication efforts are required to attract customers with an understanding of what the retailer has to offer. At later stages, more personal, in-store efforts are generally required to build relationships with the customers and to influence buying decisions.
3. Customers can be "**tracked**" through this process, as mentioned in Chapter 3. For example, a retailer could measure awareness, attitudes, trial rates, and

repeat rates for a trading area. If awareness is high, but trial is low, for example, then the problem is not so much reaching customers as it is convincing them to buy. This may indicate that the appeal is not strong enough, rather than that the media plan is inappropriate. On the other hand, if trial rates are reasonably good, but repeat rates are low, there may be a problem with the product itself, such as poor quality.

The decision process model requires the retailer to consider twelve aspects of customer psychology:

1. Customers act on their **perceptions** (of their needs, of the competitive products and retailers), which may not be the same as the perceptions of the retailer. A retailer must find a way to see the marketplace offerings through the eyes of his or her customers.

2. Customers have differing **cognitive styles**; for example, some are simplifiers and some are complexifiers. This means some customers will want lots of information and detail while others will be seeking ways to reduce the amount of information they process.

3. All customers go through a process of **information search** and **information evaluation**. This means the retailer should attempt to find out what information customers want, where they look for information (for example, prior to coming to a store, what media do they consult for information?), and how they evaluate information credibility.

4. Customers will have varying levels of **knowledge** about product–service features and benefits and store features and benefits. Sometimes, this knowledge will actually be incorrect. A retail marketer should periodically examine the extent to which target customers have accurate knowledge of his or her program offer.

5. Customers make decisions using their own **decision criteria**. A retailer should attempt to discover which criteria are being used and which are most important.

6. Customer decisions are based on perceived facts as well as **attitudes** and **opinions**. A retailer can gain great insights into customer behaviour through understanding this affective component of customers' decision process. What do customers like and dislike? What, in particular, attracts them to a store and brings them back? What do they think and feel about various competitive stores? What images do they have of the competing retailers and their marketing programs?

7. Customers make patronage and buying decisions without complete knowledge and certainty. This means there is **perceived risk** in the decision. There are at least three ways that a customer may perceive risk in a shopping situation: (*a*) the product or service might not meet performance expectations, (*b*) the product or service might not be good value for the time, money, and effort spent, especially compared to what else may be available on the market; and/or (*c*) the purchase and/or the place of purchase will be socially embarrassing when other people important to the purchaser find out about it. The extent of perceived risk will vary according to the customer's experience level with the product category and/or the retailer, with the customer's level of self-confi-

dence, and with the salience of the purchase (for example, a high-priced item will likely be seen as representing higher risk than a low-price item). This concept suggests the retailer should seek appropriate ways to reduce the level of perceived risk. This is the thinking behind test drives, "take it home and try it for the weekend" offers, money-back guarantees, testimonials, and so on.

8. Many customer decisions will be made jointly with other people, such as with a partner or with the family. In such circumstances, the retailer needs to understand the roles of each person in the **decision-making unit**. For example, a father may be concerned about the number of dials and buttons on a stereo system, whereas his son may be concerned with the power and output characteristics.

9. Often, there are **influencers** not present on the actual shopping trip. These influencers may be friends, relatives, neighbours, and so on, or they may be professional advisers (doctors, accountants, etc.), or even a more vague "reference group" of people the customer is aspiring to be like. The retailer can tailor her or his approach to customers more appropriately if the influencers are known, and especially if the influencers themselves can be reached by the retailer first. In some instances, there are identifiable "opinion leaders," that is, individuals whose opinions and behaviour provide a guide for others to follow.

10. New ideas, products, and services are not adopted by all customers at the same time. There is a process of gradual adoption called the **diffusion of innovations**. This concept, which has been extensively researched, shows that early adopters have characteristics quite different from later adopters. A retailer new to a trading area or a retailer introducing something new can benefit by targeting specifically those people most likely to adopt early.

11. Purchases are not all equal. Retailers should decide what kind of purchasing behaviour he or she wishes to encourage. For example, purchases vary according to **transaction size, frequency of purchasing**, and **recency** (time since last purchase).

12. The post-purchase stage is more important than some retailers seem to appreciate. Retailers can track customer **usage behaviour**, such as amount consumed, frequency of consumption, uses to which the product is put, handling and storage behaviour, problems encountered, and occasions for use. Retailers can also track post-purchase **satisfaction**. Customers typically go through a stage of post-purchase dissonance reduction, which means they seek reassurance that they made a good choice. This is why customers who have just bought are particularly attentive to advertising for that store and product, to other owners of the purchased product, and to the marketing offers (such as prices asked) of competing retailers for the same product or service. This is the time when an alert retailer can reassure his or her customer, follow-up with installation and usage help, and generally continue to build the relationship with the customer.

## CONCLUSION

There are many ways to identify, describe, and understand retail customers. The goal of any retailer's efforts toward customer understanding is improved ability to gain and maintain customer patronage decisions and customer purchase decisions. The main aspects of customer analysis are: (*a*) customer characteristics, and (*b*) customer decision processes. There are five dimensions of customer characteristics: geographic, demographic, psychographic, needs/wants/expectations, and shopping style/orientation. Each of these characteristics has many dimensions.

There are six stages in the decision process model: awareness, knowledge, attitudes and preferences, intentions, purchase, and post-purchase. This conceptual model points out twelve fundamentally important aspects of customer decision-making that a retailer can use to advantage in designing and refining a retail marketing program offer.

Customers are people, not statistics. While the concepts and approaches in this chapter are used extensively by retail marketers to "get closer" to their customers, they are merely tools and no substitute for actual customer contact. Neighbourhood grocers in the early part of this century did not have the computer-based information systems of today, but they kept close to customers by serving them directly, by engaging in small talk, and by being involved in their communities. Today, retailers with savvy know that the best way to stay close to the customer is still "to get out and push their own shopping carts" and stay directly involved with their customers.

## Review Questions

1. As the baby boomers get older, what adjustments in retail strategy might be appropriate for a swimwear retailer?

2. Consider a shopping centre with which you are familiar. What improvements might be made to increase its appeal to the "career-woman market"?

3. Many grocery retailers have introduced generic brands with relatively plain packaging, lower prices, and very limited item promotions. To what kinds of people might these products appeal most?

4. Surveys of the "twentysomething generation" have revealed these people report that they spent about equal time while growing up being with their parents and watching television. How might this have affected their values and their behaviour in the retail marketplace?

5. Interview a friend (or use an experience of your own) about a purchase made recently that was discretionary and cost more than $50. Trace the story of that purchase from the first idea about it through to sometime after the purchase. What were the critical stages and how do those stages relate to the decision process model in Exhibit 4.6?

## Key Terms

- basic dimensions of customers
- trading area
- census tract
- postal code analysis
- buying power
- index of retail saturation

- demographics
- age group
- gender
- age distribution
- family life stage
- household characteristics

- ability to buy
- physical traits
- psychographics
- lifestyle
- values
- cocooning
- VALS
- baby boomers
- needs
- wants
- expectations
- shopping style
- type of trip
- deliberation
- planned purchasing
- impulse purchasing
- outshopping behaviour
- loyalty
- decision process model

- problem-solving approach
- decision stages
- perceptions
- cognitive styles
- information search
- information evaluation
- knowledge
- decision criteria
- attitudes
- opinions
- perceived risk
- decision-making unit
- influencers
- diffusion of innovations
- transaction size
- frequency of purchasing
- recency of purchasing
- usage behaviour
- satisfaction

## NOTES

1. Daniel Defoe, *The Complete English Tradesman*, 1726.

2. Ken Dychtwald, and Greg Gable, "Portrait of a Changing Consumer," *Business Horizons*, January–February 1990, pp. 62–73.

3. An example is provided by Chris Peluso in "Geodemographics: Marketing by Postal Code," *The Retail Advisor*, Touche Ross, October 1989.

4. For an example of worldwide differences in spending patterns, see Neil B. Krupp, "Analysis of Spending Patterns Worldwide Shows Great Differences in Retail Markets," *International Trends in Retailing*, Fall 1990, pp. 33–39.

5. "57th Annual Report," *Progressive Grocer*, April 1990, pp. 56–61.

6. Rena Bartos, "Over 49: The Invisible Consumer Market," *Harvard Business Review*, January–February 1980, pp. 140–48.

7. See "Proceeding with Caution," *Time*, 16 July 1990, pp. 44–50.

8. Donald R. Katz, "The New Generation Gap," *Esquire*, February 1990, pp. 49–50.

9. Carole Sloan, "New Wave Retailers," *Stores*, November 1988, pp. 71–76. See also R. Lee Sullivan, "Show Me the Way to Go Home," *Discount Merchandiser*, March 1990, pp. 28–31, for an article on how home offices are growing and being served by retailers.

10. Judith Langer, *Marketing News*, August 28, 1987.

11. Canadian retail marketers wishing to understand this market should follow the work of the National Advisory Council on Aging. For example, see "Consumer Issues: The Changing Marketplace," *Expression*, National Council on Aging, Government of Canada, Spring 1990. Many other articles have appeared recently about how to appeal to the mature market. For example, see Stephani Cook "Riding the Silver Streak," *Retailing Issues Letter*, Arthur Andersen & Co., September 1989.

12. Leonard Berry, "Changing Consumer to Alter Marketplace Greatly," *Marketing News*, 1979.

13. Laurie Merckel, "Cocooning and Consuming in the 90's," *Housewares Canada*, Winter 1989, pp. 22–28.

14. "Fighting the Urge to Splurge," *Time*, 14 December 1987, pp. 86–89.

15. See also William Dunn, "Selling to Big Americans," *American Demographics*, August 1986, pp. 38–40, 55, 56.

16. Emanuel H. Demby, "Psychographics Revisited: The Birth of a Technique," *Marketing News*, 2 January 1989, p. 21.

17. Brian E. Kardon, "The Problem with Demographics: Disparities in the Coming Decade," *The Retail Advisor*, Deloitte and Touche, June 1990.

18. For example, see Faye Rice, "Yuppie Spending Gets Serious," *Fortune*, 27 March 1989, pp. 147–49; Ronald Henkoff, "Is Greed Dead?" *Fortune*, 14 August 1989, pp. 40–49; and Anne B. Fisher "What Consumers Want in the 1990's," *Fortune*, 29 January 1990, pp. 108–112.

19. For example, see Bruce Gates, "Home Is Where the Heart and Money Is," *The Financial Post*, 1 January 1990.

20. Ernest H. Risch, "The Nature of the Consumer Psyche: Implications for Merchandising Strategy, Part Two" *Retail Control*, August 1986, pp. 47–62.

21. For example, see Michael Gade, "Winning the Loyalty of Baby Boomers," *Retail Market Analysis*, Touche Ross, October 1988.

22. For an excellent summary of major demographic trends in the United States of interest to retailers, see Penny Gill, "Who's Counting," *Stores*, May 1988, pp. 33–51.

23. Kenneth Kidd, "Wooing the Working Woman," *The Toronto Star*, 8 September 1985; and Jill Curry, "Catering to Women Who Work," *Stores*, October 1985, pp. 49–52.

24. Robert P. Mark, "Ethnic Marketing: The New Opportunity," *Canadian Grocer*, January 1990, pp. 26–30.

25. For example, Barbara Buell and Neil Gross with Charles Gaffney, "The Myth of the Japanese Middle Class," *Business Week*, 12 September 1988, pp. 49–52.

26. For more information on the Japanese customer, see George Fields, *The Japanese Market Culture* (Tokyo: The Japan Times, 1988).

27. Joan Bergmann, "What Shoppers Want," *Stores*, May 1989, p. 84.

28. M.M. Lele, and U.S. Karmarkar, "Good Product Support Is Smart Marketing," *Harvard Business Review*, November–December 1983, pp. 124–32.

29. Gregory P. Stone, "City Shoppers and Urban Identification: Observations on the Pyschology of City Life," *The American Journal of Sociology*, July 1954, pp. 36–45.

30. Arthur I. Cohen, and Ana Loud Jones, "Brand Marketing in the New Retail Environment," *Harvard Business Review*, November–December, 1978, pp. 141–48.

31. "Pilot Study Finds Final Product Choice Usually Made In-Store," *Marketing News*, 6 August 1982, p. 5.

32. Cathy J. Cobb, and Wayne D. Hoyer, "Planned Versus Impulse Purchase Behaviour," *Journal of Retailing*, Winter 1986, pp. 384–409.

33. J.R. Lumpkin, J.M. Hawes, and W.R. Darden, "Shopping Patterns of the Rural Consumer: Exploring the Relationship between Shopping Orientations and Outshopping," *Journal of Business Research*, vol. 14 (1986), pp. 63–81.

34. An excellent recent summary article for retailers is Penny Gill, "Know Your Customer?" *Stores*, November 1989, pp. 31–43.

CHAPTER

# Retail Competitors

## Introduction

Every retailer faces competition, either directly or indirectly. This chapter examines how a retailer can systematically analyze his or her competition in order to make better retail marketing decisions. As discussed in previous chapters, every retailer needs to find some reason why customers should buy from him or her rather than from a competitor—in short, a competitive advantage. Gaining competitive advantage requires not only customer understanding, but also competitive understanding.

There is more to understanding competitors than simply gathering information about them. Over the past 5 to 10 years, a new business field called "competitive intelligence" has gained professional status. Practitioners of "CI" have developed a wide range of sources of information ranging from on-line databases to direct contact with a competitor's employees.[1] Competitive intelligence applies equally well to retail marketing as to other types of marketing.

A strong statement of the importance of understanding the competition appeared in a recently popular business book—a book about warfare written in China roughly 2300 years ago. The popularity of this book, and others on "marketing warfare," indicates that business practitioners seem to identify today with their messages:

> If you know the enemy and know yourself, you need not fear the result of a hundred battles. If you know yourself but not the enemy, for every victory gained you will also suffer a defeat. If you know neither the enemy nor yourself, you will succumb in every battle.[2]

Retail marketers know how exposed to competition they are; there is little need here to argue at length the need for examining competitors. In summary, the major reasons one undertakes competitive retailer analysis are as shown in Exhibit 5.1.

*Exhibit 5.1*
*Why Undertake*
*Competitive*
*Analysis?*

1. To identify one's position in the marketplace.
2. To identify areas of competitive vulnerability that may potentially be exploited.
3. To identify areas of one's own vulnerability that competitors might exploit.
4. To provide competitive benchmarks for gauging one's own performance.
5. To predict future competitive behaviour.
6. To predict competitive reaction to one's own future moves.

■
Section
■
One
■

## Four Dimensions of Competitive Analysis

This chapter is organized around four dimensions of competitive analysis as shown in Exhibit 5.2. While these steps to competitive understanding need not be done in this order, they are discussed in the sequence shown.

*Exhibit 5.2*
*Competitive*
*Analysis*

| **1. Identification of relevant competitors** | • Types of competition |
| | • Market segmentation |
| **2. Determination of information needed** | • Dimensions of differentiation |
| | • Performance differences |
| **3. Information collection** | • Marketing research |
| | • Shopping competitors |
| **4. Information analysis and use** | • Competitive profiling |
| | • Phantom-competitor planning |

Competitors may be sources of information, inspiration, awe, or frustration, depending upon how a retail marketer approaches the challenge of competitive understanding.

### Identification of Relevant Competitors

Deciding which retailers to monitor closely, which "stores to shop," is a managerial judgment. Some retail marketers narrow their scope to immediate, direct competitors (at one time, Eaton's watched Simpson's and Simpson's watched Eaton's; their respective managements largely ignored other retailers). Some retail marketers maintain that the whole world of retailing is appropriate for study (one retailer suggested that would include anything exciting being done by anyone, anywhere). The breadth of view depends on the *purpose* of the analysis and the *resources* available. For example, if one were looking for new ideas for merchandise presentation, one might learn a great deal on a European tour; whereas if one were wondering what price to charge tomorrow for a cola drink, a trip to stores in the neighbourhood would be more appropriate.

Some retailers tend to delegate responsibility for competitive analysis to a few employees, most typically buyers and store management; whereas others expect everyone to be on the alert for competitive developments at all times.

Irwin Greenberg, president of Hess's, an American department store chain, exemplifies the latter approach:

> As chief executive, certainly I shop the stores. That's how I spend Sundays. As we all know, most department stores carry the same kind of merchandise. So you better know what is going on in the market to be competitive. Our buyers and general merchandise managers are out constantly. Every one of our store managers must shop the competition every week. Our regional directors, whenever they visit our stores, must also see the competition. And the competition might be a dynamite specialty store. It doesn't have to be a department store.[3]

There are three major types of competition a retail marketer may wish to examine: intratype, intertype, and generic. Generally speaking, priority should be given to intratype, then intertype, and then generic competitors.

Most markets contain a great variety of retailers, many of whom offer similar if not identical merchandise and services; thus, customers have a choice and will select one retailer and reject another for any particular purchase. This is called **intratype competition**, meaning retailers of the same basic classification in competition with one another for any particular customer. For example, an individual embarking on a grocery shopping trip may choose Loblaws over A&P. Also, most retail competition is local, meaning it is trade area specific. Grocery shoppers seldom drive past local supermarkets to shop a supermarket in a distant city.

Retailers frequently offer merchandise that crosses over intratype boundaries. Health and beauty items (HBAs), for example, are carried by supermarkets, drugstores, and many general merchandisers. This is called **intertype competition**, that is, competition among retailers of different classifications. Our example grocery shopper may even be trading off purchasing food items in the supermarket with "eating out," which means the supermarket is competing with fast food and other restaurants.

Perhaps this hypothetical shopper is cutting back on grocery purchases this week because she plans to spend some of that money on tickets to the theatre. This form of competition is called **generic competition**, which means all competing ways in which the customer may spend his or her money and/or time, or for that matter, not spend his or her money. For example, in January 1991, Canadian department stores suffered a real sales loss of 18 percent over the same month the previous year.[4] This setback was attributed to the Gulf War, the federal goods and services tax, a deepening recession, and the growing attraction of shopping across the border in U.S. stores.[5]

A retail marketer may identify relevant competitors in three ways. One common approach is to use **managerial judgment**. Management decides (usually on the basis of its target market definition, its own knowledge of merchandise and its vendors, and its own segmentation scheme) which competitors to watch.

A second approach is to *experience* shopping as one's customers do. For example, a retailer might drive around the area, walk through shopping centres, visit stores, examine the telephone yellow pages, read the local newspapers, listen to all the local radio stations, and watch local television. The whole idea is to create a list of competitors that shoppers would ordinarily encounter.

A third approach is to *ask* one's customers and/or target customers directly about relevant competitors. A retailer might ask customers, for example, where else they shop for merchandise like his or her own (behavioural measures), what they like or dislike about other stores in the area (perceptual measures), and so on. On this basis, a retailer can develop a list of competitors from the customers' perspective, rather than his or her own perspective. (Chapter 6 includes discussion on how to design and implement such research.)

A refinement of this approach is known as **competitive structure analysis**. Kopp, Eng, and Tigert explained this idea and illustrated it with the Chicago fashion market:

> Whereas segmentation analysis forms groups of like-minded customers, competitive structure analysis employs empirical data to form groupings of similar competitors. This approach forms competitive groups of rival entities (products, brands, stores, etc.), which customers view as substitutes. Nominal industry or product category designations such as the telephone industry or the coffee market have little meaning in an empirically-based approach. In fact, such a priori designations may even mask the true nature of competition. Competitive structure analysis carries implications for short-run competitive strategies— closer competitors pose more of an immediate threat—as well as implications for longer-term competitive and product line management strategies.
>
> Competitive groups are typically formed using either perceptual data or behavioral data. . . .
>
> The combining of rivals into competitive groups, on the basis of empirical data, highlights the degree of intragroup and intergroup competition in the marketplace. . . .
>
> . . . Most retailers must attract customers from different and often incompatible market segments. Because segments differ in terms of shopping behavior, lifestyles, benefits sought, information sources used, and demographics, it is clear that different marketing strategies would be required by the same retailer should it choose to penetrate more than one consumer segment.[6]

While the above approaches aid in identifying intratype and intertype competitors, they do little for identifying generic competition. Rather than undertake elaborate research, a more straightforward approach to this problem would be to stay informed about local market conditions and events. For example, a local strike, a new plant opening, increases in property taxes, and so on, will bear on how customers will spend their money. Similarly, a special parade downtown on Saturday or a concert Friday evening may suggest that a planned sale event in a suburban mall should be scheduled for some other time since these events may be competition for target customers' attention and time. The important point to remember is that retail competition is primarily localized so attention should be focused locally. This, of course, is especially challenging for multi-unit retailers located in different trading areas.

## DETERMINATION OF INFORMATION NEEDED

Before undertaking any competitive information gathering, some thought should be given as to what information is relevant:

> Professionals in the field say that, before marketers launch a competitive intelligence program, they should first determine what information they want to obtain and how their company will use it. Otherwise, they risk wasting time in collecting unnecessary data. Responding to a competitor's new advertising campaign and evaluating another company's long-term strategy may require very different sets of information.[7]

Use of the retail marketing management model provides a framework for the kinds of information that would prove helpful. A retailer may monitor competitive assortments, service levels, prices, and so on. Generally speaking, retailers need to undertake a very thorough analysis of competition when establishing a business or when considering major changes to the marketing strategy. At other times, an ongoing "keeping up to date" kind of competitive monitoring is appropriate.

Retailers refer to checking out competitors as "**shopping the competition**." Someone visits competitive outlets to see what and how they are doing. For example, a review of several competitive shopping lists indicated that the following dimensions are typically studied:

1. Nature of the location
2. Estimated size of the store
3. Merchandise—what specifically is carried, how much of each, inventory level
4. Layout and space allocation
5. Signage and display
6. Number of customers in and passing through during a specified time
7. Type of customers
8. Prices—general impression and specifics by comparison items
9. Service levels, such as number of checkouts/cashiers
10. Condition of store and general housekeeping

This list is only indicative of what any particular retail marketer might look for when visiting competitors. The specifics will depend on the circumstances and the kinds of decisions being faced by the retailer.

Exhibit 5.3 provides a way to conceptualize competitive comparisons, using the framework developed in earlier chapters.

EXHIBIT 5.3
Competitive
Comparisons:
Some Examples

**Description and Rankings**

| DIMENSIONS | SELF | A | B | C | D |
|---|---|---|---|---|---|
| **1. Customer base** | | | | | |
| a. size | | | | | |
| b. types | | | | | |
| c. apparent satisfaction | | | | | |
| **2. Differentiation factors** | | | | | |
| a. assortment | | | | | |
| b. convenience | | | | | |
| c. information | | | | | |
| d. customer care | | | | | |
| e. value | | | | | |
| f. experience | | | | | |
| **3. Performance (past & future)** | | | | | |
| a. financial | | | | | |
| b. merchandise | | | | | |
| c. space | | | | | |
| d. people | | | | | |
| e. marketplace standing | | | | | |
| **4. Management** | | | | | |
| a. apparent goals | | | | | |
| b. skills and resources | | | | | |
| c. aggressiveness | | | | | |
| d. speed | | | | | |
| e. flexibility | | | | | |

## INFORMATION COLLECTION

There are a great many sources of information about competitors in general and in specific. (Chapter 6 is a more detailed discussion of how to design and execute marketing research, including trade sources to monitor.) All retail marketers should be continually following the developments and prospects for their particular type of retailing. This information is frequently collected and disseminated by trade associations and by trade publications. For example, Canadian supermarket operators should be reading, at minimum, publications such as *Canadian Grocer* and *Progressive Grocer*. Such publications frequently include reports on the state of the industry and articles on new trends to watch. For example, Exhibit 5.4 is an excerpt from part of the Annual Report on the Grocery Industry by *Progressive Grocer* in 1990:

*EXHIBIT 5.4*[1]
U.S. Grocery
Trends

**1.** Prospects for food retailers according to chain executives

|  | **Excellent** | **Good** | **Fair/Poor** |
|---|---|---|---|
| Superstores | 54% | 37% | 9% |
| Convenience stores | 21 | 38 | 41 |
| Superwarehouse stores | 16 | 44 | 40 |
| Combination stores | 43 | 46 | 11 |
| Specialty food stores | 13 | 31 | 56 |
| Hypermarkets | 6 | 17 | 77 |
| Wholesale clubs | 11 | 39 | 50 |
| Conventional supers | 5 | 31 | 64 |
| Warehouse stores | 1 | 21 | 78 |
| Limited assortment stores | 1 | 6 | 93 |

**2.** Outlook for specific strategies according to chain executives

|  | **Net increase** |
|---|---|
| Emphasis on perishables | +95 |
| Fresh prepared food emphasis | +95 |
| Customer services | +81 |
| In-store demos/ samplings | +79 |
| Non-foods emphasis | +51 |
| Mailers/circulars | +47 |
| Sunday openings | +44 |
| Hours open | +43 |
| Radio advertising | +41 |
| Flashy merchandising events | +37 |

| | |
|---|---|
| Hotter specials | +35 |
| Newspaper inserts | +35 |
| Private label emphasis | +25 |
| National brand emphasis | +24 |
| TV advertising | +24 |
| Store coupons | +21 |
| Half-price sales | +16 |
| Cutthroat pricing | −9 |
| Continuity programs | −19 |
| Newspaper ads (ROP) | −23 |
| Double coupons | −32 |

[1] Excerpted from "The Weapons Change, but the War Remains the Same," 57th Annual Report, *Progressive Grocer*, April 1990, pp. 28–31.

Additionally, every retailer has easy access to local and national newspapers and other media reports; the local library for government statistics; the local Planning Department for building permits, and so on; the local Chamber of Commerce; local university and college faculties, and so on. In other words, one can learn a great deal simply by keeping "eyes and ears open" about competitors in general and in specific.

As an example, suppose one were a hardware/lumber/home improvement retailer (such as Beaver Lumber or Cashway) concerned that Home Depot might

*EXHIBIT 5.5*
*Home Depot:*
*Selected*
*Information[1]*

**Number of stores:** 118   Goal: 350 by 1995

**Sales 1989:** $2.8 billion   Goal: $10 billion by 1995

**Location:** primarily Sunbelt but now moving into the Northeast; average 100,000 square feet; 7 stores in New York by April

**Assortment:** 30,000 separate items of lumber, tools, lighting, and plumbing supplies — store managers have lots of discretion; recently pushing into customized kitchen design

**Pricing:** everyday low pricing that's 30% below traditional hardware stores

**Service:** much emphasized — new hires get 4 weeks of training

**Staff:** 20,000 employees drawn from building trades; paid generously on salary

**Ad and promo:** no weekly promos; advertising is 1.5% of sales; focussed on service; 60 page catalogs mailed monthly

**Financial situation:** debt/equity 21%; earnings up 46% from 1988

[1] Excerpted from Chuck Hawkins, "Will Home Depot Be the Wal-Mart of the '90's?" *Business Week*, 19 March 1990, pp. 124–26.

enter into one's market area. How might one learn more about that organization and its likely moves? Easy-to-access sources would be annual reports and brokerage reports from a business school library. Another approach would be to search through a periodical index at a local library, seeking recent media reports about the company. Such a search would quickly reveal, among others, an article in *Business Week* in March 1990. A review of that article alone provides a great deal of information as excerpted in Exhibit 5.5.

Retail marketers can learn much by following competitive developments in comparable retail businesses in other countries. While there is no guarantee that competition will evolve at home the way it does abroad, such analysis often provides considerable insights into domestic competition. Paul Crotty, of Peat Marwick Stevenson & Kellogg, compared Canadian grocery retailing with U.K. grocery retailing with a view to suggesting avenues for improvement for Canadian firms. Whereas Canadian grocers have historically achieved after-tax profits of 1.0 to 1.5 percent of sales, U.K. grocery retailers recently reached 4 to 6 percent. Crotty detailed differences in **results** (such as U.K. grocers having three times higher sales per square foot) and **approach** (such as U.K. grocers being quicker to adopt DPP, computerized space management, EDI with vendors, and category management, and being more prone to private labels, chain consolidation, non-price competition, and in-store information control by the retailer only). However, he attributed the difference in performance as primarily the result of U.K. grocers' commitment to adding customer value:

> The U.K.'s leading grocery retailers have, since the early 1980's, shared a commitment to increasing profits by reducing operating costs whilst, simultaneously, adding value to all that they do. It is this ability to add value that is, today, the most significant difference between U.K. and Canadian grocery retailers. It is by adding value that U.K. grocery retailers achieve net profit ratios three to four times those achieved in Canada.
>
> Their ability to add value arises directly from U.K. retailers' exceptional degree of customer focus and deep understanding of customers' needs. U.K. grocery retailers have achieved their exceptional level of customer focus by employing some of the best marketers in the country and giving them the power to shape overall corporate strategy.[8]

Retail marketers have a variety of other ways to obtain information about competition. Some methods are *overt*: taking pictures, hiring competitive personnel, interviewing competitors' customers, cooperating with competitors to do mutual checkups, and asking competitive management for guided store tours. Some methods are *unobtrusive if not covert*: hidden cameras, hidden tape recorders, posing as customers or suppliers, posing as "student researchers," and interviewing store employees. There are generally "rules of the game" about shopping competition, which often include: "If you'll let us check you, you can check us," "No notetaking in the store," "No photos without asking," or "Identify yourself and we'll help, otherwise you're out."[9] Some methods of shopping the competition raise ethical questions that thoughtful, responsible retail marketers should resolve for their staff, rather than ignore in favour of the information obtained.

## INFORMATION ANALYSIS AND USE

Competitive information is worth collecting only if it is used properly. Analysis of such information can be considered for two main purposes. The first is comparison of one's own situation and marketing program with those of competitors. Questions that may be addressed include:

1. How good is one's own performance relative to competition?
2. Are there areas of particular strength or weakness?
3. Are there areas of particular opportunity or concern?
4. Why are competitors doing what they are doing?

The second reason is anticipation of future competitive developments. Questions that may be addressed include:

1. What are competitors likely to do next?
2. How are competitors likely to react to one's own future moves?
3. Are current competitors likely to exit or new competitors likely to enter?

To answer such questions requires not just information, but also insight and judgment. This is the key distinction between competitive information and competitive intelligence. Harvard professor Michael Porter, well known for his work on competition, commented:

> Analysis of competitors' goals is crucial, because it helps the firm avoid strategic moves that will touch off bitter warfare by threatening competitors' ability to achieve key goals. . . . [So] who should we pick a fight with in the industry, and in what sequence of moves? What is the meaning of that competitor's strategic move and how seriously should we take it?[10]

Two important techniques for analyzing retail marketing competitive information are competitive profiling and phantom-competitor planning.

### Competitive Profiling

**Competitive profiling** refers to gathering all available information into a composite picture of a competitor. Ideally, one wants not only to know the characteristics and methods of such a competitor, but also to have some sense of how that competitive management thinks and will likely act in the future. When possible, a retail marketer should even attempt to personalize what is discovered about competitors by learning about the key managers themselves in the competitive stores. This is often more difficult today than it was in the past, with multi-unit chains moving managers about, but it is still worth a try. Often understanding key personalities provides ways to anticipate competitive reactions to price moves, advertising efforts, and so on. Journalists are often good profilers; retail marketers could learn by mimicking the approach of an investigative reporter. Here is a brief example of the start of a profile on Penner Foods, a Manitoba-based firm:

> We're small town people who can identify with a community. The idea is to fill the gap between 2,500 square foot convenience stores and the ever-more popular superstores. The Food Marketing Institute reported the average family buys groceries 2.7 times a week. They can go to the superstores for their major orders twice a month or so and come to us for the smaller orders. Our motto is Express Foods, Fresh Foods, Fast.
>
> More and more, both husband and wife are working. They are working longer hours and want food they can pick up quickly, food that is partly prepared or ready to serve such as pizza and sliced chicken that can be warmed in the oven and served.
>
> These people like to be able to do their shopping in ten minutes and be out. If the merchandise is fresh and the pricing reasonable, we are betting they will come to us instead of a superstore for their in-between items such as milk, bread, meats and ready-made items.
>
> The "Express" store bases its prices on Safeway's price structure. We carry a lot of perishables like bread, milk and lettuce, products that can't be stored for long.
>
> We won't be selling a lot of bulky items. We are not going to go after superstores' price structure or get into any price wars. We want to run a clean, fresh operation with fast, friendly service and be customer sensitive.[11]

This profile already provides a great deal of information on Penner's competitive marketing strategy in the areas of target market, assortment, convenience, value, and, especially, customer care.

### Phantom–Competitor Planning

**Phantom-competitor planning** refers to creating a new, imaginary (or phantom) competitor that would be ideally situated to be successful in one's own market, and particularly successful competing with oneself. The basic approach is to ask someone (often a management team) to prepare a complete marketing plan for such a competitor, based on extensive customer, competitor, and self-analysis. Then this plan is examined as a competitive challenge. Questions used may be: Would it be worthwhile to emulate the phantom competitor's strategy? Should action be taken to forestall any such competitive strategy being tried by others? and so on.[12] The particular value of this approach lies in forcing a retail marketer to look at him- or herself through the eyes of a direct competitor.

Competitive analysis serves many uses. While buyers may analyze competitors to help determine assortment trends, senior executives may be watching for strategic changes in competitive positioning. Senior management, in particular, needs competitive intelligence to help formulate competitive strategies. Should a competitive move, such as a change from regular/special pricing to everyday-low-pricing, be matched or ignored? Is a new competitive private labelling program a threat? Military strategists have long classified competitive strategies into four basic types.[13] These are shown with retail marketing examples, as Exhibit 5.6, to stimulate thinking about how retail competitive intelligence may lead to competitive strategies.

EXHIBIT 5.6
Competitive
Strategies

1. Reconnaissance—ascertaining opportunities (e.g., test store)
2. Offense—attacking competitors
   a. direct (e.g., better customer service)
   b. flanking (e.g., private labelling; different size merchandise)
   c. guerrilla (e.g., opportunistic buying; low overhead operations)
3. Defense—warding off competitors
   a. deterrence (e.g., accepting competitors' coupons)
   b. passive (e.g., giving up customer segments)
   c. scorched earth (e.g., price war)
4. Surrender—leaving the market (e.g., closing stores)

A balance must be struck between too little and too much competitive analysis. Some retail marketers worry that their staff do not concern themselves enough with competition. On the other hand, some retail marketers worry that their staff rely too much on competitive analysis for ideas, that creativity is stifled when one retailer copies another. There are plentiful examples of retailer copycatting (especially in advertising and store design); this is not a necessary consequence of competitive analysis, but rather of lack of imagination and/or courage.

## CONCLUSION

Understanding one's competitors, of all types, is just as vital an undertaking as understanding one's customers: both are essential for a retail marketer to be market-driven. Competitive understanding involves gathering and interpreting information about relevant competitors to gain an understanding of the following:

1. Goals—What seems to drive competitors? How aggressive are they currently, and how aggressive will they likely be in the future? What kind of people manage these competitive operations?
2. Current strategies—What are the marketing programs, in detail, of relevant competitors and how, if at all, are these programs likely to change?
3. Current performance—How well or how poorly are these competitors performing? Why? Do customers prefer competitors and, if so, for what reasons?
4. Capabilities—What strengths and weaknesses do these competitors have? Are any changes likely in these profiles?
5. Likely reactions—How will competitors respond to various initiatives being considered by oneself?

There are many sources of information about competitors, much of which is readily accessible and inexpensive. However, it is critical to know what information one is seeking about which relevant competitors. It is especially important to motivate all of one's employees to collect competitive information and to have an organized way to analyze and disseminate such information so that it can be fully used.[14]

Retail marketers, for the most part, face intense but ever-changing competition. As markets shift, so do the relative competitive advantages (and hence fortunes) of one's competitors. Monitoring and analyzing competitors is an ongoing retail marketing management priority.

## REVIEW QUESTIONS

1. Assume that Birk's, the jewellery chain, is considering opening a new store in your area. Also, assume that Birk's does not already have a store in your area (if it does, pretend it does not exist). Birk's offers jewellery (diamonds, gold, etc.), silverware and crystal, china, and assorted expensive gifts and home furnishings. If asked to do a competitive analysis for Birk's in your area, how would you plan your approach?

2. Within the bounds of propriety and without store management help (that is, don't let them know you're doing this and if you are "caught in the act," explain, but consider yourself not a great covert analyzer), prepare a layout diagram for a local store in as much detail as possible (such as dimensions, merchandise displayed, etc.). What can you deduce from this diagram about the selected store's marketing strategy?

3. List twenty items that you feel qualify as "price sensitive groceries" for most customers. How would you do a price check on these items in area food stores? (If you have time, try it out!)

4. Suppose management of Shoppers Drug Mart, a chain of supermarket-style pharmacies, approached you to prepare a phantom-competitor plan for an operation that would prosper by exploiting Shoppers' weaknesses. How would you proceed?

5. What could be learned by analyzing competitors' classified want ads in the newspapers?

## KEY TERMS

- intratype competition
- intertype competition
- generic competition
- managerial judgment
- competitive structure analysis
- shopping the competition
- results
- approach
- competitive profiling
- phantom-competitor planning

## NOTES

1. For a good summary article on competitive intelligence, see Tom Eisenhart, "Where to Go When You Need to Know," *Business Marketing*, November 1989, pp. 38–47.

2. Sun Tzu, *The Art of War* (New York: Dell Publishing, 1983), p. 18.

3. Jules Abend, "Busman's Holiday," *Stores*, July 1982, pp. 34–41.

4. Barbara Aarsteinsen, "Store Sales Off 12.2% Due to Gulf War, GST," *The Toronto Star*, 14 March 1991, p. B1.

5. For example, same day car trips by Canadians to the U.S. jumped 15 percent in January 1991 over the same month in 1990. See "Jump in Traffic to U.S. Border Linked to GST," *The Toronto Star*, 14 March 1991, p. B3.

6. Robert J. Kopp, Robert J. Eng, and Douglas J. Tigert, "A Competitive Structure Analysis of the Chicago Fashion Market," *Journal of Retailing*, Winter 1989, pp. 496–515.

7. Tom Eisenhart, "Where to Go When You Need to Know," *Business Marketing*, November 1989, pp. 38–47.

8. Paul Crotty, "The Retail Revolution in the U.K.," *Canadian Grocer*, February 1990, pp. 22–28.

9. For some examples, see Jennifer Pellet, "Sizing Up the Competition," *Discount Merchandiser*, July 1989, pp. 84–85.

10. Michael Porter, *Competitive Strategy: Techniques for Analyzing Industries and Competitors* (New York: The Free Press, 1980), pp. 47, 57.

11. Myron Love, "Less Is More at Penner Foods," *Canadian Grocer*, February 1990, p. 118.

12. For examples, see Michael J. O'Connor "If You Were the Competition, What Would You Do?" *International Trends in Retailing*, Fall 1987, pp. 15–19.

13. See, for example, B. James, *Business Wargames* (Harmondsworth: Penguin Books, 1984); and A. Ries and J. Trout, *Marketing Warfare* (New York: McGraw-Hill, 1986).

14. John Towler, "Keeping Tabs on the Competition," *Canadian Grocer*, June 1988, pp. 26–31.

## CHAPTER

# RETAIL MARKETING RESEARCH

### INTRODUCTION

All retailers make a great variety of decisions. Typically, there is neither enough time nor information to make these decisions with certainty; or put another way, there is risk that the decision taken will be incorrect. Research is all about obtaining information in order to reduce the risk in decision-making. A retail marketer would need a great deal of information to evaluate all the choices possible when formulating, evaluating, or adjusting the marketing program. Such information would be useful to assess market potential, to assess performance, and to make choices among marketing program alternatives. For example, consider what information would be helpful in making a store location decision, a store image assessment, a decision on whether to put more money into advertising or direct mail, or a decision as to whether to change a store layout. In making each of these decisions, a marketer would benefit from knowing information about customers, competitors, costs, and so on.

The value of information in making marketing decisions does not distinguish the retailer from other marketers; however, the retailer is in an enviable position to gather information directly from customers. Increasingly, retailers are considering their stores as "laboratories" for understanding the consumer marketplace.

**Retail marketing research** is the systematic collection of any information about a retailer's marketplace and interpretation of that information to assist in making retail marketing decisions. This definition suggests that research may be both about the *marketplace* and about *marketing*. Further, this definition means that good research is problem or decision oriented. Information may come from customer surveys and advertising tests and other specific research studies, but it may also come from analyzing credit records, reviewing governmental statistics, talking to salespeople in the store, and so on.

Two ways the many kinds of retail marketing research may be classified are according to its *role in decision-making* and according to the *types of information* provided. Each of these types of research generally involves different techniques:

1. Role in decision-making:
   a. **exploratory**—identifying problems and opportunities such as determining market potential
   b. **decision-making**—evaluating alternative courses of action
   c. **evaluating**—assessing what happened and why.

2. Types of information provided:
   a. **descriptive**—reporting on what is, such as the average daily number of customers passing by a store
   b. **explanatory**—reporting on why a phenomenon occurs, such as why that number of customers passes by
   c. **predictive**—reporting on what might occur, such as forecasting traffic patterns next year after the bus route is changed in front of a store.

There are different philosophies about the whole topic of gathering information about the retail marketplace. A recent article contrasted American and Japanese approaches to marketing research:

> Japanese companies want information that is context specific rather than context free—that is, data directly relevant to consumer attitudes about the product or the way buyers have used or will use specific products rather than research results that are too remote from actual consumer behavior to be useful. When Japanese companies do conduct surveys, they interview consumers who have actually bought or used a product. They do not scrutinize an undifferentiated mass public to learn about general attitudes and values.[1]

This chapter is divided into three sections: managing research, sources of information, and primary research. It is primarily about ways to gather information directly from customers and potential customers. Exhibit 6.1 shows a summary of the major topics covered in this chapter. Topics even more specific to particular parts of the retail marketing program (such as assortment) are discussed in subsequent chapters.

## MANAGING THE RESEARCH PROCESS

**SECTION**

**ONE**

Research is only worth doing if it aids decision-making for managers. Accordingly, managers have critical roles to play in whether research is undertaken, what the

EXHIBIT 6.1
Managing the
Retail Research
Process

| | | |
|---|---|---|
| **1.** | Research objectives | Need and value of information |
| **2.** | Resources and constraints | Budget (money, time, people)<br>Standards of information quality |
| **3.** | Information sources | Internal, secondary, primary |
| **4.** | Research design | Observation, experiment, survey<br>Population and sample<br>Contact method<br>Instrument design |
| **5.** | Pre-test | Test and adjust |
| **6.** | Data collection | Staff administration<br>Respondent interaction |
| **7.** | Analysis and interpretation | Statistical analysis<br>Qualitative interpretation |
| **8.** | Report | Methodology, findings, data |

nature of that research is, and how the results are used. Drs. Scott Ward and David Reibstein aptly captured the need to blend research technique and managerial judgment as follows:

> In managerial situations, the most reasonable approach to finding out about consumer behaviour is the middle-ground: using research to test, enrich, and extend intuitive, experience-based judgements, and, conversely, interpreting research results with the benefit of managerial experience, and from the point of view of a particular marketer's situation at a given time. Unfortunately, managers often fail to do research, ignore key results and implications, or fail to see important factors bearing on the implications of research results.[2]

Typically, a retail marketer should be most involved at the beginning and end of the research process. Sometimes, the retailer may do the research him- or herself, but any manager using and/or commissioning research should always have some understanding of how research is done to avoid wasting time and money and to avoid being misled by poorly done research.

Whether research is done in making retail decisions depends on whether senior management believes it is integral to the decision-making process. Bram Bluestein, senior vice-president of Planning and Development at Montgomery Ward, spoke of the role of research in his company:

> It's almost become a way of life now. Everyone expects we will go out and do some consumer research as part of researching the business. We typically don't undertake a strategic review of our business without a focused consumer research project. We use consumer research in a variety of ways. First, to determine what consumer segments we should focus on. Second, we use consumer research to give us direct feedback on some of our latest concepts and merchandise programs. Third, we use research to make sure that the consumers are the judge of what they want, as opposed to ourselves.[3]

## RESEARCH OBJECTIVES AND CONSTRAINTS

Retail marketing research should be undertaken to accomplish specified objectives. In other words, research should be intended to answer particular questions that retail marketing managers have. A manager might, for example, phrase concerns as follows: "Traffic in the store is lower than we planned. We have been advertising in the local paper, but we don't know if the ads are really drawing customers. We don't know what kinds of people are coming into the store or what they think of us."

This manager could turn to research for help, but simply saying "Help!" would be inappropriate. The starting point is setting some research objectives and some constraints on the research effort. Our manager might say the following: "I am willing to spend up to $5000 to find out what kinds of people are our customers and where they live. In particular, I want to know what our trading area is. I need that information in one month and it must be detailed enough to shed some light on whether advertising in the city paper is a good idea."

This specification of research need could be made even more specific, but nonetheless, it provides a starting point for a researcher to design a study. The manager has said basically what information is needed, how much it is worth, when it is needed, and how it will be used. Now it is up to the researcher (or the manager him- or herself) to design and implement a study that will provide not merely interesting, but also useful, information within these constraints.

How much to spend on research is an often-asked question. Alan Andreasen offered the following cost–benefit analysis:

> Research should be viewed from a cost–benefit perspective. Its costs are usually of two types—the expenses for the research itself and the amount of lost sales and lost competitive advantage caused by delaying a decision until the results are in. The benefits result from improving the quality of decisions under consideration. Any improvement, in turn, is a function of the stakes involved and how uncertain you are about the rightness of your course of action. Note that the benefits of research are proportional to the manager's uncertainty about which way to go, not to the uncertainty of the future.[4]

## SOURCES OF INFORMATION

■
SECTION
■
TWO
■

The next major issue is the choice of which source of information to pursue. This decision dramatically affects all subsequent research design decisions. There are three basic sources of information that a retail marketing manager may access: internal, secondary, and primary.

**Internal sources**—sales records, scanning data, observations of staff, credit records, clientele books, mailing lists, want slips, contest records, continuity program records, complaint and suggestion data, and any other written or known information within the organization. This is the starting place for any research effort. For example, too often retailers hire outside consultants and research organizations to find out what their own employees already knew about the firm's customers.

**Secondary sources**—information that was gathered by someone else for other purposes. Some sources are free or relatively inexpensive, such as academic research or government publications. Most levels of government collect a great deal of demographic statistics that are readily available. Other organizations, such as The Conference Board, publish information on trends, such as consumer confidence levels. Academics regularly do research and publish it at little or no cost to the retail practitioner.

Some information is more expensive and can be obtained for one-time fees or longer-term subscriptions. There are organizations such as A.C. Nielsen that collect information on media habits, product movements, and so on. Similarly, there are firms such as Compusearch that analyze and customize enumeration data at the geographic micro-market level (the neighbourhood) providing retailers with information previously beyond their imaginations.[5]

Secondary sources have these advantages: they are immediately available at minimal cost, usually plentiful, a source of comparative data for one's own data, and they often provide data otherwise impossible for the individual retailer to collect.

There are also disadvantages: they are usually dated (that is, "old" by the time they are published, such as census reports), often not accurate enough, and often not at a level specific enough for a particular retailer's circumstances. For example, a fashion retailer would want information on specific types of apparel sales in his or her trading area, not national statistics on all apparel sales.

Consulting secondary sources is the second step a retailer should take in answering any question. The example problem posed previously can first be approached using internal sources and secondary data. Here is how one might proceed. The manager was interested in determining the **trading area** for the problem store. Each retail outlet has a geographic area from which most of its business is derived. There are a variety of ways to define this area. Often retailers define a trading area as the geographic area in which 70 percent of their customers reside or work. This guideline will be used in this example.

The physical boundaries of the trading area can be determined by plotting where the store's customers live (or work, depending on which is the point of origin for a trip to our store) on a local map. Addresses can typically be obtained in three ways: (*a*) by examining sales receipts at time of purchase or through credit records, (*b*) by asking customers directly or via an in-store contest form, or (*c*) by recording licence plate numbers of customers' cars and then paying the provincial government for the registered owners' addresses. Once obtained, these addresses can be plotted on a city map. Then, one may draw circles around the retail outlet, increasing the radius by one-half or one-quarter of a kilometre until as many of the plotted customers are included inside the outer circle as desired (usually 70 percent is the outer circle). Clearly, few trade areas are perfectly circular. There is no magic in circles so one can draw the physical shape as one likes. Physical boundaries such as rivers, streets, and so on, obviously change the shape of the area.

However it is drawn, once the trading area is defined, one can begin to examine the area more closely. For example, one might mark the census tracts, postal codes, and/or city planning districts on the map to provide a way to use secondary demographic information to characterize the areas in which most of the store's customers reside. This approach will provide an indication of income levels, housing prices, educational achievements, and so on.[6] Exhibit 6.2 provides some selected secondary sources Canadian retailers should consider.

### Periodicals and Newspapers

*Advertising Age*

*American Druggist*

*Business Quarterly*

*Business Week*

*Canadian Grocer*

*Canadian Jeweller*

*Canadian Retailer*

*Chain Store Age Executive*

*DM News: The Newspaper of Direct Marketing*

*Direct Marketing*

*Discount Merchandiser*

*Discount Store News*

*Do-It-Yourself Retailing*

*Drug Merchandising*

*Financial Post*

*Forbes*

*Fortune*

*Harvard Business Review*

*International Trends in Retailing*

*Journal of Advertising Research*

*Journal of Consumer Research*

*Journal of Marketing*

*Journal of Marketing Research*

*Journal of Retailing*

*L'Epicier*

*Le Pharmacien*

*Mass Market Retailers*

*Marketing News*

*Merchandising Week*

*Progressive Grocer*

*Retail Business*

*Retail Control*

*Sales and Marketing Management*

*Shopping Centre Canada*

*Shopping Centers Today*

*Stores*

*Style*

*Supermarket News*

*Value Retail News*

*Wall Street Journal*

*Women's Wear Daily*

*Business Periodicals Index*

*InfoGlobe*

*Readers Guide to Periodical Index*

### Government Publications Canada:

62-001 *The Consumer Price Index*

62-554 *Family food expenditure in Canada (biennial)*

62-555 *Family expenditure in Canada (irregular)*

63-002 *Department store sales and stocks (monthly)*

63-004 *Department store monthly sales by province and metropolitan area (monthly)*

63-005 *Retail trade* (monthly)

63-007 *New motor vehicle sales* (monthly)

63-008 *Wholesale trade* (monthly)

63-011 *Restaurant, caterer, and tavern statistics* (monthly)

63-014 *Merchandising inventories* (monthly)

63-015 *Service industry bulletin* (bimonthly)

63-210 *Retail chain and department stores* (annual)

63-213 *Vending machine operators* (annual)

63-218 *Direct selling in Canada* (annual)

63-223 *Annual retail trade* (annual)

63-224 *Market Research Handbook* (annual)

63-226 *Wholesale trade statistics* (annual)

63-603 *Operating results, men's clothing stores* (irregular)

63-607 *Operating results, retail drug stores* (irregular)

63-608 *Operating results, retail florists* (biennial)

63-609 *Operating results, retail jewellery stores* (annual)

## United States:

*U.S. Census of Business*

*Monthly Retail Trade*

*Survey of Current Business*

*Monthly Catalog of U.S. Government Publications*

## Associations

These are some of the major associations that concern themselves with retailing in general. There are many specialized groups as well.

American Collegiate Retailing Association

American Marketing Association

Conference Board

Direct Marketing Association

Electronic Data Interchange Council of Canada

Food Marketing Institute

International Council of Shopping Centers

International Association of Chain Stores

Marketing Science Institute

National Retail Furniture Association

National Retail Hardware Association

National Retail Federation

Point of Purchase Advertising Institute

Retail Council of Canada

Super Market Institute

## Commercial Research Firms and Directories

In addition to the above associations, there are countless research firms, consultants, brokers, and their publications. Many of their directories are particularly useful.

A.C. Nielsen

*Audits and Surveys*

| | |
|---|---|
| Canadian Directory of Shopping Centres | Operating Survey of Canadian Retailing (Retail Council of Canada) |
| The Catalogue of Catalogues | R.L. Polk |
| Compusearch | Retailing in Britain (Economist Intelligence Unit (EIU)) |
| Directory of Retail Chains in Canada (Maclean Hunter) | Retail Trade International (Euromonitor) |
| Europe's Major Retailers (Euromonitor) | Sales and Marketing Executives |
| Financial Post Survey of Markets | Selling Area Marketing Inc. (SAMI/ Burke) |
| Information Resources Inc. | Sheldon's Retail Directory |
| Marketing Research Corporation of America | The Source Book of Franchising Opportunities |

**Primary sources**—specific, customized studies undertaken by and/or for the retailer such as a customer survey, a focus group, or a site traffic study. Any retailer should undertake primary research only if internal and secondary sources are inadequate to the task.

■
SECTION
■
THREE
■

## PRIMARY RESEARCH

While internal and secondary sources of information often help a retailer a great deal, sometimes they do not provide enough insights into the problems and opportunities a retailer is examining. In such a situation, he or she may decide it is worthwhile to undertake a customized study.

## RESEARCH DESIGN ISSUES

There are many issues that a retailer will confront when considering primary research, including:

1. Who should be the population of interest?
2. Would a sample suffice? How big should it be?
3. How should the sample be selected?
4. How long will it take and how much will it cost?
5. Will it be worth it?
6. What are the best questions to ask?
7. Should I do it myself or hire someone?

The answers to these questions are dependent on the particular circumstances of the retailer. These and other relevant topics are covered in the following text.

## Population

Any research study is about somebody or something. The specification of the total group of people the research study aims to understand better is called the population. For example, an apparel retailer may decide to study current customers or potential customers who live within a five kilometre radius of the store, or university students living on campus, and so on. Each of these groups could constitute the population of interest for a study. When defined properly, this population helps determine how best to identify and reach it, much like a target market selection provides the focus for the retail marketing program. At the end of the study, the researcher expects to be able to say something meaningful about this population, not all populations.

The proper starting point is studying current customers. They are more accessible to the retailer for study and often provide valuable insights into determining how to expand the customer base; also, there are often "customer relations" benefits from visibly demonstrating one's interest in better understanding current customers.

## Sample

A researcher must decide whether to study every member of the specified population (this is called a census) or only a subgroup of this total (this is called a sample). A retailer may send a questionnaire, for example, to every person on the store's mailing list or only to every tenth name. Usually, a sample is adequate. A sample costs less to study, saves time, and done properly, represents the population surprisingly accurately.

The major concern with using a sample of the population rather than a complete census is ensuring that the sample is "representative." This means ensuring that the sample accurately portrays the whole. One may work toward this goal by the way in which the sample is selected and then measure the extent to which the selected sample was representative of the population.

## Sample Selection

Selecting a sample involves deciding how to select specific respondents and how many of them to select. In order to select from a population, such as residents in a defined geographic trading area, one needs a "sample frame," which simply means some list that represents each member of the population of interest (for example, using the telephone book as a frame for a community's households).

Then, there are several *ways to select* respondents from the frame. The most likely to provide representativeness is called **random sampling**. This approach results in every member of the population having an equal chance of being selected as a respondent. For example, to simplify the idea, one might put all the names on the store mailing list in a hat and draw names. There are times, however, when one does not want to use this random approach. A specialty retailer may wish to study upscale customers in the general trading area rather than provide every customer in the trading area an equal chance of being studied. In such a situation, a nonrandom approach (also known as non-probability sampling or judgment sampling) would be more appropriate. The retail researcher in our example may decide to specify a **quota sample** that gives upscale customers a disproportionate representation in the sample relative to their true proportion of the trading area population.

Another sampling approach often used by retailers is **area sampling**. This involves the random selection of geographic areas; for example, selecting at random certain postal codes out of the city and then certain blocks within those postal codes for the study. This approach ends up focusing on clusters of respondents to use research resources as efficiently as possible.

Yet another sampling approach is **convenience sampling**, which means respondents are chosen because they were easy to recruit. For example, a retailer may ask the first ten people into the store one day a few questions simply because that was a convenient time for the retailer to ask questions. There are other ways to select respondents as well.

The question of **sample size**—that is, the number of respondents that should be sampled—arises frequently. Unfortunately, the answer is not simple. The number may be limited at the maximum by the budget available divided by the cost per respondent and at the minimum by the accuracy of the results desired by the researcher. The required sample size is not dependent on the size of the population, as any good statistics book will explain. Rather, sample size is related to three concepts: variability, precision, and confidence. The greater the **variability** of the population (that is, the heterogeneity of its characteristics, such as demographics), the larger the necessary size of the sample taken. **Precision** refers to the measurable difference between the sample result and a complete census result. In other words, the higher the precision wanted, the larger must be the sample size. Precision is usually expressed in terms such as "plus or minus 5%" of the sample result. The way statistics work, doubling the required level of precision means having to increase the sample size by a factor of four. **Degree of confidence** refers to the probability that the true value falls in the interval created by the precision figures. For example, one may say "95% confident that the value is + or −5% of the sample result." The greater the desired confidence, the larger the sample size required.

Table 6.1 shows a simple format that should suffice to guide most research efforts. The numbers in the cells refer to the usable sample size (not the number attempted). Most researchers are content with 95% confidence with a precision of + or − 5%, which means a sample size of nearly 400.[7]

## Validity, Reliability, Meaningfulness, and Bias

Primary research should be assessed on three criteria: validity, reliability, and meaningfulness. **Validity** refers to whether or not the research examines and measures what it is supposed to. **Reliability** refers to whether or not the research does what it is supposed to do well. **Meaningfulness** refers to whether or not it addresses the right managerial questions.

TABLE 6.1
Sample Size Required

|  |  | Confidence Level | | |
| --- | --- | --- | --- | --- |
|  |  | 90% | 95% | 99% |
| Precision | +−10% | 68 | 96 | 166 |
|  | +−5% | 271 | 385 | 661 |
|  | +−2.5% | 1076 | 1537 | 2642 |

To design and conduct absolutely perfect research borders on the impossible. There are so many ways in which errors in design and implementation can occur. Two major kinds of errors may come from sampling biases or nonsampling biases.

**A sampling bias** is the difference between the observed values of a variable and the long-run average measurement one would get with repeated measurements. It is a statistical phenomenon that can be reduced by increasing sample size, as discussed previously.

**A nonsampling bias** occurs as a result of the way in which the sample was selected or processed. There are several subtypes: **nonobservation biases** refer to problems of (*a*) **nonresponse bias** (the people who responded were different in important ways from the people who didn't respond—for example, the small typeface used for the survey may have discouraged older people from responding due to difficulty in reading it), and (*b*) **noncoverage bias** (the sample did not include people that were thought to be included—for example, a telephone survey in the fall using the telephone book will not reach college students and others who moved after the telephone book was printed).

Another type of nonsampling bias is **observation bias**. Again, there are two basic subtypes: (*a*) **field collection bias** (which refers to distortions in the way the sample was selected versus the way it was supposed to be selected—for example, a mall intercept interviewer may only approach those people who appear friendly and willing to talk rather than take a random sample of people passing by), and (*b*) **processing bias** (distortions in the way the data were entered into the computer or otherwise analyzed—for example, analysts may "create" extra responses when paid per response processed or not enter data that is difficult to read).

## Observation and Experimentation

Primary information gathering may be done by observation, experimentation, or survey research. Survey research is discussed in the next section.

Watching customers or competitors is called **observation**. Such observations may be obvious (such as standing around in the store watching customers) or unobtrusive, such as analyzing scanner data, examining store security videotapes, and so on. Observation techniques focus on behaviour—on what people do rather than on their feelings, beliefs, and what they say. An observation study often does not require the respondent's permission; and there are a variety of ways to conduct one. A frequent form of observation study is a traffic count. For example, a researcher may record how many customers enter a store through a particular door at varying hours of the day on several days to reach an average "count." On the other hand, some observation studies do require permission such as gaining access to a household's pantry to see what products are kept there.

Some forms of observation are quite exotic—for example, garbage analysis, eye movement cameras, videos in mannequins, tracking customer inquiries at interactive information terminals, and so on.

Most observation methods focus on the customer directly. The most recent developments are in **single source systems**, which are complex databases created by combining purchase behaviour, media exposure, and respondent characteristics. The three major companies in the field are Information Resources Incorporated (INFOSCAN), A.C. Nielsen (SCANTRACK), and SAMI/Burke Incorporated (SAMSCAN). David Curry described the basic elements of these single source systems as follows:

> To obtain the data, each system's in-store scanners monitor prices and price promotions for all UPC scannable items, in-store audits monitor selected product placements and merchandising displays weekly, in-home meters monitor television viewing in certain panel households, and audits monitor magazine and newspaper advertising in panel cities.[8]

Some observation methods involve simulating the customer. **Mystery shopping programs** refer to individuals hired by management to pretend to be shoppers and then to observe various aspects of the retailer's operation and report about them. For example, many retailers have employed mystery shoppers to evaluate the quality of their customer care efforts (as discussed in Chapter 9).

Systematically varying the situation (that is, exposing people to varying "marketing treatments," such as different display placements) is called **experimentation**. There are several types of experiments, which may be broadly classified as field studies and laboratory studies.

A **field study** refers to an experiment that happens in the stores or their markets. For example, one might try a newspaper advertisement in one market and an in-store poster in another to see which had greater impact. A test market is a major field experiment.

A **laboratory study** is an experiment conducted in an artificial setting. For example, respondents may be asked to "shop" from a mocked-up store display to examine their reactions to varying shelf-space arrangements.

There are many types of experimental design.[9] The three most common are "after-only," "before–after," and "before–after with control group," as shown in Table 6.2.

### Survey Research

There are many different possibilities for surveying respondents, including personal face-to-face interviewing, panel studies, group face-to-face interviewing, telephone interviewing, and mail questionnaires.

**TABLE 6.2**
**Experimental Design**

| After-only | |
|---|---|
| Group 1 | exposure to stimulus A $>$ measure |
| Group 2 | exposure to stimulus B $>$ measure |

| Before–after | |
|---|---|
| Group 1 | before measure $>$ stimulus A $>$ after measure |
| Group 2 | before measure $>$ stimulus B $>$ after measure |

| Before–after with control group | |
|---|---|
| Group 1 | before measure $>$ stimulus A $>$ after measure |
| Group 2 | before measure $>$ stimulus B $>$ after measure |
| Control 1 | stimulus A $>$ after measure |
| Control 2 | stimulus B $>$ after measure |

**Personal face-to-face interviewing** is the most difficult method of all. It may take the form of a prearranged interview at the respondent's home or place of business or at some other location, such as in-store.

This approach has several advantages:

- It is the most flexible way of obtaining data because it allows probing and two-way discussion (can be lengthy).
- The interviewer controls the questions that are asked and their sequence (can tailor discussion).
- It is very private, allowing more sensitive issues to be explored without interference from other respondents (less "group think").
- Once the interview starts, nonresponse is usually very low.
- The identity of the respondent is usually known (especially when the interview is prearranged).
- It offers the possibility of controlling sample characteristics.
- Value per respondent is generally greater than in a group.

There are, however, disadvantages:

- It is usually the most expensive and time-consuming approach.
- It requires skilled interviewers.
- There are dangers of interviewer bias, interference, and even cheating.
- Questions asked may vary substantially from respondent to respondent.
- It is often difficult to get people to participate.

**Intercept studies** refer to face-to-face personal interviews that are not prearranged. This form of research has become very common. There are two basic types. **Mall intercepts** involve stopping people in the common areas of shopping malls. Bush and Hair recently examined mall intercepts versus other survey techniques, and concluded that:

- overall quality of data from the mall intercept appears to be equivalent to that of telephone interviewing
- more accurate or less distorted responses appear to be obtained
- the typical mall intercept respondent is a more frequent user of shopping centres than is the telephone respondent
- the mall intercept approach is not as well suited to probability sampling as door-to-door or telephone interviewing
- the major concern in a mall intercept survey is sampling the correct respondents.[10]

Mall intercepts have the following advantages and disadvantages, according to Katherine Smith:

### Advantages

1. They allow researchers to test visual material, product concepts, and other physical stimuli.
2. They offer an opportunity to obtain immediate response.
3. They have the potential to provide more depth of response than interviews not conducted face-to-face.
4. Researchers can use various types of equipment to analyze responses (for example, voice-pitch analysis).
5. A large number of respondents from a wide geographic area can be interviewed in a limited time.
6. Researchers can control the interviewing environment and supervise the interviewer.

### Disadvantages

1. The mall customer may have an atypical character that does not reflect the general population.
2. The intercept is not well suited to probability sampling.
3. If shoppers are in a hurry, they may respond carelessly.
4. The interview time constraint is more severe with mall intercepts than with other face-to-face methods.[11]

**Purchase intercepts** refer to intercepting people in-store, typically shortly after a purchase selection has been made, then asking them questions about it. In other words, it is point-of-purchase, face-to-face personal interviewing. This is not the same as the related technique of post-use interviewing (for example, asking satisfaction levels after a restaurant meal). The major advantage over out-of-store interviewing offered by purchase intercepts is the replacement of recall data (for example, "When did you last buy toothpaste?") with actual observation (for example, the interviewer saw toothpaste put into the shopping cart). This advantage becomes very important in low-purchase-frequency categories and low-salience situations, which may be forgotten by the time conventional surveys are done. The major advantage of purchase intercepts over scanner data analysis is the opportunity to ask "why" rather than just track "what was purchased."[12]

**Customer panels** refer to longer-term research studies. For example, individuals or families may be recruited to track their media habits or shopping habits over periods of one week to several months. One method of doing this tracking is to provide respondents with "diaries" in which to record their behaviour over time. This requirement for extensive effort on the part of the panel member has led several major firms such as A.C. Nielsen to experiment with "passive devices" to record panel members' behaviour without asking them to fill in diaries or punch buttons on a television monitoring box.

Compared to other customer contact methods, customer panels offer the major advantage of recording behaviour directly (particularly at-home behaviour) over time (called a longitudinal study) as opposed to relying on "recall" of behaviour or at-the-moment observations (called cross-sectional studies). On the other hand, it is becoming increasingly difficult to recruit people to participate in marketplace panel studies, and there is some question as to whether those who do participate are representative of those who do not. Panel studies are expensive to conduct and are usually undertaken only by major research firms that syndicate their findings to clients willing to pay substantial sums. Individual retailers, however, have the opportunity to establish their own panels of existing customers.

**Group face-to-face interviewing (focus groups)** are increasingly common. Under this approach, the researcher recruits typically 8–10 people to participate in a group discussion of 1–2 hours in duration. A moderator guides the discussion with open-ended questions, such as "Tell us how you go about buying a dress. I mean, how do you decide where to shop and things like that?" The moderator's role is to guide, to probe, to explore without looking for definitive answers to specific questions.

Focus groups have several advantages:

- They are flexible (similar to personal interviewing).
- Group members often prompt one another to comments they might not otherwise make.
- They are relatively quick to set up and to interpret.
- They are relatively inexpensive.
- The identity of the respondents is known.
- They are an excellent way to formulate and pre-test more rigorous research instruments.

Their disadvantages include:

- There is difficulty at times in recruiting participants (increasingly must compensate participants for their time).
- The interviewer is typically less able to explore very private issues.
- The group is very reliant on the moderator's skill in leading the discussion.
- They can be greatly influenced by one or two dominant participants.
- They are difficult to interpret (there is a danger in thinking that a small sample is generalizable).

**Telephone surveys** are a form of interviewing done over the phone. They, too, are becoming increasingly common. Telephone surveys may be prearranged or "cold calls." Some are made to known respondents (say, from a customer list), whereas others may be made to unknown respondents. Some researchers use computer dialling programs that conduct the entire interview without a personal operator. These are generally resisted by most respondents and are illegal in some jurisdictions.

There are several advantages to telephone surveys:

- The cost per response is relatively low.
- They are very quick to administer.
- One can control field bias by having supervisors "listen in."
- Interviewer can have two-way communication with respondent to answer questions, probe responses, and tailor the interview.

There are some disadvantages:

- It is becoming more difficult to find people at home and to get their cooperation.
- The survey must be relatively brief.
- Questions must be relatively simple.
- Interviewer is unable to reach unlisted numbers and those people who have recently moved (unless using random dialling).
- There are difficulties because of the increasing use of answering machines and call-screening devices.[13]

**Mail surveys** of many forms have been widely used. These are questionnaires addressed specifically to either individuals or households. Some are provided with instructions so that respondents "self-select." For example, a survey may be sent to Mr. and Mrs. Smith with instructions that the "principal household shopper for groceries" respond. With the amount of promotional mail being sent today, it is increasingly difficult to get people to pay attention to mail surveys, even those that are personalized. Every effort must be made to make the whole process easy for the respondent. In particular, addressed, postage-paid return envelopes are a must.

There are several advantages to mail surveys:

- There is no need for interviewers.
- Costs per respondent are lowest.
- Questions and format across all respondents are consistent.
- There is no field bias.
- The respondent may answer at her or his own speed and convenience (can think about responses, look up information, etc.).
- This may be the only way to contact some individuals.
- Respondents may be more honest on some questions (especially if responses are anonymous).

There are disadvantages:

- There is less likelihood of understanding the extent and nature of nonresponse bias.
- There is no opportunity for two-way communication.
- Response rates are generally the lowest.
- It is not always clear who actually completed the questionnaire.
- It is relatively slow to administer.

With advances in technology, variations on the mail survey (such as fax surveys, computer disk surveys, touchscreen surveys, etc.) will become increasingly common.

## Research Instrument Design

Whether designing a questionnaire, a personal interview guide, or any other script for interacting with a respondent, the researcher should observe several basic principles that help ensure that respondents will be both willing and able to answer questions. Researchers face a host of issues in the design of any data collection instrument, including how many questions to ask, how to phrase them, how to sequence them, whether to use open- or close-ended questions, and so on. Exhibit 6.3 provides some guidelines.[14]

---

*EXHIBIT 6.3*
*Guidelines for*
*Research*
*Instrument*
*Design*

1. Be clear what information is wanted and ask only for that.
2. At all times, think about how a respondent would perceive the questionnaire or interview.
3. Construct a sample set of answers and see if these would help make decisions.
4. Provide a good reason to the respondent for giving the desired information.
5. Use common words and simple grammar.
6. Be unambiguous so that questions are understood correctly.
7. Do not ask two questions at once. For example: *not*—Do you enjoy shopping at the ABC Supermarket? *but rather*—Have you ever shopped at ABC Supermarket? If so, do you enjoy it?

8. Leave sensitive demographics and other questions until the end.

9. Move from general questions to more specific questions.

10. Start with a question that the respondent will find interesting and will make him or her think "This survey applies to me so it's worth answering."

11. Use checklists and closed-end questions where possible, but be aware that such an approach may suggest responses the respondent would not think of otherwise.

12. Allow "don't know" categories wherever the respondent may not have a basis for giving a more precise response.

13. Build in cross-checks to ensure respondent consistency, but don't overdo this because respondents feel insulted if they notice much of this.

14. Switch orders of scales and response categories. Use positive and negative phrasing.

15. Leave lots of space between questions and use a reasonable size typeface.

16. Remember two basic issues for each proposed question: Can the respondent answer this question? (for example, *not* "How much did you spend on laundry detergent last year?") and, Will the respondent answer the question? (for example, *not* "Exactly how much money did you earn last year personally?")

17. Pre-test the questionnaire if at all possible.

18. Keep it as simple as possible.

---

There are many specific techniques for formulating questions. Questions may be **open-ended**, meaning the respondent answers without restraint, or **closed-ended**, meaning the respondent picks from the supplied answer possibilities (often referred to as "multiple choice"). Techniques frequently used include the following:

1. Likert scales—typically five- or seven-point agree–disagree scales (for example, strongly agree, agree, neither agree nor disagree, disagree, strongly disagree). These scales facilitate attitude questions in particular.

2. Semantic differential scales—response scales anchored by words with a range of points unlabelled between them (for example, respondents may be asked to indicate feelings about Store A and Store B on scales such as Unattractive+____+____+____+____+____+____+Attractive).

3. Projective techniques—the use of pictures, symbols, word association, or sentence completion to gain insights into respondents' thinking (for example, "Complete the sentence: Store A's customers are _____").

4. Ranking techniques—asking customers to rate or order products, stores, advertisements, etc. (for example, "Rank the following in order of importance to you: Price, Convenience, Hours . . . ").

Whatever questioning techniques are being considered, the researcher should think ahead to the analysis to be performed to ensure that the ultimate results will be useful to the decision-making objectives of the research.

**Interacting with respondents**   Conducting research is a marketing activity. In other words, the retail researcher should approach respondents as if they were customers (and often they are!), with all the same care and concern for their interests, circumstances, and motivation. For example, telephoning potential respondents during peak dinner periods is insensitive and dysfunctional; people are not interested in responding at that time and typically get angry at being asked at such an obviously bad time. This in turn leads to dislike of research in general and further deterioration in responsiveness to surveys.

All respondents should be approached as one would like one's parents or spouse to be approached: politely, truthfully, and sensitively. Similarly, questionnaires should be prepared as spoken conversations put down on paper.

One of the major issues many researchers grapple with in respondent interaction is whether to offer **incentives** to participants. There are no easy answers to this question.

The argument for incentives is that if the research is time-consuming, tedious, of no real personal interest to the respondent, and/or involves out-of-pocket expenditures by the respondent (such as baby-sitting and parking to attend a focus group session), then respondents will not only appreciate but in many cases expect (even demand) to be paid. Payments may be cash or gifts. When paying respondents, retailers should always consider using some of their own merchandise or gift certificates. In this way, the incentive offered has more "value" to the respondent than it actually cost the retailer. For example, a $25 item (selling price in the store) may have a real cost of $15 to the retailer.

The argument against incentives, on the other hand, is that if the researcher can convince the potential respondent that the research is important (to the respondent or people the respondent cares about), or that it is interesting or even fun to participate in, then only a limited incentive—or none at all—will be required. Professional appearance of people and survey instruments, polite approaches, considerate timing, follow-up thank you's, and the offer to share findings all militate against the need for monetary or other tangible incentives. Of course, a very strong reason against incentives is overall lack of funds to provide them.

**Pre-testing**   One of the steps many retail researchers ignore is pre-testing. This refers to trying the approach, the instrument, and any other aspect of the research design on a very small scale before full-scale execution. For example, one might select 10–20 customers to telephone first with the proposed telephone survey. The reason for this would be to see if there are any needed improvements in the proposed research. Pre-tests often reveal ambiguous questions, excessively ambitious surveys, inadequate incentives, and so on. Any aspect of the proposed research can be tested, including response rate. One form of pre-testing does not share with the pre-test respondents that it is a test. In other words, the pre-test is run as if it was the actual execution. In this situation, the researcher must reach his or her own conclusions about how the test went. The other basic form of pre-test involves sharing with respondents that it is a pre-test and asking additional questions to those that would be asked in a regular execution. For example, respondents may be asked: "Did you find any of the questions particularly difficult to answer?" or "How long did it take you to fill out that questionnaire." This form of pre-testing often provides better insights for the researcher. Sometimes a focus group may be used to pre-test other forms of customer contact research.

Clearly, the pre-test must be properly conducted and the researcher must be willing to adjust the proposed research according to the pre-test findings, or there is no point in having a pre-test.

**Data collection**    The actual implementation of the research can be quite complicated. Interviewers must be recruited, trained, directed, and assessed. Many excellent research designs have been undermined by poor execution. For example, if interviewers cheat in terms of who they interview or how they record responses, the whole study is jeopardized.

Studies involving interviewing should include some form of cross-checking or follow-up to ensure that the interviewers have conducted themselves properly. Some way of tracking respondents by name (or at least by phone number), as well as who interviewed whom, will be necessary to do this.

Studies using the telephone often run into implementation problems due to poor phone number lists (too many changed residences, disconnects, and so on) or due to difficulty finding respondents at home to take the call. Studies employing the mail have comparable problems, such as slow deliveries, changed addresses, and so on.

Whatever the approach taken, experienced researchers have learned that attention to detail is absolutely critical to ensuring success.

**Analysis and interpretation**    Statistical analysis of research results can be a complicated subject;[15] however, generally speaking, a retail researcher has three major concerns about the data collected:

1. Was the sample used representative of the population?
2. How can the results be summarized?
3. Do the results help with the managerial questions?

Assuming every effort was made to draw a representative sample, after the research has been completed the retailer may compare the sample's characteristics with known characteristics of the population. For example, if one knew from census data the age distribution of a city, that distribution could be compared (assuming a reasonable similarity in time frame) to the age distribution of the sample taken. Notice that if the researcher anticipated doing this, then he or she would ask about age using categories comparable to those used in the existing data (for example, 25–40 years old). Such comparisons are not perfect, but they do provide a quick and easy way to see if there are major differences in the sample taken from the population of interest.

There are many ways to summarize research findings statistically. The simplest way is to examine each question separately, recording the numbers or percentages of the different types of answers to the question. This is called **marginal analysis**. For example, on the question "How many times have you shopped in XYZ store?" the findings may be as follows:

| | |
|---|---|
| Never | 25% |
| 1–5 times | 34% |
| 6–10 times | 30% |
| More than 10 | 11% |

Some questions can be summarized with **measures of central tendency**, such as mean (arithmetic average), mode (most frequently occurring score), and median (midpoint in the range of responses). Beware of "averaging" response categories that don't make sense, such as male and female. Such categorical data should be kept separate rather than inappropriately summarized.

Data can be combined by constructing **indices**. For example, one may want to create a "customer satisfaction measure" that includes several different questions. Recently, several researchers have created "perceptual maps" and "customer satisfaction indices" by statistically combining variables.

Pieces of data can also be examined in relation to one another. One of the simplest ways to do this is by **cross-tabulation**, which refers to building matrices of information that can be analyzed by inspection. For example, one might examine age of respondent shoppers with frequency of shopping at the store, as shown in Table 6.3.

### TABLE 6.3
### Frequency of Visits to the Store

| Age \ Freq. | 0 | 1–5 | 6–10 | >10 | Total |
|---|---|---|---|---|---|
| <18 | 10 | 30 | 20 | 5 | 65 |
| 18–35 | 5 | 20 | 40 | 20 | 85 |
| >35 | 30 | 20 | 10 | 2 | 62 |
| Total | 45 | 70 | 70 | 27 | 212 |

The cells contain the number of observations. The rows and columns have been totalled. One can then analyze to see, for example, how many of the 27 who visit the store most frequently, are in a particular group, such as the 18–35-year-old category?

There are many very sophisticated statistical methods. Many are called **multi-variate statistics**, which refer to techniques such as regression, factor analysis, and cluster analysis that allow one to examine the influence of several variables simultaneously on a variable of interest (such as store patronage).

There are emerging new technologies in this field that hold great promise for making research more "management-friendly." Lodish and Reibstein commented on this as follows:

> Aside from offering exceptional detail, the consumer research techniques of the 1980's have other useful attributes. They allow data to be gathered unobtrusively, to show details about individuals, and to be ready for analysis.
>
> Another major advance is the marketing managers' accessibility to data via computers. No longer are the data relegated to the corporation's data processors. The special marketing decision software that one can easily learn to use now provides managers a way to combine modelling, statistics, graphics, flexible report generation, and data-base management.[16]

**Report**    The final step is preparing a report either for presentation to others or as a record for oneself. Here are some suggestions:

a.    Begin with a statement of the original objectives and organize the entire report or presentation as "answers" to those managerial questions. Do not necessarily organize the report in the order of the questions asked of respondents.

b.    Explain the methodology in simple terms. For example, who was contacted, what efforts were made to get a representative sample, and so on.

c.    Do not simply present the findings, but rather add some interpretation as to their meaning.

d.    Reference where the original data are kept so that they may be re-examined if necessary. For example, focus groups are typically recorded (audio or video) and then summarized by the moderator. The original tapes should be available to the manager if he or she wishes to review them.

# CONCLUSION

All retail marketers face myriad choices that must be made with very limited time and very incomplete information. Sometimes, the risks and uncertainties involved mean that market research is merited. Exhibit 6.4 provides some summary questions a retailer considering research may ask to guide the effort.[17] While this chapter may seem to have suggested that all retailers need to become research technicians, that was not its intent. Instead, it was intended to encourage retailers to use research more often than has been the general case in the past, to suggest that many retail marketers can do their own research, and to remind retailers to keep any research program in its proper perspective. It's better to work on the right problem with some flaws in methodology than on the wrong problem with perfect methodology.

EXHIBIT 6.4
Some Guidelines
for Undertaking
Research

1. What management questions are to be addressed? How much are good answers to these questions worth to you?

2. What particular respondent group (population) is to be the focus of the study?

3. Have you explored internal and secondary sources thoroughly?

4. What do you hope to be able to say at the end of the study that you cannot say now? How accurate statistically (precision and confidence) must the results be?

5. Are you planning a census of the population of interest or are you planning a sample of the population? Why?

6. If a sample, how will you identify and select which respondents to study? How many and why?

7. Do you foresee any bias as a result of your approach? If so, how will you deal with it?

8. What approach do you plan (e.g., interview at home, mail, telephone, etc.) and why? What are the major implications of this choice?

9. What plans for pre-testing your approach and instruments do you have?

10. In no particular order, write as many of the questions as possible that you may ask. For close-ended questions, provide answer categories or scales. Then, look for ways to organize them in a manner that would make sense to the respondent and be easy to ask if there is to be an interviewer.

11. Now, write your introductory, transitional, and closing comments.

12. How will you ensure that the questions are properly understood and answered by respondents?

13. Who will actually do the study and how can you be sure it will be done properly?

14. What is your schedule for this study and why?

15. How will you manage the data results?

16. What other analysis do you plan? For example, do you want percentage distributions on all questions, do you want to prepare cross-tabulation tables? Provide examples of what analysis you would do by constructing sample tables and charts you hope to complete.

17. How do you plan to present the results and communicate them to others in the organization?

18. How much do you anticipate this will cost in out-of-pocket dollars?

19. When it is all done, how will you know if it was worth it?

20. Where will the original (raw) data be kept for future reference?

## REVIEW QUESTIONS

1. Prepare a list of what a retail researcher might do to engage your cooperation in a six-page detailed questionnaire about your attitudes and behaviour with regard to your regular grocery shopping.

2. How would you discover what image a single-unit shoe store located in a mall had (*a*) among its customers, and (*b*) among potential customers?

3. How would you determine the market potential in your city for a new "home-delivery hamburger operation"?

4. List all the sources of information (such as credit records) a general merchandise retailer might use to develop a "customer information system" about his or her current customers. How might that information be used?

5. "The increasing ability and propensity of retailers to collect their own marketing research information will dramatically shift the balance of power between retailers and their suppliers." Do you agree? What examples come to mind?

## KEY TERMS

- retail marketing research
- exploratory role
- decision-making role
- evaluating role
- descriptive information
- explanatory information
- predictive information
- internal sources (of information)
- secondary sources (of information)
- trading area
- primary sources (of information)
- random sampling
- quota sampling
- area sampling
- convenience sampling
- sample size
- variability
- precision
- degree of confidence
- validity
- reliability
- meaningfulness
- sampling biases
- nonsampling biases
- nonobservation biases
- nonresponse biases
- noncoverage biases
- observation bias
- field collection bias
- processing bias
- observation
- single source systems
- mystery shopping programs
- experimentation
- field study
- laboratory study
- personal face-to-face interviewing
- intercept studies
- mall intercepts
- purchase intercepts
- customer panels
- group face-to-face interviewing (focus groups)
- telephone surveys
- mail surveys
- open-ended (questions)
- closed-ended (questions)
- incentives
- marginal analysis
- measures of central tendency
- indices
- cross-tabulation
- multivariate statistics

## NOTES

1. Johny K. Johansson and Ikujiro Nonaka, "Market Research the Japanese Way," *Harvard Business Review*, May–June 1987, pp. 16–22.

2. Scott Ward and David Reibstein, "Note on Market and Consumer Research," Harvard Business School, 1979, p.1.

3. "Market Research Put to Creative Use: Today's Retail Managers Add New Meaning to 'Business As Usual,'" *Chain Store Age Executive*, May 1988.

4. Alan R. Andreasen, "Cost-Conscious Marketing Research," *Harvard Business Review*, July–August 1983, pp. 74–79.

5. For a description of several major commercial secondary information providers, see Robert J. Dolan, "Note on the Marketing Information Industry" 9–588-027, Harvard Business School, 1987.

6. This example could be extended. For further discussion of such uses of governmental statistics, see *How a Retailer Can Profit from Facts*, Statistics Canada, 1978.

7. For further discussion of sampling statistics and other statistics, there are several good marketing research books, such as H. Robert Dodge, Sam Fullerton, and David Rink, *Marketing Research* (Columbus, Ohio: Charles E. Merrill Publishing, 1982).

8. David J. Curry, "Single Source Systems: Retail Management Present and Future," *Journal of Retailing*, Spring 1989, pp. 1–20.

9. The standard reference for experimental design is D.T. Campbell and J.C. Stanley, *Experimental and Quasi-Experimental Design for Research* (Chicago, Ill.: Rand McNally 1963).

10. Alan J. Bush, and Joseph F. Hair, Jr., "An Assessment of the Mall Intercept as a Data Collection Method," *Journal of Marketing Research*, May 1985, pp. 158–67.

11. Katherine T. Smith, "Most Research Firms Use Mall Intercepts," *Marketing News*, September 1989, p. 16.

12. For further discussion, see Shelby H. McIntyre and Sherry D.F.G. Bender, "The Purchase Intercept Technique (PIT) in Comparison to Telephone and Mail Surveys," *Journal of Retailing*, Winter 1986.

13. Thirty-six percent of U.S. households had answering machines as of mid-1990 and 17 pecent of those used their machines to screen all calls. See Jack Honomichl, "Answering Machines Threaten Survey Research," *Marketing News*, 6 August 1990, p. 11.

14. An excellent book on all aspects of survey design is D.A. Dillman, *Mail and Telephone Surveys: The Total Design Method* (New York: Wiley, 1978).

15. There are many good statistics and research books. Some are general, such as E.R. Babbie, *Survey Research Methods* (Belmont, Calif.: Wadsworth, 1973), and some are very specific, such as J.N. Sheth, *Multivariate Methods for Market and Survey Research* (Chicago: American Marketing Association, 1977).

16. Leonard M. Lodish, and David J. Reibstein, "New Gold Mines and Minefields in Market Research," *Harvard Business Review*, January–February 1986.

17. A good further reference is Vincent Barabba, "The Market Research Encyclopedia," *Harvard Business Review*, January–February 1990.

 # Cases for Part 2

CASE 2.1 Michelle's Fashions

■

CASE 2.2 Midwest Orchestra

■

CASE 2.3 Scott's Restaurants (A)

■

CASE 2.4 Scott's Restaurants (B)

■

CASE 2.5 West Oaks Shopping Centre

# C A S E 2.1    Michelle's Fashions

We've got to do something dramatic soon, or I'll have to consider closing the stores. The apparel business is awful right now; nobody seems to be making any money at it.

Michelle Thompson was lamenting the difficulties she faced with her two family apparel stores located in a major metropolitan area. Michelle was a successful lawyer in private practice and had inherited the stores from her mother two years ago. Both stores were approximately 4,500 square feet each, located in large suburban malls on the west side of the city. Each store had two entrances, one to the parking lot and the other into an interior corridor of the shopping centre. There was a cash register at each door.

Michelle's offered medium priced, middle-of-the-road apparel. About 60 percent of the assortment was for women, 20 percent for men, and 20 percent for children. Michelle's had very little to offer beyond basics to individuals aged 12-21.

Michelle's did very little advertising, relying primarily on its locations, window displays, and in-store signs to attract customers. Staff were encouraged to be extra-friendly and to create personal relationships with customers whenever possible. Still, sales had slipped below acceptable levels and Michelle didn't know why.

Michelle has approached you for help in designing some research to shed light on her situation. She wants to begin by gathering basic information on her store traffic patterns, yield rates, and reactions to her stores.

I don't really know how many people come in and out of my stores, how many of those buy something, and why or why not. I know my average transaction is $63.00 and that my weekly sales are dismal now, averaging roughly $15,000 per store. I don't know if people like what I offer, whether men are buying much, and so on. And, I have very little extra money for research. I'm wondering about an exit survey. What do you suggest?

# C A S E 2.2    Midwest Orchestra

I've got to make a decision soon about whether to move the Friday night Pops concerts to Saturday night for next season. I'm worried we'll lose a lot of our subscribers if we do this, but it makes so much sense economically that I want to do it. We did a little informal asking of people at the last Friday Pops night. We asked if they preferred Friday or Saturday night and 70% said Friday.

Roberta Howell, General Manager of Midwest Orchestra, was discussing some of her ideas with the Orchestra's Marketing Committee. This eight person committee, composed primarily of Board members and Orchestra marketing staff, was an advisory volunteer group intended to

help the Orchestra in all aspects of its marketing. Mary-Jane Morgan, Marketing Director, added:

We also need to finalize our program and program brochure within the next month. Have you decided Roberta about whether we will increase our emphasis on guest artists in next season's program?

## THE ORCHESTRA

Midwest Orchestra was located in a major Western city with a metropolitan population over 500,000 people. The Orchestra offered a variety of concerts and subscription series throughout the year. The Orchestra played most of its concerts in a 1700 seat hall in the centre of the city. Performances included symphony, chamber music, pops, light classics, and a variety of special concerts.

The Orchestra was chronically short of money despite efforts to increase box office sales (both subscription and single ticket) and to raise outside funds.

## Pops

The Pops program comprised six performances, each of which was offered both Friday night and Sunday afternoon. For the 1988-89 season, there were 2,141 subscriptions in total for the Pops program. The great majority of these subscribers lived in the city and came as couples. Thus far, Pops subscribers had been to one performance this season. The remainder of the program included both orchestral works and featured some guest artists.

## THE RESEARCH IDEA

Midwest Orchestra had not done much research on its audiences. Recently, some studies had been done on lapsed symphony series subscribers and a couple of focus groups on proposed changes to the overall program brochure. Roberta and Mary-Jane both wished to have more knowledge about their audiences, but money was tight and they had little time in their busy schedules.

Gary Boundy, a Board member and Director of Marketing for a local retailer, was emphatic:

> We shouldn't make major changes like this without some effort to see how our customers will react. Why don't we do some research?

Other members of the Marketing committee agreed, urging Roberta and Mary-Jane to conduct a study.

Roberta replied:

> It's a great idea, but we don't have the time or money. Besides, we really should move the Friday night to Saturday night to save costs on our guest artists and so on. If we ask our subscribers, they might say no, and then what do we do? I'm thinking we'll send them a letter around renewal time explaining why we're making the change.

Tom Bryant made an offer:

> OK. Roberta, let's do it ourselves. I'll offer my offices one night. I've got six phone lines we could use for a telephone survey. Let's get as many of us as we can to come in one evening next week and we'll call a bunch of the subscribers and see what they say. If Roberta and Mary-Jane get together and plan a survey, maybe David can help smooth it out and teach the rest of us how to do a survey. What about it?

David Leavens, also a Board member and a professor of marketing at the local university, nodded his agreement. He and three other committee members said they would make Wednesday evening available two weeks hence.

Roberta discussed the idea with Mary-Jane after the meeting:

> We'll need to get names and phone numbers first. Here we go again. If only we had a computerized system. Maybe Judy could make a list by hand for us from the box office records. And let's see if we can agree on what questions to ask. This could be a good opportunity to get some more information from our subscribers, see whether they're happy, and so on. Could you look after this, Mary-Jane?

# C A S E 2.3    Scott's Restaurants (A)

In January 1979 Mr. R.A. Hunter was reviewing possible alternatives for entering Scott's Restaurants (a division of Scott's Hospitality Inc.) into the pizza market. His personal preferences with respect to an entry route for pizza had evolved over the past year or so to a point where he found the two most attractive alternatives strategically inconsistent. On the one hand, he distinctly preferred to follow an acquisition route in order to penetrate the pizza market quickly with a minimum of innovative development requirement on the part of company personnel. On the other hand, he was committed to a strategy of making the best possible use of existing corporate assets, so that locating pizza outlets on company-owned land already occupied by Kentucky Fried Chicken stores also represented an attractive opportunity. Mr. Hunter felt that his recommendation to the Board of Directors should be one that made the greatest practical use of the Company's strengths while minimizing Scott's exposure in terms of what he perceived as the Company's weaknesses.

## RECENT HISTORY OF SCOTT'S RESTAURANTS

Mr. Hunter had joined Scott's in 1976 as Senior Vice President, Canadian Operations. Although his position was initially one of understudy to President Jack Leon, he was soon given an assignment which in effect made him the corporate strategist.

When Scott's had first acquired the Kentucky Fried Chicken franchise for Ontario and Quebec in 1964, it appeared to have joined the concept at a most appropriate time. The Company developed into a very effective operations unit and entered a period of growth during which little or no time was available for market research or strategic planning. The limited amount of research that was conducted had been done primarily by Scott's franchisors, and was concentrated on effective local advertising. Consumer attitudinal research had not been commissioned either by Scott's or its franchisor. As far as

potential customers were concerned, they had appeared to be so plentiful that Scott's had concentrated most of its efforts on an expansion program aimed at making KFC available to as many customers as possible within the Company's territory. In the marketplace of that time, such a strategy had been extremely successful, and Scott's had realized a compounded growth rate in sales and earnings of 15-20 percent annually.

By the time Mr. Hunter joined Scott's in 1976, the idea was taking hold within the Company that the fried chicken market would soon reach the saturation point. Meanwhile, the Company had built up nearly $50 million in retained earnings, much of which was represented by short-term deposits. Scott's had no long-term debt. In view of such circumstances, Mr. Hunter was given the assignment of familiarizing himself with all of Scott's operations and developing a complete business plan—including a thorough market segmentation study. Because of time constraints and a perceived lack of expertise in gathering market data, he contracted Roy MacNaughton, who was, president of a consulting business, Hospitality Marketing. Mr. MacNaughton and his partner, Patrick Wilson, developed market data, and Mr. Hunter used the data in the development of a business plan.

## THE BUSINESS PLAN

Approximately nine months was spent in developing the business plan. While the plan included quantitative goals by year, it was primarily designed to be an environmental size-up with respect to the outlook for the food service industry by segment including data on social, political, economic and consumer trends, etc., in order to determine the direction(s) in which Scott's should move. The plan included five-year financial forecasts, but its emphasis was on strategy and tactics designed to achieve the corporate goals. The basic strategies were summarized as follows:

1. The Company should attempt to expand by means of a major acquisition within the hospitality industry in order to utilize Scott's financial leverage (the purchase of a company in the $50 million to $60 million range would be preferred).

2. The Company should attempt to establish a presence in the United States, since management were somewhat disillusioned with the Canadian government in 1976–77, and they wanted to hedge the company's bets by geographically diversifying the company's operations.

3. The Company should continue to make the chicken business as viable as possible. This part of the Company would require continual upgrading to keep it competitive.

4. The Company should diversify into non-labour-intensive food businesses within the Canadian market.

5. The Company should diversify into non-chicken businesses within the Canadian food service market, to reduce its vulnerability to rapid changes in price and availability of its high-volume chicken.

6. New business ventures should meet the Company's R.O.I. hurdle rate.

The business plan was approved in principle by the Board of Directors in the spring of 1977.

### Early Implementation of the Plan

During the three years following its approval, Scott's Restaurants concentrated on the achievement of the major strategies identified in the business plan. The first strategy was realized by the acquisition of Commonwealth Holiday Inns, which gave the Company a major stake in the hotel business. This move was accomplished in 1979.

The second strategic objective was initiated in 1978, by the establishment of a Scott's Fried Chicken chain in Florida. The move was eventually a failure, with all of the original stores being closed. In some respects, the initial failure of this diversification was a useful learning experience. It impressed upon Scott's management the possibility that not every one of their en-

deavours would be immediately and automatically successful, the connotation being that caution and research were essential. Finally, it did leave the Company with its desired presence in the United States with some units converted to seafood operations, from which future expansion could be based.

The third strategic goal, meanwhile, was energetically followed through a continual upgrading of KFC stores in Ontario and Quebec. The red and white exteriors were largely replaced by natural stone fronts in the majority of stores, the interiors were significantly upgraded, and a comprehensive training program was initiated for unit and middle management. Simultaneously, Scott's achieved ownership of 85 percent of the KFC stores in Ontario and Quebec.

In view of the results of the Florida experience, the fourth and fifth business plan strategies were undertaken more cautiously, with a more quantitative environmental study preceding the active pursuit of food service product diversification.

### Diversification Planning

The objective of diversification toward non-labour-intensive food service operations and away from such heavy reliance on chicken involved nearly three years of planning. During this time, Mr. Hunter's thoughts on tactical procedure were influenced by the following considerations:

1. In reviewing opportunities in the red meat market (hamburgers, fast food steak, etc.), the Company decided to let McDonald's, Ponderosa, Burger King and a few other dominant participants fight it out over this sector of the market. Scott's preferred to achieve profits quickly upon opening a new store. With large competitors well located in the red meat sector, entry would be difficult and probably not profitable for some time. In addition, raw product costs were relatively high and were increasing rapidly.

2. The Company was not enthusiastic about re-entering the seafood market in Canada. It had been attempted before Mr. Hunter joined Scott's (with Davy Jones outlets) and had not been successful. As well, the busi-

ness plan size-up had indicated a high degree of risk because of inconsistency with respect to supply and price for raw materials, at least in Canada.

3. Mr. Hunter felt that Scott's lacked depth in expertise and management resources with respect to a sit-down or tablecloth type of restaurant, because of their emphasis on highly simplified take-out types of operations. On the other hand, they were quite experienced and skilled at operations which did not provide table service.

4. The business plan placed considerable emphasis on the avoidance of diversification into labour-intensive fields, such as restaurants providing table service.

5. The Company's preference for acquisitions as opposed to grass roots diversification was gradually being reinforced. The economy was slowing down, so that rapid growth was no longer available to insulate a new concept experiencing a difficult startup period. In any case, Mr. Hunter felt that the best of the new concepts had already been introduced, and with the Florida experience in mind, there was general agreement within the Company that the acquisition of a proven concept would represent significantly less risk than the attempt to introduce a new concept.

### Diversification Opportunities

Scott's size-up of the market environment suggested that the best opportunities for the Company were in pizza and Chinese food. Mr. Hunter was attracted to these market segments for the following reasons:

1. Both pizza and Chinese food were characterized by a diversity of products, and were therefore not reliant on a single raw material like chicken.

2. Both sectors involved comparatively low food costs which offered considerable profit potential after breakeven volume was surpassed.

3. Scott's limited market information suggested rapid growth prospects for both pizza and Chinese food. The pizza market for

Canada appeared to be in the range of $600–900 million of which about 60 percent was estimated to be take-out and delivery. Only 30 percent of existing operators were thought to be members of chain organizations relative to the much higher levels in hamburger (87 percent) and chicken (90 percent). Further, while apparently a popular food, pizza could not be prepared at home in quality equal to what was available at commercial establishments.

4. Finally, the environmental size-up had indicated that pizza and Chinese food should fit well with the KFC operations in terms of market segmentation. Although all ages of people were potential customers, the highest volume groups were:

Pizza: 18–24 years old (dominated by males)

Chinese Food: 25–34 years old (male and female)

Chicken: 35–50 years old (skewed towards females; but purchased for home consumption by the whole family)

This market information not only suggested that pizza and Chinese food would significantly extend Scott's customer base into the lower age groups, but it also indicated that the new products—if introduced at existing stores—should not threaten too much cannibalization of the chicken market.

5. Scott's market size-up had identified an interesting consumer trend developing in Oriental food. People were becoming very interested in nutrition, fresh foods, and wok cooking.

Meanwhile, a pizza chain in Toronto had discovered that Scott's was investigating the pizza business early in 1979, and approached Scott's. Concerned about Scott's possible entry into the pizza market, the pizza chain asked if Scott's wanted to make a deal. Scott's management passed up the opportunity, since they felt that Scott's investigation was not yet complete enough to make a major commitment. Management was quite impressed with the pizza chain's concept and system, but not very enthusiastic about their product.

Having rejected the alternative for the time being, but still with a view toward an acquisition or joint venture, Scott's approached another company in the United States. However, they found them very difficult to deal with. They ran a very successful operation—with several hundred outlets throughout the United States — but Scott's concluded that they were not really interested in making a deal.

## THE DECISION TO DO RESEARCH

By early 1979, Scott's had observed that most of the chains which were getting into the pizza business were doing so in a labour-intensive, capital-intensive manner with sit-down and table service restaurants, leaving most of the take-out and delivery business to the independents. While this approach was apparently successful, its labour and capital requirements did not fit Scott's business plan objectives. However, Mr. Hunter's market and competitive size-up also indicated that the most successful operators were doing between $7,000 and $10,000 per week of delivery sales per unit, and Scott's initial calculations suggested that a take-out and delivery volume of anything in excess of $5,000 per week per unit would provide a good return on their investment. This information encouraged Mr. Hunter to commission a fairly extensive in-house quantitative market study.

Scott's market study indicated that in spite of the success of the sit-down chains, there was an excellent opportunity in the take-out and delivery segment of the market. Because 70 percent of the pizza business in Canada was represented by take-out and delivery operations which were characterized primarily by independents and small regional operators, management concluded that there was a good opportunity for a professionally operated marketing-oriented company to enter the take-out and delivery segment. In Mr. Hunter's opinion, ". . . nobody was interested in take-out and delivery but the customer."

Scott's management felt that the most promising alternatives available were: (a) make

another attempt to identify acquisition candidates, (b) contract more thorough market research to better identify the target market and recommend the most appropriate entry vehicle, or (c) utilize the data presently available and try to enter the take-out and delivery segment of the pizza market by launching a building program to add pizza facilities to existing real estate already occupied by Kentucky Fried Chicken stores. While management did not want to repeat the Florida experience in Canada, they also did not want to sit by until some other chain achieved a dominant position in the pizza market. Scott's was interested in entering the pizza business, and appropriate funding was available to launch a modest market test entry.

In reviewing these alternatives, Mr. Hunter decided that further market research was definitely required. Scott's knew very little about the take-out or home delivery pizza consumer and was therefore not, in Mr. Hunter's opinion, in a position to launch a program designed to cater to this market segment. Having made the decision to conduct market research, he faced the issues of exactly what sort of information was required, and what means the company should utilize in order to acquire the necessary information.

## CONSUMER RESEARCH

In Mr. Hunter's opinion, Scott's did not at that time have in-house capability in conducting marketing research. Therefore, in January 1979, Mr. Hunter discussed Scott's strategic plans with an advertising agency. The agency was quite enthusiastic about the possibility of Scott's entering the pizza business, and agreed to conduct a thorough consumer research project. In conjunction with a marketing research firm, the agency arranged for a series of focus groups in the city of Toronto, segmented as follows:

14–17 years of age (male)
14–17 years of age (female)
18–21 years of age (male & female)
22–27 years of age (male & female)
28 years of age and older (male & female)

By May 18, 1979, the agency provided Mr. Hunter with a document 80 pages in length entitled "The Problems in Entering the Pizza Market". While the document is not reproduced in total here, the following excerpts (Appendix A) display almost all the basic research meth-odology, findings, analysis, implications and recommendations as presented to Scott's. Mr. Hunter was examining the research report with a view to what action to take next in the pizza field.

# APPENDIX A

## Excerpts from: The Problems in Entering the Pizza Market
### May 18, 1979

### BACKGROUND TO RESEARCH

Scott's restaurants has identified the pizza business as an area of diversification. The *problem detection system* (PDS) was recommended to develop pre-emptive positions for Scott's in the pizza market. This research technique produces actionable results and provides clear direction for the development of competitive marketing positions and effective advertising strategy. The problem detection system was carried out in two phases designed to discover the problems of heavy pizza users and then determine which problems provide the best opportunity for successful pre-emptive positioning of Scott's pizza.

### QUANTITATIVE SURVEY

Five separate focus groups composed of heavy pizza users and a quantitative survey were conducted in Toronto February through April, 1979. The quantitative survey involved 152 heavy users of delivery or take-out pizza. It was conducted by door-to-door interviews with the in-home pizza purchase decision maker utilizing problems gleaned from focus groups and the problem detection system. Respondents rated problems twice on four-point scales; once for the degree of bothersomeness of the problem and once for the degree of frequency for the problem. Respondents then rated on a two point scale whether or not they are aware of a claimed solution to each problem.

### Problem List:

(148 problems selected from nearly 200 problems gathered from the five separate focus groups conducted.)

| Rank (out of 148) | Problem |
|---|---|
| 1 | pizzerias dirty, unsanitary |
| 2 | crust soggy in centre |
| 3 | the pizza looks greasy |
| 4 | pizza tastes like cardboard |
| 5 | pepperoni filled with grease |
| 6 | pizza tastes too bland |
| 7 | crust tastes like cardboard |
| 8 | no one cares about complaints |
| 9 | pizza tastes too greasy |
| 10 | crust is undercooked |
| 11 | not enough cheese |
| 12 | not honest about delivery time |
| 13 | pizza arrives cold |
| 14 | expensive snack for one |
| 15 | crust tastes of cardboard box |
| 16 | quality of unknown pizzeria |
| 17 | delivery person does not wait to check |
| 18 | not leave party to get pizza |
| 19 | crust droops toppings fall off |
| 20 | bacon not fully cooked |

The marketer has 3 major problem areas: premises, product, and service. Cleanliness and appearance of the premises in which the pizza is prepared are *very important* to the pizza user.

| Rank (out of 148) | Problem |
|---|---|
| 1 | pizzerias dirty, unsanitary |

Service problems occur at two points: the store and at the user's door. At the store, problems are directed at store management.

| Rank (out of 148) | Problem |
|---|---|
| 8 | pizza arrives cold |
| 12 | not honest about delivery time |

At the door, the problem is with the individual making the delivery.

| Rank (out of 148) | Problem |
| --- | --- |
| 13 | pizza arrives cold |
| 17 | delivery person doesn't wait to check pizza |

The problems connected to the *product* breaks into 3 sub-groups: taste, appearance, and crust preparation. "Cardboard" is the key problem connected with *taste*.

| Rank (out of 148) | Problem |
| --- | --- |
| 4 | pizza tastes like cardboard |
| 7 | crust tastes like cardboard |
| 15 | crust has cardboard-like taste |

"Grease" is the key problem connected with appearance.

| Rank (out of 148) | Problem |
| --- | --- |
| 3 | pizza looks greasy |
| 5 | pepperoni filled with grease |

Crust preparation is of great importance to the acceptance of a pizza product.

| Rank (out of 148) | Problem |
| --- | --- |
| 2 | crust soggy in centre |
| 10 | crust is undercooked |
| 19 | crust droops, toppings fall off |

Conversely *low problem* scores *can* also indicate high opportunity areas. Pizza users are predisposed to prefer "chain operations."

| Rank (out of 148) | Problem |
| --- | --- |
| 91 | big chains part prepared before order taken |
| 99 | large chains don't care |
| 100 | big chain throw pizza together |
| 107 | big chains too impersonal |
| 119 | no "love" at large chains |

Further reinforcement for chain desirability among heavy users is provided by:

| Rank (out of 148) | Problem |
| --- | --- |
| 16 | quality of unknown pizza |
| 58 | small pizzerias put me off |

Regarding menu–pizza users *only* care about pizza.

| Rank (out of 148) | Problem |
| --- | --- |
| 146 | can't order other dishes |

Other than cleanliness, delivery and/or take-out pizza users are not highly concerned with the premises.

| Rank (out of 148) | Problem |
| --- | --- |
| 74 | some pizzerias too dingy |
| 125 | no place to eat in pizzeria |
| 144 | no atmosphere in pizzeria |
| 145 | don't trust, can't see kitchen |
| 148 | pizzeria lights too bright |

Most present high frequency pizza users feel that available pizzas are too bland rather than too spicy.

| Rank (out of 148) | Problem |
| --- | --- |
| 6 | pizza tastes too bland |
| 123 | pizza tastes too spicy |

Analysis of problem with pre-emptibility factor removed, 11 of the top 20 problems fall into the upper end of the high importance/high frequency category. In the high importance/high frequency category, cleanliness and appearance of the premises in which the pizza was prepared ranked as the number one problem. In the high importance/high frequency category, we find 7 of the top 20 problems related to service.

| Rank (out of 148) | Problem |
| --- | --- |
| 2 | pizza arrives cold |
| 5 | $1.00 too much for delivery |
| 9 | not honest about delivery time |
| 11 | delivery takes more than an hour |
| 12 | need car to pick up pizza |
| 17 | pick-up pizza not hot |
| 19 | delivery person doesn't care if satisfied |

All of the problems connected with appearance of the pizza product appeared in the top 20 high importance/high frequency category.

| Rank (out of 148) | Problem |
|---|---|
| 8 | pizza looks greasy |
| 10 | pizza tastes too greasy |
| 18 | pepperoni filled with grease |

Crust preparation also appears in the high importance/high frequency category.

| Rank (out of 148) | Problem |
|---|---|
| 6 | crust soggy in centre |
| 13 | crust is too hard |
| 25 | crust droops, toppings fall off |

The anomaly that appears in the high importance/high frequency category is the absence of "cardboard taste" problems from the top 20.

## SUMMARY OF RESULTS

There is a tremendous opportunity for a new, well-run chain to enter the pizza market. Based on norms from more than 300 PDS projects, the pizza scores rank extremely high. Results indicate a high level of interest in pizza among heavy users. The information gathered provides clear cut direction for decision making in several key areas.

Five key problem/opportunity areas are clearly defined and all are actionable:

### Cleanliness

| Oppt. Rank (out of 148) | Problem/Score |
|---|---|
| 1 | Pizzerias dirty, unsanitary/4436 |

Although other problems may have had a higher individual importance or frequency score than this, the combined frequency X importance score on this subject was 4436, some 968 points higher than the next ranking problem. This indicates a major concern on the part of the customer and provides direction for outlet design,

decor, uniforms, staff, packaging, and communications.

A note of caution must be observed when planning is being done in this area that cleanliness is not carried to the extreme so that our image becomes sterile. Our experience with consumers leads us to believe that when they select a pizza, they would probably prefer a pizzeria with a distinct character.

### Service

| Oppt. Rank (out of 148) | Problem/Score |
|---|---|
| 8 | No one cares about complaints/3071 |
| 12 | Not honest about delivery time/3056 |
| 13 | Pizza arrives cold/3468 |
| 17 | Delivery person doesn't wait/2088 |

These four problems appear in the top twenty opportunity rankings and again in the top twenty high frequency/high importance problem ranking indicating great concern with service problems. The delivery person not waiting to check the pizza ranks second in the pre-emptibility area with a score of 74.3. The highest pre-emptible problem is not sending napkins along with the order with a score of 85.5.

These problems appear to be solvable from an operations standpoint and both can be dealt with effectively in advertising.

### Grease

| Oppt. Rank (out of 148) | Problem/Score |
|---|---|
| 3 | Pizza looks greasy/3064 |
| 5 | Pepperoni filled with grease/2702 |
| 9 | Pizza tastes too greasy/NA |

Obviously grease is a "trigger" word with consumers when it comes to pizza. It occurs three times in the top ten opportunity scores and is repeated three times in the top ten opportunity scores and in the top twenty high frequency/high importance problem scores.

Again, great caution must be taken in dealing with this problem from an operations point of view because the consumer does not want a dry pizza nor a bland pizza.

### Crust Preparation

| Oppt. Rank (out of 148) | Problem/Score |
|---|---|
| 2 | Crust soggy in centre/3090 |
| 10 | Crust is undercooked/2505 |
| 19 | Crust droops, toppings fall off/2331 |

There is great concern about crust quality, taste, and texture. All of the above problems have a high score in problem importance, frequency, and pre-emptibility, indicating that the subject is key to the acceptance of any pizza product.

Again, caution must be used in attempting to correct any of the above because an *extreme shift* in texture or cooking is likely to result in an equal amount of negatives.

### Cardboard

| Oppt. Rank (out of 148) | Problem/Score |
|---|---|
| 4 | Pizza tastes like cardboard/2965 |
| 7 | Crust tastes like cardboard/2643 |
| 15 | Crust has cardboard-box taste/NA |

| | |
|---|---|
| 7 | Crust tastes like cardboard/2643 |
| 15 | Crust has cardboard-box taste/NA |

Cardboard also appears to be a "trigger" with consumers. Reference to cardboard taste has the highest frequency rating of any problem and is important to all consumers.

Here is a problem that can be dealt with directly from an operations point of view and can also be effectively communicated.

As previously pointed out an anomaly appeared in the high importance/high frequency category on the problems connected with "cardboard taste."

This anomaly is explained by the fact that "cardboard taste" problems were ranked extremely high on importance and pre-emptibility and relatively low on frequency.

This suggests that though "cardboard taste" is very important, many pizzerias are solving this problem.

---

# C A S E  2.4    Scott's Restaurants (B)

In May 1979, Scott's Restaurants received a consumer research report entitled "The Problems in Entering the Pizza Market". [Refer to Scott's Restaurants (A) for details of the report.] Several members of management read the report and considered the methodology to be quite complex and thorough. In addition, the interpretation and implications provided appeared to be reasonably straightforward, concise, and encouraging. Basically the report, as understood by Mr. Hunter, indicated that Scott's could establish a "pre-emptive" position in the take-out pizza market segment by concentrating intensely on a limited number of basic requirements. According to the study, a great deal of emphasis needed to be placed on the following:

1. Cleanliness: This aspect of an operation was rated 40 percent more important than any other factor—a rating high enough to make cleanliness by far the dominant requirement of an outlet.

2. Quality of Product: The final interpretation with respect to quality of product could be briefly summarized as emphasizing two basic characteristics: (a) the pizza should *not* be greasy; and (b) the crust of the pizza should *not* taste like cardboard.

3. Quality of Service: Again, there were two major requirements: (a) in delivery operations, the service should provide hot pizza within 40 minutes; and (b) company employees should demonstrate genuine concern in the event of customer complaints.

It appeared to Mr. Hunter that the time and money spent on consumer research represented a good investment. His interpretation of the results suggested that Scott's really should not experience too much difficulty attaining a "pre-emptive" position in the take-out pizza market. Scott's therefore set about developing and implementing a strategic plan for its entry into the pizza market.

## THE PIZZA PLAN

The primary objectives of the plan were to develop a chain of take-out pizza operations which would surpass its R.O.I. hurdle and which would realize all available growth opportunities at an acceptable level of risk.

The strategic part of the plan indicated that Scott's would set up units that directly responded to the consumer research in order to put Scott's in the position of being *dramatically* better than anyone else in the take-out and delivery segment. Management decided that every facet of the research study would be adhered to *exactly*—the outlets would be very clean, the product would not be at all greasy, and it would not taste even remotely like cardboard. In addition, the service offered would be of the highest quality attainable. Not only were such characteristics considered essential, but it was considered strategically important that they be demonstrated clearly enough to register on the customers' awareness.

The marketing plan noted that each item must be supportive of the strategy statement in order to quickly gain a pre-emptive position in the market. Several financial models were developed using worst, best and probable volume assumptions, and a forecast using probable volumes was adopted. The financial models indicated that an average volume of $5,000 per store per week would achieve the required rate of return for the type of outlet planned (i.e., clean, upscale, stores constructed beside KFC outlets on land already owned by Scott's).

In order to avoid repeating the experience of the fried chicken expansion into Florida, approval was sought from and granted by the Board of Directors for a pilot project involving five test stores in Ontario and one in Quebec. On the recommendation of a design consultant, the Ontario stores were named "The Pizza Tree"; the store layout would include a tree inside the building. However, since this name does not translate well into French, the outlet in Sherbrooke, Quebec, was named "Au Jardin De La Pizza".

During late 1979 and early 1980, the pizza plan was implemented exactly as outlined by the marketing plan. The menu was almost exclusively pizza, a new insulated delivery box was designed, price was set approximately ten percent below the local average market prices, and $1.00 was charged for delivery. Since the research report had not suggested much in terms of store design other than cleanliness and lighting, several different store types were used in the test. For example, in Whitby, where the KFC store had ample real estate, The Pizza Tree was built adjacent to the KFC store and the two were joined by a covered seating area, although table service was not offered for either. On KFC lots with less space, The Pizza Tree stores were joined to existing KFC stores with no seating provided. Exhibit 1 provides more detail. However, every store was "absolutely gorgeous". At this point, Scott's hoped to concentrate on take-out just as it did with KFC to avoid the complexity and problems associated with delivery. Company management was aware that a chain in Ottawa was operating very successfully with a sit-down and take-out restaurant, and it was hoped that Scott's could emulate this concept in time.

As the Pizza Tree project was being launched, another executive told Mr. Hunter that he had never before been involved in a new marketing venture that had been so thoroughly researched and so carefully planned. This statement reinforced the opinion that if and when a preferred acquisition route was not available to achieve market penetration, at least Scott's could pursue the desired expansion in a more professional manner than the company had exhibited in the past. In any event, Mr. Hunter was determined that Scott's would test the market thoroughly with this pilot project before making a major commitment to pizza.

## THE NEW STUDY

Early in 1981, it became apparent to Mr. Hunter that while the research report had indicated what Scott's needed to do to attain a pre-emptive position in the pizza market, it did not give any indication of where the most successful locations would be. In order to enable the company to take advantage of the locations with the greatest potential first, Scott's retained a firm of management consultants. This firm proceeded in February to conduct a study with respect to KFC, pizza and Chinese food. The study was based upon telephone questioning of 675 existing Pizza Tree customers and 992 randomly selected Toronto people about their purchasing behavior and attitudes regarding pizza, Kentucky Fried Chicken, and Chinese food. Homemade and supermarket versions of these foods were not studied. The firm provided computer analysis of an array of consumer data including age, sex, ethnic background, marital status, occupation, type of housing, education, income, etc. After analysis, the consumer data was applied against census data in Metropolitan Toronto to create a colour-coded map indicating the areas of greatest and least potential. Some excerpts are reproduced in Appendix A.

## RESULTS OF THE PILOT PROJECT

By December 1981, three of The Pizza Tree stores in Ontario had come very close to reaching their projected volumes, and two were significantly below forecasted levels as shown in Exhibit 2. Ironically, the latter two were rated best and third best in terms of location by the trading area model. In fact, the two locations which were rated "worst" by the model were first and second in actual sales as the following table prepared by Mr. Hunter indicates, although variances between model ratings and actual sales ratings were explained by Scott's personnel by such factors as unusually poor—or good—visibility of the store, advertising and promotional problems, etc.

After an initial encouraging start-up in Sherbrooke, Au Jardin De La Pizza was showing no sign of success. Mr. Hunter observed that after 1½ years, Scott's had not quite achieved the desired "pre-emptive" market position. While it appeared that half the pilot project stores might eventually reach the required R.O.I. hurdles, he was not yet prepared to recommend full-scale pizza development to Scott's Board of Directors.

In spite of being less than totally successful, the pilot stores did yield Scott's some useful information. First, in Whitby, where The Pizza

| | | | | Access to | | |
|---|---|---|---|---|---|---|
| | Fit to | Degree of | Facility | Proper | Actual | Time |
| Location | Model | Competition | Desirability | Media | Sales | Open |
| Peterborough | 4 | 1 (Highest) | 2 | 1 | 2 | 3 |
| Whitby | 5 | 5 (Least) | 1 | 3 | 1 | 2 |
| Oshawa | 3 | 2 | 3 | 2 | 5 | 5 |
| Thornhill | 1 | 3 | 5 | 5 | 4 | 1 |
| Streetsville | 2 | 4 | 4 | 4 | 3 | 4 |

Rating of 5 Ontario Test Units (from 1st to 5th)*

* All five test locations would be acceptable according to the model. Actual sales performance, however, seems to be more closely related to:
  • Degree of Competition
  • Access to Proper Media
  • Facility Desirability (seats apparently being desirable)**
** Observations from an internal company report entitled *The Pizza Tree Evaluation and Recommendations for Future Development.*

Tree was most successful (with seating provided between the pizza and KFC stores), it became apparent that The Pizza Tree was not cannibalizing the KFC store. Instead, KFC sales increased 3 percent. In addition, Au Jardin De La Pizza in Sherbrooke demonstrated that while the province of Quebec offered the highest per capita pizza consumption in Canada, the product needed to be tailored specifically for that market. It appeared that the Quebec consumer was willing to pay a premium for a more specialized pizza (more garnishments, including meat, and more seasoning, etc.).

The implications of the pilot project were not really as clear as Mr. Hunter had hoped. He was aware that Scott's had made some mistakes in the project stores, but he was not convinced that correcting those mistakes would permit the company to achieve the desired rate of return. Mr. Hunter also doubted that Scott's could achieve its objective of a pre-emptive position in the pizza market by merely increasing the number of The Pizza Tree and Au Jardin De La Pizza outlets. With these thoughts in mind, he wondered what Scott's should do next.

EXHIBIT 1

---

## DESCRIPTION OF TEST UNITS
### in order of opening

---

1. **Whitby:** free-standing pizza store, shared seating with KFC
   - take-out and delivery provided
   - blue collar area, young families, residential growth
   - limited competition

2. **Peterborough:** free-standing pizza store adjacent to KFC, no seating
   - take-out and delivery
   - small city, diverse demographics, limited growth
   - very heavy competition
   - access to local radios and newspaper

3. **Oshawa:** free-standing pizza store adjacent to KFC, no seating
   - take-out and delivery
   - medium-size city, blue collar, limited growth in immediate area
   - moderate competition

4. **Thornhill:** leased storefront adjacent to KFC leased store, no seating
   - take-out only
   - suburb, higher income, older customers within $1/2$ mile
   - rapid future residential growth to west
   - strong local competition

5. **Streetsville:** leased storefront close to KFC, no seating
   - rapidly growing suburbs, diverse demographic mix
   - adjacent to industrial and commercial developments
   - moderate competition

6. **Sherbrooke (Quebec):** free-standing pizza store, shared seating with KFC
   - small city, diverse demographics, limited growth
   - 90 percent French-speaking
   - close to university
   - moderate competition

*Exhibit 2*

## ONTARIO TEST RESULTS—YEAR ONE
### On a weekly sales basis

|  | Breakeven Volume | Actual Volume |
|---|---|---|
| Thornhill | $4200 | $2500 |
| Whitby | 5200 | 4100 |
| Peterborough | 4500 | 3400 |
| Streetsville | 4300 | 3350 |
| Oshawa | 4600 | 2150 |

# APPENDIX A
## EXCERPTS FROM
## SITE SELECTION RESEARCH REPORT
### March 30, 1981

## MANAGEMENT SUMMARY

### Consumption Characteristics of the Pizza Market

#### Highlights

- Average consumption of pizzas across Toronto was 17 times per year.
- The most important single consumer characteristic of the pizza market is age.
- The bulk of the pizza consuming market can be characterized as under 35.
- The most important combination of high frequency consumption predictors were: age, occupation, education and income.
- Our sample indicated a preference for delivery over pick-up and sit down by 2 to 1.
- Males are slightly better consumers than females.
- Singles are better consumers than marrieds.
- Within the married market, families with wife working are high consumers.
- The housing characteristics of above average consumers appears to be fairly homogeneous with some emphasis on apartments and semi-detached rental accommodations for high frequency consumers.

- Education of high frequency consumers was high school and university (students and graduates).
- Above average consumption was found in almost all occupation groups except professionals and housewives. The most frequent consumers were found to be people identified as management or unskilled.

The data which established this general profile were then subjected to a sophisticated analysis to determine if a statistically valid relationship existed between specific consumer characteristics and high consumption levels. Such a relationship was found to exist and as a result an accurate picture of the high frequency consumer can be identified.

### Customer Profile

For site selection purposes, the most appropriate customer profile would appear to be:

individuals less than 35 years of age with some high school and/or some university education achieving a household income of more than $25,000 or less than $15,000 per year.

## Highlights

- Pizza appeals to a young market, primarily less than 35 years of age.
- Delivery is preferred to pick-up.
- Average pizza consumption in Toronto was 17/year.
- Males are slightly better consumers than females.
- Singles consume more than marrieds.
- Within the married group, families with wife working are higher consumers.
- High frequency consumers were students or young people who recently entered the job market.
- A typical high consumption profile would be:
  - Individuals less than 35 years of age with some high school and/or some university and a household income of more than $25,000 or less than $15,000.
- The customer profile indicates that young adults who are still students and living at home in families with incomes of $25,000+ would be an appropriate target group. In addition, university students living away from home or young singles earning less than $15,000 and young marrieds with incomes over $25,000 are also excellent market segments.
- Dwelling type data corresponds logically to the above profiles and could be used to locate promising market areas as follows:
  - Apartments, townhouses and semi-detached homes could be used to locate singles, young marrieds, and some low income families with mature children.
  - Detached homes would be used to locate families with mature children and young marrieds, both with incomes in excess of $25,000.
- Dwelling type is useful only as a general indicator. The most important factors are the characteristics of people inhabiting the dwellings and their density.

## SITE SELECTION METHODOLOGY

Using a combination of The Pizza Tree customer profile from Phase I and the general pizza customer profile from Phase II, several predominant characteristics showed up: age 15-44; household income less than $15,000, household income greater than $25,000; some high school, some university; people living in single detached dwellings, those living in apartments. Using this profile, we deflated incomes to 1976 levels and conducted a computer-assisted area search of greater Metropolitan Toronto to find areas, by census tract, which contained the largest densities of people meeting these criteria. Each characteristic in every census tract was then given a weighting, of either greater or less than the average for Toronto. This technique enabled us to determine which areas conform to the Pizza Tree customer profile. Next, pizza consumption was determined by multiplying the average number of pizzas consumed per year per characteristic by the total population within that characteristic in that census tract. These average consumption levels were created by means of our market research. The results of these multiplications were then added up, giving the total average number of pizzas consumed per year per census tract. Finally, each characteristic, density, profile and consumption, was assigned a colour and recorded on a map.

The colours red (profile), yellow (density) and blue (consumption) create distinct secondary colours when combined. Therefore:

**Red** = high percentage of people meeting Pizza Tree customer profile.

**Yellow** = high density of people age 15–34.

**Blue** = high consumption.

**Yellow + Red** = Orange, therefore

**Orange** = high density of people aged 15–34 combined with high percentage of people meeting Pizza Tree profile.

**Blue + Yellow** = Green, therefore

**Green** = high consumption combined with high percentage of people meeting Pizza Tree customer profile.

**Red + Blue** = Violet, therefore

**Violet** = high percentage of people meeting Pizza Tree customer profile combined with high consumption.

**Red + Blue + Yellow** = Purple, therefore

**Purple** = high percentage of people meeting Pizza Tree customer profile combined with high consumption combined with high density of people age 15-34.

When these colours are reproduced on a census map, distinct market areas begin to show up. Scott's real estate department can then determine the most appropriate areas identified as promising and begin the essential final step of in-depth analysis to locate actual sites.

Therefore, in summary, our customer profile, produced by independent market research was refined to combine the high consumption characteristics of consumers. Using this data as a criterion for selecting trade areas, we then searched census data to locate the highest densities of people with high consumption characteristics.

Using the mathematical model developed by our research, individual areas can be ranked or prioritized for immediate or later development. The following discussion outlines the elements of this model.

## TRADE AREA MODEL

Three factors were used to determine the best trade areas in greater Metropolitan Toronto for location of Pizza Tree Restaurants:

1. population density of high consumption characteristics
2. profile percentage
3. average consumption levels

**1.** Population density was determined by running a computer-assisted search of Metropolitan Toronto census tract data. These numbers were then charted.

**2.** The "profile percentage" was determined by ranking each high consumption characteristic in each census tract as above or below the average for Toronto.

A computer program was run listing the percentage each number represented of the whole. For example, in census tract 311.01, there were 4,085 people between the ages of 15 and 34. This number represented 56.26% of the total population. From the profile it was established that 35.46% of the total greater Toronto population was between the ages of 15–34. Therefore;

## PROFILE OF
## GREATER METROPOLITAN TORONTO

| Characteristic | Total Population | Percentage of Population Total |
|---|---|---|
| 1976 Population 15–34 yrs. | 970,190 | 35.46% |
| 1976 Estimated household income < $6,000 | 64,958 | 7.29% |
| 1976 Estimated household income $6,000–$9,999 | 85,568 | 9.61% |
| 1976 Estimated household income $10,000–$15,000 | 121,545 | 13.65% |
| 1976 Estimated household income $15,000–$25,000 | 331,325 | 37.21% |
| 1976 Estimated household income $25,000+ | 287,120 | 32.24% |
| 1976 Population 15+ Grade 9–13 | 916,975 | 43.81% |
| 1976 Population 15+ some university | 537,905 | 25.70% |
| 1976 Apartment dwellings | 378,705 | 42.52% |
| 1976 Single detached dwellings | 345,335 | 38.77% |
| TOTAL POPULATION | 2,736,669 | |

census tract percentage – Toronto percentage divided by Toronto percentage = rank    OR

(56.26 – 35.46) divided by 35.46 = .5865 and rounded to +.59

A ranking of +1.0 means that the census tract is twice the average of Toronto. The ranks for each consumer characteristic were added up horizontally.

3.  Average consumption was determined by multiplying the population density for each selected characteristic by the average number of pizzas consumed per year by the particular group. For example, our research

indicated that people aged 15–34 consumed an average of 20 pizzas/year.

Therefore, a census tract with 4,085 people in the 15–34 age group would result in a consumption value of 4,085 × 20 = 81,700. A similar process was then carried out for each consumption characteristic and the totals summed to reveal a value for each census tract. By using these values, it was then possible to rank each census tract as well as combine them to create trading areas.

In order to effectively use the site selection methodology, it is important to use a combination of the three factors described above. By manipulating this data, a mix of highest consumption characteristics can be created.

---

# C A S E  2.5    West Oaks Shopping Centre

In mid-1988, Kathy Odegaard, Centre Manager for West Oaks Centre, was considering a proposal put to her by Ian Bramwell, a doctoral candidate from the local university. Ian summed up his ideas with:

> So, as I've said, what I'd like to do Ms. Odegaard is to make you the subject of my doctoral dissertation. I'm interested in retail research and would like to study how you are positioned in the Vanloops marketplace. I propose to do a consumer study that would tell us how you are regarded by citizens in Vanloops, how often they buy from your centre as opposed to the other centres, what they like and dislike about you, and so on. I'm willing to do all the work, but I'd need your permission and co-operation, and about $20,000 for the direct out-of-pocket costs for the research. I'm currently thinking about a mail survey and a two week shopping diary, tracking where people shop and how much they spend.

Kathy was intrigued, but Ian's request for $20,000 for expenses meant that she needed to be sure that the research was relevant to her needs and properly done. West Oaks hadn't

done any research to speak of for over eight years. She chose her words carefully:

> Ian, I'm willing to say we will go ahead with you on the condition that together we develop a complete research design that meets my needs for managing the centre. You can figure out for yourself whether that will meet your needs for your thesis. I'll give it some thought. Let's find a time when we can get together again in about a week's time.

After Ian left, Kathy began to organize her thoughts about market research for the centre.

## GENERAL DESCRIPTION OF VANLOOPS

Metropolitan Vanloops was a major city in British Columbia. With a population of 258,700 as of June 1987, Vanloops had experienced a growth in population of just over seven percent since 1981. Personal income was 12 percent above the Canadian national average, representing about $15,000 per capita. There were 105,445 private households in Vanloops and 70,210 families.

Over 90 percent of the population had English as their mother tongue. Retail sales per capita were $5,900 in 1987. There was one daily newspaper, *The Times*, and at least nine area community newspapers. Residents of metropolitan Vanloops could receive approximately 15 radio stations and 13 television stations.

## SHOPPING CENTRES IN VANLOOPS

There were 15 shopping centres in the West Oaks market area. Kathy summarized some key information about the six centres she considered her major competitors as well as information about her own, as shown in Exhibit 1. Kathy was concerned that Vanloops was becoming over-malled. She was particularly concerned about rumoured expansion plans for two of her competitors. Kathy wondered if her advertising theme "Your First Place For Fashion" was competitively powerful. She also wondered if her customers were unhappy about any aspect of the mall, such as the store assortment, parking, washrooms, strollers, etc. Kathy particularly wondered if her major competitors had some weak spots she could exploit in her own marketing campaigns.

## THE RESEARCH IDEA

Ian had suggested a questionnaire be sent to residents of Vanloops along with a "shopping diary" asking them to keep records of where they shopped and what they bought for two weeks. Kathy wondered if anybody would respond. And how many responses would be enough to have any confidence in the results? Should she offer some kind of incentive to increase the response rate? It would certainly be less expensive to hand out questionnaires in her own mall, but would that be wise? And how would she know whether a question was well-worded? She realized she had lots of questions.

Kathy felt West Oaks should work with Ian rather than let him work with her competition. She knew he had approached her first because his mother was a regular shopper at West Oaks. However, she knew her owner, Isaac Property Corporation, would insist that she proceed only if the research was very professionally handled. She wondered where she should begin.

*EXHIBIT 1*
*Selected Vanloops*
*Shopping Centres*

---

**West Oaks Centre:**
Quadrant: N
Year opened: 1963 (renovated 1984)
Type: Regional, enclosed, one level
Stores: 105
Gross leasable area: 375,000 sq. ft.
Parking: 1,800
Anchors: Woodward's 169,000; Consumer's Distributing 11,500

**Hidden Valley Shopping Centre:**
Quadrant: N
Year Opened: 1963 (renovation 1990)
Type: Regional, enclosed, one level
Stores: 14
Gross leasable area: 206,431 sq. ft.
Anchors: Woolco 125,077; Fairway Foods 24,316; Shoppers Drug Mart 5,079

**Sandwich Plaza:**
Quadrant: N
Year Opened: 1986
Type: Neighbourhood, open, one level
Stores: 22
Gross leasable area: 116,000 sq. ft.
Anchors: Save-On-Foods 75,000

**University Hill Shopping Centre:**
Quadrant: Central
Year Opened: 1987
Type: Neighbourhood, enclosed, three levels
Stores: 85
Gross leasable area: 200,000 sq. ft.
Anchors: Safeway 38,000; Kmart 84,000; Royal Bank 5,500

**Trillium Mall:**
Quadrant: W
Year Opened: 1982 (renovation 1990)
Type: Regional, enclosed, two levels
Stores: 75
Gross leasable area: 331,584 sq. ft.
Anchors: Eaton's 120,000; Zeller's 65,000; Safeway 35,000

**Coldwater Mall:**
Quadrant: E
Year Opened: 1984
Type: Community, enclosed, one level
Stores: 50
Gross leasable area: 210,000 sq. ft.
Anchors: Kmart 75,000; Fairway Foods 40,000

**Downstream Shopping Centre:**
Quadrant: S
Year Opened: 1962 (renovation 1985, 1991)
Type: Regional, enclosed, one level
Stores: 125
Gross leasable area: 398,536 sq. ft.
Anchors: Sears 118,535; Zeller's 75,090; The Market 40,000

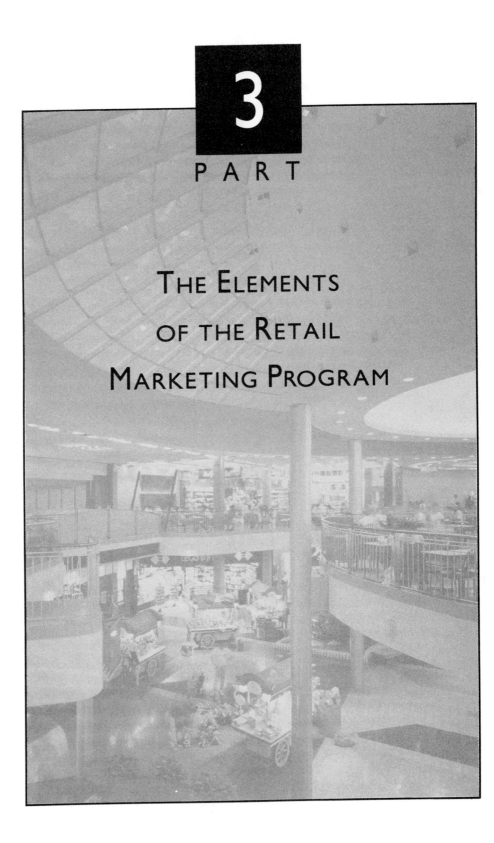

# 3 PART

# THE ELEMENTS OF THE RETAIL MARKETING PROGRAM

CHAPTER

# ASSORTMENT

Assortment is generally the major element of the retail marketing offer and is central to any effective retail marketing strategy. A well-defined and executed assortment strategy can be powerful in differentiating the total retail offering from other retailers. This chapter is about the assortment choices that retailers face.

When a customer is searching for a particular item or class of items, he or she must make a decision as to where to shop. This patronage decision is, in large part, based on expectations or experience as to which stores carry the item or selection of items and services being sought. As discussed in Chapter 4, any shopping trip involves many such decisions. The customer may be seeking a retail outlet that provides a wide selection of items in order to compare the merits of alternative products; or perhaps is simply interested in going to a store that will be sure to have the needed item in stock; or may be concerned only with saving shopping time and effort and wants a store with many related items. In other words, customers have varying perspectives on assortment that influence their decisions as to where to shop; this, of course, means that retailers may pursue many alternative assortment strategies.

Customers seek and purchase both physical products and services. Many retailers offer products along with associated services. A retail marketer may offer in addition to merchandise: delivery, credit, alterations, repairs, gift wrapping, trade-ins, personal shoppers, parking, baby sitting, fitting rooms, bridal registry, installations, and so on. Some retailers offer services, such as weight-loss counselling, bowling and billiards facilities, laundromats, copying and faxing, miniature golf and basketball shooting, beauty salons, and video games—and maybe some associated products, such as food, laundry detergent, postage stamps, and the like. Customers thus can purchase "packages of benefits" (bundles of products and services) offered by any retailer. **Assortment** refers to the merchandise and services (as distinguished from customer service) provided by the retailer to customers. This is a broader definition than that used by many commentators who tend to limit themselves to physical products only. Although assortment in this book refers to both, much of the discussion will be about merchandise assortment.

There are several levels of product assortment to consider, such as **product groups, classes, categories, lines, brands**, and **individual items**. At the finest level of detail, one refers to the **stock-keeping unit (SKU)**, which is a unique item, such as one size, colour, style, brand combination. This is the basic building block of assortment planning. The increasing ability to plan and to track performance at this level has fundamentally changed assortment management for most retail marketers.

In previous chapters, the dimensions of the retail marketer's strategy were outlined and summarized in the statement of **competitive positioning strategy**. This statement is the starting point for detailed consideration of assortment alternatives. The merchandise and service assortments largely determine most of the rest of the retailer's marketing program, such as the size and character of physical facilities required, the nature of the sales effort required, the financial strategy necessary to support this approach, and then the retailer's ultimate performance. A clear understanding of the assortment choices available is vital for any retailer. Figure 7.1 shows graphically the many aspects of assortment management that are discussed in this chapter.

---

### FIGURE 7.1
### Assortment Strategy

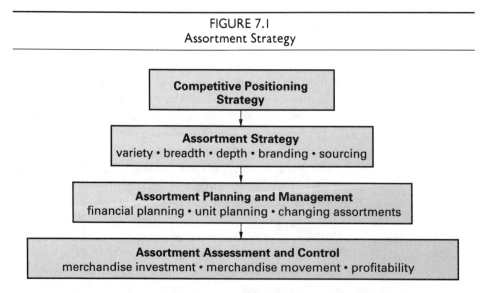

Retail marketers differ dramatically in their assortment strategies and their abilities to manage assortment. Large retail marketers have a particularly difficult time managing the details of hundreds of thousands of individual item choices, which is one of the major reasons full-line department stores have struggled in recent years. Brian Bremner and Michael Oneal wrote about Sears:

> Asks a former Sears apparel merchant: "Can any company afford the amount of time and debate that goes into Sears' assortment?"
>
> What's more, decentralized accounting methods made it difficult for buyers sitting in Chicago to track merchandise. . . . The bottom line: merchandisers had little information to work with, which made the huge retailer slow to react to its own sales patterns and larger consumer trends. By contrast, corporate buyers for competitors such as Wal-Mart place merchandise directly in their stores and keep a tight watch on inventory movement. If something doesn't sell, it is swiftly replaced with something that does.[1]

**■ SECTION ■ ONE ■**

## ASSORTMENT STRATEGY

As might be expected, the ideal assortment is the correct type and amount of merchandise on hand and on order. Many years ago, Charles Taylor stressed this point as follows:

> Serving the public efficiently requires the retailer to place continual stress upon offering assortments which are balanced to the tastes of his segment of the consuming public. To develop such assortments requires an organized, methodical system of planning and control not only for total merchandise offerings, but even more important, for every classifiable segment thereof. A retail store—or a department therein—is nothing other than the sum of its parts.
>
> Attention, hence, must continually be given to every contributing component if the total operation is to achieve successful proportions. Broad strategic plans have little value—in fact are rarely more than meaningless platitudes—unless they are implemented by the development of specific tactical maneuvers needed for the sound functioning of each subdivision of the whole.[2]

This is not an easy task to accomplish. In fact, trying to meet the needs of many different customers can lead the merchant to carry far too much stock and thus jeopardize the business. John Wingate provided the following example of how quickly an assortment can grow:

> . . . three men's shirts to be carried in only three classifications, with only three brands in each, with only three price lines in each brand, with only three materials in each price, with three cuff and front types in each material, with three collar styles within each type, with three colors in each style, with nine collar sizes in each color, with three sleeve lengths in each collar size, and with only three units in each sleeve length, there would have to be a total stock of about 177,000 units.[3]

### ESTABLISHING THE CLASSIFICATIONS

After the obvious steps of deciding what business to be in and the overall positioning strategy to follow (as discussed beginning in Chapter 2), the next step in assortment planning and management is to set up a classification system to help in buying, controlling, and presenting the merchandise.

There are several ways to classify goods, but in most sectors of retail there are conventional approaches. For example, one may set up classifications by generic department (such as shoes); by handling characteristics (such as frozen foods); by customer demographics (such as children's wear); by customer lifestyle (such as career women); by brand (such as designer boutiques in department stores); by price (such as bargain basement); by common calendar or seasonality of purchase (such as beachwear); or by supplier. The idea is not to subdivide the assortment into myriad components, but rather to segment it into meaningful, helpful parts to facilitate its management. As with customer segmentation, the customer is the ultimate guide. When in doubt, establish classifications the way a customer would view the shopping trip. For example, a shopper seeking to buy men's clothing might wish to find suits, men's furnishings (such as shirts and ties), and men's shoes all in reasonable proximity in a store and coordinated in assortment fashion and price points. This would argue for management grouping these segments of the merchandise assortment.

Gerald Smith stressed that many retailers needlessly burden themselves in assortment management by not classifying their inventory in an appropriate way. He clarified the concept of classification as follows:

> A classification is a group of merchandise which, in the eyes of the customer, is reasonably substitutable—a customer demand center. This is what a customer asks for when she comes into the store: evening dress, daytime dress, maternity dress, and so forth. Items within a classification should be perceived as being generally interchangeable, and should be able to be defined in terms commonly understood by all store employees who work with classifications. Further, a classification should be fixed in nature so that historical statistics will have current significance and be useful for future planning. . . .
>
> While a classification may be as broad or as narrow as the retailer wishes, a good general rule of thumb holds that if it comprises less than 1 percent of total sales, it probably should be merged with a broader classification. Conversely, if it comprises more than 20 percent of total sales, it should probably be split into two or more separate classifications.[4]

## Major Considerations in Assortment Management

The multifaceted nature of assortments makes decisions about them complicated. For example, a retailer may consider the following in deciding among assortment options: the nature of customer demand, what competitors are doing, vendor offerings and terms, money available for investment and the firm's financial goals, staff expertise, storage and handling capability, and so on.

All retailers should regard themselves as purchasing agents for their customers, not simply as selling agents for their suppliers. This means that the retailer must always buy with customers in mind, not simply according to statistics and market trends. It is not easy to constantly find the balance between ordering too little or too much merchandise, to select the right mix of colours, styles, sizes, and so on. When should the merchant invest inventory dollars in many different kinds of items as opposed to buying a lot of a few items? How many of an item are needed to "be in the business"; how many are needed "to make a statement"; and how many are needed to "be dominant"? Anthony Joseph offered the following guidance: "The rule should always be that if a whole-hearted commitment cannot be made to a category of goods, the department or class should be eliminated."[5]

While customers often think in terms of *selection*, retailers use three major concepts to describe their assortments: variety, breadth, and depth.

**Variety** refers to the various groups, classes, and categories of items carried. For example, a retailer offering office supplies, books, computer equipment, and copying services has a wider variety than a retailer only offering computer equipment. This is not to say that the second retailer may not have a better selection of computer equipment by virtue of specialization; however, this latter aspect of selection is termed breadth.

When retailers add variety via unrelated merchandise, this is called **scrambled merchandising**; for example, if a grocery store begins to sell motor oil or a drug store sells pool chemicals, they are scrambling their assortments.

Following are some of the many questions a retailer must ask before opting for a wide variety:

1. Will more selling space be required?
2. Will additional services be required?
3. Will the competition be capable of retailing the products better?
4. Will customers perceive a loss of expertise in the core products of the store?
5. Will financial returns be improved?

Recently, McDonalds has been experimenting with pizza. To add pizza to their menu would be to increase its variety. The implications of this change for more than 10 000 restaurants are enormous.[6]

Recent trends in variety indicate rearrangements of past approaches. Decisions on variety can be complex for any type of store. For several years department stores have been reducing the variety of their offerings for a number of reasons, not the least of which are unacceptable returns per square foot in some categories and increasing competition from specialty stores tailored toward specific market niches. On the other hand, it may appear logical for a high fashion ladies clothing boutique to begin carrying accessories like jewellery, handbags, and shoes. Similarly, as a group, supermarkets and drug stores have been attempting to widen the variety of merchandise that they offer. Supermarkets, for example, have been expanding their assortment to include in-store bakeries, delis, pharmacies, and so on in attempts to become one-stop shopping places with "destination assortments." On the other hand, most general merchandise retailers have been narrowing their merchandise mix. Even traditional "variety store" chains such as F.W. Woolworth in the U.K. have concluded that they can no longer be all things to all people. Management's solution was to eliminate 56 of 62 departments in its U.K. operations. This required a change in the firm's mission. U.K. Woolworth's now concentrates its efforts on six market-led departments through focusing on better merchandising assortment.[7]

**Breadth of assortment** refers to the selection within each group, class, and category. For example, a store might decide to offer a vast selection of men's suits to fit every size in a near endless combination of colours and styles. An obvious alternative to this approach would be to offer a narrower assortment of suits. The same store could choose to specialize in only Italian suits for the average size male. This narrower assortment strategy would permit the store to reduce inventory costs, as well as space requirements, substantially, and to simplify buying and control procedures. Breadth decisions include what lines and items in each category to buy in terms of quality, colours, sizes, price points, and brands. Breadth impacts on the number of SKU's, but it does not refer to how many of each SKU to carry. A typical convenience grocery store has wide variety and narrow breadth: there are single product items in a wide range of categories such as one brand and size of peanut butter, one brand and size of aspirin, and so on.

**Depth of assortment** refers to the inventory commitment that the retailer makes to a product category or how many of each SKU are carried. A shallow strategy implies that very few items of each SKU will be kept on hand, whereas a deep strategy implies that inventory is plentiful and turnover is anticipated to be high. An example of a depth decision is choice of the number of each size of a garment to carry, such as one dozen Size 8's. Obviously, if the retailer has only the wrong size in a shoe or a shirt, the customer won't buy, no matter how much he or she likes the price, colour, or style. Yet buying too many of the wrong sizes could be disastrous. Each retail marketer must decide on the mix of sizes based on his or her own customer base characteristics. Alternatively, a retailer may seek to provide a size range by providing alterations or special orders. Recently, Florsheim has been testing a computerized point-of-sale system with which customers can view and order unusual sizes and styles of shoes not carried in regular store inventories.

The way in which any retailer combines decisions on assortment variety, breadth, and depth reflects most of that retailer's fundamental assortment strategy. Typically, opting for more of one of these dimensions requires a reduction in the other two dimensions. Table 7.1 shows some examples.

### TABLE 7.1
### Variations in Assortment Strategies

|  | Variety | Breadth | Depth |
|---|---|---|---|
| Full-line department store | high | wide | deep |
| Specialty department store | medium | very wide | deep |
| Variety store | very high | narrow | shallow |
| Discount store | medium | narrow | deep |
| Convenience store | medium | narrow | shallow |
| Specialty store | low | medium | medium |
| Vending machine | low | narrow | shallow |
| Fast food | low | very narrow | deep |

A **dominant assortment** tells the customers that this store is a major force in the category in which it is competing. It combines breadth, and depth of product availability. It is unlikely to also mean variety unless it is a very large-scale operation. This strategy can be followed by traditional department stores in one or more product categories as well as by specialty stores, which concentrate on very few product categories. The total amount of selling space has little to do with successfully executing a dominant assortment strategy.

Assortment decisions must be consistent with other elements of the retail marketing program. A deep-discounter selecting a shallow assortment strategy will fail on points of execution: customers will be confused by the contradictory signals of "high volume/low price" being sent to them by advertising and promotion and the finding of few items in the store. Similarly, a fast food hamburger restaurant attempting to offer broad menu extensions will not only send garbled messages to its customers, but will also probably fail on an operational level.

Assortment decisions on the "package of benefits" reflect the persona of a retail establishment. It is important not only that the elements of the program be consistent, but that the assortment decisions be communicated consistently and regularly to the consumer. Shoppers Drug Mart's positioning statement "Everything you want in a drugstore" implies a dominant assortment strategy and is consistent with all the other marketing efforts of the firm. Shoppers' U.S. sister-chain, Peoples Drugs, perhaps owing to more acute competitive dimensions in the United States, has evolved a narrower assortment philosophy, preferring to emphasize "the traditional strengths of the community drug store [with] a strong emphasis on health care, convenience, value and customer service."[8] Customers are being told to expect different assortments from each chain.

An interesting approach to assortment planning is found at Toys 'R' Us. This retailer is now an international merchant of toys, games, accessories, and general merchandise for children. Toys 'R' Us has successfully used a dominant assortment strategy to provide it with the competitive advantage that has allowed the firm to capture 27 percent of all retail toy business in North America in less than twenty years.[9]

Part of the Toys 'R' Us philosophy is a commitment to the broadest and deepest selection of toys of all toy retailers. Attempts are made to carry almost every toy available on the market, which means that about 18 000 items are on stock at a time. Toys 'R' Us buyers essentially buy a limited quantity of every likely product on a trial basis. Their product tracking system, based on scanning by UPC, enables buyers to track early customer reactions to products and then to reorder quickly any items that appear promising. The firm has an unwritten policy of never being out-of-stock on high-turnover items. Backup stock is stored on shelves above the active stock in the selling area. Even with its large stores, Toys 'R' Us is required to plan space usage very carefully through the use of plan-o-grams and retail merchandising plans.

To support the cost of this assortment strategy, Toys 'R' Us has had to develop a year-round approach to toy retailing. About 75 percent of toy sales historically come in the Christmas selling season. This pattern would produce erratic cash flows and would undermine the success of the assortment approach taken by Toys 'R' Us. To create a year-round toy store, management included nontoy categories in the product mix such as diapers, baby formula and jarred food, clothing, and nontoy seasonal promotions featuring Back-to-School, Easter, and Halloween merchandise. Many of these products are sold at or below cost and are included in the assortment to create a regular flow of consumers through the store in support of the core products.

Toys 'R' Us has been successful in turning toy retailing into a year-round business. In 1989, only 47 percent of its sales occurred in the last quarter of the year; yet this is still a heavily seasonal business, which compels Toys 'R' Us management to develop sophisticated buying techniques and to centralize buying at their head office facility in order to ensure conformity across the chain.

Toys 'R' Us has become the model for many other aspiring "dominant selection" retail marketers; this includes its own venture into children's apparel retailing, Kids 'R' Us, which has been extremely successful, reaching approximately $0.5 billion in sales at the end of its eighth year in 1990.[10] Following a similar strategy are Staples, Office Depot, and Office Club; they are fast-growing U.S. discount supermarket-style office supply retailers offering up to 7000 items to small businesses and the general public.[11]

## BRANDING POLICIES

A major issue in assortment strategy is **branding**—the choice of someone else's label or one's own ("house brands") on the merchandise carried. Some retailers have no choice in the matter, being too small to do much other than resell another's brand or repackage bulk items with their own price sticker. However, many retailers do have the opportunity to have their own label or to acquire special rights to another's label. The choice of branding policy can be a difficult and contentious one. From a retail marketer's perspective, there are good reasons for and against a private or store-controlled label, as shown in Exhibit 7.1.

---

*EXHIBIT 7.1*
*Branding and Labelling from Retailer's Perspective*

**1.  Advantages of a manufacturer's label:**

    **a.**  pre-sold to customers
    **b.**  lower selling costs because manufacturer bears these costs
    **c.**  may attract new customers to the store
    **d.**  may enhance store image
    **e.**  enables customers to comparison shop and thus see store's value
    **f.**  usually includes allowances and returns privileges
    **g.**  enables carrying lower-volume items
    **h.**  many private label programs are too expensive for smaller retailers
    **i.**  better for short-lived products
    **j.**  better for items where private label "value advantage" cannot be developed

2. **Disadvantages of manufacturer's label:**

   a. lower gross margins
   b. selling restrictions
   c. pricing restrictions
   d. advertising restrictions
   e. may create more brand loyalty than store loyalty
   f. retailer is dependent on supplier who can sell to competing stores or even open own stores

3. **Advantages of private label:**

   a. greater price flexibility
   b. higher gross margins usually
   c. no advertising restrictions
   d. independence on breadth and depth of assortment
   e. enhance both store and brand loyalty
   f. can set own delivery times, pack sizes, display holders
   g. better product quality and features control through specification buying
   h. can be distinctive with no direct brand competition in other stores

4. **Disadvantages of private labels:**

   a. higher selling costs due to need to stimulate demand
   b. greater financial risk—especially if buying off-shore
   c. expanded buying and procuring responsibilities (need higher-skilled buyers)
   d. no allowances, markdown dollars, return privileges
   e. usually longer lead time in ordering and reordering
   f. earlier payments usually required
   g. usually higher minimum orders meaning higher inventory levels and risks
   h. many other retailers now seem to be doing it, which is reducing the payoff for any individual retailer

---

All retailers seek ways to differentiate their assortment from their competitors' assortments, to make it somehow unique, and to find ways to increase gross margin received. Paul Crotty explained the role of house brands as follows:

> While margin improvement remains the primary raison d'etre for many house brands, today's more sophisticated retailers also use them to attract and retain customers, to differentiate themselves from their competition, and to avoid the inevitable and easy price-point comparison that is so easy with manufacturer's brands. The retailer's own label is an integral part of the retail marketing mix; it reflects the retailer's whole positioning in a way that manufacturers' brands never can. Private label can position the retailer as an innovator, as environmentally responsible, and so on.[12]

However, any retailer opting for private labels runs some risks. First, no manufacturer who has invested in brand equity development happily steps aside in favour of store brands. Recently, several major manufacturers, such as Phillips Van Heusen, have begun to integrate forward into their own retail outlets as their retail customers have increased their purchases of private label products. Further, ultimate customers have expectations about branding policies that retailers ignore at their peril. In 1990 Management Horizons published a research study on branding in the United States:

> There are some general associations that consumers make between store and brand types in apparel. National brands are associated most often with department stores. Designer brands are affiliated most often with department stores, with local specialty stores, and with off-price apparel stores. Store brands are affiliated most often with national mass merchandise chains, but also with chain specialty stores. "No name" brands are affiliated most often with discount stores.[13]

When considering brand names, the retail marketer must not lose sight of the even more important assortment issue: having the right products and services available to the customer. From its origins, The Body Shop, an internationally successful retail chain selling natural cosmetics, followed an assortment strategy that emphasized its unique product mix. All products were originally formulated by the founder of the firm in her kitchen from natural ingredients like cocoa butter or aloe vera. Even today, 400 stores later, the owner of the firm continues to spend two months each year searching for new and unique products. The Body Shop has followed a pattern of developing and branding its own merchandise; it presents a wide variety of products, but only with its own brand names. The firm has a team of scientists whose responsibility is to continually develop new natural products.[14]

In summary, branding decisions include what percentages of manufacturer brands and house brands to carry, which name(s) to choose for house brands, who should be responsible for developing house brand characteristics, and how to position house brands as opposed to manufacturer brands.

## SOURCING DECISIONS

Decisions on which items to buy require skill, experience, information, and judgment. Buyers use a variety of inputs in making choices, including past sales data; suggestions from salespeople; their own judgment and experience as to what the customers may want next; analysis of competitive stores; vendors' offerings; trade publications; customer surveys; and want slips, which are records of what customers have asked for that the store doesn't carry. (Dollar and unit assortment planning approaches will be examined later in this chapter.) There are two basic approaches to buying: **market buying** and **specification buying**, as outlined in Exhibit 7.2.

**Security of supply** is an essential part in planning an assortment strategy. The Toys 'R' Us wide and deep philosophy is predicated upon never being out of stock in particular items. The company typically builds its own warehouses in advance of its stores in order to have rapid and assured replenishment. Erratic supply channels can shatter the success of any assortment strategy so it is incumbent upon the

EXHIBIT 7.2
*Market Buying
versus
Specification
Buying*

**1. Market buying:**

    **a.** usual approach to acquiring national brands

    **b.** buy at the store or central buying office, wholesale market centres, merchandise shows, through resident buying offices

    **c.** quick access to new products

    **d.** can buy opportunistically

    **e.** lower inventory risk

    **f.** can access a broad vendor base

    **g.** can buy in low volume

**2. Specification buying:**

    **a.** usual approach for private labels

    **b.** can be "stencil manufacturing" or can design product and all aspects of the deal

    **c.** requires closer and longer-term relationship with supplier

    **d.** usually a narrower vendor base

retailer to establish strong and ongoing relationships with suppliers as well as to cultivate more than one supplier in every category.

Single-theme retailers also face supply problems of a different sort. A retail organization like Sox Appeal is committed, by its name, philosophy and positioning, to provide the widest selection of socks and accessories available. The challenge for management at Sox Appeal is to ensure that enough variety, breadth, and depth of hosiery is always available from suppliers to fill between 500 and 800 square feet of selling space in each of its stores. Unlike Toys 'R' Us, which can temporarily shrink a product category due to supply problems, single-theme retailers have little latitude in this way. Many, like Sox Appeal, quickly develop their own design staffs and sources of supply.[15]

Another feature of the supply dimension that can influence assortment decisions is vendor power. Sometimes a retailer may be compelled to purchase products in a bundled deal to acquire the product really wanted. Similarly, a retailer may also be forced to buy in quantities that exceed planned purchases in order to secure a price competitive with other larger retailers.

**Retailer–vendor relations** vary so much that one might find it useful to consider any specific relationship along a spectrum of "conflict – tension – cooperation partnership." When retailers and vendors squabble (even fight in court) over margins, prices, delivery dates, returns, excessive inventory loading, wrong items shipped, and so on, there are clearly relationship problems. The growing prevalence, complexity, and unequal nature of deals between vendors and retailers have created much ill will in the industry:

> The proliferation of deals and allowances has spawned a rapid deterioration of manufacturer-retailer relations. Influential executives on both sides have concluded that steps must be taken to reverse the downward trend before internal

squabbling becomes so loud that what has been a family affair spills out into the public arena and wounds the industry grievously.

Fueling the deterioration are such practices as slotting allowances, street money, unauthorized deductions from invoices, diverting, and special offerings to wholesale clubs.[16]

On the other hand, when retailers and vendors share information and plans, engage in joint efforts, such as electronic data interchange (EDI), routinely cooperate in advertising and promotional programs, and so on, then the relationship is working well. There are a wide variety of ways retailers and vendors can work together for mutual gain, including cooperative advertising and promotion, allowances for shelf space and position, coupon handling, display fixtures and materials, preticketing, return privileges, market research studies, price adjustments for inventory changes, and automatic replenishment mechanisms.

Brian Goldberg of Wrangler was quoted as follows regarding vendor–retailer partnerships:

> The biggest change is working more in partnership with the retailer. Where in the past the business was more aligned toward negotiation and placing specific products for the retailer, now we are really geared with the retailer to satisfy customer needs. We are working jointly; we work together to maximize sales through the best product mix and the best product presentation and the most responsive flow of product to satisfy customer demand.[17]

Every retailer must develop criteria for what to buy, how many to buy, and who to buy it from. Most retail buyers say they want as much help from a vendor as possible and that this factor is as important or more so than simply the economics of a deal. One divisional merchandise manager was quoted at length about what she seeks from her vendors:

> One, a whole sales-stock-and-assortment-plan that is specific to each branch store. Two, in-store servicing. Training and retraining salespeople. Checking stock to make sure the facings are done properly and the department is in-stock. Three, availability of automatic re-ordering. It allows us to carry less inventory, turn it quicker, and reorder the SKU's that are selling. With automatic reorder systems, we are able to reorder so much faster than with manual counts. Four, volume is almost dictated by the number of facings on the floor so we want vendor co-op to put in improved fixturing.... Fifth, visuals.... Then, obviously, any help with advertising.[18]

There are a growing number of retailers who are **buying opportunistically**. This means they are buying special deals, end-of-seasons, close-outs, and seconds to obtain merchandise at very attractive prices. The "off-pricers" in apparel are particularly adept in this. They sacrifice assortment **consistency** and **continuity** for price- and value-driven opportunities.

Other retailers buy on a very different basis. Probably the best example of an assortment strategy predicated on specification buying and private labelling is

Marks & Spencer, the British retailing giant. Since 1928, the company has offered one brand name for all its items: St. Michael. In a fascinating review of Marks & Spencer, K.K. Tse offered the following summary:

> All of the 260 Marks & Spencer stores in the U.K. carry only one brand of merchandise—St. Michael, a sharp and striking contrast to most other retail chains. All of the products are either designed by the Company or jointly designed with the manufacturer; the Company does not buy any ready-made line from the suppliers as do most other retailers. The products thus designed are manufactured by the suppliers (none of whom are owned to any degree by Marks & Spencer) against precise and exacting specifications furnished by the Company to ensure high and consistent quality. To this end, the Company employs over 350 technical personnel in the head office who work closely with the manufacturer, advising on and monitoring such matters as the choice of raw materials, choice of production processes and techniques, quality control, production engineering, and the like. The quality of all the products sold is fully guaranteed by the Company; indeed the brand name has become a byword of quality in the British scene, with virtually no advertising whatsoever. To crown all this, over 90 percent of its merchandise is British-made, despite the fact that most of its competitors are importing heavily in comparable lines.[19]

Loblaws, a large Canadian grocery retailer, has recently followed the Marks & Spencers approach in a variety of product categories. Its President's Choice line of grocery products and its Green line of environmentally and bodily friendly products have both been very successful. Their approach is exemplified by the President's Choice Decadent Chocolate Chip Cookie. Competing in a market of roughly forty million pounds of cookies, Loblaws looked for a value-added strategy. They changed some basic ingredients, such as using butter instead of hydrogenated fat, but most importantly, they increased the number of chocolate chips to about 40 percent of the cookie. This assortment strategy resulted in Loblaws' Decadent cookie being the number one cookie brand in Ontario one year after introduction despite being sold in only 22 percent of the province's supermarkets.[20]

■
**SECTION**
■
**TWO**
■

## ASSORTMENT PLANNING AND MANAGEMENT

Retailers use two basic approaches in planning and controlling assortments: financial (or dollar) planning and unit planning. Each of these will be examined.

## FINANCIAL PLANNING

Financial planning is intended to control the investment in merchandise through budgets, sales forecasts, inventory level targets, purchases, open-to-buy budgets, and reductions planning. Financial planning is usually embodied in the six-month merchandise plan, six months being the most common planning horizon.[21] The merchandise plan is calculated in retail dollars, not cost or units. It is the basic method of financial control of assortment choices at a classification level or even at a total store level. The six-month merchandise plan involves six basic steps:[22]

1. **Overall sales forecast for next six months**—an extrapolation of past sales trends and an adjustment for anticipated market developments. The anticipated sales for the next period is the most important factor in this merchandise plan and the most difficult to predict. Basically, any retailer makes a judgment using all available information. The careful record-keeping of earlier results can help the buyer in this task:

   > It is the inherent task of any buyer to make forecasts. Every time he makes a buying decision or places an order, he is, as suggested, predicting a result. There is no escaping this responsibility; it is part and parcel of the buying process. There are however some distinct tools available to the buyer in his efforts to forecast accurately. Chief among these are the records relating to classification and unit sales and stock control. These records are maintained specifically for the purpose of furnishing an accurate history of experience with a department's merchandise—a history which hopefully will assist in predicting future patterns.[23]

   It is important to realize that forecasting for highly seasonal fashion goods differs substantially from more-stable, less-seasonal items, such as grocery products. In the former instance, the forecaster derives much less value from past records and must rely on "instinct and experience" much more.

2. **Monthly sales forecast**—breaking the six-month sales into months to account for seasonality. This may be done on the basis of last season (such as comparing last fall to the coming fall), an average of several seasons, or a weighted average giving more emphasis to recent experience.

3. **Inventory planning**—determining the opening and ending inventory levels. The establishment of planned inventory levels is typically based on the sales forecast. In principle, the retailer wishes to carry enough stock to meet customer demand (without incurring stockouts and thus missed sales), enough stock to allow for the replenishment cycle, not too much stock relative to storage capacity in the store or warehouse, and not too much stock relative to the carrying and handling costs. It is important to realize that stockouts are often different from the retailer's perspective and the manufacturer's perspective. If a manufacturer's brand is not available, a customer may switch to another brand, perhaps for a long period of time. From a retailer's perspective, having an acceptable product in stock, regardless of brand, may be adequate to retain the patronage and business of a customer. Stockouts of specifically demanded items, however, may mean walkouts and even store-switching behaviour.

   There are four ways in which dollar inventory levels are set:

   a. *Basic stock method*. This approach is typically used for staple goods with annual stock turns of less than six times and relatively predictable sales patterns. The basic idea is that a minimum level of inventory is required no matter what the sales rate. The beginning of month (BOM) inventory level is set by establishing an average stock level, then adding the planned sales for the month less the average monthly sales.

The average stock level is calculated either based on the historical performance of this category (or the performance of others in the industry) or by setting turnover goals and then calculating average inventory as seasonal sales divided by seasonal stock turn. Basic stock is average inventory less average monthly sales.

b.  *Percentage variation method.* This approach is typically used for higher turn-over classifications (more than six annually). One needs to calculate average monthly sales, divide by planned stock turn to determine average inventory, then solve the following equation for each month:

$$\text{Beginning inventory} = \text{Average inventory} \times \frac{1}{2} \times \left(1 + \frac{\text{Sales for month}}{\text{Average monthly sales}}\right)$$

c.  *Weeks of supply method.* This method is used frequently for staple items with regular sales patterns and is based on establishing a number of weeks of sales that stock can cover as of the end of each month. For example, a retailer may decide based on sales rates, lead times, and safety stock levels to aim for five weeks' supply on hand. This means that at the end of the month the retailer should plan to have on hand enough inventory to cover sales for the next five weeks. (*Note*: each six-month period contains twenty-six weeks according to the business calendar.)

d.  *Stock to sales ratio method.* This approach is used for highly seasonal merchandise. The ratio is the dollar amount of inventory on hand at a point in time (such as beginning or ending of a month) relative to the sales for a defined period of time (such as a month). A target ratio (based on previous experience of beginning of month inventory to sales calculations or on industry data) is selected for each month and multiplied by the forecasted sales for the month to determine the inventory level. This technique may be used with either retail value or cost value of inventory and is more responsive to differences in sales each month than are techniques that use averages per month.

4. **Reduction planning**—projecting expected markdowns, shortages, and discounts that will reduce the gross margin and the retail value of the inventory. Discounts, shrinkage, and markdowns can all be expressed as a percentage of sales and estimated on the basis of previous experience adjusted for expected circumstances.

5. **Purchase planning**—calculating purchases at retail and then at cost. Planned purchases at retail equal planned sales plus planned reductions plus planned ending inventory less opening inventory. Planned purchases at cost are planned

purchases at retail times (100 minus the average markup percentage). Purchases may be planned for each month of the plan this way.

6. **Open-to-buy calculations**—the amount a buyer may spend, which is the planned purchases less the merchandise already received less the merchandise on order.

   The open-to-buy calculation is designed to exercise some control over the buyer. The budget shows what the buyer has left to spend. However, it is important to allow some flexibility in this process so that buyers may take advantage of any unexpected opportunities.

## UNIT PLANNING

Unit planning involves specific decisions on what to buy and where to put it in the store(s). This is where the buyer plays a key role in making choices among all the possible items the retail operation could carry. The buyer needs to consider many factors, including customer demand and competitive activities, vendor offerings and market trends, replenishment cycles, and which stock should be on a "never-out list," to name a few. Complete books have been written on this aspect of assortment management.[24]

Space is, in most instances, the principal limiting factor in determining an assortment strategy. Robert Lusch argued:

> The influence of merchandise assortments on gross margin return on selling space (GMROS) is more important than their influence on GMROI. In merchandise assortment planning, all sku's must be examined in terms of their need for space. The sku's that contribute most to the effectiveness of the assortment plan are those that have a high inventory investment per unit of space they occupy (inventory intensity) and fortunately also have a high GMROI. In fact inventory intensity and GMROI are key correlates of retail productivity and profitability.[25]

Space may be limited because of either the physical boundaries of the store or the prohibitive cost of acquiring additional space; it may be limited for any particular category of merchandise or service to be provided, either in total or in terms of the fixtures that are available. This can restrict the scope of the merchandise decisions available to the retailer. With only 5000 square feet of leasable space, a conventional drugstore would be courting disaster if it attempted to follow an assortment strategy more conducive to the needs of a deep-discount drug warehouse operation. However, creative merchandising techniques can be used to execute a broad assortment strategy in a relatively limited space. Intent on carrying a wide variety of products but without the available space to fully merchandise important categories in its 70 000 square foot store, Rouses Enterprises Inc.'s grocery superstore in Louisiana utilizes "alcoves" to cross-merchandise product categories to create the perception of a broad assortment. They merchandise toys, for example, with breakfast cereal![26]

Since space (next to labour) is the most costly aspect of a retail operation, all retailers require a long-term merchandise plan to maximize the utilization of their space. A useful planning device is the **plan-o-gram**, which may be prepared manually or with the assistance of a computer. This is a communications link between the buyer and the personnel in the stores. It visually outlines, fixture by fixture and shelf by shelf, precise positions of merchandise, their product adjacencies, and display methods. While it has obvious uses in the store, it is also a gentle reminder to a buyer that unless a dedicated space is available for a product, it should not be purchased. (Layout and merchandising are discussed more fully in Chapters 8 and 10.)

## Category Management

The emerging quality and quantity of merchandise information that is now available to many large retailers has enabled new and more powerful organizational arrangements for managing assortments. In particular, category management has been adopted by both food and general merchandisers. Whereas a retail food buyer may be responsible for approximately ten product categories in the assortment, a category manager is responsible for the entire aisle. A buyer tends to have a very short-term focus, often weekly, and is preoccupied with replenishment and all the merchandising details. A category manager tends to be a higher level manager concerned with strategy over a longer time frame with a broader perspective of the interrelationships among all the items in the aisle. Whereas a buyer spends a great deal of time with salespeople, a category manager relies greatly on the retail marketer's information system. Daniel O'Connor and Michael Zack explained category management as follows:

> The classic retail organization often has revenue and cost centers, but in most cases profit responsibility resides only with the highest level executive. Operations and buying/merchandising are separated, with accountability for product performance split across the organization.
>
> With category management, buyers focus resources within categories instead of working across them. They "own" the long-term success of their section and are empowered to make all the strategic and tactical buying, handling, and selling decisions. Store and department managers are then leveraged away from merchandising decisions to focus on customer service and selling. . . .
>
> The key for implementing category management is to explicitly define, integrate, and manage sourcing and refining of data to create a flexible and usable supply of information. . . . A typical retailer DSS [decision support system] contains applications like DPP, shelf space management, promotion evaluation, and in the most advanced systems, expert applications to assist with pricing, new item evaluation, promotion monitoring, etc.[27]

### Changing Assortments: Quick Response

Skilled merchants have a sense of when items in the assortment are moving well and when they need some special attention. Although data (such as inventory aging reports) can help identify these situations (as discussed below), the element of judgment cannot be totally quantified even with "expert systems." Retailers need to learn their sales patterns by experience in order to know when to have merchandise and when to offer special incentives to move it out of the store to make room for new merchandise. Merchandise can be controlled in a number of ways. When to have the merchandise arrive on the sales floor involves understanding the replenishment cycle, one's own handling procedures from receipt to sales floor, and when customers will be "in the market." Nearly all merchandise is subject to some kind of seasonality.

Inventory can be managed through transfers to other parts of the store selling space or to other stores or even to close-out specialists. Sometimes, merchandise can be moved through more aggressive advertising and promotion, more attention by salespeople, or by markdowns. (The next few chapters deal with such issues.) Chain retailers frequently use "flash reports" to alert store level management of changes in merchandising strategy. The term *flash* is indicative of the usual need for immediate action. When actions to sell the assortment are not successful, sometimes merchandise can be returned to the vendor.

All facets of retailing are undergoing fundamental changes in attempts to do business "just in time." There has been much effort to improve the management of the logistics of retail assortments—the processes and procedures goods follow from factory to store floor.

**Quick response (QR)** refers to the combination of *technology* (such as bar coding, scanning, and expert systems) with *standards* (specifically for electronic data interchange (EDI) so all firms in the industry may participate)[28] with *new ways of managing* assortment strategies. The purpose is to do everything about assortments faster and smarter—sooner with more frequent deliveries of just-right merchandise in smaller quantities. To accomplish this purpose requires better assortment information and closer relationships (at least electronically) with both customers and vendors. QR is more than just information systems, more than just electronic purchase orders and standardized bar coding of merchandise and of shipping containers for item tracking. To implement QR, people's jobs must change, which is why some retail marketers are having difficulty gaining full advantage of their investments in the technology side of QR.[29] Most major retailers are involved in QR programs—one-half of medium-sized and 90 percent of large retail companies said they were committed to QR in a 1991 study of American retailers.[30] Early results of many QR programs have been very encouraging. John Nordeen, of Dayton Hudson, reported a 50 percent increase in turns and drastically reduced inventory levels:

> Our approach to QR is forward thinking. We know the battle to be competitive in retailing isn't going to be won with the traditional swords and shields. We need to be positioned for the future. . . . It's through a combination of technology, standards and vendor partnerships that QR has come to benefit retailers.[31]

## ASSORTMENT ASSESSMENT AND CONTROL

In order to achieve assortment performance objectives, retail marketers need ways to value their investment in the assortment, to monitor and control merchandise movement, and to track merchandise profitability closely.

### MERCHANDISE INVESTMENT

As discussed in Chapter 3, the investment in merchandise inventory for most retailers is a very substantial proportion of total assets and, hence, deserves careful management. Inventory may be valued in two basic ways: at cost or at retail. Each method has its advantages and disadvantages, as shown in Exhibit 7.3.

*EXHIBIT 7.3*
*Inventory*
*Valuation*

1. **The cost method**: Calculating the original cost price of each item or group of items to arrive at a total inventory cost. This cost may be reduced if current market values are less than the original costs.

   This method is typically used by small retailers, by retailers with limited number of items (especially if they are high-cost items), by service operations such as restaurants, and by retailers who negotiate final price (that is, the retail price isn't known until the deal is made).

2. **The retail method**: This approach is used by most retailers. The entire ending inventory is valued at current retail prices, then restated in cost terms by using the average markup percentage. This approach enables a retailer to calculate gross margin and profit at any time without undertaking a physical inventory count.

   a. Calculate the cost and retail value by physical count or through purchase and sales records of the opening inventory (the book-value approach). Calculate the cost and retail value of all purchases and add these to the beginning inventory figures to get cost and retail value of merchandise available for sale during the period.

   b. Add all reductions (markdowns, employee discounts, and shrinkage allowances) to net sales for the period. This figure is total deductions from inventory for the period. Deduct these from the retail value of the merchandise available for sale for the period to obtain the retail value of the ending inventory.

   c. Calculate the cost multiplier. This is 100 minus the average markup on retail of the total merchandise handled.

   d. Multiply the cost multiplier times the retail value of ending inventory to obtain the cost value of the ending inventory. One can then proceed to calculate cost of goods sold and other aspects of the income statement.

3. **Physical inventory versus book value**: Physical or actual inventory is the dollar amount of inventory on hand as determined by a count of the stock. This approach is facilitated when items are stored in standard-sized fixtures and when the inventory does not change much. Book inventory is the dollar value of inventory determined by accounting records. Shrinkage (or stock shortage) is the difference between actual and book inventory caused by theft, misplacement, inaccurate counts, or other loss.

4. **Periodic versus perpetual valuation:** Periodic valuation refers to occasional counts or calculations of inventory value, such as a year-end stocktaking efforts. Perpetual inventory is a continuous calculation of inventory value, facilitated by item movement data and continual calculations through accounting records.

5. **FIFO and LIFO:** When individual items are not tracked through purchase to sales, assumptions have to be made as to the way goods move. The First-in-first-out method of determining the value of inventory assumes that goods sell in the order in which they were introduced into the stock. Thus the goods in inventory are always the newest items. The Last-in-first-out method assumes the opposite; that the goods purchased were the most recently acquired and that the stock is a basic inventory at a fixed valuation.

---

Retailers must constantly balance merchandise investment (including carrying costs of the investment, holding costs, and handling costs) with ordering costs and time frames with stockout costs (losing sales and customers due to unavailability of the merchandise they want). It is not an easy balance to strike, even with advances in computing power, as Robert Kahn pointed out: "Scanning and computers can tell you when you have the wrong thing or too much of the right thing—but they cannot tell you when you don't have something many people want. Then we have to trust the people in the store."[32] Similarly, Dan Cooper and Frank Andrews, after studying the inventory management efforts and results of U.S. retailers, concluded:

> While most existing systems focus almost exclusively on lowering inventory, the real payoff from information technology is derived from having the right merchandise in stock rather than having the lowest inventory. Inventory turns will increase not only because inventory is lower but because sales are higher. And increasing sales, after all, is what retailing is all about. Effective inventory management supports this objective, but should not be an end in itself.[33]

## MERCHANDISE MOVEMENT

All retailers quickly learn how important it is to keep the merchandise moving through. Merchandise can and should be classified according to **rate of movement** or **velocity code**. For example, hot selling items may be candidates for priority replenishment; very slow items are usually candidates for markdowns and discontinuance from the assortment. A **traffic builder** is an item that is sufficiently popular with customers to bring them to the store. Traffic builders are usually items for which the customer knows prevailing competitive prices and availability. Careful analysis of merchandise movement data can often indicate traffic building items that may be featured in advertising and promotional efforts. Increasing use of the Universal Product Code and other systems of individual SKU identification coupled with scanning at point-of-transaction are enabling retailers to track item movement as never before. This new ability has, in turn, prompted dramatic changes in assortment, display, vendor relations patterns, and other developments.

The most common expression of merchandise movement is **turnover**, as mentioned in Chapter 3. As discussed, turnover may be calculated in four different ways:

1. number of units sold divided by average number of units carried
2. cost of goods sold divided by cost of average inventory
3. net sales divided by retail value of average inventory
4. net sales divided by cost of average inventory (this is called the sales-to-stock ratio)

It is important to remember that these turnover calculations will provide somewhat different numbers for the same circumstance; for example, the first two will be the same, the third will be lower than the first two. Care must be taken in understanding which method of calculation is being used, and that one is comparing like calculations.

Turnover provides guidance as to which stock is worth carrying and how much to order. And importantly, as discussed in Chapter 3, the combination of turnover and margin is basically how a retailer makes money. Higher turnover rates reduce the required investment in inventory, and allow the merchant to bring in new goods faster and more often. While turnover may be calculated for the entire assortment, more insights can be obtained by doing such calculations for parts of the assortment at a time.

## MERCHANDISE PROFITABILITY

As discussed in Chapter 3, there are a variety of merchandise performance assessment approaches; but the most important in terms of profitability are gross margin (and maintained markup), Gross Margin Return on Inventory Investment (GMROI), Gross Margin Return on Space (GMROS), and Direct Product Profitability (DPP).

When undertaking quantitative analysis of assortment performance, it is always prudent to remember that customers expect retailers to carry certain products in their assortments regardless of whether it may make good sense for the retailer to do so. For example, commodity items such as milk may perform poorly from a DPP perspective, but grocery managers would be foolhardy to attempt to eliminate milk and all other such poor performers from their assortment because customers may shop somewhere else to obtain not only their milk but all their other grocery needs.

## CONCLUSION

There are no clear guidelines on how to design and manage an assortment that will be a competitive winner. Assortments are constantly undergoing redefinition as retailers experiment with ways to satisfy customers. There continue to be far-reaching social, demographic, and technological changes that always have dramatic impact on the assortment decisions of retail marketers.

The growth of two-income families and the decline in time available for routine shopping will continue to affect the choices consumers make in selecting where to shop. Kmart senior management cited changing demographics as the principal reason that the firm decided in 1989 to enter into the high stakes hypermarket business, which combines food and nonfood items. The company's 244 000 square foot American Fare in Atlanta, which carries a narrow assortment of product in great depth in areas such as perishables, clothing, toys, and gardening supplies, was to be followed by more hypermarkets of similar size.[34] However, in recessions, many two-income families become one-income families—in which case, convenience and price paid may be re-evaluated for such families with dramatic impacts on the retail marketer.

As retailers face such changes, they will continue to make tradeoffs among variety, breadth, and depth of assortment. They will continue to wonder how to label their goods and from where to source them, and how to manage their assortments profitably. It is particularly vital for retail marketers to remember the need to focus on assortment management, not just assortment control. Assortment control focuses on accounting and procedures issues; assortment management focuses on overall marketing strategy issues.

## REVIEW QUESTIONS

1. What are the implications for the assortment strategies of grocery retailers of the following two statements: (a) "From 1987 to 1990 approximately 25 000 new products were added to North American supermarket shelves" and (b) "You can shelve more than 27 percent more product in the same space if the package is rectangular rather than cylindrical."

2. Wal-Mart's executive vice-president Bill Fields said, "We have a corporate concern for the environment. We are going to make a concerted effort to help clean up the environment by working with manufacturers to help promote a variety of concerns."[35] How might this affect this discounter's assortment strategy?

3. In 1988, Personics introduced a system that allows customers to select from over 5000 songs (the list is updated monthly) to compile a 90-minute cassette tape of personal choices. Customers may listen to 15-second samples of songs and then order them by number. Clerks operate a machine that can speed up rerecording to provide an average album in 5 minutes.[36] What might this mean to the assortment strategy of a record/tape/CD retailer?

4. A specialty young women's fashion retailer is musing about devoting a reasonably large area of the store to "hair goods and services." What might this assortment include?

5. If possible, visit a local supermarket to assess how house brands are integrated with manufacturer brands in the store. For example, are house brands kept separate? Are house brands given more promotionally prominent locations or not? How different are prices? Do you think the supermarket is handling house brands well?

## KEY TERMS

- assortment
- groups
- classes
- categories
- lines
- brands
- individual items
- stock-keeping unit (SKU)
- competitive positioning strategy
- classification
- variety
- scrambled merchandising
- breadth of assortment
- depth of assortment
- dominant assortment

- branding
- market buying
- specification buying
- security of supply
- retailer–vendor relations
- buying opportunistically
- consistency
- continuity
- plan-o-gram
- quick response (QR)
- rate of movement (velocity code)
- traffic builder
- turnover
- assortment control
- assortment management

## NOTES

1. Brian Bremner and Michael Oneal, "The Big Store's Big Trauma," *Business Week*, 10 July 1989, pp. 50–55.

2. Charles G. Taylor, *Merchandise Assortment Planning* (New York: National Retail Merchants Association, 1970), p. 2.

3. John W. Wingate, "What's Wrong with the Planning of Stock Assortments?" *New York Retailer*, October 1959, p. 6.

4. Gerald B. Smith, "Inventory Control and the Small Retailer," *Retail Control*, February 1991, pp. 21–24.

5. Anthony Joseph, "Inventory Planning and Control for Improved Profitability," *Retail Control*, October 1984, pp. 21–39.

6. Brian Bremner, "Two Big Macs, Large Fries, and a Pepperoni Pizza, Please," *Business Week*, 7 August 1989, p. 33.

7. Geoffrey Mulcahy, "Making of a High Street Miracle," *The London Times*, 3 September 1988, p. 31.

8. *Imasco Annual Report*, 1989, pp. 14–16.

9. "Toys 'R' Us, Kids 'R' Us," *Annual Report*, January 1989, p. 22; and F. Rice, "Superelf Plans for Xma$," *Fortune*, 11 September 1989, p. 151.

10. Penny Gill, "Kids 'R' Us Growing Up," *Stores*, March 1991, pp. 20–23.

11. Susan Caminiti, "Seeking Big Money in Paper and Pens," *Fortune*, 31 July 1989, pp. 173–74.

12. Paul Crotty, "Stocking the Aisle with Private Label," *Canadian Grocer*, August 1990, pp. 16–22.

13. Penny Gill, "Battle of the Brands: Who's Winning?" *Stores*, May 1990, pp. 77–79.

14. Deborah Cowley, "The Woman from the Body Shop," *Reader's Digest*, September 1989, pp. 159–60.

15. Denise Gallagher, "Hot Socks Shops!" *Stores*, May 1989, p. 48.

16. Steve Weinstein, "It's a Big Deal," *Progressive Grocer*, August 1988, pp. 92-108.

17. Gary Robins, "Vendor Role: Changing," *Stores*, May 1990, pp. 81-88.

18. As quoted by Susan Bass in "Hosiery: Partnerships Needed," *Stores*, November 1990, pp. 10–18.

19. K.K. Tse, "Marks & Spencer: A Manufacturer Without Factories," *International Trends in Retailing*, Arthur Andersen, Fall 1989, pp. 23–35.

20. Mark Evans, "Chocolate-Chip Contender Gets Bite of Market," *The Financial Post*, 8 July 1989, p. 1.

21. Douglas A. Louth, "How to Prepare a Six Month Merchandise Plan," *The Retail Advisor*, Touche Ross, April 1989.

22. For an excellent treatment of merchandise budgeting, see Milton Shuch, *Retail Buying and Merchandising* (Englewood Cliffs, N.J.: Prentice Hall, 1988).

23. Charles G. Taylor, *Merchandise Assortment Planning*, (New York: National Retail Merchants Association, 1970), p. 55.

24. For example, see J. Diamond and E. Diamond, *The World of Fashion* (San Diego, Calif.: Harcourt Brace Jovanovich, 1990).

25. Robert F. Lusch, "Two Critical Determinants of Retail Profitability and Productivity," *Retailing Issues Letter*, vol. II, no. 1 (April 1986).

26. Lauren Lekoski, "In Its New Superstore Rouse Wants It All: At Rouse's New Nonfood Nooks Squeeze More Variety into Less Space," *Supermarket Business*, vol. 44, no. 10 (October 1989), pp. 17A–21A, 31A, 55–58.

27. Daniel W. O'Connor, and Michael Zack, "Strategic Benefits of Category Management," *Discount Merchandiser*, July 1990, pp. 41–46.

28. For example see Warren Thayer, "The Joy of DEX," *Progressive Grocer*, May 1990, pp. 123–28.

29. Jeffrey P. Luker, "Quick Response from the Inside, Out," *Retail Control*, January 1990, pp. 3–6.

30. *Third Annual Barcode/EDI/Quick Response Survey Results* by Deloitte & Touche for the National Retail Federation, January 1991.

31. "Quick Response: The Right Thing," *Chain Store Age Executive*, March 1990, pp. 49–57. See also Penny Gill, "QR Keeps Jeans Moving," *Stores*, February 1991, pp. 23–24.

32. Robert Kahn, *Retailing Today*, December 1989.

33. Dan Cooper and Frank Andrews, "Beyond Systems: Inventory Management Takes Center Stage," *Retail Control*, January 1991, pp. 16–23.

34. Jay L. Johnson, "American Fare Opens in Atlanta," *Discount Merchandiser*, vol. 29, no. 2 (February 1989), p. 28.

35. Ela Schwartz, "Down-to-Earth Retailing," *Discount Merchandiser*, March 1990, pp. 48–52.

36. Gary Robins, "Custom Gets High Marks," *Stores*, December 1990, pp. 29–34.

CHAPTER

# CONVENIENCE

## INTRODUCTION

Early in 1990, there was an article in the *Sarasota Herald-Tribune* entitled "The Party's Over for the Formerly Shop-Happy." That article and this chapter are about the growing importance of convenience in shopping and the fact that far too many retail marketers seem to have missed the point:

> These people still shop, but not for fun. They want to get it over with as quickly and as painlessly as possible. They won't put up with lousy service or spend 20 minutes plowing through a rack of mixed-up sizes, and they refuse to trek through a million different departments in search of a simple white blouse.
> . . . Finally when they've paid, they want to get out of the store. They don't want to find that some too-clever architect has hidden the down escalator in hopes that they'll wander around lost long enough to be seduced into buying something extra."[1]

**Convenience** from the customer's viewpoint is being able to shop and buy with minimal expenditure of time and effort. These criteria can be applied to every dimension of a customer's relationship with a retail marketer and every stage of a shopping trip. Is a store easy and quick to find, to get to, to park near, and to enter? And when one gets there, is it easy to find items and information, to complete the transaction, and to leave? In short, is a retailer easy and quick to do business with? Retail marketers have a variety of ways to meet customers' convenience needs and expectations. The major ways include: location, layout, merchandise arrangement, transaction processing, hours, parking, and delivery, as shown in Figure 8.1. Each of these is discussed in this chapter.

FIGURE 8.1
Major dimensions of convenience

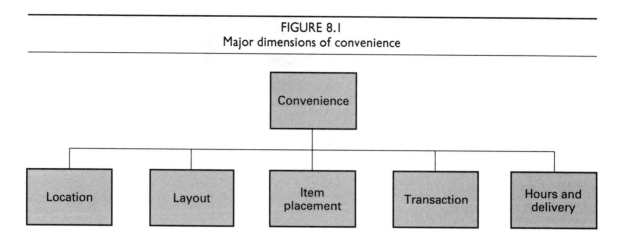

The attempt to provide convenience has even spawned some retail formats whose essential strategy is based on convenience. Perhaps most common are "convenience stores" or C-Stores. These used to be simply small neighbourhood milk, bread, etc. stores for fill-in trips between regular grocery trips to the supermarket, but now they are much more. In Canada, the number of such stores has grown to more than 5000. And the product and service selection has expanded to include prepared takeout foods, video rentals, postal and fax services, in-store bakeries, banking, and dry cleaning.[2] However, the growth in the number of convenience stores has slowed remarkably lately as a result of market saturation and high rents.[3]

Customer demands for convenience have resulted in a resurgence of home delivery operations for diapers, services of all kinds, and, of course, groceries; milk and bread delivery is once again available and you can now fax orders for groceries that will be delivered later.[4]

## LOCATION

From the customer's perspective, where the retailer is located is primarily a convenience issue. From the retailer's perspective, there are a great many other factors that must be considered when making a location decision. Retail marketers must remember that, generally speaking, customers will not exert extra effort to go shopping, but rather will patronize the most convenient retailer that can meet their needs and wants—and they will generally not travel past a close satisfier of needs to an equal facility farther away. A well-known retail phrase, "location, location, location," is the formula for retail success. In other words, a good location can compensate for other less-than-great characteristics of a store, whereas a poor location can often overshadow other marketing efforts.

Location is a retail marketing decision that is typically difficult to change frequently; yet it determines access to customers, investments in building and equipment, and many operating costs such as rent, utilities, and taxes. In short, it deserves careful attention. Too many start-up retailers are too eager to get going, or are overconfident that they can do better than others previously did at the same site, or don't feel research is really necessary. Such retailers typically make hasty and poor location decisions as a consequence.

To make the location decision, most retailers need to determine what major market area to compete in, what type of shopping area, and then which particular site. The process usually involves the steps shown in Exhibit 8.1.

*EXHIBIT 8.1*
*Steps in the*
*Location*
*Decision Process*

1. Choice of major market area
2. Division of that area into market grids
3. Mapping of competition and customers and termination points
4. Profiling of primary trading areas
5. Potential site identification
6. Detailed site evaluation
7. Actual site decision

Many of the criteria that a retailer may use will be discussed below; however, most of these criteria require detailed information. As outlined in Chapter 6, there are many sources of information available and many of them are free. Exhibit 8.2 shows sources retailers find useful for location decisions.

*EXHIBIT 8.2*
*Sources of*
*Information*
*for Location*
*Decisions*

1. National government (such as Statistics Canada census data at census tract level) and regional government (such as regional planning boards data)
2. Local government (such as city engineering and planning department data)
3. Local Chamber of Commerce
4. Real estate firms (especially commercial divisions)
5. Local developers and shopping centre managers
6. Publications of buying power (such as *Financial Post Survey of Markets*)
7. Consultants and research organization
8. One's own market research studies (such as traffic counts)

## CHOICE OF MAJOR MARKET AREA

The choice of a country, a region, or a city depends on both personal and business reasons. Exhibit 8.3 provides a list of business considerations generally found useful at this stage of analysis.

This process can be facilitated by dividing areas of a map into "grids" for more detailed examination. For each of these grids, location of competitors can be plotted, customer counts recorded, and so on. For example, one may isolate major metro-

EXHIBIT 8.3
Market Area
Considerations

1. Political/legal circumstances
2. Geographic size, climate, and extent of the market area
3. Economic growth potential
4. Population size, age composition, density, and growth
5. Income and spending levels
6. Frequency of shopping and average purchase
7. Total purchasing power and retail trade potential (adjusted for outshopping)
8. Competitive saturation
9. Labour market conditions, transportation, advertising media, financial institutions, etc.
10. Proximity to supply from vendors

politan areas and then gather information about each of these in turn. It is important to remember that the more desirable an area appears, the more likely other retailers will also be interested, and thus, the more likely that the area will become over-stored. Wal-Mart is a dramatic example of a firm that succeeded, in part, because it chose locations where its competitors were not interested in locating—small town America.

## CHOICE OF RETAIL AREA TYPE

There are a variety of retail location types, ranging from isolated, free-standing spots to locations in a megamall. When considering these options, some of the major factors to examine include:

- Access to customers
- Costs (capital and operating)
- Extent of self-determination (e.g., hours of operation)
- Image
- Neighbouring retail marketers

Exhibit 8.4 shows twelve major types of retail locations. Each of these types has numerous variations, so their definitions are somewhat general.

EXHIBIT 8.4
Major Types of
Retail Locations

### In non-enclosed shopping areas

1. central business districts
2. clusters of neighbourhood stores
3. isolated locations
4. strip malls/centres

**In enclosed shopping areas**

5. neighbourhood centres
6. community centres
7. regional centres
8. power centres
9. theme malls
10. megamalls

**In other stores**

11. concessions/leased departments

**Non-store**

12. mail order, etc.

The first group of locations is **free-standing stores**, that is, stores that are not located inside shopping centres or other stores. In such locations, retailers locate on the streetfront.

**Central business districts (CBDs)**    CBDs and downtowns are frequently "unplanned" in the sense that they have evolved over time and are not controlled by a single owner or association empowered to require conformity. This has enabled CBDs to take on characters of their own, but it has also often led them to deteriorate relative to centrally managed shopping centres. The CBD is generally the heart of the public transportation system and is frequented by pedestrian shoppers, and retailers located in the CBD will usually fight hard to keep it that way. Most CBDs contain the major branches of department, apparel, and specialty stores and, often, no major grocery outlets. CBDs are generally characterized by lots of hospitality and entertainment retailing.

In some CBDs, there has been extensive revitalization; in others, lack of political agreement and/or funds has resulted in substantial decline. Many CBDs contain major shopping centres and office complexes with ancilliary retail space. A variation on CBD development is the substantial underground shopping networks in some metropolitan areas. In Toronto's CBD, for example, there are approximately 3.5 kilometres of underground walkways linking more than 600 stores, many of which are actually located underground.[5]

The frame of a CBD is the area immediately surrounding the core, and it is characterized by less dependence on pedestrian traffic. Secondary business districts are areas servicing major portions of a city. They can be thought of as mini-CBDs. String or strip street districts develop along mass transportation lines or main thoroughfares.

**Clusters of neighbourhood stores**    There are clusters of stores located throughout neighbourhoods, yet still free-standing and not managed centrally. Such stores tend to be oriented toward providing convenience goods and they serve small trading areas.

**Isolated locations**   There are also free-standing stores along highways, in rural areas, on the fringes of cities, and so on. These are frequently occupied by either "small town variety stores" or larger "shopping goods stores" that can locate in less-expensive places (such as discount furniture stores on the edge of town).

**Strip malls/centres**   Sometimes known as plazas, strip malls typically consist of less than 150 000 square feet of space and contain 4 to 10 stores, adjacent to one another, without a common area inside (that is, there are separate store entrances from a common parking area in front of the strip but off the street). Some newer centres are putting the parking behind the stores rather than in front. Strips usually have convenience-oriented stores, such as a dry cleaner, video rental store, bank, donut shop, and convenience variety store. The number of strip malls has been growing rapidly whereas growth in the number of other types of shopping centres has slowed down dramatically. Strips cost less to build and to occupy, can "in-fill neighbourhoods" (provide locations between other retail centres), provide better identification of stores to customers, and offer in-and-out convenience to customers.[6]

The second set of locations is **inside shopping centres**, where retailers locate "on the aisle." Shopping centres are a relatively recent retail form, having evolved from "markets" of old. Harold Carlson, an eminent authority on shopping centres, has argued that shopping centres have had extraordinary impact on retailing and on society:

> However, in an operational sense, a shopping center is a management concept, not a building. As a planned collection of retail outlets, each with its own identity, each independently owned, but all working together as a single business enterprise, they have transformed the landscape of America (and elsewhere) in a little over 40 years and have had a major impact on our way of life. . . .
>
> If a marketer were seeking to be in direct contact with the largest number of Americans possible at one time, chances are the marketer's best bet would be to go to the shopping centers of the nation on any Saturday afternoon. Current research indicates that almost every American adult visits a shopping center at least once a month—that's more than 170 million people 18 years or older. Most make about two trips to a center every week. Increasingly, they are America's choice for leisure time activities and entertainment. While privately owned, many centers are the de facto hub of community life.[7]

Shopping centres can and should be managed as large stores—with both ultimate customers and intermediate customers (the retail tenants) to satisfy. For example, shopping centres have an image of their own, above and beyond the stores they include, which bears on whether shoppers patronize the centre.[8] Leonard Berry spoke of shopping centres as follows:

The right way to think about a shopping mall is to think of it as a very big store. Each of its pieces should fit together. A cohesive theme and a consistent pattern should prevail. The mall should represent an attraction, an overall bundle of benefits, that is greater than the sum of its parts. The mall should be a strong brand—a clear promise—that tells consumers what to expect. It should be an effective means for unifying otherwise independent retailers so that the promise is delivered.[9]

Definitions of enclosed shopping centres vary somewhat.

**Neighbourhood centres**    A neighbourhood centre is a small, enclosed 10 000 to 100 000 square foot shopping mall selling convenience goods and services. There are usually 10 to 20 stores, often anchored by a conventional supermarket.

**Community centres**    Community centres are the next step up from neighbourhood centres. These offer broader selections of both convenience and shopping goods in 100 000 to 200 000 square feet of selling space and 20 to 30 stores, usually anchored by a junior department store and supermarket.

**Regional centres**    Regional centres are bigger still. These are at least 200 000 square feet, with 75 to 200 or more stores specializing in apparel and general merchandise. Often, there is no supermarket, but rather one or two full-line department stores. A related form is super-regional centres, which are bigger multilevel versions of the regional centre, containing at least three main anchors and a minimum of one million square feet of space.

**Power centres**    Power centres are a new retail type, or at least the name is new. These are very large strip malls, typically anchored by 2 to 5 large promotional category leader stores (such as Toys 'R' Us) or a superwarehouse supermarket (such as Loblaws larger units). Generally, there are few stores, and most of the space is taken by the anchors. These centres are 225 000 plus square feet and usually located on or near major highways or their arteries.[10]

**Theme malls**    Theme malls can be of all sizes. They are distinct from other forms in that they focus on limited categories of goods or particular types of stores. For example, recently, many off-price malls and factory-outlet malls have been built. Home design has also been a popular theme. For example, Homeworld is under construction just outside Toronto:

> Homeworld will be the largest shopping complex in North America dedicated exclusively to the home. The 1.4 million square foot project combines retail, showcases and services. It will include indoor parking for 2,000 cars. Home World is scheduled for a fall 1991 opening.[11]

**Megamalls**    This term is used for the largest shopping centre complexes, which are millions of square feet in size. They contain at least 3 to 5 full-line department store anchors, a wide variety of 400 to 850 specialty stores (often with multiple locations in the same complex), and usually a lot of entertainment attractions. West Edmonton Mall in Edmonton, Alberta, has been a prototype. Currently under construction, the Mall of America in Bloomington, Indiana, will be 2.6 million square feet with 8 department stores; 600 to 800 specialty shops, restaurants, nightclubs; 18 theatres, and so on.[12]

Two other locational options are **concessions/leased departments** and **non-store**. Concessions/leased departments are essentially stores within stores. Many larger stores, especially department stores and mass retailers, are willing to rent space to operators of small shops. This provides a home for the smaller operator and an enhanced assortment for the bigger store. Frequent users include specialty apparel retailers and a broad range of service retailers, such as opticians, travel agents, hair salons, and financial services. Non-store locations is the miscellaneous category for all other retail marketers, such as vending machine operators, mail order vendors, and door-to-door firms.

Each of these types of locations has its own advantages and disadvantages and each has special management challenges.[13] With the 1990/91 recession and over-storing in North America, there have been fewer new locations opened (especially major shopping centres), more emphasis on renovation, and more opportunity to take over another's lease. Specialty store expansion has slowed and major operators have been exploring the possibility of making their stores "destination stores," that is, less reliant on the attraction of a centre or neighbouring retailers.[14]

All retailers, when making location decisions, face the question of whether to go where customers are (and pay higher real estate costs) or to go where customers are not (and pay higher advertising and other costs to attract customers to them). This issue and others related to choice of location are discussed on the following pages.

## TRADING AREA

Before discussing site selection, it is important to understand the concept of a trading area. Each store or group of stores has a trading area. A store's **trading area** is the geographic area where the majority of the store's customers (or potential) customers live or work. Most retailers think in terms of where customers live; however, for those retailers who rely on customers shopping near where they work (such as a restaurant in a CBD reliant on lunch-time business), it is much more relevant to concentrate on where customers are employed. A trading area can be defined in terms of distance or driving or walking time. It is often divided into zones of **core, primary, secondary**, and **tertiary shoppers**, although such division is not necessary for many retailers. For example, core shoppers may be defined as the one-quarter of the total customer base of a store comprised of the most frequent, highest volume customers. Such a definition is arbitrary.

The major reasons for determining a trading area are (*a*) to determine market potential, and (*b*) to assist in planning the scope of advertising and other marketing efforts.

There are three basic techniques used to determine the size and shape of a store or shopping centre's trading area. Some are elegant, such as gravitational and demand-gradient models; others are quite mundane, such as customer-origin recording. Whatever technique is used, it is important to undertake the effort from time to time. The size, shape, and composition of the trading area is critical to a retailer's success. If an area cannot support the retailer, sooner or later he or she will be out of business.[15] Obviously, it is much easier to determine a store's existing rather than its potential trading area. If none of the following methods can be used, a retail marketer may simply have to work out a couple of "best estimates," using whatever information is available.

## Customer Spotting

A straightforward method of determining one's trading area is to draw a representative sample of the store's customers and plot their residence or work addresses on a map.[16] The sample can be obtained in a number of ways: (*a*) *indirectly*, through credit records, sales slips, mailing list analysis, having a contest, or even licence plate analysis, and/or (*b*) *directly*, by asking customers. A common method today is the use of postal codes. In Canada, each six-digit postal code represents a very small geographic area, so using postal codes is generally sufficiently accurate for trade area identification. The trading area can be determined either by drawing lines encompassing certain proportions of the customer base (such as 50 percent, then 75 percent, etc.) or by drawing successive circles a certain distance away from the store (such as one-half kilometre, one kilometre, etc.) and seeing how many customers are in each circle. Whatever the method, the idea is to get an understanding of the source of customers relative to the store's (or shopping centre's) location.

## Retail Gravitational Models

Less straightforward for the retail practitioner is the use of gravitational models. Such models are used primarily by market geographers and planners conversant with statistics. These are generally used to predict future trading areas using such factors as population size and distance. Most models build upon the seminal work of W.J. Reilly. Reilly's Law is an equation that holds that a trading area is predictable from the size of its market centre.[17] That is, its formulation is based on the notion that the bigger the store (or group of stores), the greater its attraction power and, hence, the bigger its trading area.

P.D. Converse added a variation to this notion by examining the relative attraction of two centres to determine how customers between the centres will behave. He formulated a method of calculating the "breaking point" between two trading areas, or the point at which customers are indifferent about shopping at either of the two locations.[18] By calculating several breaking points, one can determine the boundaries of one centre's (or store's) trading area relative to surrounding competitors.

### Demand-Gradient Models

Demand-gradient models have been built on the basic assumption that the greater the number of items carried by a retail centre, the larger a shopper's expectation that a trip to the centre will be successful and, hence, the more likely he or she will travel to that centre than to another. Thus, for any one centre, there are "probability curves" that diminish outward around it where these probability curves represent the probability that customers in that "gradient" will patronize the centre. For example, a large regional shopping centre will have a larger trading area than a small strip mall, and the demand gradients will be correspondingly spread farther apart. The 50 percent gradient will be tightly drawn around a small convenience store, whereas it will be much farther away for a regional general merchandise mall.

Both gravitational and demand-gradient models are most often used for city and regional planning purposes and less by individual retailers. They require good data and statistical understanding. The assumptions behind these models should be examined whenever they are used. For example, they assume that size is an adequate proxy for all the other features of a shopping centre to determine why customers patronize one rather than another. While there is no question that size is important, increasingly it seems customers spread their shopping trips among several centres and stores, and thus do not regularly or predictably always go more to the bigger centres.[19]

Trade areas are really circles only in theory; seldom are they circles in reality. There are many factors that influence the actual trading area's physical size and shape, as shown in Exhibit 8.5.

---

*EXHIBIT 8.5*
*Factors Affecting Actual Trading Area Size and Shape*

**1.** Natural and artificial barriers, such as rivers, railways, hills.

**2.** Proximity to larger or more attractive market areas—a rural general store will have a larger geographic trading area than an equivalent store in a city.

**3.** Available transportation—ease of getting around by public and private means.

**4.** Psychology of distance prevailing in that area—some people seem to find a block too far to walk.

**5.** Existing competitive alignment—who else is close by that will impact on drawing power of the store.

**6.** Population density—in a highly dense population, such as Tokyo, trade areas can be small geographically but still contain adequate numbers of people.

**7.** Buying habits of people. For example, Europeans still do much of their shopping without a car, but this determines the range they will travel from home.

**8.** Communication—factors such as the circulation of local paper will affect who even knows about the store and its offerings.

---

## FACTORS TO CONSIDER WHEN EVALUATING A SPECIFIC SITE

Anyone considering establishing a store on a new site or acquiring an existing store has a host of factors to assess. Retailers usually have their own priorities when assessing specific sites. Some seem to place more emphasis on demand, others on competition, and still others seem to focus on costs. These leanings will influence which specific methods are used to evaluate the many characteristics of particular sites. Some techniques are simple judgmental ranking approaches, whereas others are more sophisticated statistical techniques. The intent of each approach is the same: to narrow down alternatives and to assist in making a choice with a good chance of success.[20]

Exhibit 8.6 provides a list of factors that often bear on the attractiveness of any particular site to a retailer.

---

*EXHIBIT 8.6*
*Considerations in Site Selection*

**Questions to consider, with some examples:**

1. Is the site close to a sufficient number of the target customers? If intending to attract female teenagers, how close is it to the high school? In other words, what is the volume and quality of shopping traffic (vehicular and pedestrian) by this site now and potentially?

2. Is the site easily accessible to customers? Where are public transportation stops, how wide is the street and is it divided, which side of street gets the most traffic, is there much traffic congestion, is there available parking (number of spaces, cost of parking, its distance to the store)?

3. What is the history of the site? Have other similar retailers been at the same site and failed? Is there any "stigma" attached to the site that may affect business?

4. What are conditions like around the site? Are there neighbouring retailers who are complementary in business who will increase customer traffic, are there excessive store vacancies, is there crime and/or unpleasant loitering, are sidewalks in good repair, what hours are other retailers open?

5. How strong are nearby competitors and how many are there? Are apparent sales in these stores unusually high, do customers find stores crowded and service slow, do customers have to travel farther than they want to shop?

   An index of retail saturation can be calculated as follows: number of customers in the area times retail expenditures in this category per customer, all divided by the square footage of selling area of all competitors in that category in the trading area, including the proposed new store, equals the Index of Retail Saturation per square foot. This number represents the average sales per square foot of all competitors. If this number is substantially below the level required for a profitable operation, then the area is overstored already and the retailer should be sure he or she can compete successfully with established firms before settling on the site.

6. Is the site visible? Can signs and/or the storefront be seen at an appropriate distance?

7. What are the relevant physical characteristics of the site and its building? What is the size, condition, and shape of the lot and building, what will be the investment requirements?

8. What are the terms of occupancy? How much will it cost to own or lease, to operate and maintain? Occupancy costs include rent or mortgage, overhead, common area costs, taxes, and any other costs that are directly related to doing business in that

location. What are the zoning and other local regulations (and perhaps lease terms) that will impact on what the retailer can and cannot do with the property?

9. How important is convenience of location relative to spending resources on other aspects of the marketing program to attract customers to a less convenient location? Is it better to spend extra money to locate in a high-traffic spot or to spend money advertising to draw people to a less-high-traffic spot?

---

Of course, all the preceding considerations must be translated into sales and financial projections to determine whether the site will meet the retailer's objectives. A list of selection criteria such as in Exhibit 8.6 prompts many retailers to develop a site ranking scheme. Typically, either an average or a weighted score is assigned to each site in total. Such approaches have the obvious attraction of simplifying the many considerations into an index number; however, care must be taken to avoid double-counting factors (such as including profit and factors that presumably determine profit) in the index and to identify where judgments are being made. The tradeoffs are, of necessity, judgmental in the final analysis.

## APPROACHES TO ESTIMATING MARKET POTENTIAL

One of the most challenging tasks facing any marketer is the preparation of sales forecasts. When assessing a site, a retail marketer should attempt some forecasting. There are a few basic approaches to this task.

**Analog methods**    If the retailer has had experience with a comparable site or store(s), then an approach that may be used is to develop an analog from existing experience as a basis for predicting the future at this site. For example, a chain store executive may match a proposed site with two or three existing stores most similar to the proposal. Then, based on the history of the existing store(s), projections for the proposed store are developed, making whatever adjustments seem appropriate in the numbers. Projected sales, for instance, may be calculated on a sales per square foot formula when store sizes vary.

The analog method is sometimes extended by using statistical techniques such as multiple regression analysis. Such a model may be built using many existing stores as a base. Then, using this model, any proposed store and site can be "plugged into" the model and forecasts generated. Care should be taken when using such approaches that they do not become too mechanical. Any retailer considering a new site had better include time at the site looking around, as opposed to sitting in a distant office playing with numbers on a computer.

**Share-of-space, share-of-sales methods**    If there is no comparable experience to use as an analog, a retailer must use a "market build-up" method of forecasting. If the necessary data are available or can be reasonably estimated, then the approach is straightforward. Multiply the number of households in the expected trading area by the mean annual disposable income. Then, multiply this number by the proportion of an average household's disposable income that, on average, is spent on the specific product or service category in question. This provides a rough estimate of sales in total in the area. For example, suppose for a mythical trading area that average household disposable income is $25 000, the number of households 1000, and the proportion spent on clothing is 10 percent; then the sales of clothing in that trading area is $2.5 million. (Notice, this approach does not take into account "out-shopping." If residents in a trading area do much of their apparel shopping in another city (or across the border), the local trade area potential may appear statistically larger than it really is for the stores in that trading area.)

The remaining question is how much of that total calculated potential a retailer considering a new site may achieve. In the above example, the retailer may judge that, since his or her new store will account for one-fifth of the space in the trading area devoted to apparel retailing, sales will, in time at least, be $500 000. This may not be a reasonable conclusion to reach; however, it is important to remember that the accuracy of such a judgment that may be assisted by calculating the index of retail saturation (shown in Exhibit 8.6), by assessing the relative strength of competitors, and by assessing realistically one's attractiveness to customers.

## LAYOUT

Store layout is part of the physical facility design of any retail space. Retail space is never neutral. It communicates many messages to customers and staff about what the retailer sells, cares about, and wants to be known for. Layout involves both physical and psychological dimensions. Davidson defined layout as follows: "Store layout is the spatial arrangement of selling and non-selling departments, aisles, fixtures, display facilities, and equipment in the proper relationship to each other and to the fixed elements of the structure."[21]

In this section, layout is discussed. The combination of layout and atmospherics has a powerful impact on customer traffic and buying patterns. Atmospherics is discussed in Chapter 12. Layout decisions in particular often involve making longer-term commitments and must, therefore, be approached with care. As with other dimensions of "convenience," an understanding of one's customers is absolutely essential, as Kmart has learned:

> K-Mart, for example, recently conducted an analysis of its shopper base and identified five basic types of shoppers who shop at K-Mart for different reasons and follow different shopping patterns through the store. The study revealed that two of these five shopper types, representing nearly one-half of the shoppers, never get into the softlines side of the store. Despite K-Mart's tremendous improvements in apparel merchandise over the past five years, increased advertising and heavy promotion would have little success in getting these shoppers ever to look at or try soft goods because they simply never visit that side of the store.
>
> Understanding these shoppers' specific merchandise interests enabled K-Mart to develop a new layout which uses certain "magnet" departments to draw

customers throughout the entire store, making every shopper behave like the most productive of the K-Mart shopper types, the "full-path" shopper.

K-Mart found that the most efficient layout to accomplish this is a center apparel layout with destination hardlines along the perimeter of the store, cross-aisle from related soft-goods. While this center apparel layout has caused some debate as to whether it moves too far from K-Mart's hard-hitting promotional image, the impact of full-path shopping now appears to be very compelling.[22]

Store size, layout, assortment, and other dimensions of the retail marketing program are all interrelated. For example, store sizes have been increasing for most retailers over the past two decades; but, recently, there has been downsizing for many, and growing conviction that customers do not always think bigger stores are better stores. This is the classic trade-off for customers and retail marketers between assortment and convenience. Management of Houston-based Bonham's Fiesta Mart stores has been grappling with this issue in food retailing. While their average store size had been about 85 000 square feet, they recently opened a 185 000 square foot supermarket but are now having second thoughts:

> Consumer resistance to large supermarkets has led some retailers to rethink their decisions about size. For instance, Bonham is looking for a way to remerchandise the Johnson Space Center store [185 000 square feet] to make it easier to shop. Meanwhile, Fiesta has opened two units in its normal prototype size since the big one was opened, and is readying three more about the same size. Although Bonham did not discuss the sales of the big store, he says the 85,000 square foot unit opened in November is doing about the same volume as the giant unit. . . .
>
> Fiesta found that most people have been shopping the big store only once a month. People will shop in a supermarket for only about 45 minutes, Bonham says. They want the total trip to be about one hour, including drive time. . . .
>
> "Consumers say they love the [big] store. But we are getting a lot of complaints about the 'two hour shop', and a great deal of resistance. Shoppers definitely feel it is too big, according to exit interviews," Bonham says.[23]

Most shopping centre stores are shaped much like shoeboxes: about four times as deep as they are wide. In these spaces, retail managers must decide how wide to make the entrance, whether to angle it, whether to have open or closed windows, what kind of flooring to use, where to position cash registers, and so on. While there are many techniques involved, most aspects of layout are based on a thorough understanding of customers. For example, knowing that most customers will turn right upon entering the store, go into the store about twenty feet then pause; that 75 percent of merchandise is sold from displays at heights ranging from the average customer's waist to eye level; that most people don't pay much attention to exterior store signs—all suggest that some layout alternatives are more desirable than others. It is no accident that the "power wall" is on the right wall near the entrance in most stores, that free-standing fixtures are used to encourage traffic circulation, that department stores use a "racetrack" main aisle about twenty feet from their perimeters, and so on. An astute retail marketer studies customers carefully in all kinds of stores to get insights into how to design his or her own layout. Beyond these observations, there are some general principles for layout decisions.

## OBJECTIVES

Usually, layout involves conflicting objectives: providing customer convenience while maximizing sales. Retailers faced with ever-increasing space costs must utilize space effectively and efficiently, which means exposing the customer to the maximum amount of the merchandise assortment or at least the highest margin merchandise carried. Barry Mason and Morris Mayer provided the following objectives for layout:

- Increase the consumer's ability to make intelligent decisions
- Walk the customer throughout the store if possible
- Facilitate related item selling
- Facilitate trading-up to higher quality or higher priced items
- Emphasize the full range of the assortment
- Facilitate inventory control and stockkeeping
- Enhance the appearance of the store and support the positioning strategy of the firm[24]

According to Dale Lewison and Wayne Lozier:

> For the customer, a good interior design has wide, uncluttered aisles, easy-to-find merchandise, logical merchandise groupings, and attractive surroundings. For the retailer, a well-designed store interior (1) enhances employee productivity by reducing the amount of time and effort they must spend to complete sales transactions; (2) provides maximum product exposure and encourages impulse buying by permitting the customer ease of movement and a broad view of the store's interior from any place within the store; (3) keeps product-handling requirements to a minimum by facilitating a smooth, orderly flow of goods from the time the retailer receives them to the time it sells them to the customer; (4) discourages employee and customer theft by promoting an open yet controlled environment; and (5) enhances the physical and psychological well-being of employees by creating a desirable working environment.[25]

## FACTORS

There are many interrelated factors to consider, as shown in Exhibit 8.7.[26]

*EXHIBIT 8.7*
*Layout*
*Considerations*

**Things to consider, with some examples:**

1. Type of operation. What level of service will be offered and where does this mean staff and cash registers will be located?

2. Buying habits of target market. Do customers arrive with pre-planned selections made or do they make their decisions in-store based on what they encounter, how do they tend to move around the store?

3. Size and shape of available space. Are windows and doors in such positions as to leave few options for arrangement of fixtures?

4. Nature and number of fixtures and equipment required. If displaying clothing on hanging racks, how high are the racks and how many garments will each hold.

5. Location of space needed for permanent installations. Where are the elevators, escalators, receiving areas, etc.?

6. Amount and characteristics of the merchandise to be carried. Frozen food needs to be in freezers, etc.

7. Planned atmospherics and effects. To convey an upscale image, fewer items are usually displayed with more expensive "props" to show them off, and so on.

8. Security. How do you avoid blind spots in the store that are easy for shop lifting?

---

Lusch and Dunne provided some useful specific guidelines for layout:

1. Aisles need to be wide enough that they are easy to get through, even when customers stop to examine merchandise.

2. Aisles need to be short enough that the customers aren't forced to go through a maze of goods to reach a specific item at the end of the aisle.

3. The store entrance should be free of obstacles or clutter that may interfere with the flow of customers into or out of the store; this could cause "crowding stress".

4. Try to visualize how the traffic should move to reach the entire store, then arrange the fixtures, displays, and aisles to help route the traffic this way.

5. Place staple goods in more remote areas of the store, because the traffic patterns will move to them.

6. Place impulse goods in high traffic areas.

7. Place frequently purchased goods in easy-access areas.

8. Remember your target market, especially the elderly, might have special needs that must be considered in developing traffic patterns.

9. Remember no amount of promotion or selling expertise will overcome a poorly designed store layout. If the product category is in the wrong place, the sale is usually lost.[27]

## DECISIONS

Although there are many factors to consider, most retailers have found the following steps helpful in making layout decisions:

1. Allocate total floor space on a preliminary basis.

2. Departmentalize the assortment.

3. Determine space requirements for each department or merchandise group.

4. Choose the basic floor plan for each area and in total.

**5.** Prepare a specific floor plan. Repeat previous steps if necessary.

Each of these steps is discussed in detail on the following pages.

## Allocate Floor Space

There are three major uses of space in most retail operations and, thus, a retailer must divide the total available space among these: building functions, nonselling space, and selling space. The precise amount of space for each depends on both the general type of retailer and the specific way of doing business. For example, a chain store being resupplied frequently from a nearby warehouse may need very little inventory storage area, whereas another store offering imported items may have substantial in-store storage area. The first major use is for building functions, that is, heating, air conditioning, elevators, escalators, security, and so on. These are functions almost independent of the way the retailer does business. The second major use is for nonselling services, such as receiving, marking, stock, offices, cafeteria, alterations, and workrooms. The third, and usually largest use of space is the sales area or selling floor, which includes the assortment on display, sales desks, fitting rooms, the return desk, customer service areas, and rest rooms. The selling area is typically 65–85 percent of total space (or what is often referred to as gross leasable area, GLA).

## Departmentalize

The larger the store and the assortment, the more the customer needs to encounter some kind of organization in the store to help find specific items. The usual approach in such instances is to departmentalize. A logical grouping of the merchandise helps customers find items and also helps management control the assortment by having separate buying teams, separate performance records, and so on.

There are several ways in which one might divide up the assortment (and, hence, the store). The possible criteria may include:

**a.** complementariness in use of items; that is, which items are used together and, hence, could be sold together (cross-selling)

**b.** vendor name groupings (such as designer boutiques within the store)

**c.** display or service needs (for example, merchandise that needs to be assembled, such as skis)

**d.** lifestyle groupings (for example, a working women's department)

**e.** price points (for example, a bargain floor).

A good guide for choosing among these options is what the target customer is already used to , might expect, and might like. For example, although one could arrange men's dress shirts by brand, by fit, by colour, by size, by price, or by fabric, most men prefer to find their sizes very quickly and then make their selection. (Incidentally, women are the major buyers of men's shirts.)

## Determine Space Requirements

Once the overall assortment has been departmentalized, the next step is to determine how much space is required on a category and even item-by-item basis. There are two basic approaches. One approach calculates space on rules-of-thumb relationships between space and sales. The other is a build-up method beginning from the desired stock position the retailer wishes to carry.

**Sales productivity ratios**    This method assigns floor space on the basis of sales per square foot achieved or forecasted for each category. For example, if one forecasted $50 000 in sales of shirts and if the historical average sales per square foot in one's other stores has been $125, then one might allocate 400 square feet to shirts in the new store. A retailer can choose this approach based on his or her own data or on industry averages. It is not always the best approach, especially if the merchandise is highly seasonal.

**Model stock approach**    Following this method, one calculates the amount of space necessary to carry each part of an appropriate assortment of merchandise in each category. One may proceed manually or use a computer. Exhibit 8.8 shows the steps.

*EXHIBIT 8.8 Steps in Model Stock Space Requirements Calculation*

1. Calculate the desired model stock, including list of items to be carried and desired quantity of each by colour, size, brand, etc.
2. Calculate the number of each of the SKUs to be kept both on the floor and in inventory in-store.
3. Decide how best to display the merchandise.
4. Calculate the number of fixtures required.
5. Calculate how much space is required for service functions, such as cash desk, fitting rooms, etc., and where these might be located. (The cash register desk, for example, is usually at the front to allow the customer to pay on the way out and to provide a security check between the customer and the door.)
6. Decide how to handle reserve stock (on the floor versus in storeroom) and calculate space requirements.
7. Total all the space requirements for the department or area of the store.
8. Reconcile this particular department or area with all the other departments. Repeat previous steps if necessary.

## Choose Type of Floor Plan

There are seemingly endless ways to arrange the layout of a store; however, there are two basic types that direct the flow of customer traffic: the grid and the free-flow pattern.

**Grid**   The grid is a rectangular arrangement of fixtures and aisles in a repetitive, homogeneous pattern, usually at right angles. This layout is frequently used by grocery and discount department stores. However, the aisles do not have to be at right angles to the front of the store. Sometimes, retailers angle the gondolas (the shelving units) so that a customer at the front of the store can see more of what is "down the aisle." When designing the grid pattern, one must decide where key items will be placed. For example, customers slow down when turning at the ends of aisles so these positions are good isolated spots for special displays and promotions — so valuable, in fact, that supermarkets sell this space. Also, one must decide how long the aisles will be, whether there will be cross-aisles, and how wide the aisles will be. The grid layout has become associated with high-volume, low-price stores. Accordingly, many of the "superstores/category killers" have used the grid layout to associate themselves with the image it gives. Exhibit 8.9 shows some advantages and disadvantages of the grid layout.

*Exhibit 8.9*
*The Grid Layout*

**Advantages:**

I. Customers like this for routine shopping, get familiar with it, and find it simple

2. Relatively low cost to build, fixture, and maintain

3. Facilitates self-selection selling

4. Exposes customers to maximum amount of merchandise

5. Security simplified—checkouts at entrance/exit

**Disadvantages:**

I. Tends to encourage "getting the shopping done" rather than browsing

2. Not very exciting, especially since, usually, very few fixture types used (most frequent is gondola shelving, as in supermarkets); limits creativity in decor and display

Supermarkets have long experimented with variations on the grid layout. Thomas Cullen, grandson of Michael Cullen, who founded "America's first supermarket" in 1930, was recently asked about his company's dramatic changes in layout:

> The traffic pattern is the most significant feature of the remodeling. Rather than following the conventional pattern, in which aisles run perpendicular to the front end, the gondolas are set diagonally. The design steers shoppers to high margin perishables departments at both ends of nearly every aisle. The repeated exposure—particularly to the produce section—is designed to spur sales. "We keep throwing it back in their eyes," says Cullen of produce. A shopper who picks up pasta in the grocery section and gets funnelled back to produce is likely to think, "Maybe I'll get some broccoli to go with it." says Cullen.
> . . . "after the remodelling, the volume perked up tremendously."[28]

**Free flow**  Using this layout, the merchandise and fixtures are grouped into patterns that form curving aisles. One subtype is the boutique, that is, small shops, each having its own identity. Another subtype is the loop, that is, curving aisles, often in a "racetrack" around the perimeter of the store. With the free flow approach, frequently many of the fixtures are irregular in shape. Exhibit 8.10 provides some of the advantages and disadvantages of the free flow layout.

EXHIBIT 8.10
The Free-flow
Layout

---

**Advantages:**

1. Encourages browsing lingering, and free movement
2. Visually appealing because it allows greater use of display and merchandising techniques and, in turn, facilitates impulse buying
3. Flexible
4. Promotes distinct departmental identities

**Disadvantages:**

1. May be confusing to customers
2. May require higher labour requirements if providing on-floor service
3. May be more costly because it does not use floor space as efficiently
4. Customers are exposed to less merchandise

---

## Design the Specific Floor Plan

Once the space requirements of individual departments or areas have been estimated, the next step is to arrange all of the parts into the whole, much like putting a jigsaw puzzle together. There are many issues to consider. For example, allocation of specific space should be done after considering how much effort customers will expend for specific items (recall discussion in Chapter 4), sales and margin returns expected, display and other requirements, seasonality, staffing, and other factors. Of all these factors, customer behaviour is most important. For example, "contemplative goods" (goods that customers need time to consider, such as jewellery and furniture) should be located where customers can deliberate without being rushed or jostled. Some areas of the store have more customer traffic and, therefore, are more valuable for certain items. In a multi-level store, for example, the main floor is best and the top floor worst. In most stores, the front is better than back (one rule of thumb is that only one-quarter of all customers go more than one-half way into an average store). Other good areas are near elevators, escalators, and entrances. Most people turn right when entering. Also, inside corners are generally avoided.

Layout decisions are interconnected, that is, rearranging one department often leads to rearranging others. Layout choices should be made with recognition that some areas are traffic generators, that space adjacent to high-traffic areas is most appropriate for high-turnover promotional impulse items, that shopping goods are typically best placed in nonprime areas, that support services are usually best in nonprime but easily accessible areas, and that secluded areas (where visibility of merchandise and customers is poor) present security problems. Here are some more decisions to make about the actual layout:

1.  How close should product displays and stored inventory be to each other?
2.  Where should seasonal products be placed?
3.  How can customer crowding around the cash register be avoided by using "surge areas" (areas that are relatively larger to accommodate peaks in traffic, such as long weekend lineups of shopping carts in supermarkets)?
4.  Which products should be displayed at the front and which at the back of the store?
5.  Where should promotions be placed?
6.  How should the special needs of the physically challenged and elderly be accommodated?

## ITEM PLACEMENT

Although more details of merchandising are treated in Chapters 10 and 12, it is important to recognize the convenience aspect of item arrangement in this chapter. As shown in the Kmart story above, shoppers develop patterns of moving around in stores that can have a profound effect on the retailer's sales and profitability. Good item placement follows the same basic principles as departmental layout, but on a smaller scale, of course. There are many ways to arrange items within departments and on displays, such as by size, by colour, and by brand name. Generally speaking, the retailer needs to find the dimensions of most interest to customers and use that as the basis for item arrangement. For example, if customers find it most convenient to select blouses on the basis of size first and then colour, organizing blouses by brand name would be inappropriate.

A good general rule for item arrangement is as follows: "Each item should earn the space that it occupies by producing a sales volume and gross margin contribution that is commensurate with the quantity of space, weighted by its location value within the department."[29]

This rule has to be abandoned at times (such as for very high-turnover items that can be restocked frequently), but it should be set aside knowingly. Item-movement, item-cost, and item-profitability information is necessary to make such decisions (recall the discussion of merchandise performance in Chapter 3).

Items should be arranged to make shopping easy for customers, to encourage them to buy related items, and, when appropriate, to encourage trading up. In supermarkets, this system is seemingly down to a science. Eye-level shelf position and end-of-aisle cappers are prime locations and are usually given to the best sellers and most profitable items. Some supermarket operators even put larger-sized versions of items on the right side of smaller items (as the customer looks at the shelf), reasoning that more people are right-handed and thus more likely to pick up the larger sizes.

Beyond such ideas, most retailers use one form or another of the **plan-o-gram**, which is a schematic of a shelf or fixture or department, showing the exact locations of each item of merchandise. This kind of planning (especially practised by major supermarket and mass merchandiser chains) enables careful experimentation with shelf positions for products, helps shelf restocking, and ensures a greater measure of management control over store presentation (especially important with multiple units).

Computer-assisted shelf management techniques (such as Spaceman and Apollo) are designed to use item-movement and item-profitability information to provide suggested shelf arrangements. These programs allow simulations and, among other outputs, produce realistic photos as plan-o-grams for in-store use. The use of such computer programs is growing rapidly.

> Space management systems are to merchandising what the introduction of spreadsheets were to financial planners because "what if" scenarios can be developed. Simply input information on package size, past sales history, projected sales, store deliveries, and other relevant data and out comes an exact representation of the planogram schematic—including pegboard layouts and shelf-space allocations.
>
> Computerized planogramming works by constructing a product data base that includes package size, digitized images of each product, product part numbers/UPC numbers as well as movement data, price/cost information, profit margins, shipment information, and other relevant information.
>
> From the data base, the computer works to establish merchandising placement based on products that have the highest turnover, products with higher gross margins or other criteria that will allocate shelf space to best influence the consumer's behavior.[30]

Our understanding of the impact of store layout and item placement is growing, with more and more research being reported. For example, Park, Iyer, and Smith reported:

> This study demonstrates that consumers' store knowledge and the time available for shopping affect many types of in-store shopping decisions. Both factors have an effect on levels of unplanned buying, brand switching due to difficulty in locating preferred brands/products, and the level of purchase volume deliberation. Knowledge of a store's layout, irrespective of time available for shopping had a positive effect on absolute levels of brand/product switching. Time pressure primarily had an effect on frequency of failure to make intended purchases. . . .
>
> To avoid the potential pitfalls of relying on one particular strategy, a coordinated approach to store environment, which considers in-store aisle and display configurations, product display arrangements, and in-store presentation of information, needs to be taken. These strategies may include (1) arrangement of aisles

based on customers' prior knowledge or expectations of product location, (2) arrangement of product displays for non-staple items in prominent locations to reduce purchase failure rates, (3) joint display of substitutable products to encourage brand-switching as opposed to purchase postponement when a preferred brand/product is not available, and (4) prominent displays of brand or product information to promote the recognition of previously unrecognized needs that encourages unplanned purchasing.[31]

## TRANSACTIONS

A retailer can influence how customers perceive the convenience provided by careful attention to each stage of the shopping trip, from the customer's perspective. For example, a longstanding customer grievance in supermarkets is the time spent waiting in line to check out. In such circumstances, a retailer has three choices: ignore the complaint (and hope for the best), spend money to speed up the delay in reality (such as by having more checkout lanes, rescheduling help, automating the front ends with scanners, hiring extra baggers or asking customers to do their own bagging or even their own checking out),[32] or distract the customer so that the time spent waiting doesn't seem so long. The Checkout Channel is a recent example of an attempt to distract waiting customers. This system involves a series of television monitors placed above the waiting shoppers' heads.

> Checkout Channel will consist of 70% editorial content, on a feed from Atlanta-based Turner Broadcasting System's Cable News Network (CNN). . . . It will be live all the time, customized for the supermarket in-line audience.
> The balance of the eight minute cycle will be national advertising. The monitors will be placed at the checkout section. They will be equipped with sound sensitive directional microphones that will limit the sound portion of the broadcasts to a radius of 4–6 feet, with the speakers positioned away from the checkout personnel to avoid distracting them.[33]

There are many ways to speed up transaction time, including:

1. Having sufficient staff available to serve the number of customers
2. Training staff in all procedures of cash register, credit authorization, etc.
3. Enabling every staff member to authorize cheques
4. Using magnetic-strip readers and automatic dialers for credit card authorization calls
5. Asking only for the necessary information of customers, rather than using the "checkout" as another sales-attempt or market-research venue
6. Doing paperwork on one's own time rather than the customer's time (for example, some banks have many forms to fill out for foreign exchange procedures that are for internal purposes only and could be finished in between serving customers)
7. Paying more attention to the needs of checkout personnel to keep them fresh, motivated, and efficient

8. Providing on-line customer information to avoid asking "the same questions" again and again (Pizza Pizza has long used this approach to speed up orders of pizza from repeat customers, using telephone numbers as customer identifiers). Weber's, a takeout hamburger operation located north of Toronto on Highway 11, speeds up the transaction by having employees work along the customer waiting line. One staff member asks customers for the order, filling in a preprinted form that covers all the menu options. Another staff member follows up by taking the money and returning change. The order goes to the master cook so that, as the line moves along, one's hamburger, fries, etc., are ready approximately at the same time one reaches the counter. The novelty of the approach and its efficiency (one small unit with one grill can serve up to 900 people per hour at peak times) strike customers as sincere attempts to meet their convenience needs. Arby's has approached the same goal of increased convenience with a high-tech solution. Arby's Touch 2000 is a touch-screen computer system that allows customers to place orders. Customers can order in two languages, see what they have ordered, receive a running total of their bill, get prompted for add-ons, and find the whole system faster and easier.[34] Similarly, airlines, car rental firms, dry cleaners, video rental stores, and others have moved recently to speed their transactional operations for the time-conscious customer with "express services."

## HOURS AND DELIVERY

Convenience, from the customer's perspective, also includes the hours that the retailer is available for business. This has become, again, a controversial issue with the debate about Sunday shopping. Generally, the North American trend has been to longer and longer hours of business for all retailers, with some open twenty-four hours a day, seven days a week. Even chartered banks, once content to open their doors at their own convenience, have shifted to "customer-friendly hours." However, it is not clear that longer hours mean more convenience from the shopper's perspective. The convenience of being able to shop at an unusual time (such as the middle of the night or Sunday morning) will be traded off against the kind of service available. European retailers still routinely close their doors at lunchtime, allowing all staff to go for a lengthy lunch. When the doors open, all staff are back on duty. In North America, the tendency seems to be to think the convenience of having the store open (albeit perhaps thinly staffed) is the same as providing good service.

While most store owners are looking at expanding hours, some are going the other direction. Bondar's Four-Day Outlet in Calgary is open 39 hours a week, from 10 a.m. to 9 p.m. Thursdays, Fridays, and Saturdays, and from noon to 6 p.m. on Sundays. This store, modelled after the 4-Day Tire Store in the United States, offers furniture with two-thirds the staff it would need to stay open seven days a week.[35]

There are many related convenience issues, such as delivery and alterations. For example, some car dealerships are now moving to having an evening shift for repair service and providing pickup and delivery service to customers who find regular service times inconvenient.

Automatic banking machines (ABMs) are a good example of finding new ways to offer convenience. The growth of ABMs has been explosive and not confined simply to banks:

> Automated teller machines are found in about 90% of 7-Eleven's Canadian stores. The average ATM does 4,000 transactions a month, is essentially self-serve and generates increased traffic for 7-Eleven without major financial or staffing requirements. At this stage, most banks have installed ATM's in any branches they think are suitable. To expand the ATM network and met the consumers' on-going demand for ever-greater accessibility, c-store installations are seen as a logical step for all parties.[36]

Vending machines, direct mail, telephone and fax ordering, 1–800 lines, and so on are all ways in which retailers are attempting to competitively meet the convenience needs of their customers.

## CONCLUSION

*Convenience is as it is perceived by customers.* Is it easy, quick, and "inexpensive in time and money" to do business with a retailer? The best way to ascertain the answer to this question is to examine all aspects of the customer–retailer interaction from this perspective. Periodically, every retail marketer should undertake an audit of all aspects of his or her retail offering with convenience in mind. Too often retailers have made trade-offs in favour of their own interests instead of their customers' interests. There are too many instances where washrooms are hidden, wanted items are in the back of the store instead of the front, there are no chairs on which to sit, signs are cryptic rather than descriptive, and so on—all indicating a conscious or unconscious lack of effort to meet customers' needs and expectations for shopping convenience. (The next chapter deepens this discussion of "encounters" and "customer relationships" under the heading of customer care and service.)

### REVIEW QUESTIONS

1. If shopping centres should be regarded as large stores, what principles of store layout would you use if asked to design a two-floor regional shopping centre that will have 200 stores offering a very broad range of products and services?

2. Recalling your last shopping trip, what aspects could have been made more convenient for you? What are the implications of your experience for retail marketers?

3. Some retailers have opened stores for the "time-pressed customer." Where would you put such a store? What would its assortment be? How would you lay out the store? What other ways might you operate it to reinforce this positioning?

4. Evaluate "at-home banking" from a convenience standpoint. Electronic home banking means being able to communicate with your bank from your personal computer at any time of the day.

5. If many two-income families become one-income families as a result of a recession, what is the impact, if any, on the importance customers attach to convenience when assessing retail alternatives?

## KEY TERMS

- convenience
- free-standing stores
- central business districts (CBDs)
- clusters of neighbourhood stores
- isolated locations
- strip mall/centres
- neighbourhood centres
- community centres
- regional centres
- power centres
- theme malls
- megamalls
- concession/leased departments
- non-store locations
- trading area

- core (shoppers)
- primary (shoppers)
- secondary (shoppers)
- tertiary (shoppers)
- customer spotting
- retail gravitational models
- demand-gradient models
- analog methods
- share-of-space, share-of-sales methods
- sales productivity ratios
- model stock approach
- grid (floor plan) pattern
- free-flow (flow plan) pattern
- plan-o-gram

## NOTES

1. Patricia McLaughlin, "The Party's Over For the Formerly Shop-Happy," *Sarasota Herald-Tribune*, 19 March 1990, p. 1.

2. Mark Evans, "The Old Milk Store Evolving into One-Stop Shop," *The Financial Post*, 30 October 1989, p. 47.

3. James Careless, "Crossroads: The Canadian Corner Store Has Reached a Turning Point," *Canadian Grocer*, September 1990, pp. 26–30.

4. There are lots of examples. A recent local effort was Tell-A-Cart, which allowed customers to use their modems or fax machines to order home-delivered groceries. See Dominique Lacasse, "Convenience Crunch Spurs Grocery Man," *London Free Press*, 30 January 1989, p. 3.

5. Chris McConvey, "A Study of the Retail Structure of Toronto's Underground Pedestrian System" (term paper for Retail Marketing Management course, Western Business School, The University of Western Ontario, 1990).

6. For example, see Randy Fisher, "Strips are 'Taking Off' Once Again," *Financial Post*, 31 August 1987, p. 5; and Eric C. Peterson "Strip Centers: Changing?" *Stores*, March 1990, pp. 53–54.

7. Harold T. Carlson, "How Shopping Centers Reshape Retailing: Past, Present, and Future," *International Trends in Retailing*, Arthur Andersen, Spring 1990, pp. 33–44.

8. Carman Cullen, "Involvement as a Moderator of Image-Patronage Relationships" (Ph.D. dissertation, Western Business School, The University of Western Ontario, 1989).

9. Leonard L. Berry, "Editors Corner" in Francesca Turchiano, "Farewell, Field of Dreams," *Retailing Issues Letter*, November 1990.

10. Eric C. Peterson, "Power Centers! Now!" *Stores*, March 1989, pp. 61–66.

11. "Canada Centers: Overbuilt, Underanchored," *Chain Store Age Executive*, March 1990, pp. 34–38.

12. Debra Hazel, "Twin Cities Overcome Retail Neglect," *Chain Store Age Executive*, July 1989, pp. 25–31.

13. For example, for an overview of mall management issues, see Marvin J. Rothenberg, "Mall Marketing Principles That Affect Merchandising," *Retail Control*, October 1986, pp. 2–36; and Peter G. Martin, *Shopping Center Management* (London: Spon Publishing, 1982).

14. David P. Schultz, "Specialty Expansion Slowing," *Stores*, December 1990, pp. 35–38. See also, Mike Reynolds, "Revamps on the Rise," *Stores*, July 1990, pp. 34–40.

15. For a good treatment of trade area analysis, see Avijit Ghosh, *Retail Management* (Chicago: Dryden, 1990), chapter 9.

16. Customer spotting techniques are generally credited to William Applebaum. For example, see William Applebaum, "Methodology for Determining Store Trade Areas, Market Penetration, and Potential Sales," *Journal of Marketing Research*, May 1966, pp. 127–41.

17. W.J. Reilly, *Law of Retail Gravitation* (1931).

18. Paul D. Converse, *A Study of Retail Trade Areas in East Central Illinois* (Chicago: University of Illinois, 1943).

19. Michael R. Pearce, Chow-Hou Wee, Carman Cullen, and Donna Green, *The London Retailing Study* (London, Ontario: The University of Western Ontario, 1984).

20. For a particularly good treatment of site selection techniques, see Ken Jones and Jim Simmons, *Location, Location, Location* (Toronto: Methuen, 1987), chapter 10.

21. William R. Davidson, Daniel J. Sweeney, and Ronald W. Stampfl, *Retailing Management*, Fifth Edition (New York: John Wiley and Sons, 1984), p. 197.

22. Randall Gebhardt, "Merchandising the Store," *Discount Merchandiser*, May 1989, pp. 84–86.

23. Steve Weinstein, "Are Bigger Stores Better?" *Progressive Grocer*, May 1990, pp. 141–46.

24. J. Barry Mason and Morris L. Mayer, *Modern Retailing Theory and Practice*, Fifth Edition (Homewood, Ill.: Irwin, 1990), p. 616.

25. Dale M. Lewison and M. Wayne DeLozier, *Retailing*, Third Edition (Columbus, Ohio: Merrill, 1989), p. 298.

26. See also *Store Design and Display—For Sales*, Retail Council of Canada, 1986.

27. Robert F. Lusch and Patrick Dunne, *Retail Management* (Cincinnati: South Western Publishing, 1990), p. 485.

28. Stephen Bennett, "King Kullen Polishes Its Crown," *Progressive Grocer*, September 1990, pp. 152–60.

29. Davidson, Sweeney, and Stampfl, *Retailing Management* (see note 21), p. 420.

30. Tom Steinhagen, "Space Management Shapes Up with Planogram," *Marketing News*, 12 November 1990, p. 7.

31. C. Whan Park, Easwar S. Iyer, and Daniel C. Smith, "The Effects of Situational Factors on In-Store Grocery Shopping Behavior: The Role of Store Environment and Time Available for Shopping," *Journal of Consumer Research*, March 1989, pp. 422–33.

32. Safeway has been experimenting with self-checkouts. See "Do-It-Yourself: Grocery Chain Introduces New Checkout Scanners," *Marketing News*, 12 November 1990, p. 1.

33. Howard Schlossberg, "Checkout Channel Targets Those Long Lines of Shoppers," *Marketing News*, 25 June 1990, p. 6.

34. Cyndee Miller, "Arby's Adds Technology to Boost Service," *Marketing News*, 12 November 1990, p. 1.

35. Barry Nelson, "Four Day Week Caps Rising Retailing Costs," *Calgary Herald*, 15 June 1990.

36. Kara Kuryllowicz, "C-Stores Coming of Age," *Canadian Grocer*, March 1989, pp. 35–40.

CHAPTER

# CUSTOMER CARE AND SERVICE

## ■ INTRODUCTION

This chapter is about customer care: what it is and how to manage it in a retail operation. Customer care, often referred to as **customer service** or just **service**, has recently become a very popular subject for retail consultants and commentators because retail managers and customers alike have discovered that customer care just doesn't happen; retail customer care must be designed, delivered, and controlled. Customer care is a complicated matter, much more involved than "being nice to the customer," yet many retailers have not given it the same managerial attention as inventory or real estate—no more complicated nor important matters. Terrence Smith, senior vice-president of Platinum/Gold Card operations for American Express, stated his company's position as follows:

> At American Express, service is our differentiator—outstanding, superior service quality. It's part of our contract with our customers. If something goes wrong, we view it as an opportunity to demonstrate our ability to exceed our customers' expectations. We don't want our customers to be simply satisfied—we want them to be delighted![1]

Section One deals with the nature and importance of customer care and service. Section Two describes the details of the four-part task of customer care management shown as Figure 9.1.

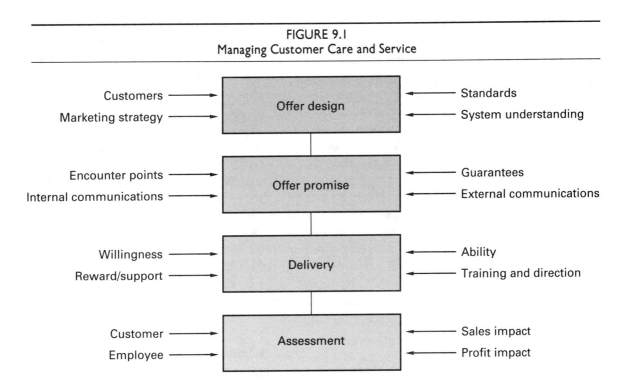

FIGURE 9.1
Managing Customer Care and Service

## THE NATURE OF CUSTOMER CARE AND SERVICE

When retailers use the term "service," two different ideas can get confused; we need to make a distinction between the services offered to customers and customer care and service.

In addition to products (goods, such as apparel and food), retailers offer *services*. These might include parking, alterations, credit, installation and instruction, delivery, repairs, cleaning, child care, layaway programs, gift wrapping, washrooms, consultation, monogramming, and bridal registry. Such services are part of the overall package of benefits the retailer provides to customers in general, and the costs are either built into general overhead or shared partially (such as fee for alterations) with using customers. These services are intended to help sell the product assortment and may be termed **patronage-building services**. Other services offered might include beauty salons, optometrists, leasing, insurance, and travel assistance. While these services are also part of the overall package of benefits the retailer offers, they are sold directly to customers and often don't involve the direct purchase of any product. These services may be termed **revenue-producing services**. Thus, a retailer may use the term "service" to refer to one of these patronage-building or revenue-producing services. *Marketing services* is in many ways similar to marketing products as far as a retailer is concerned, and thus the earlier discussion in Chapter 7 applies.

*Managing customer care* is a very different task from providing services and is the subject of this chapter. The other meaning of service is the retailer's side of managing the relationship with customers, both in general and in specific circumstances. To avoid confusion, this notion will be termed **customer care**. Some people may regard use of the term "care" as inappropriate, as a term more relevant to health services. However, the term connotes serious attention, taking responsibility, liking, and performance. These are exactly the dimensions most often missing from the "customer service" provided by many retail marketers.

When customers recount shopping experiences, they often begin with such phrases as "I thought their service was really great" or "You can't get service like you used to." When probed for details, they reveal there are many dimensions to customer care. It's more than finding a salesperson, more than getting something delivered, and so on. With such statements, customers are referring to the specific attributes of any **customer care encounter** and to the overall feeling they have about how well the retailer is managing the *relationship* with them as individuals. Do they feel that their time and patronage are respected and appreciated? Do they feel anyone cares? Once that overall feeling is gone, adding specific services will not improve a retailer's "customer care rating" with customers. This distinction is very important.

A key concept in customer care is **relationship**. Relationship refers to the myriad perceptions, expectations, emotions, and experiences people have when they interact with one another. People have relationships with one another and with organizations such as retailers, and have a natural tendency to personalize such relationships. Stanley Marcus captured this idea as follows:

> Management is so busy today with the mechanics of merchandising that merchandising itself and customers themselves get lost. The customer gets translated into an abstract statistic called consumers. I've seen many customers, but I've never seen a consumer. Consumers don't get their feelings hurt; customers do. Today's merchants have become so intrigued with computers that they find them more exciting than going down on the floor and waiting on customers. The computer doesn't say one thing about whether the customer is happy.
>
> Take good care of your customers and they'll come back. Take good care of your merchandise, and it doesn't come back.
>
> Every business depends on repeat sales. We are all customers, and we go back where we're treated right.
>
> If we were selling exclusively to customers who come in knowing what they want, vending machines would be just as good as salespeople.
>
> The only thing about the customer today that's changed is that he or she has less time.[2]

It is unfortunate, therefore, that, for the past century, most North American retailers have sought ways to impersonalize their relationships with customers, to remove the human dimension from the shopping experience. Too many potential "customer care encounters" are "encounters without care."

Berry and Gresham wrote about what they called "relationship retailing," which they defined as "attracting, retaining, and enhancing client relationships." They argued that some retailers have more opportunity to practise relationship retailing than do other retailers; that is, relationship retailing is most appropriate when:

- The consumer periodically rebuys in the product classifications sold by the retailer (for example, buying fashion apparel rather than a cemetery plot);
- The consumer has alternatives from which to choose (for example, buying housewares rather than electricity);
- The consumer is ego-involved (for example, buying home furnishings rather than frozen foods);
- The consumer requires personal service and/or selling (for example, buying an automobile rather than a light bulb).[3]

The notion of "managing the relationship with the customer" must not be allowed to become abstract. It must be given operational meaning for any particular retailer. The management of Federal Express once defined service as "all actions and reactions that customers perceive they have purchased." This definition contains some important ideas.

First, the customer's perception of customer care is the ultimate measure of customer care. It's not whether a salesperson smiles during the "approach" to a customer so much as what that smile means to the customer—is it perceived as sincere and friendly or insincere and plastic?

Second, from the customer's standpoint, customer care is part of what is paid for in a transaction. Whereas a retailer may think the acronym POS stands only for Point-of-Sale, the customer would think (or hope that) POS stood for Point-of-Service. Even in so-called "self-service" stores, customers expect some service.

Third, customer care is the summation of the many ways a retailer may interact with a customer to encourage patronage. These ways may be reactive to customer requests as well as proactive, such as offering "extras" not expected or available from competitors. These extras, such as loyalty reward programs (or continuity programs) like Zellers' Club Z, must be valued by customers to be real competitive advantages for the retailer. When a retailer customizes his or her approach to individual customers (or clients), then customer care is perceived by customers to be especially high. Berry and Gresham said that relationship customization "involves learning the preferences of individual clients, capturing this information so that it can be readily accessed, and then using it to best advantage in merchandising and serving client requirements."[4] Many retailers use client books and computer technology to track individual customers. Hotels, travel agencies, and upscale specialty stores are among those who keep customer profiles as to preferences in order to serve customers in more customized ways.

All retailers, by definition, are concerned with customer care; the nature of that care varies tremendously, as will be discussed.

## THE IMPORTANCE OF CUSTOMER CARE

Customer care is important because customers say it is; retailers say it is; and retailers who have focused on improving customer care have generally fared well.

Over the past ten years, there have been plenty of articles and speeches lamenting declines in the quality of retail customer care and cataloguing the problems in improving it. There have also been many research studies, especially of public opinions, about service levels. Some presaged growing retailer awareness of the critical importance of customer care to competitive strategy. For example, it is now widely accepted that most conventional North American department store organizations reduced the level of customer care in the early 1980s to reduce costs. This strategic move has since been criticized severely. However, customer care levels in North American department stores were already below customer expectations.

A Touche Ross study in 1989 polled 370 retailers in the United States and Canada, a sample reasonably representative of the many types of retailers in both countries. Asked what were the major issues facing them today, retailers responded: first, increased competition and, second, improving customer care. These respondents went on to identify the difficulty in obtaining good sales people as central to their problems with customer care:

> 96% of the total respondents believe that obtaining experienced, reliable sales personnel today is either a critical problem (51% say it is) or somewhat of a problem (45%). While the percentages vary from one region to another, labour is a problem for retailers in just about every geographic area in North America. In geographic areas where the majority of respondents consider obtaining experienced, reliable sales personnel to be a critical problem, the jobless rate is lower than that of the national average.[5]

Increasingly, executives believe the cost of poor customer care is high; the payoff of excellent customer care is high. One retail executive, commenting on poor customer care, put it bluntly: "If an employee takes $10 from the till, that's theft and justifies firing. If an employee upsets a customer, that costs us lots more than $10 and I feel totally justified in firing that employee."

Stories of turnarounds in company performance based on a dedication to customer care have greatly intensified attention to care management. In particular, Karl Albrecht and Ron Zemke have told the stories of SAS and British Air (to name only two of their examples) in such a compelling way that some of the terminology, such as "moments of truth," has become part of the customer care jargon.[6]

It is readily apparent to most people that customer care is not what it could be. It seems retailers have all too many ways to upset customers and, thus, encourage them to shop the competition. For example, one might change the layout without explanation or warning, disrupting established shopping patterns; one might make it difficult to find or access merchandise, have poor signs, have poorly informed or impolite salespeople, discontinue products and services without explanation or warning; or one could charge fees for services that were once "free," have empty checkout stands, allow staff to chat with one another rather than helping customers, and so on. An examination of these many ways reveals that a large number of them are simply diminished customer care. Customer care is not a neutral topic: high levels of customer care win and retain customers; low levels of customer care—especially when customer care is expected—lose customers.

Customer care should be regarded as an expression of the retailer's corporate culture. This is one dimension of culture that becomes very obvious to everyone.[7] A very simple way to assess the overall real marketing orientation of any retailer is to test the level of customer care. Customer care in the store, on the telephone, or through the mail indicates management's commitment both to customer care and to the customer. Jim Williams, president of the National Retail Federation, put it this way:

> Customer service problems do not begin on the selling floor. They are merely symptoms that something is wrong with the way a firm manages the customer service function. A firm noted for good service invariably has a clearly defined customer service strategy. It knows how to select and hire people who enjoy helping others. It knows how to develop employees who have skills in dealing with customers. Most important, it recognizes the basic ingredient in dealing with people is courtesy!
>
> In a store noted for courteous service, ask any manager what the company's customer service strategy is and chances are he or she can tell you. In firms where poor or indifferent service is the norm, even senior level executives will be hard put to describe the service policy. In firms with no clear strategy, executives assume that customer service is the responsibility of sales people and put only one executive in charge of service.[8]

### Customer Care Initiatives

Many retailers have undertaken a variety of initiatives to improve their customer care. These initiatives can be characterized on a spectrum of intensity: "back-to-basics" good personal selling; operations analysis and change; organizational change; and strategic embrace of customer care.

**Improved personal selling**   Many retailers have re-emphasized personal selling skills, believing that better training and better sales management would be instrumental in improving customer care. Revitalized training programs based on "greet, ask, suggest, thank" are underway everywhere. For example, Higbee's initiated a new concept in June 1988 called "Service in the Aisle," which called for salespeople (when they were not waiting on customers) to be positioned in highly visible locations, usually near the main aisle, to greet customers and offer customer service—administrative and clerical duties were taken away from noon until closing. Management reasoned it would be hard for salespeople not to greet customers when in such locations in the store. For some retailers, this renewed focus on personal selling entailed seemingly minute changes, such as replacing salespeople's name tags with ones that customers can actually spot and read from a distance.

**Operations analysis**  Some retailers have wondered if their salespeople were not doing a better job in delivering customer care because there were impediments to doing so. For example, at Marshall Field, beginning about 1984, management identified what they called "task interferences"—things that salespeople and supervisors were having to do (such as running off the floor for cheque approvals) that got in the way of providing good customer care. Analysts found about sixty task interferences. Management then set to work to reduce these. They focused one step at a time on improving customer care once these interferences were attended to: first, courtesy skills (approach, greet, proper name tags), then suggestion selling, and so on.[9] Other retailers have also redesigned their in-store operations to facilitate customer care. Some retailers, for example, have begun to prepare merchandise for display before it arrives on the selling floor in order to reduce the amount of time salespeople spend on-floor, putting merchandise away. Some are even focusing on building the service right into the product, such as by offering boneless chicken, more prepared foods, single servings, and reclosable packages. At Boscov's, management reduced the number of departments (giving more flexibility to everyone) and used sophisticated scheduling software to match salespeople with customer traffic patterns. Similarly, building on research studies that show transaction speed is increasingly important to customers, many retailers are forging ahead with investments in front-end registers that scan products. Toys 'R' Us found that scanning registers reduced ringing-in time by 40–60 percent.

Such changes in operations have worked. For example, in 1984 Gimbel's Midwest created a customer care program called CARE, Customers Are Really Everything. Management wanted to increase yield from store traffic and had studies that showed 50 percent of their salespeople's time was spent on other functions requested by management and little time was spent on selling and customer care. In fact, a salesperson couldn't even tell from the register at the end of the day how much had been sold. During this program, on a typical day, management instructed no counts, no talking with buyers, no filling the floor, etc.—and sales went up 75 percent.[10]

**Organizational changes**  Some retailers have concluded that customer care must be conceived of as part of the product assortment, not as peripheral. Following this thinking, customer care deserves its own organization parallel to the merchandising organization and its own resources. Why shouldn't there be a Vice-President Customer Care? For example, Kmart has put in 1–800 numbers for customer feedback, has hired a Vice-President Human Resources and Customer Service, has five regional customer service managers, has some in-store greeters, and displays photos in each store of the manager and the regional customer service manager. Further, if the role of all employees is to provide customer care, why is the "customer service department" usually in some out-of-the-way location in the store? Berry made this point strongly:

> Retail companies should not label in-store departments that handle credit applications, perform gift-wrapping services, or perform other specialized functions

as "customer service" departments. To do so suggests to employees and customers alike that a handful of store employees are responsible for customer service, and that all other employees are responsible for other things.[11]

**Customer care as core strategy** A few retailers have seized on customer care as the essential core of their strategy. Nordstrom's customer care strategy was mentioned in Chapter 3. Brettons, American Express, Disney, and others have all made much greater efforts to manage customer care and service than most retailers.

## Some Problems

Customer care is a critical topic for retail managers. Jules Abend, after researching this topic for *Stores* magazine, concluded:

> With increased competition, many retailers are placing greater emphasis on "customer service" to differentiate themselves from the competitive pack. The traditional approach to "customer service", however, is not broad enough to accomplish this objective or to satisfy the needs of today's consumer. To find new areas of opportunity, retailers must go beyond customer service to a customer-focussed culture.[12]

It is not easy to implement an integrated approach to customer acquisition and customer care. There are two basic reasons. First, many retailers apparently haven't carefully conceptualized the task prior to trying to operationalize it. For example, they may be quick to implement "mystery shopper" surveys before deciding what their customer care strategy is or should be. Second, managing customer care is essentially managing people, which is often much harder than managing money, goods, and physical assets. Albert Bates summed up the problem of getting improvements in people productivity as follows:

> The basis of this problem is that the service sector does not lend itself to easy productivity gains, that is, increasing physical output per employee. In fact, many perceived productivity gains are really workload shifting to either customer or suppliers. Self-service and vendor pricing are only two examples. The difficulty in generating productivity improvement has led cost-pressured management to maintain a price position by gradually eroding service.[13]

The remainder of this chapter addresses two issues: conceptualizing the customer care offer and managing its delivery.

## A CONCEPTUAL MODEL OF CUSTOMER CARE

In a recent *Fortune* article, Leon Gorman, president of L.L. Bean, commented on customer care as follows: "A lot of people have fancy things to say about customer service, including me, but it's just a day-in day-out, on-going, never-ending, unremitting, persevering, compassionate type of activity."[14]

SECTION
TWO

Such a statement may mislead some into thinking that customer care is simply being nice to the customer; it is far more complicated. What are the dimensions of customer care, and isn't it just a matter of service or self-service?

For many years, it has been customary to classify retailers according to four differing levels of customer service provided. This classification scheme is only a start toward understanding customer care distinctions. **Self-service** refers to the circumstance in which the customer does all the work of selecting items to purchase, completing the transaction with the retailer, transporting the item home, and perhaps even assembling or installing it. Few retailers other than vending machine operators are true self-service operations. Rather, many retailers are **self-selection** retail operations where the customer selects the item from the assortment displayed in the store or catalogue and then the retailer offers assistance with the transaction itself, such as with a cashier at a front-end checkout in a grocery store. Some retailers offer more than this rudimentary level of customer care by providing limited assistance in product selection, delivery, installation, and so on. These **limited service** operations are characterized by a relatively few salespeople offering a low level of routine selling and customer care. At the opposite end of the spectrum from self-service is **full-service**. In these retail operations, salespeople are plentiful, and presumably attentive, engaging in creative selling ranging from clientele development to post-sale problem solving. Such salespeople spend time with customers, get to know their individual characteristics, and use this knowledge to customize their relationships.

Retailers who conceive of their customers as masses of people to be dealt with impersonally call them *consumers* and *customers*. Retailers who conceive of their customers as individuals call them *clients*. Leonard Berry said clients are served by specific personnel who handle their account in a personalized way.[15]

Certainly, not all retail circumstances require a high level of customer care. Customer care is expensive and time-consuming. Sometimes, speed and lack of personal contact are preferable. On the other hand, there are circumstances when a high level of customer care is not only appropriate, but also expected. For example, when one buys a car or real estate, one usually expects a higher level of care than when one buys groceries or basic clothes. From the customer perspective, higher customer care levels are expected and valued when product knowledge is low in the face of a complicated product or service, when the perceived risk of an incorrect purchase decision is high, when the product or service needs to be customized to the individual, and when there is a need to negotiate the price (or trade-in). Further, if the customer has experienced high customer care levels in the past, he or she may well expect that level of care again.

Kevin Coyne has provided a useful distinction across customer care encounters. According to him, there are three types of encounters:

1. Environmental encounters—In these situations, the service level is rarely noticed unless it is performed so badly as to be intrusive. The customer expects service to be performed adequately without needing to be consciously aware of it. (Example: airline baggage handling)

2. Transactory encounters—These are entirely routine re-enactments of customary interactions with retailers. The customer expects to "get what he came for" after exerting a certain amount of effort. (Example: grocery checkout)

3. Assistance-based encounters—These are circumstances in which the customer cannot precisely define desired outcomes in advance because of lack of knowledge (and therefore high perceived risk) and thus needs the input of the service provider to make the best decision. The customer expects to exert some effort but also expects the service provider will be ready and able to help through providing information and reassurance. (Example: furniture buying)[16]

In each of these encounters, customers have expectations of the nature of the customer care interaction with the care provider. If the customer care provider errs by providing too little care or service (for example, treating an assistance-based situation as a transactory encounter), the customer will be upset that customer care was "poor." If the customer care provider errs by providing too much service (for example, treating a transactory encounter as an assistance-based encounter), the customer will be upset that customer care was "intrusive." The customer care provider is thus constantly challenged to match what is offered to what is expected.

Further to this issue of how much customer care and service a retail marketer should provide is the question of how much customer care the customer generally expects and values. In every country, people are socialized as "consumers," which includes learning how their retail marketplace works. This leads to specific expectations about customer care. For example, in North America we expect to do our routine grocery shopping with a minimum of personal contact with retail staff; it is possible to buy groceries for weeks without having a word of conversation with store staff. This would seem absolutely incredible in other countries who are habituated to buying their groceries in markets where conversation, haggling, and lots of personal contact are the norm. (This important topic of determining customer care and service expectations will be addressed in greater detail later in this chapter.)

The simple secret to being perceived to offer high levels of customer care is to *always exceed somewhat customer expectations of customer care* for one's particular type of store or operation. The concept may be restated as "pleasant surprise." Wal-Mart is essentially a self-selection discount retailer, but in many stores they employ older or retired staffers as greeters at the door. Many full-service retailers do not do as good a job of acknowledging and approaching customers in-store. People going into Wal-Mart, at least initially, do not expect that level of customer care so they are pleasantly surprised. People going into a full-service department store who are frustrated trying to find someone to give money to for their purchases are unpleasantly surprised. It's all a matter of expectations.

These expectations are shaped by a great number of factors, not the least of which are experiences with comparable retailers and the messages conveyed in advertising and promotion. When there is a gap between what one expects and what one experiences in customer care, there is a customer care problem, or, more optimistically, a customer care opportunity. A. Parasuraman, V. Zeithaml, and L. Berry used this notion of gaps in their "service quality model."[17]

There are many dimensions of customer care (or attributes of the customer care encounter); Exhibit 9.1 shows several collected from numerous sources[18] and organized according to apparent groupings.

*EXHIBIT 9.1*
*Dimensions of*
*Customer Care*

1. **Courtesy and empathy**—politeness, respect, consideration, friendliness, smiling, helpfulness, saying "thanks," avoiding arguments, fairness, conveying a caring attitude, conveying an understanding of the customer, recognizing and conveying appreciation to the repeat customer

2. **Appearance of staff**—clothing, grooming, name identification

3. **Communication skills**—keeping customers informed, listening skills, eye contact, body language, concentration and attention, vocabulary, and grammar

4. **Product and store knowledge**—ability to explain product characteristics, use, and care; ability to relate product and service to marketplace trends (e.g., fashion); knowledge of store policies and procedures; overall competence

5. **Responsiveness**—apparent willingness and readiness to provide customer care; time to acknowledgement, approach, and after-sale follow-up; initiative and creativity in solving customer problems and taking customer's "side" of the issue

6. **Access**—accessibility by phone or mail: accessibility for personal visit (location); waiting time to receive help or to process the transaction; hours of operation; ease for physically challenged customers

7. **Product and service assortment**—variety, breadth and depth; in-stock position; appropriateness to apparent store type and to customers attracted

8. **Reliability and assurance**—consistency of performance (dependability); reputation for honesty and fairness; record-keeping accuracy; trustworthiness; guarantees and return procedures (what is promised and what is delivered); keeping promises made in advertising and promotion and by store personnel

9. **Security**—protection against physical risk, financial risk, and breach of confidentiality; privacy

10. **Respect for customer's time**—convenience of layout; appropriateness of signs and displays; adequate staffing and staff being easy to find (such as at checkout islands); adequate equipment to provide customer care; "customer-friendly" policies and procedures (such as cheque authorization); policies regarding treatment of in-store customer versus telephone calls; keeping promises, such as having repairs or alterations ready when promised and doing them right the first time

As mentioned previously, not all of these dimensions are equally important to any particular customer at all times, or equally important to all customers. Further, some of these dimensions are central to the encounter, whereas others may be used by customers as "indicators" of customer care. Thus, the importance of each of these dimensions varies by customer and by circumstance. This makes the retail marketer's task of deciding just which care dimensions to emphasize difficult.

Some commentators have concluded that there are generalizations about high-customer-care providers compared to low-customer-care providers. For example, George Reider distinguished between service winners and losers, as shown in Exhibit 9.2.[19]

*EXHIBIT 9.2*
*Reider's Service*
*Distinction*

**Service Winners:**

1. Noticeably more friendly, courteous, and seem to care
2. Go out of their way to understand customer needs
3. Have integrity
4. Know the business well and how to get things done quickly and accurately
5. Shine under pressure
6. Pay attention to small details
7. Exhibit genuine appreciation for patronage

**Service Losers:**

1. Dehumanize the transaction by inattention or plastic professionalism
2. Regard questions and requests as interruptions and nuisances
3. Often do not keep promises
4. Are poor trouble-shooters and unskilled in problem solving
5. Appear disorganized, inefficient, and waste customers' time
6. Don't seem to care
7. Communicate in vague language

Another way used to analyze customer care is on two dimensions: perceived care content value to customers (high and low) and cost to provide (high and low), which leads to four types of services: support services, disappointers, basics, and patronage builders. Using this notion, Albert Bates classified services into a four-cell matrix that distinguished between the value of the service to customers (high or low) and the cost of providing that service (high or low). Such a scheme helps set priorities for service program design.[20] However, it is important to realize that Bates and many others have mixed customer care with providing services for customers—the distinction made at the beginning of this chapter.

Albrecht and Zemke provided a simple-appearing but helpful model of customer care management that they called the "service triangle," which formed the conceptual framework of their entire book.[21] Their model is shown as Figure 9.2. The lines connecting each of the four areas in this diagram represent the necessary relationships to manage in their conception of service management.

Despite all the speeches, books, and articles, most commentators and practitioners have at best only conceptualized the dimensions of customer care. Few have attempted to research the validity of these conceptualizations or the relative importance of the dimensions as far as customers are concerned. There have been exceptions: most notably, Berry, Parasuraman, and Zeithaml. They researched service quality in four industries and concluded there were five major customer expectations for service, in this order:

- reliability—the ability to perform the desired service dependably, accurately, and consistently
- responsiveness—the willingness to provide prompt service and help customers
- assurance—employees' knowledge, courtesy, and ability to convey trust and confidence
- empathy—the provision of caring, individualized attention to customers
- tangibles—the physical facilities, equipment, appearance of personnel.[22]

Efforts to conceptualize customer care are the first step toward the design, promise, delivery, and assessment of a customer care strategy.[23]

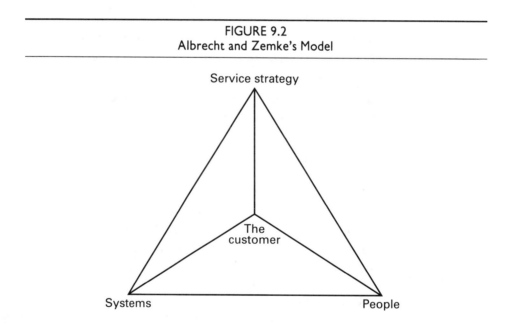

**FIGURE 9.2**
**Albrecht and Zemke's Model**

Service strategy

The customer

Systems

People

### OFFER DESIGN

Designing the customer care program begins with an overall care or service strategy. Albrecht and Zemke defined a service strategy as follows: "A service strategy is a distinctive formula for delivering service; such a strategy is keyed to a well-chosen benefit premise that is valuable to the customer and that establishes an effective competitive position."[24]

In order to formulate such a strategy, several factors must be considered: these may be classified as customer issues and operational issues. The starting place is with the customer.

A complete customer care strategy embraces all aspects of the relationship the customer has with the retailer—including first impression, acknowledgment, selling, transacting, follow-up, and returns. Accordingly, by examining each of these relationship dimensions, the retailer can learn what customers need, want, expect, perceive, and experience. Christopher Lovelock suggests (a) flow-charting the process as the customer experiences it (a kind of "methods analysis" of each step), (b) having focus groups to see how they think about and experience the process, and (c) monitoring the competition on the same basis.[25] A related concept gaining popularity is "moments of truth," which Scandinavian Airlines president Jan Carlzon originated as: "an episode in which a customer comes into contact with any aspect of the company, however remote, and thereby has an opportunity to form an impression."[26]

However management proceeds with this research and inquiry, the goal is to understand in some detail how customers make patronage choices; how they get cues about customer care quality; what their customer care expectations, experiences, and hopes are; and what changes are occurring in these dimensions over time, because customer expectations of customer care seem to increase over time.

Management should always be looking for **customer care opportunities**, that is, opportunities to provide differentiated, appropriately extra care to customers at critical stages in the relationship. Bernie Fuchs of Palais Royal in Texas said they discovered the most frustrating part of a woman's shopping experience in apparel happened in the fitting room when sales staff were inattentive. They installed call buttons in the fitting rooms and required each sales associate to answer a call within five minutes. Sales associates responded by being more attentive to customers in the fitting rooms, in effect trying to beat the call, so the buttons have rarely been used.

General research provides some guidance about customers and customer care. For example, Kevin Coyne has provided several useful insights into how customers view customer care, which are summarized in Exhibit 9.3.[27] While these insights may be used to guide a marketing research effort for a specific retail marketer, one must remember that customer expectations of care level vary by store, merchandise category, and, of course, by customer.

---

*EXHIBIT 9.3*
*Some Customer Views of Service*

1. Service, in the customer's view, consists of many separate interactions with the company (encounters) and each encounter has a number of attributes. Each encounter and attribute must be analyzed separately.

2. Customers' expectations vary according to the type of encounter: environmental, transactory, or assistance-based.

3. Individual service encounters produce one of five states of satisfaction:

   a. OK—expectations are met but not exceeded; no strong positive feelings toward the service provider

   b. Irritated—transaction succeeds but service provider overly intrusive by trying to provide too much or inappropriate kind of service

    **c.** Dissatisfied—transaction does not succeed or requires more than the expected level of effort

    **d.** Angry—transaction does not succeed, despite substantially greater than expected effort or because of a mistake by the service provider that clearly (in the customer's mind) should have been avoided

    **e.** Excited—customer is pleasantly surprised by the encounter; the level of effort required is substantially below expectations or the expectations of success are low or the success of the transaction is redefined upward (e.g., upgrade on an airline flight)

**4.** Links exist between service and customer behaviour but they are not always straightforward. There are two thresholds for service, below one customer loyalty drops dramatically and above the other customer loyalty increases dramatically. In between, behaviour is not affected much. This means the retailer should first ensure reaching the minimum service threshold and then decide if investing in service to exceed the next threshold is a worthwhile strategic investment.

**5.** Behaviour lags behind satisfaction, especially if there are barriers to switching from one service provider to another (such as transferring bank accounts).

**6.** Service strategies can, thus, have three basic objectives, in ascending order of difficulty of achievement: achieving competitive parity, retaining the loyalty of current customers, and acquiring new customers.

---

Some retailers involve customers actively in the design and other stages of their customer care program. Customers may be asked to volunteer as "customer care advisers" in a variety of capacities. Dave Ulrich believes that involving customers in a firm's human resources practices—but in ways he describes as "voluntarily, publicly, and irreversibly"—increases their commitment to dealing with the firm. He gives examples of customers participating in product and customer care design, participating in meetings and award ceremonies, communicating with employees through internal newsletters, acting as temporary company representatives and advisers to management, helping with training programs, and participating in employee performance assessment.[28]

Before formulating a customer care strategy, management must also examine various aspects of the operation and interact with employees. Management must know what tasks employees in customer-contact roles are performing. Store visits by management with meetings to reinforce management's commitment to customer care, providing opportunities to hear directly from employees what barriers are in the way to providing better customer care, soliciting and rewarding suggestions, working the floor with them, and any other approach to involving employees in the customer care offer design all increase the likelihood that good ideas will be brought forward and that commitment to them will follow.

A useful customer care strategy must be more than a statement of philosophy and good intentions. It must express **customer care standards**. These are clear, meaningful (to everyone) statements of what the retailer will do for the customer.

Standards must be precise even for issues such as product knowledge. For example, one might say each men's suits salesperson must know that there are five basic silhouettes for men's suits (American, British, European, Italian, and Classic) and how each of these fits certain body types better than the others.

Some customer care standards might be for internal use only, such as "All customers will be acknowledged within five minutes of entering our stores"; others may be both for staff and for customer knowledge, such as "Your lunch pizza delivered to your table within five minutes of your order or you eat free." Customer care standards must be specific enough to provide a basis for performance assessment.

Customer care standards can be made into customer care guarantees, which are both part of the customer care offer design and its promise. Customer care guarantees are discussed in the following text.

## PROMISE

When customer care standards are expressed directly or indirectly to customers, a promise is being made. Many retail marketers do not manage this process well. Some firms don't seem to consider the opportunities of using customer care in their communications program; others dismiss it, fearing that "you can't attract people on service, you need to use merchandise and price." It is not clear that this assumption always holds true; it should be examined.

A first issue in promising customer care is whether customer expectations should be accepted as "given" or whether the retailer should attempt to influence them. Most customers do not have clear expectations of any particular retailer's customer care level. Karl Hellman gave the following advice:

> For those customers who don't have clear expectations, you can influence their expectations:
> - tell them what to expect
> - explain what is going on inside your company so they appreciate what you are doing for them
> - get information from them that helps you give them what they need
> - know what they need better than they do, give it to them, and help them understand that they have received what they needed
> - tell them what they need to do to get full benefit from your products and services.[29]

**Customer care guarantees** not only promise customer care, but also help ensure that it is delivered. Timothy Firnstahl, owner of a chain of restaurants, attributes much of his success to his service guarantee. He described his approach as follows:

> It starts with a guarantee—not that moth-eaten old promise of a cheerful refund—but a guarantee that customers will be satisfied with their whole experience of the company's products and services. It moves on to a system for giving employees complete responsibility and authority for making the guarantee stick.

It ends with a process for identifying system failures—the problems in organization, training, and other internal programs that cause customer dissatisfaction.[30]

According to Christopher Hart, a service guarantee has five major benefits for the company and avoids three major problems for customers:

First, it pushes the entire company to focus on customers' definitions of good service—not on executives' assumptions. Second, it sets clear performance standards, which boost employee performance and morale. Third, it generates reliable data (through payouts) when performance is poor. Fourth, it forces an organization to examine its entire service-delivery system for possible failure points. Last, it builds customer loyalty, sales, and market share.

. . . [without a service guaranty] consumers who receive poor service are often left with no evidence to support their complaints . . . customers don't know their rights . . . there is often no one to complain to—at least no one who looks capable of solving the problem.[31]

Hart described a good service guarantee as having five characteristics:

1. Unconditional—no exceptions, no quibbling
2. Easy to understand and communicate—simple, clear, unambiguous
3. Meaningful—guarantees service dimensions important to customers, doesn't simply promise what customers already expect, calls for significant payout when the service promise is not kept
4. Easy (and painless) to invoke—customers don't have to make special efforts to get attention when service promise not kept
5. Easy and quick to collect—no special effort, on-the-spot if possible.

Hart also stated that a service guarantee is appropriate when one or more of the following conditions exist:

a. The price of the service is high
b. The customer's ego is on the line
c. The customer's expertise with the service is low
d. The negative consequences of service failure are high
e. The industry has a bad image for service quality
f. The company depends on frequent customer repurchases
g. The company's business is affected deeply by word-of-mouth
h. The company is not already providing such a high level of service that a guarantee would be perceived to be at odds with its market image.

In 1990, Xerox announced a "Total Satisfaction Guarantee" for all its equipment: if the customer is not satisfied, Xerox will replace the product free of charge, and the customer is the sole arbiter of "satisfaction."[32]

There are a great variety of ways to communicate care promises. It is important to communicate the customer care strategy everywhere the retailer "touches a customer." For example, one may use advertising and promotion, signs, personal selling efforts; encourage referrals; and use price levels and merchandise quality to create expectations. One of the worst ways is to have a "Customer Service Desk" in an out-of-the-way location in the store as the indicator of "we're here to serve." In all customer care promises, it is important to remember that there are two major audiences to be reached: customers and employees.

## DELIVERY

Delivery of customer care refers to the execution of the customer care strategy. Retail employees will deliver excellent customer care when (*a*) they are willing to do so, and (*b*) they are able to do so. It is very important to distinguish between willing/unwilling and able/unable. For example, often retail personnel would like to give better care but are unable to because they have been constrained by policies and procedures, not provided with enough equipment or time to serve customers, and so on.

The willingness/unwillingness dimension is one of attitude and personality. Some people really do not enjoy much people-contact; others relish it. Accordingly, a retail marketer concerned about customer care must begin with careful recruiting. Prospective customer contact people should be screened for willingness to serve. Further, this retailer should ensure that the atmosphere in the company continues to encourage this positive attitude toward providing care. A negative corporate culture can quickly overwhelm individual employees' willingness to serve, changing them into cynical nonservers, who avoid responsibility for providing customer care and shift blame for poor customer relationships to others in the firm.

Central to creating and reinforcing this "customer care culture" is a customer-focused culture. Roy Burns stated this thought as follows:

> . . . the key factor that initiates and nurtures a customer-focussed culture is a statement of customer focus. That will produce the drive, incentive, and awareness and must include:
> - Top management commitment
> - Clear organizational goals
> - Specifically assigned responsibilities to each area
> - A focal point for questions and problems
> - On-going communication and positive examples[33]

Albrecht and Zemke were unequivocal about the most important advice they have about the management of customer care:

> Unless the shared values, norms, beliefs and ideologies of the organization—the organization's culture—are clearly and consciously focussed on serving the customer, there is virtually no chance that the organization will be able to deliver a consistent quality of service and develop a sustained reputation for service.[34]

There is, of course, a relationship between willingness and ability to serve. Training and positive reinforcement are essential first steps in ensuring that employees predisposed to customer care learn how to do it and are encouraged to take responsibility for doing so. For example, too many retail marketers do not spend the necessary time engendering positive customer care attitudes, but rather just train in policies and procedures for completing transactions. Training should include improved understanding of customer expectations of customer care, greater appreciation of customer characteristics in general; the firm's customer care strategy; and, of course, the many specific skills a customer-contact person should have, such as acknowledgment, approach, personal selling skills, problem-solving, post-sale follow-up, and how to personalize and customize all aspects of the relationship with customers. There is much to learn. The post-sale stage involves more, for example, than sending a thank-you postcard.[35]

The ability to provide care can be enhanced or hampered by the systems in place. Employees required to seek approvals from distant supervisors for cheques, who are required to ask embarrassing questions of customers making returns, who are on the floor doing housekeeping instead of in the "service/checkout desk," and so on, are hampered from providing customer care. As mentioned earlier, many major retailers have found that customer care and sales productivity increase dramatically when systems are improved.

There are a number of ways to improve the management of customer care through organizational design. Some firms are experimenting with "service quality circles"; that is, small groups of employees are given the responsibility to care for customers on a profit-and-loss basis. Other firms have created "customer service committees" comprised of store people and head office people. For example, Younkers Department Stores did this in 1986 and attributed the subsequent 20 percent sales increase to the program:

> The committee worked hard defining customer service as it pertained to Younkers and developed a clear, complete set of customer service standards for every position within the organization. The Steering Committee examined functions, positions, policies and procedures to determine what roles all associates should perform in order to provide Younkers with service superior to that of our competitors. They also sighted various obstacles in the way of achieving these standards and offered recommendations and a plan to overcome them.
>
> The real impact of the committee was to create a general awareness about customer service. Since the committee was made up of a diverse group from all functions and levels of the business, this awareness took place both horizontally and vertically.[36]

Further, enlightened retailers realize that the employee–customer dynamic can put a lot of pressure on the customer care employee. Sometimes, "being nice to people all day" gets to be too much for employees. There may be too much customer contact and too little contact with fellow workers to balance this out. In such circumstances, according to research, it is normal for employees to try to gain control of customer encounters in order to avoid abuse before it happens. For example, employees may ignore customers' requests, may engage in a pre-emptive conversation, or may even be more responsive to customer feedback than management direction.[37] It is usually a mistake to increase pressure on staff and to mechanize and control customer care too much. Usually, it is better to give individuals some discretion and flexibility in solving customer problems, that is, to encourage and "empower" the staff to do it. In this sense, the retail marketing organization exists to serve the people who serve the customers.

Other retail marketers have focused on the pivotal role of the store manager in customer care. There seems to be broad agreement that the traditional role of the store manager must change to ensure delivery of customer care. Who is in a better position to be the "customer care champion"? Hensel expressed this thought as follows:

> Marketing-oriented retail companies need to view store management as a localized customer satisfaction management system. In the past, the store manager's emphasis has been on facilities, merchandise, and/or expense management. The store manager's job must be re-defined and emphasis placed on customer service management. How can store personnel best help customers find what they want? Make a purchase decision? Execute a transaction? What can be done to attract more local trade area shoppers to the store and convert them to buyers and satisfied customers? What improvements can be made that might enhance the quality of the customer's experience with the store and help get an edge on competition? These are the questions store managers must ask—and answer—as customer service managers.[38]

Hensel further advised that store managers do the following to ensure customer care:

> . . . convince customer contact personnel that serving shoppers in the store takes precedence over all other aspects of their job.
> . . . wander around the store, maintaining an open-door policy with respect to ideas and suggestions and remaining highly visible, heavily involved and actively solicitous of inputs in the daily coaching of customer contact personnel
> . . . reward and recognize outstanding performances of customer contact personnel on a regular basis
> . . . demonstrate through actions . . . the importance of the customer contact role
> . . . provide adequate preparation and training for store personnel
> . . . isolate as many potential problem situations as possible (such as phone calls to sales personnel when customers are in the department) and provide guidelines on how they can be best handled
> . . . set performance standards and periodically evaluate the quality of the customer's experience
> . . . be alert for shopping problems . . . such as customer difficulty in locating items
> . . . welcome customer complaints as an opportunity for positive communication with the customer

... design and manage the store's complaint and inquiry system to ensure fully satisfying responses

... make it as easy as possible for customers to lodge complaints and make inquiries. The customer should be able to answer the question "What do I do if I am not satisfied?"

... help communicate to higher levels of management the customer's preferences, likes and dislikes.[39]

## ASSESSMENT

Assessing customer care quality is a complicated matter. While some retailers rely on complaints and suggestions as performance measures, these are merely indicators of the extremes of customer reactions. A more representative sample of customer perceptions and experiences is necessary for a reliable assessment of customer care quality. The starting point is with the customer. There are many ways used to research customer care quality. For example, L.L. Bean has developed a well-deserved reputation for extraordinary customer care:

Some 96.7% of 3,000 customers L.L. Bean recently surveyed said that quality is the attribute they like most about the company. Bean executes a customer-driven quality program by:

Conducting regular customer satisfaction surveys and sample group interviews to track customer and non-customer perceptions of the quality of its own and its competitors' products and services.

Tracking on its computer all customer inquiries and complaints and updating the file daily.

Guaranteeing all its products to be 100% satisfactory and providing a full cash refund, if requested, on any returns.

Asking customers to fill out a short, coded questionnaire and explain their reasons for returning the merchandise.

Performing extensive field tests on any new outdoor equipment before listing it in the company's catalogues.

Even stocking extra buttons for most of the apparel items carried years ago, just in case a customer needs one.[40]

An advertisement in *The New York Times* by L.L. Bean suggested that only when the customer has used up the product and is totally satisfied is the sale complete. Delivering against such customer care standards is not always easy. In 1988, dissatisfied Bean customers returned $82 million in goods, prompting management to update size information in the catalogues and ordertakers' computers and to retrain 3200 employees in order to improve customer care to previous standards.[41]

Any customer care quality assessment program begins with the retailer's customer care strategy and standards. The assessment program should be designed to see to what extent these standards are being met and, if they are not, why not. If customers are being lost, the retailer needs to know why.

Whether customers are interviewed, surveyed, or whatever, the questions are basic: "Are we easy to do business with? Are we responsive? Do we keep our customer care promises? Do we listen? Do we seem to care?", and so on. The retail marketer should compare customer expectations of customer care with customer perceptions of the customer care experienced, in his or her own store and in those of competitors.

As discussed in Chapter 6, there are a variety of research designs to choose from when designing customer research. One popular approach is to use trained **"mystery shoppers"** who simulate customer behaviour and then report to management on their experiences. This approach has the advantages of being more systematic, consistent, and detailed than asking regular customers to recount their experiences. It has the disadvantages of "mystery shoppers" being more attuned to looking for what management is interested in than what "real" customers are interested in, and of becoming too mechanical (e.g., using stopwatches to measure acknowledgment time without taking into account circumstances in the store at the time). While useful, mystery shopper programs should not be the only method of gauging customer care quality. Some firms regularly survey their customers. For example, Levi Strauss attaches questionnaires to its Dockers apparel, and Nissan surveys customers shortly after purchase and again one year after purchase.

In customer care "satisfaction" research, it is quite likely that customer problems and dissatisfactions will be uncovered. Those doing the research should attend to these, not simply record them.

The other side of customer care quality assessment is examining managerial and employee perceptions and suggestions. There are a variety of approaches, ranging from employee suggestion (and reward) programs to extensive interviewing of employees. Sometimes, external consultants examine basic attitudes and even the language used by employees. John Graham put it this way:

> Interestingly, language plays a key role in how we provide service. If we really think like a customer, our language will reflect that view. Our words become an expression of how we view the person who buys our products or services. There is only one goal when it comes to service: to instil confidence in the customer. When the right words are used, the organization begins to behave as if they were true. Use the wrong words and the opposite is true. Here are the words:
>
> "I'll take care of that for you"
> "I take full responsibility"
> "We want your business"
> "Thank you for thinking of us"
> "Consider it done."[42]

According to consultant Sybil Stershic: "In addition to using the results of customer satisfaction measurement, it's important to assess the internal service culture through employee interviews, focus groups, and surveys."[43]

Berry and colleagues suggest asking customer care employees "What is the biggest problem you face in trying to deliver quality care day in and day out?" and "If you were president and could make only one change to improve service quality here, what change would you make?"[44] Any efforts to assess customer care quality should involve careful attention to the distinction between customer care system performance and the performance of the people providing care. Berry, Bennett, and Brown suggested four rules for any customer care quality performance measurement system: relate the measures directly to customer care standards; train customer care employees so that they have the knowledge and skills they need to do well in the measurement system; carefully communicate the "rules of the game" to those being measured; and use more than one measure to get different angles on customer care performance.[45] For example, mystery shopper programs should be shared with employees, including the criteria that mystery shoppers are using and the reports they prepare.

It is also important to assess senior management's behaviour toward customer care. George Rieder suggests management keep a time log for a while to see whether they are really devoting time to customer care quality management as opposed to simply talking about it:

> Calculate the percentage of time and energies devoted to: clarifying key quality factors and standards of performance; measuring efficiency and effectiveness in meeting quality standards; reinforcing and rewarding service quality performance; hiring, placement and promotion decisions where service quality factors play a principal part; orientation, training, and development activities that communicate a company's basic beliefs and values of customer service; and finding innovative ways to improve service levels through simplified systems, automation, and customer education.[46]

It is important to compare and link customer feedback and employee feedback. The first question is whether management and employees are "in tune" with customers. If employees feel they are delivering excellent customer care but the customers disagree, this is obviously a major problem. As well, the retailer can use customer feedback in her or his management of people. For example, one can tell employees what customers say, use customer feedback as basis for reward or incentive programs, or even use customer feedback as direct link to regular compensation. According to Chris Lee:

> A small, but growing number of companies are attacking the prickly challenge of delivering customer satisfaction by practising a simple maxim: What gets rewarded gets done. Top management make sure that they are rewarding performance that customers want, they tie employees' incentives or bonuses to ratings given by the customers.[47]

Ultimately, of course, the acid test of any customer care program is its effects on sales and profits. As with many other dimensions of the total marketing program, calculating the impact of investments in customer care on the "bottom line" is a very difficult task. It is far easier to reduce investments and costs (such as by reducing on-floor salespeople) to see dollar savings than it is to maintain that increases in these investments and costs paid off in increased profits. Yet, this inability to quantify results will be overcome in time with creative efforts. In the meantime, it is important to make decisions consciously about the level of customer care that will be provided and to begin the difficult task of assessing how that level relates to one's marketing objectives of acquiring and retaining customers.

Reward, recognition, and incentive programs are very important reinforcers of customer care strategy. In other words, a positive human relations environment helps immensely in accomplishing customer care objectives. According to Gordon Segal, the CEO of Crate and Barrel, "If top management doesn't care about staff, staff won't care about customers."[48] Staff generally won't treat customers any better than they are treated.

Some retailers have been using a recognition program designed to sustain a care culture. Such programs may include putting stars on badges or giving gold name tags or business cards so that employees and customers recognize a "customer care performer." Tom Amerman, Parisian's senior vice-president of Personnel and Loss Prevention, explained his company's emphasis on individual recognition of its sales professionals:

> How many CEO's today know the actual names, or have met face-to-face in a store, with their top producers? How many GMM's call their top producers to find out why something is or isn't selling? Or know how much volume they sold last month? How many buyers know? How does it make a person feel to be recognized only once a year?
>
> You can have all the banquets you want. But when a division gets a report and can call a sales person, and knows that Sally Jones was the top producer in juniors last month, that's quite an ego trip.[49]

Some retailers also use newsletters and meetings to highlight "acts of customer care heroism" where individual employees went beyond management's expectations to serve customers.

## ■ CONCLUSION

Customer care expectations are constantly changing, which means that, as commendable as any retailer's level of customer care may be, it is always important to seek ways to make it better. Exhibit 9.4 shows the major questions a retailer may use to formulate, implement, and evaluate a customer care strategy. These questions should be addressed if one hopes to use customer care as a competitive edge, not just a "me too" effort.

Customer care and service is an exciting possibility for competitive advantage because quality customer care is hard to find; it is highly valued by customers; and it allows a retailer to focus productively on the best target market available—those people already in the store.

Customer care must be a managed program of design, promise, delivery, and assessment. Above all, customer care requires careful and powerful **internal marketing**. Customer care providers must be both willing and able to provide superior customer care and service.

---

*EXHIBIT 9.4*
*Customer Care*
*Management*
*Questions*

**Customer care strategy design:**

1. Is there an identifiable customer care strategy?
2. Does the strategy distinguish between customer care and services?
3. To what extent does the customer care strategy include the notion of relationship management?
4. Is the language used appropriate (e.g., customers versus clients)?
5. To what extent does the strategy include efforts to customize relationships with customers?
6. Does the strategy provide for competitive advantage by focusing on meaningful dimensions of customer care in ways superior to those of competitors?
7. Does the strategy encompass the many dimensions of customer care?
8. Does the strategy fit with what is known about customer expectations of care, ways in which customers make patronage decisions and get customer care quality cues?
9. In designing the customer care strategy, were all steps in the customer experience/ interaction charted and examined? Was the strategy designed to provide levels of customer care appropriate to the nature of the customer care encounter type?
10. Has there been an attempt to identify especially meaningful customer care opportunities?
11. Have customers been involved in the customer care strategy design?
12. Have the relevant aspects of the employees' jobs been examined to ensure that the procedures, equipment, and other aspects of the "system" are appropriate for the customer care strategy?
13. To what extent have employees been involved in the customer care strategy design?
14. What are the customer care standards? Are they specific and communicable?

**Customer care promise:**

1. Is the stance that customer expectations are a "given" or that they can be influenced?
2. To what extent is customer care being promised in advertising and promotion? In in-store signage, etc.? In employees' interactions?
3. Is the customer care strategy apparent at all points of interaction with customers?
4. What is the impact of the "customer care desk" in terms of location, staffing, etc.?
5. Are there customer care guarantees? If so, are they well handled?

**Customer care delivery:**

1. To what extent are employees willing to give the customer care desired? Is this built into recruiting decisions?

2. Does the company culture and reward/punishment system foster delivering superior customer care? Who are the customer care quality champions and do they have stature in the company?

3. To what extent are employees able to give superior customer care by virtue of their training and management?

4. To what extent are employees able to give superior customer care by virtue of the staffing levels, equipment, layout, expectations of their job function, etc.?

5. Are employees divided into workable groups and given responsibility for customer care delivery?

6. Are store managers in particular responsible for customer care?

**Customer care assessment:**

1. Is the customer care assessment task given emphasis?

2. Is the assessment effort properly related to the customer care strategy and standards?

3. Are customers, competitors, and employees surveyed regularly and thoroughly?

4. If mystery shoppers are used, what efforts are made to calibrate their findings with customer perceptions and experiences?

5. Are the aspects of customer care that are most important to customers being measured?

6. Are employees encouraged and rewarded for customer care quality improvement suggestions and superior performance?

7. Are employees periodically asked "What are the barriers preventing you from offering better customer care?"

8. Do employees believe top management is really committed to customer care?

9. Are store managers in particular ensuring that customer care is given priority?

10. How much time is spent on customer care quality versus pricing, inventory, and other matters in meetings and discussions?

11. Is customer care quality "reported" at management meetings with the same vigour as inventory levels, sales, etc.?

---

## REVIEW QUESTIONS

1. In your experience, which retail marketer provided you with the most customer care? What exactly was done to lead you to this conclusion?

2. Consider all the stages involved in planning, arranging, and undertaking a one-week holiday requiring air travel, car rental, and hotel accommodation. What are the "customer care encounter points" in this trip? (You may find drawing a flow chart useful.)

3. Continuing this example, supposing you were the traveller, what would be the most important encounter points and how would you distinguish good customer care and service from poor at these points?

4. Many apparel retailers have begun sending "thank you" postcards to customers after the purchase. Is this a good idea? Why?

5. Ernst & Young's 1990 *Human Resources in Retail* survey examined 86 U.S. retail organizations. Two-thirds of store managers were male and 70 percent were over 30 years old. A typical sales associate was female (56 percent), over 20 years old (82 percent), worked full time (58 percent), had been on staff for less than two years (60 percent), and was paid on a salary-plus-incentive basis (92 percent).[50] What are the implications of these findings for managing customer care programs in these organizations?

## KEY TERMS

- customer service
- service
- patronage-building services
- revenue-producing service
- customer care
- customer care encounter
- relationship
- self-selection (operation)

- limited service (operation)
- full-service (operation)
- customer care opportunities
- customer care standards
- customer care guarantees
- mystery shoppers
- interval marketing

## NOTES

1. Terrence J. Smith, "Nurturing a Customer Service Culture," *Retail Control*, October 1989, pp. 15–18.

2. Stanley Marcus, "Fire a Buyer and Hire a Seller," *Journal of International Retailing*, Fall 1985, pp. 49–55.

3. Leonard L. Berry and Larry G. Gresham, "Relationship Retailing: Transforming Customers into Clients," *Business Horizons*, November–December 1986, pp. 43–47.

4. Berry and Gresham, "Relationship Retailing" (see n. 3), pp. 43–47.

5. H. Braun, C. Cohen, and I. Cohen, "U.S./Canadian Retailers Worried About Customer Service," *The Retail Advisor*, Touche Ross, February 1989, p. 2.

6. Karl Albrecht and Ron Zemke, *Service America!* (Homewood, Ill.: Dow Jones Irwin, 1985).

7. Jackie Bivins, "Corporate Cultures," *Stores*, February 1989, pp. 9–15.

8. James R. Williams, "President's Letter," *Stores*, September 1984, p. 80.

9. Jules Abend, "Focus on Customer Service: Are There Better Ways?" *Stores*, December 1988, pp. 56–72.

10. Jules Abend, "Aiming to Please," *Stores*, October 1984, pp. 50–54.

11. Leonard L. Berry, "Delivering Excellent Service in Retailing," *Retailing Issues Letter*, Arthur Andersen and Co., April 1988.

12. Roy Burns, "Customer Service Vs. Customer Focussed," *Retail Control*, March 1989, pp. 25–35.

13. Albert D. Bates, "Rethinking the Service Offer," *Retailing Issues Letter*, Zale Corporation, June 1986.

14. Bro Uttal, "Companies That Serve You Best," *Fortune*, 7 December 1987, pp. 98–116.

15. Berry and Gresham, "Relationship Retailing" (see n. 3), pp. 43–47.

16. Kevin Coyne, "Beyond Service Fads— Meaningful Strategies for the Real World," *Sloan Management Review*, Summer 1989, pp. 69–76.

17. A. Parasuraman, V. Zeithaml, and L. Berry Servqual, *A Multiple-Item Scale for Measuring Customer Perceptions of Service Quality* (Cambridge, Mass.: Marketing Science Institute, August 1986).

18. See, in particular, A. Parasuraman, Valarie Zeithaml, and Leonard L. Berry, *A Conceptual Model of Service Quality and Its Implications for Future Research*, Marketing Science Institute Working Paper, 1984.

19. George A. Rieder, "Show Me: The Secret to Building A Service-Minded Culture," *Retailing Issues Letter*, Zale Corporation, June 1986.

20. Albert D. Bates, "Rethinking the Service Offer" (see n. 15).

21. Albrecht and Zemke, *Service America!* (see n. 8), chapter 3.

22. Leonard L. Berry, A. Parasuraman, and Valarie Zeithaml, "The Service-Quality Puzzle," *Business Horizons*, September–October 1988, pp. 35–43. See also, James M. Carman, "Consumer Perceptions of Service Quality: An Assessment of the SERQUAL Dimensions," *Journal of Retailing*, Spring 1990, pp. 33–55.

23. For a review of how American Express has approached customer care, see Richard T. Garfein, "Evaluating the Impact of Customer Service Delivery Systems," *The Journal of Services Marketing*, Fall 1987, pp. 19–25.

24. Albrecht and Zemke, *Service America!* (see n. 8), p. 64.

25. Christopher H. Lovelock, "Competitive Advantage Lies in Supplementary, Not Core Services," *Marketing News*, 30 January 1989, p. 15.

26. As quoted by Albrecht and Zemke (see n. 8), p. 27.

27. Coyne, "Beyond Service Fads" (see n. 18), pp. 69–76.

28. Dave Ulrich, "Tie the Knot: Gaining Complete Customer Commitment," *Sloan Management Review*, Summer 1989, pp. 19–27.

29. Karl Hellman, "Don't Just Meet Customer Expectations—Exceed Them," *Marketing News*, 13 March 1989, pp. 5, 10.

30. Timothy W. Firnstahl, "My Employees Are My Service Guarantee," *Harvard Business Review*, July–August 1989, pp. 28–34.

31. Christopher W.L. Hart, "The Power of Unconditional Service Guarantees," *Harvard Business Review*, July–August 1988, pp. 54–62.

32. "Xerox Guarantees 'Total Satisfaction,'" *Marketing News*, 15 October 1990, p. 2.

33. Roy Burns, "Customer Service Vs. Customer Focussed," *Retail Control*, March 1989, pp. 25–35.

34. Albrecht and Zemke, *Service America!* (see n. 8), p. 102.

35. Theodore Levitt, "After the Sale Is Over . . .," *Harvard Business Review*, September–October 1983, pp. 87–93.

36. Jack Prouty, Gerald Roth, and Chuck Nelson, "An Evolving Obsession with Customer Service," *Retail Control*, September 1988, pp. 2–12.

37. For example, see Anat Rafaeli, "When Cashiers Meet Customers: An Analysis of the Role of Supermarket Cashiers," *Academy of Management Journal*, vol. 32 (1989), pp. 245–73.

38. James S. Hensel, "Store Managers Should Be Customer Satisfaction Managers," *Retailing Issues Letter*, Zale Corporation, October 1985.

39. Albert D. Bates, "Rethinking the Service Offer," *Retailing Issues Letter*, Zale Corporation, June 1986.

40. Hirotaka Takeuchi, and John A. Quelch, "Quality Is More Than Making a Good Product," *Harvard Business Review*, July–August 1983, pp. 139–45.

41. Stephen Phillips, Amy Dunkin, James Treece, and Keith Hammonds, "King Customer," *Business Week*, 12 March 1990, pp. 88–94.

42. John R. Graham, "Keep Customers by Using the Right Words," *Marketing News*, 24 October 1988, p. 4.

43. Sybil F. Stershic, "Internal Marketing Campaign Reinforces Service Goals," *Marketing News*, 31 July 1989, p. 11.

44. Berry, Parasuraman, and Zeithaml, "The Service-Quality Puzzle" (see n. 25), pp. 35–43.

45. Leonard Berry, David Bennett, and Carter Brown, *Service Quality: A Profit Strategy for Financial Institutions* (New York: Dow Jones Irwin, 1988).

46. George A. Rieder, "Show Me: The Secret to Building a Service-Minded Culture," *Retailing Issues Letter*, Zale Corporation, June 1986.

47. Chris Lee, "Using Customers' Ratings to Reward Employees," *Training*, May 1989, pp. 40-46.

48. Speech given at Texas A & M, Fall 1987.

49. Jules Abend, "Service: Shaping Up?" *Stores*, September 1986, pp. 74–87.

50. "Study: Store Management," *Stores*, September 1990, pp. 48–49.

CHAPTER

# Information

## Introduction

Customers need and want **information** to help in making choices about where to shop and what to buy. Retail marketers need and want to create customer **incentives to patronize and to buy** from them; these are created and nurtured by images, ideas, thoughts, and feelings that customers have about themselves and about relevant competing retailers and their offerings. How customers make choices about where to shop and what to buy is a complex and somewhat contentious field of study. Most observers agree, however, that all of us seek information and process it in one form or another, and that that information greatly impacts on our behaviours in the marketplace.

The purpose of this chapter is to discuss several key elements of **information exchange between the retailer and the customer**. It encompasses the many related activities retailers undertake to provide incentives to patronize and to buy, such as providing information about store location, hours, ease of parking, products carried, prices, and so on, and the ways customers respond to such information. Although most of the information flow is directed *from* the retailer *to* the potential customer, the customer also communicates *back* to the retailer by his or her choices and behaviour, and, of course, through comments, complaints, and involvement in market research. Retailers need to manage all of the many aspects of their information programs as a coordinated set of activities to achieve maximum impact.

A related topic is **information exchange between the retailer and the vendor**. With the remarkable changes in information technology (such as point-of-sale capture of product movement) that has occurred in retail marketing, retailers now increasingly find themselves as the locus of informational power in their channels of distribution. Where once manufacturers were the centre of information about what customers wanted or what they were buying, retailers now have this position. With market information comes market power and, hence, dramatically changed retailer–vendor relationships; however, while this shift of informational control is extremely important, it is not the topic of this chapter.

From the customer's perspective, access to appropriate, timely, and credible information is valuable because it helps one make decisions about shopping. Although any one individual may not be considering the purchase of a particular product from a particular store at the same time the retailer is providing information about it, this information may nonetheless have a later impact on that person.

Information is a controllable dimension of the retail marketing effort, and includes five key dimensions, as shown in Figure 10.1: advertising, promotion, signs and displays, personal selling, and direct marketing. Each of these dimensions is discussed in turn in this chapter; and although the chapter is lengthy, it is important to examine the many different ways that retail marketers convey information and incentive to buy to customers.

FIGURE 10.1
Elements of Information

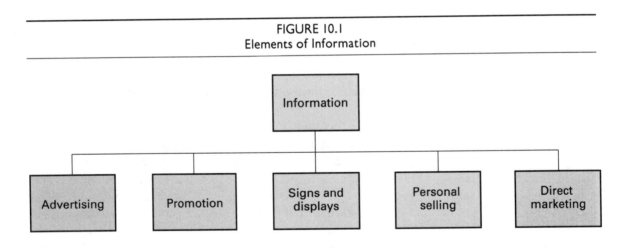

## RETAIL ADVERTISING

■
SECTION
■
ONE
■

Retail advertising is intended to communicate to potential customers some of the benefits of the offer being made by the retailer. It occurs *outside* of the store, is paid for directly (unlike publicity), and is designed to bring customers into the store primed to buy. One of Canada's earliest and most effective retail advertisers was Timothy Eaton. In 1890, he had a simple way of expressing what his advertising was intended to do: "Tell your story to the public what you have and what you propose to sell . . . that every article will be found just what it is guaranteed to be."[1]

Broadly speaking there are three types of retail advertising: store or company advertising, product/service advertising, and co-operative advertising. Advertising, like all other parts of the information program, involves decisions about:

1. Objectives
2. What to say
3. How much to spend
4. What media and scheduling to use
5. How to evaluate it

## What's Different about Retail Advertising

Unlike manufacturer advertising, which encourages consumers to focus on brand choices, retail advertising must also encourage customers to select one retailer over another. Traditionally, many observers have argued that retail advertising has been less sophisticated than manufacturer product advertising; however, the gap is narrowing. Whereas a company like Procter and Gamble has had more than seventy years to refine and adapt advertising techniques to its target market, national retailers entered the national-advertising fray much later, and have, therefore, had much less time to do so. Sears, for example, did not pursue consistent national advertising and pricing decisions until the mid- to late 1970s. Before that time, Sears' regional managers exercised a great deal of autonomy in the direction of Sears' local advertising programs.[2]

Furthermore, the structure of the retail environment is one that allows relatively small independent operators to survive and flourish in niches not exploited by national retailers. Many cities in North America can boast an indigenous local retailer who is as good if not better than the national chains at attracting and winning customers. Such retailers have found ways to overcome their size and budget limitations to communicate effectively with their markets.

Retail advertising, as compared to manufacturer product advertising, is also typified by shorter lead times for creation and execution, more use of local media, more use of print media, and a broader range of objectives being served, such as trying to motivate in-store customer-contact staff as well as customers.

## Advertising Objectives

It is important to have concrete objectives for any form of information campaign, including retail advertising. Objectives help guide creative efforts, select media and schedules, and evaluate the results of the campaign. One approach to setting objectives is to think about moving customers through their decision process from "unaware" to "repeat purchase," as shown in Exhibit 10.1. Different aspects of the information program are usually more effective for customers at different stages. For example, advertising is typically more effective at generating awareness, whereas personal selling is more effective at closing sales.

This approach must be tempered by an understanding of the specific circumstances facing one's customers. If the choice facing the customer is one that requires significant information or learning about the product or service and carries with it perceived high risk to the consumer (such as purchases of major appliances, new cars, homes, stereo equipment, computer technology), then it is in the interest of the retailer to emphasize in the advertising information about the store and product

EXHIBIT 10.1
Stages of
Customer
Purchasing
Process[1]

- Awareness
- Knowledge
- Liking
- Preference

- Conviction
- Purchase
- Post-purchase
- Repeat purchase

[1] This "hierarchy of effects" model is generally credited to Robert Lavidge and Gary A. Steiner, "A Model for Predictive Measurements of Advertising Effectiveness," *Journal of Marketing*, October 1961, p. 61.

differences such things as staff competence, store reputation, and product guarantees to reassure the customer that the risks of buying such a product are significantly reduced at that store.

Several specific objectives may be part of a retail advertising program, including:

1. Increase awareness of the store, its products, services, prices, and so on.
2. Find new customers by generating sales leads and referrals.
3. Increase the usage of a particular product.
4. Increase store traffic.
5. Increase unit sales to customers to pre-empt competitor advertising and promotion.
6. Reduce inventory (such as a post-Christmas clear-out of seasonal merchandise to improve cash-flow and pay receivables).
7. Announce store changes, price changes, new merchandise arrivals, seasonal promotions, and so on.
8. Instil pride and responsibility into front-line staff.

It is usually necessary to focus on only one or two of these objectives at a time to avoid diluting the message being sent in the advertising. Whatever objectives are chosen, it is helpful to be as specific as possible: "to increase sales" is not as specific as "to increase sales by 10 percent over the same period last year." The latter objective provides a clear, measurable target against which actual results can be assessed.

## WHAT TO SAY

Deciding what to say (also known as the creative or copy strategy) is a challenging task. Even if an advertising agency is used, the retailer should provide some guidelines for the message strategy. Having clear objectives for the advertising campaign helps greatly in selecting among the many possible messages and executions of those messages. Further, a thorough understanding of customers, competitors, and one's own offering provides the basis for crafting a message for an advertisement or series of advertisements. The message should be both informational and motivational. Essentially, an advertisement is a promise about some benefit(s) a customer will get from buying from the retailer. It may be a general promise (such as, what it is like to shop at that store) or it may be specific (such as, the nature of a particular product's performance).

There are many appeals that may be used, including: factual, positive or negative incentives, comparative, social, humorous, emotional, lifestyle, and sexual. These may be executed in several ways including: product demonstrations, torture tests, product or store as hero, product or store comparisons, testimonials by customers, endorsements by well-known people, product or store personification, slice-of-life (that is, showing a common life situation), and fantasy characters. Because the possibilities are endless, the following guidelines may be helpful when evaluating creative ideas:

1. Will customers understand the basic message and remember it?
2. Is the message about something that matters to customers? Does it focus on benefits?
3. Is it believable? Has every opportunity to "localize" the ad been used?
4. Has it been used a lot by others already?
5. Is it true and in good taste? Are there any legal concerns?[3]
6. Is it well made and does it reflect well on the retailer? Is the retailer well identified with wanted information, such as location, hours, and telephone number?
7. Is there any evidence that it works (pre-tests, etc.)?

Retailers who understand the dynamics of societal change will make better decisions on the messages and images they want to impart to their audience. For example, as social values change about women, marriage, sex, and so on, retail advertisers need to adapt their approaches to remain tasteful and appropriate.

The choice of what to say and how to say it is the essence of message design. A retailer who selects twenty-five items to feature in a cluttered half-page newspaper ad trumpeting price reductions will very likely convey the impression of a discount store, whether or not that was intended.

There are many tough questions retailers face about what to say and do in their advertising. Is it better to advertise the store or its products or both at the same time? Which of the many products carried should be advertised? How many at a time? Can customer care and service be advertised effectively? These and other questions go to the heart of the advertising (and information) strategy for any retailer. They cannot be answered with pat "textbook solutions," but rather must be decided upon according to the particular circumstances of the retail marketer.

## How Much to Spend

The question of how much to spend on retail information campaigns, such as advertising, also remains largely unanswerable. A retailer must decide how much to spend in total on providing information, and then how much to allocate to retail advertising and its various aspects, such as media. There are five methods to determine how much to spend:

1. A **fixed ratio formula** is a rule-of-thumb approach that usually relates the size of the advertising budget to forecasted sales levels. This approach is simple, but fails to adjust for changing circumstances. In other words, when sales go down, advertising will go down, yet there may be good reason to increase advertising when sales begin to decline.

2. **All-that-can-be-afforded approach** is one that relates the advertising budget more to the resources available than to the specific advertising needs of the retailer.

3. **Competitive benchmarking** refers to the retailer selecting some competitors to watch, then spending more, the same, or less than these competitors either in absolute terms or in relative terms. The major problem with this approach is that it assumes competitors know what they are doing with advertising.

4. The **task method** begins with some specific objectives (such as raising the retailer's awareness levels by 10 percent in the trading area over the next three months), then determines how much it will take to achieve these objectives. Unfortunately, it is often difficult to determine ahead of time just what will be required to accomplish any particular task.

5. **Experimentation** refers to basing decisions on controlled tests and then adjusting expenditures accordingly.

All of these approaches have their merits and shortcomings. Many retail marketers use at least two of these methods at a time to estimate a rough budget figure, and then fine-tune this number over time. Retailers may regard advertising (and other information program activities) spending as either an expense or an investment, regardless of how the accountants treat the spending on the firm's statements. An *expense viewpoint* regards advertising's impact as very short-term and thus results in treating advertising as a discretionary variable cost. An *investment viewpoint* regards advertising's impact as longer-term and cumulative (due to "carry-over effects") and thus results in treating advertising as a less-discretionary fixed cost.

## WHAT MEDIA AND SCHEDULING TO USE

One of the dilemmas facing any retail marketer is how to allocate what seems to be always a too small advertising budget to too many different media. The choices seem endless and include those shown in Exhibit 10.2.

Some criteria that a retailer can use to help determine media selection and allocation include:

1. Does the medium reach target customers in sufficient numbers with sufficient impact to be cost effective?

2. Will the type of message sent be more appropriate in one medium than in another?

*EXHIBIT 10.2*
*Retail*
*Advertising*
*Media*

## 1. Print

a. periodicals

b. newspapers (regular, supplements, inserts/pre-prints)

c. magazines

d. shopping publications

e. school papers

f. neighbourhood papers

g. telephone and other directories, directory jackets

## 2. Broadcast

a. radio commercials and on-site broadcasts

b. television (national, regional, and local)

c. cinema and videos

d. video trailers

e. loudspeakers

## 3. Signs

a. outdoor (billboards, posters, transit shelters, litter-disposal boxes)

b. transit (public, taxi, other)

c. banners

d. skywriting, airplane trailers

e. kites, blimps, balloons

f. benches, shopping carts, portasigns

g. sandwich boards

h. T-shirts and other clothing and accessories

i. retailer's own signs, exterior and interior

j. retailer's own trucks and delivery vehicles

## 4. Direct

a. mail (statement stuffers, individual flyers)

b. circulars, flyers, handbills

c. package or bag inserts

d. wrapping paper, shopping bags

e. catalogues

f. telephone (telemarketing)

g. electronic (computer, fax)

3. Does the cost of the exposure in the media outweigh the payoff expected?

4. Is the lead time required consistent with the time frame of the retailer? Is there adequate flexibility for last-minute changes?

5. Does the medium provide the image, graphics, colour, and demonstration capability sought?

6. Do any media leave a more permanent image in the minds of the consumers (if permanence is an objective)?

Each medium has specific strengths and weaknesses. Morris Saffer, founder of Saffer Advertising, a major retail advertising agency, has characterized some of the major media retailers might use, as shown in Exhibit 10.3.

*EXHIBIT 10.3*
*Saffer's Views of*
*Retail Media[1]*

## 1. Newspapers

### a. Strengths

- good for reaching a broad cross-section of the adult market
- flexible—can get in and out quickly and don't need to make long-term commitments
- good for presenting a lot of factual information such as items and prices
- good for generating quick response
- good for establishing credibility
- good for gaining audience involvement in the message—there is some evidence that customers read newspapers because of the ads, which is in contrast to broadcast where the advertising is regarded as an intrusion
- relatively low production costs

### b. Weaknesses

- relatively poor reproduction despite recent improvements
- poor ability to segment an audience except regionally
- no longer capable of delivering total mass market since percentage reach has been declining
- less ability than tv to create an overall mood or image
- generally conservative management that does not provide as good marketing research information as the broadcast media

## 2. Radio

### a. Strengths

- excellent ability to target, especially on young people
- good choice for frequency
- good for creating image and mood
- good for presenting a single big concept

- reasonably good for generating fast response
- easy to update quickly
- relatively low production costs
- tremendous creative potential—"theatre of the mind"

### b. Weaknesses

- no visual factor
- relatively poor ability to communicate a lot of factual information—hard to remember it all
- relatively poor ability for a single station to deliver a mass market
- not as good an environment as a newspaper since music is often background not being actively listened to
- can be difficult to buy well—lot of negotiating off rate card

## 3. Television

### a. Strengths

- tremendous impact despite criticism of irritation of commercials
- excellent ability to deliver mass audience although this is diminishing with more and more stations
- excellent for creating mood and image
- excellent for demonstrations
- good ability to generate fast response

### b. Weaknesses

- less flexible than radio or newspapers—requires longer-term commitment and planning
- relatively poor ability to communicate a lot of factual information
- irritation factor—zipping, zapping, time shifting
- relatively high production costs
- usually difficult to buy well without lots of experience

---

[1] Morris Saffer, in class discussions when visiting at the Western Business School, The University of Western Ontario, 1986, 1987.

Whatever media are used, the retailer must always consider the context in which a customer finds the advertisement. For example, a retail newspaper ad should not be designed as a "free-standing" message, but rather as one of many such ads found in the newspaper any particular day: will it stand out from the crowd for the reader?

**Scheduling** refers to when the advertising will be shown to customers. Scheduling decisions involve choices about time of year, time of season, time of week, and time of day. Scheduling also involves deciding whether to advertise relatively steadily or with "ups and downs" in frequency and/or weight (meaning, for example, size of the advertisement). Some scheduling decisions are dependent on the media availability. For example, if the local weekly newspaper is published on Thursdays, and this paper is judged to be the best medium for a small local retailer, then this will strongly impact the scheduling for that retailer's sale announcements.

Most retail marketers maintain an **advertising and promotion calendar** on which they plan their year's informational campaigns. Choices are then made about sale events, what to do around seasonal holidays, and so on, such that adequate planning time is allotted and the total budget is allocated over the many competing demands for it. Most retailers have developed their advertising calendar over time with experience, learning, for example, how far ahead to promote Valentine's Day, and so on.

## How to Evaluate the Contribution of Advertising

Deciding whether informational expenditures, such as advertising, are worthwhile is difficult; predicting their impact even more difficult. Nonetheless, every retail advertiser should attempt to assess the impact of his or her advertising, if for no other reason than ensuring appropriate use of usually large amounts of money, which would otherwise go directly into profit. To assess the impact of advertising, one may compare results with the objectives that were set at the outset; or one may simply seek to discover what, if any, impact advertising had on customers.

In simple terms, retail advertising ultimately should contribute more to gross profit dollars than was spent on advertising. To illustrate, if the gross margin were 35 percent and the advertising budget were $50 000, then incremental sales of $142 857 would be required just to cover the costs of the advertising (50 000/.35). Only after achieving that sales figure would advertising begin to pay off.

Unfortunately, assessing advertising is seldom so simple as adding up incremental sales and comparing those with a sales target required to break even on the advertising budget. Some retailers are able to track sales directly from advertising by using coupons, specially coded ads that customers are asked to redeem at purchase, and so on; but this is the exception rather than the norm. Most retailers must rely on less-direct assessments of the impact of their advertising. In order for advertising, or any form of information, to be effective, it must be seen, it must be read, it must be believed, it must be remembered, and it must be acted upon.[4] This provides several dimensions of advertising that may be assessed; for example, how many people saw the ad and how many remembered seeing it. Retail advertisers cannot assume that because they placed an ad in a newspaper, everyone in town saw it, read it, and so on. All of us filter the barrage of information directed at us every day. There are four filters that an individual uses to block advertising: one selectively exposes oneself to places advertising is; one selectively perceives advertising (we do not all see messages the same way); one selectively remembers what one saw; and one selectively decides whether to act upon the advertising.[5]

Advertising performance assessment typically begins with determining *who* actually had an opportunity to be exposed to the advertising. Various measures can be used for media to indicate the number and the nature of the audience for those media. For example, in print media, **circulation** refers to the one time physical distribution of a publication to any individual in a household. There may, of course, be some secondary effects where the medium (such as a magazine) is read by more than one individual, and some media attempt through research to determine their readership. Circulation can then be compared with reach. **Reach** is the cumulative unduplicated target audience exposed to the advertiser's message, by media, expressed as a percentage of the target group population in a defined geographic area (the term "penetration" is sometimes used). Thus, if a particular newspaper was read by 50 percent of the retailer's target market, reach would be 50 percent.

If more than one occasion is used for the advertising, then frequency should be tracked as well. **Frequency** refers to the average number of occasions that the persons reached have been exposed to the ad in a given period of time. Reach and frequency can be combined for print media into **impressions**, that is, the total number of ads scheduled times the total target audience exposed to each occasion. One relative measure of efficiency of media is the **cost per thousand impressions (CPM)**, that is, the cost of delivering one thousand impressions to the target audience. With broadcast media, the approach is much the same. **Audience size** can be defined as anyone tuned into a station once or more often in a week. Reach and frequency then can be applied to this audience. However, in broadcast, the combination of reach and frequency is referred to as **gross rating points (GRPs)**. A one-point (GRP) rating is 1 percent of the total target audience tuned to a specific station at a specific time; thus, the total GRPs for a schedule are the sum of all ratings for a defined time period. Most media and advertising agencies can provide detailed information to assist a retail advertiser in planning and in evaluation of results.

These audience assessment techniques, which can be highly quantitative and sophisticated, can provide an estimate of the number of people who were exposed to the advertising message, but they do not indicate the success of the message itself in communicating an incentive to patronize or to buy. Therefore, the next level of analysis is the **impact** the advertising had on the people exposed. For example, one may use measures of change in the level of customer awareness of the store or its offering, in understanding, in recall (aided and unaided), in attitudes and acceptance, in intentions, in actual traffic, in inquiries, in coupon redemptions, in sales of advertised items, in overall sales, in image, and in referrals. These impact measures can be taken before, during, or after a particular advertising campaign is run. By comparing before and after measures, a retailer can gain some understanding of the supposed impact of the campaign—it is seldom possible to isolate the real impact of advertising from the impact of the many other influences on customers during any period of time. While sales measures of the impact of advertising are oriented more to the "bottom line," communications measures (such as recall) are often easier to use. Further, the longer the time period between advertising and its likely effect on sales, the better it is to use communications measures.

Most retail marketers have concluded that the best way to assess advertising is to assess it constantly, to use multiple measures, and to realize that there are no perfect performance methods at present. As with research, if possible it is a good idea to pre-test advertising impact. For example, a few focus groups may be asked their reaction to a proposed brochure before it is mass distributed. Other informational activities can be assessed in comparable ways.

## CO-OPERATIVE ADVERTISING

**Co-operative advertising** refers to advertising that is jointly sponsored by a retailer and a supplier (or another partner such as a shopping centre or even a group of retailers), but directed at the final customer. Co-operative arrangements may also include sales promotion and other information vehicles, such as catalogues; these arrangements are usually contractual, specifying what the retailer must do, what the vendor/manufacturer will pay for, and all the procedures that must be followed for the retailer to be reimbursed.

Co-operative advertising must serve the interests of both the retailer and the vendor. The *retailer* may be interested to participate in cost sharing, to find ways to extend the advertising budget, to associate the store image with the vendor's image, to build awareness that the store carries a well-known brand, or to build a better relationship with the vendor by engaging in joint efforts. The *manufacturer* may be interested to improve trade relationships, to add to the advertising support the product otherwise would receive, to lower his or her advertising costs, to find a way to get the retailer to carry particular products or more of a product or put the product in particular places in the store, or to build sales by associating the product with the retailer's image.

While co-operative advertising may be desirable in many situations, it seems most appropriate in situations that may be characterized as "retailer-dependent," as follows:

- Selective distribution—relatively expensive shopping goods infrequently purchased, low brand loyalty
- Contemplative purchase—ego-involving
- Customer expects personal service—retailer has relatively large impact on purchase choice
- Both retailer and vendor believe there is value in sharing the campaign costs in order to increase the total amount spent.

There are some problems with co-operative advertising.[6] For example, in Canada and many other jurisdictions, co-operative programs must be proportionately available to all the vendor's customers and the vendor must inform them all of the availability. In many instances, the problems with co-operative programs are largely attributable to an overly complex or onerous set of administrative procedures as to what the retailer must do in order to be reimbursed and what the manufacturer must do to avoid paying nonqualifying claims. Often, difficulties arise because of disagreements about exactly how the money should be spent. Such issues sometimes cloud the more important strategic question: how does one trade off the value of co-operative advertising with one's own advertising?[7]

## SUMMARY

Retail advertising is an important aspect of retail information, and the issues involved in managing advertising typify other information program components. To summarize this section, here are some retail advertising principles from Warren Kornblum, the principal of MMB/Kornblum International Inc., a Canadian retail advertising agency:[8]

1. Great advertising begins with a sound strategy.
2. Singularity of purpose and theme must precede the creative act.
3. Research, while a valuable tool, is no substitute for sound judgment.
4. The greatest advertising achieves not merely share of mind but share of heart.
5. With the big idea, you can outsmart the competition; without it, you may have to outspend them.
6. Advertising that rewards the attention of the customer builds business.
7. People don't count the number of ads you run—they simply remember the impression you made.
8. Safe advertising is risky business.
9. The best advertising is good salesmanship—otherwise what's the point.
10. Nothing is more cost effective than the creativity that makes one ad do the work of ten.
11. An ad agency is only as good as the results it produces for its clients.
12. Talk with, not at, the customer.

**SECTION**

**TWO**

## RETAIL SALES PROMOTION

Retail sales promotions include a wide range of techniques intended to provide short-term or immediate incentives to patronize a particular retailer and/or to buy particular products. Sales promotion is often the "all other" category after considering the advertising, signs, displays, and personal selling aspects of the information program. The dividing line between advertising and sales promotion is often quite arbitrary, particularly since many information programs now combine both to increase the impact on customers.

Sales promotion approaches used by retailers include, but are not limited to, the following: gifts and samples, premiums and prizes, coupons, price reductions and rebates, contests and sweepstakes, events, tie-ins, and continuity programs.

**Gifts and samples**    Gifts and samples are usually products offered to the customer either to provide a "no cost" trial of the product or in some cases to instil a sense of obligation to buy in the shopper. Gifts and samples are not conditional on purchase.

**Premiums and prizes**    Premiums and prizes are conditional on purchase or at least doing something the retailer values, such as providing information that may in time be used as a mailing list. There are many types of premiums. Two frequent types are "purchase with purchase" (such as being able to buy another product at a much-reduced price) and "gift with purchase." Premiums and prizes either may represent a cost to the retailer or be "self-liquidating," which means customers cover the direct costs of the promotion through paying some money. For example, if the retailer can purchase T-shirts at a very low price and then offer them to customers for that low price as a purchase-with-purchase premium, then the promotion would be essentially self-liquidating.

**Coupons**    Coupons are basically certificates that entitle customers to price reduction. While couponing is used a great deal by major food and beverage manufacturers, store-specific couponing is also being used by stores to create sales within their own stores by coupons that are redeemable only at a particular store or group of stores. The most common type of retailer coupons are price reduction coupons and "discount money." The former are coupons entitling shoppers to special prices on specific items. The latter can be used like cash to reduce the prices paid on any items in the store on subsequent visits. Canadian Tire has used such coupons for many years. Coupons may be distributed by mail or by media (such as newspapers), or they may be provided at point-of-purchase.

**Price reductions and rebates**    Price reductions are another method of sales promotion. They can be either part of an offer presented in an advertising campaign with a specific "deal" period offered the customer; or they can be unannounced, but routine, in-store specials. The objective of both approaches is to increase traffic to the store as well as stimulate the sales of a particular brand. Often pricing promotions like these will be undertaken with the financial help of the manufacturer whose brands will be featured. Price reductions refer to direct decreases in the price paid in-store. The customer receives either the same amount of product for less money or more product for the same money. Price rebates require the customer to apply, usually by mail, for a refund from the price paid. Rebates are more frequently used by manufacturers than retailers.

**Contests and sweepstakes**    Contests and sweepstakes refer to theme promotions enabling customers an opportunity to win prizes, trips, cash, or other rewards. In **contests**, customers compete for a limited number of prizes and premiums. There are legal issues about skill testing and "consideration" (that is, what the customer must do to participate, such as providing a proof of purchase). **Sweepstakes**, on the other hand, are simply "games of chance." These are increasingly favoured, as evidenced by the many "scratch and win" and other sweepstakes programs being offered.

**Tie-ins**    A tie-in promotion involves tying the purchase of one product or service to another. It is intended to build sales of one through the proven success of another.

Tie-in promotions may involve several products or services for one retailer, or even two or more retailers. For example, Sears and McDonald's very successfully ran a tie-in promotion for McKids, a line of children's apparel. Many retailers, from gasoline retailers to department stores, have been actively exploring these "cross-merchandising" opportunities.

**Events**    Events can include a great variety of happenings. Many retailers offer store events such as "anniversary sales," "liquidation sales," and so on. Other events may include parades, sidewalk sales, "tent sales," and "midnight madness extravaganzas." Events may also be co-operative such as getting together with other retailers in a shopping centre. Some events may be sponsored by the retailer (such as a local sporting event); others may be actually orchestrated by the retailer (such as a fashion show). There seem to be endless possibilities in terms of what and where to do something unusual to increase sales.

**Continuity programs**    Continuity programs are intended primarily to increase patronage. There have been many types, most notably trading stamps, collectibles, and frequent buyer programs. For example, gas service stations traditionally have made available complete sets of glassware or tableware, but multiple visits to the company offering the promotion were necessary to complete a set because only one unit was available per purchase. Some grocery chains still offer trading stamps, which can be collected by the customer in return for some future gift of the customer's choosing from a catalogue of items available at varying numbers of stamps. Zellers' "Club Z" is a variation of the trading stamp promotion approach: a frequent buyer program modelled after the airlines' frequent flyer programs. Regular purchases at Zellers over time are rewarded by a gift chosen by the card-carrying customer. This "frequent shopper program" has had astounding penetration of the Canadian market—nearly 50 percent of homes had a Club Z card as of early 1990—and has been credited as a main contributor to Zellers' dramatic sales and profit growth in recent years.[9]

The purpose of all these continuity efforts is to encourage regular shopping habits at the same retailer. In each instance, there is a "hook" that may force the customer to continue a shopping pattern in order to win a contest, collect a prize, or complete a set of dishes.

**Other types**    There are of course other types of sales promotions, such as charity sponsorships, seminars, and participation in community events.

Also, there has been an increasing use of technology in sales promotion, both in delivering the offer to customers and in tracking the impact of the promotion. Electronic discount systems that provide coupons in-store or even deduct price reductions at the checkout are becoming increasingly common. An article in *The New York Times* characterized the three major electronic discount systems as follows:

- Post-purchase discounts: Readers, printers, and video screens interface with scanning equipment at cash registers and issue coupons for designated products.

These are based on what the customer has bought or is expected to buy in the next visit.

- Pre-purchase discounts: Machines that dispense coupons are in the shopping areas, and consumers choose coupons for the products they want, often by touching the screen of the dispensing machine. They then select the products they want and take them and the coupons to the checkout counter.
- Frequent shopper programs: Customers who use the same store regularly sign up for plastic identification cards. A shopper gives the card to the check-out clerk, who inserts it in a machine that records the shopper's identification number and all of the purchases. When certain quantities or products have been bought, customers get either free merchandise or cash rebates.[10]

## MEASURING THE IMPACT OF SALES PROMOTIONS

All of these efforts are designed to produce a short-term incentive to buy at a specific retail outlet. Measuring the exact impact is a formidable task, although one that has become significantly easier with item tracking capability in many retail operations. Essentially, a retailer needs to be able to track pre-promotion, during-promotion, and post-promotion data on product movement, prices, costs, and vendor allowances and discounts taken. An alert retailer would add to this list display space and location, sales and profits of related items in the category, and maybe even overall store traffic and results.[11]

For sales promotions to be effective, several conditions must prevail, including:

1. The basic product or service must be of some interest to customers.
2. The promotional reward must be perceived as having adequate value to merit changing patterns of behaviour.
3. The effort required of the consumer to get the reward must not be too burdensome.
4. The firm must meet the promises made—not fulfilling rebates, etc. can be very negative.
5. The promotion must pay for itself, including taking into account any negative impact on category sales or longer-term patterns (such as customers stocking up this week due to a promotion and then not buying as they regularly would next week).

Calculating the economic impact of promotions can be complicated because of all the variables to consider.[12]

■
**SECTION**
■
**THREE**
■

## SIGNS, DISPLAYS, AND POINT-OF-PURCHASE INFORMATION

There are a myriad of ways to convey information and incentive to buy *at and in-store*. These methods range from straightforward printed signs to "motion-sensitive" devices that activate a pre-recorded message as the customer nears a display. Every aspect of the store can be looked at in terms of how well it provides information to customers and, of course, whether that information is consistent with customer needs and the retailer's marketing strategy. Viewing the store this way, the alert retailer approaches product tagging, shelf signs, bags, uniforms, mannequins and fixtures, props, and so on, as communication methods and devices, deserving as much or more care and attention as media advertising and sales promotion.

## SIGNS

Signs are critically valuable pieces of retail information that communicate quickly to the public:

> For too long, signing has been at the bottom of the store presentation considerations. But in fact, a sign is as much an extension of the corporate image as is an ad, poster, or a store logo. More sales are generated at the point of purchase by instore presentation than all other media combined. The merchandise picture augmented by consistently attractive and informative signs adds credibility to the sales floor.
>
> Good signing is good selling—signage in your store is one of its most important elements. Your signs are your silent communicators to your customers; they start off the sale before the salesperson gets to the customer, and they act in place of the salesperson in a self-service or self-selection store. They should be carefully chosen and designed to conform with your store image.[13]

There are several types of retail signs:

1. *exterior signs*
   a.   store name
   b.   hours, services provided, credit cards taken, etc.

2. *interior signs*
   a.   department
   b.   category
   c.   point-of-purchase or item (sometimes called "shelf-talkers")
   d.   event (such as anniversary sale, Valentine's Day).

Signing can direct traffic, suggest products, and dramatize a display. For example, department stores in mall settings can use signing, exposed to the mall traffic, to draw attention to products that customers might not normally associate with the department store offer: "Come and view our patio furniture on the 6th floor." Retailers can also pre-sell an upcoming seasonal offer: "Watch for our garden centre to be opened in the north parking lot on April 15."

Signing can cross-sell merchandise and suggest purchases to consumers that they may otherwise have overlooked. A grocery manager may place signs in the fresh produce section reminding customers not to forget to pick up a bottle of their favourite salad dressing before leaving the store.

Signing can add to the decor of a store, augment its image, and enhance its display. A promotion for beachwear may create a mood that helps the customer think about vacations rather than the miserable late winter weather outside.

Good signing is distinctive, informative, recognizable as coming from a particular retailer, durable in the case of permanent signing, and flexible in the case of nonpermanent signing.

## DISPLAYS

The way in which merchandise is displayed and presented can have a great impact on customers, both in terms of the information conveyed and the feelings generated. For example, if customers seek information about how a product works or how to assemble or install it, a retailer may place photos, pamphlets, or even a video running on a monitor adjacent to the product display. Management of KinderZimmer, a toy and children's furniture store operating in San Francisco, decided that it was important to get children directly interacting with their merchandise while in the store. Therefore, there are sandboxes, puppet theatres, and an open-stock display throughout the store. Said Jim Abrams, KinderZimmer president: "Children have to be able to touch and play with the merchandise. It is important both for the parent and for us. We want to see the way children relate to the toys."[14]

There are two basic types of displays: **special displays** of products to attract customers into the store (such as window displays) or a department; and **selection displays** from which merchandise is expected to be sold (such as an item display). Each of these types of display have many variations. For example, windows may be open to the exterior or closed (only visible from the exterior), may be of varying sizes, may be in varying locations, and so on. Similarly, mannequins may be full-figure, half-figure, bustforms, heads, and so on; they may be selected to as closely resemble target customers as possible or they may be forms more reminiscent of the latest popular science fiction movie. Displays are intended to generate customer interest, inform customers about the retailer's assortment, suggest items or combinations of items the customer may not have thought of, and motivate purchase.

There are many ways to present merchandise, ranging from simple tables, shelves, and pegboards to elaborate lifestyle, room-style displays. The devices on which merchandise is piled, hung, or otherwise placed are called **fixtures**. There are a great variety of these and experts in the field will extol the virtues of each. Recently, many retailers are using computers to assist them in store design and fixturing. Ideally, fixtures present and enhance the merchandise and provide any appropriate information (such as signs), yet the fixtures themselves are largely unseen and flexible enough to permit easy rearrangement. Good fixtures enable efficient use of the retailer's space (for example, by utilizing vertical space as well as horizontal space—which is called "merchandising the cube"), and also make it easy for the customer to locate appropriate merchandise (for example, by facilitating display by size or colour). Fixtures include:

1. Units on or in which goods sit: gondolas (the open shelving used primarily by large self-service retailers); showcases (the closed shelving typically used by

retailers offering higher priced items sold with service); wall shelves; display cubes; drawers; tables and other flat surfaces; and even their own shipping cartons (called "cut case displays")

2. Units on which goods hang: pegboards, wall and ceiling hooks, T-stands, rectangular racks, round racks, quad racks ("Bloomingdales"), S-racks, and many others.

There are, of course, many variations in displays. For example, in super-markets, the end-of-aisle display has become a popular place to offer "specials" and merchandise the store management particularly wants to sell in volume. Not only are these natural places to highlight items because they are set apart from the rest of the items along the gondola, but also customers slow down as they turn corners to enter the next aisle. In fact, these locations have become so associated with "price deals" in customers' minds that many customers now assume any item at end-of-aisle is on sale. These locations in the grocery store, as well as others (such as "eye level"), have become so valuable that grocery operators now can sell these spaces to manufacturers; the fees collected are called "slotting allowances."[15]

Merchandise presentation is an art and a science. Latest developments include new angles on fixtures (30 and 60 degrees), motion displays (allowing animation), greater flexibility in fixtures, and more mature mannequins to reflect the aging baby boom generation. The choice of fixtures and the ways in which these fixtures are arrayed and merchandise placed on them can make the difference between success and failure for a retailer. Even retailers reliant on a value strategy have paid increasing attention to display and merchandise presentation. Elliot Jaffe, president of Dress Barn, a U.S. chain of 455 career-apparel stores, put it this way in 1990:

> Fixturing is particularly important for the presentation of goods now, as opposed to just stacking them up as we used to five or more years ago. Fixtures should tell stories. It's the use you make of the fixtures rather than simply the fixtures themselves. There really is nothing dramatically different that we've bought lately in the way of fixturing. Most have been around at least 10 years—T stands, two-arm verticals, four-ways—they're quite standard. But we try to use them to make them points of interest, stories unto themselves—or exclamation points even.[16]

There are many guidelines used in merchandise presentation. For example, here are a few tips from the Retail Council of Canada:

- Use waterfall face-out bars to show fronts of garments, housing the back-up quantities behind, making sure they have the same sleeve lengths, silhouette and style and are color blocked.

- Hang all apparel on round racks within groups of the same color.

- Arrange patterned merchandise within color groups, using the color spectrum or color wheel as a guide.

- Make the hook of all hangers face to the left. Most of your customers are right-handed, and when removing a hanger to look at an item of clothing, they naturally tend to move it from left to right.
- Merchandise presentation should be done by commodity (e.g. lingerie), divided by look (e.g. pyjamas, slips), style (e.g. long, short), color, and size (where appropriate), in that order of priority.[17]

## POINT-OF-PURCHASE INFORMATION (P-O-P)

Point-of-purchase material refers to information provided to customers where the product is displayed. It is usually very product or service specific and is intended to act as a "silent salesperson." P-O-P has become much more important and sophisticated in the retail environment over the past fifteen years as the on-floor sales staff in most stores has been reduced in numbers. P-O-P can suggest product usage, provide information about product characteristics, dramatize the display, and, of course, help close the sale. There are three broad types of P-O-P material: shelf-talkers, product packaging, and product display units.

**Shelf-talkers** are visual devices, often provided by the product manufacturer, that are positioned on the edge of the shelf in front of a product. They are more than simply price signs. Shelf-talkers are usually integrated into a display by means of their colour coordination and can offer a discount, provide a coupon, direct the customer to more information ("ask our pharmacist about our complete line of vitamins"), or reinforce an advertising message. Recently, there has been experimentation with electronic shelf-talkers where prices and other information can be sent to the shelf from a remote computer.

**Product packaging** can also be used as P-O-P. "Billboard packaging"—a technique that extends the useful cardboard component of a package in order to gain more visual space—is a technique often used by manufacturers of small items to include more information on product packages. The resultant packages are mixed blessings to the retailer. They may be displayed on pegboards and they discourage shoplifting of small items; however, they present difficulties in handling product and stacking shelves.[18]

Product shippers and custom-designed **display units** can also be utilized as P-O-P. They can be either permanent (such as for L'Eggs pantyhose) or temporary (such as for Coppertone); they may be supplied by a manufacturer or created especially by the retailer (such as dump bin displays); they may be large and free-standing (such as a Coca-Cola display) or small and sit on a counter (such as Bic lighters).

Excellent P-O-P materials have the following characteristics:

- Capture attention and arouse interest
- Are selective in what is displayed
- Are visually and/or sensually appealing (such as new displays that allow the customer to smell the product)
- Are informative

- Integrate colour, style, size, and design into the display to complement the product's packaging features
- Are simple to setup, maintain, and remove for the retailer.

*Manufacturers* often provide P-O-P free of charge to retailers to generate increased awareness of a brand; to help the retailer with merchandising and stock-keeping; to improve sell-ins because of the simplicity of prepackaged orders (merchandise displays are usually sold with a predetermined amount of stock that may be above the amount the retailer would otherwise buy); to provide an information vehicle for the manufacturers in-store; and/or to prevent competitors from gaining an advantage in-store.

*Retailers* like P-O-P because it provides information at less cost than sales staff; it facilitates self-service; it may enhance the image of the store; and, more importantly, it may encourage impulse purchasing.

*Shoppers* like P-O-P because it may provide helpful information to choose among products, thus speeding up shopping time, reducing confusion, and avoiding the need to interact with salespeople.

Most retailers are deluged by manufacturers seeking to promote their own products in the retailer's stores with manufacturer-provided P-O-P. Some manufacturers spend a large portion of their own promotional budgets in hiring the best graphic artists and packaging engineers to develop new and unique P-O-P, so it is not surprising that retailers will be tempted to use it. However, the retailer must ask whether vendor-provided P-O-P supports his or her own information program. For example, if the P-O-P conflicts with the retailer's colour scheme, or is disproportionate in size, or makes shopping difficult for consumers, or occupies too much valuable selling space, it should not be used.

Doug Leeds, president of Thomson-Leeds, a New York advertising agency, summed up well why only good supportive P-O-P should be used: "P-O-P is not just merchandising the product, it's merchandising information."[19]

## PERSONAL SELLING

Retailers may be classified according to the nature of the personal selling they provide, ranging from none at all (in the extreme, vending machines) to a great deal (full service). Along this spectrum, the types of personal selling provided are low complexity (transaction processing at checkouts), medium complexity (routine selling situations), and high complexity (creative problem solving through customizing offers).

Personal selling offers retailers the opportunity to build personal relationships, to provide a human touch to the exchange through personal attention and two-way communications. Personal selling is usually face to face either in-store or at the customer's residence or place of work, although it can also occur over the telephone. Personal selling is particularly important when customers need more than just information—advice, reassurance, and help in customizing the product or service.

For example, while some customers may be willing to serve themselves when buying home furnishings, others prefer the assistance of a salesperson skilled in home decorating, colour coordination, and so on.

## RETAIL PERSONAL SELLING PROCESS

The job of a retail salesperson may be defined to include a variety of tasks ranging from stocking floor displays to selling to basic housekeeping to market research, but the core of the job is selling. Exhibit 10.4 shows the nine major skill sets a retail salesperson must have. Each of these topics will be briefly discussed.

*EXHIBIT 10.4*
*The Retail Selling Process*

| | |
|---|---|
| 1. Preparing | 6. Handling concerns |
| 2. Prospecting | 7. Closing |
| 3. Approaching | 8. Concluding |
| 4. Qualifying and determining needs | 9. Following-up |
| 5. Presenting | |

**Preparing**   The salesperson needs to have information in order to be able to provide it. He or she needs information about the store, the market, and the product/service assortment. For example, an apparel salesperson should know the store's policies on alterations, layaways, and so on; fashion trends and local competitors; as well as how the products carried were made, how they should be cared for, how the products will perform, when the products should be worn, what other products would complement the products being considered, etc.

**Prospecting**   Some salespeople are expected to seek out customers rather than wait for customers to approach them. The door-to-door salesperson is an example of one who must continually seek customers before being able to engage in the "selling process." Prospecting may be done on the basis of inquiries to advertising, on the basis of referrals from current customers, on the basis of good customer records indicating who might be ready to repeat purchase, or on a "cold call" basis.

**Approaching**   Acknowledging customers are in the store (or department), greeting them, and beginning the sales process are all part of the "approach."
   According to Michael Bunyar, a Canadian retail consultant specializing in sales training, many retailers fail in the approach stage:

> Studies in different parts of the country reveal a similarity in customer approach patterns:
>
> In specialty shops, 3.5 customers out of 10 are approached by a salesperson.
>
> In department stores, drug stores, hardware stores, 1.8 customers out of 10 obtain the services of a salesperson.

In a grocery store, only .3 customers are served.

And in most of the above mentioned cases, the customer will be asked the usual question: "May I help you?" and 80% of the time "No, thank you" will be the answer.[20]

Some possible approaches and examples include (a) the **salutation approach**, "Hello. How are you?" (b) the **salutation-plus-comment approach**, "Hello. Nice day isn't it?" (c) the **merchandise approach**, "That's our new line of keyboards. They have some wonderful new sounds." (d) the **acknowledgment approach**, "Hello. Please make yourself at home. I'll be with you shortly." and (e) the **presumptive approach**, "So you're looking for a new suit." The salesperson has to decide which approach to use. For example, the merchandise approach is often useful when a shopper is closely examining some products when approached. The purpose of the approach is to make the customer feel noticed and welcomed without feeling intimidated and pressured.

**Qualifying and determining needs**   Some customers are simply "recreational browsers" with no serious interest in the product and/or no ability to pay. If the salesperson can identify such shoppers, then the decision can be made whether there is any point in continuing to interact with such a shopper. Unfortunately, too often salespeople do this "qualifying" on the basis of appearance such as by age or kind of clothing worn. Such assumptions are often far from the truth.

In order to determine customer interest and needs, a salesperson should ask a series of nonthreatening questions. It is very important at this stage to remain customer-oriented rather than product-oriented. A product-oriented salesperson launches prematurely into a sales pitch about the product without determining if the product is at all what the customer is seeking or likely to value.

At this stage, the salesperson should listen and observe closely, not talk. Eye contact, open body language, and active listening are critical skills in order to show interest and to obtain information from the customer. Active listening refers to checking with the customer; for example, "So you're interested in finding a sports coat that will travel well and go with your grey flannels, is that right?"

The salesperson needs to remember that, for the customer, buying is problem solving and that a good salesperson is a problem solver. This means that sometimes the salesperson confronts situations where the store's assortment does not meet a customer's needs. Some salespeople in such situations will still help this customer find what is being sought by referring them to competitors. This extra effort in helping the customer solve problems usually leads to creating excellent goodwill with a customer, and chances are good the customer will return another time.

Asking open-ended questions that are easy to answer, especially ones that lead to positive answers, increases the possibility that the salesperson will acquire some useful information about the customer needs, the customer's current knowledge of products, preferences, and ability to pay. With this information, the salesperson can build a more effective sales presentation rather than launching into a standardized "pitch."

**Presenting merchandise**   Whenever possible, merchandise should be presented in terms of its benefits to the customer rather than its inherent characteristics and features. Demonstrations provide important information for customers, and aid in reducing perceived risk. There are many suggestions for how to present merchandise, such as:

- Show no more than three pieces of merchandise at one time so you don't confuse the customer.
- Begin by showing the customer items in the medium or slightly higher price range rather than merchandise that is either the most expensive or the cheapest.
- Show the customer merchandise that illustrates the range of items that you carry in the merchandise category.
- Get the customer involved directly with the merchandise by allowing her to touch, see, hear, smell, or taste it for herself.
- Handle the merchandise with respect and in appropriate manner.
- Stand either beside or behind the product you are presenting. This allows the customer to be involved with the merchandise yet still follow your presentation. It also allows you to observe the customer's reaction.[21]

Whatever is being presented should not be the focal point of discussion, but rather attention should always be on the customer. There's a world of difference between saying: "That dress looks nice" and "You look nice in that dress."

**Handling concerns**   Reluctance to buy may be expressed by shoppers in a number of ways. Legitimate concerns may be expressed as **indifference** (in which case the salesperson should probe for more information); as **doubt** (in which case the salesperson should offer evidence for claims made); or as **objection** (in which case the salesperson should show understanding and concern but provide a direct answer). In this way the salesperson will be able to separate concerns from excuses, and respond to concerns as appropriately as possible.

**Closing**   Closing is a critical skill for salespeople. A trained salesperson picks up cues from the customer as to when and how to close. Dale Lewison and Wayne DeLozier provided the following guidelines as to when a close is appropriate:

*Physical cues provided by customers:*

1. The customer closely re-examines the merchandise under consideration.
2. The customer reaches for his billfold or opens her purse.
3. The customer samples the product for the second or third time.
4. The customer is nodding in agreement as the terms and conditions of sale are explained.
5. The customer is smiling and appears excited as he or she admires the merchandise.
6. The customer intensely studies the service contract.

*Verbal cues provided by customers:*

1. The customer asks "Do you offer free home delivery?"
2. The customer remarks "I always wanted a pair of Porsche sunglasses."
3. The customer inquires "Do you have this item in red?"
4. The customer states "This ring is a real bargain."
5. The customer exclaims "I feel like a million bucks in this outfit!"
6. The customer requests "Can you complete the installation by Friday?"[22]

Closing may be done in a variety of ways, including (*a*) the **alternative close**, "Will that be cash or on your credit card?" (*b*) the **assumptive close**, "Would you like this gift wrapped?" (*c*) the **direct close**, "Would you like to buy this?" and (*d*) the **summary close**, "It appears that this pair of shoes best meets your needs for comfort and durability." Again, the salesperson has to decide which close seems most appropriate in the circumstances.

**Concluding**   Concluding involves processing the sale, wrapping or bagging, thanking for the sale, reassuring the customer of the appropriateness of the purchase, and inviting the customer back in the future. This is an opportunity to get the customer's name on a mailing list, to begin building towards the next visit and the next purchase.

**Following-up**   Thorough retail salespeople follow up post-sale to ensure their customers are satisfied. This may take the form of phone calls or letters inquiring about the product's performance, whether the customer has operating questions, and so on. Such follow-ups emphasize the salesperson's interest in the individual customer and can lead to follow-up sales. A reasonable balance must be struck between too little and too much follow-up. Too much post-sale contact may annoy customers and prevent them from returning.

During the selling process, the salesperson may see opportunities for **up-selling** (that is, for moving the customer to a higher priced or higher margin product) or for **horizontal selling** (that is, for selling the customer related items such as ties and shirts for a suit).

There are some **legal issues** involved in retail personal selling that retailers should be aware of. For example, most jurisdictions have laws forbidding misrepresentation, laws governing bait-and-switch selling (attracting the customer with a special deal but only using that as a come-on to sell something else), and laws allowing a cooling off period for sales occurring outside the retailer's premises during which time the customer can cancel the sale entirely.

## RETAIL SALES FORCE MANAGEMENT ISSUES

Personal selling goes beyond the tasks outlined in the job descriptions of retail sales personnel. Personal selling can be viewed as a mind-set of the *entire* retail organization. The manner in which the telephone is answered — even in credit departments — reflects on the organization. Do merchandising and housekeeping tasks take precedence over customer attention? Are retail personnel fully attentive to the needs of the customer even when not serving a customer? Do salespeople on breaks remove their name tags and pass by customers without an acknowledgment? Do managers (when on the sales floor) help out when regular staff are busy and customers are waiting? These are all ways in which one retailer may differ from another.

There are four major dimensions of the retail sales management task: organization and deployment (including scheduling); recruiting and selecting people; training and direction; and evaluation and compensation.

**Organization and deployment** of the retail salesforce refers to deciding how many sales staff are required, how they will be used in the store or in the field (''territories''), what the particular sales jobs will be, and when they must be done. This planning stage determines how many of what kind of people to seek and how to schedule their use. Scheduling is becoming increasingly important with the cost of salespeople rising and the patience of customers decreasing. Low productivity of the salesforce may be more a function of inappropriate scheduling than of training or motivation.[23]

**Recruiting and selecting** can be a difficult task. Retail selling remains for many people a relatively low-status job with little career attraction. Yet retailers seek enthusiastic, knowledgeable, motivated people and ask them to perform what may be a relatively difficult set of tasks. Selecting is frequently done more on the basis of attitude and personality, apparent customer sensitivity and similarity, than on sales skills and product knowledge. Most retailers believe that selling skills and product knowledge can be learned in training programs.

**Training and direction** involve equipping salespeople with the knowledge, skills, self-confidence, and sense of direction and purpose that they will need to perform the defined sales task. Such training ranges from how to operate the cash register to complete programs in product design and manufacture. Training may be done in the classroom or on the sales floor. Increasingly retailers are using professionally prepared videos and other instructional aids and techniques, such as role playing, to periodically train their salespeople. Turnover in retail salespeople is so high that many organizations are constantly training. Too often retail marketers fail to see the connection between inadequate training and poor sales staff productivity, preferring instead to blame the salesperson.

**Evaluation and compensation** refer to assessing performance and rewarding or correcting it. Such efforts may involve supervisors observing sales skills, or electronic tracking of cashiers' speed and accuracy at checkouts, mystery shoppers reporting on interactions with salespeople, or simply review of daily or weekly sales figures. Whatever the approach, evaluation can be threatening to salespeople. Salespeople under stress and feeling spied upon will not be relaxed and comfortable with customers, leading to poor customer care, as discussed in Chapter 9.

Compensation is a difficult issue. Most retailers decide between straight salary (often an hourly rate) and commission. Many blend the two. Some add in bonuses, profit-sharing plans, and so on. There are no simple answers as to the right method that combines administrative simplicity, ease of understanding for the salespeople, and sends clear signals as to what the salespeople should do and not do with their time. For example, straight commission may lead to very aggressive, non-teamplaying salespeople who line up at the door to pounce on customers as they enter the store. Straight salary may lead to lackadaisical efforts and a "let someone else deal with the customer" attitude. Or if there are individual as opposed to group commissions, how does the retailer handle cross-department selling situations, such as a customer who has just bought a suit and now wants a shirt and tie and shoes to go with it from the next department?

Notwithstanding the efforts of leading firms like Nordstrom's to provide unusual performance incentives for retail salespeople, the opportunity for acceptable compensation has not generally been available in the retail environment. Most retailers believe there simply aren't adequate margins to pay sales staff high wages, and many seem to think that such wages aren't deserved in any event. Still, it seems ironic that perhaps the most critical point of contact between the customer and the store is often given to one of the lowest-paid positions in the organization—that of the salesperson.

All retailers, large and small, struggle with sales management issues. During periods with very slow sales, retail marketers wonder what to do to increase salesperson productivity and whether (and how) to keep good salespeople when sales levels are so low. Some retailers lay off salespeople, while others use these slow selling times to engage their people in extra training programs to improve product and selling knowledge, to institute new clientele programs, and to encourage new efforts to prospect for customers.

## ■ SECTION ■ FIVE ■

## DIRECT RETAIL MARKETING[24]

One of the fastest growing methods of providing customers with information and incentive to buy is known as direct retail marketing. The Direct Marketing Association has defined direct marketing as follows: "An interactive system of marketing which uses one or more advertising media to effect a measurable response and/or transaction at any location."[25]

Direct retail marketing can be a *complement* to store-based retailing (for example, by extending the store's reach to customers who cannot or will not come to the store) or as a *replacement* for store-based retailing (for example, by eliminating the need for even having a store). In fact, direct marketing even allows manufacturers to deal directly with final customers without using retailers, a fact not lost on retailers.[26] Direct retail marketing differs from other methods of providing information and incentive to buy as follows:

1. It communicates directly with the customer or prospect, rather than using nonaddressable mass media.

2. It personalizes out-of-store communications between the retailer and the customer.

3. It specifically requests that the customer perform a specific action.

4. It typically utilizes a comprehensive database from which some customers are selected for any one campaign to drive the marketing program.

5. It can provide quantifiable, measurable results.

6. It can allow the retailer to conduct relatively invisible campaigns and, frequently, several parallel campaigns.

**Direct advertising** is similar but not the same as direct retail marketing. The former uses addressable media such as the mail to communicate directly to potential customers, but lacks the critical characteristic of a specific mechanism to take immediate action to buy, such as a toll-free number to place an order, a business reply card, a prepaid return address envelope with attached order form, or a salesperson at the other end of the telephone, waiting to take an order. In other words, direct retail marketing involves a complete program of outbound solicitation of customers and inbound fulfilment of orders.

Direct retail marketing includes use of printed and electronic media as well as telephone and personal solicitation. Common forms are catalogues, telemarketing, direct mail, door-to-door selling, vending machines, videotext and home shopping clubs, and, recently, computer and fax selling. The range of methods of communicating offers and then allowing customers to respond are limited only by technology and customers' willingness to use that technology. The most frequent ways customers respond are mail order, telephone order, visit to the store, and electronically with faxes and computers. Direct retail marketing then is simply a variety of ways retailers and customers can interact directly, usually outside the confines of the retail store. By the same token, retail marketers can very successfully combine "store-marketing" and "direct marketing" in one operation. For example, Talbot's, Sears, Radio Shack, and Canadian Tire—and, of course, Nieman Marcus with its Christmas Book—all use catalogues to convey store image, to expand their product offerings, to extend their store trading areas, and, obviously, to sell. Combining catalogue operations with store operations is not always easy or profitable, as many companies, including Sharper Image, have discovered.[27] The trend, however, is to targeted direct marketing as opposed to "one catalogue mass mailings to everyone."[28]

## Program Steps

There are several steps in a direct retail marketing program:

1. Product/offer selection
2. List selection and targeting
3. Outbound solicitation
4. Testing

5. Inbound fulfilment

6. Evaluation

### Product/Offer Selection

An **offer** can be defined as the complete proposition made by a retailer to a prospective customer. It is what will be provided in return for taking the action requested. The type of offer must be carefully chosen, as a change in the offer will affect the response rate, and a small difference in the response rate can have a huge impact upon campaign profitability. From the customer's point of view, the offer must be easily understood and the response mechanism easy to use. The offer must include the product, price, length of commitment, ways to respond, and terms of payment.

The length of commitment can be structured as a fixed term, automatic shipment, or a club or continuity program, such as the Book of the Month Club. The terms of payment can also be important; studies show that when customers use credit cards, the average size of the order is typically 15 percent to 30 percent greater than if credit cards are not used.

Often an incentive, such as a free gift or sample, or a price discount is used to increase the response rate; however, these should be used judiciously as they decrease the profitability per transaction. Incentives are usually limited-time offers to encourage the customer to respond immediately. Another technique used to increase the response rate is a risk reduction mechanism, such as a guarantee, warranty, or free trial period.

Another option is to use multiple offers or multi-stage offers. Multiple offers may attempt to cross-sell the customer an additional product that the firm sells. Conversely, one creative piece may offer numerous products manufactured by several competitors. Multi-stage offers may involve an inquiry, a detailed mail package, a qualifying phone call, and a personal sales call.

What kinds of products would consumers comfortably purchase from a direct marketer? One might expect that low-risk, routine purchases requiring little personal involvement would be the most likely kinds of products that customers would want to purchase since these require little demonstration or little contact with an experienced salesperson for information. This is not always the case. For example, the earliest large-scale attempts at direct marketing in the computer age were grocery warehouses claiming to relieve the drudgery of routine grocery shopping. Surprisingly they failed in large part because:

a.  They lacked the managerial skills required to operate a high volume warehouse operation dependent on quick turnaround.

b.  They were under-financed.

c.  They failed to satisfy consumer needs by requiring time-consuming double checking of the typically large number of units ordered by customers on a routine grocery order.

**d.** They did not offer low prices. The grocery business survives on very low margins and the additional costs of these warehouses (delivery, etc.) translated into marginally higher costs for the consumer.[29]

Products that have a relatively higher risk and require more learning on the part of the customer *can* be sold directly, even if in some cases a physical demonstration is required. Three conditions must exist to sell high-risk products through direct retailing:

1. The customer must be totally assured of product satisfaction through either an open returns policy or liberal customer support.
2. The customer must be an "expert" on the products sold or have completed preparatory comparison shopping at in-store retailers or be totally familiar with brand reputation.
3. The direct marketer must have the ability to provide comprehensive technical information on the products being sold.

Successful mail-order retailers such as L.L. Bean and Nieman-Marcus have focused much product attention on the high end of the market. American Express routinely promotes televisions, VCRs, video cameras, and stereo equipment via mail to its cardholders. These organizations have impeccable reputations for standing behind the products that they sell to their customers. Computer hardware, software, and peripheral direct marketers grew quickly during the 1980s. The leading direct seller of microcomputer technology, Texas-based DELL Computer Corporation, sells turnkey systems through the mail in North America and Europe for prices in excess of $11 000. Guaranteeing next-day deskside service if required, by the XEROX Corporation, DELL has been acknowledged by corporate volume buyers as the best microcomputer supplier for customer satisfaction.[30] High-end products can be sold successfully through precise targeting and segmentation. DELL Computer Corporation advertises only in magazines that have a sophisticated microcomputer readership: DELL does not want to sell to the novice computer buyer. American Express targets its own cardholders, who have already passed the financial requirements to hold an American Express Card. And the general trend in the catalogue business has been one of specialization with the "decline of the mega-catalogue" and the rise of segmentation.[31]

## List Selection and Targeting

Direct retail marketing is driven by a marketing database, which is an organized collection of client information and relationships needed to make effective marketing decisions. A database can include information from internal records and/or external sources. Marketing databases are frequently referred to as **Customer Information Files (CIFs)**.

A database is capable of providing a list, but a list cannot provide a database. Specific campaign lists can also be referred to as **Marketing Information Files (MIFs)**. Databases constantly evolve over time as additional information is added to them and often they are managed on-line computer systems. In contrast, lists represent information from a database at a particular point in time, for example, the subscriber list for *Maclean's* as of this week.

Database marketing uses the information in the marketing database to match products and services to the needs and wants of individual customers and prospects. By storing detailed information about customers and prospects, database managers are able to segment lists by specific criteria. Thus, only the most promising individuals are contacted with any particular offer in order to maximize profitability.

Creating a database opens up many marketing opportunities for firms that are willing to invest the necessary time and dollars. A database should allow the following functions:

- Identify the most profitable customers to obtain more business from them.
- Identify and qualify the best prospective customers to convert them to actual customers.
- Identify past customers who are still prospects to reactivate them.
- Identify the organization's most profitable products to develop appropriate promotional and pricing policies.
- Identify new market opportunities to develop new strategies to tap these markets.
- Measure the effectiveness of advertising and promotion to reduce waste and increase productivity.
- Evaluate the effectiveness of channels of distribution and individual channel members to decrease costs and increase sales volume.

The superiority of direct retail marketing over other methods of contacting customers lies in its ability to communicate directly with individuals who, from past behaviour, are known to be *active* prospects for the product or service that the retailer is selling. In achieving this selection the retailer relies heavily on lists of potential customers.

How can a retailer compile a useful list of prospects? Broadly speaking, lists can be developed *internally* from past or existing customers or *externally* by purchasing a list or lists from another firm in the same business or from a firm that specializes in compiling lists of potential customers with common profiles.

**Internal lists** can be compiled through a number of sources. Any credit purchases usually provide a complete profile of the customer with information such as name, address, and home telephone number. If the retail operation is large enough to have its own internal credit card system, the organization will have comprehensive credit and personal data on all of its customers who hold their credit cards, including data pertaining to income, size of family, age, types of products purchased on credit, and payment history. Cash paying customers can be asked to provide home address information in order to receive future information from the organization.

The benefits of internal lists are that they are more reliable than externally built lists because store personnel are responsible for compiling them. They reflect the interests of customers that have made active decisions to shop from this retailer (rather than others), and they may allow building specific customer profiles, tastes, and dislikes. The shortcomings of developing internal lists are that they may take too much time and be too small in number. Furthermore they are limited by the retailer's past ability or inability to attract customers.

There are many **external lists**. A thriving business exists in the sale of customer lists. Magazine publishers and mail-order houses sell subscription lists to a variety of firms. Although a purchased list gives a direct marketer quick and easy access to a potentially large database, there are shortcomings associated with this method. Since the lists are sold for profit, there is a possibility that the competition is using the same list, and there is no guarantee that the supplier of the list has conscientiously built the list to the specifications of the purchaser. In fact, since lists are sold on a per name charge, it can be in the interest of the seller to include as many names as possible.

**Mass compiled lists** produce the largest database of names as they are compiled from a variety of sources, such as telephone directories, automobile registration records, voter registration records, drivers' licence records, and credit bureaus. This type of list spans across a number of industries. **Vertically compiled lists** consist of names with a common denominator, such as new homeowners, association members, or new mothers. For example, Kimberly-Clark sends new mothers coupons for Huggies disposable diapers with a lullaby audio cassette with the baby's name in the lyrics.[32] **Response lists** are individuals or firms that have previously responded to DM solicitations, for example, catalogue buyers. This type of list is considered to be the best; there is less resistance to purchasing by mail or phone and, in the case of a firm's own customers, such lists represent prime opportunities for repeat sales. Those firms that use response lists are often known as "frequency marketers."[33]

In Canada, there are 600–700 commercial lists available presently, with the size of the larger subscription lists reaching four million names.

The Canadian postal system allows direct marketers to target specific households for mailings. The first three digits of a postal code are referred to as the Forward Sortation Area (FSA), and the last three digits as the Local Delivery Unit (LDU). The various digits represent the following information:

TABLE 10.1
Breakdown of Postal Code Designations

| FSA | first digit | • provinces, from east to west |
| | second digit | • urban (1–9) or rural (0) |
| | third digit | • potential to assign 3600 FSAs |
| LDU* | three digits | • indicate blockface,** apartment or office building, large firm, rural route, general delivery, or post office box |

\* assigned from north to south and, then, east to west within a FSA

\*\* A blockface is one side of a city street between consecutive intersections with other streets.

As of September 1988, there were 621 000 urban postal codes, 5700 rural postal codes, and 3000 special postal codes, such as for the House of Commons. Each urban postal code is comprised of 30–35 people or 10–15 households. Each rural postal code represents 1000 people or 350 households. Canada Post has extensive guidelines for companies wishing to take advantage of rate reductions, in exchange for pre-sorting their mailings. These guidelines are outlined in a publication called *The National Distribution Guide* (NDG), which is available from Canada Post. In practice, large mailers employ lettershops to address and stuff their mailings and these firms are also experts at interpreting the *NDG*.

As postal rates rise, retail marketers are increasingly turning to methods other than the postal service to deliver their message to customers. One popular method is to employ part-time help or professional service companies to deliver material direct to customer homes.

The key to any form of direct retail marketing is targeting, rather than simply blanketing every known name with every offer. American Express is very careful about this:

> The danger of course is that too many direct marketing pitches might junk up the relationship. Linen [head of Amex direct marketing] says that careful targeting helps the company avoid mass solicitations. His computers maintain and update weekly a profile of 450 attributes — such as age, sex, and purchasing patterns — on every cardholder. That way the company will send out information about home health care products only to people of a certain age with a certain pattern of medical charges on their card. Amexco might also pitch furniture and insurance to those whom an esoteric computer program deems likely to move in the near future.[34]

Therefore, database retail marketing means keeping enough information about customers to allow good targeting. For example, first time customers may differ considerably from repeat heavy-user customers and therefore merit a separate treatment, such as a welcoming letter. This notion of targeting combined with the addressable nature of direct retail marketing enables a retailer to engage in differentiated campaigns for different parts of its customer base. Exhibit 10.5 shows some of the common items of information kept in a customer database.

*EXHIBIT 10.5 Common DM Database Fields*

- original source of name
- individual's name
- salutation (Mr., Mrs. etc.)
- company name
- title
- address
- city
- province
- postal code
- home phone number
- business phone number
- fax number
- telex number
- account number
- demographic information
- date of last purchase

- amount of last purchase
- total dollar purchases
- number of purchases
- purchase history by product category

- method of purchase
- return history
- cancellation history
- customer service history

## Outbound Solicitation

Outbound solicitation refers to the message and the method(s) the retailer chooses to make contact with the customers. The most common direct media used are direct mail and telemarketing.

**Direct mail**    There are many strong personal positions about direct mail, ranging from "junk mail" to "the most profitable form of direct marketing." During 1990, over 63 billion pieces of third-class mail were sent in the United States (4.2 billion pieces in Canada), about 39 percent of U.S. postal volume (it's 46 percent in Canada)—leading one observer to estimate that the average U.S. professional will spend eight months over a lifetime just sifting through mail solicitations. However, the technique is so powerful that even environmentalists protesting the waste of resources use direct mail to convey their message.[35]

A **personalized offer** can be achieved through careful attention to the format of the communication. For example, mailing labels on envelopes convey a mass-produced image. If possible, a retailer should use a first-class stamp rather than a postage meter for the same reason.[36] There are many tips that direct retail marketers have learned over the years through trial and error. For example, on the main proposal to the offer—typically a sales letter in direct mail campaigns—the salutation should be different than the envelope. For example, a mailing directed to

Mr. John Smith
123 Elm Street
Anytown, USA 98765

should not begin with a salutation like "Dear Mr. John Smith," or "Dear John Smith," because it is impersonal and easy to conclude that this is only one letter being produced from a large database. A salutation like "Dear Mr. Smith," or even "Dear John," is more forceful, effective, and personal. In any database it is easy to include a "Known As" field or "salutation" field adjacent to the mailing address to make the sales letter more useful. The direct marketer may even want to use a high-quality impact printer rather than a laser printer to convey the image that the letter was personally typed and addressed to the recipient. Since direct marketing cannot provide the *personal* attention that traditional in-store retailers have been able to offer customers, it is critical that the direct marketer take steps to *appear* to be communicating on a personal one-to-one basis with the potential customer.

A direct mail offer must also contain a coherent and reasonable argument to take action. It must convey benefits to the reader and suggest appropriate solutions to achieve these benefits. Tired, hackneyed clichés and a preaching tone should be avoided. Consider the following two examples of sales letters for their effectiveness:[37]

Dear Reader:

**Boost profits higher than ever before** with the proven procedures found in this handy marketer's guide.

Whether you're introducing a new product, promoting an established one, or positioning your product among its competitors . . . you'll see how to design and implement a pricing strategy that attracts customers and keeps them buying!

Page after page author Thomas T. Nagle tells the secrets of strategic price-setting, a task which rates among "Fortune 500" executives as the *single most critical* aspect of product marketing today.

Would this sales letter be effective in encouraging marketing professionals to buy? The following letter is a more tempered approach to a specific clientele and illustrates how to raise interest by asking a closed question, which if the readers answer positively, the writer politely thanks them for their time and informs them that they do not require the product. It is not as upsetting or strident as the first letter and because it is targeted at a specific group would probably generate more response than the first letter.

Dear Executive:

When do you use "skim pricing" ? When do you use "penetration pricing" ? If you know the answers you probably don't need any help from us in formulating your pricing strategies. But just in case you don't. . . .

*Pricing* is the single most critical aspect of marketing today. That isn't my opinion. It's the solid opinion of "Fortune 500" executives.

**Telemarketing**  Telemarketing presents different challenges than direct mail. Telemarketing has touched almost every household in North America. Much of the public attention toward telemarketing has been centred on the negative aspects of the industry: automatic dialers that tie up telephone lines, calls made at inconvenient times for the consumer, and aggressive tactics promoted by telephone "sweatshops" where the only goal is to sell rather than to fairly represent the product or service. In fact there have been legislative attempts in North America to curtail the activities of telemarketing organizations, and the American Telemarketing Association has responded with a nine-point code of ethics that it hopes will address some of the concerns of the public.[38]

If a firm wishes to engage in telemarketing, it has two major options. It can either create its own telemarketing centre or hire an outside telemarketing agency. This decision involves a trade-off between allocation of resources (dollars, people, and time) and control over the telemarketing campaign.

How can a retailer telemarket effectively, given the general level of hostility toward the industry from the public? First, the retail offer must be well conceived as far as product selection is concerned. A product that requires physical demonstration will probably meet with some resistance in a telemarketing campaign. Second, as with direct mail, a concerted segmentation effort must be mounted. Mass telephone campaigns directed at individuals who have no interest in the product or service being sold will drive up total marketing costs, and drive down response rates, as well as create a bad feeling among customers.

Third, since product demonstration is not possible over the telephone, the telemarketers must be well trained in suggestive selling. Telemarketing is not order-taking, but rather proactive selling in which the telemarketer must determine customer needs and meet them. The telemarketer should have a script but it must not be delivered like a "canned" presentation because that will sound insincere and nonpersonal. The telemarketer should engage in a conversation with the prospect to put the customer at ease and through the conversational tone should attempt to greet the customer, probe for his or her needs, acknowledge those needs even if they do not correspond with the products being sold, attempt a trial close, and begin the loop again if the first trial close is not successful. It is important that the telemarketer smile when speaking with prospects because the voice changes and becomes more pleasant to the ear when a person is smiling. Finally, it is important that the telemarketer remain pleasant even in the event of a lost sale because the reputation of the firm (as well as the industry) rests upon the impression made by the key contact person with the individual prospect.

A **script** is an essential part of the preparation for telemarketing and door-to-door solicitation. This acts as a checklist to ensure the person undertaking the contact covers the key points in an order found to be effective with most people. A script is a selling device and thus should contain an introduction of self and retailer being represented, an attention-getter such as a special time-limited offer or sale, some possible replies to information requests or concerns raised, a close, a protocol for collecting order information, a fallback close (such as "I'd be happy to mail you our brochure" ), and a conclusion to the call.

Here are some more tips:

- The number of choices given customers should be limited so that customers do not get confused and hence delay making any decisions.
- Teaser copy on the envelope may seem cute, but it is used by customers to decide whether or not the envelope should be thrown away unopened because it is just "more junk mail."
- Guarantees and other risk-reducing techniques (such as testimonials) help because many customers distrust dealing with retailers, except in-store.

Briefly, other types of direct retail marketing media would include:

- Broadcast Media: combining traditional broadcast media with a direct response device, such as a television commercial with an 1–800 number for placing orders

- Print Media: combining traditional print media with a direct response device, such as a magazine ad with a mail-in order form
- Interactive Media: for example, video kiosks that combine a product videotape, a touch-sensitive interactive screen for purchase selection, a phone hook-up to a computer to process the order, a magnetic strip reader for payment by credit card, and a printer for a receipt
- Catalogues: considered to be part of direct retail marketing as the purchaser may never be required to enter a traditional retail outlet.

## Testing

Once target list, message, and media decisions have been made, costs are largely fixed for the program, whether is it successful or not. It is advisable to field test direct marketing campaigns, much the same as advertising campaigns are tested. It is important to test only variables that can materially improve the likelihood of the success of a direct program. They are: the product or service offer itself, product positioning alternatives, target list selection, variations of the offer, media options, format of the promotional piece, creative alternatives, and timing. In general, there are two types of tests: (*a*) a **dry test** that is not supported by adequate inventories at the time of the test, and (*b*) a **wet test** for which inventories are purchased prior to knowing the response rate.

## Inbound Fulfilment

The customer's perception of the service they receive is closely tied to fulfilment issues; thus, although this function is often neglected, it is extremely important. The fulfilment process consists of the following steps:

1. order placed by customer
2. order received by firm
3. order verified (credit, completeness)
4. data entry (computer updates database, billing system, inventory system)
5. order picked, packed, and shipped
6. product received by customer
7. returns and problems handled by customer service

## Evaluation

Campaign evaluation is tied to campaign objectives. Some sample objectives are listed below, along with the corresponding method for evaluating results. In practice, response rates are often used to assess campaign success. In direct marketing, to increase the response rate, retailers experiment with various components of the package, including the copy, the graphics and reply formats, the incentives, etc., and then track the impact on measures such as follows:

## TABLE 10.2
### Campaign Objectives and Evaluations

| Objective | How Results Are Measured |
| --- | --- |
| Generate x % response rate | Number of orders/Number of solicitations |
| Acquire new customers | Cost per customer |
| Acquire new leads | Cost per lead |
| Acquire new inquiries | Cost per name |
| Convert leads and inquiries | Cost of conversion |
| Convert one time buyers | Growth of multibuyer file |
| Maximize number of mailings | Number of customer mailings per year |
| Make a profit | Return on sales and investment |
|  | Value of a customer over certain time period |

The concept of **lifetime value** is important for retail direct marketers. It can be defined as:

$$\text{Lifetime value} = (\text{Number of customers} \times \text{Number of purchases per customer} \times \text{Gross margin per purchase}) - \text{Expenses}$$

For example, suppose a company implemented a campaign that attracted 500 new customers and each customer over his or her lifetime was expected to purchase an average of five products, with the average gross margin on the product bundle equivalent to $25. Each customer's account would cost $75 to service over his or her lifetime. Then, the lifetime value of those 500 customers would be:

$$\text{Lifetime value} = (500 \times 5 \times \$25) - (500 \times \$75) = \$25\ 000$$

Exhibit 10.6, following, shows a sample profit and loss statement for a direct marketing campaign. All revenue and expenses are quoted as cost per thousand potential customers. This format is typical in the industry as list prices are quoted as cost per thousand names. All costs are amortized over the total number of pieces mailed out.

Most direct retail marketers maintain records by customer name of frequency, recency, and amount of purchases. These three measures help a great deal in determining best prospects for subsequent campaigns.

## ELECTRONIC RETAILING

The ongoing technological developments in electronic retailing have brought some of the biggest retailers in North America into this form of retail direct marketing. Firms such as Sears, Kmart, Levi-Strauss, J.C. Penney, and Kroger have been experimenting with new techniques.[39] If there is any generalization about electronic retailing, it would be that market acceptance for it has not developed anywhere nearly as fast as has the technological ability to deliver information and products. The marketers seem constantly too far ahead of the customers.

EXHIBIT 10.6
Profit and Loss
Statement

## Assumptions

**1.** 125 000 direct mail pieces mailed out

**2.** 10 000 responses (calls) received

| | |
|---|---|
| *Revenue (per 000)* | |
| $36 000 in sales × 7 % gross margin | $2 520 |
| | |
| *Expenses (per 000)* | |
| Outbound solicitation (including production, postage, design and creative) | 1 000 |
| Inbound response (including telemarketing line charges, script development, systems development, telemarketing training and overhead) | 300 |
| Fulfilment | 160 |
| Profit | |
| Per Thousand | 1 060 |
| Total Profit ($1060 × 125) | $132 500 |

There are three main types of electronic retailing. They include: at-home shopping; public access terminals in office buildings, airports, and so on; and in-store systems.

Electronic retailing may be **vendor controlled** (providing one-way information) or **buyer controlled** (such as interactive shopping machines that allow customers to browse the database at will). Some customers seem only to want information while others seem to wish to be able to consummate transactions.

At-home shopping is a phenomenon that some experts predict will generate sales in the United States in excess of $4 billion by 1993.[40] At-home electronic shopping can be divided into four distinct categories:

1. Telephone-assisted catalogue buying
2. Direct response television advertising
3. Home video shopping
4. Videotext experiments

The widespread use of WATS lines has given at-home shoppers the inexpensive alternative to in-person shopping.[41] Falling long-distance charges have been the impetus for retailers like L.L. Bean to offer 24 hour a day, 365 days a year telephone shopping with liberal return policies.[42] Also, utilizing the cost efficiencies of WATS, many direct marketers began to use direct television advertising with a prominent 1-800 number.

In 1982 the Home Shopping Network was founded and began to broadcast on a cable television network in Florida. Since that time there have been many imitators with similar formats. Medium-quality goods are promoted to viewers who are requested to telephone via a WATS line and place their orders for immediate shipment. Most of the shopping networks suffer from two key weaknesses: shoppers have no control over which products they get to examine and many of the products are not presented in sufficient detail to enable confident shopping.

These three categories of home shopping have utilized common existing technology, and their future success appears to be dictated by the interest that consumers show in the *products* that these firms are marketing or in the nature or in the entertainment value of their message. Videotext experiments, on the other hand, involve newer technology. The acceptance of the technology itself will be the key factor in the success of some of these systems, and to date the acceptance has been slower than the system providers had hoped.

An example is PRODIGY, a joint venture between Sears and IBM that allows home computer users—for a flat fee of $9.95 a month—to access information on news, sports, weather, and stock quotations through the use of a modem. The shopping dimension allows users to review prices, analyze product differences, conduct banking, make travel arrangements, and purchase products from many well-known retailers such as Sears, Kmart, J.C. Penney, Sam Goody, D'Agostino's, The Broadway, Lechemere, Kroger, and Wolf Cameras. In the words of a senior vice-president responsible for marketing PRODIGY, it will "move the POS terminal into the home" in the future.[43]

Unlike the other existing shop-from-home technologies, videotext services are "customer driven," and because of this, the future of services such as PRODIGY is linked to the growth of personal computers in the home. IBM has entered an agreement with Sears to market its low-end newly released PS/1 to novice computer buyers in the hopes that home computer penetration will double to 30 percent by 1994.[44] But PRODIGY will still have some technical problems to overcome if it is to become a method of shopping choice for consumers. As of this writing, it could not download information from the screen nor was it possible to save or print information acquired from on-line sources. Its screen only allowed for text to be displayed in 12 line windows and the time to redraw a screen on a machine like a PS/1 was about 10 seconds.[45] These technical drawbacks may be sufficient enough to inhibit the successful mass appeal of this attempt at home shopping. It would not be unusual because there have been many disastrous entries into home shopping.[46]

## THE FUTURE OF DIRECT RETAIL MARKETING

Sales from direct marketing have been growing at a 15 percent yearly rate in Canada. Much of this growth can be attributed to social and demographic changes in North American lifestyles. Dual-income families with less time to devote to traditional routine shopping excursions, older individuals who find it physically difficult to shop, and the explosion in the use of credit cards has fuelled the demand for the direct retail marketing alternative. This demand has been accompanied by a corresponding development in the technology required to market directly to customers in an efficient and sophisticated manner. Relational databases and the falling cost and increasing power of desktop computers have put the power to reach a wide audience at the hands of even the smallest retail operator. Increasing costs of marketing in more traditional methods have edged retailers toward the direct communication alternative.

Direct retail marketing is not really a new concept, but its profitable application requires considerable sophistication. The relatively low cost of some kinds of direct marketing has led some retailers to develop a "shotgun approach." Nontargeted lists have been used; nonpersonalized mail solicitations have been sent; telemarketers have used local phone books to approach everyone with a listed phone number for product sales. The result has been a growing scepticism by the public toward the direct retail marketing industry.

In formulating a product offer, the direct retail marketer must carefully prepare the total program. It has been suggested that as a rule of thumb, 40 percent of the planning effort should go toward determining if the product or service a firm is attempting to sell is appropriate for the target audience and then structuring the offer to maximize the response rate. An additional 40 percent of the planning effort should be directed toward selecting the best list and media to reach the target audience, and the remaining 20 percent should focus on designing an effective creative presentation.

## McDonald's Restaurants: A Marketing Success

McDonald's Restaurants is acknowledged as one of the great marketing success stories of the 20th century. Fast food consumers patronize McDonald's more than any other restaurant chain because McDonald's has successfully communicated benefits to consumers in a way that no other chain has been able to do. Since the tremendous expansion of the firm in the mid-1960s, McDonald's advertising and other efforts to provide information have captivated the North American consumer.

McDonald's has consistently attempted to develop new images, sentiments, slogans, ideas, and messages in all its communications with customers. For example, at times, management has utilized television advertising in a subtle way by reaching out to special-interest groups (women working outside of the home, teenagers, senior citizens, blue-collar workers, and others) by portraying these individuals as favourable "stars" of television commercials. At other times the commercials are unabashed straightforward item advertising: "The Big Mac Combo" and so on.

McDonald's puts a premium on its public image by funding Ronald McDonald House, a nonprofit organization devoted to supporting the financial needs of families with sick children. Management believes that it is important to communicate to the public a corporate image of good citizenship. In 1987, McDonald's launched a print advertising campaign the intent of which was to demonstrate and promote the values, standards, and behaviours that McDonald's stands for. By following the careers of young ex-McDonald's in-store employees—one had become a physician, another an airline pilot, and another a lawyer—McDonald's was attempting to communicate to its public much more than product features or benefits. It was an attempt to personify McDonald's as the catalyst in the career choices made by these individuals. Copy indicating that lessons learned at McDonald's led to the physician's interest in practising medicine in a third-world country spoke eloquently that McDonald's does more than sell hamburgers.

McDonald's has perfected sales promotion techniques by utilizing consumer coupons to generate increased sales at the retail level. Advertising during the Christmas season and at Hallowe'en promotes gift coupons for children, such as a booklet of five coupons for five free small french fry orders for a nominal cost of fifty cents. The intent is to encourage children to bring the family for a meal at McDonald's in return for the nominal loss on each coupon redeemed.

McDonald's also provides a total information package for customers through its signing and P-O-P material. The golden arches outside each restaurant signify consistency and a known menu. Some stores feature life-size statues both inside and outside of the McDonaldland characters, communicating fun and excitement to children. Some stores even have interior playgrounds.

Large exterior banners spanning the length of the restaurant announce current promotions and giveaways. Drive-through menus are large, easy to read, illuminated, and provide all of the price and assortment information that is found inside on the regular menu.

Inside each restaurant, promotional timing is executed with military efficiency. Cross-promotions with movie releases are designed to tie-in popular interest in a theatrical release with a particular McDonald's promotion. For example, order a "packaged" meal such as cheeseburger, fries, and a small drink and receive a popular character image or souvenir for free or at a nominal charge. All signing and P-O-P material in the stores during these promotions are directed toward only the current promotion. Decor kits hanging over the customer service counters not only add to the atmosphere of the restaurant, but also provide customers with the information that they require to make product decisions. Place mats on all food trays serve an informational purpose and are changed regularly to support the current promotion in the store and/or to inform customers of upcoming McDonald's programs.

Utilizing a largely teenage workforce—notwithstanding recent attempts to recruit seniors with a lifetime of work experience—McDonald's has raised the level of personal selling in the fast food environment to an art. Through intensive training efforts, McDonald's capitalizes on suggestive selling at every opportunity by requiring customer service staff to ask customers after an order has been placed if they would like to order an item on the menu that the customer did not include in the original order. This approach focuses on only one product at a time across all the stores in the chain. In one month, apple pie may be the product promoted, whereas french fries may be suggested the following month. This approach allows McDonald's management to monitor the customer service activities of all staff because the messages being communicated to the customers are the same and more importantly, to measure the effectiveness of the program on sales of the product being promoted against a month when no suggestive selling was used in support of the product.

Other subtle techniques are used to provide customers with a complete package of information on McDonald's. All staff wear uniforms and buttons announcing current promotions or deals on specific menu items. Cleanliness and sanitation concerns of the corporation are communicated to customers through constant observation of employees cleaning the store as well as signs in washrooms announcing the daily cleaning schedule of the washrooms. The self-service concept is illustrated through strategically placed self-serve napkin and straw dispensers and by separate and extra-large refuse containers with directions to the customer on how to dispose of trash.

Much of McDonald's success can be attributed to the uniformity of its programs and the tight controls that the firm exercises over all dimensions of its activities—from site selection, franchisee selection, menu preparation, product testing, training, and customer satisfaction.[47] As part of its persona, McDonald's management believes its *consumers want to be informed* about what the firm is doing for the customer.

## CONCLUSION

Managing information provided to customers is a critical and complex retail marketing task. Some aspects of information are intended to communicate the store's presence and image and to bring customers to the goods (such as advertising and promotion); other aspects are to bring the goods to the customer (such as in-store merchandising and display); and others are to bring the customers and the goods together (such as personal selling and direct marketing).

Information is a critical component in the retail marketer's marketing program. Retailers promise their assortments, care, convenience, and so on. Without such promises (and reassurances), customers may never patronize a particular store or may never consider issues other than price.

All too often, retailers have a tendency to fragment the information program task, divide responsibilities for its management, and thus to dilute the potential impact of an integrated effort. Managing the information program should be integrated around the purpose of providing appropriate and motivating information to targeted customers at the right times in the right places.

It is crucial to remember why this chapter is entitled "information" as opposed to "selling techniques." If the retail marketer focuses on advertising, he or she is concerned about his or her own needs to sell merchandise. If the retail marketer focuses instead on providing needed and wanted information to customers, then he or she is concerned about customers. This latter approach is consistent with the theme of this book and results in better performance in the longer term. Information is intended to provide customers with reasons to patronize the retailer and incentives to buy products and services.

Perhaps symbolic of the overall theme of this chapter are recent reports that managements of shopping centres have discovered the marketing power of information: "The most notable single service innovation by [shopping center] managements is the upgrade of previously half-hearted attempts at information booths, where they even existed, to highly visible, full scale service centers that give shoppers a focal point."[48]

## REVIEW QUESTIONS

1. Don Watt, head of the Watt Group, an international consulting firm in Toronto, is perhaps best known for his store signage work with Loblaws. He recently said:
   Store signage can last much longer than a print ad campaign. We want to do something that is much more of an image statement for the business long-term. ... The fact that most people have thrown bad taste at the walls, along with money, and not ever decided to tell the customer anything, that's great because the very few people who do use signs as part of an integral marketing mix to position a company and its product, those people are going to outperform the others."[49]
   Do you agree with him? What examples have you seen of good and poor store signage in terms of meeting customer expectations for information?

2. Sears Canada launched its Sears Club program in early 1991. Membership was open to all Sears credit card holders. Each dollar charged to the Sears card earned one point and could be accumulated for two years or until the program was cancelled by Sears. Points could be redeemed for merchandise only by the cardholder. For example, as of February 1991, 9000 points resulted in a certificate worth $200 toward a purchase of a microwave oven or a bicycle. Particularly from the perspective of material in this chapter, what are the advantages and disadvantages of such a continuity program for Sears?

3. According to the U.S. House Energy and Commerce Committee in late 1990, 180 000 businesses use automatic dialing systems to deliver prerecorded sales pitches to as many as 7 million people each day, and 2 million American offices employ fax machines to transmit more than 30 billion pages of information, much of it unsolicited, per year.[50] What is your position on "unsolicited information," particularly if the customer must pay, as in the case of fax machines and cellular telephones?

4. Remember the last time you encountered a particularly good retail salesperson. What did that person do or say that was so unusual? What are the implications of your observation for other retailers?

5. How would you evaluate the contribution, if any, made by retail store image advertising?

## KEY TERMS

- information
- incentives to patronize and buy
- information exchange between the retailer and the customer
- information exchange between the retailer and the vendor
- fixed ratio formula
- all-that-can-be-afforded approach
- competitive benchmarking
- task method
- experimentation
- scheduling
- advertising and promotion calendar
- circulation
- reach
- frequency
- impressions
- audience size
- cost per thousand (CPM)
- gross rating points (GRPs)
- impact
- co-operative advertising
- contests
- sweepstakes
- special displays
- selection displays
- fixtures
- shelf-talkers
- product packaging

- display units
- salutation approach
- salutation-plus-comment approach
- merchandise approach
- acknowledgment approach
- presumptive approach
- indifference
- doubt
- objection
- alternative close
- assumptive close
- direct close
- summary close
- up-selling
- horizontal selling
- direct advertising
- internal lists
- external lists
- mass compiled lists
- vertically compiled lists
- response lists
- personalized offer
- script
- dry test
- wet test
- lifetime value
- vendor controlled (electronic retailing)
- buyer controlled (electronic retailing)

## NOTES

1. Joy L. Santink, *Timothy Eaton and the Rise of His Department Store* (Toronto: University of Toronto Press, 1990), chapter 6.

2. Arthur I. Cohen, and Ana Loud Jones, "Brand Marketing in the New Retail Environment," *Harvard Business Review*, September – October 1978, p. 141.

3. For example, most jurisdictions have laws prohibiting false and misleading advertising, deceptive price advertising, bait-and-switch advertising, and other unfair advertising and promotional practices. Such laws may be criminal, civil, or both. Advertisers should also be aware of relevant "intellectual property" legislation. For example, recent changes in U.S. law may change the nature of comparative advertising. See Bruce Buchanan and Doran Goldman, "Us vs. Them: The Minefield of Comparative Ads," *Harvard Business Review*, May–June 1989, pp. 38–50.

4. Timothy Joyce, "What Do We Know About Advertising," The British Market Research Bureau (undated), p. 3.

5. Donald F. Cox, "Clues for Advertising Strategists," *Harvard Business Review*,

November–December 1961, pp. 160–82.

6. Robert F. Young and Stephen A. Greyser, *Co-operative Advertising: Practices and Problems* (Cambridge, Mass: Marketing Science Institute, June 1982).

7. For an excellent guide to co-operative advertising, see *The Retailer's Guide to Supplier Support Funding*, Television Bureau of Canada, 1987.

8. Warren Kornblum, shared with the author in conversation.

9. Pat Corwin, "Zellers — Canada's Own," *Discount Merchandiser*, January 1990, p. 40.

10. Leonard Sloane, "Electronic 'Coupons': Savings but No Scissors," *New York Times*, 21 April 1990, p. 16.

11. For example, see John C. Totten and Martin P. Black, *Analyzing Sales Promotion: Text and Cases*, Commerce Communications, 1987.

12. Rockney G. Walters, "Retail Promotions and Retail Store Performance: A Test of Some Key Hypotheses," *Journal of Retailing*, vol. 64, no. 2 (Summer 1988), p. 173.

13. *Store Design and Display — For Sales*, The Retail Council of Canada, Toronto, 1986, p. 23. See also Harry Spitzer and Richard Schwartz, *Inside Retail Sales Promotion and Advertising* (New York: Harper and Row, 1982), p. 226; and Charles M. Edwards, Jr., and Carl F. Lebowitz, *Retail Advertising and Sales Promotion*, 4th ed. (Englewood Cliffs, N.J.: Prentice-Hall, 1981), p. 251.

14. "KinderZimmer: A Scientific Approach to Toys," *Chain Store Age Executive*, March 1989, pp. 121–22.

15. For example, see Lois Therrien, "Want Shelf Space at the Supermarket? Ante Up," *Business Week*, 7 August 1989, pp. 60–61.

16. Pat Corwin, "Fashion-Forward Presentation," *Discount Merchandiser*, March 1990, pp. 58–62.

17. These and many other guidelines are in *Store Design and Display* (see n. 13).

18. Tina Kyriakos, "Cutting the Clutter," *Drug Merchandising*, April 1989, p. 25; "Sentinels of the Supermarket," *Modern Packaging*, vol. 42, no. 2 (February 1969), pp. 82–86.

19. Cyndee Miller, "P-O-P Gains Followers as 'Era of Retailing' Dawns," *Marketing News*, 14 May 1990, p. 2.

20. Bunyar, Malenfant & Associates Ltd., *The Professional Retail Sales Training Course*, (Toronto, 1979), pp. 9–10.

21. *How to Train to Sell*, Retail Council of Canada, Toronto, 1986.

22. Dale M. Lewison, and M. Wayne DeLozier, *Retailing*, 3rd ed. (Columbus, Ohio: Merrill Publishing, 1989), p. 639.

23. Douglas A. Louth, "Better Salesperson Scheduling Should Cut Costs While Improving Service," *The Retail Advisor*, Deloitte & Touche, September–October 1990.

24. This section owes much to the Direct Marketing Industry Note prepared by Helen Liigsoo under the author's supervision, in fulfilment of MBA course requirements at the Western Business School, 1990.

25. Terence A. Shimp, *Promotion Management and Marketing Communications*, 2nd ed. (Chicago: The Dryden Press, 1989), p. 439.

26. Robert D. Kestnbaum, "Retailing vs. Direct Marketing: Competitors or Confederates?" *International Trends in Retailing*, Arthur Andersen & Co., Autumn 1984, pp. 25–30.

27. "Tough Choice for Catalogs: Mail or Mall?" *Chain Store Age Executive*, October 1990, p. 35.

28. Penny Gill, "Targeting Direct Mail," *Stores*, July 1990, pp. 42–57.

29. John A. Quelch and Hirotaka Takeuchi, "Nonstore Marketing: Fast Track or Slow?" *Harvard Business Review*, July–August 1981, pp. 76–77.

30. *PC Magazine*, vol. 9, no. 12 (June 26, 1990), p. 513.

31. Lynn Wunderman, "A Mail-Order Addict Looks at Today's Catalogs," *Viewpoint*, March–April 1987, p. 11.

32. Lynn Coleman, "Data Base Masters Become King of the Marketplace," *Marketing News*, 18 February 1991, p. 13.

33. Recently a newsletter was established on frequency marketing, called *Colloquy*. If you are interested, call (513) 248-9184.

34. John Paul Newport, Jr., "American Express: Service That Sells," *Fortune*, 20 November 1989, pp. 80–94.

35. Jill Smolowe, "Read This!!!!!!!!," *Time*, November 1990, p. 49.

36. Harry Spitzer, and Richard Schwartz, *Inside Retail Sales Promotion and Advertising* (New York: Harper and Row, 1982), p. 155.

37. Both examples are taken from Herschell Gordon Lewis, "Do Sales Letters Still Work?" *Direct Marketing*, February 1990, p. 31.

38. *Marketing News*, 9 October 1987, p. 23. For a review of telemarketing in Canada, see James Domansk, *Direct Line to Profits* (Montreal: Grosvenor House Press, 1991).

39. Cosmo Ferrara, "Electronic Retailing 89: Heavy Hitters Taking Over," *Retail Control*, September 1989, p. 15.

40. Ibid.

41. Mark S. Albion and Walter J. Salmon, "The Emergence of the Electronic In-Home Shopping Industry," Harvard Business School, 1987, p. 2.

42. John A. Quelch, *How to Market to Consumers* (New York: John Wiley and Sons, 1989), p. 133.

43. Ferrara "Electronic Retailing 89" (see n. 39), p. 16.

44. *Globe and Mail*, Report on Business, 27 June 1990, pp. B1-2.

45. *PC Magazine*, vol. 8, no. 17 (17 October 1989), pp. 399–400.

46. Gary Robins, "On-Line Service Update," *Stores*, February 1990, p. 24.

47. Robert F. Hartley, *Marketing Successes* (New York: John Wiley, 1985), p. 151.

48. Jules Abend, "New Amenities Set to Improve Service," *Stores*, May 1990, pp. 30–39.

49. Hilary Forrest, "The Watt Way," *Canadian Retailer*, December–January 1990–91, p. 11.

50. Jill Smolowe, "Too Many Busy Signals," *Time*, November 1990, p. 49.

CHAPTER

# VALUE AND PRICE

## INTRODUCTION

Value means much more than simply price, more than the money the customer pays and the money the retailer gets. **Value** is the perception that customers have (or may be convinced to have) of the total package of benefits received at a price from the retailer. Price from the customer's perspective then becomes an indicator, a measure of the promised value. If the benefits appear to be substantially higher than the "cost" (the price being asked), the customer perceives the retailer to be offering "good value" and a sale is likely. On the other hand, if the cost is perceived as higher than the benefits, the value is not there for the customer. When customers say "the price is too high" they may mean "the value is too low."

This cost–benefit comparison is made relative to alternatives available to the customer. Competitive prices are easily compared; value is not so easily compared. Retail marketers can offer customers added value when they are in the top left three cells of the cost–offer matrix shown as Exhibit 11.1. As discussed in previous chapters, the total offering is compared to competitive offerings; and costs to provide it are relative to competition. The point of this chart is to challenge an individual retail marketer to demonstrate whether and how he or she can provide added value to a customer. Without added value of some kind—such as closest location—there is no reason for customers to choose the retailer.

Value perceptions will vary from customer to customer and are not simply a matter of comparing prices charged for like merchandise from store to store. Retailers who focus excessively on price alone miss opportunities to affect the "value" perception in other, less easily imitated ways. For example, as discussed in Chapter 9, customer care can add value to the merchandise purchased—so can

EXHIBIT 11.1
Cost–Offer
Matrix

**Relative Offer (assortment, care, etc.)**

| Relative Cost | | Better | Parity | Worse |
|---|---|---|---|---|
| | **Better** | + value | + value | ? value |
| | **Parity** | + value | = value | - value |
| | **Worse** | ? value | - value | - value |

convenient location, hours, wide assortments, and so on. Central to any retail marketing strategy should be a statement of what value the retailer adds for customers and how to ensure customers perceive it. Walter Loeb, an American retail analyst, discussed the importance of value as follows:

> The 1990's will be a more hostile environment for the consumer. He will have to bear the brunt of higher taxes, his discretionary spending power will be impacted, and employment opportunities will grow at a reduced pace. As a result, he will be very value sensitive and will shop where he perceives the greatest value. Value can be divided into two separate categories: value, because the price is lower, or because the quality of the item is so superior that it saves him a lot of time at the repair shop.[1]

Figure 11.1 shows the major topics about retail pricing that will be discussed in this chapter.

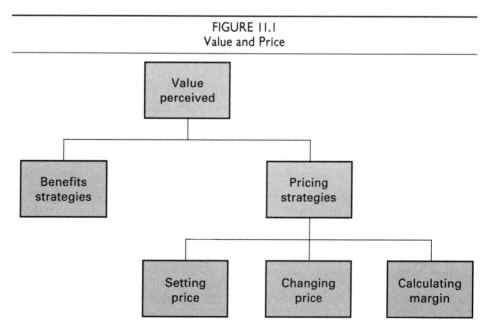

FIGURE 11.1
Value and Price

## BASIC PRICING STRATEGIES

There are several basic pricing strategies retail marketers may follow to affect value perceptions. First, one may keep the retail offering the same as competition, but with lower average prices than the competition to offer perceived incremental value to customers. This may entail better buying to lower merchandise costs, maximizing volumes, and/or keeping overhead lower. Some retailers manage to keep some prices lower and others higher, concerning themselves with the overall margin of the sales mix. The essence of this strategy is **cost advantage**.

Second, one may add benefits while retaining parity price levels to offer perceived incremental value. This might involve providing exclusive products, redesigned products, or improved communication of the benefits inherent in the products, services, or other aspects of the retailer's total program. The essence of this strategy is **program differentiation**.

Third, one may flaunt the price in an attempt to separate price from the value perception. In such instances, price is so unrelated to cost that it can become a value adder itself. The essence of this strategy is **price as a value adder**.

Fourth, one may bargain price in each instance to allow the customer to find the acceptable balance between benefits and price in order to buy. The essence of this strategy is **price negotiation**.[2]

## THE NATURE OF RETAIL PRICING

Pricing decisions for retailers can be more complicated than for manufacturers. First, the number of items involved makes it very difficult to give each item pricing decision the attention it might deserve to price according to the demand sensitivity of customers. Accordingly, retailers often resort to more "automatic" rule-of-thumb pricing methods.

Second, because most items are sold one at a time to final customers, the price sensitivities that the retailer faces are far more diverse than a manufacturer selling in large quantities to relatively few customers.

Third, because of seasonality and other pressures, retailers frequently adjust the "regular" asking price for their merchandise. This is called "breaking the price."

Finally, the prices charged not only for each item but for the whole assortment reflect on the total store image a retailer has, resulting in the need to manage overall price very carefully. Often, retail marketers charge relatively less for some items and relatively more for others, intent on having the sales mix generate the desired overall margin.

Price is a very visible, quantitative, and flexible part of the retailer's marketing program. However, it has been overstressed as a competitive weapon in retailing, although this is not surprising given the overstoring that has occurred in most markets, the willingness of suppliers to help support retail price wars, and downturns in the economy. Unfortunately, customers have now been conditioned to wait for someone to break price—why buy anything at regular price any more, especially if retailers have regular predictable sales times? Leonard Berry captured this as follows:

> Successful retailers deliver value to their customers. Customers "win" rather than "lose", by doing business with these companies. Going on sale is only one way for a retailer to deliver greater value to its customers. A well-conceived sale may generate significant additional—and immediate—cash flow. It may burnish a retailer's image as a source of "good values". It may allow a retail firm to get money back for merchandise that is not moving at higher price levels. The "sale" is an important retailing tool. But it is not retailing's only tool. Today, many retailers are overusing, or improperly using this tool. In the process, they are lessening its impact, sacrificing the trust of customers, and competing on a basis most easily matched by competitors. It is not too late to reflect on the implications of "too many sales" and to change the course of tomorrow's retail history.[3]

There are many reasons why a retailer should carefully examine the pricing strategy he or she intends to follow rather than simply make price decisions mechanically or "on the basis of the competition." Robin Peterson argued that there are ten reasons retailers shouldn't overrely on price cutting.

1. Demand may be inelastic.
2. Price reductions can set off a price war, particularly in oligopolistic industries.
3. Consumers may become trained to be habitual price shoppers.
4. Most customers who patronize the retailer mainly because of low prices are not loyal customers.
5. Persistent price reductions may create an undesirable image.
6. The retailer's costs may be higher than those of competitors.
7. Variable cost may be a high percentage of total cost, meaning higher volumes at lower margins may be worse than lower volumes at higher margins.
8. Rivals may be vulnerable to non-price competition.
9. Some retailers keep prices low because they fear potential competition.
10. Retailers can run afoul of the law through relentless price cutting.[4]

Joan Bergman, editor of *Stores*, commented in October 1989 about the growing problem of confusing customers with retail pricing practices:

> The data show that in 1988, 53.8% of the dollars shoppers spent for apparel went to merchandise that was on sale. The figure was 54.3% for women's apparel and 54.8% for men's apparel . . . What does all this activity about pricing portend? It seems to point out the fact that we as retailers don't know whom we want to be, where we want to go, and what we want our customers to think of us. And that leads to catastrophe when consumers lose faith and trust in us.[5]

The prevailing "price wars" in retailing will stop only when all major participants have the will to stop them:

The price war in Canadian retailing should not, and certainly need not, drag on interminably. Peace and greater prosperity for all can most swiftly be established by retailer and manufacturer working together, in partnership, to create and keep a customer. That will require outstanding customer marketing by the retailers and outstanding trade marketing by manufacturers.[6]

## FACTORS TO CONSIDER IN RETAIL PRICING DECISIONS

Since the price of any good or service is the summary assessment a retailer places on the fair market value of all his or her efforts to provide that particular good or service, it can be a complicated decision. In some parts of the world, retailers make decisions on price in direct negotiations with customers, whereas in North America it is now generally customary for retailers to set prices and then offer their goods and services on a "take-it-or-leave-it basis." There are, of course, exceptions ranging from real estate to automobiles, to antiques, to garage sales.

Our "set pricing" approach has evolved over time and is actually a relatively recent way to conduct retail marketing. In the previous century, price ticketing, and particularly placing priced merchandise in store windows, was regarded as less than genteel, only for lower-class stores.[7] And a century ago, negotiating was common; fixed pricing was not:

> Frank Winfield Woolworth was a 21-year old variety store clerk in Watertown, N.Y., when his boss decided to try to move unwanted inventory by displaying it on a "five cent counter." Woolworth thought the idea could support a store of its own.
>
> His first effort, "The Great Five-Cent Store" in Utica, N.Y., did lukewarm business, so Woolworth closed it and 10 days later, on June 21, 1879, opened another in Lancaster, Pa. The circus had just arrived, and townsfolk in a spending mood promptly bought one third of the inventory—$127.65 of biscuit cutters, fire shovels, linen thread, and other nickel notions sold on the first day of business.
>
> Woolworth had stumbled on a marketing truth. In an age when bargaining with clerks was still the retailing norm, customers would flock to buy goods at a low fixed price; a price so low that the price itself was an inducement.
>
> To offer more merchandise, Woolworth inched up his top price to 10 cents. It stayed there, in the face of stiff competition, until 1932, 13 years after his death. (Stores west of Missouri and in Canada could price items at 15 cents because of higher freight costs.)[8]

There are many factors to consider when arriving at original prices and when adjusting those prices over time. Some of the major considerations follow.

### Factors External to the Retailer

**Consumer demand and sensitivity to price**   As discussed in Chapter 4, there are many factors bearing on customers' interest and willingness to buy, of which price is only one. The choice of customer target will determine the price sensitivities that an individual retailer faces; or, the choice of pricing strategy may determine the kinds of customers that can be attracted. But even for the most price-sensitive customers, a retailer would be well-advised to remember the old adage (here rephrased): "The customer doesn't want a cheap suit, he wants a suit cheap."

A 1990 study of 802 supermarket shoppers in Columbus, Ohio, raises questions about the assumptions retail marketers make about the price sensitivities of their customers. Professors Dickson and Sawyer discovered:

- Only 49.1% of shoppers interviewed knew the item they had just selected was on special.
- If shoppers believed an item was on special (whether it was or not), they were more inclined to feel that both the store and the brand had low prices.
- Slightly more than half of shoppers checked the price of the item they'd just selected.
- The average time spent in the area of the product category was less than 12 seconds. About 42% of shoppers spent five seconds or less.[9]

**Competition**     As discussed in Chapter 5, there are many types of competitors, both direct and indirect. Their pricing strategies can have a big impact on a retailer, especially if their assortments or other characteristics make their offer quite similar. Clearly, the more differentiation that exists on dimensions of importance to customers, the more pricing latitude an individual retailer will have. In many instances, a retail marketer has little option but to price at the "going rate." In 1991, Taco Bell and Wendy's reduced their prices in many locales throughout North America. McDonald's quickly responded by reducing its hamburger prices—in some areas as low as $0.49—as part of its "value menu." Burger King's immediate reaction was to stay away from "permanent reductions," relying instead on specials, discounts, and premiums. As of this writing, this latest development in "Burger Wars" remains unresolved.[10]

**Legal environment**     There are many laws and regulations that bear on retail pricing practices. All retailers should be aware of the applicable laws on price fixing and conspiracy, resale price maintenance, and suggested retail prices, misleading price advertising, two-price ticketing, price discrimination, and promotional allowances. Generally speaking, the legal environment involves laws intended to protect customers from unfair practices and competitors from predatory competition.

**Economic conditions**     Many retailers find their business—and the price sensitivity of their customers—highly related to the ups and downs of the economy. Those retailers offering necessities encounter price sensitivity, especially in difficult economic times. Retailers offering mid-range nonnecessities are the most prone to price sensitivity in difficult times while those offering high-end luxuries are least sensitive to price. The combination of economic slowdown and new federal sales taxation in 1991 resulted in Canadian retailers paying much greater attention than usual to pricing decisions.

**Suppliers**    The terms and conditions offered or imposed by suppliers fundamentally impact both the cost incurred and the pricing discretion a retailer has. For example, a retailer may have obtained exclusive merchandise for his or her trading area and, thus, have considerable flexibility in pricing. Similarly, some suppliers protect their retail dealers to some extent against price wars. Franchise agreements may stipulate the prices that will be charged for merchandise and services across the franchise system, thus curtailing the retailer's freedom to price. For example, Canadian Tire sets maximum prices for its dealers. Dealers are unable to raise prices, but they can lower them.[11] Similarly, pre-ticketing by manufacturers may set the upper bound for pricing of merchandise by any particular retailer.

Purchasing arrangements, including discounts and allowances, may provide a particular retail marketer with more latitude than her or his competitors have for pricing.

### Factors Internal to the Retailer

**Nature of product offered**    As discussed in Chapter 4, customers will expend differing amounts of effort to obtain merchandise. This notion led to product classifications of convenience, shopping, specialty, emergency, and other types. Convenience goods typically offer the retailer relatively little latitude in pricing, whereas, at the other end of the scale, emergency goods offer lots of potential. For example, shoppers caught in a sudden rainstorm will pay more for umbrellas, and new parents out of diapers late at night will pay more for them at the nearby convenience store than they might on a stock-up trip next day. Similarly, the more differentiated the product or service, the less likely price comparisons will be made.

**Costs**    For many retailers, costs are the prime determinant of prices, as will be discussed below. It is important to distinguish between fixed and variable costs. Fixed costs do not change with alterations in volume of goods sold, at least for a reasonable range of volume (costs such as heat, light, occupancy, management salaries), whereas variable costs change directly with volume sold. Those retailers with high fixed costs are very sensitive to volume level changes and must be particularly careful with their pricing to ensure they reach and exceed "break-even," which is the point at which volume just covers fixed costs and no profit is made.

**Other retail program dimensions**    A retailer's location, service, decor, overall assortment, and so on all impact on the prices that can be charged. While these factors influence the retail marketer's total costs, they also help the customer decide on what would be a suitable price for the product or service offered.

The role of price in retail marketers' strategies varies greatly. For example, Japanese department stores do not emphasize price; in fact there is little difference in price across comparable merchandise in comparable stores. Rather, these stores compete on assortment (such as fashionability and tradition), customer care, and amenities. This lack of price competition is reflected in very infrequent sales events.

Japanese department stores operate on slimmer margins (about one-half North American levels) and use consignment selling to reduce assortment risks.[12]

**Pricing objectives**    Pricing decisions can be taken on the basis of differing objectives such as sales volume maximization, profit maximization, image setting, cash generation, competitor discouragement, traffic generation, and seasonal changes. A retailer should have in mind what objective is being sought before getting deeply involved in the details of price setting and adjusting.

## SOME MAJOR APPROACHES AND ASPECTS OF RETAIL PRICING

### Four Ways to Set Price

Any retailer may begin the task of setting price from four different reference points: cost, competition, customer demand, or flat versus variable usage. Each of these approaches has advantages and disadvantages.

**Cost-plus pricing** refers to establishing prices based on invoice or allocated costs of the item. This approach is often used when there are a large number of relatively inexpensive items with known costs, such as grocery items. It has the advantage of being simple, fast, mechanical, and it can be flexible (by changing formula for different classes of items). It has the disadvantage of not taking into account varying customer price sensitivities or varying competitors' prices. If competitors have different costs or different markup formulas, then the resultant prices can be very different. This technique is reliant on suppliers setting good price levels.

**Competitor pricing** refers to establishing prices depending on what relevant competitors are doing. A retailer may price above, at, or below the prevailing market price by a predetermined amount. For example, one could price above the market if there were no strong competitors nearby, and one had a good location or hours, better service or assortment, exclusive lines (such as private labels), etc. It all depends on whether one has competitive advantages valued by customers.

**Demand-oriented pricing** refers to attempting to price according to known or suspected customer sensitivity to price. This can be difficult. One variation on this is to negotiate price with each customer, either individually, such as many auto dealers do, or via "Dutch auctions" where the price is lowered until a buyer appears. Negotiated prices are particularly common when the "ticket price" is high and when trade-ins are likely involved.

Another demand-oriented approach is to charge different customer groups different prices either based on customer characteristics (such as lower rates for senior citizens) or on differences in the product or services offered (such as seats farther back in a theatre), or depending on the time of purchase (such as bakery goods at the end of the day).

Many of these demand-oriented approaches can be called price discrimination. This is legal in most jurisdictions and most instances, except where similar customers in identical circumstances are charged different prices.

**Flat versus variable rate pricing** refers to service pricing in particular. Some retail marketers prefer to charge every customer a standard price (such as Disney charging one price for admission and rides on attractions at Disney World) whereas others charge a fixed flat rate plus extra based on usage (such as the local telephone company). Finding the right mix of flat versus variable rates to maximize profits can be a complicated matter.

## Pricing Merchandise Groups

One of the issues a retailer faces when establishing prices for an assortment of goods is whether to price every item individually or whether to group the items into price zones. There are three basic options: price each item separately, price line, or one price.

**Price lining** refers to establishing a few price levels or points at which groups of merchandise will be sold. In other words, one determines the price of several related items (such as blouses) on cost-plus basis then collapses all the prices into 3 or 4 price points, such as $29.95, $39.95, and $49.95, by moving each price (such as $38.17) to the nearest point (such as $39.95). These levels should be meaningful to the customer. Often, retailers establish three price zones: good, better, best, to provide three basic choices for customers. The idea is to simplify shopping for customer by grouping merchandise and also to induce trading up from the "basic" price point. The retailer often will then buy for each of these price points, trying to get the best value for each. In many instances, the "best" price point is dispropor-tionately higher than the "good" or "better" price points, thus cross-subsidizing the products or services in the assortment mix. Price lining also makes it easier for sales people to know prices of the merchandise on the floor and to trade customers up to the next highest zone. Price lining does not preclude circumstances where addi-tional features and options may be added to the product at extra prices, a common situation in higher priced durables such as automobiles.

**One price** refers to offering the same price throughout a department or throughout the whole store. Every now and then, some retailers attempt to sell all or nearly or their assortment at one price point. The five-and-dime variety store, the penny candy store, and others have had their day in North America. Lately, major retailers have offered single price points as sales promotions, such as Woolco's $1.44 Day. A relatively new version of this pricing strategy is the emergence of "one-price clothing stores" (also known as ceiling-price stores) in the United States. In these stores, all the clothing is at the same price, typically $6, $8, or $9. Many of the store names express their approach: $5 Clothing Stores, One Price Clothing, and Ten Below. From the customer's standpoint, there is no "Why did I pick out the most expensive item in the store?" feeling. From the retailer's viewpoint, there is tremen-dous discipline required to source good values that can be sold at such low price points. Several one-price operators have come and gone because they have not been able to manage the tight operations required. One of the largest chains is Simply 6.

Jay Kline, CEO of this chain, commented on their merchandise and pricing as follows:

> There is always a lot of cheap merchandise available for cheap prices. But, those in this business will really suffer if what they are really offering their customers is not truly a good value. These days it is really a trick to be able to offer customers those values for $6 and $8, but we are helped by the fact that there is always an oversupply of merchandise to choose from. . . . We are close-out buyers in the truest sense when it comes to the merchandise we purchase and we are always looking for deals both at the beginning of the season as well as out of season. We will even warehouse a large amount of goods if necessary. For example, we were able to get our entire early fall inventory very, very early at a time when manufacturers were dumping merchandise at ridiculous prices just to generate cash. We have the financial strength to take advantage of anything that comes our way and we use the cash we have as a commodity. Most retailers are short-term thinkers, but we are not.[13]

### Special and Everyday Pricing

All retailers face the challenge of pricing over time. One approach is to set "regular" prices and then offer reduced **special prices** during sales events. The idea is to induce sales and generate traffic. For example, grocery and discount department stores often have "weekly sales" promoted in the newspaper.

A variation on the above approach is loss leader pricing. **Loss leader pricing** refers to pricing an item below its cost in hope of generating traffic for the store and recovering the losses through increased sales of other items. This approach works best with items with high demand that are not easy for the customer to inventory. Such items should be ones whose prices are well known by customers such that the deal is obvious. These items are often known as "football items" (such as bread, soft drinks, and coffee) because their prices are "kicked around" so much. Loss leader items are best if they are not directly competitive with other items in the retailer's assortment.

Instead of regular/special pricing, the retailer may choose **everyday-low-pricing (EDLP)**, which means that a price is selected that the retailer expects to use for a longer period of time. Retailers such as Wal-Mart, Kmart, Toys 'R' Us, Eatons, and Sears have been using this approach.[14] This technique hopefully thwarts customer behaviour of "waiting for the sale" and promotes a "low price image." Further, the retailer saves money making price changes, on handling inventory fluctuations, and on advertising specials. And presumably, there is less ill-will when customers who bought at higher prices realize they missed the sale.

### Price Comparisons and Promotions

Not all prices are well known by customers, so retailers use a number of techniques to facilitate price comparisons. One method is **comparative ticketing** whereby a regular, manufacturer's suggested list price or a competitor's price is shown along with the asking price.

Another approach is unit pricing. **Unit pricing** refers to showing the total price of an item and then a price per unit of weight or volume to facilitate comparison across items differing in size or brand. This technique is most widely used in supermarkets.

There are several ways to induce purchase by reducing apparent price other than simply changing the price on the item. **Couponing** refers to providing the customer with a piece of paper entitling him or her to a price reduction. Such coupons may be distributed through advertising or direct mail, or even through electronic distribution in store. **Free goods** refers to various deals such as "buy one, get one," "two for one," half-price sale, and one-cent sale.

## Consignment Selling

When consignment selling is used, such as by pantyhose and sunglass manufacturers, the manufacturer retains title to the good while on the retailer's premises. Although this is a safer approach to inventory management for the retailer, the manufacturer retains complete pricing control.

## Psychological Considerations

Price and value are more than just an economic calculation for customers. For example, **price as an indicator of quality** is often used when product/service knowledge is low, when price is consistent with other marketing cues, and when the customer is attempting to reduce perceived risk. In such circumstances, customers will typically buy the mid-range priced item or even the higher-end item. For this reason, some retailers carry items they never expect to sell, but which provide an image for the retailer and a sense of value for other items in the assortment. A common example is the wine list of a fine restaurant: those extraordinarily expensive rare vintages are not really for sale, but rather for positioning the rest of the wine assortment.

**Prestige pricing** refers to pricing items especially high just to ensure that many people will find them too high for "value." In other words, for a select few, the value of the item or the service is in large part the snob appeal of knowing many people simply couldn't afford to buy it.

The actual digits used in expressing the price also often have a bearing on customers' reactions. **Odd pricing** refers to prices that end in digits other than 0 (especially, 7, 8, 9), such as $29.99. The idea is to convey the impression that the item is less expensive than it really is. This is premised on the belief that shoppers generally focus on the first digit of the asking price. Most North American retailers seem to favour odd price endings. **Even pricing** refers to prices that end in 0 such as $500. With even pricing, the idea is to convey the impression that the price was rounded off and is not something the customer is expected to quibble about, nor is it a matter of great concern to the retailer.

**Multiple unit pricing** refers to offering a discount if more than one item is purchased at a time, such as "two for $0.39 instead of $0.20 each". The hope is to encourage multiple item purchases by conveying an impression of savings that is greater than the actual savings. This approach is most often used by convenience good retailers.

**Taxation pricing** refers to decisions as to how to handle sales and other taxes levied at retail. A recent example of taxation pricing occurred in Canada with the introduction of the federal goods and services tax. This 7% tax, levied at retail, required retailers throughout the country to make pricing policy decisions: Should the new tax be included in the ticketed price (GST-in prices) or added at the cash register (GST-out prices)? Should retailers struggling for sales absorb some or all of the tax increase? Should margin percentages be changed since retailers were dealing with new, lower merchandise costs? Should prices be altered to new endings to reflect traditional psychological levels and, significantly, to reduce the need for pennies in making change?

Despite some limited focus group research indicating that customers generally preferred GST-in prices for convenience and understandability, many retailers worried that customers would not be able to sort through the varying approaches and would incorrectly compare GST-in prices with GST-out prices of competitive retailers. Many managers worried that the GST itself would dissuade buying, even though in many instances retail prices should go down with the removal of the previous manufacturer's tax levied at wholesale. Consequently, when the new tax was introduced in January 1991, pricing policies between competitive stores varied greatly. Commentators argued over the impact of the new tax and retailers scrambled to institute new systems and price tickets. In time, these policies will converge again, and will probably settle to a GST-in approach.

## CALCULATIONS FOR ESTABLISHING AND VARYING PRICE

Retailers are vitally interested in the relationship between retail selling price and the cost of the merchandise sold. In simple terms, the difference between the two is called **markup** (or markon, the older term); however, matters can get confusing because both price and cost are subject to various definitions and markup is not the same as gross margin.

### Establishing Sales Retail Price

**Retail price** may be the original price placed on the goods when first offered for sale or the current price (perhaps reduced), or it may be the price actually received when the item was sold. **Initial retail price** refers here to the price asked when the item was first offered, whereas **sales retail price** refers to the price at which the item was actually sold.

The difference, if any, between initial retail and sales retail is called **retail reductions**. Retail reductions may include markdowns, employee or customer discounts, and/or shortages. There may also be **retail additions**, representing additional markups if these occurred. These would be added to the initial retail.

Sales retail = initial retail + retail additions − markdowns − employee/customer discounts − shortages

## Establishing Cost of Merchandise

The **cost of merchandise** is the base invoice price the retailer pays to obtain the item plus any delivery charges minus any payment or other discounts granted by the vendor. Sometimes this gets more confusing because **alteration and workroom costs** may be added to obtain a net cost of merchandise for sale figure. It is important to determine how each individual retailer has decided to calculate the cost of merchandise figure.

The typical cost of goods sold section of a retailer's income statement would be as shown in Exhibit 11.2.

| | |
|---|---:|
| *EXHIBIT 11.2* | |
| *Income Statement (cost of goods sold)* | |

| | |
|---|---:|
| Beginning inventory | $42 547 |
| Merchandise purchases | 16 050 |
| Less returns and allowances | 1 265 |
| Net purchases | $14 785 |
| Transportation inward | 275 |
| Total merchandise handled | $57 607 |
| Ending inventory | 38 305 |
| Gross cost of merchandise sold | $19 302 |
| Discounts earned | 1 022 |
| Net cost of merchandise sold | $18 280 |
| Workroom and alteration costs | 205 |
| Total merchandise costs | $18 485 |

## Calculating Markup and Margin

There are different ways to calculate the differences between prices and costs. **Initial markup** is the planned difference; **maintained markup** is the achieved difference. Both numbers are important to the retailer for planning and control purposes. **Markup in dollars** is calculated as follows:

Initial $ markup = initial retail − invoice cost of merchandise

Maintained $ markup = sales retail − invoice cost of merchandise

It is important to remember that total markup is the sum of individual markups, each weighted in proportion to the total sales of items at that markup. Thus, a retailer may increase total dollar markup by improving the mix of markups obtained.

The calculation of maintained markup may not quite represent the actual gross profit the retailer has realized because there may be other relevant costs to deduct. Retailers commonly use the term "gross margin" to signify the achieved gross profit. **Gross margin** is not exactly the same as dollar maintained markup, although sometimes it can be the same number. Gross margin is sales retail less all relevant costs of the merchandise sold, not just the invoice cost.

$$\text{\$ Gross margin = sales retail} - \text{invoice cost of merchandise} - \text{alteration}$$
$$\text{and workroom costs} + \text{discounts earned}$$

This formula for gross margin provides important suggestions for ways to improve gross margin. Albert Smart summarized these ways as follows:

1. The merchant can increase gross margin by increasing initial markup percentage or by raising the retail price of an item.
2. The gross margin can be increased if the retail merchant is able to sell a larger proportion of higher markup items.
3. The retailer's gross margin can be improved by buying merchandise at lower cost and by keeping the retail prices the same.
4. The retail merchant can cut back on retail reductions which means taking smaller markdowns, and giving smaller discounts to special customers and employees.
5. If the merchant has a policy of offering free alterations, he may charge a fee for these services.
6. If the retailer has been negligent about taking advantage of cash and other discounts available from suppliers, he may begin doing so.[15]

Markups are frequently expressed in **percentages**. Markup percentages may be on cost or selling price. Most retailers today use selling price, but both methods are used, so care must be taken to distinguish them.

$$\text{\% Markup on cost} = \frac{\text{\$ markup}}{\text{\$ invoice cost}} \times 100$$

$$\text{\% Markup on selling price} = \frac{\text{\$ markup}}{\text{\$ selling price}} \times 100$$

These formulas can be used for either initial markup or maintained markup. There is one important distinction, however, between calculating initial and actual markup. Since initial markup is based on the initial retail price, not the sales retail price, it is calculated on a base that includes both net sales and reductions, as follows:

$$\text{Initial markup \%} = \frac{\begin{array}{c}\text{expense \% + profit \% + reductions \% +}\\\text{alteration costs \% − discounts received \%}\end{array}}{100\% + \text{reductions \%}}$$

For example, if expenses are 42% (on net sales), profit 2%, reductions 15%, alteration costs 3%, and discounts received 5%, the formula is as follows:

$$\text{Initial markup \%} = \frac{42 + 2 + 15 + 3 - 5}{100 + 15} = 49.6\%$$

Frequently, one may wish to convert from one expression of markup to another.

$$\text{Markup \% on cost} = \frac{\text{markup \% on retail}}{100 - \text{markup \% on retail}}$$

$$\text{Markup \% on retail} = \frac{\text{markup \% on cost}}{100 + \text{markup \% on cost}}$$

$$\$ \text{ Retail} = \frac{\$ \text{ cost}}{100 - \text{retail markup \%}}$$

$$\$ \text{ Cost} = \frac{\$ \text{ retail}}{100 + \text{cost markup \%}}$$

## Calculating Controllable Contribution

Often it is helpful to calculate the amount of margin that a particular unit or category or manager contributes to the overall operation. To make this calculation meaningful, the relevant gross margin is calculated and then those expenses directly attributable to that unit or category or manager's responsibility are deducted to arrive at the controllable contribution.

$$\$ \text{ Controllable contribution} = \$ \text{ gross margin} - \$ \text{ controllable expenses}$$

## Calculating Breakeven and Profit Target Volumes

Knowing the contribution figure enables calculation of breakeven and profit target volumes. The basic question being addressed is as follows: If fixed costs are known, and the contribution percentage is known (or $ average contribution per unit sold or average $ contribution per transaction), how much sales revenue (or units in volume or number of transactions) must be realized to cover all the fixed costs? The answers can be calculated as follows:

$$\text{Breakeven sales revenue} = \frac{\text{Total fixed costs}}{\text{Contribution \%}}$$

$$\text{Breakeven sales volume} = \frac{\text{Total fixed costs}}{\text{Avg. \$ cont. per unit}}$$

$$\text{Breakeven transactions} = \frac{\text{Total fixed costs}}{\text{Contrib. per transaction}}$$

$$\text{Revenue to realize profit target} = \frac{\text{Total fixed costs} + \text{target profit}}{\text{Contribution \%}}$$

Figure 11.2 summarizes this section on prices, costs, and markups.

## PRICING ADJUSTMENTS

Continuous price adjustments are common in retailing and typically include markdowns, employee and customer discounts, and additional markups.

## FIGURE 11.2
### Prices, Costs, and Markups

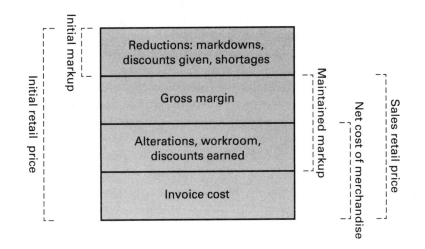

### Markdowns

A reduction in price from the initial retail level to help an item sell is a **markdown**. Markdowns may be taken because goods are not moving well and price reductions are thought to be helpful, or markdowns may be taken to reduce general price levels to promote increased customer traffic. **Dollar markdown** is the dollar amount subtracted from the initial retail price. Dollar markdown appears in the retailer's books, whereas percentage markdown is helpful in presenting pricing changes to customers.

There are several ways to express markdown in percentages. The customer thinks in terms of **markdown off initial retail percentage**. Thus, if an item selling originally at $10 is reduced to $8, the markdown off initial retail is $2 divided by $10 or 20%.

$$\text{Markdown off initial retail} = \frac{\$ \text{ markdown}}{\text{initial retail price}} \times 100$$

A different percentage results if, instead of initial retail, sales retail is used as the base in the calculation. The ratio obtained is commonly called markdown percentage, but will be called **markdown off sales retail percentage** in this book to avoid confusion.

$$\text{Markdown off sales retail} = \frac{\$ \text{ markdown}}{\text{sales retail price}} \times 100$$

A third markdown percentage is useful to determine what proportion of goods sold in a store during a period were at marked down prices. This is called **markdown goods percentage**.

$$\text{Markdown goods percentage} = \frac{\$ \text{ sales of goods marked down}}{\$ \text{ total sales}} \times 100$$

To illustrate, suppose in a week $200 in markdowns were taken on goods originally retail priced at $1000 (that is, they sold for $800) and the total sales for the store were $5000 for the week. The markdown goods percentage would be $800 divided by $5000, or 16 percent. Matters are simplified if the same amount of markdown goods is assumed in opening and closing inventories for the period, although one could make the necessary adjustments to the calculation.

While it is important to be able to calculate markdowns (and other formulas), it is even more important to be able to assess their meaning for the retailer's performance. There are many reasons one may markdown merchandise. For example, the goods may have been priced too high to begin with; they may have been bought in error, such as in the wrong sizes or colours; it may be time for a season change and old stock must be moved out to make room for the new; one may want to generate additional traffic; or there may have been poor advertising or sales efforts on the floor. Therefore, it is important to regard markdowns as a possible *signal* that something did not occur as planned rather than regard them as inevitable and mechanical.

The tendency for many retailers in recent years has been to break price, that is, take markdowns, earlier than traditionally. For example, there have been "January Sales" in December. Similarly, members of the Swimwear Industry Manufacturers Association (SWIM) were so concerned with retailers breaking price long before the summer selling season that they took out full-page ads asking retailers to hold price into the most favourable weather conditions.[16]

Markdowns can be taken across board (that is, on all merchandise in a department or a store) or selectively by picking the items in the assortment that most would benefit. Some retailers have used an automatic markdown procedure where merchandise so indicated is reduced steadily according to its age in stock. Filene's Basement has long been known for this practice, which creates excitement among its customers. The question is whether to buy the item today or wait until it goes down in price but risk someone else buying it in the meantime. The actual timing of markdowns can be as critical or even more critical than the actual amount.

## Employee Discounts

Employee discounts may be provided to retain employees' patronage and loyalty, to have them use the store's products so they may have more credibility with customers, and to show off the store's products (such as by having employees wearing the store's clothing). As discussed above, employee discounts are a retail reduction, that is, they reduce the initial retail price.

## Customer Discounts

Often retailers offer discounts directly to customers, such as to seniors, charitable organizations, preferred customers, or associated business people. Customers may receive discounts because of the circumstances, such as for damaged items, or on the basis of who they are, such as for patronage loyalty. Customer discounts are retail reductions, but should not be confused with markdowns.

## Additional Markups

While less common than markdowns, sometimes retailers are able to increase their markups. For example, when wholesale prices increase, or demand increases, or there are supply shortages, or when competitors lead prices up, a retailer may be able to take an additional markup on inventory already owned. The current craze for sporting celebrities' cards provides an example of when a retailer's stock may appreciate due to "current market value." A signed Nolan Ryan baseball card has been escalating in value. Additional markups are treated the opposite way to markdowns in the formulas above.

## REACTING TO COMPETITIVE PRICING INITIATIVES

Most retail marketers prefer to compete on other bases than price; however, competitors have a tendency to force retailers into price competition regularly. Much of the effort spent on shopping the competition (as discussed in Chapter 5) is devoted to price comparisons. Few retailers can afford to be unaware of prevailing prices in their competitors' stores.

Some retailers are regarded by virtue of their size and market dominance as **price leaders**. These marketers—such as Sears, Wal-Mart, and Toys 'R' Us—are watched for signals as to how to price in a market. Some retailers have little choice but to follow the dominant price leader. Another form of leadership is **barometric leadership**, which is to say a retail marketer whose pricing policies are regarded as worth following because that retailer has a good record of pricing appropriately for the market. Size need not be a factor for such a price leader.

**Price wars** are extremely common because many retailers believe that price is the dominant criterion for customer choice. Sagging demand, surplus inventory, apparent "sleepiness" of competitors, and a belief that a price reduction will lead to a more than offsetting volume increase all are common preludes to a price war. One retailer can begin a price war; price wars end when everyone stops fighting with price.

One of the most interesting retail price wars occurred in the early 1970s when A&P launched its WEO campaign. A&P, the largest grocery chain in the United States as of 1970, was suffering from levelling sales and sagging profits. The new CEO, William Kane, decided on a bold change to discounting. The "Where Economy Originates" (WEO) program began in 1972. Prices were lowered on 90 percent of A&P's merchandise, and the selection was reduced by nearly 30 percent. Heavy advertising began to tell customers about WEO. Competitors reacted with a wide variety of initiatives: price cuts, extended hours, extra service, increased advertising, and so on. A&P did gain sales and share for a while, but at a tremendous cost: the gained volume was at a loss. Strong competitive reaction, shareholder pressure due to missed dividends, rising food prices, and very narrow margins all combined to force A&P to raise prices sooner than planned. The tremendous dislocations this campaign brought to the grocery industry demonstrate that price wars seldom provide lasting advantage, even to the initiator. A&P lost its leadership position to Safeway during this time and could never regain its former status in the industry.[17]

When competitors change prices from previous levels, the retail marketer must decide whether to respond or not. Responses may include matching or exceeding price cuts or raises. All of the factors that should be considered in establishing price levels in the first place are again relevant, but competitive analysis in particular becomes even more critical. For example, questions to consider include:

1. What is the competitor attempting to accomplish? How long might this pricing change last?

2. How far will all the affected competitors go? How far can they afford to go, for how long?

3. Is there any evidence that customers are responding?

4. What are the economics of the battle? Will a lower price (and margin) require an increase in volume that is unrealistic to expect?

5. Are there ways to mitigate the price war with generics, private labels, extra customer care, and so on?

## VALUE RETAILING STRATEGIES

While all retailers may reduce their prices from time to time, some retailers, as a matter of strategy, price below the market. This form of retailing is typically called discounting, although there are various forms of discounters, including: discounters, wholesale/warehouse clubs, deep discounters, catalogue showrooms, close-outers, off-pricers, and hypermarkets and superstores. Each of these store types relies on buying items less expensively than its direct competitors, on selling higher volumes and/or at higher turnover rates, and on having a lower cost structure.

Discounting began roughly in 1960 when large numbers of customers were given the option to trade off assortment breadth and variety, locational convenience, personal service, and upscale ambience for reduced prices. Discounters expanded as quickly as possible across North America, typically with standardized units. These units tended to be in the 40 000 to 80 000 square foot range and were predominantly housewares, hardware, apparel "basics," and some electronics and appliances.

The discount retailers thrived, growing from about $2 billion in 1960 to $161 billion in 1989 in the United States. Discounting began with hard goods, but it has spread to all aspects of retailing. The discount industry has fragmented too: in 1988, there were seven major classifications and traditional discounters accounted for only one-half of total discount industry sales.

A report released July 1989 showed that discount stores are the big winners in U.S. retailing recently, posting gains in shopping trips of 17 percent over 1988, while all other retailers declined.[19]

Among all the discounters, the types getting the most attention lately are off-pricers, wholesale clubs, hypermarkets, and supercentres. The last three are all large surface area retailers selling a combination of food and general merchandise, typically at discount prices, and have been termed by this author as "hyper-marketers."[20] Off-pricers, wholesale clubs, hypermarkets, and factory outlet malls are described next to provide examples of value retailing strategies.

| | % of Total U.S. Sales in 1989[18] |
|---|---|
| Discount Stores | 50.2 |
| Specialty Stores | 18.7 |
| Wholesale Clubs | 10.8 |
| Combination Drugstores | 8.3 |
| Combination Supermarkets | 5.9 |
| Catalog Showrooms | 3.2 |
| Deep Discount Drugstores | 2.8 |

## Off-pricers

Off-price retailing is an interesting variation on discounting characterized by a regular, everyday sale of medium-to-high quality products at deep discount prices. Off-pricers occupy a position somewhere between full-service retailing and discounting. Off-price retailers carry nationally recognized brand names (mostly in soft goods) in no-frills, pipe rack style stores. This mode of retailing was encouraged in the late 1970s and early 1980s by customers feeling the need to save money, by oversupply of goods, by department and conventional stores emphasizing "brand names" versus their own brand names, by manufacturers actively advertising their names, by slow buying and physical distribution by conventional stores, by the high margin/price umbrellas of conventional retailers, by disenchantment with conventional retailers who were cutting back service, by the availability of second use space such as vacant old supermarkets, and by the excessive "sale" emphasis in all stores that encouraged price sensitivity and skepticism regarding "regular price." The off-price customer turned out to be price sensitive, but not economically downscale. In off-price stores, discounts typically range from 20 to 40 percent off the prices charged for the same goods by "conventional" retailers. There are a limited number of SKUs—with a focus on high turnover, high volume. There is low overhead through less-convenient, less-costly facilities and amenities. The inventory ranges from last season and surplus to this season with the emphasis on opportunistic buying of closeouts, end of season, slightly damaged, special runs, etc., at favourable prices, which means assortment continuity may be low. In Canada, there are many examples, such as in clothing (BiWay, Bargain Harolds) and in drugs (Howies, Hy&Zel's, Herbies).

## Wholesale Clubs

In 1976, Sol Price began an experiment in discount retailing that was to have a profound impact. He began a store called Price Club in San Diego, California, which was a membership store for wholesale customers only. After a disappointing start, Price broadened his offering to regular retail customers, but the wholesale customer has been the key to success for this concept. His idea was that small business customers in particular were not being well served by conventional wholesalers.

These wholesalers were more interested and indeed more geared to serving bigger business customers. Price reasoned that these customers purchased often and in far greater quantities than retail customers. Accordingly, his concept was built on high volume, low margin. Price Club became the prototype for what are variously called wholesale clubs, warehouse clubs, or membership clubs.

Wholesale clubs are not simply variations on supermarkets and general mass merchandisers, but rather quite different formats and operations. Exhibit 11.3 is a brief description of a wholesale club.

*Exhibit 11.3*
*Description of a*
*Wholesale Club*

- average 100 000 square feet in size, nearly all of which is selling area
- in a low-cost, out-of-the-way location
- offering a very limited assortment of high velocity items (brand leaders)
- typically 3000–5000 SKUs
- opportunistic buying; more committed to categories than particular brands
- good deal of seasonal merchandise
- direct buying, no warehousing other than right in the store
- food about one-third of assortment, rest general merchandise
- initial product offerings especially in food were very basic but now experimenting with fresh food and big ticket items
- prices typically 20–40 percent below those of other retail outlets
- no individual price marking
- average weekly sales about $750 000 per unit
- depend on high inventory turns, typically need over 17x (at 15x they are operating on negative inventory investment, which is critical to their success)
- large institutional package sizes; or multiples shrink-wrapped and sold together
- membership only, although over time operators began waiving fees; wholesale members must be licensed small business operators; retail customers typically pay 5 percent more
- advertising and promotion limited to store opening time only
- cash and carry, no credit, no delivery
- bare facilities, no frills, no amenities, warehouse building
- inventory on floor on pallets and warehouse shelving
- no on-floor service help
- cost about $10 million to start
- typically need about $30 million in sales to breakeven

Today, Price Club remains the leader in this industry in terms of profitability. Price operates on average gross margins about 7.5 percent with a narrower assortment than most other wholesale clubs—about 2400–2500 SKUs as of 1989. As a comparison, the average Kmart at the same time offered about 125 000 to 150 000 SKUs. In 1990, Price Club sales from 57 units were about $6 billion. The average store was expected to generate about $1150 sales per square foot that year with average customer transactions of about $112.

Wholesale clubs have developed quite separately from the grocery industry and for the most part have not seemed to have had a major impact on conventional supermarkets. They haven't all been successful by any means. After a period of rapid expansion, many wholesale clubs found themselves competing with other wholesale clubs. There followed a shake-out period, which is still underway today. This sector has grown dramatically from $2 billion in 1980 to $17.3 billion in 1988. U.S. sales were about $22 billion in 1990 with just over 400 units. Stephen Mandel, Jr., of Goldman, Sachs & Co., in an extensive 1988 study of wholesale clubs, predicted wholesale clubs will become the fourth largest form of mass distribution in the United States behind supermarkets, discount stores, and department stores.

Surprisingly, retail analysts have found that the wholesale club customer is an affluent customer looking for low prices—not the lower income households, as some people had assumed. Wholesale club members are most often married, between the ages of 25 and 44, consider their occupation professional or managerial, and have annual household incomes of $20 000 or more. Even so, the most successful wholesale clubs have a solid small business base. Accordingly, much of the competitive impact of wholesale clubs is on wholesalers, not on other retailers, such as supermarkets.

Wholesale club managements continue to experiment. For example, new classes of membership have been created, assortments have become increasingly retail-oriented, and consolidation of firms has continued.

## Hypermarkets

Hypermarkets have come to North America in two waves, the latest beginning in October 1984, with the opening of Bigg's in Cincinnati. This was a joint venture between SuperValu (a supermarket chain) and Euromarché (the French hypermarket chain). Each of the major French hypermarket operators has come to the United States: Euromarché with SuperValu, Auchan with Cub, and Carrefour with Costco (and then on its own). Other hypermarkets followed, most notably: Hypermarket USA, Franklin Mills, and American Fare. The general profile of a hypermarket is shown in Exhibit 11.4

It is perhaps still premature to pronounce on the future for hypermarkets, but this author has argued in early 1990 that their future is not particularly bright because:

1. There isn't enough customer appeal.
2. They need too much market share
3. Too much is expected of nonfoods in providing margins
4. Operating expenses will likely climb faster than prices and volume can absorb.

5. Owners have alternate uses for their money and time, such as supercentres and wholesale clubs.

6. Wholesalers won't willingly support them.

7. Manufacturers will give limited support.

8. Organizationally, they will be difficult to manage.[21]

In short, there is a growing opinion that only the very best operators will make any significant money with hypermarkets.[22] After opening four hypermarkets, Wal-Mart chairman Sam Walton announced in spring 1990 that Wal-Mart would not be opening any more. Carrefour and Kmart have also been disappointed by hypermarkets.[23]

*EXHIBIT 11.4*
*General Profile*
*of a Hyper-*
*market*

- 150 000–200 000 square feet of selling space (not including leased areas)
- a 20–40 acre location
- in a trade area of 1 million plus within 30 minutes driving time
- high variety of items (about 60 000 SKUs) and good depth, but limited breadth (not a lot of choice within product categories)—food selection about the same or even less than a conventional supermarket
- low cost of goods sold because large quantities purchased directly from suppliers
- everyday-low-pricing (with some specials)
- gross margin 9–15 percent
- very low labour costs at 6–8 percent
- very low advertising costs

## Factory Outlets and Cross-border Shopping

"Direct from the factory" stores have been popular for some time, but, until recently, not a major retail format. Such stores were once relatively rare, in isolated locations, and confined largely to seconds and surpluses. However, the creation of factory-outlet malls—shopping centres themed around discount outlets, often owned and managed by manufacturers—has spawned a major new type of value retailer. Sawgrass Mills, described as the world's largest outlet mall, was profiled in late 1990 as follows:

> Situated 25 km west of Fort Lauderdale, it boasts 200,000 square meters of name-brand shopping at no-name prices. The parking lot alone covers 70 hectares. Three kilometers of store fronts, 150 in all, include outlets for such status labels as Ann Taylor, Maidenform, Van Heusen, American Tourister, and Athlete's Foot, plus such familiar discount stores as Brands Mart and Marshalls.
>
> All offer goods at 20% to 60% off the usual retail price, a requirement that is specified in the stores' leases and that distinguishes such discount centers from ordinary malls.
>
> . . . Sawgrass Mills has a Disneyesque ambiance that offers fun along with bargains.[24]

There are many strong feelings about factory-outlet malls. For example, many conventional retailers feel their suppliers are unfairly and unreasonably going into competition with their own customers. However, the greatest controversy from a Canadian perspective has been their great appeal to Canadian shoppers when located just inside the American border close to Canadian centres of population. Cross-border shopping has not been confined to factory-outlet malls by any means, but these value retailers are in the forefront of the U.S. stores attracting Canadian customers, much to the dismay of Canadian retailers and governments.

Currently, there are but a small handful of factory-outlet malls in Canada, although more are planned. The appeal of finding a broader selection of name brand merchandise at significantly lower prices—even when paying appropriate duties and taxes—has been enough to prompt thousands of bargain seekers to drive over the border. Two out of every five Windsor residents shop in the United States. Canadians made 27 percent more border crossings in February 1991 than in February 1990. Mayors have argued that senior levels of government should do something to stop the flow; economists have estimated tremendous costs to the Canadian economy; Canadian retailers have wondered how to lower prices when their costs are so much higher; and citizens have taken strong positions on all sides of the issue.[25] Out of all this, one point is very clear, providing added value is a very powerful retail marketing strategy.

## CONCLUSION

Value is critical in customer choices about where to shop and what to buy. Value is a perception of the relationship between benefits provided and the price charged. Retail marketers must approach pricing and other marketing activities that affect value perception with great care. Price is only one part of the marketing program a retailer offers to customers to attract their business on a value strategy. Sol Price put retail pricing into perspective as follows:

> Price is important, but the most important lesson my son, Robert, and I have learned during our years in retailing is that it's really not hard to be a successful merchant or manager if you just remember one thing and act on it. That one thing is the golden rule: Look at everything you do from the viewpoint of the customer. I mean everything. If you were the customer, would you want to be treated this way? If you went into a place and the toilet was dirty, how would you feel about it? If a sign were misleading, how would you react? If you just apply the golden rule to every aspect of operations, you aren't going to go very far wrong. That's easy to say, but when you have thousands of employees, it's not easy to do.[26]

A retail marketer should not make pricing decisions in isolation from other marketing program decisions. Woolco management in Canada recently exemplified this point:

> Recent Woolco advertising has shifted its focus from price to service and brand-name exposure. "We've spent quite a bit of our advertising money projecting a service image because that's one differentiation we have from our closest com-

petitors," says Whitell [President and CEO of F.W. Woolworth Canada].... "Price Is Just The Beginning" is the basic slogan of the Woolco advertising campaign.[27]

Price is the only element of the retail marketing program that is directly related to revenues. Changes in price can have tremendous impact on a retailer's financial success. Therefore it is important to understand the many factors—economic, competitive, and psychological—that bear on setting price and changing price.

## REVIEW QUESTIONS

1. For how many supermarket items can you remember the price? Supposing you are typical of supermarket shoppers, what is the implication of your memory for prices for supermarket operators?

2. Recalling the last time you negotiated a price, how did you go about it? What would happen if more retailers in North America negotiated price?

3. What is the difference between initial markup and maintained markup?

4. If markdowns are higher than normal for a season, what might you suspect?

5. What is your position on cross-border shopping? For example, should the level of duties be changed? Should inspections be increased? Should customs inspectors collect retail sales taxes? How might Canadian stores compete with U.S. stores? Why do the same products cost more in Canada?

## KEY TERMS

- value
- cost advantage
- program differentiation
- price as a value adder
- price negotiation
- cost-plus pricing
- competitor pricing
- demand-oriented pricing
- flat versus variable rate pricing
- price lining
- one price
- special prices
- loss leader pricing
- everyday-low-pricing (EDLP)
- comparative ticketing
- unit pricing
- couponing
- free goods
- price as an indicator of quality
- markdown off initial retail percentage
- markdown off sales retail percentage
- markdown goods percentage
- prestige pricing
- odd pricing
- multiple unit pricing
- taxation pricing
- markup
- retail price
- initial retail price
- sales retail price
- retail reductions
- retail additions
- cost of merchandise
- alteration and workroom costs
- initial markup
- maintained markup
- markup in dollars
- gross margin
- (markup) percentages
- markdown
- dollar markdown
- price leaders
- barometric leadership
- price wars

## NOTES

1. Walter F.Loeb, "The Outlook for Retailing," *Discount Merchandiser*, May 1988, pp. 80–82.

2. For further thoughts on value and pricing strategies, see Albert D. Bates, "Pricing for Profit," *Retailing Issues Letter*, Arthur Andersen & Co., September 1990.

3. Leonard L. Berry, "Reflections on Retailing's Price War," *Retailing Issues Letter*, vol. 1, no. 1 (undated).

4. Robin T. Peterson, "Price Cutting Can't Be Sole Strategy" *Marketing News*, 23 October 1987.

5. Joan Bergman, "What Price a Sheet?" *Stores*, October 1989, pp. 11, 70.

6. Paul Crotty, "Beyond 'the' Price War . . . ," *Canadian Grocer*, February 1989, pp. 48–56.

7. Joy L. Santink, *Timothy Eaton and the Rise of His Department Store* (Toronto: University of Toronto Press, 1990), chapter 3.

8. Eugene Carlson, "Woolworth's Big Idea Began as a Nickel Notion," *Wall Street Journal*, 14 February 1989.

9. Warren Thayer, "Do Your Customers Know What's on Special? Do They Care?" *Progressive Grocer*, May 1990, pp. 81–86.

10. "McDonald's Cuts Prices in 'Value Menu' Move," *Marketing News*, 1 April 1991, pp. 12–13.

11. Ela Schwartz, "Canadian Tire's Leading Edge," *Discount Merchandiser*, January 1990, pp. 50–57.

12. Susan Bass, "Japan Eyeing New Areas," *Stores*, August 1990, pp. 66–78.

13. Jacquelyn Bivins, "One Price Clothing Stores," *Stores*, October 1989, pp. 39–42.

14. For example, see Francine Schwadel, "The 'Sale' Is Fading as a Retailing Tactic," *Wall Street Journal*, 1 March 1989, p. 1.

15. Albert Smart, *Retail Pricing Policies and Procedures* (New York: Lebhar-Friedman Books, 1982), p. 61.

16. "The Case for Later Sales," *Stores*, August 1990, pp. 37–38.

17. Robert F. Hartley, "A&P's WEO: A Price Offensive Backfires," *Marketing Mistakes*, 2nd ed. (Columbus, Ohio: Grid Publishing, 1981), chapter 13.

18. "The True Look," *Discount Merchandiser*, June 1990, pp. 48–72.

19. Rick Gallagher, "Where America Shops," *Chain Store Age Executive*, July 1989, pp. 18–19.

20. Michael R. Pearce, *Hypermarketing* (Working Paper 90-01), The School of Business Administration, The University of Western Ontario, February 1990.

21. Ibid.

22. This view was shared by Steve Weinstein in "The Hypermarket Jury Is Still Out," *Progressive Grocer*, January 1990, pp. 68–74.

23. Kevin Kelly and Amy Dunkin, "Wal-Mart Gets Lost in the Vegetable Aisle," *Business Week*, 28 May 1990, p. 48.

24. Cathy Booth, "The Price Is Always Right," *Time*, 17 December 1990, pp. 38–40.

25. For example, see " The Borderline Shopping Binge," *Maclean's*, 29 April 1991, pp. 36–46.

26. Richard S. Bragaw, "Price Club: One of California's Best Retailing Ideas," *International Trends in Retailing*, Spring 1990, pp. 23–31.

27. Debra Chanil, "The Woolco Way," *Discount Merchandiser*, January 1990, pp. 44–48.

CHAPTER

# SHOPPING EXPERIENCE

## INTRODUCTION

The notion "shopping experience" may at first seem somewhat redundant after the five previous chapters, but it is a concept that goes beyond these five other ways of customer–retailer interaction. When asked about shopping experiences, individuals typically have little difficulty in recounting personal stories of shopping trips that were memorably good or bad, enjoyable or not, and so on. Such stories frequently centre on whether the shopping trip was successful, e.g., "I couldn't find a thing I liked in the whole mall "(assortment); whether the service was good, e.g., "Nobody was around to even take my money" (customer care); whether the trip was easy, e.g., "Imagine putting a store there without a parking space for blocks?" (convenience); whether the customer got the information he or she wanted, e.g., "It took me forever to find the right place in the store. Why don't they put up better signs?" (information); and whether the customer felt the value was good, e.g., "You know, for the kind of money they charge in that restaurant, I expected a better meal!" (value). These are all the common, if sometimes vague, understandings customers have of the term "shopping experience," and certainly they all are part of the experience. Yet, beyond these dimensions, more happens in a retail establishment or shopping area, such as a mall, that shapes how customers feel and behave. Why do customers seem to feel more comfortable in some stores than in others? Why do customers seem to buy more than intended in some stores? In short, what is the impact of the retail surroundings or retail environment on customers?

Shopping is not the same as buying. Some people shop for the fun of it, not for the accomplishment of purchasing something. These people in particular appreciate the theatre of retailing: the sights, sounds, smells, and other stimuli that set a visit to Harrod's, or the West Edmonton Mall, or the local fish market apart from the act of purchasing a product by telephone or mail order. Sandra Harris, writing for British Airways, captured the experience of shopping as follows:

> Unfortunately, what buyers will never understand is that shopping is not lining up behind a whole lot of harassed people in a supermarket for a trolley full of pre-packaged food squashed into submission under plastic. Neither is it replacing a tired, but much loved sweater with another that will eventually have to be replaced in turn. Nor is it trudging around looking for precisely the same boots Uncle Harry had in 1952 and have stood him in good stead ever since. These errands are chores. Shopping is entertainment.
>
> Shopping is finding something special, something new and different in some funny, dusty little shop way off the beaten track. It's luxuriating in the atmosphere of some of the world's greatest shopping emporiums; it's trying on a wildly unsuitable evening gown, cut up to here and down to there, and actually entertaining the thought, for all of seven minutes, that you might buy it. Shopping is fun.[1]

All retailers, from small stores to megamalls, know that the atmosphere and surroundings in which goods are displayed and transacted can impact customers psychologically and physiologically. While customers often pay scant conscious attention to atmospherics, retailers with savvy take great care. This is an aspect of retail marketing that gives full scope to creativity as retailers attempt to stay "fresh and different," to "make a statement." Just as a play gains from the set and costumes and a fine meal gains from quiet music and soft lighting, most, if not all, retailers can gain by "stage-managing the retail theatre" in which they operate.

**Managing the shopping experience** refers to providing comfortable, or novel, or exciting, or pleasantly appropriate sensory stimulation to affect customers' feelings positively toward the store and its merchandise and to convert shoppers into buyers. In this chapter, we will examine several techniques used to do this, in addition to the techniques discussed in the previous five chapters. The discussion is organized according to the five senses of sight, hearing, smell, taste, and touch, as shown in Exhibit 12.1, because it is through these senses that shopping experience can be affected.

## SENSORY STIMULATION IN THE RETAIL OUTLET

■
SECTION
■
ONE
■

Sensory stimulation through managing the retail atmosphere impacts on the image held by customers of a store and shopping area; store and centre choice; customer emotional or psychological state (such as arousal and pleasure); and customer behaviour (purchase and repeat visit).[2] The impacts are by no means uniform or predictable, especially since these stimuli are mediated by individual personalities and life experiences. In other words, once again it is imperative to understand one's customers. Rodney Fitch, chairman of a British design consultancy firm with international offices, put it this way:

Successful design is about capturing the consumer's imagination and through this, the consumer's loyalty, time, and disposable income. Design is about needs and desires, about social circumstances; it is about touching people in their hearts as well as their pockets. It is sensory as well as practical.

Customers experience design directly, so in order to master the realities of customer preference, retail designers must first gain expertise in the retailer's present and future markets. And this expertise should be broader and deeper than conventional market research. Designers should be concerned with what people want, rather than just with what can be sold to them. A good designer will conduct a continuous enquiry into the consumer's visual, tactile, and spatial consciousness. That way, designers can create the kind of design ideas that will persuade tomorrow's consumer with substantial arguments—feelings and motifs that will stand the test of time, while remaining relevant and contemporary.

In providing this dimension, good design offers the retailer a strategic vantage point on the consumer. Its starting point must be people. In retail environments, people like to be where they will be stimulated not bored, where they are satisfied rather then frustrated, where they find solutions not problems.[3]

| | | |
|---|---|---|
| *Exhibit 12.1*<br>*Experiential*<br>*Ways to Affect*<br>*Customers*<br>*Physiologically*<br>*and Emotionally* | **1.** Through what they see: | ▪ Architecture<br>▪ Lighting<br>▪ Colour<br>▪ Display and presentation<br>▪ Demonstration |
| | **2.** Through what they hear: | ▪ Music, water, other sounds<br>▪ Acoustics |
| | **3.** Through what they smell: | ▪ Odours and fragrances |
| | **4.** Through what they taste, touch, do, use: | ▪ Sampling and involvement<br>▪ Events<br>▪ Amenities and facilities |

## Sight

The most important set of sensory stimulation techniques are targeted at the sense of sight. Retailers catch the eye through distinctive architecture, comfort and direct shoppers with lighting, influence moods with colour, and evoke purchasing with display and demonstration.

### Architecture

One of the best-known features of the North American retail landscape is the "golden arches" of McDonald's Restaurants. For thirty years the company has consistently held fast to its beliefs that consistency of design would result in a distinctive signature, with the benefit of immediate identification. The exterior of a store—its overall architecture and exterior signage—should tell potential customers at a glance what type of store it is and who it is for, and identify it uniquely. The initial impression provided by the exterior may determine who enters the store and with what expectations. Department stores and upscale specialty stores have long believed—as have banks—that an imposing exterior is well worth the investment in creating appropriate impressions upon customers. As discussed in Chapter 11, exterior signs and window displays play an important role in attracting customers into a store. An adult walking at a normal pace can travel about twenty feet in five seconds. Whether inside or outside a store the retailer has very little time and/or opportunity to capture the attention of the prospective shopper.

Size is an important visual cue for customers. Large stores are thought to be indicators of success, of importance, of stability. Prices are perceived as more likely to be reasonable and the selection broader. Small stores are thought to be more personal, more likely to be operated by the owner. Size can be conveyed through design as well as through actual construction.

Interior architectural design and use of space are important not only for the functional requirements of the retailer (many of these were discussed in Chapter 8), but also for the psychological impact on customers. The choice of materials such as smoked glass, wood, and marble, all have effects on the images formed in customers' minds. There are also effects on store employees. For example, some retailers have found their sales staff can be expected to vacuum, but seem very resistant to mopping a hard-surface floor.

Retail marketers can use space creatively to convey an image of the store or shopping environment, but they face a series of decisions with regard to the skilful planning of space. For example, even though space is expensive, retailers should generally avoid the temptation to cram product into every nook and cranny to maximize returns. The exception, of course, is those stores whose special atmosphere is created by being overstuffed with odds and ends, such as second-hand stores and rural general stores.

Space conveys images to consumers about the store. Customers of a teahouse may value intimacy in space, whereas the target audience of an upscale women's fashion store may value a sense of privacy and bigness. Mirrored walls, partitions, alcoves, false ceilings, room dividers, and other articulated architectural methods are used by retailers to reconfigure space actually and in the minds of customers. The intent is to make the customer feel comfortable and to focus attention on the merchandise in any one area. A smaller store can use an open concept with low fixtures if it is trying to expand the perception of its space. Ceiling height can be adjusted to provide a sense of expansiveness. The unused space from the ceiling down to about ten feet from the floor can be used for aesthetic display purposes— signage, fabric banners, and merchandise to move the customer's eyes upward from a more congested selling area on the floor itself.

## Lighting

Most customers tend to pay very little attention to lighting unless the lighting is of a very poor quality. From the retailer's perspective, lighting often represents 60 percent of the total electrical costs of a typical retail operation.[4] However, effective lighting presentation can (a) attract attention and enhance the presentation of merchandise, (b) create a pleasant visual impact and stimulate interest, and (c) generate sales.

Lighting can be either natural or artificial and can play either a functional or an aesthetic role in a retail store. Natural ambient lighting can be obtained from windows, skylights, and doorways; however, it cannot be relied upon in some geographical areas. Artificial light can be produced by incandescent methods (light produced by tungsten bulbs), photo-luminescent methods (fluorescent light), HID (high-intensity discharge) methods, or halogen/quartz lighting.[5]

**Functional lighting** can include lighting designed for the exterior and interior of the store to draw the customers' attention to it, to light the store in order to ensure safety, to provide protection of merchandise from theft, and to create a healthy environment for staff and customers. **Aesthetic lighting**, on the other hand, can be used to accentuate the features of products and highlight creative displays.

Among the important considerations in selecting an appropriate form of lighting for a store are colour integrity, cost, quality, and maintenance. Retailers are in the business of selling merchandise and it is important that customers be given the opportunity to evaluate merchandise under fair conditions. It is generally still believed that incandescent lighting best approximates natural light,[6] but the relatively lower cost of fluorescent lighting—which now includes technological developments that permit better colour integrity—make it the most popular choice among retailers as a general or blanket lighting source.[7]

Lighting can be a major cost for a retailer and, thus, alternatives should be considered, such as energy saving lightbulbs, reflectors, and other devices:

> Interior lighting accounts for up to 60% of the electricity used in retail establishments. Exterior lighting can add another 20% on top of that. Retail lighting, because it places such a large demand on the utility, is a major target of energy conservation programs.[8]

Although aesthetic lighting is functional from the retailer's point of view, its goal is to do more than simply light an area. Retailers are becoming more reluctant to rely simply on blanket lighting to cover an entire area, preferring instead to use accent lighting to draw attention to specific areas and displays. Some stores use high-intensity lighting on the displays abutting aisles, while using lower-intensity lighting to light the aisles themselves. This has the effect of visually emphasizing the areas where the products are displayed.

Lighting can also create a mood: bright, high-intensity lighting can create a festive atmosphere, whereas low-intensity lighting can have the opposite effect. However, too much light is uncomfortable and one's eyes will seek the dimmer areas of a store for rest. Some retailers use coloured lighting, but care must be taken to use the same coloured lights as the merchandise; otherwise the merchandise will appear a different colour. There are a wide variety of lighting possibilities and most retailers would be wise to consult a lighting specialist.[9]

## Colour

Even though each of us is faced with a barrage of colours every day of our lives, most of us seem largely unaware of the impact colour has on us psychologically. Thus, colour is a retail marketing tool that should be considered carefully in the design of a store or a department. Colour's power is derived from its ability to affect people physiologically, emotionally, and symbolically through conscious or unconscious associations.

Each major colour has significance. For example, red is generally received as warm, exciting (and is regarded by many retailers as the best colour to use when communicating value); blue (the usual favourite) as calming; yellow as bright and cheerful and for children; purple as dramatic and royal; green as restful; orange as warm and earthy. Yet, too much of these is a problem too. Prolonged exposure to red can raise blood pressure and can be very irritating. Purple can generate a subdued mood.[10]

According to the Prang Colour System, colours differ from one another along three dimensions:

1. **hue** or name of the colour—warmth or coolness (blue, green, and purple are cool, whereas red, orange, and yellow are warm)
2. **value** of the colour lightness (tints) or darkness (shades)
3. **intensity** or chroma of the colour—brightness or dullness

For example, hue distinguishes blue from green, while value distinguishes light blue from dark blue, and intensity distinguishes between bright blue and dull blue.

Colour planning should be done with the entire store in mind: this includes floors, walls, ceilings, fixtures, signage, and, of course, product. For example, warm colours have the effect of moving space in, and cool colours have the illusory effect of moving space out. Walls and floors should be different colours to provide a contrast—this is especially important for older customers whose visual acuity has diminished. In general, the retailer must take into account many of the same factors that should be considered for any marketing decision: (*a*) the target market; (*b*) the intended image (jewellery stores often use blue or purple to convey stability and status); (*c*) competition; and (*d*) the nature of the product (bakeries often use warm, natural tones). The retailer must consider the impact of colour symbolism, association, and visibility. For example, yellow is more visible than blue. Each season has colours associated with it, as do major holidays and events. For example, orange is associated with Hallowe'en and green with St. Patrick's Day.

Because the appeal of colour is largely an emotional one, the retailer should understand the preferences of his or her target customer. Women may prefer different colours than men, and children are attracted to warm and bright colours (consider the colour schemes of McDonald's Restaurants), whereas older individuals appear to be attracted to subdued shades. Upscale fashion stores tend to use very subdued colours and shades, whereas mass retailers like Kmart and T.J. Maxx purposely use bright, bold colour schemes. The image that a retailer is attempting to convey can be helped by appropriate colour selection and coordination. A store intending to convey images of thriftiness, savings, and economy would normally avoid cool passive colours in favour of those that generate a sense of arousal and activity.

Identifying and assessing the colour strategy of the competition is important if the retailer wants to establish a distinctive identity. Colour selection is one step in developing a total identity system to differentiate one retail offer from another. Loblaws is known for its use of yellow, whereas Birks is known for its blue. The nature of the product refers to the categorization of products sold in a store, such as impulse items or shopping goods. Impulse items, which rely on visibility, are usually displayed with bright pure colours. On the other hand, products that require time to sell are best presented in an environment that predisposes the customer to feel relaxed and unhurried.

### Display/Presentation

Displays are discussed in Chapter 10, but it is important to note their importance here on the customer's overall shopping experience. Displays and in-store presentation do more than simply show products—they also set the tone of the store. Good displays of all types follow basic principles of interior design: visual balance, emphasis (or focal point of attention), proportion, rhythm (the eye moves easily from one part of the scene to the next), and harmony (everything fits together cohesively).[11]

Well-conceived and well-constructed visual displays and presentations aid in the process of selling product and in affecting the shopping experience. Display techniques include selection displays (also known as point-of-purchase displays) and special displays.

**Selection displays** are the primary methods of display and presentation used by retailers. It is the merchandising of normal goods found in the retailers' assortment on shelves, racks, tables, pegboards, counters, etc. Often "specials" occupy the end-of-aisle position to create customer awareness of the product and increase unit sales.[12] Merchandise can be displayed in cut cases (the shipping cartons sheared open to display the contents), in bin displays, or as an "impact" display with the product piled high to create a sense of dramatic presence. Effective selection displays can be cross-merchandised promotions to accentuate the relationships between two or more products and encourage customers to make multiple purchases.[13] (Selection displays are discussed in more detail in Chapter 10.)

**Special displays** go beyond products to set the theme or event for a store or area of a store. Special displays can be part of the long-term image building of the store. In these displays, the intent is to make a positioning statement to the customer rather than actively attempting to sell particular products. An upscale men's store selling Ralph Lauren's "Polo" line could develop a display related to the sport of polo, complete with polo accessories and life-size replicas of horses. The purpose would be convey images of exclusivity, wealth, power, and prestige, and to encourage targeted customers to associate with the image as well as the store. Special displays frequently use artifacts (such as "found" or borrowed objects), unusual mannequins, and a host of "theatrical props" to create settings of real or fantastic impact. S.S. Retail Stores opened their first Sesame Street store in a California shopping mall in mid-1990. Designed to entrance children, the store features many special displays:

> Once inside, they're greeted by full-sized cutouts of Cookie Monster, Big Bird, Oscar the Grouch, and Bert and Ernie. And if they feel a need to take a break from all their shopping, enterprising tykes can draw on the "art wall", hang out at the soda fountain in Mr. Hooper's store, or even make an appearance on the stage in the Sesame Street Theater.[14]

Plants are also an important part of store and shopping centre presentation. Not only is greenery restful, it offers associations with the outdoors—an effect most malls seem to seek. Real plants and trees also help put oxygen back into the air and to clean the air of odours, such as from cigarette smoke. There are also advantages to using artificial plants and trees, most notably low maintenance and ability to place them in low-light locations. A relatively new option is "preserved palm trees," which are real trees whose fronds have been chemically preserved and trunks hollowed out and reinforced. These trees offer the best of the appearance of real foliage and the low maintenance and flexibility of artificial plants.[15]

## Demonstration

Most of us are fascinated by demonstrations of even the simplest procedures and items. Pitchmen at country fairs have long known this and have developed carefully designed patter and movements to gather and keep a crowd entranced. In a store setting, increasingly retailers engage customers with live and recorded demonstrations. For example, piano and organ stores have musicians demonstrating products; hardware stores show videotapes of products in use and handymen at work. A new trend has been to show customers the product in preparation: Stew Leonard's in Connecticut allows customers to see through a glass wall into the dairy area; Black's allows customers to get close to the photofinishing machine to see their prints being developed; food areas in malls cook products on grills under the customers' noses. On the other hand, many retailers miss opportunities to use demonstration. For example, many telephone stores do not have their telephones "live" so customers cannot try their sound qualities.

Activity is important in a retail setting. It animates people and is thought to influence purchasing. There are lots of ways to do this other than simply hoping for crowds of people. Xtra Super Food Centers, a superwarehouse operation in Florida, was described as follows:

> But it's more than just the look of the stores that makes Xtra special. There are unusual features everywhere. Hydroponic gardens, located on the produce selling floor, are used to grow alfalfa and bean sprouts; juice factories produce hundreds of gallons of fresh-squeezed orange juice every week; peanuts are

roasted in the bulk food department; deli meats and cheeses are vacuum packed in the middle of the deli department; and in one of the stores, a coffee factory roasts coffee beans.

The stores buzz with activity. Employees are everywhere, stocking shelves, handing out product samples and helping customers locate items. Some employees are even on roller skates. "A lot of super warehouse stores leave customers cold because there is no interaction with employees" said Burmeister [corporate vice-president]. "But we make sure that customers are constantly meeting employees throughout the store."[16]

## SOUND

There are many opportunities to use sound to influence the shopping experience. Silence (dead sound) is very upsetting and unsettling to most people, as is too much noise or unpleasant sounds. The retail marketer's challenge is to find sounds that are appropriate in quality and intensity for its particular customers. While few retail outlets are designed with acoustics in mind, specialists in this field can make dramatic changes in the ability of the retailer to affect customers through sounds.

In any shopping setting, there are a variety of "background sounds" ranging from conversation to machinery sounds. These background sounds can be masked by running water, music, or other controlled sounds. Shopping centres frequently use fountains and moving water to soothe shoppers, not just to provide a pleasant view. Some retailers take advantage of their particular operation to produce sounds—stereo retailers play their radios and stereo sets; popcorn stands operate their poppers; discount stores use their loudspeakers to announce in-store surprise specials; and so on. However, the most common form of sound employed by retailers is pre-recorded music.

Retailers can use music to create appropriate moods and to develop the image of their store. Retailers of denim jeans targeted at teenagers seem inevitably to play rock music, believing their target audience would immediately identify with their store. A women's fashion store targeted at the expectant mother, on the other hand, would likely select music that conveyed a more restful, soothing environment.

There are many sources of music. There is no rule of thumb for the retailer to follow in selecting a source of music; however, if music is to be utilized, its selection should be given the same attention as other elements of the retail marketing program. For example, radio, while inexpensive, should be avoided if possible. The retailer loses control over the content of the material and avoids the embarrassing problem of occasionally inadvertently broadcasting commercials for competing retailers.

Professionally produced musical selections ranging from pre-recorded cassettes and CDs to specially designed selections tailored to the needs of his or her store are the retailer's best choices. Muzak is widely used because it has been found to be very effective. The nature of the music (classic, contemporary, country and western, etc.), its intensity or level (quiet to loud), and its tempo (slow to fast) all have an impact on customers. For example, slower music has been found to keep people in a store longer. Music can add to the experience in the retail establishment.

For example, restaurateurs have long known the incremental value a violin or piano player can add to an expensive meal.

Pre-recorded music is now available in a wide variety of formats, allowing the retailer considerable flexibility:

> Retailers not only have more variety, but new technology allows them to automatically change their music at certain times during the day to reflect customer demographics. A store might have adult contemporary piped in during the morning and then switch to Top 40 when teens start coming in after school. Ritter [Marketing Manager at Muzak] estimated that almost half of Muzak's clients use the dayparting service.
>
> Technology also allows large department stores to play different types of music in different parts of the store.[17]

Music can also be used in unique ways to discourage unwanted behaviour and/ or customers. In 1985 Southland Corporation began experimenting with the use of "middle of the road" music *outside* of its 7 Eleven stores to discourage teenagers from loitering. Staff controlled the volume levels. If management perceived that a group of teenagers was gathering outside of the store, the volume was increased. The company believes that this technique has been effective in reducing loitering, keeping entrances clear, and reducing littering. It also appears that regular customers did not find the music offensive.

Retailers should realize that, in most jurisdictions, playing music (even as broadcast on the radio) at a place of business is legally subject to paying royalties to the writers/artists (or their licensing organizations). While this has not been actively enforced, it is likely coming. The only exceptions are stereo and record stores playing the music with the intent of selling the recordings.[18]

## SMELL

The most acute human sense is the sense of smell: most of us can distinguish thousands of odours. All of us have learned from an early age to make immediate judgments on products and environments based on their fragrances and odours. And, odours can evoke emotional reactions because they arouse memories of other occasions and affect moods. For the retailer, the challenge is to avoid unpleasant odours and to use pleasant odours creatively to enhance the customer shopping experience.

Routine housekeeping and adequate ventilation are essential to keep a store clean and odour-free. It is incumbent on the retailer to ensure that potential customers are not turned away from the store because of unpleasant odours. Related to odours is the problem of allergies. Apparently more and more North Americans suffer from allergies of all kinds, so care must be taken that the air in a store is not allergenic to customers. Too much perfume, too much dust, etc., can send customers running from the store.

On the other hand, opportunities are available to most retailers to use **scent appeal** to create an environment that the customer will find enticing. Restaurants, florists, bakeries, popcorn stores, and delis are examples of stores that have built-in opportunities to attract customers with the pleasant smell of their products. Such smells not only attract customers, but also prompt them to buy and to create associations. Supermarket operators routinely vent the bakery aromas into the store because the smell of fresh baked bread encourages people to think of "Grandma's baking" and to buy all kinds of food throughout the store. Other retailers, as well, can capitalize on different opportunities. Any retailer can buy fresh flowers or bring them from their own garden to enhance both the visual and olfactory appeal of their establishments. Any store that sells leather goods—luggage stores, fashion stores selling leather garments, shoe stores—can train retail salespeople to sell using suggestive techniques, such as "Can you smell the genuine leather?" to create an image in the mind of the consumer that denotes product quality and assurance. Some stores even dispense perfume automatically into the air at intervals, while others go to great lengths to clean their air of odours and particles.

There are very few studies of the role of odours in marketing. Some researchers are beginning to offer prescriptions, such as Alan Hirsch of the Smell and Taste Treatment and Research Foundation:

> For example, retailers should use a spicy odour if they're targeting men in their 30's, but to attract females in their 60's, a mixed floral with a higher note of lily of the valley would be more appropriate. Retailers should also choose odours to suit the area of the store and the time of the day.[19]

## TASTE AND TOUCH

There are also a variety of ways retailers engage the sense of taste and touch. **Sampling** is very common in food stores. Not only does this approach engage customers (such as slowing down the shopper wheeling a cart around a super-market), but also it often results in additional sales of the sampled item. Similarly, customers in North America tend to shop more on carpeted floors than on hard floors; they have been trained to regard hard floors as aisles between the carpeted selling areas.

Retailers with savvy look for ways to get customers involved with their merchandise. Computer games, or suggestions such as "Feel this fabric," "Sit on this sofa," "Test drive this car," and so on are all ways to overcome resistance by customers. Merchandise that can't be touched and tried often stays on the shelf.

The temperature and humidity level in a store is another way in which customers are "touched." Beyond a "comfortable level" (found to be 18–20°C), retailers sometimes move their thermostats a little up or down to encourage sales of particular items such as swimsuits and sweaters. Touch is also engaged with choice of floor covering. Carpets are frequently used not only to reduce noise, but also to convey walking comfort and upscale look.

Retailers also engage customers' senses with extra amenities ("try our coffee while you're waiting"), areas for kids (such as a "ball-room"), clean restrooms, automatic doors, lockers, and so on. Giving customers things to do while they are waiting, getting them involved in the store, are tried-and-true ways of keeping them in the store longer. Shopping centre managers have learned the value of food courts and benches to keep shoppers in the mall longer. Some retailers add costumed characters roaming the store to greet children, "greeters" at the door, periodic contests and events to generate excitement, and so on.

A recent trend has been the construction of "entertainment malls." These shopping centres, in addition to the usual assortment of stores and services, offer rides and other entertainment activities for the whole family. Such attractions provide new ways for shopping centres to differentiate themselves. One proponent of such malls, Daniel O'Connell, director of leasing for Time-Out Family Amusement Centers, put it this way:

> Entertainment has become an integral part of the enclosed regional mall experience. Over the years, developers have added food courts, theaters, and other attractions to extend the mall's leisure-time activities. The entertainment anchor is the next step in the evolution of mall development. . . . Most enclosed regional malls offer the same fare these days—The Gap, The Limited, food courts, etc., are standard, but a destination entertainment anchor can make a real difference in that it makes a mall stand out from the competition.[20]

## MONEYSWORTH AND BEST: A TOTAL EXPERIENCE

To one degree or another all retailers employ the techniques discussed above in attempts to create an atmosphere and experience in their places of business. Those that are most successful are those that effectively carry through their strategy from overall positioning decisions through to store design and execution. One such retailer is the highly successful and growth-oriented Moneysworth and Best Shoe Repair Inc.

Begun in 1985 as the brainchild of a packaged-goods marketing executive who believed that shoe repair was a traditional service that everyone used yet was not being fulfilled, Moneysworth and Best offers quality shoe repair in nontraditional settings such as shopping malls and railway stations.

The original concept was to provide quick economical shoe repair—a fairly mundane and unappealing service—with a theatrical flair. Evoking an earlier age when service was king, Mr. Van Sant, the founder of Moneysworth and Best, introduced an old-fashioned value-added service—shoeshines—to his product mix. To "theatricalize" the basic service, he hired a choreographer to develop the "Chattanooga Shoe Shine, a virtuoso performance of rag-snapping, toe-tapping exuberance" and "train(ed) shoeshiners to ensure that the rags snapped right and the toes tapped in time."[21]

Believing that traditional shoe repair was largely carried on in "dirty, messy, lousy looking stores that you wouldn't go into . . . ,"[22] Mr. Van Sant decided to present the service within a period setting. All Moneysworth and Best stores are set at about the turn of the century and convey the image of old-fashioned craftsmanship and tradition. High-intensity discharge (HID) track lighting, which casts shadows and gives a soft three-dimensional look to the merchandise and machinery, is used in all of the stores. It accentuates the warm brown glow of the rich oak chairs and countertops and gives a sparkle to the brass accessories.[23]

Following through this period setting, all stores have big band music playing in the background, which is set against the quiet hum of the brightly painted red machinery. All staff wear bright green aprons with the Moneysworth and Best logo. The smell of leather and shoe polish wafts out into the common shopping areas beyond the leaselines.

What Moneysworth and Best has done is carefully position their retail offering. With traditional shoe repair outlets raising questions about the quality of service, Moneysworth and Best has suggested to the consumer that the consumer has in fact moved back in time to a period when quality workmanship was more available.

Moneysworth and Best stores average only about 300–400 square feet and their return per foot is reputed to be among the highest of all franchise operations. Stores average yearly sales of about $300 000–$400 000, with some of the flagship operations generating as much as $600 000 per year.

## CONCLUSION

Experience refers to the ways customers feel as a consequence of the physical and sensory environment of the retail establishment. It is different from what many retail commentators mean when they use the term "experience" as a generalized expression of the interaction of the retailer and the customer. In this book, experience refers to sensory stimulation, not whether the customer had a pleasant interaction with salespeople or was able to find a parking space. Retail marketers attempting to provide appealing, even compelling, experiences must engage customers through each of the five senses: sight, sound, smell, taste, and touch.

Customers have experiences with retail stores whether or not retailers consciously attempt to affect those experiences. Accordingly, it makes more sense to stage-manage the retail theatre than to leave it to happen haphazardly. The starting point is to identify all the dimensions of experience and then to examine a store as media and as art from the customer's perspective. If all the store's a theatre, how does the show appear from the customer's viewpoint? Retailers can conduct visual, aural, and other sensory audits of their store environments.

A common trap for store management is to build and operate a store for their own tastes, rather than those of their customers. Young salesclerks may enjoy rock music, but older customers may not. In fact, an emerging challenge is modifying store environments to meet the needs and desires of aging customers.

In order to provide a noticeable and sales-effective experience, retail marketers need to be both appropriate and different. For example, Mark Endres, the grocery manager of a Save Mart store in California, tripled sales of candy with mass displays of candy bars at the back of his store, and a trail of candy wrappers pasted to the floor from front to back of the store. Gary Wood, meat coordinator for Piggly Wiggly in Kentucky, developed a local "Groundhog Week" promotion in conjunction with pork producers.

We had the kindergarten class of Mayfield Elementary School draw pictures of groundhogs with numbers on their backs. These were then handed out to customers. Every 30 minutes, we'd call out a number. If the number matched the one on the customer's groundhog picture, he or she would win a pork sausage or what we call "real ground hog."[24]

A store is not supposed to be a temple to management's liking, but an efficient, appealing, and fun experience for customers who enjoy it so much they come often and spend both time and money in the store. Few retailers have appreciated the strong customer desire to enjoy the shopping experience.

## REVIEW QUESTIONS

1. The first Barnum & Bailey Circus Store opened in the fall of 1990 in Fairfax, Virginia. The 4000 square foot store was designed to offer children's apparel and merchandise as well as memorabilia from "The Greatest Show on Earth." What would you do to create a shopping experience for customers at this store?

2. Considering a local shopping centre with which you are familiar, what could that centre do to add more "experience" to your shopping trips?

3. In your experience, what store is the most fun to shop in? Why?

4. In what ways can a store be designed to send an architectural message of "Please come in"?

5. What is the impact of special events and activities on a retailer's own staff?

## KEY TERMS

- managing the shopping experience
- functional lighting
- aesthetic lighting
- hue
- value

- intensity
- selection displays
- special displays
- scent appeal
- sampling

## NOTES

1. Sandra Harris, "Shopping for the Fun of It," *British Airways High Life*, June 1990, pp. 12–22.

2. Robert A. Westbrook, "Sources of Consumer Satisfaction with Retail Outlets," *Journal of Retailing*, vol. 57, no. 3, Fall 1981, pp. 68–85; Robert J. Donovan and John R. Rossiter, "Store Atmosphere: An Environmental Psychology Approach," *Journal of Retailing*, vol. 58, no. 1, Spring 1982, pp. 34–

57; Francis Buttle, "How Merchandising Works," *International Journal of Advertising*, vol. 3, no. 2, Winter 1984, pp. 139–48.

3. Rodney Fitch, "The Role of Design in Retailing Strategy," *International Trends in Retailing*, Arthur Andersen & Co., Spring 1989, pp. 35–40.

4. Mimsie Bohanon and Ken Wallington, "A Retailer's Approach to Lighting

and Colouring," Retail Merchants Association, 1983, p. 14.

5. For a recent comparison of various lighting methods, see Jennifer Pellet, "The Power of Lighting," *Discount Merchandiser*, February 1990, pp. 71–77.

6. Adolph Novak, *Store Planning and Design* (New York: Chain Store Publishing Corp., 1977), p. 134.

7. Jennifer Pellet, "The Power of Lighting," *Discount Merchandiser*, February 1990, p. 72.

8. Gordon E. Kirkland, "How Energy Efficient Is Your Store?" *The Retail Advisor*, Deloitte & Touche, February 1991.

9. It is important to follow both the technical and legal trends in lighting and energy management. For example, see "More Choices in Lighting in the 1990's," *Chain Store Age Executive*, March 1990, p. 90.

10. Harriet Goldstein, and Vetta Goldstein, *Art in Everyday Life* (New York: The Macmillan Co., 1954).

11. For more detail, see J. Diamond and E. Diamond, *The World of Fashion* (San Diego, CA: Harcourt Brace Jovanovich, 1990), chapter 14.

12. Jean Paul Gagnon, and Jane T. Osterhaus, "Research Note: Effectiveness of Floor Displays on the Sales of Retail Products," *Journal of Retailing*, vol. 61 (Spring 1985), p. 115.

13. Francis Buttle; see n. 2.

14. "Sesame Street Opens Store," *Marketing News*, 15 October 1990, p. 2. See also Penny Gill, "The Disney Store Blends Retailing and Entertainment," *Stores*, June 1991, pp. 20–24.

15. Rick Telberg, "Palm Trees: Are They or Aren't They?" *Stores*, April 1991, pp. 40–43.

16. Priscilla Donegan, "An Xtraordinary Experience," *Progressive Grocer*, March 1989, pp. 86–94.

17. Cyndee Miller, "The Right Song in the Air Can Boost Retail Sales," *Marketing News*, 4 February 1991, p. 2.

18. "Mall Music: No Free Lunch," *Stores*, May 1990, p. 41.

19. Cyndee Miller, "Research Reveals How Marketers Can Win by a Nose," *Marketing News*, 4 February 1991, p. 1–2.

20. As quoted in "Entertainment Anchors: New Mall Headliners," *Chain Store Age Executive*, August 1989, pp. 54–65.

21. *Canadian Business*, January 1987, p. 34.

22. Ibid., p. 35.

23. "Shoe Repair—With a Flair," *Canadian Footwear Journal*, August 1989, p. 110.

24. These ideas and many others were found in "Merchandising Ideabook," *Progressive Grocer*, September 1990, pp. 70–92.

# ■■■■ CASES FOR PART 3 ■■■■

CASE 3.1  Jouets du Monde

■

CASE 3.2  Atom Foodstores

■

CASE 3.3  Sarah Leavens

■

CASE 3.4  The Arrow Company and the Bay:
Bin Stock Proposal

■

CASE 3.5  Burger King Canada Inc.

■

CASE 3.6  Simpsons: Men's Furnishings

■

CASE 3.7  La Maison Simons

■

CASE 3.8  Stewart Shoes

■

CASE 3.9  Central Guaranty Trust: Telemarketing

■

CASE 3.10  Fisher and Cooper

■

CASE 3.11  Loblaws Supermarkets Limited:
You Can Count On Us!

■

CASE 3.12  Some Exercises in Retail Pricing

■

CASE 3.13  La Maison de Drogue

# **C A S E** 3.1  Jouets du Monde

In March 1987, M. Henri Jolivet, the buyer for Division 4 (metal, plastic, and wood model kits, construction toys, etc.) of Jouets du Monde, was considering what action to take on his Hi-brix line of construction toys, which were now facing new and significant Korean competition. Decisions were required soon so that orders could be placed and plans firmed up for the fall selling season.

Jouets du Monde was a Canadian chain of toy and hobby stores with eight locations spread through the major urban centres in Eastern Canada—Toronto, Ottawa, Montreal, Quebec, St. John's and Halifax. The company had been immensely successful in the decades of the 1970's and early 1980's and had developed a reputation for both breadth and depth in toy merchandising. It was, some observers noted, the only place in Eastern Canada where certain specialty toy and hobby lines could be obtained. While still profitable, the company in the early 1980's had come under increasing competitive pressure, particularly in the higher-volume standard toy lines, from department stores, other specialty retailers, warehouse type outlets, and so on. As a result, sales growth had slowed, and profitability as a percent of sales and return on operating assets had dropped. Attempts to find noncompetitive or unique lines had made some progress but at the cost of greater inventory investments due to slower turns and the emergence of what some called a cluttered look in the stores. Pressed by these circumstances, management was asking all personnel to give greater attention to return on inventory investment and shelf space.

## *HI-BRIX*

The Hi-brix line of construction toys was based on a miniature rubber interlocking brick patented by a European manufacturer. By means of these bricks and several small accessories, such as windows, doors, etc., a child could construct model homes, castles, vehicles, even space ships. By purchasing progressively larger sets, more elaborate structures could be built.

The Hi-brix line had been marketed in toy stores and department stores in Canada for many years and was very well known as a high-quality high-priced toy that had certain educational benefits for the child. The European manufacturer had always provided advertising and promotional support and had controlled distribution to the end that recommended retail prices were by and large observed by all outlets. Sales were made throughout the year with a peak in the pre-Christmas period.

## *HI-BRIX AT JOUETS DU MONDE*

Jouets du Monde imported the Hi-brix line direct from Frankfurt, ordering the bulk of its estimated annual requirements in March for the subsequent year. Smaller orders could be placed throughout the year to fill in popular items, but this tended to be expensive in terms of shipping and order processing costs.

In preparation for placing his 1988 order, M. Jolivet compiled some historical data on the aggregate performance of the Hi-brix line (Table 1).

As M. Jolivet well knew, the Hi-brix line had come under competitive fire in the past two years from the entry of a Korean toy set, which was apparently copied from the Hi-brix line. The Korean product, branded O-hio, was of good quality and resembled Hi-brix in many ways, except that it was not compatible in use because square rather than round studs were used to interlock the pieces. It was imported by a distributor who operated in Western Canada and was priced to sell at retail at approximately two-thirds of the price of an equivalent Hi-brix line.

In the first year after introduction, the O-hio line achieved distribution largely through non-traditional outlets for toys; but in the past year

<table>
<tr><td colspan="5" align="center">Table 1</td></tr>
</table>

| Fiscal Year End Jan. 30 | Units Sold | Average Per Unit Retail Price ($) | Gross Margin*($) | Closing Inventory at Cost ($×1000) |
|---|---|---|---|---|
| 1982 | 17,100 | 20.15 | 9.91 | 94.1 |
| 1983 | 19,700 | 17.50 | 8.58 | 98.9 |
| 1984 | 21,600 | 16.80 | 8.08 | 127.4 |
| 1985 | 23,200 | 19.10 | 8.88 | 130.8 |
| 1986 | 21,400 | 17.20 | 7.77 | 153.4 |
| 1987 | 16,100 | 18.40 | 9.02 | 139.7 |

*After transportation, brokerage, etc., but before promotional allowances.

several department stores and other direct competitors had taken the line, and, in the process, some had dropped Hi-brix. M. Jolivet had discussed the Korean line with the distributor and determined that the full line would be available to Jouets du Monde. Taking the average of several similar items, M. Jolivet came up with the following comparisons.

sale materials. There was no promotional allowance available on the O-hio brand.

Up to this point, M. Jolivet had rejected the notion of stocking both brands. He realized that if he did, unit inventories would have to be almost doubled (because most of the inventory was located on or under the shelves in the stores) and that shelf space as well would have to be

| HI-BRIX | | O-HIO | |
|---|---|---|---|
| Current Retail Price | Current Cost* | Recommended Retail Price | Current Cost |
| $17.40 | 9.40 | $12.60 | 5.40 |

*After transportation, brokerage, etc., but before consideration of promotional allowances.

M. Jolivet had appealed to the European manufacturer for lower purchase prices to meet the new competition, initially to no avail. Then, in the past year, the promotional allowance for Hi-brix had been increased from 5 to 15 percent of purchases. Jouets du Monde had traditionally spent the full promotional allowance provided for the line on media advertising and point-of-

expanded. M. Jolivet estimated that in fiscal 1987 Hi-brix inventory was stored in 175 square feet and that 100 linear feet of shelf space was given to the Hi-brix line. Table 2 shows comparable data for previous years. He felt it very unlikely that sales would increase correspondingly, although there was some hope for modest unit sales increases.

<table>
<tr><td colspan="3" align="center">Table 2</td></tr>
</table>

| Fiscal Year End Jan. 30 | Inventory Space (sq. ft.) | Shelf Space (linear feet) |
|---|---|---|
| 1982 | 100 | 80 |
| 1983 | 120 | 90 |
| 1984 | 170 | 100 |
| 1985 | 160 | 100 |
| 1986 | 180 | 100 |
| 1987 | 175 | 100 |

# C A S E 3.2    Atom Foodstores

Sam Reynolds, category manager for Atom Foodstores Limited, faced several decisions that had been triggered by a new product-listing proposal and by the vice president of merchandising's concerns about the profitability of the Yoodle category.* The Yoodle category was one of thirty categories under Sam's control. However, before making the decisions on the number of brands, pricing, merchandising, and shelf space, a review of the entire Yoodle category was necessary. Such a category-review meeting was scheduled for two day's time.

After reviewing the category data, Sam would have to decide whether or not to list the new product, whether or not to delist one of the existing products, and whether or not to change the amount of space allocated to the category. Improving the category's financial performance by increasing merchandising dollars was another option. He could do this by negotiating for better promotional discounts and more over-and-above promotional money from suppliers. His merchandising-strategy decision of whom to support would have a definite impact on total merchandising dollars generated from the category. His final decision would have to take into consideration Atom's store positioning, the competition, and, of course, Atom's customers.

## THE COMPANY

Sam had just read an article in the business press that contained several quotes from his CEO, John Cooper, who was calling for improved relations with suppliers. In an attempt to break down communication barriers with suppliers, he had recommended, "If at any time, at any level, you feel you're not being treated justly, move up to a higher level of management." He then went on to say that in regard to over-and-above payments, volume discounts, and trade spending, he felt that in some cases his chain had not received the best deal. "Our suspicions were not entirely unfounded," he continued.

He also called for more realistic pricing that would tend to reduce the need for deal making. He said, "Drastic reductions from regular prices affect our credibility and our price image, and it makes it look like we're gouging the customer." He then went on to justify promotional allowances and trade discounts for the efficiencies of higher volume that they created for the manufacturer.

Apart from strained supplier relations at the present, Atom Foodstores was doing relatively well for a regional grocery chain. Atom had achieved more than $1 billion in sales during 1986 and an operating margin of 1.85 percent. Exhibits 1 and 2 show the financial performance of the 62-store chain. In recent years Atom had become much more sophisticated in terms of retail technology. The chain was just beginning to make use of detailed point-of-sale information on category and brand performance provided by Atom's online scanning stores. For the first time, attempts were being made to gauge the effectiveness of certain merchandising promotions.

Chain executive had abandoned the "cookie cutter" approach to assortments. Merchandising in specific site locations was being adapted to the local market. Chain executives anticipated that scanning would refine each location even further by providing point-of-sale information that would customize each store's planogram. Atom had 35 percent of the chain's stores on-line and planned to have the entire chain equipped with scanners by 1989.

---

*This case has been simplified in terms of size and selection for each brand. A nonexistent category was developed to prevent any bias on the part of the reader.

EXHIBIT 1
Atom Foodstores:
Ratios

| | Selected Financial Performance $ Million | | | | |
|---|---|---|---|---|---|
| | 1986 | 1985 | 1984 | 1983 | 1982 |
| Sales | 1037 | 966 | 896 | 788 | 708 |
| Percent Change | +7.3 | +7.8 | +13.7 | +11.3 | +13.7 |
| Operating Income | 19.2 | 18.8 | 16.5 | 12.0 | 10.0 |
| Percent of Sales | 1.85 | 1.95 | 1.85 | 1.52 | 1.41 |
| Percent Change | +2.0 | +13.9 | +37.5 | +20.0 | +22.0 |
| Net Income | 6.5 | 8.83 | 7.67 | 5.83 | 4.33 |
| Percent of Sales | .6 | .9 | .9 | .7 | .6 |
| Percent Change | −26.0 | +15.0 | +31.0 | +35.0 | +44.0 |
| Cash Flow from Operations | 19 | 18.5 | 16.3 | 12.5 | 10.2 |
| Percent of Sales | 1.83 | 1.92 | 1.82 | 1.59 | 1.44 |
| Capital Expenditures | 1.3 | 15.5 | 23.0 | — | — |
| Percent of Sales | 1.1 | 1.6 | 2.57 | — | — |
| Fixed Assets Renewal Rate | 6.7 | 4.6 | 2.9 | — | — |
| Shareholders Equity | 57.0 | 53.0 | 46.0 | 40.0 | 32.0 |
| Long Term Debt | 22.0 | 16.0 | 16.5 | 18.3 | 17.0 |
| | | | | | |
| KEY RATIOS | | | | | |
| Working Capital | 1.2:1 | 1.23:1 | 1.22:1 | 1.23:1 | 1.23:1 |
| Inventory Turn | 12.8 | 12.4 | — | — | — |
| Accounts Payable/ Inventory | 1.02:1 | .99:1 | .89:1 | — | — |
| Return on Net Worth (%) | 11.3 | 16.7 | 16.7 | 14.5 | 13.7 |
| Return on Investment (%) | 8.2 | 12.8 | 12.2 | 9.9 | 8.9 |

Sophistication was increasing in management methods as well. Financially, the company had clear goals in place combined with rigid profitability criteria. The chain had recently completed the closure of unprofitable locations and the renewal of remaining assets.

Operations were very efficient with sophisticated computer assists for buying, warehousing, and individual store management. Merchandising skills were being sharpened with the development of a strong private label assortment of more than one thousand items.

Atom Foodstores had moved away from a mass-marketing approach toward a more segmented one. Three store formats were in use: box store, traditional, and super store. Different store formats enabled Atom to target various segments.

The limited-assortment box store was positioned to appeal to price-conscious consumers who were willing to forego service and atmosphere to stock up on deal items. Atom used these sites to increase velocities for national brands purchased on deal.

Atom tried to target an upscale market in the traditional store format. Stores were clean and modern. Service levels were comparable to those of competitors. Although approximately nine thousand items were stocked, efforts were constantly being made to reduce slow-moving, undifferentiated items without adversely affecting customer loyalty.

EXHIBIT 2
Atom Foodstores:
1986 Income
Statement ($ Million)

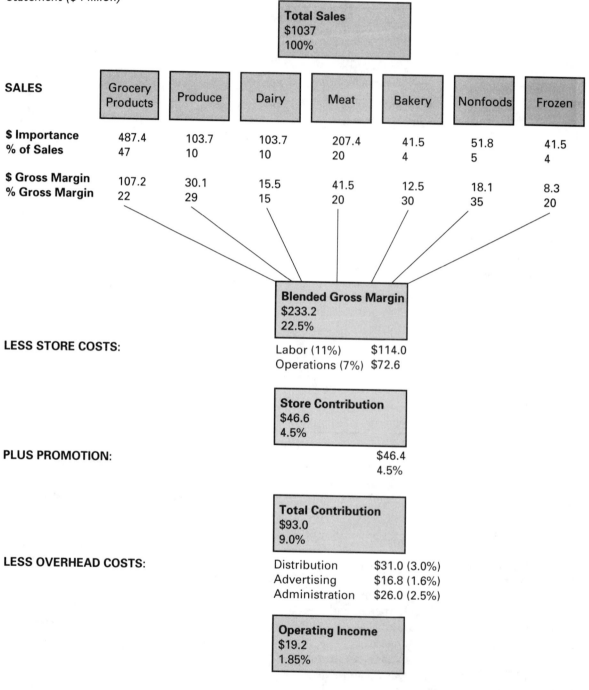

**Total Sales**
$1037
100%

**SALES**

| | Grocery Products | Produce | Dairy | Meat | Bakery | Nonfoods | Frozen |
|---|---|---|---|---|---|---|---|
| **$ Importance** | 487.4 | 103.7 | 103.7 | 207.4 | 41.5 | 51.8 | 41.5 |
| **% of Sales** | 47 | 10 | 10 | 20 | 4 | 5 | 4 |
| **$ Gross Margin** | 107.2 | 30.1 | 15.5 | 41.5 | 12.5 | 18.1 | 8.3 |
| **% Gross Margin** | 22 | 29 | 15 | 20 | 30 | 35 | 20 |

**Blended Gross Margin**
$233.2
22.5%

**LESS STORE COSTS:**    Labor (11%)    $114.0
Operations (7%)  $72.6

**Store Contribution**
$46.6
4.5%

**PLUS PROMOTION:**    $46.4
4.5%

**Total Contribution**
$93.0
9.0%

**LESS OVERHEAD COSTS:**    Distribution    $31.0 (3.0%)
Advertising    $16.8 (1.6%)
Administration    $26.0 (2.5%)

**Operating Income**
$19.2
1.85%

The super store was hard to pin down in terms of customer focus. It was in essence a very large, traditional store with a blend of upscale and deal items. Wednesday feature pages for both the traditional and the super stores were very slick and highlighted several good deals. Effective feature advertising emphasized what a good deal it was to shop at Atom. Ads featured a limited number of products with deep discounts.

One of the most significant events for Atom was the formation with two other regional chains of a large buying group called Awesome One. Beyond the sizeable volume discounts, the three chains were able to obtain excellent information regarding prices and deals that suppliers were offering across the country.

## THE BUYING GROUP

Atom was in strong competition with other grocery chains and Sam's group was under constant pressure to buy better. To keep up, deals were essential. Because the retail grocery trade earned 1–2-percent profit before tax, the effect of improving gross margin by 1 percent could increase the bottom line by 50 percent. Constant effort was made to increase margins, turns, and ROII (Return on Inventory Invested; formula is contained in Exhibit 3). Particular attention was paid to improving trade terms and increasing merchandising dollars from suppliers.

Until recently, category-manager performance was evaluated on the basis of increases in sales, margins, turns, and co-op money, all of which had separate performance targets. More recently, category-manager performance was measured against particular category-performance plans. The category plan combined gross-profit dollar performance with merchandising funding. The primary objective of the new plan was to meet "net gross-profit dollars after allowances" targeted for each of the categories under the buyer's control. At Atom, the term "net gross-profit dollars after allowances" meant gross-profit dollar contribution from each product category, including annual trade allowances and discounts. This term also included special periodic and over-and-above merchandising dollars.

## THE YOODLE PRODUCT CATEGORY

The Yoodle category was part of the larger Grocery Products category at Atom. Of the eight lines on the market in the Yoodle category, Atom carried three national brands and its own private label. All Yoodle brands were almost identical in physical package size and servings. Sam had looked at Nielsen brandshare data and was confident that he had the right selection of existing

EXHIBIT 3

### Grocery Products: Subcategory velocity report: Yoodle
### (Period 8: 4 weeks ending August 31, 1987)

| SLOT | CODE | BRAND/ ITEMS PER CS | CASE COST | UNIT RETAIL | NET MARGIN% | TURNS | ROII $* | DATE RCVD | YTD SALES | PDB SALES | OH INV | WKS INV |
|------|------|---------------------|-----------|-------------|-------------|-------|---------|-----------|-----------|-----------|--------|---------|
| K370 | 422513 | A BRAND/12 | 17.18 | 1.79 | 20.0% | 15.5 | 388 | 6/13 | 24667 | 3083 | 2350 | 3.3 |
| J555 | 422513 | C BRAND/12 | 14.88 | 1.59 | 22.0% | 12 | 338 | 5/29 | 14664 | 1883 | 550 | 1.3** |
| K532 | 422515 | B BRAND/12 | 15.35 | 1.65 | 22.5% | 13 | 377 | 7/06 | 19328 | 2416 | 1285 | 2.3 |
| J472 | 422516H | HB BRAND/12 | 11.61 | 1.29 | 25.0% | 18 | 600 | 6/27 | 8664 | 1083 | 1000 | 4.0 |
| SUBCATEGORY TOTALS | | | | | 21.8% | 14.3 | 399 | | 67323 | 8415 | | |

*ROII (Return On Inventory Invested)

$$ROII = \frac{Net\ Margin}{1 - Net\ Margin} \times Inventory\ Turns$$

**422515 Brand C had fallen below reorder point, on wait list for delayed shipment.

EXHIBIT 4

| Yoodle Category Analysis (Based on 1986 Category Data) | | | | | |
|---|---|---|---|---|---|
| | **BRANDS** | | | | Z (proposed) |
| **SEPTEMBER 4, 1987** | A | B | C | HB | (e = estimates) |
| SUPPLIER | ALPHA FOODCORP | BETA FOOD MFG | COLONIAL BRANDS | PRIVATE LABEL | ZETA INDUSTRIES |
| Total Market Units Per Month = 100,000 | | | | | |
| Total Market Units Per Year = 1,200,000 | | | | | |
| Market Share of Units | 37 | 29 | 22 | 12 | 10 e |
| Retail Price Per Unit | 1.79 | 1.65 | 1.59 | 1.29 | 1.65 |
| Units Per Case | 12 | 12 | 12 | 12 | 12 |
| Case Price | 21.48 | 19.80 | 19.08 | 15.48 | 19.80 |
| Case Cost | 17.18 | 15.35 | 14.88 | 11.61 | 15.44 |
| Trade terms: | | | | | |
| Cash (all 2/10 net 30) (%) | 2 | 2 | 2 | 2 | 2 |
| Freight (all prepaid) | PPD | PPD | PPD | PPD | PPD |
| Regular Co-op Advertising (%) | 2 | 5 | 5 | — | 5 |
| Volume Incentive Plan (VIP) (%) | 1 | 2 | 3 | 3 | 3 |
| Margin (Percent, *Including* above Terms) | 20 | 22.5 | 22 | 25 | 22 |
| Annual Unit Volume (000s) | 444 | 348 | 264 | 144 | 120 e |
| Annual Dollar Sales ($000s) | 795 | 574 | 420 | 186 | 198 e |
| Gross Profit $Pre-Allowance ($000s) | 159 | 129 | 92 | 46 | 44 e |
| Deal Frequency/Year | 3 | 4 | 5 | 2 | 4 |
| Average Deal Dollars/Case | 2 | 3 | 3 | 1 | 3 e |
| Over & Above Co-op Average $/Case | 0 | 1 | 1 | 1 | 3 e |
| Total Deal and Over-and-Above Ave./Case | 2 | 4 | 4 | 2 | 6 |
| Pct of Annual Vol Purchased in Deal (%) | 60 | 80 | 90 | 60 | 80 e |
| Average Deal Dollars/All Cases | 1.20 | 3.20 | 3.60 | 1.20 | 4.80e |
| Total Deal Dollars (000s) | 44 | 93 | 79 | 14 | 48 e |
| Gross Profit After Allowances (000s) | 203 | 222 | 171 | 60 | 96 e |
| Average Case Inventory (000s) | 2.3 | 2.2 | 1.8 | .7 | .7e |
| Turns | 15.5 | 13 | 12 | 18 | 14-15e |
| ROII (Percent) | 388 | 377 | 338 | 600 | — |
| Consumer Advertising | Strong | Strong | Weak | None | Promised |
| Consumer Promotions | Yes | Yes | None | None | Promised |
| Traffic Builder | Yes | Mild | No | No | ? |
| Units on Shelf (Typical Traditional) | 36 | 24 | 24 | 24 | — |
| Shelf Space (sq/ft) (Trad. Planogram) | 4 | 2.66 | 2.66 | 2.66 | — |
| Linear Facings (feet) (Trad. Planogram) | 3 | 2 | 2 | 2 | — |

national brands. Exhibit 4 provides profiles of the four brands and the proposed new product. Sam's 1987 budgeted category target for Yoodles was a gross profit after allowances of $720,000. This target was 10 percent higher than the previous year's performance. The target did not specify sales or gross-profit dollar amounts.

Prior information on the category indicated stable performance with no significant external factors, as shown in Exhibit 5. Sales to the end of August, however, indicated no volume growth over the same eight-month period in 1986, so unless Sam made some changes, he expected GPDAA for Yoodles in 1987 to be the same as in 1986. The weighted net-margin average for the category was 21.8 percent, slightly below the overall margin of 22 percent for grocery products. Inventory turn for the Yoodle category was 14.3 times, slightly below the grocery-product

average of 15 times.

Grocery-product category growth and margins closely mirrored overall category growth of 5 percent and blended margins of 22.5 percent for the entire chain. This low growth figure could at times be misleading. A few stars existed within the grocery products category. For example, breakfast foods were growing at 16 percent and had gross margins averaging 21 percent. Snack foods were growing at 14.7 percent and provided average margins of 29 percent. Diet and low-calorie foods were growing at 28 percent and offered average margins of 27 percent.

Growth and margins in the grocery-product category were not as attractive as they were in other categories such as Produce, Bakery, and Nonfood. Produce experienced 7-percent growth with a 19-percent margin. Bakery goods were growing at only 5 percent but had a 30-

*Exhibit 5*

| | | Yoodle Subcategory Gross Profit Dollars for 1986 | | | | |
|---|---|---|---|---|---|---|
| BRAND | UNITS PER MO. | UNITS PER YR. | RETAIL PRICE | RETAIL SALES | NET MARGIN* | GROSS PROFIT DOLLARS |
| A | 37000 | 444000 | $1.79 | $794,760 | 20.0% | $158,952 |
| B | 29000 | 348000 | $1.65 | $574,200 | 22.5% | $129,195 |
| C | 22000 | 264000 | $1.59 | $419,760 | 22.0% | $ 92,347 |
| HB | 13000 | 156000 | $1.29 | $201,240 | 25.0% | $ 50,310 |
| TOTALS: | | | | $1,989,960 | 21.8% | $430,804 |

| | | | |
|---|---|---|---|
| Sales: | Subcategory sales . . . | | $1,989,960 |
| | Percent of total sales . . . | | 0.19% |
| | Percent of grocery product sales . . . | | 0.41% |
| Gross profit: | Gross profit dollars . . . | | $ 430,804 |
| | Percent of total gross profit . . . | | 0.185% |
| | Percent of grocery-product category gross profit . . . | | 0.40% |

*Net margins include terms of payment discounts, volume rebates, freight terms, and VIP and regular co-op advertising. Not included are special deal and over-and-above co-op monies.

percent margin. Nonfood was growing at 7 percent and had an astounding 35-percent average gross margin.

In spite of sporadic competition between brands, the Yoodle category had not yet become a commodity. There was still room for differentiation of the products. Competing chains had promoted the category from time to time, resulting in some peaks and valleys in sales and inventories, but brand shares remained fairly constant.

Brand A's 37-percent market share and 15.5 turns, combined with the lowest net margin, bothered Sam. He wanted to get a better deal, but A's management refused to increase total ongoing trade terms beyond 5 percent. The product was highly differentiated and managed by a very professional company. He thought that A's executives were quite cocky about their number-one seller.

Brand B's net margin of 22.5 percent was the highest received from a national brand in the Yoodle category. Brand B's product management was aggressive in its attempts to gain share. Brand B's ongoing trade terms totaled 9 percent, four points higher than Brand A's. B's management offered the brand on deal four times a year. Sam believed that supporting B made good sense

and might put some pressure on A's management to improve terms and allowances. Brand B was reasonably differentiated from Brand A and other brands and had an excellent consumer-ad program.

Brand C's performance concerned Sam. C's ROII (at 338 percent) was the lowest of the four brands listed. Brand C was not differentiated and was of similar quality to the House Brand. Two months earlier, Sam had called in C's executives and warned them of potential delisting. In response, they gave Atom an off-invoice allowance that effectively raised the net margin to 22 percent.

Sam suspected that Brand C was the victim of poor management because of the high number of stockouts and erratic product strategy. What made matters interesting was a $25,000 over-and-above co-op advertising proposal just received from C's product manager. The proposal would certainly put Sam's gross dollars for Brand C back on target.

The House Brand (HB) had a 25-percent margin and was turning eighteen times, resulting in a staggering 600-percent ROII! Sam was wondering if he should try to increase unit volume by getting together with merchandising to run a big store promotion on the House Brand.

*EXHIBIT 6*

| New Product Test Market Results | |
|---|---|
| **BRAND Z** | |
| SUPPLIER: | Zeta Food Industries |
| MARKET SHARE RESULTS: | Performed very well in test market with 6-percent market share projected in nine months |
| | Projected 12 percent in one year and 18 percent by year two |
| PROJECTED TURNS: | Anticipated turns of between fourteen and fifteen times by end of year two |
| PRODUCT QUALITY: | Excellent |
| | Consumers able to differentiate |
| CONSUMER BENEFIT: | Unique product |
| | Strong appeal to a large segment of potential customers |
| TEST PRICE: | Same as proposed |
| | $1.65 against national brand B |

## THE NEW PRODUCT PROPOSAL

Sam had just received a new product proposal from Zeta Food Industries. Zeta was a highly reputable manufacturer, offering Brand Z, a product in a category new to them. The company had a very professional approach and a strong track record of supporting their products. Exhibit 6 shows the test results from a fellow chain member in the Awesome One buying group. Consumer research testing indicated the product was strongly differentiated from other brands. Brand Z offered a benefit that could cause consumers to view this as a unique product. At least Sam believed that this was no "me too" brand, and believed that competing chains would give the new product serious consideration.

Brand Z was to be priced at $1.65, positioned directly opposite Brand B. The proposed net margin would be 22 percent, after taking into account payment terms of 2 percent/10 net 30 days, a 3-percent volume rebate and 5 percent for co-op advertising. Zeta was planning an intensive launch with TV-ad support and a coupon drop. Sam believed that a minimum of $75,000 should be required for the introductory promotion allowance. The introductory listing fee would have to cover various services such as listing on the store's computer, making the appropriate space on shelf, in-store promotional material and displays, and feature-ad promotion. Zeta management had countered with a proposed listing fee of $50,000 which Sam felt was comparatively low when he considered his budgeted gross profit and merchandising dollars for the category.

## ALTERNATIVES AND PROBLEM REVIEW

Sam had several options and variables to consider. He could accept or reject Brand Z. He had to decide which brand to support and what the impact would be on his private label. It was also time to give serious consideration to assessing the viability of Brand C. Should he maintain C's listing and accept the new over-and-above proposal? Deciding who to accept, who to reject, and who to support would upset the present balance and hopefully create some pressures on all the players in the category to improve their co-operative merchandising efforts. Sam's schedule was very tight until the category review meeting in two day's time. He figured that he could devote possibly two hours, at best, to the problem.

## C A S E  3.3    Sarah Leavens

Sarah Leavens had just been appointed the assistant buyer for lingerie at Holt's, a mid-sized department store chain headquartered in Montreal. After some weeks of training she was given her first merchandise planning assignment. Sarah was asked by her buyer, Janet Morgan, to prepare a dollar merchandise budget for Exhibit major classifications of lingerie for the spring-summer season. She was to do a budget for each of these, Good and Best, and then total the two. She was most anxious to do a good job on this assignment so she gathered a good deal of historical data about these lines (Exhibits 1–3), obtained Holt's budgeting worksheets (Exhibits 4–6) and spent time talking with other assistant buyers who had been through this assignment before.

Sarah reviewed the steps and information she had gathered:

1. Prepare a sales forecast. Janet had suggested she work with a total net sales increase of 3.5 percent over the comparable season in 1987. She also said that she expected net sales of Good to fall to 45 percent of the department's total net sales. Sarah was to work with that

assumption in her calculations. Janet wouldn't give Sarah any guidance on how to forecast net sales at the monthly level saying "I'd rather see what you come up with, Sarah."

2. Forecast retail reductions first at the seasonal level and then by month for each of the classifications. Janet suggested that retail reductions could be estimated as the average of the past three years expressed as a percentage of net sales for both Good and Best. Gross sales = net sales + retail reductions.

3. Calculate beginning of month (BOM) inventory valued at retail. This department values inventory using the basic stock method. Basic stock = average inventory at retail − average net monthly sales. Average inventory at retail for the season = planned season net sales divided by planned season inventory turnover rate. BOM (retail) = planned net sales for the month + basic stock (at retail). Janet suggested Sarah aim for a seasonal stock turn of 3.0 for Good and 2.5 for Best.

4. Calculate end of month (EOM) inventory at retail. EOM is BOM for the next month. For the last month of a season Sarah planned to follow the conventional practice of using average monthly inventory for the season.

5. Prepare a projected income statement for each of Good and Best and then their totals. In 1987, Good had the following ratios: initial markup 61.1 percent, cost of goods sold 56.3 percent, maintained markup before discounts earned 43.7 percent, operating expenses 43.2 percent, and classification profit 6.5 percent. In 1987, Best had the following ratios: initial markup 59.3 percent, cost of goods sold 55.5 percent, maintained markup before discounts earned 44.5 percent, discounts earned 6.0 percent, gross margin 50.5 percent, operating expenses 43.2 percent, and classification profit 7.3 percent. Initial markup percent = (expenses % + profit % + reductions % − discount %) divided by (net sales % + reductions %). Janet's best estimate of total operating expense increases for Good and Best was 5

*EXHIBIT 1*

| | Net Sales History | | | | | | | | |
|---|---|---|---|---|---|---|---|---|---|
| | 1985 | | | 1986 | | | 1987 | | |
| | GOOD | BEST | TOTAL | GOOD | BEST | TOTAL | GOOD | BEST | TOTAL |
| February | $ 35,000 | $ 15,000 | $ 50,000 | $ 30,360 | $ 20,240 | $ 50,600 | $ 25,400 | $ 25,400 | $ 50,800 |
| March | $ 39,128 | $ 19,272 | $ 58,400 | $ 32,780 | $ 26,820 | $ 59,600 | $ 30,600 | $ 28,200 | $ 58,800 |
| April | $ 57,524 | $ 21,276 | $ 78,800 | $ 55,380 | $ 29,820 | $ 85,200 | $ 44,350 | $ 42,050 | $ 86,400 |
| May | $ 68,040 | $ 29,160 | $ 97,200 | $ 59,040 | $ 39,360 | $ 98,400 | $ 49,600 | $ 51,200 | $100,800 |
| June | $ 51,992 | $ 25,608 | $ 77,600 | $ 49,890 | $ 30,510 | $ 80,400 | $ 42,050 | $ 43,150 | $ 85,200 |
| July | $ 42,036 | $ 15,564 | $ 57,600 | $ 32,230 | $ 26,370 | $ 58,600 | $ 30,800 | $ 32,800 | $ 63,600 |
| Total | $293,720 | $125,880 | $419,600 | $259,680 | $173,120 | $432,800 | $222,800 | $222,800 | $445,600 |
| February | 11.9% | 11.9% | 11.9% | 11.7% | 11.7% | 11.7% | 11.4% | 11.4% | 11.4% |
| March | 13.3% | 15.3% | 13.9% | 12.6% | 15.5% | 13.8% | 13.7% | 12.7% | 13.2% |
| April | 19.6% | 16.9% | 18.8% | 21.3% | 17.2% | 19.7% | 19.9% | 18.9% | 19.4% |
| May | 23.2$ | 23.2% | 23.2% | 22.7% | 22.7% | 22.7% | 22.3% | 23.0% | 22.6% |
| June | 17.7% | 20.3% | 18.5% | 19.2% | 17.6% | 18.6% | 18.9% | 19.4% | 19.1% |
| July | 14.3% | 12.4% | 13.7% | 12.4% | 15.2% | 13.5% | 13.8% | 14.7% | 14.3% |

EXHIBIT 2

| | | 1985 | | | 1986 | | | 1987 | |
|---|---|---|---|---|---|---|---|---|---|
| **Net Retail Reductions History** | | | | | | | | | |
| | GOOD | BEST | TOTAL | GOOD | BEST | TOTAL | GOOD | BEST | TOTAL |
| February | $ 13,664 | $ 5,856 | $ 19,520 | $ 12,568 | $ 6,767 | $ 19,335 | $11,321 | $ 9,263 | $ 20,584 |
| March | $ 20,044 | $ 8,590 | $ 28,634 | $ 19,370 | $10,430 | $ 29,800 | $16,008 | $13,098 | $ 29,106 |
| April | $ 18,059 | $ 7,739 | $ 25,798 | $ 20,654 | $11,121 | $ 31,775 | $17,914 | $14,656 | $ 32,570 |
| May | $ 18,711 | $ 8,019 | $ 26,730 | $ 22,102 | $11,901 | $ 34,003 | $19,488 | $15,945 | $ 35,433 |
| June | $ 24,957 | $10,696 | $ 35,653 | $ 22,246 | $11,979 | $ 34,225 | $18,291 | $14,966 | $ 33,257 |
| July | $ 21,329 | $ 9,141 | $ 30,470 | $ 17,467 | $ 9,406 | $ 26,873 | $16,400 | $13,417 | $ 29,817 |
| Season | $116,764 | $50,041 | $166,805 | $114,407 | $61,604 | $176,011 | $99,422 | $81,345 | $180,767 |
| PERCENT REDUCTIONS | | | | | | | | | |
| February | 39.0% | 39.0% | 39.0% | 41.4% | 33.4% | 38.2% | 44.6% | 36.5% | 40.5% |
| March | 51.2% | 44.6% | 49.0% | 59.1% | 38.9% | 50.0% | 52.3% | 46.4% | 49.5% |
| April | 31.4% | 36.4% | 32.7% | 37.3% | 37.3% | 37.3% | 40.4% | 34.9% | 37.7% |
| May | 27.5% | 27.5% | 27.5% | 37.4% | 30.2% | 34.6% | 39.3% | 31.1% | 35.2% |
| June | 48.0% | 41.8% | 45.9% | 44.6% | 39.3% | 42.6% | 43.5% | 34.7% | 39.0% |
| July | 50.7% | 58.7% | 52.9% | 54.2% | 35.7% | 45.9% | 53.2% | 40.9% | 46.9% |
| Season | 39.8% | 39.8% | 39.8% | 44.1% | 35.6% | 40.7% | 44.6% | 36.5% | 40.6% |

EXHIBIT 3

| | | 1985 | | | 1986 | | | 1987 | |
|---|---|---|---|---|---|---|---|---|---|
| **End of Month Inventories History** | | | | | | | | | |
| | GOOD | BEST | TOTAL | GOOD | BEST | TOTAL | GOOD | BEST | TOTAL |
| January | $ 81,000 | $43,500 | $124,500 | $ 71,280 | $ 59,595 | $130,875 | $61,300 | $ 71,514 | $132,814 |
| February | $ 75,000 | $40,500 | $115,500 | $ 65,250 | $ 52,650 | $117,900 | $54,810 | $ 68,445 | $123,255 |
| March | $ 94,500 | $53,100 | $147,600 | $ 84,105 | $ 72,747 | $156,852 | $73,170 | $ 80,020 | $153,190 |
| April | $105,000 | $70,500 | $175,500 | $ 93,450 | $ 88,125 | $181,575 | $80,367 | $105,750 | $186,117 |
| May | $115,500 | $82,500 | $198,000 | $100,485 | $103,125 | $203,610 | $88,425 | $123,750 | $212,175 |
| June | $123,000 | $85,500 | $208,500 | $108,240 | $111,150 | $219,390 | $90,922 | $122,265 | $213,187 |
| July | $ 99,000 | $67,500 | $166,500 | $ 89,100 | $ 92,475 | $181,575 | $76,626 | $124,841 | $201,467 |
| AVERAGE INVENTORY | | | | | | | | | |
| February | $ 78,000 | $42,000 | $120,000 | $ 68,265 | $ 56,123 | $124,388 | $58,055 | $ 69,980 | $128,035 |
| March | $ 84,750 | $46,800 | $131,550 | $ 74,678 | $ 62,699 | $137,376 | $63,990 | $ 74,233 | $138,223 |
| April | $ 99,750 | $61,800 | $161,550 | $ 88,778 | $ 80,436 | $169,214 | $76,769 | $ 92,885 | $169,654 |
| May | $110,250 | $76,500 | $186,750 | $ 96,968 | $ 95,625 | $192,593 | $84,396 | $114,750 | $199,146 |
| June | $119,250 | $84,000 | $203,250 | $104,363 | $107,138 | $211,500 | $89,674 | $123,008 | $212,681 |
| July | $111,000 | $76,500 | $187,500 | $ 98,670 | $101,813 | $200,483 | $83,774 | $123,553 | $207,327 |
| Season | $ 99,000 | $63,300 | $162,300 | $ 87,416 | $ 82,838 | $170,254 | $75,089 | $ 99,512 | $174,601 |

percent in total over 1987's total. Each year operating expenses were allocated to Good and Best according to the ratio of each classification's net sales to the total of the department's net sales. Discounts earned were expected to stay at 6 percent of net sales for both Good and Best. Janet asked Sarah to aim for an improvement in classification net profit for Good to 6.9 percent of net sales and for Best to 7.8 percent of net sales.

6. Calculate monthly purchases at retail and at cost. Planned purchases at retail = planned monthly sales + EOM inventory at retail + monthly planned reductions − BOM inventory at retail. Planned purchases at cost = planned purchases at retail × (100 − initial markup percentage).

Sarah had recently been learning spreadsheet analysis on her computer and wondered if it was worthwhile for her to try out that software for her calculations or whether she should use her hand calculator.

EXHIBIT 4
Good Budget

| | Dollar Net Sales | Retail Reductions | B.O.M. Retail | E.O.M. Retail | Purchases At Retail | Purchases At Cost |
|---|---|---|---|---|---|---|
| February | | | | | | |
| March | | | | | | |
| April | | | | | | |
| May | | | | | | |
| June | | | | | | |
| July | | | | | | |

Total Season:

| | | |
|---|---|---|
| Gross Sales | $ _____ | xxx |
| Reductions | $ _____ | % |
| Net Sales | $ _____ | 100% |
| Initial Markup | $ _____ | % |
| Cost of Goods Sold | $ _____ | % |
| Maintained Markup | $ _____ | % |
| Discounts Earned | $ _____ | % |
| Gross Margin | $ _____ | % |
| Operating Expenses | $ _____ | % |
| Profit | $ _____ | % |

EXHIBIT 5
Best Budget

| | Dollar Net Sales | Retail Reductions | B.O.M. Retail | E.O.M. Retail | Purchases At Retail | Purchases At Cost |
|---|---|---|---|---|---|---|
| February | | | | | | |
| March | | | | | | |
| April | | | | | | |
| May | | | | | | |
| June | | | | | | |
| July | | | | | | |

**Total Season:**

| | | |
|---|---|---|
| Gross Sales | $ _____ | xxx |
| Reductions | $ _____ | % |
| Net Sales | $ _____ | 100% |
| Initial Markup | $ _____ | % |
| Cost of Goods Sold | $ _____ | % |
| Maintained Markup | $ _____ | % |
| Discounts Earned | $ _____ | % |
| Gross Margin | $ _____ | % |
| Operating Expenses | $ _____ | % |
| Profit | $ _____ | % |

---

*EXHIBIT 6*
*Good and Best*
*Total Budget*

| | Dollar Net Sales | Retail Reductions | B.O.M. Retail | E.O.M. Retail | Purchases At Retail | Purchases At Cost |
|---|---|---|---|---|---|---|
| February | | | | | | |
| March | | | | | | |
| April | | | | | | |
| May | | | | | | |
| June | | | | | | |
| July | | | | | | |

**Total Season:**

| | | |
|---|---|---|
| Gross Sales | $ _____ | xxx |
| Reductions | $ _____ | % |
| Net Sales | $ _____ | 100% |
| Initial Markup | $ _____ | % |
| Cost of Goods Sold | $ _____ | % |
| Maintained Markup | $ _____ | % |
| Discounts Earned | $ _____ | % |
| Gross Margin | $ _____ | % |
| Operating Expenses | $ _____ | % |
| Profit | $ _____ | % |

# C A S E 3.4   The Arrow Company and the Bay: Bin Stock Proposal

In November 1980, representatives of The Arrow Company and the Bay were preparing to meet about a proposed change in their relationship. Mr. David Whitehead, Principal Buyer for Men's Furnishings at the Bay, had proposed a men's dress shirt buying programme called bin stock, which would mean changes for both his company and for the vendor, The Arrow Company. Mr. Whitehead was examining the merits of this programme for the Bay, while Mr. Lionel Griffith, Vice-President, Sales at The Arrow Company, was doing the same for his organization. Both gentlemen had discussed the idea recently, sounding one another out; both knew a decision had to be made this month for the 1981 fall selling season.

## THE PRINCIPALS

The Arrow Company was a division of Cluett, Peabody and Company of Canada, a large clothing manufacturer. The Arrow Company manufactured and sold under its own name a wide range of shirts as well as pajamas, boxer shorts, and handkerchiefs. Its shirts were classified into several categories: dress (including formal wear), sports, and knits. Within dress shirts, Arrow offered a wide variety by colour and style, by fabric, and by cut. As of fall 1980, Arrow offered 332 different cutting ways (style, colour, fabric, cut combinations) in its dress shirt line. A large department store such as the Bay typically carried roughly one-fifth of this dress shirt line at any one time. Mr. Griffith described his company as the best-known shirt producer in Canada among consumers and as a well-regarded resource among Canadian retailers. "We're a very service-oriented company," he said, "and this is the key to our success. We're not simply bookers and shippers." Arrow's manufacturing was in Kitchener, Ontario, while its marketing offices were in Toronto, Ontario.

One of Arrow's major customers was the Bay, a full-line department store with 50 stores across Canada. With headquarters in Winnipeg, Manitoba, the Bay was a division of The Hudson's Bay Company, a very large, diversified company with major holdings in the Canadian natural resources sector. "I've heard different views on our position in the marketplace," said Mr. Whitehead, "but internally we view our major competitors to be Eaton's, Simpsons and Woodwards, followed by Sears and others." The Bay, similar to many large department store operations, was organized with a central office, the General Merchandising Office (GMO) in Montreal, Quebec, and a field operations group, consisting of seven regions with focal points in Vancouver, Calgary, Edmonton, Winnipeg, Toronto, Ottawa, and Montreal. The key people in the Bay organization concerned with men's dress shirts were (1) at GMO, Gloria Ben-David, Group Merchandising Manager—Men's Wear; David Whitehead, Principal Buyer—Men's Furnishings; and Ron Gross, Buyer—Men's Shirts and Neckwear; and (2) in the field, the seven Regional Department Managers, who had responsibility for shirts and other merchandise.

## DRESS SHIRTS AT THE BAY

"We have three merchandise categories for dress shirts," said Mr. Whitehead, "330: regular cut, long sleeve; 331: regular cut, short sleeve; and 332: tapered shirts. These categories accounted for about 70 percent of our total men's shirt and neckwear volume in 1980. We've changed over the past few years in our buying from being almost completely decentralized to a mixed system where GMO and the regionals each have major inputs into commitments."

As of 1980, GMO was responsible for all assortment planning; but all budgeting, and hence ability to commit funds, rested with the regional department managers. GMO staff prepared assortment strategies, based on their understanding of style and fashion directions, for each region and then each store. A commodity marketing plan was developed for each category detailing a recommended blend of products and resources, sales and margin histories and projections, turnover and average inventory statistics, and a buying plan detailing the required commitment of funds, nature of agreements with resources, advertising and promotion plans, and product knowledge training for the sales staff. In addition, GMO staff suggested for each store an opening model stock, replenishment schedules, methods of replenishment, and a variety of suggestions on how to present the category for merchandising impact. The GMO staff had established an assortment classification scheme called National Stock Assortment List (NASL), which enabled them to set priorities for each store in its assortment. Priorities ranged from "core" (all stores must carry the item), to "core large store" (the big downtown stores must carry), to "complementary" (an optional category of distinctly fashion-oriented items, usually offered only in the very high-volume stores). "We've all got the message," said Mr. Whitehead, "that senior management wants us to put top priority on reduced inventory investment and improved return on that investment. This means we need an improved flow of business, which will require that we work even harder on our relationships with our resources. We've had traditionally somewhere over 1000 SKU's in dress shirts alone; we're trying to bring that down dramatically."

The assortment parameters and plans formulated by GMO staff were discussed at length with the regional department managers. "This approach has had its problems," said Mr. Whitehead. "As one might expect, it has been difficult to get consistency in our assortment and merchandising, to get economies in our buying, and so on. Even our inventories are completely decentralized. Each region keeps its own item records. But I think we're getting much better now. The commodity marketing planning system really helps."

Dress shirts were purchased from five major sources: Arrow, Forsyth (best known lately for the Pierre Cardin line), Yves St. Laurent, Hathaway, and the Far East on a direct import programme. The Bay carried both manufacturer brands (such as Arrow) and its own Baycrest line. As of 1980, Arrow and Forsyth were very close together as the leading suppliers in terms of dollar volume sales at the Bay. Dress shirts was the third largest volume department in Men's Wear, and Mr. Whitehead had hopes of making it the leader in the near future. The dress shirt category had been growing recently at an annual average of 18–20 percent.

Actual procurement was typically done in one of two ways for dress shirts. The traditional method was a seasonal commitment. GMO would send out an assortment strategy and suggested quantities. The regions would commit for a season, tying up dollars for the season. A typical flow of events would be as follows for a fall season: preliminary discussions with the vendor in November, a preview in December, commitments in March for delivery in the summer. "This worked reasonably well, I suppose," added Mr. Whitehead, "but in addition to the problems of getting everybody on side, the OK growth rate and profit rate is really getting crunched as interest rates climb. We've had limited repeats; our money has been in inventory for the whole season."

The second method of procurement was vendor-assisted automatic reorder programmes. This was added to the seasonal commitment approach. The regional representative of the vendor met with the Bay regional department manager to ratify a vendor assistance agreement, which in part meant that the vendor sales representative became responsible for physical counting of store inventories and for repeats based on rate of sale in the store. The intent of this arrangement was to provide a more constant flow of merchandise from the resource into the individual stores. This system required more tasks of the vendor's sales force and shifted some of the inventory risks to him. As of 1980, approximately 40 percent of all dress shirts were on this "automatic" reorder system basis at the Bay.

## BAY RELATIONSHIPS WITH DRESS SHIRT VENDORS IN GENERAL

"Like any other retailer, I guess, we've had our share of problems over the years with our resources," said Mr. Whitehead. "Whenever our relationships weren't open, trusting, and backed up with a flow of information, we've had misunderstandings about the terms of our agreements." The Vendor Assistance Agreement (VAA) was regarded by Mr. Whitehead to be absolutely critical to the relationship the Bay had with its resources. The VAA spelled out what the Bay required of all its major suppliers and was an integral part of all purchases with them. Excerpts from the basic VAA are shown as Exhibit 1. "We have additional attachments as part of the agreement spelling out any specifics," commented Mr. Whitehead. "We also add a copy of pertinent sections of our commodity marketing strategy. We share this strategy with the vendor because we now believe that it is critical the vendor knows where he stands with us, what he can expect of us, and how we intend to grow this business."

Mr. Whitehead went on to say that one of the key issues in the Bay's relationship with any large resource is that vendor's ability to provide timely, accurate in-store item counts. "If a vendor stopped doing this, we'd be very unhappy, but we could do it ourselves. In fact, I suppose as our electronic systems capability increases, that item counting service will no longer be necessary," said Mr. Whitehead. "Overall, we know each vendor has strengths and weaknesses on dimensions such as service, fashion, etc. In fact, our quarterly assessment of each vendor, based on our GMO files and regional reports, shows this clearly. We also have different needs in each merchandise category. So we try to match vendor strengths with our particular needs in each category in our vendor selection."

EXHIBIT 1
*Excerpts from the*
*Bay's Vendor*
*Assistance*
*Agreement*

### Vendor Responsibilities

1.  Representatives will call on stores as per schedule determined by the Regional Merchandise Information Manager, Department Manager and representative. The representative will report to each store's Item Records Office upon arrival and sign the vendor register (a record of representatives' visits showing date of visit, vendor, and representative's signature).

2.  All regular merchandise in vendor's line will be regularly and accurately counted. Counting will be done once a month or more often if indicated in the agreement.

3.  Merchandise return privileges will be exercised 2 times a year or as noted in the agreement.

4.  Unless otherwise arranged by the General Merchandise Office (GMO), counts will be made in Hudson's Bay Company Item Records Books.

5.  All new products, colour changes, price changes, etc., must be presented to GMO for authorization. GMO, through a National Stock Assortment List revision, will advise the Regions of changes.

6.  The Item Records Office is charged with determining reorder quantities by using the Company's standard reorder formula. Representative suggested order quantities are subject to Item Records Office review. Normally, representatives should work with IRO clericals in preparing suggested orders.

## Hudson's Bay Company Responsibilities:

1. Department Manager or designate must acknowledge and cooperate with Vendor's representatives when they call.

2. Arrangements other than those specified in the National Agreement will not be made in the Regions unless GMO, the Office of the Vice-President, Department Stores, and the representative's head office are notified.

3. Problem stocks, overstocks, etc., must be reviewed when representatives call.

4. Under normal circumstances, representative will receive his order (if merchandise is required) the day the count is made.

5. No returns will be made to supplier without authorization.

6. HBC staff will count:

   (a) between supplier visits if rate of sale warrants action.
   (b) if representative does not appear for a scheduled count.

7. Stock levels must be reviewed by the Department Manager or Sales Manager in conjunction with Vendor's representative every third month.

8. Any complaints or problems arising from VAA will be made in writing by the Regional Merchandise Information Manager to GMO to be taken up with supplier.

---

## ARROW RELATIONSHIPS WITH RETAILERS IN GENERAL

"There are many dimensions to our relationships with retailers," said Mr. Griffith, "but the key one that's really important is that all our programmes are available to everyone. We know independents are different than major department stores—they have different problems but different capabilities too. We have lots of programmes, but we're always careful to remember that two-thirds of Arrow's business is with independents."

Arrow management regarded itself as a "one-price house," meaning that their terms were one wholesale price for everybody, net 30, no cash discounts and no advance order discounts. Arrow's competitors varied in the terms they offered, for example, some offered 9–10 percent discount for early orders. As was industry practice, Arrow offered quantity discounts. Orders were F.O.B. Kitchener with some exceptions when delivery problems occurred. Unlike its one-location competitors, Arrow maintained regional warehousing in Vancouver and Winnipeg to expedite repeat orders on basic items.

Arrow did not offer push money or display space money, and according to Mr. Griffith, it was against company policy to provide markdown money or to buy display fixtures for retailers.

Arrow's practice of putting a suggested retail price on its shirts was contentious. All its shirts were so marked except some higher-priced sportshirts and other specialty items. Some retailers liked this practice, especially the independents, while some retailers apparently did not. According to Mr. Whitehead, this practice was of no concern one way or another to the Bay. Arrow was undecided about the future of suggested price marking. "We've also had conversations about doing price ticketing for some retailers using their tickets, but we haven't done this yet," added Mr. Griffith.

"Our greatest competitive strength," Mr. Griffith commented, "is our experienced field sales force." Arrow salesmen were spread across the country (nine of them dealt with the Bay), constituting a very experienced group in Mr. Griffith's opinion. "Unlike the big retailers such as the Bay who are constantly moving their people around, we leave ours in place," he added. "The average experience base of our sales representatives is 20 years. They know the business. Their job involves continuous data gathering. We want field reports constantly on business conditions in all their stores, in all their territories." The sales job included item counting whenever a retailer would allow it. "Even if the Bay's VAA didn't require this, we'd want to do it," said Mr. Griffith. "It tells us what's happening with each item in our line on a store-by-store basis for all our customers in the nation."

Arrow offered many services to its customers, which will be detailed further with specific reference to the Bay-Arrow relationship. A source of great pride to Mr. Griffith was Arrow's strong consumer marketing programme. Arrow engaged in extensive consumer mass media advertising, promoting both the Arrow name and specific Arrow products such as the Mark II collar line. Mr. Griffith felt this was a definite advantage in obtaining retailer support. "There's no question in my mind he's right," commented Mr. Whitehead. "Our last Bay market survey showed that brand recall in shirts was 67 percent. We've interpreted that as meaning the customer cares about shirt brand names, especially national brands. While we care about growing our Baycrest line, we also believe we should be strong in the names the customers want. That's why Arrow has roughly 80 percent of our volume in 330, 70 percent in 331, and 40 percent in 332."

## THE BAY-ARROW RELATIONSHIP

"I'd say we have a good relationship with the Bay, from the top on down," ventured Mr. Griffith, "and I'm pleased they have a principal buyer in place now who cares about what's happening to them and to us." Mr. Whitehead added, "Arrow has grown with us at about or above the departmental average rate, because they've demonstrated flexibility in meeting our changing requirements." Asked to elaborate on the specifics of their relationship, Mr. Whitehead and Mr. Griffith identified ten important dimensions of it.

1. *New product development.* Arrow and the Bay typically worked closely together in the very early stages of new product development. The Bay formulated their dress shirt strategy in part on price-point segmentation. Ron Gross, the buyer, commented: "I spend a lot of time with Arrow discussing specifications on cloths, qualities, etc. We want appropriate products in our assortment, so we tell them exactly what we want based on our sales and even on our in-house testing programmes." For its part, Arrow sought early comments from its major customers like the Bay on innovations such as the Mark II collar in order to design better products and marketing programmes.

2. *Preview meetings.* For the past six to seven years, Arrow had made a practice of having preview meetings with all its major customers approximately three months before a line was released to Canadian retailers in general. Such meetings allowed discussion of a new line, thus encouraging early commitments by retailers in return for good selection and higher certainty of on-time delivery. Arrow normally did not offer previews to smaller customers unless requested to do so by them.

3. *Backup stock.* Arrow ordinarily provided some limited backup stock for its major customers. This meant that Arrow allowed a margin of error for such customers by keeping aside extra inventory on an order, earmarked for a specific customer. This stock was owned by Arrow, and the retailer was not obliged to take it.

4. *Stock adjustments.* All retailers have peaks and valleys in sales. Arrow allowed its customers to build inventories for a peak selling period such as Christmas, then to bring inventories back down to agreed-upon predetermined levels by returning goods to Arrow. Arrow limited this privilege to those categories of merchandise that usually had some seasonal carryover. This service, which Arrow also provided to all its customers, sometimes involved a cost to the retailer. If Arrow had to refurbish shirts to bring them back to salable quality, the company charged $12 a dozen to stock adjust.

5. *Product knowledge sessions.* Both the Bay and Arrow staff felt that the periodic (at least annual) sessions offered by Arrow salesmen and management to Bay employees, especially in-store selling staff, were most valuable. These sessions typically were done in the regions to keep the Bay staff up to date on fashion directions in general, qualitative dimensions of shirts, Arrow product features, and Arrow advertising and promotional developments. "If we get their selling staff nodding their heads about our merchandise before it even gets to the store, we're way ahead of the usual lack of commitment and understanding a supplier's merchandise receives by in-store personnel," explained Mr. Griffith.

6. *Advertising, promotion, and visual presentation.* According to Mr. Whitehead, all the major dress shirt resources offered essentially the same co-operative advertising and promotional programmes. Such programmes, from Mr. Whitehead's viewpoint, were expected of the vendor by the retailer, but their offer was not critical in the selection of vendors. "Besides," he added "we're continuously negotiating on this. Arrow appears to have overall parameters, and we move inside these depending on the opportunities we mutually see." In conjunction with Arrow's national consumer advertising programme, Arrow offered its retailers advertising mats to enable them to tie into that campaign. Further, Arrow had two separate co-operative programmes, catalogue and media advertising. Each was a percentage contribution to the retailer's advertising expenditures based on the dollar volume of regular ("first") quality shirts sold. In other words, these programmes did not apply to off-price sales. As Exhibit 2 indicates, the Arrow co-operative advertising programme applied only to advertising in newsprint and on radio and television. Arrow also generally offered point-of-sale promotions such as signs and racks (which remained Arrow's property), although its activities in dress shirts had not been as extensive as in sportshirts and knits. Recent promotional programmes had included giveaways of Polaroid cameras and free monogramming. In the latter instance, Arrow loaned monogramming machines to participating stores. The Bay had offered this service to customers at its downtown stores.

7. *Special promotions.* Special promotions referred to jointly preplanned, controlled offers of off-price merchandise. Arrow and the Bay arranged such deals on a "buy to sell-out basis" for promotional events such as Father's Day. "Probably the best way to think of this is we're jointly supporting some off-price business, which gives each of us a quicker turn but a lower margin," explained Mr. Whitehead.

---

*Exhibit 2
Excerpts from
Arrow's
Co-operative
Advertising
Programme*

### THE ARROW COMPANY
45 St. Clair Avenue West, Toronto, Ontario M4V IK9

CO-OPERATIVE ADVERTISING PROGRAMME
EFFECTIVE—January I through June 30, 1980

The Arrow Company offers to you and all retailers of Arrow shirts in your trading area, a co-operative advertising plan for Spring 1980.

**BASIS OF COMPENSATION:** The programme provides an allowance for advertising, based on a percentage of your total purchases of first quality shirts purchased from

The Arrow Company. This allowance is based on the preceding corresponding season (i.e., January 1, 1979 to June 30, 1979).

**NEWSPAPER ADVERTISING:**  Arrow will pay, up to the limits of your allowance, 50% of the actual and reasonable net rate paid to the newspaper (after any discounts or rebates). Supporting newspaper invoice(s) and tearsheets must be submitted.

Newspaper inserts, supplements, rotogravure inserts, or reprints distributed in the paper are paid on the same basis as any other newspaper advertising.

PRODUCTION COSTS ARE NOT COVERED

ONE EXTRA COLOUR will be additionally compensated (within the limits of your allowance) at 100% of the newspaper's actual colour surcharge; providing that at least 60% of the colour advertisement is devoted to products carrying the ARROW label.

**TO QUALIFY, ADS MUST**

1. DISPLAY THE ARROW LOGO in a headline or sub-headline.
2. MUST NOT include products competitive to those offered by The Arrow Company.
3. FEATURE ARROW merchandise exclusively. Should other merchandise appear in the same ad, there must be clear separation of Arrow advertising in both copy and illustration. Arrow's participation will be determined on a pro rata basis.
4. APPEAR IN ANY NEWSPAPER that publishes in an approved marketing area, between January 1, 1980, and June 30, 1980.

   Every consideration will be given to requests to use other suitable newspapers, e.g., weeklies. Submit a copy of a recent issue of the paper, a notarized statement of circulation, and local rate card, to The Arrow Company.

**CANADIAN RADIO AND TELEVISION:**  Up to the limits of your allowance, The Arrow Company will pay 50% of the actual reasonable cost of air time, for spot commercials featuring ARROW merchandising, which are aired in an approved marketing area. Sponsorship of programmes is not covered. Net local rates (after any discounts and rebates).

PRODUCTION COSTS ARE NOT COVERED

The Arrow name must be prominently mentioned in the audio. T.V. commercials must also include the Arrow logo.

**TO QUALIFY, COMMERCIAL MUST**

1. The radio or television commercial must be supplied by The Arrow Company.
2. Any other commercials must have approval of The Arrow Company's Advertising Department prior to airing.

**OTHER CO-OP ADVERTISING**

1. Any customer may participate, up to the limits of their allowance, in any or all of the advertising media or material described in this programme.

**2.** Favorable consideration will be given any other advertising media or point of sale promotions in which the values are comparable to Arrow's promotional values and to those specifically available under this programme.

NOTE: In these instances, PRIOR APPROVAL MUST BE OBTAINED from Arrow's Advertising Department.

**LIMITATION:** Arrow's share of the cost of all advertising and advertising materials on any season's merchandise lines shall not exceed the dollar value equal to the established percentage for co-operative advertising in your region. Only Net Shipments on first quality shirts are used in calculating co-operative allowances. "Net Shipments" means merchandise invoiced, less returns. Excludes: Close-outs, Clearances and Special Production.

**HOW TO COLLECT FOR ADVERTISING:** All claims are to be sent to:

The Arrow Company
45 St. Clair Avenue West,
Toronto, Ontario M4V IK9
Attn: Co-operative Advertising Department

**FOR NEWSPAPER ADS—SEND:**

**1.** Full tearsheet with the invoice claim.
**2.** An invoice based on the rate sheets or an invoice for 50% of the actual amount paid to the newspaper, net of discounts or rebates, with supporting newspaper invoice(s).

**FOR RADIO AND T.V.—SEND:**

**1.** Copy of Radio or T.V. script aired.
**2.** Copy of station's invoice for time with log of spots aired.
**3.** Station's affidavit of performance.

*CLAIMS SHOULD BE SUBMITTED WITHIN 60 DAYS FROM THE DATE ADVERTISING IS RUN.* Credit will be issued within 60 days of receipt of an approved claim. DO NOT DEDUCT FROM MERCHANDISE REMITTANCES.

No "deductions" or "credits" for the cost of advertising are permitted to be taken against any outstanding indebtedness to The Arrow Company. Any such deductions from merchandise invoices will be considered a violation of this programme and may result in withdrawal of this offer.

If your purchases from the preceding corresponding season are not approximately in line with your current purchases in relationship to other merchants in your marketing area, Arrow will adjust your allowance accordingly.

Your Arrow representative will be able to advise you of the allowance available to you.

Retail promotional programmes are also available.

8. *Contact with Arrow sales organization.* "We try to have points of contact at several levels with the Bay," said Mr. Griffith. "For example, our regional representatives call on the stores monthly or even weekly in the major centres while I'm in contact much less often with their PB and buyer in Montreal. That much would be usual in our business, but in addition we have a fulltime man called our Regional Sales Manager located in Montreal. His job is to be in virtual constant contact with our key accounts at the buyer and PB level. He's almost a Bay employee, he works so closely with them." "Their man in Montreal is important to us too," added Mr. Whitehead, "because he's at a sufficient level in Arrow's organization to make important decisions quickly. Other suppliers either don't have such an individual or, if they do, have him in a less convenient location for us; for example, Forsyth's man is in Toronto."

9. *Arrow local warehousing.* Arrow shipped shirts directly to the Bay's seven regional receiving centres, either from Kitchener or its warehouses in Vancouver or Winnipeg. "This is a definite plus that Arrow offers," commented Mr. Whitehead, "because none of the other sources have such warehouses." "We try to stock the automatic reorder merchandise in the warehouses," added Mr. Griffith. "Anything special, we source directly from Kitchener."

10. *Merchandise flow improvements.* "An extremely important aspect of our relationship," said Mr. Whitehead, "is our efforts to improve the information flow between us and in that way improve the flow of merchandise." Typically, the Arrow salesperson in conjunction with the Bay department managers set up a model stock programme for each store and established a replenishment procedure. When the salesperson visited the store, he would count the Arrow inventory, then record it for the Bay in its store item record books and also send it to Arrow management in Toronto. Some-

times the salesperson received a fill-in order based on rate of sale figures on the spot and sometimes the Bay staff followed up later. "Our salespeople telephone in their orders each night to our computer," explained Mr. Griffith, "in order to get our process moving as quickly as possible."

The data gathered by the regional salespeople was an integral part of the quarterly or bimonthly review discussions between the Bay and Arrow management. Arrow prepared by hand movement statistics for each commodity item on a national, regional, and store-by-store basis for the Bay management. Further, these reports were used to identify the blend of regular and off-price goods, any problems in receiving or delivery of orders, etc. "This system provides both of us with invaluable information," added Mr. Griffith, "and we probably know at a national level what's happening in the Bay's shirt departments faster than they do." "We also share general marketing information based on our market research here, our activities in the U.S., and our trips abroad to Europe and other sources," said Mr. Whitehead.

## THE BIN STOCK PROPOSAL

"We're looking at a variety of options to improve our ROI and to increase flexibility in our relationships with vendors," said Mr. Whitehead. "We're looking now at three options, but there are probably more. First, we might negotiate a slight variation in our seasonal commitment approach. We would predetermine with Arrow some promotional programmes on selected cuts, styles, and patterns. We would commit system-wide for an inventory from which the regionals would draw repeats. We've done something like this with other vendors in other merchandise categories. There would be a lot of details to work out. Second, we might focus on vendor deals. Arrow occasionally has off-price offers intended for deal-selling. Ideally, we'd get these in early, sell at regular prices during the peak season, then go with promotional dumps when sales slackened off. We do this, too, with some of our other vendors. Third, we could try again the bin stock programme. Essentially, we would sit down with Arrow earlier than usual in the sequence of events to select specific items. We would get an exclusive on a few items in terms of cloth, style, cut, etc. We'd commit the entire Bay system to these items and put them on an automatic reorder basis, based on rate-of-sale in our stores. The usual VAA terms would apply. We'd be assured of repeats being available, even though we'd have unique merchandise. There are lots of details to work out, but the big question is whether Arrow wants to do this again after our at best semisuccessful attempt at bin stock in 1976 with them. I suspect they're less than enthusiastic."

Mr. Whitehead was referring to earlier experiments with forms of a bin stock programme with Arrow and other shirt vendors. The first such trial was in 1976 when the Bay and Arrow agreed to try three items (eight cutting ways) in category 330. The idea came up just before the usual buying commitment point for the fall 1976 season. The major question posed to Arrow as Mr. Griffith recalled was not what items would be best, but rather what items could be obtained in sufficient quantity to support such a programme. "In retrospect," said Mr. Griffith, "we should never have agreed. We tried to do too many numbers in too short a time. The fabric and style choices were wrong." "I wasn't in this job at the time," explained Mr. Whitehead, "but the files show that we sold only 52 percent of what we expected to sell. A lot of inventory was left over."

Both men advanced a variety of additional opinions why that bin stock programme failed and was discontinued. Mr. Whitehead: "Our organization was in limbo, which meant there was no continuity, no systemwide support for the programme. We weren't really into planning. Our regionals just didn't repeat as we'd expected." Mr. Griffith added: "Somehow their regionals never really understood the programme or supported it. The items didn't get the exposure they needed. I mean, the Bay didn't make a strong statement to its customers about these numbers. Not only wasn't there enough

volume to make this attractive to us, but the repeat rate was below what we would normally get. The programme would have been even less successful had we not told our salespeople to really birddog. We were often in the middle, between what GMO said would happen and what the regional people actually did. So we got stuck with a lot of inventory, which we had to move ourselves."

Another experiment by the Bay was with Forsyth in 1979 buying for fall 1980. GMO felt that Pierre Cardin shirts, in category 332, were a "trending commodity," which they were having trouble keeping in stock. A line budgeting system was established whereby the Bay made a seasonal commitment but held only opening inventory orders. Rates of sale parameters were set for each item for repeat purchases guidelines. This programme, somewhat similar in concept to bin stock, was arrived at largely by GMO and Forsyth on a national basis. According to Mr. Whitehead, Forsyth was an easier company than Arrow with which to establish this kind of buying arrangement, but harder than Arrow to maintain it once under way. "Forsyth's performance on our VAA was hit and miss at the time, but they've been improving their regional representation." This programme was judged by Mr. Whitehead to be a success. "We've only had some experience last spring and this fall, but it looks like sales will be up by a third. I think we'll talk to other resources about this kind of arrangement," he said, "but each deal will be different because the suppliers are different."

"The Bay's proposal is somewhat unique for us," said Mr. Griffith. "We have several issues to consider, such as timing, and order quantities. If we do this again, we need more than the usual lead time and full details on all their plans. I see some advantages for production in larger cuts and more certainty in scheduling. We would probably aim to stay one month ahead of their sales, gearing our buying and production to initial order plus a system of fill-ins adjusted as we go by rate of sale information. We haven't talked any numbers yet, so it's premature to get out my calculator. We haven't talked number of items, types (basic or more fashion-oriented), prices, advertising and promotional programmes, or, very importantly, about who bears the inventory risk."

The inventory issue was yet to be resolved. If the quantity ordered was insufficient, then several options were possible. For example, the Bay might agree to accept a substitute, or if plans and materials were in place, some of next season's numbers might be moved ahead to fill the quantity shortfall. A more difficult question was a surplus. Each party wanted the onus on the other for a surplus. "Somebody would have to carry it over to the next season or liquidate it through markdowns," stated Mr. Griffith, "and this must be worked out. Our carrying costs are no longer 11 percent, like they used to be."

"This whole idea bears careful consideration, first in concept, then we can get into the numbers," concluded Mr. Whitehead, "but the whole thing depends on the evolving relationships we have with Arrow and our other resources."

---

# C A S E 3.5    Burger King Canada Inc.

Mr. Victor Wood, newly appointed President of Burger King Canada Limited, was examining a difficult site selection problem in the Montreal, Quebec, market in early Spring, 1981. Mr. Wood and two of his executives, Mr. Peter Calore, Director of Development, and Mr. Clay Doucette, Area Operations Manager, had decided that Burger King Canada would seek to penetrate fully the metropolitan Montreal market. The existing franchised single Burger King unit in Montreal would be joined as soon as possible with many more units (or stores). As of Spring, 1981, six promising sites had been identified. Although six or more sites might be developed, Mr. Wood and his colleagues realized that they could only proceed one unit at a time because of existing funds and management time. Therefore, they were engaged in the task of rank ordering the six possibilities in order to know where to begin actual development activities.

## BURGER KING— WORLDWIDE

Burger King, a wholly owned Miami-based subsidiary of the Pillsbury Company, was a U.S. multinational fast-food hamburger chain. At the end of fiscal 1981 (May 31st), Burger King had 3,022 restaurants worldwide. Approximately 100 of these were in Europe, Latin America, and the Far East; and 65 were in Canada. Overall, 85 percent of the units were franchised and 15 percent company-owned. System-wide, Burger King sales were $2.1 billion in fiscal 1981, a 16 percent increase over 1980. Operating profit to sales was 11.5 percent.

U.S. Burger King management had three main objectives for 1982:

- to increase the total number of units to 3,700
- to increase current average unit sales to over U.S. $1 million
- to increase current unit operating profit margins to 15 percent of sales.

Achieving such objectives was regarded as a challenge by senior Burger King managers, who believed that the fast food business had matured. Major gains, it was thought, would have to come from taking market share from major competitors such as McDonald's, Wendy's, and others.

The Burger King system strategic plan through fiscal 1983 included the following:

1. Menu development—Management intended to retain the emphasis on hamburgers, but also to pursue gains in traffic at all times of the day (breakfast, lunch time, dinner, snack, and late-night) by introducing new menu items.

Exhibit 1 illustrates a typical menu in Canada as of 1981 and the mix of sales by item. Exhibit 2 provides a weekly and hourly sales distribution. Exhibit 3 displays a typical Burger King unit monthly profit and loss statement.

2. Upgrading of facilities—Management planned to continue the emphasis on upgrading both to increase productivity and to enhance Burger King's image.

3. Aggressive marketing—Management en-

visaged an expanded marketing program not only to hold current customers, but also to expand the customer base by increasing child and adult perception of Burger King as "the quality fast food alternative".

4. Operational consistency—Management planned to emphasize further programs to improve decor, quality of product, and speed of service in all units to ensure consistent performance throughout the system.

EXHIBIT 1

| Burger King Canada Incorporated Typical Unit Canada Menu and Product Mix* | | | | |
|---|---|---|---|---|
| Sandwiches | | Price | % of Sandwiches | % of Sales |
| Burgers: | Whopper | $1.50 | 14.5% | 10.9% |
| | Whopper w/cheese | 1.70 | 7.7% | 6.5% |
| | Whopper Jr. | 1.05 | 9.0% | 3.9% |
| | Double Cheeseburger | 1.40 | 9.4% | 6.1% |
| | Cheeseburger | .75 | 20.0% | 6.6% |
| | Hamburger | .65 | 18.6% | 5.4% |
| | Other | | 4.0% | 2.3% |
| Specialty: | Roast Beef | $1.99 | 3.4% | 3.3% |
| | Chicken | 1.99 | 6.2% | 5.9% |
| | Veal | 1.99 | 2.5% | 2.2% |
| | Fish | 1.79 | 4.7% | 3.5% |
| | | | 100.0% | |
| Fries: | Regular | $ .50 | | 9.4% |
| | Large | .60 | | 7.6% |
| | Onion Rings | .65 | | 3.6% |
| Beverages: | Shakes[a] | $ .75 | | 5.6% |
| | Soft Drinks[b] – small | .42 | | 4.3% |
| | – medium | .49 | | 5.8% |
| | – large | .59 | | 3.0% |
| | Other | — | | 3.4% |
| Desserts: | Apple Pie | $ .40 | | .7% |

[a]Vanilla, Chocolate, Strawberry
[b]Coke (66% of soft drinks), Root Beer, Orange, Seven-Up
*Breakfast will not be served initially at any of the proposed Montreal sites.

EXHIBIT 2

### Burger King Canada Inc.
### Daily and Hourly Distribution of Sales

**A. Distribution of Sales Throughout Week Spring 1981.**

| Day | % of Week's Customers | % of Week's Sales | Check Average |
|---|---|---|---|
| Sunday | 11.9% | 12.8% | $2.74 |
| Monday | 12.6% | 11.9% | 2.34 |
| Tuesday | 12.3% | 11.4% | 2.28 |
| Wednesday | 13.2% | 12.5% | 2.35 |
| Thursday | 16.6% | 16.5% | 2.45 |
| Friday | 17.4% | 18.0% | 2.56 |
| Saturday | 16.0% | 16.9% | 2.67 |
| | 100.0% | 100.0% Average | $2.49 |

**B. Distribution of Sales Throughout Day Spring 1981.**

| For Hour Ending at | % of Day's Sales | Check Average |
|---|---|---|
| 11 a.m. | 2.0% | $2.33 |
| 12 | 8.7% | 2.58 |
| 1 p.m. | 17.9% | 2.61 |
| 2 | 10.7% | 2.44 |
| 3 | 6.3% | 2.16 |
| 4 | 4.3% | 2.62 |
| 5 | 6.5% | 3.05 |
| 6 | 10.4% | 2.96 |
| 7 | 9.9% | 2.45 |
| 8 | 7.0% | 2.20 |
| 9 | 5.5% | 2.08 |
| 10 | 4.3% | 2.03 |
| 11 | 3.1% | 2.17 |
| 12 | 3.4% | 2.10 |
| | 100.0% | $2.49 |

This overall strategic plan was adapted in each geographic area because of the unique characteristics of each market. For example, development strategies in Europe and Asia focussed on storefront locations in major cities, unlike the traditional free-standing, inside seating and drive-through units in North America. At the same time, in the relatively more saturated U.S. markets, Burger King's development strategies focussed on interstate highway exchanges and smaller cities and towns.

### BURGER KING CANADA INC.

Burger King Canada Ltd. was established in 1976 to assume control of four corporate stores already existing in the Windsor and Toronto, Ontario, markets. The corporate name was changed in November, 1980, to Burger King Canada Inc.

to comply with Quebec language law. From the original base of four stores in 1976, Burger King Canada Inc. had grown to 66 stores by spring, 1981, with 10 more stores under construction. The mix of franchise to corporate-owned restaurants was three to one. Management planned to achieve a mix of seven franchised stores to three company stores during 1982. By December, 1981, Burger King had units in every Canadian province except Saskatchewan, as shown in Table 1.

In management's view, the development strategy for Burger King Canada differed from Burger King U.S. Management believed that the Canadian market lagged behind the U.S. market; for example, the 1980 Canadian market was thought to be at the same stage of maturity as the U.S. market in the early 1970's. The initial development strategy for Burger King Canada had involved emphasis on Southern Ontario and the Maritime provinces, which contained populations somewhat familiar with the Burger King name and product from the U.S. and were very familiar with fast food concepts in general. Ac-

cordingly, Burger King Canada management had focussed especially on metropolitan areas of Ontario. Mr. Calore defined a metropolitan area to include a city and neighbouring areas that were within the communications radius of the city's media.

Burger King system-wide espoused the notion of market penetration, which meant the identification and utilization of all sites in a key market area. Such key sites included major traffic intersections, termination points such as large shopping malls, and other areas of major residential and commercial activity. Development in Canada was frequently delayed, awaiting greater penetration of U.S. border markets by Burger King U.S. In this way, it was hoped, the Canadian market would be prepared by media overflow and other experience with Burger King.

By 1980, Burger King Canada had placed very high priority on penetrating Canada's major metropolitan markets, such as Toronto, Winnipeg, and Vancouver. The second largest metropolitan market, Montreal, was virtually untapped. The single Burger King store in the

Table 1
Burger King Canada Inc.
Restaurants by Province

|  | F-1976* | | F-1980 | | F-1981 | | F-1982** | | F-1983 (est.) | |
|---|---|---|---|---|---|---|---|---|---|---|
|  | CO. | FR. | CO. | FR. | CO. | FR. | CO. | FR. | CO. | FR. |
| British Columbia | — | — | 1 | 1 | 3 | 2 | 3 | 5 | 4 | 7 |
| Manitoba | — | — | — | — | 1 | — | 4 | 1 | 5 | 1 |
| Alberta | — | — | — | 3 | — | 3 | — | 3 | — | 4 |
| Ontario | 4 | — | 10 | 22 | 11 | 33 | 21 | 31 | 21 | 40 |
| Quebec | — | — | — | — | — | 2 | — | 4 | 1 | 6 |
| Maritimes | — | — | — | 6 | — | 6 | — | 7 | — Ⓐ | 8 |
| Newfoundland | — | — | — | — | — | — | — | 2 | — | 2 |
| TOTALS | 4 | 0 | 11 | 32 | 15 | 46 | 29 | 53 | 31 | 68 |
|  | 4 | | 43 | | 61 | | 82 | | 99 | |

* Fiscal year for Burger King Canada Inc. ends 31 May.
** Some sites in these categories were under construction as of summer 1981.
Ⓐ Changes in Co./Fran. store numbers accounted for in the proposed sale of company Stores to Franchises.

*EXHIBIT 3*

| Burger King Canada Inc. Typical Restaurant Profit & Loss Statement | | |
|---|---|---|
| Line Item | Amount | % of Sales |
| Sales | $100,000 | 100.00% |
| Food | 31,500 | 31.5% |
| Waste | 800 | .8% |
| Condiments/Shortening | 1,500 | 1.5% |
| Paper | 4,500 | 4.5% |
|  | $ 38,300 | 38.3% |
| Gross Profit | $ 61,700 | 61.7% |
| Hourly wages | 15,000 | 15.0% |
| Salaries | 4,000 | 4.0% |
| Fringes | 3,500 | 3.5% |
| Other controllable expenses | 3,200 | 3.2% |
|  | $ 25,700 | 25.7% |
| Controllable Profit | $ 36,000 | 36.0% |
| Utilities | 3,000 | 3.0% |
| Sales Promotion | 1,500 | 1.5% |
| Occupancy | 8,000 | 8.0% |
| Advertising | 4,000 | 4.0% |
| Other | 3,000 | 3.0% |
|  | $ 19,500 | 19.5% |
| Store Operating Profit | $ 16,500 | 16.5% |

downtown core of Montreal, which opened in December, 1980, was quite successful. There were no corporate owned Burger King stores in Quebec as yet.

Exhibit 4 provides background information on the Metropolitan Montreal market.

## SITE SELECTION PROCESS AND CRITERIA

Burger King Canada management selected cities for development and penetration in relation to media coverage with special attention to spill-over television advertising from the U.S. border stations. One of the reasons Burger King Canada had not developed the Montreal market was management's belief that U.S. television adver-tising had relatively little effect on Montreal's French-speaking population.

Within a city, Burger King Canada manage-ment began the process of specific site selection with a one-year plan of total investment funds available. In general, management used one half of its development funds in new markets and one half to penetrate further into existing market areas. Burger King Canada generally entered new metropolitan markets with a dispor-tionately high percentage of company units. Once the market was partially penetrated, sec-ondary and outlying sites were more easily franchised.

Management typically identified several sites and followed a standardized timetable of

EXHIBIT 4

---

## Burger King Canada Inc.
## Metropolitan Montreal, 1979 Data from Financial Post Survey of Markets

---

**Market:** 1% above national average

| | |
|---|---|
| Retail sales, 1978 ................. | $ 8,196,100,000 |
| % Canadian total ................ | 12.14 |
| Per captia ...................... | $2,900 |

**Income:** 7% above national average

| | |
|---|---|
| Personal disposable income, 1978 ....................... | $20,069,000,000 |
| % Canadian total ................. | 12.87 |
| Per capita ...................... | $7,110 |

**Current Growth Rate:** 5% per decade

| | |
|---|---|
| Population, June 1, 1978 ........... | 2,822,900 |
| % Canadian total ................. | 11.99 |
| % Change, '71-'78 ................ | +3.43 |

### HOUSING

| | 1976 Census | % Total |
|---|---|---|
| Occupied dwellings, no. ........ | 924,635 | 100 |
| Owned .................... | 353,225 | 38 |
| Rented ................... | 571,410 | 62 |
| Type of Dwelling: | | |
| Single detached ........... | 223,365 | 24 |
| Double ................. | 34,130 | 4 |
| Row ................... | 19,905 | 2 |
| Apartment .............. | 603,740 | 65 |
| Duplex ................. | 38,870 | 4 |
| Mobile ................. | 2,375 | ... |

### MOTHER TONGUE

| | 1976 Census | % Total |
|---|---|---|
| English .................... | 607,505 | 21.7 |
| French .................... | 1,831,110 | 65.3 |
| Chinese & Japanese ........... | 10,585 | 0.4 |
| German ................... | 18,705 | 0.7 |
| Greek .................... | 34,015 | 1.2 |
| Italian ................... | 120,595 | 4.3 |
| Polish ................... | 10,550 | 0.4 |
| Portuguese ................ | 16,390 | 0.6 |
| Spanish .................. | 11,570 | 0.4 |
| Ukrainian ................. | 10,070 | 0.4 |

### RETAIL TRADE

| | |
|---|---|
| Total stores ..................... | 7,348,016 |
| Combination .................... | 1,569,934 |
| Grocery, confectionery ........... | 470,376 |
| Other food ..................... | 203,705 |
| Department .................... | 810,680 |
| General merchandise .............. | 88,545 |
| General stores ................... | 3,484 |
| Variety ........................ | 85,957 |
| Motor Vehicles .................. | 1,175,689 |
| Used car dealers ................. | 25,285 |
| Service stations ................. | 416,784 |
| Garages ....................... | 64,842 |
| Automotive parts & access. ......... | 114,413 |
| Men's clothing .................. | 94,223 |
| Women's clothing ............... | 148,762 |
| Family clothing ................. | 113,400 |
| Specialty shoe .................. | 12,135 |
| Family shoe .................... | 102,103 |
| Hardware ...................... | 145,394 |
| Household furniture .............. | 164,357 |
| Household appliances ............. | 22,513 |
| Furniture, TV, radio & appliance ..... | 67,111 |
| Drug stores .................... | 205,602 |
| Book & stationery ............... | 41,933 |
| Florists ....................... | 25,137 |
| Jewellery ...................... | 71,062 |
| Sporting goods & access. ........... | 111,994 |
| Personal access. ................. | 174,534 |
| Miscellaneous .................. | 815,062 |

### POPULATION

1976 Census:

| | |
|---|---|
| Total .................... | 2,802,485 |
| Male .................... | 1,367,755 |
| Female ................... | 1,434,730 |

| Age groups: | Male | Female |
|---|---|---|
| 0-4 ...................... | 94,345 | 89,545 |
| 5-9 ...................... | 106,675 | 101,780 |
| 10-14 .................... | 131,235 | 125,140 |
| 15-19 .................... | 137,545 | 134,720 |
| 20-24 .................... | 128,565 | 132,825 |
| 25-34 .................... | 235,920 | 242,055 |
| 35-44 .................... | 176,165 | 178,610 |
| 45-54 .................... | 159,845 | 169,220 |
| 55-64 .................... | 109,365 | 126,960 |
| 65-69 .................... | 37,535 | 49,045 |
| 70+ ...................... | 50,570 | 84,830 |

### FAMILIES

| | 1976 |
|---|---|
| No. ........................... | 715,775 |
| Aver. no. per family .............. | 3.3 |

## CONSUMER PRICE INDEX

(1971 = 100)    Montreal
1978 (May) .......... 169.4
1977 (May) .......... 155.9
1976 (May) .......... 144.2

## BUILDING PERMITS

| | 1977 | 1976 | 1975 |
|---|---|---|---|
| | | –$000– | |
| Value .............. | 1,151,599 | 1,427,874 | 1,109,303 |

## LABOUR FORCE BY INDUSTRY

| 1971 Census | Male No. | Female No. |
|---|---|---|
| All industries ................ | 643,700 | 336,730 |
| Manufacturing .............. | 193,500 | 83,010 |
| Clothing .................... | 14,815 | 28,495 |
| Construction ............... | 46,870 | 2,720 |
| Transportation & Communication .............. | 85,710 | 17,770 |
| Transportation ............... | 60,800 | 6,950 |
| Trade .................... | 108,370 | 52,305 |
| Retail .................... | 69,905 | 39,975 |
| Finance & Insurance .......... | 32,135 | 29,125 |
| Services ................... | 124,540 | 134,750 |
| Education .................. | 29,380 | 36,670 |
| Health welfare ............. | 20,010 | 44,750 |
| Business mgmt. ............. | 24,495 | 22,110 |
| Accommodation & Food ....... | 22,385 | 16,215 |
| Government ................ | 41,770 | 11,705 |
| Local .................... | 22,270 | 2,955 |

## LABOUR FORCE BY OCCUPATION

| | 1971 Census | % of Total |
|---|---|---|
| Mgmt. admin. ................ | 65,050 | 6.0 |
| Eng. & science ............. | 34,410 | 3.2 |
| Law & soc. science ........... | 11,545 | 1.1 |
| Religion ................... | 2,485 | 0.2 |
| Teaching ................... | 42,625 | 3.9 |
| Med. & health .............. | 41,805 | 3.9 |
| Art & literary .............. | 14,945 | 1.4 |
| Clerical ................... | 213,285 | 19.7 |
| Sales .................... | 108,505 | 10.0 |
| Service ................... | 108,090 | 10.0 |
| Primary ................... | 7,575 | 0.7 |
| Processing ................. | 34,125 | 3.2 |
| Machining .................. | 29,430 | 2.7 |
| Product fab. ............... | 105,595 | 9.8 |
| Construction .............. | 50,430 | 4.7 |
| Trans. equip ............... | 40,755 | 3.8 |

| | | |
|---|---|---|
| Materials hand. ............... | 21,675 | 2.0 |
| Miscellaneous ................ | 147,445 | 13.7 |
| All occupations .............. | 1,079,785 | 100.0 |

## EARNINGS

| | Av. weekly earnings $ | |
|---|---|---|
| | Montreal | Canada |
| 1973 ...................... | 174.54 | 160.46 |
| 1974 ...................... | 201.49 | 178.09 |
| 1975 ...................... | 224.18 | 203.34 |
| 1976 ...................... | 243.86 | 228.03 |

## EMPLOYMENT

| (1961 = 100) | Montreal | Canada |
|---|---|---|
| 1973 ...................... | 126.0 | 135.9 |
| 1974 ...................... | 130.9 | 142.8 |
| 1975 ...................... | 130.8 | 141.1 |
| 1976 ...................... | 132.3 | 144.1 |
| 1977 ...................... | 127.6 | 144.3 |

## TAXATION STATISTICS

| Income class: | 1976 |
|---|---|
| Under $2,000 .................... | 86,385 |
| $2,000 – 3,000 ................. | 72,174 |
| 3,000 – 4,000 ................. | 70,192 |
| 4,000 – 5,000 ................. | 61,686 |
| 5,000 – 7,000 ................. | 146,771 |
| 7,000 – 10,000 ................ | 209,536 |
| 10,000 – 15,000 ............... | 248,247 |
| 15,000 – 20,000 ............... | 122,920 |
| Over $20,000 .................... | 112,148 |
| Total returns, no. ................ | 1,130,059 |
| Total inc., $000 ................. | 12,315,665 |
| Average income, $ ............... | 10,898 |
| Total fed. tax, $000 .............. | 1,092,729 |
| Average fed. tax, $ ............... | 1,355 |

## MANUFACTURING INDUSTRIES

| | 1975 | 1971 |
|---|---|---|
| Plants ..................... | 5,128 | 5,625 |
| Employees .................. | 280,883 | 297,137 |
| | –$000– | |
| Salaries, wages ...................... | 2,819,921 | 2,118,800 |
| Mfg. materials cost ...................... | 7,877,132 | 4,317,364 |
| Mfg. shipments, value .................... | 13,580,866 | 7,868,522 |
| Total value added .................... | 5,876,232 | 3,769,299 |

site consideration. The first step was review of the market and selection of several generally acceptable sites for further in-depth evaluation. This process took about 90–180 days. The second step was determination of the best, second best, etc., sites to arrive at a site development priority list. This step was regarded as very crucial, usually requiring approximately ten days. Following this decision by senior Burger King Canada management, the actual development of a site began. This involved obtaining permits, easements, and building plans; letting tenders for construction, and so on. This stage usually required up to 180 days. Finally, construction required about another 100 days. Thus, the whole process of site selection through to opening required 12–15 months.

Management had developed a set of criteria to assist in evaluating potential sites. Priority was given to selecting the best sites rather than the most readily available ones and to selecting the sites with the best prospective return on investment rather than the least costly ones to develop.

Burger King Canada management utilized in sequence the following procedure and criteria to make site selection decisions:

1. A map of the whole market area was divided into grids by tracing the major arteries and transportation points (i.e., expressways, highways, bridges, and tunnels). Each grid was then sectioned by streets with 20,000 vehicles per day or more.

2. The competition was mapped as well as termination points and traffic generators such as shopping centres, arenas, civic and art centres. Competition was defined on two levels. The first and primary level was fast food operations such as McDonald's, A&W, Harvey's. The second level included any restaurant operation that served the same demographic or geographic area.

*EXHIBIT 5*
*Freestanding Burger*
*King Unit*

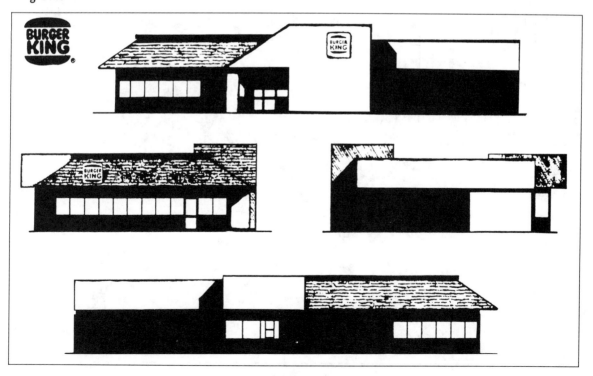

*Exhibit 6*
*Proposed Site*
*Locations Montréal,*
*Canada*

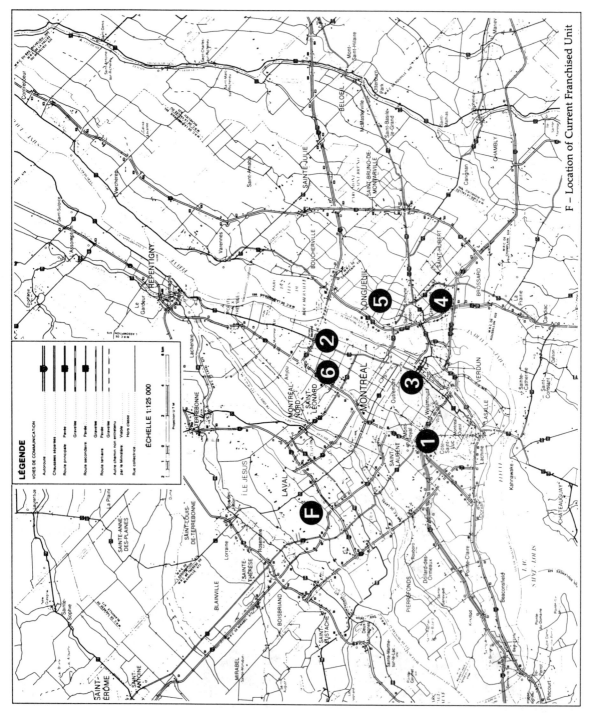

F – Location of Current Franchised Unit

3. The relationship between local employment patterns, local population demographics such as age, occupation and median income, residential density, traffic generators and natural or man-made barriers was examined to provide an idea of the traffic flow and patterns leading to the identification of primary trade areas. Burger King Canada management noted that their customer demographics indicated an age group of 18–34 years and maturing, blue collar or white collar occupations, family and singles, and an income above the national per capita average.

4. In order to qualify for serious consideration, a location had to be:

   (a) adjacent to a residential area that was growing and had at least 30,000 people in the unit's trade area; (b) close to a termination point such as shopping malls, major road intersections, or a recreational facility; (c) close to a white collar and light industry working population; (d) immediately accessible to a normal traffic flow of over 20,000 vehicles per day.

5. The physical requirements of the site depended on the trade area which was to be penetrated. The Burger King trade area would include a travel time of approximately 5 minutes by foot and 10 minutes by car, taking into account natural barriers such as rivers, interstate highways, etc. Suburban locations called for large sites to accommodate a free-standing restaurant with adequate parking space and drive-through traffic potential. Downtown locations had to be planned for large pedestrian traffic, possibly a storefront operation with little or no parking. Requirements for Burger King sites generally called for 30,000–40,000 sq. ft. The major exception to this was center city non-parking storefront units. Exhibit 5 shows a picture of a typical free-standing Burger King Unit.

6. Management considered corner locations as ideal for several reasons. Visibility was good, traffic slowed down allowing drivers time to react, and access could be four-way. A secondary choice after a corner was an L-shaped site which wrapped around a corner allowing frontage on two different roads.

7. Additional considerations included availability of utilities, subsoil conditions, zoning regulations, and other factors which affected construction and profitability.

8. Management calculated volume and profitability projections for a site on several bases:

   (a) initial volume estimates were established based on other Burger King Canada units in comparable locations and trading areas;

   (b) adjustments to these estimates were made to allow for any differences in demography, accessibility, local market conditions, etc.;

   (c) the competition's volume was examined by observation as another base on which to assess volume projections;

   (d) once the sales volume was averaged for each of the three years of operation, this figure was then compared to the total cost of development over a three year time period using a 10 percent per year estimated sales growth;

   (e) the estimated average annual sales volume for the first three years divided by the cost of development gave a fraction which was compared to a pre-established rule-of-thumb standard to give a summary picture of feasibility of site;*

---

* The rule-of-thumb calculation also known as investment turnover (ITO) was based on sales forecast inputs from the real estate representative, the Operations Manager and Peter Calore. This averaged figure was divided by total investment. In a franchised unit, this investment figure would not include equipment cost. For rental property, the capitalized lease value was obtained by multiplying the annual rental by a factor of 10. The minimum standards were 1.2 for a company-owned unit and 1.65 for a franchised unit.

(f) a projected internal rate of return was required to meet or exceed the standard internal rate of return of 16 percent.

## The Decision to Be Made

Six sites had been identified as potentially promising for Burger King Canada in Montreal, as shown on the map in Exhibit 6. These sites are profiled on the basis of the site selection criteria outlined above in Exhibit 6. Management had agreed that all possible speed should be taken to penetrate the Montreal market and that all the necessary data for making priority site selection choices had been gathered. Mr. Wood had arranged a meeting for tomorrow with Mr. Calore and Mr. Doucette to select the priorities for site development.

EXHIBIT 7

| Burger King Canada Inc. Proposed Montreal Burger King Sites | | |
|---|---|---|
| | 1 | 2 |
| Burger King Site Selection Criteria | COTES-DES-NEIGES AT BARCLAY | SHERBROOKE EAST |
| FIT TO MARKET GRID FOR AREA | City proper, Barclay one way st., east to west | City east end; major commercial artery |
| COMPETITION | MCDONALD'S—HARVEYS | MCDONALD'S—no drive thru |
| PRIMARY TRADE AREA | Residential base; shopping centre 400,000 sq. ft. across st., busstop all four corners | Two shopping centres; One adjacent, residential base, 85% French. Adjacent strip mall less than 100,000 sq. ft. Near by shopping mall 400,000 sq. ft. |
| TYPE OF TRADE AREA | Traffic 32,000 Pedestrian 6,000 + | Traffic 35,000 Minimal pedestrian |
| TRADE AREA POPULATION | 50,000 | 40,000 |
| SITE PHYSICAL REQUIREMENTS | Zoned—2 story bldg.; Size: only 31 parking spaces; 26,000 sq. ft. available | Zoned—2 storey bldg., Access-parking good with adjacent shopping centre, further easements required for access, sign and utilities. Meets site space requirements |
| VISIBILITY/CORNER LOT | From south—very good From north—fair. Sign visibility very good, corner lot | Excellent both directions |
| SITE CONDITIONS | Water main across four lane highway; drive-thru possible | No foreseeable site work requirement |
| SITE LAND/COST LEASE TERMS | Land cost $420,000 | Ground lease 20 yr. plus 2-5 year options. 1st five years $51,000/yr. Escalator every 5 years. |
| SALES PROJECTION (YEAR ONE) | $1,400,000 | $1,300,000 |

EXHIBIT 7 (cont'd)

| TOTAL SITE DEVELOPMENT COST—BUILDING, SITE AND EQUIPMENT | Building and site $460,000 Equipment (co. only) $310,000 | Building and site $460,000 Equipment $300,000 |
|---|---|---|
| FORM OF OPERATION PROPOSED | Company or Franchise | Company |
| BUILDING PROPOSED | BK 120 | BK 90 |

### Burger King Canada Inc.
### Proposed Montreal Burger King Sites

| | 3 | 4 |
|---|---|---|
| Burger King Site Selection Criteria | ST. CATHERINES WEST | GREENFIELD PARK |
| FIT TO MARKET GRID FOR AREA | City proper major core intersection | Suburb south shore near 2 main bridges |
| COMPETITION | HARVEYS—MCDONALD'S Five minute walk to hotels/theatres | HARVEYS—ST. HUBERT, MCDONALD'S—WENDY'S—LUM'S |
| PRIMARY TRADE AREA | Major office area, shopping complexes; hotel & entertainment area—light residential | Commercial district, shopping centre enclosed more than 300,000 sq. ft. |
| TYPE OF TRADE AREA | Pedestrian—20,000; vehicular—no information | Traffic—30,000 |
| TRADE AREA POPULATION | Not available, Near university | 40,000 |
| SITE PHYSICAL REQUIREMENTS | Zoning—ok, 5,000 sq. ft. ground floor of abandoned Woolworth's. No parking or delivery space. Site space requirement n.a. | Zoning ok, excellent access, site on shopping centre pad; Meets site space requirements |
| VISIBILITY/CORNER LOT | Corner lot frontage total of 140 ft. visibility excellent | Corner lot signaled Break in median Excellent visibility |
| SITE CONDITIONS | Structural analysis required for building; venting for equipment not adequate; utility capacity not sufficient | No foreseeable site work required; utility availability not conclusive. |
| SITE LAND COST/LEASE TERMS | Store lease 20 yr. term, Rent $75,000; escalations not yet determined | Ground lease w/restrictive covenants i.e. no pizza sales, hours of operation, protection of visibility for other tenants signs. 20 year term $35,000 rent. Escalation every 5 years; 3% sales over 1.5 million/year. (escalation clause on sales) |
| SALES PROJECTION (YEAR ONE) | $1,200,000 | $1,250,000 |
| TOTAL SITE DEVELOPMENT COST—BUILDING, SITE AND EQUIPMENT | $280,000 Bldg. (no site costs) | $350,000 Bldg. and Site $300,000 Equip. |

*Exhibit 7 (cont'd)*

| FORM OF OPERATION PROPOSED | Franchise | Company |
|---|---|---|
| BUILDING PROPOSED | Storefront model | BK 90 |

### Burger King Canada Inc.
### Proposed Montreal Burger King Sites

| Burger King Site Selection Criteria | 5<br>LONGUEVIL CHAMBLY RD. | 6<br>JEAN TALON |
|---|---|---|
| FIT TO MARKET GRID FOR AREA | Suburb south shore, major north shore artery | City east end; major east/west artery |
| COMPETITION | MCDONALD'S—ST. HUBERT—WENDY'S 1 mile south in new commercially developed area | ST. HUBERT—MCDONALD'S |
| PRIMARY TRADE AREA | Residential shopping centre, strip mall 300,000 sq. ft. | Shopping centre strip mall; less than 200,000 sq. ft. |
| TYPE OF TRADE AREA | Traffic—27,000 | Traffic—21,000 mainly rush hour |
| TRADE AREA POPULATION | 40,000 | 30,000 |
| SITE PHYSICAL REQUIREMENTS | Zoning ok—site on shopping centre pad, only shopping centre in area. Restrictive covenant on building site to 5,000 sq. ft. BK can meet this requirement | Zoning ok; located on new small shopping centre pad; meets site space requirements |
| VISIBILITY/CORNER LOT | Excellent visibility/accessibility | Good visibility; BK must share major sign pylon w/one other shopping centre business |
| SITE CONDITIONS | No foreseeable site work | No foreseeable site work |
| SITE LAND COST/LEASE TERMS | Ground lease 20 yr. term $30,000 per year; escalations every 5 years | Ground lease 20 yr. term 2-5 options $32,000/year, escalator every 5 years. |
| SALES PROJECTION (YEAR ONE) | $1,250,000 | $1,175,000 |
| TOTAL SITE DEVELOPMENT COST—BUILDING, SITE AND EQUIPMENT | $350,000 building and site $300,000 equipment | $350,000 building & site |
| FORM OF OPERATION PROPOSED | Company or Franchise | Franchise |
| BUILDING PROPOSED | BK 90 | BK 90 |

NOTES TO EXHIBIT 7

1. All units except St. Catherines West (site 3) would have a Drive-In window.

2. If a unit was franchised, the I.T.O. would not use an equipment cost in the calculation as the franchisee would be responsible for this investment expense.

3. The building model number (which refers to seating capacity) is based upon estimated sales.

| | |
|---|---|
| BK 50 | 800,000 – 1 million |
| BK 90 | 1 million – 1.3 million |
| BK 120 | over 1.3 million |
| STOREFRONT | generally based on facility to be renovated and trade area size. |

4. St. Hubert offered BBQ chicken—full service and takeout. Lum's was a coffee shop with a takeout.

---

# C A S E 3.6    Simpsons: Men's Furnishings

Mr. Adrian Herschell, Divisional Sales and Merchandising Manager (London) for Simpsons Limited, sat before a desk stacked with floor plan blueprints, computer printouts and other papers. Mr. Herschell was co-ordinating a team effort to change the layout of Simpsons' 210,000 square foot (selling space) London, Ontario, store. "Right now, I'm working on our men's wear area," said Mr. Herschell in June, 1981. "We must have our plan completed and approved by senior management at head office by July 1st in order to have the plan implemented by the end of August for the fall season. The pressure is on all of us."

Mr. Herschell and other Simpsons regional and London store executives were in the midst of extensive changes to the London store. Known as the flagship of the Ontario region, the London store was expected to set the pace for the other four stores in its region. For a variety of reasons, however, very little investment in fixture improvements and major layout changes had been made in the London store for several years. Mr. Herschell and others in Simpsons' management had determined that the store needed rejuvenation in order to implement the merchandising plans for the various departments and in order to improve the image London shoppers had of Simpsons. "At the outset," Mr. Herschell said, "we knew profit improvement was critical and that we should be concerned with return on investment in each department. However, everyone seems to accept we have to make a substantial investment to turn this store around. So, we began our thinking without any ceiling

on investment in mind, but rather a commitment to do whatever we did in the best way possible."

The changes in store layout were addressed simultaneously at several levels of merchandise aggregation. Planning was done by floor (five floors plus a basement level), by merchandise group (men's and youths' fashion, women's fashion, women's fashion accessories, home, and leisure) and by department (for example, within men's and youths' fashion: men's furnishings, men's clothing, men's active wear, boys' wear, young men's wear, men's footwear, and the West End Shop). Mr. Herschell and his colleagues had made the major decision that all men's wear should be relocated onto the same floor, rather than being on three floors. Exhibit 1 shows the existing layout of the main floor.

An initial allocation of 25,000 square feet was made for all of men's wear on the first floor, an increase of 40% over the previous amount of first floor space allocated. As shown on Exhibit 2, this allocated space was divided up by department and an attempt made to locate departments within the space in a way that made sense to a customer. See also Exhibit 3(a).

Mr. Herschell was relatively comfortable with this tentative layout. The next step was to look at each department in detail to decide on layout and fixtures. "There are many factors to consider," said Mr. Herschell. "First, whatever we do must be flexible. We'll be changing all the time as seasons change and as merchandise strategies change. Our floor plan has to be changeable. Our fixtures have to be multi-purpose. We're going to replace many of the fixtures

**EXHIBIT 1**
*Current Layout*

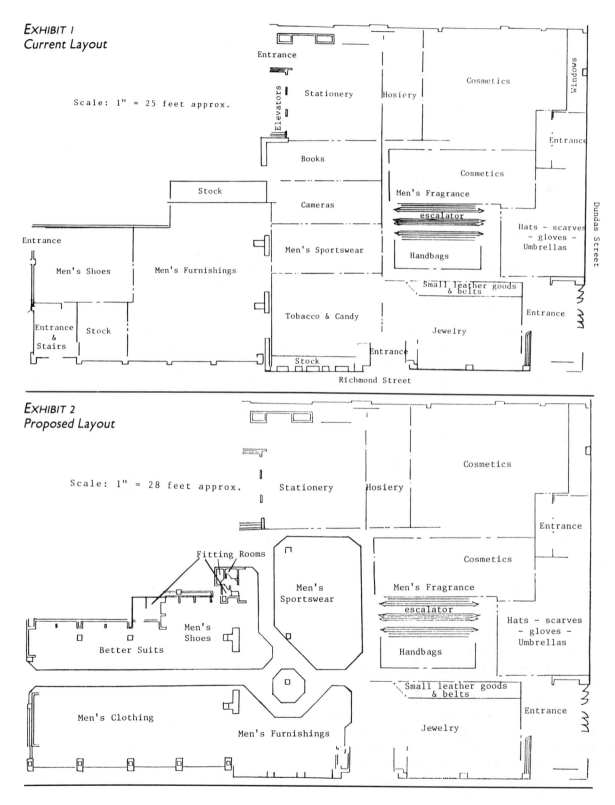

Scale: 1" = 25 feet approx.

**EXHIBIT 2**
*Proposed Layout*

Scale: 1" = 28 feet approx.

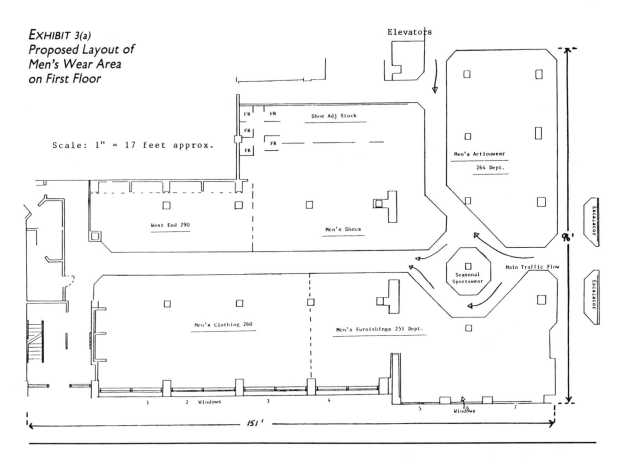

EXHIBIT 3(a)
Proposed Layout of
Men's Wear Area
on First Floor

Scale: 1" = 17 feet approx.

we're using now. They're not multi-purpose enough and the new fixtures available also provide a better presentation of our merchandise."

"Second, we must remember our customers. We have a solid core of regular customers who buy basic, utilitarian, middle-of-the-road clothes. In fact, roughly one-third of our merchandise is sold while on promotion, or off-price as we say. We typically use 6 promotional tables (4′ × 4′ × 52″ high) at any one time for this featured merchandise. Our merchandise planners want us to move into a more fashion-oriented mode, but we'll have to be careful not to lose our core, middle-income customers by going overboard in our layout and visual merchandising. They also want us to sell more of our merchandise at regular rather than sale prices."

"Third, we must decide in each department what merchandise to feature, to dominate and

how to allocate space to each product category. We'll look at sales, markup and inventory turn figures to help us make such decisions plus we'll look at the evolving plans of the department in the principal buyer's marketing plan."

"Finally, we'll have to keep in mind what our alternatives are within sound merchandising practices. We have a variety of new fixtures available and have to be sure we lay them out so that it makes sense on the floor, not on paper. For example, we can't put high displays at the aisle; that would only block vision into the department. We have to leave space for aisles and at least three feet between fixtures for customers; have high volume items near high traffic areas and so on."

Department 251, men's furnishings, consisted of dress shirts, ties and other neckwear, pajamas, robes (gowns), hats and umbrellas, belts, underwear, gloves, and socks (hosiery). As

*EXHIBIT 3(b)*
*Proposed Space for*
*Department 251*

Scale: 1" = 10 feet approx.

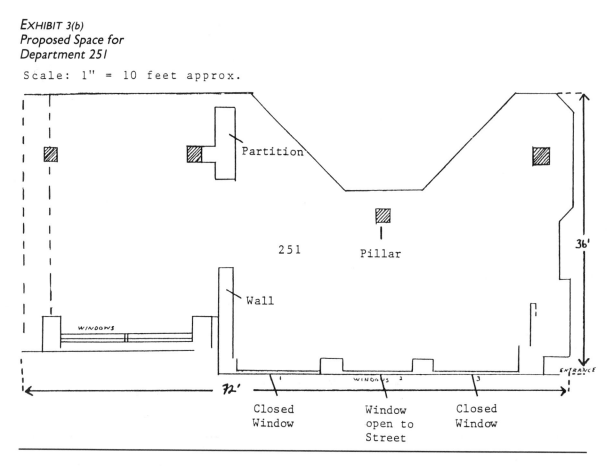

Closed
Window

Window
open to
Street

Closed
Window

currently planned, Department 251 would remain on the first floor, but be moved to a higher traffic area, more accessible to the middle of the store. It would be adjacent on two sides to other men's wear assortments, as shown in Exhibit 3(a). Latest figures available to Mr. Herschell showed that dress shirts were the largest volume items in Department 251, but not the highest markup items. See Exhibit 4 for more details on inventory and display. Mr. Herschell had also carefully read the 251 Department Marketing Strategy, prepared in late 1980 by the principal buyer for 251. Excerpts of this plan are shown in Exhibit 5.

Mr. David Free, Regional Visual Merchandising Manager, had been working closely with Mr. Herschell on the layout of all the London store departments. He had provided Mr. Herschell with some background material on the major types of fixtures they would likely use in

the 251 layout (Exhibit 6) and was prepared to assist Mr. Herschell in the preparation of displays once Mr. Herschell had made the major decisions on layout design for 251. "We'll use fewer, but better fixtures," said Mr. Free, "and I hope better use of our wall space too. We've got to get the merchandise out of display cases customers can't reach and on to the floor for self-selection. I suspect we'll have only one sales desk," added Mr. Free, "that will take 64 square feet of space including register, bags, and some small display cases for handkerchiefs, etc."

"I've spent a lot of time down on the floor just watching customers so that I have some feel for layout," said Mr. Herschell. "All of us do that; we don't just sit in our offices pushing paper. But, I can't study much longer. I've got to do a first cut at this 251 department to get Dave going on visuals."

EXHIBIT 4

| Merchandise Statistics for Department 251 | | | | | | | | | |
| --- | --- | --- | --- | --- | --- | --- | --- | --- | --- |
| 1980 YEAR | | | | | | | | PLAN | |
| Category | $ Sales | Average Markup | Gross Profit (%) | Invent. Turns | Square Footage | Average Retail Per Item | Comments Re Display | Planned Items in Store Stock | % of Items on Display |
| Dress Shirts | 320,000 | 39.2% | 33.4% | 6.1× | 1,260 | $23.00 | | 3,500 | 60% |
| Pyjamas | 84,000 | 38.6 | 34.3 | 3.8 | 310 | 20.00 | | 1,400 | 60 |
| Gowns | 80,000 | 41.1 | 38.0 | 5.8 | 285 | 45.00 | | 350 | 80 |
| Hats | 31,000 | 42.7 | 39.8 | 4.4 | 43 | 28.00 | Intend to display on wall with face-out brackets. | 170 | 80 |
| Ties and Handker-chiefs | 145,000 | 40.0 | 34.6 | 6.1 | 165 | 11.00 | Sales mostly ties. Handkerchiefs & scarves will be in display case as part of sales desk. | 2,500 (ties) | 75 |
| Belts | 44,000 | 43.8 | 40.5 | 6.5 | 150 | 10.00 | | 600 | 100 |
| Under-wear | 140,000 | 39.5 | 35.8 | 4.0 | 828 | 4.50 | | 6,000 | 75 |
| Gloves & Umbrellas | 58,000 | 41.6 | 35.1 | 5.0 | 150 | 18.00 | Mostly gloves. Umbrellas in sales desk display or on wall. Gloves usually in 2 cubes like shirts. | 650 (gloves) | 100 |
| Hosiery | 140,000 | 41.0 | 37.8 | 5.6 | 756 | 3.50 | | 5,000 (pairs) | 75 |
| TOTAL | 1,042,000 | 40.2 | 35.4 | 5.4 | 3,952 | | | | |

EXHIBIT 5
Excerpts from 251
Department
Strategy
Fall 1980

**Department Profile**
To supply the general male population, age 16 and over, with their basic furnishing needs, with emphasis to be placed on the age group of 25 to 50 years of age. It is to this contemporary age group that our fashion merchandise groupings are aimed. Our merchandise offerings will appeal to customers with a moderate to upper income.

**Customer Profile**
Due to the large percentage of basic everyday merchandise sold within the furnishings department we have a highly varied customer.

The 'Conservative Customer' (50%) is the oldest and possibly the largest segment of our customer mix. He has a passive attitude to wearing apparel, is concerned with comfort and practicality. This is an average income group.

The 'Young, Casual Customer' (10%) is the youngest and the smallest segment of our customer mix. Preferring Jeans and T-shirts, many of this group are still students, but this group shops for underwear, hosiery, pyjamas within the furnishings department. This is the lowest income group.

'Main Stream Customer' (25%) is in the 25 to 50 year old age group. Well educated and employed in both white and blue collar jobs, he has an average to above average income. This customer group has a middle of the road taste level, will accept fashion changes once established, but is not an innovator.

The 'Updated Customer' (15%) is in the 25 to 50 year old age group, is well educated and in a professional or 'semi' professional occupation. This is the highest income group of customers, leads a more sophisticated life style, dining out, travel, theatre. This customer enjoys fashion apparel; is concerned with look, not wearability; is an innovator in his dress; and is fast to pick up on new fashion trends.

It is towards the last two customer groups that our merchandising direction should be aimed, not neglecting entirely our conservative customer in the process.

• • • • •

## Market Appeal
Upgrading our budget price points and styling as well as increasing one fashion selection on the main floor. We are and will increasingly move towards development of house brands, improving mark-up, profitability, and offering our customer tested (Seal of Approval) value and fashion for dollars spent.

• • • • •

## Classification Emphasis
Items will be selected within these high growth classifications for volume fashion trends and narrow and deep items. In general the selections will be made narrower eliminating fringe items from all but the Flagship Stores.

• • • • •

## Inventory Management
We have four major selling periods, which are May Sale, Father's Day, Anniversary Sale and Christmas. Stocks should be peaked for the events. In addition, we have highly seasonal commodities, gloves, scarves, winter underwear. This winter merchandise would open in October, peak in November, and close in February.

• • • • •

## Visual Presentation
Because of the amount of colour shown in all commodities, it is necessary to present lines by colour. Presentation by size has the effect of turning the merchandise into an

odds and ends display. Outposts should be created for seasonal items such as Gloves and Scarves, Short Sleeve Shirts and Gowns. Other than at Christmas when a Gown outpost should be created, during the balance of the year Gowns and Pajamas should be shown in a 'Sleep Shop'. Greater use must be made of show cards for the identification of size, fit and designer label. Displays must be created with items from the clothing dept. to illustrate to our customers how the various items can be worn, all displays fully accessorized from within our department.

• • • • •

It is vital that the visual merchandising standards be maintained at the highest possible level. The following should be used to maintain this level:

- brand identification
- prominent well-accessorized displays
- signing — in house or vendor provided
- 'Sleep Shop' signing
- outposts signing
    - gloves
    - robes
    - scarves
    - short sleeve shirts
- prominent colour displays for major items
- colour blocking
- fit and size identification

---

*EXHIBIT 6*
*Description of*
*Major Fixtures*
*Planned*

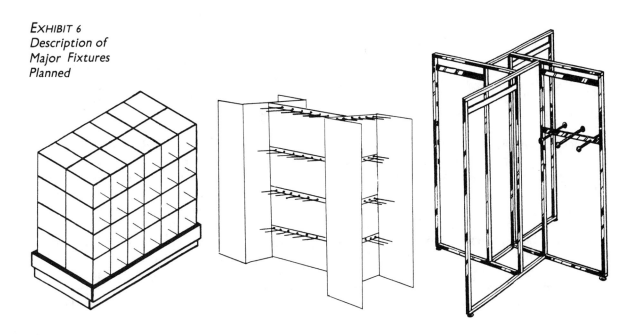

*Exhibit 6 (cont'd)*

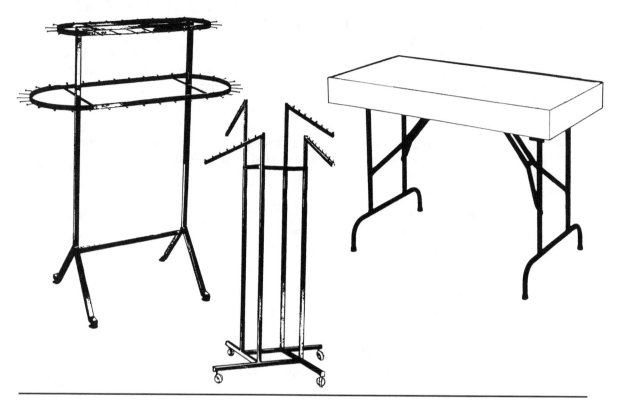

# C A S E 3.7   La Maison Simons

Peter Simons, Merchandise Manager for the Junior Misses department for La Maison Simons, sat at his desk thinking about the advertising themes he wished to use for the upcoming spring 1988 season. It was February 26 and he had just returned from a buying and scouting trip to Europe. Madame Lebrun, from the firm's advertising department, had just called to inform him that an advertising slot for the Junior Misses department had been reserved for March 4. Mr. Simons realized he would have to get together soon with his buyer to decide upon the items which they wanted to promote. Together, they would also have to develop some preliminary copy to describe the fashion message that they wanted to convey to their customer in order to complete the firm's requisition for advertising, as shown in Exhibit 1.

## HISTORY AND EVOLUTION

La Maison Simons was founded in the heart of Vieux Quebec City, Quebec, five generations ago, in 1875, by John Simons. The original store still stood in the square facing City Hall. Over time, La Maison Simons became well known for importing fine linens and domestics from Europe, earned a very good reputation, and boasted customers from all over Canada as well as the United States. In the 1950's, Donald Simons, Peter's father, took over operation of the store. Under his direction, La Maison Simons began to move away from linens toward importing European fashions. Representatives from La Maison Simons began to go to Paris in search of fashionable clothing. This was a natural progression since much of the linen buying was done in

Ireland and Scotland. In the 1950's, the company opened another outlet (25,000 sq. ft.) in the suburb of St. Foy in a shopping centre. At the time, it was one of the first shopping centres in Quebec City.

In 1983, another store (25,000 sq. ft.) was opened at Galerie de la Capitale, a newly constructed mall. This mall was located in Charlesbourg, one of the fastest growing regions of Quebec City. The two mall stores carried a full assortment whereas the downtown store, due to space limitations (10,000 sq. ft.), carried only certain high turnover items. The downtown store contained all Simons centralized offices including Merchandising, Graphics and Publicity, Accounting, Data Processing and Inventory Control. Plans to expand the St. Foy store to 60,000 sq. ft. were in the advanced stages and the building beside the downtown store had just been purchased. This would add another 5–10,000 sq. ft. to the existing floor space.

*EXHIBIT I*

## Publication Request

Date of Publication: _____Dept.: _____By: _____

Advertising:        Fashion Sale:        Special Purchase:        Mail Pamphlet:

Clothing being advertised: _____

Style: _____    Classification: _____    Company: _____

Imported: Yes _____    No _____    Exclusive: Yes _____    No _____    Designer: _____

**Main Fashion Theme:**

Introduction Title: _____

     Sub-title: _____

Why do we like it? _____

What is new about item? _____

What is different? _____

**Outline importance of:**

The silhouette: _____

The fabric: _____

The colors: _____

The shape: _____

The length: _____

Skirt: _____

Jacket: _____

Sleeve: _____

EXHIBIT 1 (cont'd)    Neckline: _____

Other Details: _____

Regular Price: _____    Special Price: _____

Sizes: _____

Colors: _____

Available at: _____

We like to wear it with: _____

_____

Any other special information: _____

_____

_____

_____

EXHIBIT 2

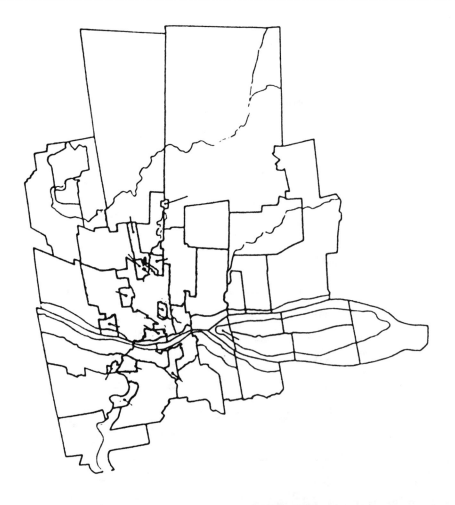

## THE QUEBEC CITY MARKET

As of 1988, the population of Quebec City and its surrounding suburbs was approximately 600,000. The city served as the seat of the Quebec provincial government. Quebec City's population was composed of a large proportion of middle income, dual career families with jobs in the civil service or at Laval University. The average income per household for Quebec City was $24,616. Management felt several specific characteristics of the Quebecois population existed which presented a unique opportunity for a fashion retailer:

1. People in Quebec were very advanced in their taste and yet were very open to new fashion.

2. Quebec City was the capital of the province of Quebec which meant its economy was largely white collar based. Its population had a stable income that didn't fluctuate with recessions, which meant they had the money to purchase apparel fashions.

3. Social interaction was very casual. There was not a lot of demand for very dressy, formal clothing (e.g. tuxedos or ball gowns). The upper end of the market was characterized by fine sports wear.

More information on Quebec City and its surroundings is provided in Exhibit 2.

*EXHIBIT 2 (cont'd)*

**MARITAL STATUS***
1986 Census:
(age 15+)

| | |
|---|---|
| Singe (never married) | 153,460 |
| Married (incl. sep.) | 284,600 |
| Widowed | 27,550 |
| Divorced | 17,745 |

**MOTHER TONGUE***

| | 1986 Census | % Total |
|---|---|---|
| English | 10,750 | 1.82 |
| French | 575,395 | 97.27 |
| Chinese | 415 | 0.07 |
| Dutch | 75 | 0.01 |
| German | 360 | 0.06 |
| Greek | 140 | 0.02 |
| Hungarian | 100 | 0.02 |
| Indo-Pakistani | 40 | 0.01 |
| Italian | 660 | 0.11 |
| Japanese | 30 | 0.01 |
| Korean | 10 | 0.00 |
| Polish | 175 | 0.03 |
| Portuguese | 330 | 0.06 |
| Scandinavian Languages | 10 | 0.00 |
| Ukrainian | 30 | 0.01 |
| Vietnamese | 530 | 0.09 |
| Other | 2,520 | 0.43 |

**FAMILIES***
1988 Census:
Families in Private

| | |
|---|---|
| Households. Total | 158,580 |
| Husband-wife families | 134,985 |
| Lone-parent families | 23,595 |
| Aver. no. persons per family | 3.1 |
| Aver. no. children per family | 1.3 |

**MANUFACTURING INDUSTRIES**

| | 1984 | 1979 |
|---|---|---|
| Plants | 575 | 555 |
| Employees | 18,860 | 20,960 |
| | –$000– | |
| Salaries wages | 443,771 | 312,677 |
| Mfg. materials, cost | 1,784,176 | 1,119,703 |
| Mfg. shipments value | 3,180,425 | 1,929,202 |
| Total value added | 1,405,939 | 814,752 |

**LIFESTYLES**

| | No. of Hhlds. | % | Index |
|---|---|---|---|
| Markets: | | | |
| Affluent | 2,800 | 1.3 | 103 |
| Upscale | 22,000 | 10.1 | 148 |
| Upper Middle & Middle | 63,000 | 28.8 | 183 |
| Working class | 55,600 | 25.5 | 166 |
| Lower Class | 25,100 | 11.5 | 156 |
| Young Singles | 9,000 | 4.1 | 94 |
| Young Couples | 13,600 | 6.2 | 177 |
| Empty Nesters | 14,000 | 6.4 | 71 |
| Old & Retired | 7,800 | 3.6 | 87 |
| Ethnic | 0 | 0.0 | 0 |
| Total | 218,400 | 97 | |

Note — Rural households have been excluded from total.

**BUILDING PERMITS**

| | 1986 | 1985 | 1984 |
|---|---|---|---|
| | | –$000– | |
| Value | 662,626 | 545,267 | 378,041 |

**CAPITAL EXPENDITURES**

| | 1987 | 1986 | 1985 |
|---|---|---|---|
| Manufacturing | —$ | Millions | |
| Total exp. | 109.7 | 115.9 | 180.0 |
| Capital exp. | 72.5 | 79.4 | 138.9 |

| | | | |
|---|---|---|---|
| Construction | 16.4 | 20.7 | 18.3 |
| Mach. & equip. | 56.1 | 58.7 | 120.6 |
| Repairs | 37.2 | 36.5 | 41.1 |
| Construction | 11.5 | 10.9 | 12.0 |
| Mach. & equip. | 25.7 | 25.6 | 29.1 |

**CONSUMER PRICE INDEX**

| (1981 = 100) | Québec |
|---|---|
| 1987 (Apr.) | 138.6 |
| 1986 (Apr.) | 133.3 |
| 1985 (Apr.) | 126.8 |
| 1984 (Apr.) | 122.1 |
| 1983 (Apr.) | 117.3 |

**AVERAGE WEEKLY EARNINGS**
(including overtime, industrial aggregate)

| | Quebec, CMA | Canada |
|---|---|---|
| Feb., 1987 | $401.69 | $438.20 |
| Feb., 1986 | $396.55 | $428.50 |
| Feb., 1985 | $373.14 | $417.08 |
| Feb., 1984 | $365.54 | $404.10 |

**DAILY NEWSPAPER(S)**

| | 1987 Circulation Total pd. excl. bulk |
|---|---|
| Le Journal de Québec | |
| Mon.-Fri. | 103,127 |
| Sat. | 106,350 |
| Sun. | 91,533 |
| Le Soleil | |
| Mon.-Fri. | 111,575 |
| Sat. | 136,621 |
| Sun. | 87,859 |

*EXHIBIT 2 (cont'd)*

### INCOME

**1981 Census**

| | |
|---|---|
| Average total | $ |
| Male | 17,184 |
| Female | 9,014 |
| Average employment income: | |
| Male | 17,734 |
| Female | 10,358 |
| Average census family income | 27,305 |
| Average household income | 24,616 |

### NUMBER OF EMPLOYEES
(industrial aggregate)

| | |
|---|---|
| Feb., 1987 | 204,900 |
| Feb., 1986 | 181,500 |
| Feb., 1985 | 193,200 |
| Feb., 1984 | 176,100 |

### HOMES BUILT

| | 1986 | 1985 | 1984 |
|---|---|---|---|
| No. | 7,541 | 4,413 | 4,462 |

### COMMUNITY NEWSPAPER(S)

| | 1987 Total Circulation |
|---|---|
| Beauport: Beauport Express | 32,800 |
| Lévis: Le Peuple-Tribune | 20,680 |
| Lévis, Lauzon, Saint-Romuald-d'Etchemin, Charny: Rive Sud Express | 31,049 |
| Quebec: Chronicle Telegraph | 7,000 |
| Sainte-Foy/Metro Quebec, L'Elan, L'Eventail, L'Envol | n.a. |
| Sainte-Foy, Sillery, Cap-Rouge: L'Appel | 36,716 |

### RADIO STATION DATA

| | | | Mon-Sun 5 am.-1a.m. All Persons 7+ | |
|---|---|---|---|---|
| Station | Market | Format | Weekly Reach % | Aver. Hrs. Tuned |
| All Stations | | | 95 | 24.1 |
| CJRP | Québec | MOR | 22 | 8.9 |
| CITF-FM | Québec | MOR | 31 | 9.6 |
| CJMF-FM | Québec | Progressive Rock | 44 | 11.4 |
| CKCV | Québec | MOR | 12 | 5.0 |
| CHRC | Québec | Adult | 46 | 13.2 |
| CBV | Québec | Multi-format | 17 | 7.8 |
| CFLS | Québec-Lévis | Top 40, Rock | 15 | 16.0 |
| CHOI-FM | Québec | MOR, Contemp. | 15 | 4.6 |
| CHIK-FM | Québec | Contemp., MOR | 10 | 7.7 |
| CBV-FM | Québec | Multi-format | 5 | 6.9 |
| CBVE-FM | Québec | Multi-format | 1 | 7.1 |

Note — MOR stands for Middle of Road,
AOR stands for Album-oriented Rock

### TV STATION DATA

| | | | Mon-Sun 6 a.m.-2 a.m. All Persons 2+ | |
|---|---|---|---|---|
| Station | Market | Network Affiliation | Wkly. Reach % | Aver. Hrs. Tuned |
| All Stations | | | 98 | 23.9 |
| CFCM | Québec | TVA | 84 | 10.7 |
| CBVT | Québec | CBC | 92 | 8.6 |
| CIVQ | Québec | ORTQ | 56 | 2.6 |
| CFCF | Montréal | CTV | 10 | 2.9 |
| WCAX | Burlington, VT | CBS | 9 | 2.1 |
| CKMI | Québec | CBC | 29 | 1.8 |
| WVNY | Burlington, VT | n.a. | 13 | 1.8 |
| WPTZ | Plattsburg, NY | NBC | 8 | 2.9 |
| CKTM | Trois Rivières | Ind | 11 | 2.4 |
| TVFQ | Montréal | Pay TV | 12 | 1.5 |
| CFTM | Montréal | TVA | 3 | 8.9 |
| CFAP | Québec | n.a. | 50 | 2.9 |
| TVJQ | Montreal | n.a. | 8 | 2.9 |
| ECRAN | NA | Pay TV | 8 | 5.3 |

## Quebec, V

*In census division Québec.*

**N.B.:** *Information marked* * *is based on boundaries revised in 1986; all other information is based on 1981 boundaries.*

### POPULATION

| | |
|---|---|
| 1981 Census Total | 166,474 |
| 1981 Census. Adjusted Total | 165,908 |

| 1986 Census: * | |
|---|---|
| Total | 164,680 |
| Male | 76,680 |
| Female | 87,905 |

| Age groups. | Male | Female |
|---|---|---|
| Under 4 | 4,030 | 3,730 |
| 5-9 | 4,040 | 4,075 |
| 10-14 | 4,355 | 3,935 |
| 15-19 | 5,175 | 5,090 |
| 20-24 | 8,325 | 8,315 |
| 25-29 | 8,925 | 8,755 |
| 30-34 | 7,295 | 7,375 |
| 35-39 | 6,230 | 8,325 |
| 40-44 | 4,960 | 5,360 |
| 45-49 | 4,110 | 4,570 |
| 50-54 | 3,895 | 4,670 |
| 55-59 | 4,020 | 5,120 |
| 60-64 | 3,625 | 5,175 |
| 65-69 | 2,860 | 4,695 |
| 70-74 | 2,210 | 4,180 |
| 75+ | 2,620 | 6,525 |

### MARITAL STATUS*
**1986 Census:**
(age 15+)

| | |
|---|---|
| Single (never married) | 52,320 |
| Married (incl. sep.) | 69,565 |
| Widowed | 11,500 |
| Divorced | 7,020 |

### MOTHER TONGUE*

| | 1986 Census | % Total |
|---|---|---|
| English | 2,915 | 1.8 |
| French | 155,520 | 94.5 |
| Other | 6,145 | 3.7 |

### HOUSING*
1988 Census:

| Occu. Priv. Dwellings, | |
|---|---|
| Total | 70,030 |
| Owned | 21,395 |
| Rented | 48,635 |

| | |
|---|---|
| Single detached | 10,100 |
| Apart., 5 or more storeys | 7,110 |
| Movable dwellings | 20 |
| Other dwellings | 52,800 |

## PRIVATE HOUSEHOLDS*
1986 Census

| | |
|---|---|
| Private Households, Total ..... | 70,030 |
| Pop. in private households .............. | 158,850 |
| Aver. no. per household .... | 2.3 |

## FAMILIES*
1986 Census:

| | |
|---|---|
| Families in Private Households, Total ................. | 40,700 |
| Husband-wife families ...... | 32,160 |
| Lone-parent families ....... | 8,540 |
| Aver. no. persons per family ... | 2.9 |
| Aver. no. children per family ... | 1.1 |

## LEVEL OF SCHOOLING

| | 1981 Census |
|---|---|
| Population, 15 years + .............. | 138,045 |
| Less than Grade 9 .......... | 36,340 |
| Grades 9–13 .............. | 49,660 |
| Trades certificate or diploma ........... | 5,030 |
| Other non-university, with certificate .......... | 17,560 |
| University degree .......... | 11,390 |

Note — Level of Schooling refers to the highest grade or year completed by the person. Those currently enrolled reported their present grade or year.

## LABOUR FORCE
1981 Census

Males:

| | |
|---|---|
| In the labour force ........ | 45,260 |
| Employed ............. | 39,310 |
| Not in labour force ........ | 17,830 |
| Participation rate: | |
| 15-24 years ........... | 65.7 |
| 25 years + ............. | 73.7 |

Females:

| | |
|---|---|
| In the labour force ........ | 35,035 |
| Employed ............. | 30,625 |
| Not in labor force ........ | 39,920 |
| Participation rate: | |
| 15-24 years ........... | 64.5 |
| 25 years + ........... | 41.7 |

## INCOME
1981 Census

| | $ |
|---|---|
| Average total income: | |
| Male ................. | 14,433 |
| Female ................ | 8,626 |
| Average employment income: | |
| Male ................. | 15,483 |
| Female ................ | 10,286 |
| Average census family income .............. | 23,467 |
| Average household income .............. | 19,936 |

## BUILDING PERMITS

| | 1986 | 1985 | 1984 |
|---|---|---|---|
| | | —$000— | |
| Value ... | 225,021 | 220,987 | 128,517 |

## HOMES BUILT

| | 1986 | 1985 | 1984 |
|---|---|---|---|
| No. ........ | 1,696 | 825 | 1,094 |

## MANUFACTURING INDUSTRIES

| | 1983 | 1979 |
|---|---|---|
| Plants ............ | 200 | 228 |
| Employees ........ | 7,932 | 9,152 |
| | —$000— | |
| Salaries, wages .......... | 198,003 | 144,141 |
| Mfg materials, cost ........... | 442,196 | 334,413 |
| Mfg. shipments, value | 981,547 | 727,716 |
| Total value added ......... | 507,306 | 387,485 |

## TAXATION STATISTICS

| Income Class: | 1985 | % of Total |
|---|---|---|
| Under $2,500 ...... | 13,079 | 12.22 |
| $2,500–$5,000 .... | 7,505 | 7.01 |
| $5,000–$7,500 .... | 8,951 | 8.36 |
| $7,500–$10,000 ... | 9,009 | 8.42 |
| $10,000–$12,500 .. | 8,373 | 7.82 |
| $12,500–$15,000 .. | 7,789 | 7.28 |
| $15,000–$20,000 .. | 14,997 | 14.01 |
| $20,000–$25,000 .. | 11,464 | 10.71 |
| $25,000–$30,000 .. | 8,476 | 7.92 |
| $30,000–$40,000 .. | 9,540 | 8.91 |
| $40,000 plus ...... | 7,838 | 7.32 |
| Total returns no. .... | 107,021 | 100.0 |
| Total inc., $000 ...... | 1,911,711 | |
| Average income $ ... | 17,863 | |
| Total tax, $000 ...... | 201,970 | |
| Average tax, $ ...... | 2,637 | |

## COMMUNITY NEWSPAPER(S)
See Quebec, CMA.

## OCCUPATIONS BY MAJOR GROUPS

| 1981 Census: | Male | Female |
|---|---|---|
| | —000— | |
| All occupations ..... | 43.3 | 33.8 |
| Managerial etc. ...... | 4.9 | 1.7 |
| Teaching .......... | 1.7 | 2.0 |
| Health ............ | 1.2 | 3.7 |
| Technological social & relig. ..... | 4.7 | 2.6 |
| Clerical ........... | 5.5 | 14.1 |
| Sales ............. | 4.1 | 2.4 |
| Service ........... | 7.1 | 5.4 |
| Primary ........... | 6 | — |
| Processing ........ | 1.4 | 4 |
| Fab. & repair ....... | 4.1 | 9 |
| Construction ....... | 3.2 | — |
| Transport ......... | 2.9 | — |
| Other ............ | 2.0 | .6 |

# Sainte-Foy, V

In census division Québec.

N.B.: *Information marked * is based on boundaries revised in 1986; all other information is based on 1981 boundaries.*

## POPULATION

| | |
|---|---|
| 1981 Census Total ........ | 68,883 |
| 1981 Census, Adjusted Total ........... | 68,889 |

| 1986 Census: * | |
|---|---|
| Total ................. | 69,615 |
| Male .................. | 32,675 |
| Female ................ | 36,940 |

| Age groups. | Male | Female |
|---|---|---|
| Under 4 .......... | 1,585 | 1,490 |
| 5–9 ............. | 1,910 | 1,820 |
| 10–14 ........... | 2,060 | 1,985 |
| 15–19 ........... | 2,650 | 2,730 |
| 20–24 ........... | 4,150 | 4,750 |
| 25-29 ........... | 3,810 | 3,785 |
| 30-34 ........... | 2,765 | 3,165 |
| 35–39 ........... | 2,335 | 2,645 |
| 40–44 ........... | 2,125 | 2,740 |
| 45–49 ........... | 1,800 | 2,285 |
| 50–54 ........... | 1,900 | 2,200 |
| 55-59 ........... | 1,750 | 2,080 |
| 60–64 ........... | 1,445 | 1,775 |
| 65–69 ........... | 1,050 | 1,305 |
| 70–74 ........... | 705 | 930 |
| 75 + ............. | 635 | 1,065 |

## MARITAL STATUS*
1986 Census:
(age 15 +)

| | |
|---|---|
| Single (never married) ....... | 20,690 |
| Married (incl. sep.) .......... | 32,925 |
| Widowed ................. | 2,720 |
| Divorced ................. | 2,425 |

## MOTHER TONGUE*

| | 1986 Census | % Total |
|---|---|---|
| English ........... | 2,035 | 2.9 |
| French ........... | 64,435 | 92.6 |
| Other ............ | 3,145 | 4.5 |

## HOUSING*
1986 Census:
Occu. Priv. Dwellings

| | |
|---|---|
| Total ................. | 27,355 |
| Owned ................ | 12,835 |
| Rented ............... | 14,520 |

## EXHIBIT 2 (cont'd)

| | |
|---|---|
| Single detached . . . . . . . . . . . | 9,835 |
| Apart., 5 or more storeys . . . . . | 2,925 |
| Movable dwellings . . . . . . . . . | 20 |
| Other dwellings . . . . . . . . . . . | 14,580 |

### PRIVATE HOUSEHOLDS*
**1986 Census:**

| | |
|---|---|
| Private Households, Total . . . . . | 27,355 |
| Pop in private | |
| households . . . . . . . . . . . . . | 68,675 |
| Aver. no. per household . . . . | 2.5 |

### FAMILIES*
**1986 Census:**

| | |
|---|---|
| Families in Private | |
| Households, Total . . . . . . . . . | 18,525 |
| Husband-wife families . . . . . . | 15,545 |
| Lone-parent families . . . . . . . | 2,980 |
| Aver. no. persons per family . . . | 3.0 |
| Aver. no. children per family . . . | 1.2 |

### LEVEL OF SCHOOLING

| | 1981 Census |
|---|---|
| Population | |
| 15 years + . . . . . . . . . . . . . | 56,550 |
| Less than Grade 9 . . . . . . . . . | 5,155 |
| Grades 9–13 . . . . . . . . . . . . . | 16,865 |
| Trades certificate | |
| or diploma . . . . . . . . . . . . | 1,625 |
| Other non-university | |
| with certificate . . . . . . . . . . | 10,010 |
| University degree . . . . . . . . . . | 11,205 |

Note — Level of Schooling refers to the highest grade or year completed by the person. Those currently enrolled reported their present grade or year.

### LABOR FORCE
**1981 Census**

| | |
|---|---|
| Males: | |
| In the labor force . . . . . . . . . | 20,995 |
| Employed . . . . . . . . . . . . . | 19,120 |
| Not in labor force . . . . . . . . | 5,100 |
| Participation rate: | |
| 15–24 years . . . . . . . . . . . | 66.3 |
| 25 years + . . . . . . . . . . . | 86.6 |
| Females: | |
| In the labor force . . . . . . . . . | 17,770 |
| Employed . . . . . . . . . . . . . | 15,475 |
| Not in labor force . . . . . . . . | 12,690 |
| Participation rate, | |
| 16–24 years . . . . . . . . . . . | 65.6 |
| 25 years + . . . . . . . . . . . | 55.4 |

### HOMES BUILT

| | 1986 | 1985 | 1984 |
|---|---|---|---|
| No. . . . . . . . . . | 1,147 | 504 | 698 |

### INCOME
**1981 Census**

| | |
|---|---|
| Average total income: | $ |
| Male . . . . . . . . . . . . . . . . | 20,592 |
| Female . . . . . . . . . . . . . . . | 10,304 |
| Average employment income: | |
| Male . . . . . . . . . . . . . . . . | 20,242 |
| Female . . . . . . . . . . . . . . . | 11,084 |
| Average census family | |
| Income . . . . . . . . . . . . . . . | 33,424 |
| Average household | |
| income . . . . . . . . . . . . . . . | 28,698 |

### BUILDING PERMITS

| | 1986 | 1985 | 1984 |
|---|---|---|---|
| | | —$000— | |
| Value . . . | 117,966 | 99,556 | 47,120 |

### MANUFACTURING INDUSTRIES

| | 1984 | 1979 |
|---|---|---|
| Plants . . . . . . . . . . . . | 73 | 64 |
| Employees . . . . . . . . | 1,260 | 1,133 |
| | —$000— | |
| Salaries, | | |
| wages . . . . . . . . . . | 27,349 | 15,247 |
| Mfg. | | |
| materials, | | |
| cost | 65,820 | 37,261 |
| Mfg. ship- | | |
| ments, value . . . . . . | 123,517 | 66,888 |
| Total value | | |
| added | 59,648 | 30,057 |

### COMMUNITY NEWSPAPER(S)
See Québec, CMA.

### OCCUPATIONS BY MAJOR GROUPS

| **1981 Census:** | Male | Female |
|---|---|---|
| | —000— | |
| All occupations . . . . . | 20.5 | 17.2 |
| Managerial etc. . . . . . | 4.3 | 1.2 |
| Teaching . . . . . . . . . . | 1.4 | 1.4 |
| Health . . . . . . . . . . . | .8 | 2.4 |
| Technological | | |
| social & relig. . . . . . | 3.6 | 1.7 |
| Clerical . . . . . . . . . . | 1.8 | 6.6 |
| Sales . . . . . . . . . . . . | 2.3 | 1.6 |
| Service . . . . . . . . . . | 2.3 | 1.8 |
| Primary . . . . . . . . . . | .3 | .1 |
| Processing . . . . . . . . | .3 | .1 |
| Fab. & repair . . . . . . | 1.1 | .2 |
| Construction . . . . . . . | .9 | —— |
| Transport . . . . . . . . . | .7 | —— |
| Other . . . . . . . . . . . | .7 | .1 |

# Charlesbourg, V

*In census division Québec.*

**N.B.:** *Information marked * is based on boundaries revised in 1986; all other information is based on 1981 boundaries.*

### POPULATION

| | |
|---|---|
| 1981 Census Total . . . . . . . . | 68,326 |
| 1981 Census: | |
| Adjusted Total . . . . . . . . . . | 68,320 |

| | | |
|---|---|---|
| 1986 Census * | | |
| Total . . . . . . . . . . . . . . . . | 68,995 | |
| Male . . . . . . . . . . . . . . . . | 33,555 | |
| Female . . . . . . . . . . . . . . . | 35,440 | |
| Age groups: | Male | Female |
| Under 4 . . . . . . . . . . | 1,985 | 1,855 |
| 5–9 . . . . . . . . . . | 2,450 | 2,330 |
| 10–14 . . . . . . . . . . | 2,640 | 2,530 |
| 15–19 . . . . . . . . . . | 2,975 | 2,895 |
| 20–24 . . . . . . . . . . | 3,295 | 3,190 |
| 25–29 . . . . . . . . . . | 2,930 | 3,010 |
| 30–34 . . . . . . . . . . | 2,665 | 3,010 |
| 35–39 . . . . . . . . . . | 2,850 | 3,110 |
| 40–44 . . . . . . . . . . | 2,780 | 3,145 |
| 45–49 . . . . . . . . . . | 2,245 | 2,295 |
| 50–54 . . . . . . . . . . | 1,995 | 2,055 |
| 55–59 . . . . . . . . . . | 1,655 | 1,740 |
| 60–64 . . . . . . . . . . | 1,230 | 1,380 |
| 65–69 . . . . . . . . . . | 835 | 1,090 |
| 70–74 . . . . . . . . . . | 540 | 850 |
| 75+ . . . . . . . . . . | 495 | 940 |

### MARITAL STATUS*
**1986 Census:**
(age 15+)

| | |
|---|---|
| Single (never married) . . . . . . . | 16,425 |
| Married (incl. sep.) . . . . . . . . . | 34,445 |
| Widowed . . . . . . . . . . . . . . . | 2,485 |
| Divorced . . . . . . . . . . . . . . . | 1,845 |

### MOTHER TONGUE*

| | 1986 | % |
|---|---|---|
| | Census | Total |
| English . . . . . . . . . . | 695 | 1.0 |
| French . . . . . . . . . . | 66,625 | 96.6 |
| Other . . . . . . . . . . . | 1,680 | 2.4 |

### HOUSING*
**1986 Census:**

| | |
|---|---|
| Occu. Priv. Dwellings, Total . . . | 23,370 |
| Owned . . . . . . . . . . . . . . . . | 14,655 |
| Rented . . . . . . . . . . . . . . . | 8,720 |
| Single detached . . . . . . . . . . . | 12,865 |
| Apart., 5 or more storeys . . . . . | 1,095 |
| Movable dwellings . . . . . . . . . | 60 |
| Other dwellings . . . . . . . . . . . | 9,370 |

### LEVEL OF SCHOOLING

| | 1981 Census |
|---|---|
| Population, | |
| 15 years + . . . . . . . . . . . . . | 51,915 |
| Less than Grade 9 . . . . . . . . . | 8,900 |
| Grades 9–13 . . . . . . . . . . . . . | 20,595 |

| Trades certificate or diploma | 2,215 |
| Other non-university, with certificate | 8,290 |
| University degree | 4,395 |

Note — Level of Schooling refers to the highest grade or year completed by the person. Those currently enrolled reported their present grade or year.

**INCOME**
**1981 Census**

| Average total income: | $ |
| Male | 18,445 |
| Female | 9,129 |

| Average employment income: | |
| Male | 18,757 |
| Female | 10,267 |
| Average census family income | 29,027 |
| Average household income | 27,651 |

## SIMONS' STRATEGY

Peter Simons described Simons' strategy as follows:

First of all we are a junior department store dealing medium volumes. We don't compete on a price basis with merchandisers and we can't compete in exclusivity and personalized service either. Although we want to be first in fashion, this has to be clarified. In terms of first in fashion it would have to be defined in a merchandising sense and this means testing articles of clothing in each classification in order to identify fashion cycles early on. When these cycles are identified the merchandiser tries to coordinate his assortments and his selection in order to maximize the sales and profit potential of this particular cycle which represents a consumer desire. I would say that the goal of the whole game, if you would like to look at it that way, is to try to develop a monopoly in a fashion cycle because this is where there is no price cutting, there are no limitations on the profit that can be made in the cycle. A monopoly can be developed by ordering large quantities and tying up a certain resource. A monopoly early on is often developed simply by being the first one to identify the trend and to offer it to the customer. A monopoly can be developed simply by default because you identify the trend earlier and you stick with it when others think it has terminated. So the whole game is to identify and to try as much as possible to develop a monopoly. However, the majority of trends I would say are hardly monopolistic. This is the ideal. Instead, you identify the fashion trend, so does everyone else, and you try to merchandise your assortments and your selection and the amount of money invested in that sort of merchandise so as not to be caught at the end with a lot of merchandise that the customer no longer wants. I would say our key strength is our merchandising philosophy. It's a philosophy based on this theory of merchandising that I just outlined. It's also a philosophy based on very much paying attention to what the customer wants and identifying her needs and then fulfilling those needs. It's a volume philosophy because we feel that each purchase is a vote for what the customer wants and we try to follow her as closely as possible and fulfil her needs as closely as we can.

Our second strength is really that we have a scientific approach to merchandising. As much as possible we try to eliminate the chance in selecting merchandise and following fashion trends. We do this using a complex inventory control system and we reduce fashion trends down to very basic statistical analysis and sales forecasting. This is successful because, although a lot of people don't see it this way, buying fashion merchandise in part is an art and it depends on taste, but another part depends on being organized and scientifically numerically aware of where your customer is and what her wants are.

Our third strength is certainly that we can compete with the mass merchandisers in the major department stores in Canada because we are focussed on a geographical niche in the country. Quebecers are very unique in their tastes and their acceptance of fashion and we service this market whereas the majors service all sorts of different markets. The market out east and the market in the far west are extremely different. Even Ontario and Quebec are very, very different. Inside this geographical niche we service a customer niche which is the development of our brand name such as TWIK which gives us added strength, even more focus in the Quebec City market.

The fourth strength is obviously our computer control program where we're exclusive owners of a certain type of retail program that we developed with IBM that allows us to know what our customer is purchasing. I can find out every day exactly what I've sold and track every sku in all my departments and believe me there's tens of thousands of sku's.

I think a fifth strength is just the fact that we're very mobile. Although we're not as big as the major chains, we are large enough to support the overhead involved in sourcing worldwide, be it in the Orient directly, or in Europe, or in developing other markets such as India, Madagascar, Mauritius, and Taiwan. Due to smart moves in the past we also have taken control of key retailing locations in the city that are all on long-term leases.

In general, I would say that we pride ourselves on being alert merchants that are tuned in to what our customers want and we make our living by giving them the things that they desire, and not by trying to teach them about fashion and not by getting our egos too inflated. We're merchants. We're there to provide the right product, the right value at the right time and at the right place. And if you start thinking that you're anything more than that, that's when trouble starts.

## TARGET MARKETS AND THE SIMONS OFFER

Simons carried merchandise at higher level price points than some of its competitors, but did not compete at the highest level price points in the market. Several well-known designer names were offered as well as a significant number of private labels. La Maison Simons was divided into four main departments and several smaller service departments:

1.  Linens and Domestics—This department offered leading edge fashion, higher price point items in linens and domestics of good quality.

2.  Junior Misses (TWIK)—Junior Misses merchandise was targeted at women aged 18–25 who shared common attitudes toward life. According to management this woman was very active, kept in shape and looked for a bit of fun in life. She was very flexible, loved fashion and was always seeking out new trends. She may be just finishing high school or just beginning her first full-time job. She need not necessarily have an independent income. The higher end of this department was characterized by such brand names as Fiorucci, Marithe et François Girbaud, Mexx, Esprit. This department also carried the house brand name TWIK which was well known in Quebec City. The brand had become synonymous with La Maison Simons and represented fun, quality fashion at an affordable price.

3.  Contemporary—Contemporary merchandise was targeted at women 30–40. This customer was thought to be more sophisticated than the Junior Misses customer. She was confident and knew what she wanted. She still followed fashion, but was looking more for investment pieces. She may be a career woman and married but would still have her own independent income. Brand names were Calvin Klein, Anne Klein, exclusive Ralph Lauren, Perry Ellis, Giorgio Armani. Many exclusive items of clothing bearing the Simons label were also carried in this department.

4.  Men's—The target market in this department was not as focussed. Management believed the majority of customers were professionals aged 25–40. The men's department carried everything from casual wear to business suits and ski wear. The higher end of this department included brand names such as Hugo Boss, Giorgio Armani, Ralph Lauren, and Perry Ellis.

5.  Accessories—This department included gloves, handbags, belts, scarves, sunglasses and costume jewelry, and was intended to serve both the women's departments.

6.  Active Sports Wear—Simons carried ski wear in the winter and swim wear in the summer.

7.  Lingerie—This department included hosiery, sleep wear and undergarments. La Maison Simons had one of the largest programs for house brand underwear in the country. Most of the hosiery carried bore the Simons brand name.

## SERVICE

La Maison Simons offered a lifetime guarantee on all its products. All items could be returned: no exceptions and no questions asked. For example, if a pair of pants were returned three years later because the zipper had broken, the customer would receive a full refund. The company also offered its own credit card with interest rates lower than that of other major department stores.

Sales staff were paid a straight salary. Management believed sales staff were attentive and helpful, but not overly so. Management believed this was appropriate because their customers wanted to browse and try out new fashions without a lot of sales pressure.

## ORGANIZATION

Donald Simons, great-grandson of the founder, was the President of La Maison Simons. He had earned a reputation as an excellent merchandiser and was responsible for successfully refocusing Simons' strategy on high quality fashion clothing in the 1950's. In 1988, Donald Simons still included merchandising for the Men's and the Linens and Domestics departments as part of his direct concerns. Reporting to him were the managers of Advertising and Publicity, Accounting and Personnel, as well as two other managers in charge of Merchandising: Peter Simons and David Simons. David was responsible for the Contemporary, Lingerie and Accessories departments. Peter was responsible for the Junior Misses (including TWIK) and Active Sports Wear departments.

Peter was also responsible for starting up "The Studio". This was a small manufacturing facility located in the same building as the old store. The Studio produced small runs of fashionable clothing that Simons' buyers could not find elsewhere.

## ADVERTISING AND PROMOTION

The majority of La Maison Simons advertising budget of approximately $750,000 was spent on print ads in Le Soleil, one of Quebec City's daily newspapers as well as on the Graphics Department, staff salaries, equipment and so on. The person in charge of the Graphics Department was a woman artist who was well-known in North America. In 1987, she won an award for the best color newspaper ad in Canada. Simons placed black and white or color ads on the second page of Le Soleil every day. Management believed this enabled Simons' customers to know where to look for the firm's advertising, easily recognizing the familiar Simons' logo and layout. Each department had its particular advertising style and place in the weekly slot. For example, Junior Misses (including TWIK) was usually featured on Fridays and its ads promoted a very young, energetic style as shown in Exhibit 3. Junior Misses (including TWIK) had approximately 25 percent of the total advertising budget spent on space in Le Soleil for the year. For the Spring season of three months, Junior Misses (including TWIK) would have approximately 25 percent of their year's budget. Peter Simons elaborated on the advertising policy as follows:

Our advertising policy is I would say quite liberal. Certainly expenses have to be controlled and we aim for a certain percentage of sales to be spent on advertising.

However, if you can show your merchandise manager that you have a good product, a good value to show, and that in advertising it you both believe that you can quadruple or sell 10 times as much in the two weeks following the ad, it certainly becomes a profitable venture to spend the money on the advertising. In such a situation, the gross contribution from increased sales due to advertising would more than cover the cost of the ad. Therefore, although we may have a fixed amount of space, we're always flexible and if there are problems or good products that we want to advertise, we will make space.

I would characterize our advertising philosophy as very pragmatic. Every ad is monitored by a computer-generated report that looks at volume three weeks prior to the ad and two weeks after. And then the increase in volume due to the ad is gauged. Here's an example. Let's assume it's 100 units above the pace that we were selling the three weeks prior to the ad. Therefore, two weeks after the ad we've sold 200 units assuming a gross contribution of $25 that would be a $5,000 increase in gross contribution and that is how the ad is evaluated. Our advertising philosophy is pragmatic because we tend to put money where we feel the potential is and we evaluate the potential of an article by its sales prior to advertising. So, it just means that if something is selling well, it probably means that people have seen it and passed by that item and have like it, and because some people have liked it probably more people will like it. In the past we have tended to select items that have had proven sales ability before being advertised. My buyers and I wonder sometimes about this approach because although it seems a profitable way to advertise, we feel that it is also difficult to fit image advertising and fashion advertising into the success criteria.

We have standard layouts for our newspaper ads that are never changed dramatically [as shown in Exhibit 4]. They evolve very slowly so that the customer can always recognize them. There are no major changes. The layout represents the image of

the department and the image in the newspaper and to change this dramatically would just cause confusion on the part of the customer. We are well known for our color ads.

The cost of the ad obviously depends on its size. In black and white, Junior Misses/TWIK format A is $1,251, format B is $2,002, format C is $500, format D is $334, and format E, like format B, is $2,002. Color is available in ad sizes of 600 lines or more, and adds about $1,500 in color separation and 4-color printing costs to the space cost. Advertising expenditures are not charged directly to the department, but an ad is evaluated by a number of

EXHIBIT 3
TWIK
Advertising

droites.
à fronces,
à plis...

## les jupes courtes

c'est la saison court-circuit... twik pense court, twik coupe court, twik rit court... ses jupes sont définitivement au-dessus du genou et dévoilent des jambes bien galbees dans des collants opaques, noirs de préférence.

à droite: la jupe courte à larges plis creux cousus de la taille aux hanches, en lainage prince-degalles noir et blanc ou noir et brun. 5 à 13. 50.00

au centre: la jupe courte en velours cotelé, emplacement froncé à la taille, boutonnage au devant. noir, cannelle, taupe, vert. 5 à 13. 58.00

à droite: la jupe courte et droite en jersey de coton, taille extensible. noir, manne, vert foncé. p.m.g. 36.00

la maison
⊘ simons

TROIS MAGASINS...   PLACE STE-FOY,   GALERIES DE LA CAPITALE

*Exhibit 3 (cont'd)*

merchandise managers and the profitability of the ad reflects on the buyer's ability to do her job and to spend her advertising money appropriately.*

In addition to print ads, some of the advertising budget was used on a limited direct mail campaign to credit card holders.

## THE MERCHANDISING FUNCTION

Merchandising was done on a classification basis. Each department was divided into demand centres. For example, TWIK was divided into sweaters, sports wear (including blouses, shirts, pants and jackets), dresses and coats, and

---

*The space on a newspaper page is defined horizontally by "columns" and vertically by "agate lines", or lines for short. The page size of the Quebec City *Le Soleil* was 9 columns wide by 300 lines high. There are 14 agate lines per inch (25.4 mm). Column width can vary. Each of the *Le Soleil* columns was 1½ inches (38.1 mm) wide. Thus each page contained 2,700 (300 × 9) lines. The sizes of the ads in Exhibit 4 are described in lines and columns. "A" is 225 lines by 4 columns wide, or 900 lines or ⅓ of a page in size. At $1.39 per line, that's $1,251.

*Exhibit 3 (cont'd)*

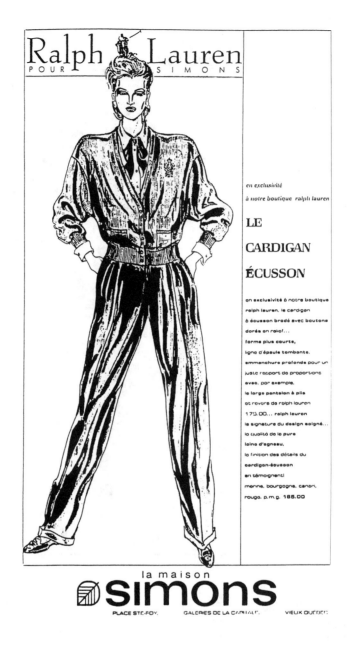

active sports wear. Each buyer was responsible for certain classifications. Budgets were drawn up for each of the classifications and buyers developed their buying schedules within these constraints. The buyer took into account several factors when determining the merchandise mix for the upcoming season. Peter Simons explained as follows:

We focus on past successes and we use these past successes to guide our purchases. We feel these past successes represent viable fashion trends that can continue to be exploited sometimes from season to season. After repeating the best items we always try to return to our best suppliers. We feel that long term loyalty has its benefits. For a good department there's so many suppliers out there that you have to merchandise your suppliers before

*Exhibit 3 (cont'd)*

you merchandise your items. If not, you would be doing business with hundreds of people and it would be impossible to control you sku's in a profitable manner. And only thirdly then after repeating the best items and sticking with the best suppliers do we go out and really search for new fashion impact such as those things that were successful in Europe and New York. Fourth, after the initial placement which is for tests, we save our money to repeat items. Repeats are money spent to

buy more of the things that the customers are purchasing.

The buyer prepared an initial buying plan. This included an allowance for changes as the season progressed. Once this plan was confirmed, the buyer would begin to place orders. Most often, she would have to make changes to her plan due to lack of availability with manufacturers.

*Exhibit 4*

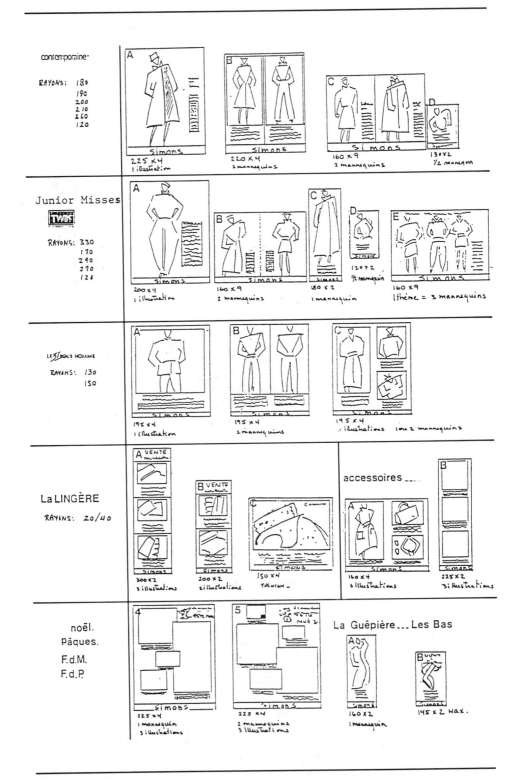

## PETER SIMONS

In 1986, Peter Simons had graduated from The University of Western Ontario with an Honours degree in Business Administration (HBA). Although he had received several job offers upon graduation, he decided to enter the family business. As Merchandising Manager for the TWIK and Active Sports Wear departments, Mr. Simons found his job both hectic and challenging.

When Mr. Simons returned from his recent trip to Europe, he was very excited about the fashions he had seen in the showrooms and in the stores. He was certain that the spring line that he had ordered would be very successful with his TWIK customers. His main concern was that he might have hesitated too long when ordering which would mean some of his merchandise would be late in getting to the floor.

As Mr. Simons sat at his desk, tentatively sketching out an advertising schedule for March and April, he thought about the various factors that would influence his decisions and mused as follows:

> The problem is when to shift from item advertisements to fashion advertisements. It's relatively easy to evaluate the ads that are geared toward sales volumes. They either produce volume or they don't.
>
> But image is a much more nebulous affair and much more difficult to measure our return. I know it's important in any advertising to have some way of measuring our return. Without it we have no sense of whether our money is being spent profitably.
>
> My advertising decisions are aggravated by uncertainties about deliveries. The problem of late deliveries is quite important for us. I could go out and place my lines earlier which would please our manufacturers. However, we want to be a high-fashion retailer which means we want to place orders as close as we can get to the season. We'll have more information about certain fashion trends and a better idea about what to place and what we think will be strong next year. So it's a real balance to find between placing orders early versus waiting long enough to still have a good selection and to allow time to find the best value and to find the best items on the market. In the meantime, I have to decide what to do about our advertising.

Peter Simons was considering advertising a number of specific items which he categorized as either "mainstream" or "fashion-forward". In the mainstream category: a nautical sweater, a blouse imported directly from the Orient, a dress purchased from a direct importer from India, and a cardigan T-shirt in a range of colours which was also a direct importation from the Orient. In the fashion-forward category: a zebra skirt made in the Simons Studio, a neoprene plastic jacket made in Paris, and which was part of a collection, a fisherman knit sweater from the Orient with roses sewn on it in the Simons Studio, Bronx pants ("one size fits all") from a supplier in Montreal, and a cropped sweater.

Peter thought he might sell the nautical sweater in the hundreds of units at $43.00 with an approximate margin of 55 percent on retail price. The blouse he thought might sell in the thousands of units at $39.95 with an approximate margin of 66 percent. The dress he forecasted in the hundreds of units at $29.95 with an approximate margin of 58 percent. The cardigan T-shirt he expected would sell in the thousands at $35.00 with an approximate margin of 60 percent. Peter explained the margin structure as follows:

> Where there are higher margins, these usually involve items where we have imported directly thus eliminating the distributor in the middle. The margin that the distributor would usually take, we take in part ourselves to finance the overhead that we occur in importing directly and we pass part of it on to the customer. This in turn allows us to give extremely good values to all our customers.

Peter elaborated on his forecasts for the fashion-forward items:

> For the zebra skirt the cost of production at The Studio is still quite expensive; therefore, the margin is approximately 50 percent and I expect sales in the 1–2 dozen unit range at $70.00. The plastic jacket is an extremely high-fashion idea which was imported from Paris. On such an item we don't even attempt to take our regular margin of approximately 50 percent so we'll aim at 30 percent. We are really just trying to convey an idea and entertain the client, not make money. I estimate we'll

sell 1–10 of these at $350.00. As for the sweater with the roses on it produced at The Studio, applying the roses was at minimal cost and again here we have our higher margin due to direct importation.

So, I estimate sales in the hundreds of units at $29.95 with a margin of about 66 percent. We have an exclusive on the Bronx pants but we have to go with the margin determined by the supplier and ourselves when we negotiated our terms of doing business with him. That was 50 percent. I guess we'll sell in the hundreds of units for this item at $65.00. Finally, the cropped sweaters should sell in the 10–100 range at $75.00 with an approximate margin of 50 percent.

Peter Simons knew that he would have to coordinate any new TWIK advertising with the themes run in previous ads. Last year, Mr. Simons had decided to convey fashion statements to his TWIK customers in the initial ads. As the season continued, he had placed more emphasis on items that were big sellers rather than making fashion statements. If he repeated this formula, he would have to decide when to make the shift and which items to promote when. (Easter would be April 3rd and the store would be closed Good Friday.) In selecting the items, Mr. Simons would have to decide which items would have the most incremental sales potential. In addition, Mr. Simons was given the option to run several of his ads in color. Which ads should those be and what type of message did he want to convey?

---

# C A S E 3.8  Stewart Shoes

Founded in 1953, Stewart Shoes had grown to six similar sized outlets by 1990, headquartered in Nova Scotia. For the past year, management had been debating the value of money being spent on advertising and promotion.

"I'm convinced we should simply stop advertising altogether," said Malcolm Gibbings, the Controller. "We're facing tough times and all that money could simply go to the bottom line. John hasn't shown us that it really pays for itself."

"Well, I don't known how I can convince you Malcolm," said John Andrews, the Marketing Manager, "but I can't imagine maintaining our presence in our markets without advertising. Our major competitors all advertise about the same percentage of sales that we do as best we can figure out. And how would our customers ever learn about our special sales? No, we shouldn't cut advertising, we should increase it by 50 percent."

"That's a lot more money, about $285,000 if I'm not mistaken," said Lynn Graham, Manager of Stores. "Why not put more of our emphasis on direct mail efforts or even just do a better job with our in-store signs and displays? We've got 53,000 names on our total mailing list across all stores now. It's pretty evenly divided across the stores. We could mail to them for a lot less than we spend on advertising and probably have a bigger sales impact. It costs us about $.65 to send a simple letter to each person. And our in-store merchandising can be done for about $28,000 per event, about $10,000 in production and $3,000 per store to implement."

"I'm tired of this disagreement," said Janet Stewart, President. "It's time we resolved this. We've got our Father's Day event coming up in six weeks and there's a couple of items we were going to promote heavily. Then there's the Canada Day sale a little after that. Let's try some testing of these ideas around these two week-long events to find out just which way is best for us to spend our advertising, direct mail and merchandising dollars. Now, I know that none of our store managers or buyers will want less than a total ad and promo effort for their area, but I think we can convince them if we have a good test design. We had originally set aside $40,000 for advertising and $28,000 for merchandising in total for these events. John, please design a test or two and get back to me by the end of the week."

# C A S E 3.9    Central Guaranty Trust

In April 1989, Joel Posluns, the Assistant Vice-President of Direct Marketing at Central Guaranty Trust (CGT), was contemplating how to promote CGT's Personal Line of Credit (PLC) product. He felt direct marketing would be an ideal marketing approach. Therefore, he needed to plan the campaign details to support his concept in time for a scheduled launch date of August 1989. The August launch date was crucial. If the campaign were delayed, the increased PLC sales would not be reflected in the 1989 statements. Also, the end of October was traditionally a busy period for the branches due to Canada Savings Bond sales; therefore, if the branches were required to help with campaign, their role would be limited during the late fall.

## THE FINANCIAL SERVICES INDUSTRY IN CANADA

As of 1989, the Canadian financial services industry was composed of "the four pillars," namely, banks, trust companies, insurance companies and investment dealers. Deregulation had blurred the distinction between these institutions. Also, there was a trend towards "financial supermarkets," whereby institutions were being allowed to offer financial products which they were previously restricted from selling. For example, most of the major banks had formed alliances with large investment dealers and were selling brokerage services through their branch network.

CGT's competition was primarily the major chartered banks—Toronto Dominion, Scotia-Bank, Bank of Montreal, Canadian Imperial Bank of Commerce and Royal Bank—as well as the two major trust companies—Royal Trust and Canada Trust. These financial institutions competed in both the corporate and retail (individuals) markets. All of these competitors offered a similar retail product line which typically included:

1. Deposit Products:
   — chequing and savings accounts
   — short term deposits—Guaranteed Investment Certificates, Canada Savings Bonds, term deposits and T-bill accounts
   — Registered Retirement Savings Plans (RRSP's) and Registered Retirement Income Funds (RRIF's)

2. Lending Products:
   — credit cards
   — Personal Line of Credit (PLC)
   — various types of loans (for car purchases etc.)
   — mortgages

Trust companies were governed by the Trust and Loan Companies Act while banks were governed by the Bank Act. This distinction had encouraged banks to offer a broader range of products, particularly to the corporate market which they traditionally had dominated, although banks were not allowed to offer fiduciary (i.e. trust) products. The major banks were significantly larger than the trust companies in terms of their branch network size, the number of employees and sales. In the 1980's many of the major banks began to focus more upon marketing issues, but many observers believed they still lagged behind the trust companies, who had responded to the changing market by extending their hours of operation and running numerous promotions to attract new customers.

## BACKGROUND OF CENTRAL GUARANTY

The Central Guaranty Trust Company was officially formed December 31, 1988, with the amalgamation of Central Trust, Guaranty Trust, Yorkshire Trust and Nova Scotia Savings and Loan, with Financial Trust added on December 31, 1989. The company was based in Halifax and Toronto. Its mission statement was to provide "consistently impressive customer service". In terms of size, CGT had 183 branches, the second largest network of retail branches of any trust company with only Canada Trust being larger with 531 branches. Joel commented on CGT's rapid growth:

> In the last two years Central Capital bought up so many companies that we now have $26 billion in assets in insurance companies, trust operations, mortgage holding companies and fund management companies and just under the legal limit of 10 percent of publicly owned companies in the United States.

There were aggressive plans for further short run expansion through internal growth and through acquisitions.

## DIRECT MARKETING DEPARTMENT (DMD) AT CGT

Traditionally, CGT branches had been oriented towards taking orders, as opposed to cross-selling products. According to Joel, "The branches do not view sales as part of their job, whereas in direct marketing, our whole mandate is to sell and cross-sell". The organizational culture of the branches was shifting slowly towards a more proactive approach, but many CGT staff felt it could be an evolutionary process, with changes in compensation, career paths and job descriptions necessary for reinforcement. In Joel's opinion, the attitude and motivation of people in CGT's branches varied widely depending upon the location (rural vs. urban, east and west coast vs. central Canada), the branch history (particularly which predecessor company it originated from) and the goals of the individual branch manager. In contrast, some of the branch managers resented the formation of the DMD as they viewed product sales and service as their exclusive mandate.

In Joel's view, the branches operated like a batch shop, selling a mix of products and performing various administrative duties. In contrast, the DMD operated like an assembly line, focusing on sales of one product at a time and performing less administrative functions overall.

Central Guaranty's DMD was formed in early 1988 by Denis Nixon, the Executive Vice-President of Marketing. He strongly believed that direct marketing was a vital way in which CGT's geographic and product coverage of the financial marketplace could be expanded. Expansion via construction of new branches was becoming increasingly expensive and many of the prime locations had already been taken. Direct marketing allowed CGT to solidify relationships with current customers (helping to prevent them from migrating to competitors) and allowed CGT to cross-sell products and services thus increasing CGT's share of its customers' business. CGT spent approximately $2.5 million to establish the DMD.

Joel Posluns was first extensively exposed to direct marketing in 1983, when as the Manager of Advertising and Merchandising at Xerox Canada, he had been responsible for developing an alternative distribution network for the Commercial Markets Division. After leaving Xerox in 1985, he became the Director of Marketing Services for a major direct marketing service bureau which developed comprehensive direct marketing programs for such clients as Nissan, Ford, Chrysler, American Express and ScotiaBank.

Joel Posluns was recruited to head CGT's DMD in 1988. By mid-1989, the department had grown to 30 people (see Exhibit 1). The DMD was organized into three functional areas: telemarketing, production, and database management. The DMD worked closely with product managers in the Retail Marketing Department but typically, the DMD took a very pro-active approach to designing campaigns (see Exhibit 2). The implementation of any direct marketing campaign was solely the responsibility of the DMD. Previous campaign information is shown in Exhibit 3. Development and implementation of any campaign could include the following steps:

- develop campaign concept and objectives
- preliminary data analysis
- telemarketing script development
- systems work for telemarketing script

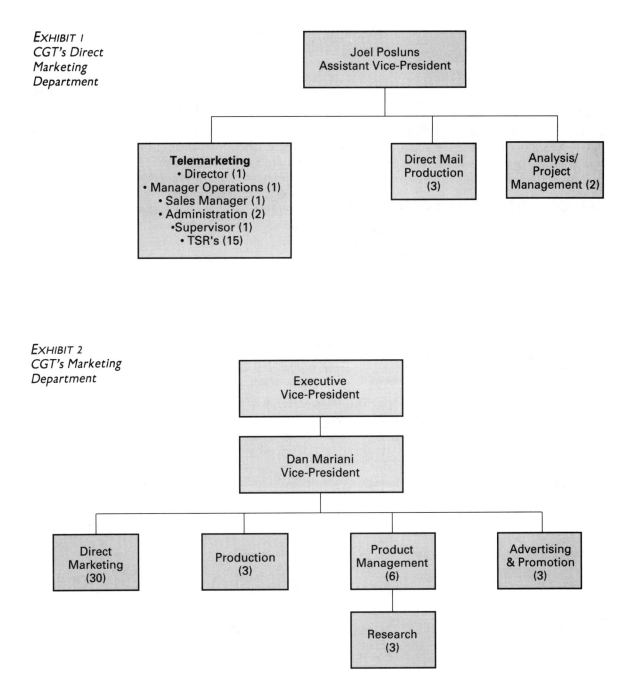

*EXHIBIT 1*
*CGT's Direct Marketing Department*

Joel Posluns
Assistant Vice-President

**Telemarketing**
• Director (1)
• Manager Operations (1)
• Sales Manager (1)
• Administration (2)
•Supervisor (1)
• TSR's (15)

Direct Mail Production (3)

Analysis/ Project Management (2)

*EXHIBIT 2*
*CGT's Marketing Department*

Executive Vice-President

Dan Mariani Vice-President

Direct Marketing (30)

Production (3)

Product Management (6)

Advertising & Promotion (3)

Research (3)

- test script using live data
- design creative and copy for mail piece
- develop fulfilment process
- produce mail piece

- select lettershop to insert information into envelopes, sort envelopes etc.
- design tracking format and internal reports
- final sign-off

- communicate campaign details to branches
- Telemarketing Service Representatives (TSR) training
- drop mail piece (outbound)
- implement fulfilment process

Each of the steps included several more levels of detail. A sample of a portion of a campaign timeline is shown in Exhibit 4. The next part of this case describes some of these steps in more detail.

## THE FORMATION OF THE CGT DATABASE

A marketing database serves as the engine for database marketing. It is an organized collection of data about individual customers and prospects that is accessible and actionable for the purposes of selling. Database marketing, then, is the process by which information in the marketing database is used to match products and services to the needs and wants of individual customers and prospects.[1]

Joel's first priority was to create and maintain a state-of-the-art marketing database or Marketing Information File (MIF) before any actual campaigns could be implemented. The MIF was used to fulfil the marketing goals of customer retention, activation, upgrading, cross-selling and acquiring. The MIF included extensive customer and product information which was up-

*Exhibit 3*
*CGT Direct*
*Response Campaigns*

| Product | Date | Outbound | Inbound | List | Offer | Results |
|---------|------|----------|---------|------|-------|---------|
| Term Deposits | Sept/Oct 1988 | Direct Mail Telemarketing | N/A | CGT Fee-Cutter customers | quarter point bonus | Incremental $23 million in outstanding deposits |
| RRSP's | Jan/Feb 1989 | Direct Mail Telemarketing | N/A | CGT customers without RRSP's | quarter point bonus | Incremental $12 million in outstanding deposits |
| Money Market Fund | Spring 1989 | Direct Mail | N/A | CGT Fee-Cutter customers | free video on investments | Fund increased by approx. $45 million without additional marketing support |
| Fee-Cutter | Spring 1989 | Direct Mail | N/A | National white pages list (external list) | free rosewood pen | Incremental $1 million in outstanding balances (did not break even) |
| Term Deposits | Summer 1989 | Direct Mail | N/A | Regional white pages list (external list) | quarter point bonus | Incremental $2 million in outstanding balances (break even) |
| Mortgages | Fall 1989 evenings only | Direct Mail Telemarketing | N/A | Non-CGT mortgage renewals (external list) | 60 day rate guarantee | Objective is incremental $15–$18 million in outstanding balances |

[1] *Canadian Direct Marketing News,* May 1989.

EXHIBIT 4
Campaign Timeline
Sample

**Schedule Name: DIRECT MARKETING - RRIF PROGRAM**
**Responsible    :**
**As-of Date      : 5-Jun-89  4:00pm    Schedule File: C:\USR\TL3\RRIF**

| Task Name | Resources |
|---|---|
| BUSINESS CASE | |
| Project Outline | JP |
| Reports: #, Distr., Content | MM, SL |
| Schematic | SL |
| MEETING WITH CLIENT | CL, DM |
| DATA ANALYSIS | |
| Input Format | HS |
| Data Flow/Capture | SL |
| Output | |
| Reports: Dist., #, Content | SL, HS, MM |
| Variable copy data | MS, MM |
| Output Layout | SL, MM |
| DEFINE EXTRACT REQUIREMENTS | HS |
| ISD PROJECT REQUIREMENTS DOC. | SL |
| PERFORM EXTRACT | |
| Develop & Compile extract prog. | ISD |
| Test program | ISD |
| Extract Data | ISD |
| Verify Extract Data | ISD |
| Forward tapes to supplier | ISD |
| PERFORM DATA WORK | ER |
| SCRIPT DEVELOPMENT | |
| Detailed Screen Design | SL |
| Client Approval | CL, TM |
| Sign-off | BO, LE, PR |
| TCS DEVELOPMENT | |
| CONSTRUCT DATA DICTIONARY | ISD |
| CONSTRUCTION OF SCRIPTS | |
| Scripting of verbage | SL |
| Routing | ISD |
| Logic/User Exits | ISD |
| Translation Tables | ISD |
| Queue Mgmt. Development | ISD |
| SET UP RND/CICS TABLES | ISD |
| RE-GEN REGION | TS |
| COMPILE SCRIPT | ISD |
| ISD TESTING | ISD |

Legend: Detail Task, Summary Task, Milestone, (Started), Conflict, (Slack), Resource delay

TIME LINE Gantt Chart Report, Strip 1

dated on a continual basis by the Customer Service Representatives (CSR's) and Telemarketing Service Representatives (TSR's), as individual customer transactions were made (see Exhibit 5). The CSR's worked in the branches and the TSR's operated in the telemarketing unit of the DMD.

In November 1988, the first version of the MIF was created for the Smooth Switch Mailings to communicate merger information with the customers of the initial four amalgamated trust companies. Since each company had numerous systems developed for their individual products and they did not interact with each other, compiling a master mailing list was a difficult task. Each system had a different file format and even within a particular company, there was no continuity of the input from branch to branch, or even employee to employee.

EXHIBIT 5
Sample MIF
Fields

Transit number
Product key
Issuing company code (Central Trust/Guaranty Trust/Yorkshire Trust/Nova Scotia Savings and Loan/Financial Trust)
Branch number
Name
Address
Home telephone number
Business telephone number
Sex
Date of birth
Social Insurance Number
Language flag (French/English)
Marital status
Account balance
Minimum monthly balance
Account accrued interest
Interest rate
Account status
Start date
Maturity date
Term
Mail flag (Yes/No depending on whether customers have asked not to receive mailings)
Deceased flag

The MIF was improved in June 1989 when unique customer identifier numbers were added to the data to facilitate campaign tracking and measurement by individual customers or households. In addition, the MIF data was supplemented with taxfiler database information purchased from StatsCan which identified the average age, income, RSP contribution and dividend and interest income received within postal walks.[2] The file did not include individual taxfiler information. In the long term, Joel intended to add data from many sources to the MIF to allow him to identify further market opportunities.

Future plans for the MIF information included housing the MIF on one desktop personal computer so that an analyst within the DMD would be able to analyze market opportunities without tying up mainframe time and systems personnel. Down the road, Joel planned to use cluster analysis to identify attributes which would help predict a customer's or household's propensity to purchase a particular product. Once target clusters had been identified, the next step would be profitability modelling of these clusters.

## THE TELEMARKETING UNIT

Joel believed CGT's telemarketing unit was extremely sophisticated as it utilized computerized scripts and tracking. In fact, the TSR's did not have any paper on their desks. Early Cloud, a telemarketing software package which CGT owned, automated the scripts and scheduled the call sequence. Early Cloud was used in the United States by Coca-Cola, Chase-Manhattan Bank, Mattel, Sears, Montgomery-Ward, and

---

[2] A postal walk is defined as one route followed by a postal carrier and typically included 200 to 400 households.

EXHIBIT 6
*Sample Early
Cloud Screens*

## Additional Information Menu

### *Objections*

PF1  Already changed address

PF2  Why did I receive X letters

PF3  Does not want to give Social Insurance Number

PF4  Does not want to give birth date

*Already Changed Address Objection Screen*

It is unfortunate, but sometimes, due to the volume of transactions that a branch must deal with, addresses are not updated as quickly as we would like. However, I would like to take this opportunity to obtain this information from you at this time and ensure you that we will make the necessary changes to our files.

*Multiple Mailings Objection Screen*

Yes Mr/Mrs (customer's name), I can understand how annoying it must be to deal with multiple mailing on the same topic. Problems arise due to keypunch errors, different registrations and clients dealing with multiple branches. Currently, we are implementing strict controls to overcome some of the problems which have led to multiple mailings. This program represents one way in which we hope to reduce the frequency of this. By providing us with one standard name and address format for all your accounts, along with your Social Insurance Number and birth date, we will be better able to reduce or eliminate the duplicate mailings that you receive.

*Does Not Want to Give Social Insurance Number Objection Screen*

Please be assured that any information given to us will be held in the strictest confidence. The reason that we are requesting your Social Insurance Number is that the federal government has passed legislation that will fine the institution if they have failed to make a reasonable effort to obtain the Social Insurance Number from the customer. Similarly, the customer will be fined if they refuse to provide their Social Insurance Number.

*Does Not Want to Give Birth Date Objection Screen*

Please be assured that any information given to us will be held in the strictest confidence. The reason that we are requesting your birth date is to help us to better determine your needs. As an example, by having your birth date on file, we will be able to exclude you from inappropriate mailings for example, you may be too young or too old for RSP information. Also, we will be able to send you literature that is more appropriate to your needs.

Allstate. CGT was the only Canadian company currently using Early Cloud. Scripts were developed in-house. Extensive lead time was required to develop the scripts because they included application forms and "objections screens" which provided the TSR's with specific information to counter potential customer objections (for example see Exhibit 6). In addition, the automatic call distributing system (ACD), which CGT had purchased as part of their PBX switching system, was capable of generating statistics on the number of calls received, the number of calls disconnected, how long it took for each call to be answered, when the calls were received, etc. Each telemarketing campaign cost CGT an average of $25,000 in line charges. On the terminals that housed the Early Cloud package, it was also possible to access CGT's electronic mail system and some product systems. In the future, all TSR's would be able to access each product system.

## THE PERSONAL LINE OF CREDIT PRODUCT

A personal line of credit was a revolving loan targeted towards individuals who had fluctuating needs and wanted easy access to credit. A personal line of credit could be used to meet a variety of needs including home renovations, investments, children's educations, purchases of major items and debt consolidation. CGT's PLC offered the following features:

- interest as low as $1/2$% over prime if secured
- interest paid just for the actual days the balance is outstanding and not charged automatically over the full month like other forms of credit
- maximum loan amount limited only by customer's repayment capability, minimum of $10,000
- one time application, subject to periodic review (see Exhibit 7)
- access by cash advance at any branch of CGT or by a cheque written to a third party
- variable interest rate

- can use any of the following as collateral security: cash, time deposit, GIC's, CSB's, stock, government and corporate bonds and real estate
- minimum monthly payment is 3% of outstanding balance or $50, whichever is greater if line is unsecured; minimum payment is interest only if line is secured
- monthly statement
- minimum withdrawal of $100
- can be used as overdraft protection for customer's CGT chequing account

CGT's product compared favourably to competitive products in general in terms of the product features; however, CGT had been a late entry into this market and thus, many customers had already purchased their PLC from another financial institution. For unsecured PLC's, other competitors offered special rates for professionals, such as, doctors who often used their PLC in effect as a business operating loan. For unsecured PLC's, CGT's rate was prime plus $1^1/2$%, whereas, other institutions offered prime or prime plus 1% to professionals (see Exhibit 8). On secured PLC's, CGT's rate was prime plus .5% versus 20.25% for a VISA card or 15.25% for a car loan. On the whole, CGT's rates were comparable to those of competitors.

From the branch's perspective, this product was easy to administer as the PLC application took approximately fifteen minutes to complete. Verifying documentation and credit checks could take up to an additional hour, depending on how complicated the customer's credit history was. The PLC product earned a spread of 75 basis points for CGT (excluding fixed costs) and the average outstanding balance was $4,000 to $5,000.

## THE PERSONAL LINE OF CREDIT CAMPAIGN

In April 1989, Dan Mariani, the Vice-President of Lending Products, and Joel Posluns felt an opportunity existed to use direct marketing as well as the branch network to launch CGT's PLC product. A market research study had been performed in March to provide direction for the PLC marketing strategy. The specific goals of the research study included:

1. To prioritize potential customer target groups

2. To compare the proportion of CGT lending customers who had a line of credit vs. lend-

ing customers of other institutions to determine if CGT customers had lower than average product usage levels

3. To measure interest levels in the product, once respondents were told about it, among specific customer target groups (i.e. Visa, loan and mortgage customers)

4. To determine whether a CGT offering would

EXHIBIT 7
PLC Application

---

**Central Guaranty Trust Company**                                    CENTRAL Ⅱ GUARANTY
**Personal Line of Credit Application**

| Unique Identifier | Branch # | Transit # | Branch Address |
|---|---|---|---|

| | | | | | | | |
|---|---|---|---|---|---|---|---|
| **M A I L I N G** | Honorific | Applicant's First Name | Applicant's Last Name | Social Insurance # | Date of Birth Y/M/D | Home Phone No. | Marital Status |
| | Honorific | Co-Applicant's First Name | Co-Applicant's Last Name | Social Insurance # | Date of Birth Y/M/D | Home Phone No. | |
| | Address | | | | | Own/Rent | |
| **A D D R E S S** | City/Town | | Province | Postal Code | Length of Residence year(s) | | No. of Dependents |
| | Previous Address (if less than three years at present address) | | | | | | |
| | City/Town | | Province | Postal Code | Length of Residence year(s) | | |

| |
|---|
| Name of Relative, Close Friend Not Living With You |
| Address of Relative, Close Friend Not Living With You |

| | | | | | |
|---|---|---|---|---|---|
| **E M P L O Y M E N T** | Applicant's Employer | Occupation | Gross Monthly Income | Business Phone No. | |
| | Employer's Address | | City/Town  Province | Postal Code year(s) | How Long year(s) |
| | Previous Employer | Occupation | Gross Monthly Income | How Long year(s) | |
| | Co-Applicant's Employer | Occupation | Gross Monthly Income | Business Phone No. | |
| | Co-Applicant's Employer's Address | | City/Town  Province | Postal Code year(s) | How Long year(s) |

VISA (CGT)  American Express  MasterCard

CGT Branch Transit Savings Account #   CGT Branch Transit Chequing Account #

| | | | | |
|---|---|---|---|---|
| **C R E D I T  R E F E R E N C E S** | Branch Name & Address | Account # | Name & Address | Account # |
| | Creditor | Purpose | Account # | Date / Present / Monthly Incurred / Balance / Payments<br>$   $<br>$   $<br>$   $ |
| | Central Guaranty Car Loan Creditor | Make & Model | Present Balance<br>$ | Monthly Payments<br>$ |

| | | | |
|---|---|---|---|
| **O T H E R  R E F E R E N C E S** | Mortgage Holder or Landlord's Address<br>Central Guaranty Trust<br>Monthly Mortgage           Mortgage Balance           Account #<br>$                    1st $        2nd $ | | **ASSETS**<br>Home, Savings,   Market<br>Vehicles,    Value<br>Investments   $<br>$<br>$<br>$<br>$ |
| | Monthly Rent      Monthly Mortgage      Mortgage Balance  Account #<br>$          $          1st $    2nd $<br><br>Name Registered in | | |

In this credit application the words you and your mean the applicant and co-applicant. We and us mean Central Guaranty Trust Company. By signing below, you are applying for a personal line of credit from us in the amount of $_____. You also affirm that the information you have given is true and complete and you have not withheld any information. We will rely on the information you have given us to decide on your application. You authorize us to obtain further information about you and check the information you have given us. We can also give information about you to credit bureaus and other credit grantors as permitted by law. Note: In British Columbia, your authorization allows information on your spouse to be included in any report even if your spouse is not the applicant.

Date _____   Applicant _____   Co-Applicant's Signature _____

**OFFICE COPY**

appeal to customers who currently had a line of credit with a competitive institution

Over 400 CGT clients and non-clients participated in the telephone survey. All respondents had either a VISA card, personal loan, mortgage or any combination thereof outstanding with either CGT or a competitive institution. In total, CGT presently had 68,000 mortgage customers, 102,000 VISA customers and 45,000 personal loans customers. Joel had reviewed the research and had selected the results which he felt would be most useful to designing and implementing a PLC campaign (see Exhibit 9).

## PLANNING THE DIRECT MARKETING CAMPAIGN FOR PLC

Joel was excited about designing and implementing a direct marketing PLC campaign as he

EXHIBIT 8
Competitive
PLC Rates

| Financial Institution | Secured | Unsecured |
|---|---|---|
| **Banks** | | |
| Bank of Montreal | 13.75 | 15.25 |
| Cdn. Imperial Bk. of Commerce | 13.50 | 15.50 |
| Royal Bank | 14.50 | 16.00 |
| Scotia Bank | 14.00 | 15.50 |
| Toronto Dominion Bank | 13.75 | 16.25 |
| **Trusts** | | |
| Canada Trust | 13.50 | 14.50 |
| Royal Trust | 13.50 | 15.25 |

EXHIBIT 9
Market Research

INCIDENCE OF LINE OF CREDIT HOLDING*

| | Type of Product Held | | | |
|---|---|---|---|---|
| | | | Loan | |
| | Visa | Mortgage | Term | Demand |
| **Customer Type** | % | % | % | % |
| CGT | 16 | 23 | ---13--- | |
| Any Trustco | 18 | 24 | 13 | 13 |
| Any Bank | 14 | 21 | 9 | 9 |
| Total market | 14 | 22 | 8 | 9 |

*Data via Market Facts' Household Flow of Funds 1988

AWARENESS OF LINE OF CREDIT PRODUCT

| | Total |
|---|---|
| **Total respondents** (100%) | 400 |
| | % |
| **Not aware** | 24 |
| **Aware** | 76 |
| Very familiar with | 18 |
| Somewhat familiar with | 26 |
| Heard the name, but don't know much about it | 32 |

EXHIBIT 9 (cont'd)    IMPORTANCE RATING OF LINE OF CREDIT (LOC) FEATURES AMONG
CUSTOMER GROUPS

| | % Rating Very Important | | |
| --- | --- | --- | --- |
| | Visa | Mortgage | Loan |
| **Total respondents** (those without a LOC) | 137 | 120 | 60* |
| | % | % | % |
| Lower interest rate | 81 | 83 | 87 |
| Flexibility to pay off when want | 69 | 70 | 72 |
| Interest paid on days balance outstanding | 64 | 70 | 67 |
| Having control/you decide when to use or pay off | 64 | 56 | 67 |
| No need to reapply | 51 | 53 | 63 |
| Security for an emergency or the unexpected | 49 | 55 | 48 |
| Convenience of buying on the spot | 45 | 34 | 43 |
| No need to justify purchases | 37 | 33 | 42 |
| It is confidential | 33 | 34 | 28 |

*Caution small base

PROFILE OF THOSE INTERESTED IN A LINE OF CREDIT

| | Total Sample | Very Interested | Somewhat Interested |
| --- | --- | --- | --- |
| **Total respondents** (100%) | 400 | 41* | 127 |
| | % | % | % |
| **Sex** | | | |
| Male | 54 | 56 | 49 |
| Female | 46 | 44 | 51 |
| **Age** | | | |
| Under 34 years | 33 | 44 | 35 |
| 35 to 44 years | 34 | 24 | 29 |
| 45 to 54 years | 17 | 17 | 13 |
| 55 to 64 years | 10 | 10 | 11 |
| 65+ years | 6 | 5 | 11 |
| **# Years had Mortgage** | | | |
| Less than 5 years | 34 | 41 | 30 |
| 5 to 9 years | 24 | 21 | 30 |
| 10 to 14 years | 20 | 14 | 27 |
| 15 to 19 years | 12 | 10 | 9 |
| 20+ years | 10 | 14 | 3 |

**# Times Obtained Loan (past 5 years)**

| | | | |
|---|---|---|---|
| 0 | 32 | 20 | 25 |
| I | 30 | 39 | 39 |
| 2 | 18 | 10 | 19 |
| 3 | 10 | 24 | 10 |
| 4+ times | 10 | 7 | 6 |

**Household Income**

| | | | |
|---|---|---|---|
| $25,000 or less | 11 | 22 | 16 |
| Over $25,000 to $35,000 | 15 | 20 | 20 |
| Over $35,000 to $45,000 | 34 | 32 | 38 |
| Over $45,000 to $75,000 | 17 | 10 | 13 |
| Over $75,000 | 13 | 12 | 6 |
| Refused | 9 | 5 | 7 |

*Caution small base

## USAGE OF INSTITUTIONS AMONG LINE OF CREDIT HOLDERS

| | Line of Credit | Chequing Account | VISA | Mortgage | Loan |
|---|---|---|---|---|---|
| **Total respondents** (100%) | 111 | 110 | 101 | 86 | 65 |
| | % | % | % | % | % |
| Total CGT | — | 23 | 54 | 76 | 34 |
| Canada Trust | 5 | 4 | 2 | 2 | 3 |
| Montreal Trust | 1 | 2 | — | 2 | — |
| National Trust | — | — | — | — | — |
| Royal Trust | 4 | 4 | 2 | 2 | 2 |
| Other Trust | 2 | — | — | — | — |
| Bank of Montreal | 14 | 12 | 5 | 1 | 11 |
| Bank of Nova Scotia | 19 | 11 | 11 | 1 | 14 |
| CIBC | 10 | 14 | 7 | 5 | 6 |
| Royal Bank | 11 | 16 | 17 | 2 | 11 |
| T.D. Bank | 10 | 7 | 10 | 1 | 8 |
| Other Bank | 7 | 7 | 6 | 1 | 5 |
| Credit Union | 14 | 12 | 2 | 2 | 9 |
| All Other Institutions | 8 | 4 | — | 7 | 3 |

## FREQUENCY USE LINE OF CREDIT

| | |
|---|---|
| **Total respondents** (those who had/have a LOC) | 111 |
| | % |
| Once a month or more often | 25 |
| Once every two to three months | 26 |
| Once every six months | 15 |
| Once a year | 4 |
| Less often than once a year | 28 |

*Exhibit 9 (cont'd)*    PROFILE OF LINE OF CREDIT HOLDERS

| | Total Sample | Line of Credit Holders |
|---|---|---|
| **Total respondents** (100%) | 400 | 111 |
| | % | % |
| **Sex** | | |
| Male | 54 | 63 |
| Female | 46 | 37 |
| **Age** | | |
| Under 34 years | 33 | 23 |
| 35 to 44 years | 34 | 44 |
| 45 to 54 years | 17 | 20 |
| 55 to 64 years | 10 | 13 |
| 65+ years | 6 | 1 |
| **# Years had Mortgage** | | |
| Less than 5 years | 34 | 37 |
| 5 to 9 years | 24 | 16 |
| 10 to 14 years | 20 | 21 |
| 15 to 19 years | 12 | 21 |
| 20+ years | 10 | 9 |
| **# Times Obtained Loan (past 5 years)** | | |
| 0 | 32 | 26 |
| 1 | 30 | 23 |
| 2 | 18 | 22 |
| 3 | 10 | 9 |
| 4+ times | 10 | 20 |
| **Household Income** | | |
| $25,000 or less | 11 | 5 |
| Over $25,000 to $35,000 | 15 | 9 |
| Over $35,000 to $45,000 | 34 | 32 |
| Over $45,000 to $75,000 | 17 | 25 |
| Over $75,000 | 13 | 23 |
| Refused | 9 | 5 |

## FEATURES A NEW INSTITUTION WOULD NEED TO OFFER TO STIMULATE SWITCHING FROM CURRENT INSTITUTION

| **Total respondents** (those who had/have a LOC) | 111 |
|---|---|
| | % |
| Lower interest rates | 49 |
| No collateral | 5 |
| Larger credit limit | 5 |
| No/lower fees | 4 |
| Less collateral | 2 |
| Flexibility/pay when you want | 3 |
| Overdraft protection | 2 |
| Don't know | 18 |
| Nothing/satisfied with current institution | 18 |

believed he could generate substantial sales for this product. Inputs would be required from the Legal Department, Consumer Services, the Internal Audit Department and Dan Mariani in Marketing. Consumer Services encompassed the branch network while Branch Operations was a Head Office group responsible for ensuring branch operating procedures were as streamlined as possible (see Exhibit 10). While it was in Joel's long term interests to co-operate with the other departments, ultimately he had full responsibility and control over the campaign.

Reflecting back on previous campaigns, he felt the following issues had to be resolved:

1. Whom did he want to target?
2. What would be an appropriate offer for this group?
3. What was the best method to reach this group?
4. How should he assess campaign results?

As Dan was still extensively involved in many merger related issues, he would have little time to devote to this project. However, it was common for the product group to assign sole responsibility for direct marketing campaigns to the DMD, once the initial concept had been approved.

## DEFINING THE TARGET MARKET

Joel knew that choosing the appropriate target market would be critical to the success of the campaign. "We want to look for opportunity segments," he kept saying. As CGT already had an internal database capable of generating customer lists, one option would be to use an internal list of customers for any other CGT product or combination of products. The PLC market research on CGT VISA, loan and mortgage customers would help determine if those product lists were appropriate to use. Intuitively, it seemed that there would be a high response rate from these customers as they were not credit adverse. However, these customers had purchased their previous products through the CGT branch network and might not respond favourably to a mail or phone solicitation, particularly as some potentially sensitive information (such as income level) would be necessary to gather for the credit application. If an internal list were to be used, certain criteria might still have to be imposed on the list to make it as responsive as possible. For example, it would be desirable to select the list so that the majority of the respondents would be likely to pass the required credit check, but due to the time lag between the data work and the campaign launch, it was inevitable

*Exhibit 10*
*CGT's Consumer*
*Services*

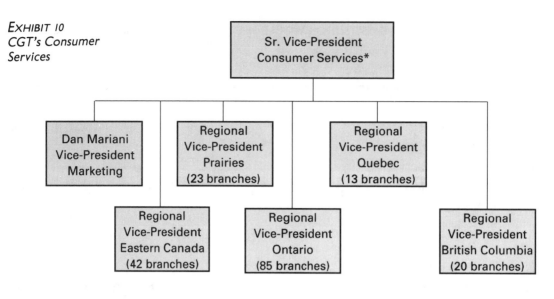

*Most Regional Vice-Presidents had an Assistant Vice-President and several District Managers reporting to them.

that certain people who were solicited would not qualify because their financial situation had changed.

The MIF would allow the list to be customized on any of the variables it contained. For example, only French-speaking customers could be selected. Typically, the Information Systems Department performed the extract work or raw data dump. Then, the file was sent to an outside supplier for data manipulation into the MIF or for a specific campaign. Joel estimated that he spent $200,000 per year on external data work and the lead time for campaign related data analysis would take a minimum of one month.

An alternative option would be to use an external list. Numerous list brokers existed that would readily rent lists of almost any customer profile required. List brokers rarely sold lists; their fee was based on the number of times a company used a list and the complexity of the data work required to manipulate a list to match the customer's needs. Each name would typically cost between four to twelve cents with the average cost per thousand names roughly $40 to $120. If an external list existed (that after manipulation would be suitable for the campaign), the data work would require three to four weeks.

Developing a list from scratch would take much longer. One example of a potential list would be to mail to university graduates who presumably would be in a higher income bracket than average Canadians.

## REACHING THE TARGET MARKET

Once the target market was identified, Joel knew the next step would be selecting the method of contacting them which he called "outbound solicitation". The possibilities included direct mail, telemarketing or the branch network. If outbound direct mail were used in conjunction with inbound telemarketing (i.e., customers responding by telephoning CGT), there would be a constraint on the number of calls each TSR could handle. Joel estimated that each TSR could handle a maximum of six presentations or calls per hour. This problem might be circumvented if mailing waves were used which meant not all of the mail pieces would be sent at once, allowing the incoming responses to be staggered.

No data were available on what type of a response would likely be generated if the branches were used. Typically, the branches were supported by advertising and promotion campaigns where tracking the number of people receiving the marketing message was almost impossible to determine. Joel was somewhat concerned about involving the branches in any substantial fashion because during the merger, the branches had incurred a high turnover rate and there were already numerous demands placed on branch staff time.

"There has to be something to attract the customer because we are asking them to change their purchasing behaviour whether it be 'Buy now and do not delay' or 'Buy with us and not with them'," Joel commented. One option would be to offer a discount on the PLC interest rate. In the past, DMD had offered individuals whom they identified as being a good prospect for a product an improved or discounted rate. "We know that we want to induce trial by giving an offer; however, we do not want to offer a discount on a product that is not used," said Joel. The branches were under no obligation to match this rate; in fact, they were discouraged from doing so as the offer was only valid if the individual presented the personalized voucher which they had received in the mail from the DMD along with a solicitation letter (see Exhibit 11). These vouchers were redeemable in the branch only and resembled a high quality certificate with the terms and conditions listed on them.

---

*EXHIBIT 11*
*Previous DMD Mail Piece Including Voucher*

# Central Guaranty Trust Company

### CENTRAL ⅠⅠ GUARANTY

## You could win $25,000* and get—compliments of Central Guaranty— a superbly crafted *Rosewood* and brass fountain pen. FREE!**

Dear Neighbour:

It's easy. Better than easy, it makes obvious financial sense.

Here's what you do. Take the enclosed FeeCutter Gift Certificate to any Central Guaranty Trust Company branch. Using a personal cheque or bank draft on a competing financial institution (better still, complete a Balance of Account Transfer Request and we'll handle the paperwork), make a minimum transfer of $1,000 to a FeeCutter account before June 30, 1989, and you'll get:

1. A magnificent natural Rosewood-finished fountain pen with a solid brass interior, absolutely FREE**
2. The chance to win one of three $25,000* cash prizes

You've probably heard about our FeeCutter account. It's Central Guaranty's way of saying enough is enough with the high-off-the-hog service charges most financial institutions make you pay.

The enclosed brochure tells the story. And, by checking the branch location guide inside the brochure, it will take you just seconds to find the Central Guaranty branch most convenient to your office or home! By reading the brochure, you'll find more about how you could win $25,000* in cash. Plus everything you need to know about our FeeCutter account's remarkable money-saving features. Here are just a few of them:

- No Fee Unlimited Chequing
- No Fee Stop Payments
- No Fee VISA
- No Fee Withdrawals

- No Fee for using our Money Machine
- No Fee NSF cheques payable to you

**Maximized Daily Interest on Every Dollar!**

The FeeCutter. Open one and discover that it's the only account you need for your daily transactions and savings needs! Like we've been saying. It's time to stop the nickel and diming.

Sincerely,

Stephen W. Stewart
Senior Vice President, Consumer Services

P.S.   Your FREE** Rosewood-finished fountain pen with brass interior will be mailed to you — by speedy First Class delivery — upon opening a FeeCutter account and transferring a minimum deposit of $1,000.

*Complete details available at your branch.

**You must bring in the enclosed FeeCutter Gift Certificate for branch validation to ensure you receive this handsome gift.

---

**FeeCutter GIFT CERTIFICATE** You could win $25,000* and get this Rosewood fountain pen — FREE!**

This handsome Rosewood and brass fountain pen is yours FREE** just for opening a FeeCutter account with a $1,000 minimum balance.

CENTRAL⊥GUARANTY

999999

John Datamark
50 Valleywood Drive
Unit # 3
Markham, Ontario          (R)
L3R 6E9

*Complete details available at your branch.
**Bring this FeeCutter Gift Certificate into any Central Guaranty branch. Use a personal cheque or bank draft drawn from a competing financial institution or complete a Balance of Account Transfer Request and make a minimum transfer of $1,000 into a Central Guaranty FeeCutter account before June 30, 1989.
• Offer Expires June 30, 1989
• This FeeCutter Gift Certificate is Non-Transferable

**CENTRAL⊥GUARANTY**
Central Guaranty Trust Company

Branch Number     New Account Number     Account Opening Balance

EXHIBIT 11 (cont'd)

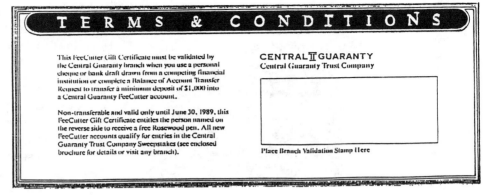

T E R M S   &   C O N D I T I O N S

This FeeCutter Gift Certificate must be validated by
the Central Guaranty branch when you use a personal
cheque or bank draft drawn from a competing financial
institution or complete a Balance of Account Transfer
Request to transfer a minimum deposit of $1,000 into
a Central Guaranty FeeCutter account.

Non-transferable and valid only until June 30, 1989, this
FeeCutter Gift Certificate entitles the person named on
the reverse side to receive a free Rosewood pen. All new
FeeCutter accounts qualify for entries in the Central
Guaranty Trust Company Sweepstakes (see enclosed
brochure for details or visit any branch).

CENTRAL ℡ GUARANTY
Central Guaranty Trust Company

Place Branch Validation Stamp Here

Joel was also considering using a value-added offer. When CGT's mortgage product was launched, a Home Investment Savings Package which offered discounts on various home care products was used to attract customers. This coupon book had a value of $5,000 if all the coupons were redeemed and companies, such as, Chubb Security Systems, Lennox Air Conditioning and Heating and Allied Van Lines participated in it. Extra copies of this coupon book had been printed and were available for use with the PLC campaign.

Much of the information on the PLC credit application was the same as that required for a VISA application. Joel was considering attempting to cross-sell VISA cards at the same time as the PLC. While he did not want to antagonize any customers by trying to sell them too many products at once, any additional revenue generated would only help campaign results. Each VISA account generated approximately $8 per year, net of transaction costs. Exhibit 12 describes CGT's VISA product in further detail.

If direct mail was used, the cost per package of designing, producing and mailing it first class would average one dollar apiece. The cost would decrease to $.80 for a third class mail package, but a first class mail package would take three days to deliver, whereas, a third class package could take 21 days. In order to mail third class, a minimum of 10,000 mail pieces were required. Typical packages included a two page cover letter describing the offer along with a product brochure and activation voucher to track re-

sponse. The mailing would have to be externally produced and would take three to four months to develop from the initial design to production.

In the past, Joel had not had time to pre-test any direct mail packages in order to determine if changes to the package would produce a higher response rate, although pre-testing was a common industry practice. If he decided to use direct mail, he wondered if he should pre-test packages for this campaign and how he might go about doing this.

## FULFILLING THE OFFER

Joel's philosophy about fulfilment was as follows:

> Fulfilment must be customer driven and allow the client to follow the path of least resistance. One of the things we are offering underneath is support for the customer's decision. Therefore, we have to make it easy for them.

The key fulfilment issue was whose role it should be: should the branches be responsible for fulfilment or should DMD? If the branches handled campaign fulfilment, Joel was concerned about the volume of customers they could manage. The fulfilment for this product was relatively straightforward; however, the branches sometimes resented servicing customers that had been acquired by the DMD, in spite of the fact that all sales would be credited to the branches. Also, customers might phone the DMD to check on the status of their PLC application. Assuming the application had been for-

*EXHIBIT 12*
*VISA Product*
*Information*

### The first NO-FEE VISA card in Canada

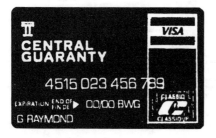

### is the only card you need.

If you don't have a VISA card, this is the one to get.

If you do, this is the one to switch to.

Because the Central Guaranty Trust VISA card was the first NO-FEE VISA card in Canada.

That means **no service charges. And no yearly fees. None.**

In addition, we give you competitive interest rates, overdraft protection on any Central Guaranty Trust personal chequing account, and free life insurance against accidental death on balances of up to $10,000.*

So why have any other card?

Especially when no card is more widely accepted than VISA.

And good for instant cash at any Financial Institution displaying the VISA symbol.

### Why have a credit card at all?

How many times have you passed on a sale item you needed because you didn't have the ready cash?

If you'd had a VISA card handy, you wouldn't have ended up paying the regular price a few weeks later.

Also, if you pay the full amount of your statement every month you'll pay absolutely no interest. Not to mention the fact that you'll be paying with one cheque.

Even the statement itself has its advantages. By telling you exactly what you spent for what, you can keep tabs on your budget.

### Do I have to be a Central Guaranty Trust Customer?

No. But when you consider what we have to offer, you might like to become one.

As shown by innovations like the Super T-Bill and Fee-Cutter accounts, we're unusually responsive to customer needs.

Our "Guaranteed Best Rates" policy assures you of unbeatable rates on GICs and GIC-RSPs.

### Getting our NO-FEE VISA card is no trouble.

Simply fill out the attached application form, and send it or present it to your nearest Central Guaranty Trust branch.

Your new card will arrive with two VISA cheques with which to transfer any outstanding balances from your old VISA card to ours.

**So, as you can see, switching to Canada first NO-FEE VISA card is no trouble.**

*See your Branch Manager for details.

warded to the branch for fulfilment, the DMD would be unable to give the customer an immediate answer as they would have to contact the branch to determine the status.

Joel was willing to have DMD handle fulfilment, but he felt there would be resistance from Consumer Services. If fulfilment was handled centrally, the final documentation would have to be sent via mail to the customer for completion and both the documentation and voucher would have to be returned to Head Office.

Regardless of who handled the fulfilment process, the customers would have to receive similar responses to their campaign or product-related question, whether they went to the branch or communicated with DMD. Certain clients might require additional information, in which case, one alternative would be to mail them a more detailed product information package which Joel estimated would cost about $2 per package for first class mail. A first class turnaround time would probably be necessary because of the offer expiry date.

## ASSESSING THE RESULTS

Joel believed, "We have an opportunity cost if we spend the campaign budget unwisely so it is extremely important to track results." In the past, CGT had used vouchers, which were sent to the client to track their responses. "When we send someone a voucher or an activation device, once they have the voucher in their hand, it is not just a piece of paper. It represents the offer. It makes an intangible product tangible."

Any information required for post-campaign analysis had to be identified now so that it could be collected during the campaign. Joel wanted to review the appropriateness of past tracking efforts, particularly since he planned to ultimately house the MIF on a desktop PC. In the past, information had been tracked for the following types of items:

- sales by dollars and by number of accounts/ transactions
- the number of vouchers mailed and the number redeemed

- response rate
- average transaction size

As well, data could be tracked by various time periods (daily, weekly, monthly, cumulative for the campaign) and by various levels of responsibility (TSR, CSR, branch, regional, telemarketing only, overall company).

The total budget for the campaign was between $200,000 to $250,000. In the past, campaign guides had been produced for the branches regardless of whether they were actively involved so that they could respond to any campaign-related questions that came to them. The campaign guides typically cost $1700. Exhibit 13 illustrates an index for a previous campaign guide. Historically, DMD campaigns were evaluated based on the incremental level of outstanding deposits or loans they generated, although Joel was now working on profitability modelling for individual campaigns.

## THE CHALLENGE

To the best of Joel's knowledge, no other financial institution used both direct mail and telemarketing to market PLC's. He thought it was probable that some companies sent a PLC application out in the mail. Then, the client would complete this at home and submit it either to the Head Office to be centrally administered or send it directly to the appropriate branch. To his knowledge, no other company had CGT's ability to take the application over the phone using a telemarketing unit.

Upon reflection, Joel determined that his goal for the campaign was to achieve a 10% response rate accompanied by a 60% PLC activation rate. In other words, 10% of the customers receiving the offer would reply and of those, 60% would utilize their line of credit. As August was fast approaching, he knew he had to make some decisions soon. There would be long lead times required from either his staff or external suppliers to finalize the details and he realized the more time he was able to give them, the smoother the campaign would run.

*EXHIBIT 13*
*Campaign Guide*
*Index*

## TABLE OF CONTENTS

# C A S E 3.10    Fisher and Cooper Ltd.

Jo Ann Fisher and Pat Cooper sat down for a cup of coffee at the end of the day. Their days had been busy since they had opened their women's clothing store, Fisher and Cooper, a few months ago. They had not really had time to determine how well the store was doing, what was making it successful (or unsuccessful) and what they should be doing with it in the future. They knew that their total concept was unique in London and felt that there was a real need for the services they offered their customers. They were surprised when a woman approached them interested in franchising their operation. The offer was on their minds but they really didn't know too much about franchising and its advantages and disadvantages to them. They were not sure how to evaluate whether or not franchising was feasible to them.

## COMPANY BACKGROUND

Jo Ann and Pat met in 1981 at a Mary Kay Cosmetic Convention. Both were sales representatives for London, Ontario, and surrounding area. The two began to work closely while supplying each other with any cosmetics items when either was out of stock. In addition to selling cosmetics at this time, Jo Ann was also managing a woman's retail store in London and training as a colours' consultant (see Exhibit 1). Tired of managing someone else's store for minimum wage, she approached Pat in the spring of 1985 with the idea of opening their own retail operation. Jo Ann saw a need for a service to help women become more professional in their dressing and feel better about themselves: "An image is very necessary for every individual, and basically that's what being well-dressed is all about." Though Pat had no previous retail experience, Jo Ann felt that together they could pool their "image creating" resources.

Fisher and Cooper identified their target market as professional women. The concept they developed was to provide women with a total package in one location: wardrobe consulting, colours' analysis, personalized shopping and retail merchandise (see Exhibit 2). Jo Ann and Pat would perform the colours' analysis, personalized shopping and merchandise selling. However, due to the amount of time these activities required, Jo Ann felt that they had to recruit a third person for wardrobe consulting. Through her retail contacts, she decided that Alita Kraven was very suitable. Alita had been a professional model and had recently compiled a book and organized a full seminar on fashion consulting. It was decided that while Alita performed wardrobe consultations, either Jo Ann or Pat would sit in on the seminars to become familiar with each customer's appropriate clothing style. It was hoped that the wardrobe consulting and colours' analysis would not only help establish close relationships with customers, but also act as feeders for their retail merchandise. Once appropriate clothing styles and colours were determined for a customer, Jo Ann and Pat would be able to draw from their merchandise and put together a clothing capsule consisting of various separates (eg. skirt, jacket, blouse and scarf). This capsule would enable the professional to reflect her best image and save time in the process. Jo Ann and Pat had identified London as a conservative city. In terms of merchandising, they felt that work classics such as jackets, skirts, blouses and basic dresses, as opposed to trendy items, would be suitable for the London market.

In June 1985, before securing a store location, they began establishing relationships with a few suppliers in Toronto. By July 2, they had begun consulting and buying outfits for various Mary Kay customers. The merchandise for these customers was secured not only from suppliers, but, from feeder stores throughout London. These feeder stores provided Fisher and Cooper with a 15% commission on total sales.

On August 1, 1985, Jo Ann and Pat signed a three year lease for a four room house located on

EXHIBIT I

_____

The Concept of Colour Analysis: Excerpts from _Color Me Beautiful_ by Carole Jackson

"Discover your Natural Beauty through the Colors that Make You Look Great and Feel Fabulous!"

The seasonal color theory was inspired by the studies of artist and colorist Johannes Itten of the famous Bauhaus school in Germany. He discovered the power of physical coloring in directing a student's personal colors in his paintings. He noted that a student's personal colors were consistently those complementary to his skin tone, hair and eyes, in both tone and intensity. After years of observation and documentation, he emphatically states in his book, _The Elements of Color_, that "Every woman should know what colors are becoming to her; these will always be her subjective colors and their complements". So Itten concluded that our personal palette, the one to which we are drawn naturally, consists of the very colors that look best on us.

In adapting Itten's theory to fashion we have developed the four seasonal palettes as guides for clothing, make-up, and wardrobe planning. You don't have to be a brilliant colorist or fashion coordinator yourself, though you will look as if you are. Simply determine which palette fits your coloring, wear those colors, and enjoy the compliments.

Each season presents a distinct array of colors, and your coloring is in harmony with one of these palettes. We could call your coloring "Type A", "Type B", and so on, but comparison with the seasons provides a more aesthetic and poetic way to describe your coloring and your best colors.

Some women are their most beautiful in the clear, true primary colors or the icy colors of Winter, while others are flattered more by the softer shades of Summer. Autumns come to life in the rich, warm tones of fall, and the Spring woman's coloring is most enhanced by clear, warm colors, like the budding growth and fresh fruit tones of springtime. When you wear your special colors, you are indeed the fairest of them all.

The genes that determine your skin tone, hair, and eye color also determine what colors look best on you. When you study your coloring, you will find that your skin, hair and eyes have either blue or golden tones. Your inherited skin tone does not change; it simply deepens with a tan and fades with age. The same colors will always look the best on you.

In our classes, we drape each client in all the colors of her season, contrasting wrong colors for the sake of comparison and illustration. The right color brings out the best, while the wrong shade detracts. It's exciting to see the differences. Many women do not know how pretty they are.

_____

Richmond Street, just south of St. Joseph's Hospital. The owner of the house had operated a successful woman's retail store and hairdressing salon from the location. Thus, few renovations were necessary: the dressing rooms were large, the pink and grey colouring conveyed a warm feeling and a four room division provided separate facilities for the wardrobe and fashion consulting.

During the month of August, they prepared for their grand opening. This included securing additional suppliers, designing the layout, pricing and sending out personalized store information flyers to their present 800 Mary Kay customers. They also rented out one of the rooms to a combined hair dresser and esthetician team. They felt that this would be an obvious extension to their "image creating" operation, as well as providing additional traffic flow.

On September 2, 1985, Fisher and Cooper officially opened. Other than the flyers, there was no other source of advertising. At least over the short term, the owners knew that they would have to rely on word of mouth as their main

EXHIBIT 2
Price List

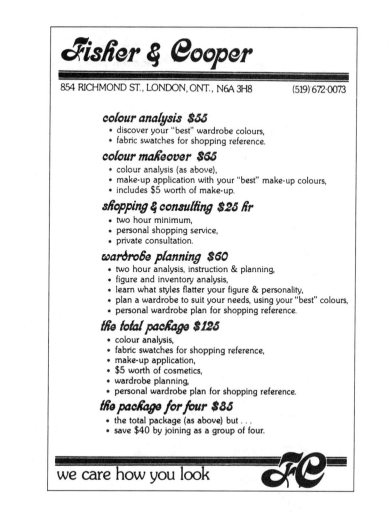

## Fisher & Cooper

854 RICHMOND ST., LONDON, ONT., N6A 3H8          (519) 672-0073

**colour analysis $55**
- discover your "best" wardrobe colours,
- fabric swatches for shopping reference.

**colour makeover $65**
- colour analysis (as above),
- make-up application with your "best" make-up colours,
- includes $5 worth of make-up.

**shopping & consulting $25 hr**
- two hour minimum,
- personal shopping service,
- private consultation.

**wardrobe planning $60**
- two hour analysis, instruction & planning,
- figure and inventory analysis,
- learn what styles flatter your figure & personality,
- plan a wardrobe to suit your needs, using your "best" colours,
- personal wardrobe plan for shopping reference.

**the total package $125**
- colour analysis,
- fabric swatches for shopping reference,
- make-up application,
- $5 worth of cosmetics,
- wardrobe planning,
- personal wardrobe plan for shopping reference.

**the package for four $85**
- the total package (as above) but . . .
- save $40 by joining as a group of four.

we care how you look

source of promotion due to the costs of radio and newspaper advertising. During the opening week, Jo Ann and Pat served wine, cheese, tea and coffee to all their customers in order to further emphasize the personalized attention and friendly atmosphere. They also organized a fashion show that was held in conjunction with a London restaurant. All tickets were sold and Jo Ann and Pat both felt that the event was a great introduction for women to their store.

## A TYPICAL DAY AT FISHER AND COOPER

Jo Ann and Pat were rushing around; they were having a busy day today. The store had been open since 10 a.m. but they had been there since 9 a.m., sorting through some stock and updating customer file cards. Two women were in the change rooms and Jo Ann and Pat wanted to make sure that they had found what they were looking for and were completely satisfied before Mrs. Cook, a customer from Tillsonburg, came in at 11 a.m. for her wardrobe consulting appointment.

Both Pat and Jo Ann greeted Mrs. Cook when she arrived. Pat took her back into the consulting room and introduced her to Alita. Mrs. Cook sat down and felt very much at home while they served her coffee and crackers.

A couple of hours later, Mrs. Cook had a good understanding of what clothing items looked good on her. She had previously had her colours done and had brought her palette with

EXHIBIT 3
Financial
Statements

**Statement of Income**
**September 30, 1985**

|  | Year to Date | % sales |
|---|---|---|
| Revenue |  |  |
| Clothing sales | $13,208.88 | 82.38 |
| Commissions & consulting | 486.75 | 3.03 |
| Jewellery & make up | 790.45 | 4.92 |
| Other income | 1,547.40 | 9.65 |
| Total Revenue | $16,033.48 | 100.00 |
|  |  |  |
| Cost of Goods Sold |  |  |
| Opening inventory | 1,005.00 | 6.26 |
| Purchases | 38,040.65 | 237.25 |
| Freight | 140.96 | 0.87 |
|  | 39,186.61 | 244.40 |
| Closing inventory | (29,111.00) | 181.56 |
|  | 10,075.61 | 62.84 |
| Gross Margin | $ 5,957.87 | 37.15 |
|  |  |  |
| Expenses |  |  |
| Accounting and legal | 36.76 | 0.22 |
| Advertising and promotion | 1,949.58 | 12.15 |
| Bank charges and interest | 422.57 | 2.63 |
| Credit card discounts | 49.47 | 0.30 |
| Wages and benefits | 634.73 | 3.95 |
| Insurance | 100.00 | 0.62 |
| Office supplies and postage | 2,005.51 | 12.50 |
| Supplies and cleaning | 22.00 | 0.13 |
| Rent and taxes | 3,972.50 | 24.77 |
| Telephone | 214.76 | 1.33 |
| Utilities | 150.00 | 0.93 |
| Total expenses | $ 9,557.88 | 59.61 |
|  |  |  |
| Net income (loss) before taxes | $(3,600.01) | 22.45 |

**Balance Sheet**
**as at September 30, 1985**

**Assets**

| Current assets: |  |
|---|---|
| Cash | $ 1,321.20 |
| Accounts receivable | 551.19 |
| Inventory | 29,111.00 |
| Total current assets | $30,983.49 |

|  | | |
|---|---|---|
| *EXHIBIT 3 (cont'd)* | Fixed assets — at cost | |
| | Furniture and fixtures | 1,928.35 |
| | Equipment | 5,546.24 |
| | | 7,474.59 |
| | Less accumulated depreciation | 0.00 |
| | Total fixed assets | $ 7,474.59 |
| | Incorporated costs (net) | 250.00 |
| | Total assets | $38,708.08 |

## Liabilities and Shareholders' Equity

| | |
|---|---|
| Current liabilities: | |
| Due to bank on demand | $18,000.00 |
| Accounts payable | 13,948.00 |
| Accrued charges | 7,551.20 |
| Sales tax payable | 859.68 |
| Due to shareholders | 2,004.34 |
| Total current liabilities | $42,363.22 |
| | |
| Shareholders' equity: | |
| Common shares | 20.00 |
| Retained earnings | (75.13) |
| Net income (loss) for the period | (3,600.01) |
| Total shareholders' equity | $(3,655.14) |
| | $38,708.08 |

| | | Year to date (24 days) |
|---|---|---|
| *EXHIBIT 4* *Financial Analysis as of September 30, 1985* | | |
| | Total Sales/ft.$^2$ | $14.52 |
| | Clothing Sales/ft.$^2$ | $11.96 |
| | Gross Margin/ft.$^2$ | $ 5.40 |
| | Net Profit/ft.$^2$ | $(3.26) |
| | GMROI | 39.6% |
| | Clothing Transactions/ft.$^2$ | 0.05 |
| | Sales/Inventory Dollar | 0.88 |
| | Inventory Turnover | 0.67 |
| | Accounts Payable/Inventory Dollars | 12.63 |
| | Gross Margin Percentage | 37 % |
| | Net Profit to Net Sales | (22)% |
| | Net Profit to Total Assets | (9.3)% |
| | Working Capital | $(11,380) |
| | Days Receivables | 0.8 |
| | Days Payables | 8.8 |
| | Current Ratio | 0.73 |
| | Acid Test Ratio | 0.04 |

her. She started talking to Pat, who had sat in on the consultation, about what she had and she did not have in her wardrobe to fit in with what she had learned. Pat showed her around the store and Mrs. Cook saw a few items that interested her and that she wanted to try on. While she was in the dressing room, Pat and Jo Ann continued to bring in items that they thought would look nice on her. She was surprised that she liked many of these items once she tried them on, since she would not have chosen them herself after seeing them on a hanger.

Mrs. Cook would put on an outfit and then come out into the store, where there were other customers also trying on clothes. The atmosphere was friendly and comfortable with not only Pat and Jo Ann giving opinions but also the other customers expressing their views. With each outfit she came out in, either Pat or Jo Ann would add accessories to complete the look.

Mrs. Cook ended up buying two skirts, a jacket, a blouse, a sweater, beads and a scarf. She felt happy and confident about the way she looked in those outfits and knew that she had purchased quality items that made her look well dressed and could be combined into many different outfits. Pat wrote down all of the relevant information, such as her season, size and preferences on a file card. This information would help them if her husband ever came in looking for a gift for her or when Fisher and Cooper received merchandise because they could keep her in mind when sorting through it.

When the store closed at 6 p.m., the day was not yet over for the owners. At 6 p.m., Pat had an appointment to do make-up and at 7 p.m., Jo Ann and Pat were running a seminar for a group of twenty women to explain their concept. It was around 10 p.m. before they finally left for home.

## PERFORMANCE TO DATE

Both Jo Ann and Pat had been pleased with the performance of the store. Selected financial data on Fisher and Cooper is presented in Exhibits 3 to 7.

The concept of personalized attention combined with total image creation had been well received. The average total sales per day over their 60 day working period was $946.41. Over the last two weeks in November, this figure was $1,361.68 (see Exhibit 5). Though weekly sales had been somewhat erratic, the general trend was upward (see Exhibit 6).

The number of wardrobe consultations performed had increased steadily. November's average consulting sales per day exhibited a 40% increase over October (see Exhibit 5).

Pat and Jo Ann were satisfied that each and every customer who had been in their store had left feeling "special". The increase in the sales of accessories, such as jewellery and scarves, indicated that Pat and Jo Ann had spent time with customers and provided them with a total look. The scarf sales in particular emphasized the amount of trust developed between Fisher and Cooper and their customers. No scarves were displayed in the store. Instead, the scarves were custom made by a woman in London who designed them according to each customer's outfit. No customer had seen her scarf prior to the sale.

Judging by the number of skirts, jackets and blouses sold as a percentage of total articles, it appeared as though customers were looking for basics (see Exhibit 7). As well, this trend indicated Fisher and Cooper's success in providing "value" to their customers. A large percentage of sales were wardrobe capsules consisting of 4 or 5 items that could be combined into possibly 10 different outfits.

An interesting trend was evident in the volume of Mary Rose sets sold. These sets consisted of inexpensive cotton pieces that provided both comfort and style. Jo Ann felt that this line acted as a sales feeder: "If a customer is in the mood to buy, yet does not want to spend a great deal of money at the time, she will buy some Mary Rose and hopefully return later."

Word of mouth was quite instrumental in promoting Fisher and Cooper. An analysis of the store's trading area showed that customers were dispersed throughout London in clusters (see Exhibit 8). Jo Ann expressed interest in future advertising on the radio and in the newspaper to increase their volume of customers within London. However, at this point in time, the store's

EXHIBIT 5
Sales Breakdown
and Daily
Averages

| | Total Daily Sales | Total Cloth-ing Sales | Total Make-up | Total Colours | Other | # Cloth-ing Trans-actions | Avg. Sales/ Cus-tomer | Total Feeder Sales | Total Jewel-lery | Total Consul-ting | # of Days |
|---|---|---|---|---|---|---|---|---|---|---|---|
| Pre-October | $12,350 | 11,187 | 260 | 130 | — | 52 | 215.13 | 160 | 513 | 100 | 25 |
| % Total Month Sales | | 91% | 2% | 1% | — | — | — | 1% | 4% | .8% | |
| October 1-31 | $28,095 | 23,298 | 634 | 1145 | 865 | 124 | 187.89 | — | 1122 | 1031 | 23 |
| % Total Month Sales | | 83% | 2% | 4% | 3% | — | — | — | 4% | 4% | |
| November 1-16 | $16,340 | 13,832 | 414 | 455 | 165 | 64 | 216.12 | — | 884 | 590 | 12 |
| % Total Month Sales | | 85% | 3% | 3% | 1% | — | — | — | 5% | 4% | |
| TOTAL | $56,785 | 47,317 | 1308 | 1730 | 1069 | 240 | 197.15 | 159.15 | 2519 | 1721 | 60 |

$$\text{Transactions/Customer} = \frac{240 \text{ transactions}}{127 \text{ customers}} = 1.9 \text{ over 60 days}$$

Averages Per Day (eg. Average Total Sales/Day)

| | Total Sales | Clothing Sales | Make-up Sales | Colours Sales | Other Sales | Feeder Sales | Jewellery Sales | Consul-ting | Trans-actions |
|---|---|---|---|---|---|---|---|---|---|
| Pre October | 494.00 | 447.48 | 10.40 | 5.20 | — | 6.40 | 20.52 | 4.00 | 2.08 |
| October 1-31 | 1221.52 | 1012.96 | 27.57 | 49.78 | 37.61 | — | 48.78 | 44.83 | 5.39 |
| November 1-16 | 1361.68 | 1152.67 | 34.51 | 37.92 | 13.75 | — | 73.67 | 49.17 | 5.33 |
| TOTAL | 946.41 | 788.61 | 21.80 | 28.83 | 17.82 | 2.66 | 41.99 | 28.68 | 4 |

financial resources were limited. Fisher and Cooper also seemed to be drawing a substantial customer base, at least 21%, from outside London.

## COMPETITION

Within London, there were many people who did colour consulting. There were four establishments listed in the London Yellow Pages (Fisher and Cooper was not currently listed there) where a customer could have both colour and wardrobe consulting done:

(a) "Colour and Style—Visual Image Analysis" performed colour analysis, wardrobe con-sulting, figure analysis, make-up and personal shopping.

(b) Another woman who did consulting in colours and wardrobe was Ethel Harper from "Colour By Design". She did it by appointment only and offered a 6 week course on wardrobe analysis. She had been consulting for 5 years and trained in California in 1978-79 with a colour analyst.

(c) "Colours" did colours and style consultations. They were franchised and trained by Colours in Toronto and had cosmetics in their store. They did not do personal shopping and they did not have any clothing in their store.

*EXHIBIT 6*
*Weekly Sales*
*Activity*

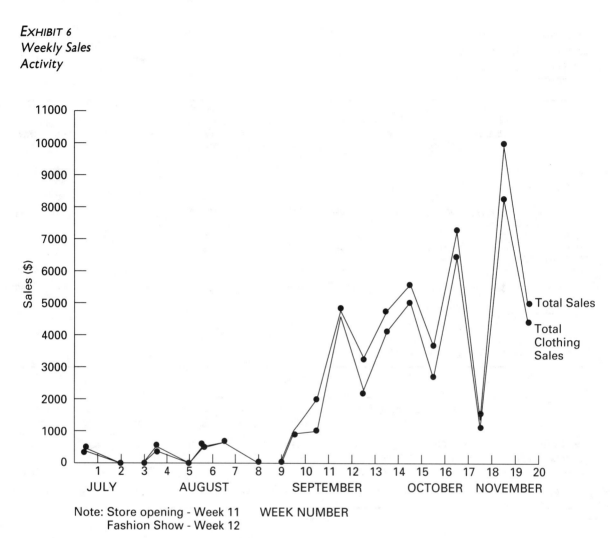

Note: Store opening - Week 11
Fashion Show - Week 12

*EXHIBIT 7*
*Breakdown of*
*Articles Sold*
*July 2 – Nov. 16,*
*1985*

| Articles Sold | July 2 – Oct. 31 | Nov. 1 – Nov. 16 | TOTAL |
|---|---|---|---|
| Top | 18 | 33 | 51 |
| Skirt | 52 | 34 | 86 |
| Jacket | 30 | 15 | 45 |
| Pant | 20 | 15 | 35 |
| Scarf | 14 | 12 | 26 |
| Mary Rose Set | 47 | 8 | 55 |
| Dress | 33 | 14 | 47 |
| Shorts | 3 | 0 | 3 |
| Sweater | 18 | 12 | 30 |
| Blouse | 44 | 19 | 63 |
| Cardigan | 1 | 0 | 1 |
| Tie | 5 | 1 | 6 |
| Vest | 2 | 0 | 2 |
| Belt | 12 | 1 | 13 |
| Sweatshirt | 0 | 2 | 2 |
| Camisole | 0 | 1 | 1 |
| | 302 | 164 | 466 |

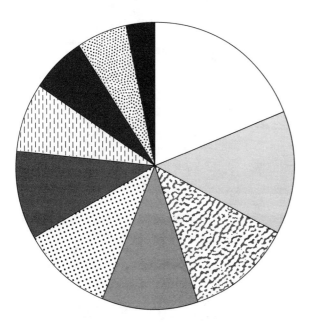

Skirts 18.5%
Blouses 13.5%
Mary Rose Sets 11.8%
Tops 10.9%
Dresses 10.1%
Jackets 9.7%
Pants 7.5%
Sweaters 6.4%
Scarves 5.6%
Other 3.1%

*EXHIBIT 8*
*Trade Area Analysis*
*Within London*

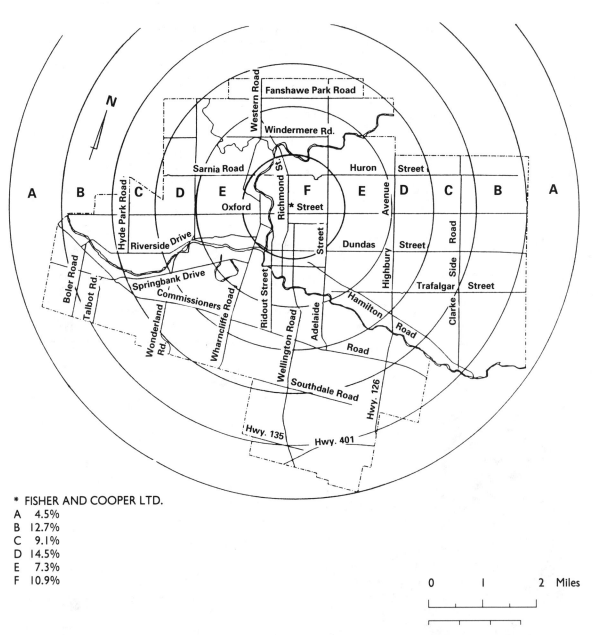

\* FISHER AND COOPER LTD.

A  4.5%
B  12.7%
C  9.1%
D  14.5%
E  7.3%
F  10.9%

EXHIBIT 9
Trade Area Analysis
Outside London

| City/Town | # Customers | Distance from London (km) | % of TOTAL (110) |
|---|---|---|---|
| Belmont | 3 | 20–35 | 2.7 |
| Collingwood | 1 | 100+ | .9 |
| Dorchester | 2 | 20–35 | 1.8 |
| Embro | 1 | 36–50 | .9 |
| Lakeside | 1 | 36–50 | .9 |
| London (RR. #1 to 7) | 5 | 20–35 | 4.5 |
| Lucan | 1 | 20–35 | .9 |
| New York City, New York | 3 | 100+ | 2.7 |
| Port Stanley | 1 | 51–65 | .9 |
| Sparta | 2 | 36–50 | 1.8 |
| St. Thomas | 6 | 36–50 | .9 |
| Sunnydale | 1 | 20–35 | .9 |
| Thamesford | 1 | 20–35 | .9 |
| Thorndale | 2 | 20–35 | 1.8 |
| Thornhill | 1 | 100+ | .9 |
| Tillsonburg | 9 | 100+ | 8.2 |
| Toronto | 1 | 100+ | .9 |
| Union | 1 | 36–50 | .9 |
| Wallacetown | 2 | 66–80 | 1.8 |
| Woodstock | 1 | 51–65 | .9 |

EXHIBIT 10
Total Trade
Area Analysis
(Both Within and
Outside London)

| | 2 km | 2–4 | 4–6 | 6–8 | 8–10 | 10–19 | 20–35 | 36–50 | 51–65 | 66–80 | 81–99 | 100+ | TOTAL |
|---|---|---|---|---|---|---|---|---|---|---|---|---|---|
| Number | 12 | 8 | 16 | 10 | 15 | 5 | 15 | 11 | 2 | 2 | 0 | 15 | 110 |
| % of Total | 10.9 | 7.3 | 14.5 | 9.1 | 12.7 | 4.5 | 13.6 | 10 | 1.8 | 1.8 | 0 | 13.6 | 100 |
| Cumulative % | 10.9 | 18.2 | 32.7 | 41.8 | 54.5 | 59 | 72.6 | 82.6 | 84.4 | 86.2 | 86.2 | 99.8 | 100 |

Note: Total percentages may not equal 100 due to rounding.

(d) The fourth location for colour and wardrobe analysis was "The Magic of Colours and Line" at Stretch and Sew Fabrics in Masonville Place Mall. They offered colour, figure and wardrobe analysis from their fabrics store. Staff were trained in New York by Stretch and Sew Franchise people.

Exhibit 11 gives Fisher and Cooper's price list and also lists competitive prices.

Thus, in combining the colour and wardrobe consulting with a clothing store, Jo Ann and Pat felt they had a unique concept in London. Even though there were many high quality, high price women's clothing stores in London, none offered the "total package" concept of Fisher and Cooper. The competition did, however, offer personalized service within their stores. Accessories, at 481 Richmond, was willing to have one saleswoman spend a lot of time within the store with a customer helping her set up a wardrobe that looked good on her. Similarly, The Village Shop in London Mews had given seminars on wardrobes but they did not offer any kind of appointment service. They felt that any one of their sales staff could help the customer with anything they might need.

## FRANCHISING

In October, 1985, Mrs. Nancy Oatman came to Fisher and Cooper for a colours and wardrobe analysis consultation. She had seen a Fisher and Cooper price list that a co-worker had put up in Elgin General Hospital where she worked, so Nancy came with a group of four. She really liked the concept of the store and brought her husband, an optician, back to see it with her. Nancy's background was as a food supervisor but she was thinking about a career change. Nancy considered the idea of opening a Fisher and Cooper franchise in St. Thomas, where she lived:

> Fisher and Cooper is what I've been looking for for years. I like the concept and the style here. There is no hard sale. I like the concept because I'm interested in self-improvement and I want to find out what looks good on me. I've been considering a career change and if this is what I decide to do, I want to do it well or not at all. I would like to know exactly what to expect. Before I decide what I'm going to do, I have to look at my own time and money. I have two children under the age of 5. If I decide to go into retail, this would be my first choice. I like the hours, the fact that there are appointments and that I'd be working a couple of hours a day.

Nancy felt that her lack of retail experience would be a problem even though her husband runs an optical store in Elgin Mall and she has his support. She felt that she would like to have a lot of training to feel confident that she knew what she was doing. She would also like help choosing and hiring the sales staff and the hairdresser. Nancy could not be away a lot right now so she would want someone else to do the buying, but she would eventually want to be part of this. She was eager to learn and would take any courses in retailing or business that would help her.

Nancy felt that the Fisher and Cooper concept should be feasible in St. Thomas because currently the store had a lot of customers from St. Thomas who drove to London for the special service but would prefer the store to be closer. She thought that there were two types of shoppers in St. Thomas: those who now shopped in St. Thomas and were not really willing to pay a high price for high quality clothing, and those who were willing to pay for quality and currently shopped in London and Toronto for their clothes. She described people in St. Thomas as being careful where they spent their money and felt that the less expensive clothing lines, such as the Mary Rose line, would do well. Nancy was not sure what kind of consumer a St. Thomas store should target, but said that 10% of the people she had spoken with had been really interested in the concept. They were professional people who liked quality but did not have the time to shop.

Nancy said that in the clothing stores which were open in St. Thomas, the inventory had moved slowly. However, there was a fairly new lingerie store which was working well in St. Thomas. It had survived through a tough period

EXHIBIT 11
Competition's
Prices

### Colour and Style — Visual Image Analysis
— 349 Princess Ave.

| | |
|---|---|
| Complete Package (inc. colours, wardrobe, figure, style, makeup) | $150 |
| Colour Analysis | $ 80 |
| Figure and Style | $ 80 |
| Client Shopping | $ 25/hr. |

### Colour By Design
— 210 Dundas

| | |
|---|---|
| 6 week Wardrobe Course (group of 12) | $ 40 |
| Closet Cleaning | $ 40/hr. |
| Colour Analysis | $ 85 |
| Figure Analysis | $ 65 |
| Personal Shopping | $ 40/hr. |

### Colours
— 363 Queens Ave.

| | |
|---|---|
| Colours Analysis | $ 75 |
| "Your Style" Consultations (wallet included) | $ 75 |

### The Magic of Colour and Line — Stretch & Sew Fabrics
— Masonville Place Mall

| | |
|---|---|
| Colours, Wardrobe and Line | $ 75 |
| Wardrobe and Line | $ 35 |
| Colour analysis | $ 45 |

for the town. It had average to high quality items and personalized service. She saw this store as having a similar style as Fisher and Cooper and since it had been successful, she felt Fisher and Cooper might also be.

"I would not be ready to start into this until the end of this year," Nancy concluded, "but I'm interested because it would be a total change for me, fun, and a good feeling to help people out."

### FRANCHISING FROM FISHER AND COOPER'S PERSPECTIVE

Jo Ann and Pat were both surprised when Nancy approached them with the franchise offer. They felt that their concept had been well received in London and wanted to expand "sometime" in the future. However, over the past few months

they had been too busy trying to organize their own operations to even consider expansion.

Nancy appeared enthusiastic about Fisher and Cooper's concept. "We may be missing an opportunity," Jo Ann wondered, "And, if we don't franchise, there is the threat that Nancy will open her own store, since training is available, that would compete with us." Pat, however, wondered about Nancy's suitability. If she did not work out it would create more problems. She felt that Fisher and Cooper might consider waiting until sometime in the future when both herself and Jo Ann felt more organized and therefore able to choose the appropriate candidate.

Despite their apprehensions, Pat and Jo Ann both agreed that franchising represented a viable expansion alternative for their business. An outline of both the franchisee's and the franchiser's obligations is given in Exhibit 12. Jo Ann commented:

> The concept will work anywhere. There will always be women searching to portray themselves to their utmost advantage. The key is going to be in training the franchisee so that both the franchisee and the staff are aware of colours, fashion and the total look.

Another advantage for Fisher and Cooper was the increased buying power that franchising offered through centralized buying. Neither Pat nor Jo Ann felt that centralized buying would be contrary to their concept. Currently, they bought according to seasons. For example, they noticed that in general those persons whose best colours were autumn shades tended to be bigger boned and wear sizes 10 or 12. Jo Ann and Pat did not usually buy according to individual customers.

Instead, if a piece of merchandise arrived that they felt was well suited to a particular person, they would contact her.

Jo Ann and Pat felt differently about the timing and location of the franchise. Jo Ann, who imagined Fisher and Cooper franchising after a full season, commented: "It is difficult to attract customers from St. Thomas and surrounding districts on a regular basis. This is especially true with Fisher and Cooper's limited advertising budget." On the other hand, Pat felt that St. Thomas was too close: "Windsor or Tillsonburg maybe, but not St. Thomas. I don't know if we will be prepared to franchise until another 5 years or so, yet, I still wonder whether this concept will be applicable to St. Thomas." In her view, currently St. Thomas did not have an upscale woman's store.

Overall, Pat and Jo Ann had many questions with respect to the franchising issue. Jo Ann expressed concern over the effects on their own

---

*EXHIBIT 12*
*Franchise*
*Obligations*

Typically, franchisors are obligated

- to locate or open new locations
- to stock new locations with equipment and inventory
- to train the operating staff
- to provide operating and accounting systems and manuals
- to coordinate purchases for franchisees and/or to act as a supplier
- to coordinate advertising.

Franchisees are usually subject to more contractual obligations. They must:

1. conduct periodic maintenance of the premises (i.e., redecorating or remodelling)
2. follow mandatory personnel policies
3. use suppliers approved by the franchisor
4. permit unscheduled inspections by the franchisor
5. use a standard accounting system
6. maintain uniform operating hours
7. carry minimum insurance coverage
8. obtain advertising approval from the franchisor
9. agree to territorial restrictions
10. accept quota clauses
11. follow pricing policies
12. make appropriate payments.

store: "I'm not sure how much time Pat and myself have to devote to another operation. And, if it's not done right and the franchise is unsuccessful, will the image of Fisher and Cooper suffer?" Both owners wondered whether someone without the experience in image creation and fashion retailing would be able to provide the same service that their customers seemed to enjoy.

### The Franchise Location

Total retail sales in London in 1982 were $1.286 billion ($4,497 per capita), 10% above the national average. Personal disposable income was $3.027 billion ($10,583 per capita) which was 8% above the national average. London's current growth rate was 10% per decade. According to the London Retailing Study (Pearce, Cullen, Green, Wee, 1984), London was overstored and retailing in London would become even more

aggressive as rivals competed for market share in a limited total market.

The tentative franchise location was in St. Thomas, approximately 45 kilometres south of London. St. Thomas had a population of 28,400 (1982) which was 10% the size of London. In London, 20% of the people had been to university while in St. Thomas, this number was 10%. The average income was $13,673 for London and $12,431 for St. Thomas. Further statistics for both London and St. Thomas are given in Exhibits 13 and 14.

Jo Ann and Pat wondered whether the store's concept was as viable in St. Thomas as it was in London.

There were many questions going through their minds, but they knew that they had to decide soon. Pat and Jo Ann realized that before they could answer these questions they had to understand how their own store was performing and what, if any, changes they should make.

| EXHIBIT 13 London Statistics | **Population:** | | |
|---|---|---|---|
| | Population, June 1, 1982 | | 286,000 |
| | % Canadian total | | 1.16 |
| | % Change, '76–'82 | | +5.77 |
| | **1976 Census:** | | |
| | Total | | 270,385 |
| | Male | | 131,820 |
| | Female | | 138,565 |
| | Age Groups: | Male | Female |
| | 0–4 | 10,005 | 9,330 |
| | 5–9 | 10,795 | 10,020 |
| | 10–14 | 12,600 | 12,030 |
| | 15–19 | 13,075 | 12,835 |
| | 20–24 | 13,550 | 14,860 |
| | 25–34 | 21,515 | 22,425 |
| | 35–44 | 15,210 | 15,235 |
| | 45–54 | 14,430 | 15,365 |
| | 55–64 | 10,965 | 11,845 |
| | 65–69 | 3,720 | 4,650 |
| | 70+ | 5,950 | 9,960 |

| Level of Schooling: | 1976 Census | % Total |
|---|---|---|
| Population, 15 years + | 205,570 | 100 |
| Less than Grade 5 | 4,845 | 2 |
| Grades 5-8 | 29,960 | 15 |
| Grades 9-10 | 38,790 | 19 |
| Grades 11-13 | 58,375 | 28 |
| Post secondary non-university | 33,545 | 16 |
| University only | 24,350 | 12 |
| University & post-secondary, non-university | 15,715 | 8 |

**Retail Trade:**

1971 Census

| | 1976 Census | |
|---|---|---|
| Total Sales, $000 | 478,163 | |
| Stores, no. | 1,789 | |
| Year-end inventory, $000 | 55,801 | |
| Employees, no. | 9,756 | |
| Payroll, total, $000 | 51,306 | |

| | Stores, No. | Sales, $000 |
|---|---|---|
| General Merchandise | 92 | 87,849 |
| Department | 8 | 65,476 |
| General Merchandise | 13 | 9,826 |
| Variety | 65 | 11,935 |
| Apparel & Accessories | 204 | 32,229 |
| Men's & Boys' Clothing | 33 | 8,490 |
| Women's & Misses' | 42 | 8,080 |
| Family Clothing | 19 | 4,522 |
| Family Shoe | 37 | 5,227 |

**Taxation Statistics:**  Total income = $2,261,025,000
Average income = $13,673

| Income class: | 1980 | % of Total |
|---|---|---|
| Under 2000 | 20,890 | 12.5 |
| 2000-4000 | 13,473 | 8.1 |
| 4000-6000 | 14,130 | 8.5 |
| 6000-10,000 | 26,485 | 16.0 |
| 10,500-15,000 | 30,903 | 18.7 |
| 15,000-20,000 | 23,544 | 14.2 |
| 20,000-30,000 | 24,183 | 14.6 |
| 30,000-40,000 | 7,129 | 4.3 |
| 40,000 plus | 4,609 | 2.8 |

| | | |
|---|---|---|
| *EXHIBIT 14*<br>*St. Thomas*<br>*Statistics* | | |

**Population:**

| | |
|---|---|
| Population, June 1, 1981 | 28,400 |
| % Canadian total | 0.12 |
| % Change, '76–'82 | +4.39 |

**1976 Census:**

| | |
|---|---|
| Total | 27,205 |
| Male | 12,840 |
| Female | 14,365 |

| Age Groups | Male | Female |
|---|---|---|
| 0–4 | 1,120 | 1,125 |
| 5–9 | 1,125 | 1,075 |
| 10–14 | 1,165 | 1,185 |
| 15–19 | 1,125 | 1,210 |
| 20–24 | 1,095 | 1,285 |
| 25–34 | 2,170 | 2,140 |
| 35–44 | 1,365 | 1,340 |
| 45–54 | 1,280 | 1,480 |
| 55–64 | 1,150 | 1,415 |
| 65–69 | 465 | 620 |
| 70+ | 780 | 1,490 |

| Level of Schooling: | 1976 Census | % Total |
|---|---|---|
| Population, 15 years + | 20,405 | 100 |
| Less than Grade 5 | 405 | 2 |
| Grades 5–8 | 3,635 | 18 |
| Grades 9–10 | 4,615 | 23 |
| Grades 11–13 | 5,960 | 29 |
| Post secondary<br>non-university | 3,605 | 18 |
| University only | 1,095 | 5 |
| University & post-secondary<br>non-university | 1,020 | 5 |

**Retail Trade:**

1971 Census

| | |
|---|---|
| Total Sales, $000 | 52,380 |
| Stores, no. | 210 |
| Year-end inventory, $000 | 5,604 |
| Employees, no. | 1,000 |
| Payroll, total, $000 | 5,104 |

|  | Stores, No. | Sales, $000 |
|---|---|---|
| General Merchandise | 13 | 5,357 |
| Department | n.a. | n.a. |
| General Merchandise | nil |  |
| Variety | 8 | 1,780 |
| Apparel & Accessories | 34 | 3,598 |
| Men's & Boys' Clothing | 5 | 1,056 |
| Women's & Misses' | 7 | Confidential |
| Family Clothing | 1 | Confidential |
| Family Shoe | 9 | Confidential |

**Taxation Statistics:** Total income = $284,126,000
Average income = $12,431

| Income class: | 1980 | % of Total |
|---|---|---|
| Under 2,000 | 3,024 | 13.2 |
| 2,000–4,000 | 1,862 | 8.1 |
| 4,000–6,000 | 1,929 | 8.4 |
| 6,000–10,000 | 3,897 | 17.1 |
| 10,500–15,000 | 4,632 | 20.3 |
| 15,000–20,000 | 3,553 | 15.5 |
| 20,000–30,000 | 2,937 | 12.8 |
| 30,000–40,000 | 641 | 2.8 |
| 40,000 plus | 380 | 1.7 |

# C A S E 3.11    Loblaws Supermarkets Limited: You Can Count on Us!

Mrs. Ineke Zigrossi, Director of Staffing and Development and Coordinator of the Customer Relations Program, Loblaws Supermarkets Ltd., Toronto, Ontario, was preparing for the upcoming meeting of the Customer Relations Advisory Board. During the meeting the Board planned to review the test store results and finalize the strategy for the Customer Relations Program. Mrs. Zigrossi had three main concerns: how the company's employees would react to the new program, how she could measure the program's results, and how she could maintain employee enthusiasm levels past the introductory stage.

The Customer Relations Program was scheduled for launch at the upcoming Annual Store Managers Conference on March 29, leaving only two weeks to resolve these implementation issues and make any final adjustments to the program.

## COMPANY BACKGROUND

Loblaws Supermarkets Ltd. (Loblaws) began in 1921 as a single grocery store in Toronto. By 1989 Loblaws included 105 stores in southwestern, central, and eastern Ontario. Loblaws position within George Weston Ltd. is shown in the organization chart in Exhibit 1. From 1986 to 1988 Loblaw Companies Ltd.'s eastern Canadian operations accounted for 40–45% of its sales and the portion had increased over that period. Loblaw Companies Ltd. was Canada's largest food distributor and operated in every province, except Quebec, and in the St. Louis and New Orleans regions of the United States. Its sales and operating income were the largest within George Weston Ltd.

From 1979 to 1987 Loblaw Companies Ltd. experienced consistent growth in both sales and profits (see Exhibit 2). Loblaw Companies Ltd. officials attributed the disappointing 1988 performance to strong price competition in the United States and central Canada along with Ontario consumers' rejection of the new Super-Centre concept. The SuperCentre concept combined food marketing with hard goods typical of department stores to create a one-stop shopping environment of up to 12,000 m² (about four times as large as a typical Loblaws store). In 1988 a number of Ontario SuperCentres were sold or reduced to Loblaws Warehouse Superstores (large food and drug outlets). The SuperCentre concept remained very successful in western Canada.

## Strengths Of The Organization

Over the years Loblaws developed a number of innovative retail grocery store concepts. First was the No Frills outlet: a low price, low service store targeted at price conscious consumers. During the 1980s Loblaws also introduced Warehouse Superstores, Garden Markets, and SuperCentre stores.

The variety of new store concepts reflected Loblaws' operating strategy. Mr. David Stewart, President of Loblaws Supermarkets Ltd., felt that the company's future depended on its ability to become the best target marketers in the business by meeting the specific needs of a customer in any given area:

> We have to tailor not only the selection, but the ambience of the store, the pricing strategy, and the level of customer service. We have to target all these things towards specific customers.

Loblaws also differentiated itself by introducing new and innovative products, especially with its Loblaws' private labels: No Name and President's Choice. The approximately 1,800 No Name products were targeted at price conscious consumers, providing similar quality to national brands at discount prices. The 750 President's Choice products catered to more affluent customers, offering extremely high quality, unique items. No Name products were introduced in 1978, a period of high inflation and high unemployment; President's Choice products became available in the early 1980s, a period of rapid economic growth. These private label lines enjoyed outstanding consumer reputations and awareness levels.

Loblaws published and distributed *Insider's Report*, a public relations newsletter, disguised as a comic book, that described new and innovative products. In 1989 Loblaws planned to introduce a line of superior nutritional products under the Nature's Choice label and a line of environmentally low hazard non-food items under the GREEN label. These two new product lines responded to consumers' growing concerns over environmental and health issues.

Loblaws' other innovative ideas included a full-colour mail order Christmas catalogue, a program of corporate gift baskets, a new wedding and floral business offering home delivery, a counter-ready vacuum-packed meat program at 'No Frills', an all natural beef program, and Ziggy's, an in-store delicatessen providing a full range of prepared foods. Loblaws also invested a lot of effort developing unique store designs, unlike the grocery industry's traditional standard approach to layouts.

## Employee Relations

Loblaws' management described the relationship with their employees as relatively healthy for the grocery industry. Management had a long-standing reputation of fostering open communication with their unions. Both held consistent goals aimed at preserving job security and corporate health. Loblaws had never had a work stoppage.

*EXHIBIT 1*
*Loblaws Companies*
*Ltd. Organizational*
*Chart*

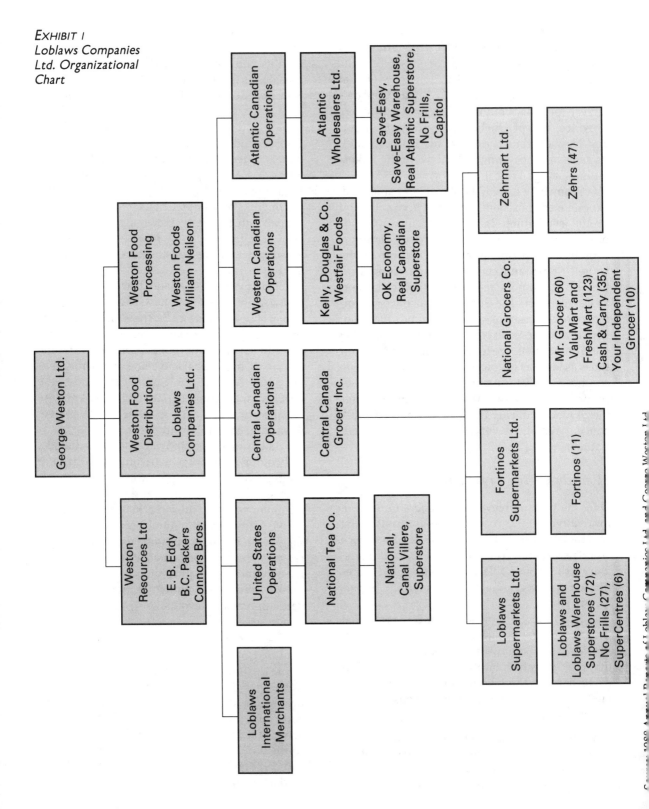

EXHIBIT 2
Loblaws Companies
Ltd. Ten Year
Financial
Performance

| Operating Results ($Millions) | | 1979 | 1980 | 1981 | 1982 | 1983 | 1984 | 1985 | 1986 | 1987 | 1988 |
|---|---|---|---|---|---|---|---|---|---|---|---|
| Eastern Canada: | Sales | 1,800 | 2,070 | 2,250 | 2,410 | 2,540 | 2,690 | 2,780 | 3,070 | 3,600 | 3,710 |
| | Operating Income[1] | 29 | 52 | 53 | 56 | 62 | 70 | 72 | 74 | 107 | 78 |
| Western Canada: | Sales | 1,300 | 1,420 | 1,600 | 1,710 | 1,580 | 1,700 | 1,890 | 2,030 | 2,090 | 2,340 |
| | Operating Income[1] | 24 | 29 | 36 | 33 | 36 | 38 | 48 | 61 | 52 | 61 |
| United States: | Sales | 1,600 | 1,890 | 1,950 | 2,100 | 1,970 | 2,030 | 2,260 | 2,740 | 2,940 | 2,260 |
| | Operating Income[1] | 26 | 31 | 31 | 32 | 32 | 34 | 35 | 33 | 37 | 29 |
| Corporate: | Sales | 4,730 | 5,380 | 5,800 | 6,220 | 6,090 | 6,420 | 6,930 | 7,840 | 8,630 | 8,310 |
| | Operating Income[1,2] | 72 | 99 | 113 | 115 | 128 | 138 | 152 | 163 | 190 | 160 |
| | Net Earnings[3] | 46 | 53 | 39 | 53 | 64 | 64 | 67 | 74 | 74 | 26 |
| **Financial Position ($Million)** | | | | | | | | | | | |
| Total Debt | | | 195 | 231 | 220 | 253 | 223 | 283 | 390 | 569 | 686 | 623 |
| Total Shareholders' Equity | | | 242 | 277 | 317 | 344 | 413 | 466 | 521 | 655 | 690 | 651 |
| Total Assets | | | 868 | 962 | 1,034 | 1,111 | 1,151 | 1,264 | 1,530 | 1,978 | 2,214 | 2,004 |
| **Changes in Financial Position ($Millions)** | | | | | | | | | | | |
| Cash Flow From Operations | | | 75 | 98 | 111 | 114 | 118 | 124 | 132 | 204 | 182 | 158 |
| Purchase of Fixed Assets | | | 99 | 92 | 92 | 69 | 98 | 148 | 192 | 289 | 232 | 186 |
| **Financial Ratios** | | | | | | | | | | | |
| Return on Common Equity | | | 15.2% | 16.9 | 16.3 | 15.3 | 16.3 | 16.3 | 15.6 | 14.6 | 12.5 | 5.9 |
| Pretax Return On Sales | | | 1.1% | 1.4 | 1.4 | 1.4 | 1.7 | 1.7 | 1.7 | 1.5 | 1.5 | 0.8 |
| Return On Capital Employed | | | 14.8% | 17.3 | 18.0 | 17.5 | 18.6 | 18.1 | 17.0 | 14.3 | 13.6 | 11.2 |
| Working Capital Ratio | | | 1.23 | 1.22 | 1.23 | 1.20 | 1.24 | 1.26 | 1.20 | 1.27 | 1.17 | 1.12 |
| Total Debt To Equity Ratio | | | 0.81 | 0.83 | 0.70 | 0.74 | 0.56 | 0.61 | 0.75 | 0.87 | 0.99 | 0.96 |

Notes: [1] Operating Income = Sales − Costs of Sales − Selling and Administrative Expenses.
   [2] The corporate rate income includes some small negative figures originating in head office.
   [3] Net Earnings = Operating Income − Interest Expense − Capital Lease Obligation − Income Tax − Extraordinary Items.
Source: Loblaw Companies Ltd. 1979–88 Annual Reports.

The company employed about 12,000 people in its stores and 400 at head office. Part-time employees accounted for 70% of the Loblaws labour force and 50% of the total hours worked. The part-time employees tended to be young and unskilled, with an annual turnover rate of about 35% (which Loblaws officials felt was low for the industry). Part-time labour offered significant cost and scheduling benefits over full-time employees: the company did not have to

*EXHIBIT 3*
*Grocery Store*
*Market Share*
*Information for*
*the Ontario*
*Market*

| Chains | 1979 | 1980 | 1981 | 1982 | 1983 | 1984 | 1985 | 1986 | 1987 | 1988 |
|---|---|---|---|---|---|---|---|---|---|---|
| Loblaws | 21.6% | 20.6% | 18.7% | 16.9% | 15.1% | 15.3% | 12.1% | 12.3% | 12.0% | 12.9% |
| Dominion and A&P | 39.4 | 38.6 | 38.0 | 36.1 | 31.9 | 28.7 | 25.7 | 23.8 | 22.4 | 19.9 |
| Steinberg & Miracle | 13.8 | 12.8 | 12.3 | 10.9 | 10.7 | 12.0 | 14.8 | 15.6 | 15.7 | 14.9 |
| Food City | 4.2 | 4.7 | 4.7 | 4.8 | 5.4 | 5.8 | 7.9 | 8.0 | 7.8 | 8.5 |
| Safeway | 3.2 | 3.8 | 3.7 | 3.9 | 3.4 | 3.0 | 2.1 | 1.0 | 1.1 | 0.0 |
| Total Chains | 82.8 | 80.5 | 77.4 | 72.6 | 66.5 | 64.8 | 62.6 | 60.7 | 59.0 | 56.2 |
| **Independents** | | | | | | | | | | |
| I.G.A. | 4.1 | 4.4 | 4.7 | 5.2 | 6.4 | 7.9 | 9.8 | 11.3 | 10.6 | 11.7 |
| Convenience Stores | 13.7 | 15.1 | 17.9 | 22.2 | 27.1 | 27.3 | 27.6 | 28.0 | 30.4 | 31.2 |
| Total Independents | 17.8 | 19.5 | 22.6 | 27.4 | 33.5 | 35.2 | 37.4 | 39.3 | 41.0 | 42.9 |

Note: Data are from surveys conducted in several major Ontario markets on behalf of Loblaws by an independent market research firm. The 1988 data are for the first quarter only.

Source: Loblaws Supermarket Ltd. files.

pay the higher wage rates or benefits required by full-time employees and had the flexibility of scheduling short or split shifts.

## RETAIL GROCERY INDUSTRY

The Ontario retail grocery industry remained very competitive; pretax profits averaged only 1–2% of sales. The industry had reached maturity because of slowing population growth rates, low food price increases, and declining per capita expenditures on groceries (people were more frequently eating outside of their homes). In 1988 the corporate unionized chains, such as Loblaws, A&P, Dominion, Miracle Mart, Safeway, and Food City, had about 56% of the market. The smaller independents and franchises, including IGA, Mr. Grocers, Fortinos, Your Independent Grocers, and the growing number of convenience stores, held the balance (Exhibit 3). The independents' market share was steadily increasing.

Success in this competitive market depended on a grocery store's location and the variety, quality, and selection of its products. A successful grocery store also had to establish a strong relationship between prices and quality, and create an attractive shopping environment. The competitive strength of the large chains was in their ability to invest heavily in real estate, merchandising, and communication programs. Independent chains were less complex and required less investment in computer systems or communication campaigns giving them better cost structures because of lower labour and overhead expenses. Many independents had an added competitive advantage because they provided a higher level of customer service and a more personal atmosphere than the large chains.

## CUSTOMER SERVICE AT LOBLAWS

Mr. Stewart had been aware before of the need for Loblaws to develop superior customer service, but other issues had taken priority. He also realized that management's previous efforts to increase store level labour efficiency had often taken employee attention away from the customer. Although customer surveys indicated that Loblaws was the number one rated grocery chain in two large Ontario metropolitan areas, the company still lagged behind some of its major competitors in services offered (see Exhibit 4 for the February 1989 results).

Mr. Stewart realized that any successful attempt to change customers' perceptions would require a large commitment of human and financial resources. However, in 1988, he felt confi-

EXHIBIT 4
Results from
Customer Surveys,
February 1989

| COMPETITIVE POSITION | Loblaws | I.G.A. | Dominion | A & P | Miracle & Steinberg | Food City |
|---|---|---|---|---|---|---|
| Rank | 1 | 2 | 3 | 4 | 5 | 6 |
| Last Shop Share | 35 | 20 | 9 | 6 | 5 | 5 |
| Most Often Shopped | 38 | 18 | 9 | 5 | 7 | 6 |
| Short List | 63 | 38 | 20 | 21 | 17 | 11 |
| Conversion Ratio | 56 | 53 | 45 | 29 | 29 | 45 |
| Average Best Rated | 36 | 15 | 5 | 4 | 5 | 5 |
| Overall Bestdex | 104 | 75 | 58 | 68 | 97 | 105 |
| **Bestdex Profile** | | | | | | |
| Location | 78 | 119 | 64 | 110 | 120 | 140 |
| Food/Grocery Selection | 128 | 21 | 64 | 58 | 110 | 90 |
| New/Different Products | 128 | 53 | 29 | 46 | 70 | 80 |
| Private Labels | 142 | 27 | 36 | 39 | 70 | 80 |
| Featured Specials | 71 | 78 | 50 | 93 | 130 | 120 |
| Overall Prices | 80 | 85 | 21 | 89 | 140 | 120 |
| Value for Money | 109 | 72 | 64 | 66 | 130 | 90 |
| Quality and Freshness | 112 | 61 | 86 | 75 | 80 | 90 |
| Specialty Departments | 122 | 36 | 64 | 70 | 100 | 110 |
| Modern and Trendsetting | 136 | 36 | 50 | 73 | 60 | 110 |
| Trustworthy | 93 | 80 | 71 | 66 | 100 | 100 |
| Enjoyable to Shop | 108 | 108 | 57 | 60 | 70 | 100 |
| Check-out Speed | 69 | 107 | 64 | 59 | 100 | 130 |
| Staff | 74 | 117 | 71 | 45 | 80 | 110 |
| Cleanliness | 108 | 80 | 79 | 83 | 90 | 110 |

Notes: All figures are expressed as percentages. The data are based on periodic surveys of shoppers by an independent market research firm. The 'short list' figures are the portion of respondents who indicated that they ever shop at the respective store. The 'conversion ratio' is 'last shopped share'/'short list'. The survey asked respondents to indicate which store is 'best' in various categories making up the 'bestdex profile' — the ratio of 'best rated'/'last shop share' in each category. The 'overall bestdex' is the simple unweighted average of the 'bestdex profile' scores for each store and is close to the ratio of 'best rated'/'last shop share'.
Source: Loblaws Supermarket Ltd. files.

dent that Loblaws was in a position to address the issue. In order to begin generating ideas on customer service issues Mr. Stewart invited two customer service consultants, Ms Anne Mitchel and Mr. Dave Bolton of two well-known human resources consulting firms, to join a Loblaws senior executive think tank session. Ms Mitchel and Mr. Bolton helped develop a customer service program for a major U.S. grocery chain, regarded as one of the best in the industry. Mr. Bolton commented on the importance of generating open management-employee dialogue on customer relations issues:

> Employee relations mirror customer relations as there is a strong correlation between customer and employee views of service quality and the internal climate for service.

He also emphasized the powerful benefits of superior customer service:

1. Five times as much effort, energy, time and money are spent to attract a new customer as to retain a current client.

2. The average service business loses between 10 and 15% of its customer base yearly because of poor or inattentive service.

3. A customer with a satisfactorily resolved problem will produce three times the revenue of a customer whose problem remains unresolved.

4. Ninety percent of the time the customer will request an adjustment that will be quite reasonable compared to what you are willing to offer.

5. Each happy customer tells at least five others of the experience.

6. Ninety-six percent of unhappy customers never complain but:
   a. Ninety percent never return,
   b. He or she tells nine others,
   c. Thirteen percent tell at least 20 others.

The July 1988 session exposed senior management to a variety of perspectives on customer service, a subject that Mr. Stewart hoped would become a number one priority within the organization.

Loblaws senior management team began to search for ways to improve customer service. They perceived service at Loblaws to include clean stores, neat appearance of staff, fast checkouts, prices on or near products, and courteous, helpful staff. Senior management chose to concentrate on the human interaction aspects of service as the other factors were already addressed on a daily operational basis. The focus of Loblaws efforts would be on customer *relations*, rather than customer *service*, emphasizing the need to understand and improve the relationship between employees and customers. Mr. Stewart said:

> Understanding customer satisfaction is the most important thing we can do. It will affect each and every one of our actions during the day. Loblaws cannot control how an employee acts or reacts to situations; the reaction must come from within. At Loblaws we want to prepare individuals in terms of attitudes, beliefs, and self-confidence. We want to encourage them to use their own initiative, make their own judgements, and follow their own instincts when it comes to dealing with customers.

Under Mr. Stewart's initiative and Mrs. Zigrossi's coordination the company committed itself to ensure that employees were competent at handling customer relations, to highlight outstanding customer service, and to invite customers to participate in Customer Appreciation Days. Loblaws' senior management believed that they could not change the customer so the change target would have to be the employees. The company planned to provide employees with the following elements of service training:

1. Explain the importance of good customer relations and how the individual contributes to the service impression.

2. Suggest techniques for dealing with customers.

3. Offer participative skills training and practice sessions.

## THE CUSTOMER RELATIONS PROGRAM

In September 1988 Mrs. Zigrossi set out to fulfil her mandate of coordinating the design and implementation of the new Customer Relations Program. Ultimately, Mrs. Zigrossi hoped to instill customer relations as Loblaws' most important corporate value, both at head office and the store level. She believed this change would have to come through employee training and hired Ms Mitchell to assist her in redesigning and improving Loblaws' training program.

In November 1988 Mrs. Zigrossi and Ms Mitchel presented their first recommendation to Mr. Stewart: establish an Advisory Board responsible for implementing a chain-wide Customer Service Program. The Board would be chaired by Mrs. Zigrossi and would report directly to Mr. Stewart. By December 1988 Mr. Stewart had invited 13 individuals (store level to head office staff with varying degrees of seniority) to join the Advisory Board, thus ensuring input from all levels of the organization (see Exhibit 5).

At its first meeting in January 1989, Mr. Stewart emphasized his expectations for the Board: enthusiasm, problem solving, and a long-term commitment to make customer relations the number one priority at Loblaws. The Board also developed a theme for the new Customer Relations Program: *You Can Count On Me!*, emphasizing the importance of individual employee contributions to the customer relations process.

The Advisory Board realized that changing employee perspectives on customer relations would involve training thousands of people including all store and head office personnel. The number of people affected by the Customer Relations Program dictated that the Advisory Board prioritize its efforts. Store level employees were given first priority for training because of their daily interaction with customers. Head office staff would be included in the program by September 1989; it was equally important that head office employees develop skills to improve service for suppliers and the various Loblaws departments, as well as for their main customers, the store employees.

The Advisory Board established four subcommittees (Store Involvement Committee, Employee Feedback Committee, Standards and Training Committee, and Communications Committee) with responsibilities to launch the new Customer Relations Program. Each subcommittee consisted of three or four members of the Advisory Board and, under the direction of Mrs. Zigrossi and Mr. Stewart, each Subcommittee met and defined its role, range of responsibilities, and priorities.

### Store Involvement Committee

The Store Involvement Committee was responsible for implementing the customer relations program at the store level. The Committee suggested establishing In-Store Committees within each store to link the store, its employees, and the Store Involvement Committee. The store manager would oversee the In-Store Committee and encourage enthusiastic employees to become involved. The In-Store Committees would enable every Loblaws' employee to participate in the new Customer Relations Program and give them the opportunity to submit 'ground level' suggestions, preferably ones that would be practical and easy to implement. The Store Involvement Committee also developed plans for two trial 'Customer Appreciation Days' to encourage interaction between customers and employees and to promote a feeling of loyalty among customers. These days are described in more detail below.

### Employee Feedback Committee

The Employee Feedback Committee was responsible for monitoring employee suggestions or questions related to customer service or customer relations. They designed suggestion cards that read 'Getting it Right' (see Exhibit 6). Suggestion boxes would be located in every store and the In-Store Committees would review the suggestions, implement them if possible, or send them along to the Employee Feedback Committee. The Employee Feedback Committee would then take action or forward the suggestion to the appropriate department. The Employee Feedback Committee would ensure that every employee received a quick response to his or her recommendation or question.

*EXHIBIT 5
Invitation to Join
the Customer
Service Advisory
Board*

**Loblaws**

MEMORANDUM

Date: December 21, 1988

To:
| | |
|---|---|
| Doug Boylin | Sr. Manager, Sales Merchandising Planning |
| Reno Cramarossa | Pricing Manager |
| Mary Dalimonte | Special Projects Manager |
| Marcella Fellin | Front End Specialist |
| Bill Hazlitt | Store Manager #206 |
| Elroy Kranz | V.P. Operations |
| Jan Phillips | Back-Up Head Cashier #194 |
| Susan Poulter | Sr. Manager, In-Store Marketing |
| Shad Qadri | Dell Specialist |
| Fred Roult | Director, Systems Audit |
| Marie Saffery | Director, Public Relations and Store Communications |
| Jack Semple | Store Manager, #205 |
| Mima Summers | Sr. Co-ordinator, Front End Training |

From: David Stewart

As part of Loblaws' commitment to service excellence for our customers, I invite you to participate on an Advisory Board that will be responsible for the implementation of a chainwide Customer Service Program. The Board will report to me and be under the direction of Ineke Zigrossi, our Director of Operations Staffing and Development.

Details for participating on the Advisory Board will be forwarded to you under separate cover from Ineke. The first meeting is scheduled for January 5th from 2:00 to 6:00 p.m. in the Penthouse at 6 Monogram. Also, please plan to attend training for the Customer Service Program, the following day from 8:30 a.m. to 4:30 p.m.

I'm excited about the possibilities the customer service effort provides and I welcome your support.

Regards,

David Stewart
President
Loblaws Supermarkets Ltd. and
Combined Merchandisers Inc.

cc: R. Bureau
C. Whitney
I. Zigrossi

LOBLAWS SUPERMARKETS LIMITED
6 MONOGRAM PLACE,
WESTON, ONTARIO, CANADA M9R 4C4

EXHIBIT 6
Getting It Right
Employee
Suggestion
Forms

*GETTING IT RIGHT*

Questions/Suggestions: _____

_____

_____

_____

_____

Employee Name: _____     Department: _____

Store Number: _____     Store Address: _____

Date: _____

*Working With You To Improve Customer Service*

Source: Loblaws Supermarket Ltd. files.

## Standards and Training Committee

The Standards and Training Committee would assist Mrs. Zigrossi in scheduling and monitoring the new training program. The Committee also developed a set of corporate standards that ensured excellent service for each Loblaws customer. These standards included guidelines for staff appearance, enthusiasm, and product knowledge:

1.  Look your best!
2.  Be friendly!
3.  Make enthusiasm work for your!
4.  Give the customer your full attention!
5.  Do it now!
6.  Know your store!
7.  Be a team player!

## Communications Committee

The objective of the Communications Committee was to promote, throughout the organization, a clear understanding of the importance of superior customer relations and make customer relations a personal commitment for every Loblaws' employee. The ultimate goal was to achieve demonstrable improvements in the area of customer relations and enable the company to advertise and promote these improvements (see Exhibit 7).

The Communications Committee became the public relations force behind the customer relations campaign. To assist it in this task the Communications Committee hired the services of a marketing and corporate communications company which designed the *You Can Count On Me!* customer relations training handbook to be fun and easy to read. The company also created the format of a newsletter that focused on employee and customer relations, and monitored the activities and progress of the Customer Relations Program. Loblaws used an outside communications firm to ensure that the material developed for the program would be consistent and professional.

## Training Program

Mrs. Zigrossi and Ms Mitchel designed the new training program to emphasize human interaction skills. In order to tailor the program specifically to Loblaws' employees, both Mrs. Zigrossi and Ms Mitchell travelled to many Loblaws' locations and interviewed a large number of employees; they were determined to integrate employee perspectives into the new program.

*EXHIBIT 7*
*Customer
Relations
Communications
Program:
Objectives and
Strategies*

## OBJECTIVE

Create a clear understanding of the importance of superior customer relations throughout the organization and make it a personal commitment for every Loblaws person.

## STRATEGY

### I. Nothing is more important.

Move customer relations up the agenda, both corporately and personally. Emphasize to each Loblaws person the significance of customer relations superiority to the success of the business and therefore to his/her own success. Attitude breeds performance and excellence is expected.

### 2. Commitment to superiority.

Communicate to Loblaws people the commitment of top management to an attitude which will result in demonstrably superior customer relations. This is an enduring commitment, not the flavour of the week.

### 3. Individual buy-in.

Isolate the role of the individual in contributing to the whole service impression: convert corporate intention into personal commitment.

### 4. Customer awareness.

Provide for expansion of the communication program to the customer level when appropriate: first through in store osmosis, then, only when results are demonstrable, through advertising and promotion.

Source: Loblaws Supermarkets Ltd. files.

Ms Mitchel tested the training program on the 13 member Advisory Board and proceeded to teach the training techniques to six trainers. The trainers then tested the new program from January 16 to February 11 at the Agincourt Mall store in suburban Toronto and the Cataraqui Mall store in Kingston. They planned to visit the remaining stores over an 18 month period starting after the Annual Store Managers Conference. Loblaws chose the Agincourt and Cataraqui stores as test sites because they were well-established, stable stores, they represented both a large and a smaller community, and each had a well-respected manager who served on the Advisory Board.

The first part of the four hour training program consisted of an employee questionnaire that probed the individual's feelings about customer relations and their role at Loblaws (see *Exhibit 8* for the Cataraqui Mall store results). This information was intended to provide the Committee with an understanding of current employee perspectives and the potential areas for improvement.

The next stage of the training program introduced the participants to each other, the new Customer Relations Program, the role of the committees, and the reasons why they were there. Each training workshop included about 20 people chosen from a variety of store departments and job descriptions. The workshops were held at varying times throughout the day and night so that employees could participate during their regularly scheduled shifts.

The trainers and workshop participants then discussed the seven standards for superior customer service and, after a short break, discussed the judgements and distractions that are a part of everyday life in the retail grocery industry. Recognizing these factors would enable employees to become more open-minded towards the public. Mrs. Zigrossi realized that prejudices would never be totally eliminated, but felt that the workshops would encourage employees to give customers the benefit of the doubt. The trainers gave employees both suggestions for managing the daily distractions that could negatively impact their job performances and a three-step process for dealing with customer complaints:

1. Acknowledge customers and make them aware that they count.

2. Explain the reasons for the problem.

3. Provide a workable compromise, offer the customer a solution that is acceptable for both parties.

The participants practised these skills using role plays during which each employee had the opportunity to be either a manager, another employee, or customer faced with a unique customer relations problem.

At the end of the session each employee received a copy of the *You Can Count On Me!* training manual and filled out a Seminar Evaluation Form which asked for their thoughts on the appropriateness of the program and any suggestions for improvement (see *Exhibit 9* for the Cataraqui Mall store results). Mrs. Zigrossi commented on the similar feedback they received from both test stores:

> We got fairly consistent responses to the question: 'How can Loblaws, as a company, recognize employees who give good customer service?' on the Participant Survey. Employees commonly suggested that management praise or just saying thank you for a job well done was the way to go. Other

suggestions included bonus plans or other monetary incentives, employee of the week or month awards, customer evaluation forms being passed around to all employees, and customer feedback to individual employees. Another comment that appeared a number of times was that staff shortages made it difficult to serve customers properly. Some participants also mentioned the importance of improving the relationship between staff as well as with the customers.

> The feedback we got from the Seminar Evaluation Forms was very positive. The participants said that they had a great time and that the trainers did a super job. They found the role plays very effective and said that the experience of being someone else gave them a unique perspective on their own jobs. In fact, a number of people recommended spending more time on the role plays.

### Customer Appreciation Days

The Customer Appreciation Days were to consist of a sign welcoming the customer, 'We are happy you are here!', and give-aways that included: coffee, President's Choice cookies, a piece of cake decorated to read 'You Can Count On Us!', Pepsi, $0.50 hot dogs, Teddy's Choice Raisins for the kids (Teddy was a Teddy Bear designed to appeal to children that appeared on Loblaws packaging), carnations, and special coupons. Customer Appreciation Days were developed to expose store employees and management to some of the elements available in creating a fun day of shopping.

The Customer Appreciation Day concept was tested on March 2 at the Agincourt Mall store (see *Exhibit 10*) and on March 3 at the Cataraqui Mall store. Funds to pay for these and future Customer Appreciation Days were provided by head office, each store having a budget of $1,500 per event. Mrs. Zigrossi described the Customer Appreciation Days:

> The goal behind the Customer Appreciation Days is to give the store employees a chance to practise some of the skills that we taught them during the training sessions. We want the In-Store Committees to try and have their Customer Appreciation Day within 8 weeks of completing their training workshops. This helps keep enthusiasm levels high and maintains interest in the Customer Relations Program.

EXHIBIT 10
Customer
Appreciation Day
Promotional
Material

We give each In-Store Committee a set of guidelines, a budget, and suggestions on how to run the Days, but we leave the fine-tuning up to them. We want to encourage them to be creative and get everyone involved. We also supply them with flyers to leave around the store and use as bag-stuffers. We don't use any form of external advertising because we want it to be a special day for our regular customers. We want our employees and our customers to get together and have a fun day at Loblaws! We also try and encourage the In-Store committees to get other members of the community involved in Customer Appreciation Days. For example, all proceeds from hot dog sales go to a local charity.

In my view the two test store Days were a great success. Employees came in on their own time to help set-up and run the special give-away counters. Our customers loved it! The kids had a great time presenting their Teddy's Choice Credit Cards for free cookies. The kids get to keep their cards. Every time they come to the store in the future they can get another free cookie. Everyone was really excited! Both stores had an above average number of customers during the Appreciation Days. We got a lot of positive comments. People wanted to know when the next day was going to be held!

We also got some very positive feedback from our employees. Their comments included trying to tie in more promotions with the give-aways. For example, give out coupons with the President's Choice coffee or hot dogs. They also recommended more signs to clearly explain to customers what the Day was all about. The only complaint I heard was that employees would have liked to have been more involved in serving the food, they felt that there were too many visiting head office people working at the give-away counters.

## IMPLEMENTATION ISSUES

Mrs. Zigrossi found the development of the Customer Relations Program a relatively smooth process. The enthusiastic support of senior management and the Advisory Board meant that she did not have to spend time trying to sell the

EXHIBIT 8
*Participant Survey*
*Form and Test Store*
*Results*

| | Strongly Agree 5 | Agree 4 | Un-certain 3 | Disagree 2 | Strongly Disagree 1 | Weigh-ted Average Score |
|---|---|---|---|---|---|---|
| 1. Courtesy is a skill that can be learned. | 44% | 54% | 0% | 2% | 0% | 4.40 |
| 2. What is going on in my personal life often affects how I deal with customers. | 15 | 41 | 10 | 31 | 3 | 3.34 |
| 3. I am responsible for whether or not a customer interaction is pleasant. | 24 | 51 | 8 | 16 | 0 | 3.80 |
| 4. I know that different kinds of customers get different kinds of treatment from me. | 10 | 41 | 8 | 23 | 10 | 2.94 |
| 5. I feel that Loblaws is truly committed to customer service. | 15 | 46 | 23 | 13 | 0 | 3.54 |
| 6. It's possible to be courteous while telling customers that they are mistaken. | 29 | 59 | 8 | 3 | 1 | 4.12 |
| 7. I put aside my judgements when dealing with customers. | 11 | 52 | 26 | 10 | 0 | 3.61 |
| 8. Work frustrations often affect how I deal with customers. | 16 | 43 | 16 | 20 | 5 | 3.45 |
| 9. I view my job as important to Loblaws. | 43 | 44 | 10 | 2 | 2 | 4.27 |
| 10. I feel differently about different kinds of customers. | 6 | 38 | 16 | 26 | 10 | 2.92 |
| 11. My ability to be courteous rarely depends on the customer's behaviour. | 10 | 37 | 16 | 26 | 10 | 3.08 |
| 12. When I'm distracted it affects how I deal with customers. | 11 | 37 | 20 | 23 | 8 | 3.17 |
| 13. Loblaws views my role as important. | 29 | 34 | 26 | 8 | 2 | 3.77 |

How can Loblaws, as a company, recognize employees who give good customer service:

Other comments or suggestions:

Optional: (Used only for statistical research): 50 people responded to these questions.

| Age: (years) | 16-19 10% | 20-30 36% | 31-40 36% | > 40 13% | Length of Service: (years) | < 1 16% | 1-2 8% | 2-4 10% | 4-10 22% | > 10 44% |
|---|---|---|---|---|---|---|---|---|---|---|

Note: A total of 61 employees from the Cataraqui Mall store completed this survey. Percentages may not total 100% because some respondents did not answer all questions.

Source: Loblaws Supermarkets Ltd. files.

*EXHIBIT 9*
*Seminar Evaluation*
*Forms and Test Store*
*Results*

This questionnaire will be used to evaluate the workshop you have just completed. It will not be used to evaluate participants, and you are not expected to identify yourself.

The questionnaire is divided into two sections. In the first one, you simply circle numbers in order to express your opinions. The second section gives you an opportunity to make comments or suggestions.

## Section 1:  Seminar Content and Delivery

Circle the number that comes closest to expressing your opinion. Notice that the words written above numbers 1 and 6 are not the same for every question.

|  |  |
|---|---|
| 1. What was the overall value of the seminar to you? | No Value        Extremely Valuable<br>1   2   3   4   5   6<br>Weighted Average Score = 5.2 |
| 2. Was the course content relevant to your job? | Not at All        Extremely<br>1   2   3   4   5   6<br>Weighted Average Score = 5.7 |
| 3. How would you rate your level of participation? | Low Participation    Active Participation<br>1   2   3   4   5   6<br>Weighted Average Score = 5.1 |
| 4. Were you satisfied with the results you achieved in the seminar? | Not at All        Extremely<br>1   2   3   4   5   6<br>Weighted Average Score = 5.2 |
| 5. Do you feel you can do your job better because of this seminar? | Not at All        Definitely<br>1   2   3   4   5   6<br>Weighted Average Score = 5.6 |
| 6. Would you recommend this seminar to others in your organization? | Not at All        Highly<br>1   2   3   4   5   6<br>Weighted Average Score = 5.7 |

## Section 2:  Comments and Suggestions:

Please answer the following questions. This section provides data that is essential for improving our seminars.

1. Which information was of most value to you?

2. What sections of the seminar do you consider to be weak areas? Why?

3. What suggestions would you make to improve the seminar?

4. How effective was the staff leadership of the workshop?

5. Additional comments.

Note:  A total of 61 employees from the Cataraqui Mall store completed this survey.
Source:  Loblaws Supermarkets Ltd. files.

project; instead she progressed quickly to the implementation stage. The feedback from the test stores seemed very positive but she wondered if Loblaws' remaining 12,000 employees would react with similar enthusiasm. The Advisory Board planned to review the test store results at their next meeting.

Mrs. Zigrossi realized that she would have to develop some criteria and methods for measuring the success of the Customer Relations Program. She considered using consumer surveys, focus groups, employee surveys, or supervisor feedback forms. Should she look for some sort of quantitative measure such as increased sales, reduced employee turnover, or absenteeism? If so, how could she set target levels? Who should be responsible for taking measurements, one of the Advisory Board's subcommittees or an outside research consultant? When should measurements be made and how often? When would Loblaws be confident enough to advertise its improved customer relations to the public?

Given the organization's reliance on part-time labour and its high turnover rate, Mrs. Zigrossi was also concerned about maintaining employee motivation and enthusiasm levels. Should a reward and recognition program be incorporated to ensure success? Who should administer the program? How long could the organization reasonably expect to keep interest levels high — six months, one year, three years, five years? The coordination required to train over 12,000 people seemed like an insurmountable task.

The Board planned to discuss these implementation issues and finalize the program's strategy at its upcoming meeting. Mrs. Zigrossi had only two weeks to make final program adjustments before the planned launch at the Annual Store Managers Conference. With a program budget of over $1,000,000 in the first year, she knew that senior management in both the Loblaws and Weston organizations would be carefully watching this new customer relations effort.

# C A S E 3.12   Some Exercises in Retail Pricing

1. A buyer paid $24 a dozen for golf balls and planned to obtain a $1.00 markup on each ball. What should the initial retail price be? What is the initial markup percentage on cost? What is the initial markup percentage on retail?

2. A tennis racquet costing $5 is to be sold with a markup of 45 percent on retail. What should the initial retail price be?

3. A markup of 40 percent on cost is equivalent to what percentage on retail?

4. A buyer finds a dress in a manufacturer's showroom and estimates it should retail at $120. She needs a markup of 42 percent on initial retail. How much should she pay for the dress to realize her objectives?

5. What dollar gross margin would result from the following operation:

| | |
|---|---|
| gross sales | $30,000 |
| invoice cost | $20,000 |
| alteration expenses | $   600 |
| discounts to employees | $   400 |
| stock shortages | $   500 |
| discounts earned | $ 2,000 |
| markdowns | $ 4,000 |

6. You have been buying a line of clothing at an average of $60 a unit and selling it for an average of $105 a unit. The manufacturer has raised the price to $66, but you don't want to change your retail price because of a promotional campaign you have begun. What percentage must your sales increase to maintain the same dollar markup you are now realizing?

7. From the following information, calculate the percent of markup on retail Dept. B would need if the store were to achieve an average 45 percent markup.

| | % Markup | $ Net Sales |
|---|---|---|
| Dept A | 40 | $30,000 |
| Dept B |  | $40,000 |
| Dept C | 42 | $50,000 |
| Dept D | 39 | $20,000 |

8. A buyer purchased 500 lamps at $60 each to retail for $99.95 each. 300 lamps sold at $99 and the remaining lamps were sold at $79.95. If all the lamps had been sold at $99.95 what would have been the initial markup in dollars and in percentage on retail? What was the maintained markup in dollars and in percentage on retail? What was the dollar markdown on lamps? What was the markdown as a percentage of initial retail price (markdown off %), and the markdown goods percentage (sales of goods marked down as a % of total net sales)?

9. A national brand shoe costs $54 and sells for $90 per pair. Last year 3,000 pairs were sold in your store, but of these 500 were marked down and sold for $60 per pair. The brand is charged for 75 square feet of space at $24 per foot per year. Interest is also charged for the carrying cost on the inventory at 20 percent per year. Half of the shoes were delivered to customers at an average cost of $1.50 per pair. Other handling costs charged to this product were estimated at $.75 per pair. Variable costs on net sales included 6 percent for selling and 2 percent for advertising, after deducting advertising allowances from the vendor. Opening inventory at cost was $81,000 and closing inventory was $64,800. Returns to the vendor at cost were $2,160. The vendor offered a cash discount of 2 percent on purchases and all such discounts were taken. Returns from customers were all sold at the marked down price or returned to the vendor. What was the percentage initial

markup on retail and the percentage maintained markup on retail? What was the markdown as a percentage of the actual selling price (markdown %), and the markdown as a percentage of total net sales (cumulative markdown %)? Considering space, interest, delivery and other direct costs as controllable expenses, what was the controllable margin as a percentage of net sales?

10. The stationery department has a markup of 38 percent, an operating profit of 12 percent on sales, and a stock turn of 3.1. The book department has a markup of 42 percent, an operating profit of 10 percent, and a stock turn of 2.6. Based on these numbers alone, if your objective is GMROI, which department is performing better?

11. The chart below shows simplified data for three consumer packaged goods products being carried in your supermarket. Not all Direct Product Costs have been included in the chart. The manufacturer of Brand C is offering a special deal. Brand C will be delivered directly from the manufacturer to the stores rather than going through your warehouse, in pre-packaged displays to put in your stores at end of aisle. Brand C will be pre-priced at $1.69, with an off-invoice allowance of $5.00 per case. Your Direct Product Costs will change in a net fashion down 30%. Anticipated volume for the two weeks you expect to have Brand C at end-of-aisle position is eight times normal. The previous two weeks are expected to be at normal volumes while the two week post-feature period would be at 50% normal volume at the regular retail price. For the six week period, the retailer would have a reduced purchase price, but would have the normal DPC's for the first two and last two week periods. You anticipate that increased sales of Brand C would reduce sales of Brand A 20% and Brand B 10% during the feature period. Given these changes, you're wondering whether this deal is a good one in terms of impact on Direct Product Profit.

| | Brand A | Brand B | Brand C |
|---|---|---|---|
| # SKU's | 10 | 2 | 4 |
| Linear shelf space | 5 | 3 | 4 |
| Retail price | $2.19 | $1.77 | $1.99 |
| Case cost (24) | $47.76 | $37.20 | $43.20 |
| Weekly unit sales | 1425 | 976 | 648 |
| Direct Product Costs/unit | $.052 | $.043 | $.056 |

# C A S E 3.13   La Maison de Drogue

*"Nobody* beats Montreal Drugs on their flyer pricing," commented Pierre Tremblay as he shuffled the piles of paper on his oversized oak desk in search of the latest Montreal Drugs promotional flyer. "Here it is. I knew I had it somewhere. These guys at Montreal Drugs have started to advertise NutriVite. And look at the price: $8.99 a bottle!"

Pierre Tremblay was the President of La Maison de Drogue, a deep-discount drug warehouse located in Montreal. He was in the middle of his twice monthly regular meeting with a Pharmex Ltd. sales representative, Bill Taylor. Pharmex was a key supplier of several leading ethical OTC products as well as a number of other pharmaceutical preparations to the retail pharmacy business as a whole. The purpose of today's meeting was to discuss the quantity of NutriVite, Pharmex's pre-natal vitamin supplement, that Pierre should purchase during the current deal period. Pierre was faced with a decision on how to price NutriVite given competitive pricing approaches. This decision was linked closely to the commitment he had to make on the quantity to purchase.

"What's the best price I can get per unit during this deal period, Bill?" Pierre asked.

BILL: OK Pierre, let's get the pricing issues out on the table to begin with. If you order a minimum of a gross[1] your net will be $8.77 a bottle. We have a smaller deal with a six dozen minimum that will price out at $9.21 a unit but that will put your pricing way out of the competitive picture and anyway the analysis that I've done on the movement of the product in your store over the last eight weeks (Exhibit 1) suggests that an order of 1.5 to 2 gross would be appropriate for this deal period. Here, let me show you my unit planner.

PIERRE: Are there any allowances available?

BILL: Just the differential pricing on the deal quantities and the 2% discount you will take by paying within 10 days. This will bring your net down to $8.61.

PIERRE: What about co-op?[2]

BILL: Pierre, we don't support advertising on this kind of a product. The marketing dollars are spent detailing physicians and, to a certain extent, nurses, so all sales are generated from their recommendations. These are not self-medicated products. And . . .

PIERRE: OK, OK. Do you have any car stock?[3]

BILL: No, we don't carry any car stock.

PIERRE: We sell a lot of your products and we devote a lot of space to them. I want to do a good job with NutriVite and I'd like to increase the facings on the shelf but this will take more space. I really

---

[1] A gross is 12 dozen or 144 bottles.

[2] Co-operative advertising was advertising, usually in newspapers or promotional flyers, that would be supported financially partially by the manufacturer in return for the retailer agreeing to feature the product in his store as well as include it in some of his advertising programs.

[3] Car stock was a vernacular term used to imply that a representative would provide free merchandise out of his car to sweeten a deal for an important retailer for the purpose of getting the retail price below that of the competition.

[4] Display money was an allowance paid to the retailer by the manufacturer for displaying the product in a better location or for increasing the number of product facings. Usually paid by the sales representative in the form of a cheque, specific performance terms were usually attached to the written agreements. Examples would be to position the product on the top shelf to the right of the market leader for a specific period of time, or to display at least 10 facings of the product in a specified location.

EXHIBIT 1

## INVENTORY CONTROL SHEET

| DATES | | 2-Feb | 23-Feb | 16-Mar | 6-Apr | 27-Apr | 18-May | TOTAL |
|---|---|---|---|---|---|---|---|---|
| PRODUCT | | | | | | | | |
| | O/H* | 321 | 266 | 214 | 155 | 111 | 55 | |
| NutriVite | Sold** | 55 | 55 | 52 | 59 | 44 | 56 | 321 |
| | Order | 0 | 0 | 0 | 0 | 0 | 449 | |

\* O/H means inventory on hand
\*\* Sold is the total # of units sold since last sales call

need some display money[4] from you to do the kind of job that I can do with this product!

BILL: If it was up to me I'd give you display money but you have to understand that I can't just write you a cheque without the approval of the company. Our program with this product is to encourage doctors to recommend NutriVite over the competition. From our perspective, sales cannot be increased overall by advertising or merchandising. As I said before, this is not a self-medicated product!

Pierre leaned back in his swivel chair and stared at the ceiling for about a minute. He broke the silence by leaning forward and saying in a very serious tone: "This just isn't good enough. I need a better price. What are you offering the wholesalers?"

BILL: Now Pierre, the price will obviously be better but the trade-off you'll have to make in the quantity of inventory will be substantial. Our minimum deal to the wholesalers is 15 gross with a net of $8.06 per bottle, less the 2% of course. I've suggested that you need about two gross until the next deal period. I don't think we've ever had an individual store order a wholesale deal. Our best accounts would rarely get above three gross. I really think that you should plan your buying based on unit needs rather than on pricing needs.

## LA MAISON DE DROGUE

La Maison de Drogue was controlled by two major shareholders which were key players in the Canadian retail environment. L'Investeur Inc. controlled 48.5% of the common shares and The Capital Group Ltd., an organization involved in the retail drug store business controlled 48.5% of the common shares. The remaining 3% was owned by Pierre Tremblay. L'Investeur Inc. had been interested in diversifying away from its traditional base in the retail fashion business. The growing strength of drugstore sales attracted L'Investeur Inc. management as did the appearance of an explosion in the relative shares of the deep-discount outlets. Deep-discounting was attractive to L'Investeur Inc.: the corporation felt it could use its expertise in high volume retailing to make La Maison de Drogue very profitable. Management had aggressive expansion plans: within three years it was expected that an additional 10 La Maison de Drogue stores would be in operation in the Montreal area. All would be targeted towards middle to lower income families with the intention of offering 'Rock Bottom Prices.'

## DEEP-DISCOUNTING

All deep-discounters like La Maison de Drogue did not offer what is traditionally understood to be full-line service. The prevailing philosophy of a deep-discounter was to do very little to create a pleasant shopping environment for the customer although stores were laid out to make shopping convenient. Product was merchan-

EXHIBIT 2

## UNIT PLANNER

| | |
|---|---|
| Total Units Sold Since Last Deal | 321 |
| Anticipated Unit Percent Growth | 10% |
| Lost Sales (Percent)* | 2% |
| Planned Inventory (Units)** | 144 |
| **Total Suggested Order** | 449 Units |
| | 37 Dozen |

\* Lost Sales are calculated based on 'out of stocks', poor shelf displays, failure to restock shelves. An arbitrary percentage—usually under 5%—is chosen.

\*\* Planned inventory is the number of units—at minimum—required to successfully merchandise the product. At La Maison de Drogue 6 facings, two high and twelve deep was the shelf display used.

dised utilizing a warehouse format. Goods would normally be stacked on the selling floor in their shipping cartons which were sheared open to display their contents. Fixtures were industrial warehouse-type shelving, lighting was strong direct fluorescent, colors were garish and bold, product assortment was usually very narrow, in-store signage announcing promotions were hand made and shouted at the shopper, and service personnel were usually in short supply. These were trade-offs that customers usually made gladly in return for the price discounts offered by the deep-discounters.

Deep-discounters were able to offer savings to their customers by buying most merchandise on manufacturers' deals or discounts, and also by selling the merchandise at lower markups than those of conventional retailers. Almost all of the merchandise was name brand, but usually only the most popular or economical labels and sizes were stocked.

A typically deep-discounter would offer a merchandise mix which included prescription drugs, non-prescription drugs, health and beauty aids, cosmetics, fragrances, film and film processing, tobacco products, reading materials,

greeting cards, giftwrap, stationery, toys, some hardware items, luggage, video rentals, seasonal goods and other general merchandise and in some cases a wide variety of food products. About 20% of the floor space would be used for storage of merchandise and for personnel facilities, with the balance used as selling space. The capital cost of fixturing a new store would be about $10 per square foot. To become operational a 30,000 square foot store would require about $2–$2.5 million in inventory.

Deep-discounters competed against others using the same merchandising format as well as conventional drugstores, super drug warehouse stores, discount and department stores, supermarkets, convenience stores, variety stores and other general merchandisers.

### PIERRE TREMBLAY AND LA MAISON DE DROGUE

The young President and CEO of La Maison de Drogue, Pierre Tremblay, had been raised in a retail environment. His father had risen through the ranks of Shoppers Drug Mart to the point where he was the CEO of one of Imasco's leading divisions. Retail was in Pierre's blood. As a child, dinner-table conversation frequently revolved around conceptual and practical issues in retailing. Pierre's intuitive grasp of the retail environment belied his youth (he was under thirty) and his lack of formal business training.

La Maison de Drogue operated two stores in the east-end of Montreal. One had opened about six weeks before the meeting described above and the other had been in operation for several years. Both were excellent locations for their target markets, provided ample parking, easy access and long hours. There were immediate plans for expansion over the next eighteen months. La Maison de Drogue was committed to at least one store in North Montreal and one in Quebec City. Other locations were possible, but these two were confirmed expansion sites.

By the mid-1980's, industry analysts were unanimous in predicting the rise of the deep-discounter at the expense of the traditional drug store. There had been a proliferation of deep discount drug outlets. All were free-standing warehouse stores averaging between 15,000 and 40,000 square feet. Herbie's, Howie's, Hy & Zel's and La Maison de Drogue were among the most prominent entrants in this category. Traditional full-line chains like Shoppers Drug Mart, Pharmaprix, Jean Coutou and Boots had suffered reversals in market share and were beginning to scramble in an attempt to redefine their strategies. Heavy advertising and rock bottom prices had contributed to the allure of the deep-discount drug outlets.

## MANUFACTURERS' DEALS

Manufacturers of health and beauty aids, ethical OTC's, proprietary medications, snack foods and pharmaceuticals normally sold "on deal". This meant that price discounts would be available to trade customers in return for the purchase of certain quantities of the goods. Many firms had different levels of quantity discounts: as the orders got larger, the discounts got larger.

Selling on deal was beneficial to the manufacturer because it allowed for the planning of production, shipping, sales forecasting, and marketing. It was beneficial to the retailer because it provided an opportunity to buy the product at the lowest available price. Retailers had to plan their buying carefully because if they under-bought and sold out before the next deal period they would be forced to purchase additional stock at full manufacturers' cost. It was not uncommon for 'deal' prices to be as much as 25% to 50% below the regular prices stated on the manufacturers' price lists.

## THE RETAIL BUYING PROCESS

As for most deep-discounters, the buying process was critical to the success of La Maison de Drogue. All the buying was done by Pierre Tremblay who was extremely aggressive in buying situations. La Maison de Drogue competed on price. Pierre's main attack in any buying situation was to get the best price available. His deep-discount competitors generally bought centrally for many stores and could get the lowest prices by virtue of being eligible for the largest deals. Even a conventional chain like Montreal Drugs, with 110 stores, had a central buying office and warehouse facility. Shoppers Drug Mart, on the other hand, the largest drug chain in Canada, with over six hundred stores, did not buy centrally: each store had its own merchandise manager who was responsible for purchasing and inventory control in his or her own store.

## THE PRODUCT

There were at least six brands of pre-natal supplements sold in Canada although two or three of these brands were really insignificant in terms of market presence. NutriVite was the leading pre-natal vitamin supplement in Canada with about 40% of the total market. In the Montreal area it had a somewhat stronger position with about a 50% market share. It was estimated in the industry that perhaps 50–60% of all pregnant women used a pre-natal supplement on the recommendation of their physician.

Physicians who recommended pre-natal supplements usually did so at about the third month of pregnancy. Some suggested that the woman continue to use the supplement until three months after the birth of the baby if the woman was breast-feeding, but this was not uniformly agreed upon in the medical community. NutriVite and the other two competing brands were packaged in bottles of 100 and the dose of all three was one tablet a day. All pre-natal supplements were manufactured with a three year expiry date and that date was printed on each bottle.

The suppliers of pre-natal supplements faced no competitive threat from other vitamin products. Pre-natal supplements contained the precise quantities of vitamin and mineral ingredients required by pregnant women such as elemental iron, folic acid and stool softeners and no other commercially available vitamin preparation could match this chemical composition. The unique combination of ingredients also precluded the use of pre-natal supplements for other therapeutic conditions or treatments. Furthermore, it was understood in industry circles that the verbal recommendation of a doctor carried sufficient weight to convince a woman to purchase the specific product recommended.

NutriVite was available on deal only twice a year for a two week period per deal. Deal price represented a 33.3% discount off full manufacturer's price.

## THE COMPETITION

In addition to NutriVite there were two other key products competing in the pre-natal vitamin supplement market in Montreal. Materna by Lederle and Nutrifer by Ayerst were products of similar chemical composition. In the Montreal market, Materna held about a 35% share and the remaining 15% was held by Nutrifer. All three products were priced at about the same levels by their manufacturers, although small periodic price spreads occurred based on unsequenced price increases from the manufacturers.

## PIERRE'S DECISION

Pierre Tremblay faced a difficult decision. He knew that full-line drug stores like Shoppers Drug Mart usually worked on a 22–24% retail markup and that their net cost could be no less than $8.77 a bottle. His concern was with Montreal Drugs at $8.99 a bottle and the anticipated pricing strategies of the other deep-discounters in his market who he felt would price at about the $9.00 mark as well.

As a rule he liked to aim for a 10% gross margin in all his product categories. In certain situations he worked with less than 10% gross margin: paper products were often sold below cost and in some other categories he priced at or below the competition for strategic reasons, although he wanted this to be the exception rather than the rule. He had to make a decision today. The deal period ended on Friday—two days from now—at which point pricing on NutriVite reverted to full cost for another four months.

**4**

PART

RETAIL MARKETING
PLANNING AND
IMPLEMENTATION

CHAPTER

# Retail Marketing Planning and Plans

Introduction

The concept of retail strategy and its major components are discussed in Chapter 2 as a prelude to the next ten chapters, which are more detailed examinations of these issues. The intent throughout is to illustrate how retailers manage to stay close to their customers, make choices among assortment strategies, and so on, to outperform their competitors. In short, Chapters 2 to 12 are discussions of the basic retail marketing management model used in this book. This model has been rearranged into the planning model shown in Figure 13.1, which is discussed in this chapter.

This final chapter is an examination of the overall issues in using this approach to formulate and implement retail marketing plans, including what is different about retail marketing planning, why plan, what goes into a plan, and how to manage the planning process. In the Appendix, franchising is examined as a special example of predetermined marketing plans, which guide many retail businesses.

## Planning and Plans

### Why Retail Marketing Planning Is Different

As has been mentioned several times, retail marketing is generally more complicated than manufacturer product marketing in terms of the need to deal with both product and patronage motivation. This is not to minimize the difficulties of planning for any marketer, but rather to suggest that retailers need to plan on several interrelated levels:

1. Overall firm — finding a viable position in the competitive marketplace
2. Store level — competing in the local marketplace with comparable stores
3. Category level — competing in the local marketplace with others who offer the same category of goods or services
4. Item level — competing in the local marketplace with others who offer the same or comparable items

Retailers, unlike manufacturers, typically sell their goods and services one at a time to individual customers. A retailer's marketing program, in the final analysis, is the summation of all the activities undertaken throughout the organization to attract and satisfy hundreds, or thousands, or millions of individual customers, generally one at a time. Imagine the complexity of planning an ever-changing assortment of goods and services of 200 000 to 500 000 items to be sold to millions

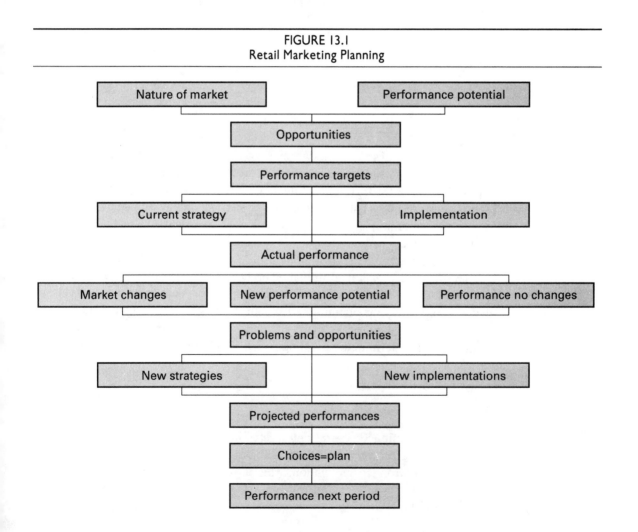

**FIGURE 13.1**
**Retail Marketing Planning**

of customers about whom little is generally known, in widely differing but highly competitive local markets in differing regions of the country, and all this on a relatively slim profit margin. This is a job most marketing planners would find daunting, yet national department store marketers face exactly this task. In comparison, preparing the annual plan for the manufacturer of a toothpaste brand seems relatively straightforward.

## THE NEED FOR PLANNING AND PLANS

**Marketing planning** is defined in Chapter 2 as systematic thinking about managing the future relationship with the retailer's customers and potential customers. This definition properly focuses the attention of planning on the future, not the past, although the lessons of the past are often very useful in preparing for the future. This definition also points out that planning is not simply vague thinking about what one might do, but rather disciplined, hard work with a formalized process underlying it. Unfortunately, the person who wouldn't dream of having a contractor build his or her new dream home without architectural drawings and lots of discussion often goes to work in a retail organization and operates with no comparable blueprints and planning process.

Managers have been asked repeatedly whether they use planning and whether it is valuable. They have reported back consistently that planning provides five key benefits, whether in marketing or any other part of an organization:

1. A disciplined and somewhat detached look at the future of the organization or part of the organization.
2. A focus on key activities when there are too many activities competing for the manager's time and attention.
3. A clarification of mission, objectives, strategy, implementation responsibilities, etc.
4. Help in making marketing activity choices, setting priorities, and in making resource allocations.
5. Help for all levels of employees in understanding the competitive environment, the organization, and their own role and tasks in achieving organization objectives and goals.

These sorts of benefits are particularly apparent and meaningful when organizations face more turbulent circumstances and when those circumstances are complex, the stakes are high, and/or the people and operating units are geographically dispersed. In fact, when change is most pronounced, the more valuable is the planning process itself as opposed to the actual plan.

By the same token, when times are very turbulent, there is a natural tendency to think any planning is a wasted effort.[1] And, some will argue that, despite planning efforts, not all planning results in good decisions, nor do all who plan have successes. However, such arguments miss the point because performance is based on both planning and execution, and, of course, not all planning is good planning.

For example, recent studies of Canadian retailers entering the United States and failing (unfortunately, to date more have failed than succeeded) indicated that failing Canadian retailers did not plan well their entry strategies. They simply did not understand market conditions in their new markets and did not anticipate the full import of their entry and, therefore, did not plan particularly well for it.[2]

Are retailers engaging in marketing planning? While there has been relatively little research and writing on retail marketing planning, there is growing evidence that it is being undertaken, particularly as more and more firms switch from a merchandising focus to a marketing focus. Barry Mason, Morris Mayer, and Anthony Koh conducted a survey for presentation to the National Retail Merchants Association Annual Convention in 1984. Their survey detailed many dimensions of current practice in retail marketing planning among department stores. Two-thirds of the respondents indicated they had formal market plans. The authors summarized some of their findings as follows:

> This research has documented that functional marketing plan development in retailing tends to be a year or less in duration, the same time period which has been identified in other types of organizations. The primary responsibility for marketing plan development tends to reside with the general merchandise manager, although final approval authority for such plans normally resides with the president or chief executive officer. Firms with formal marketing plans also tend to have larger sales levels and to be located in larger communities than firms without formal marketing plans.
>
> The formal marketing planning efforts of the marketing executive, in spite of their short term nature, however, do reflect a keen awareness of strengths and weaknesses of competitors and of the desirability of spelling out issues involving profit planning, sales promotion expenditures planning, merchandise addition/ deletion decisions, and issues involving inventories/physical distribution.
>
> A variety of different marketing plans tend to be developed including separate marketing plans for each store or for each division of a multi-unit organization, and more comprehensive market plans in what are apparently larger retailing organizations. Also, separate plans are developed by merchandise lines in many organizations. In essence, many firms seem to have a micro-marketing plan as well as inter-regional formalized marketing plans which may vary by geographical area and by merchandise line. The firms with a single marketing plan seem most likely to operate primarily in a local trading area.[3]

Increasingly, retail managers are viewing planning as an integral part of being a professional manager. Kenneth Gilman, executive vice-president of The Limited, spoke of the need for increased professionalism among retailers as follows: "The Eighties demonstrated that you need real skills to prosper as a retailer. You have to be expert in your product, understand your customer, and know how to add the most value to that combination."[4]

There are many ways to increase one's professionalism; few offer as focused an opportunity as formalized marketing planning. However, planning is not easily or universally accepted, particularly by retailers who have operated with a less formalized method. Retail marketing planning, done properly, requires senior executives to be willing to manage less personally, a requirement that often runs directly counter to the dominant personalities that often lead our major organizations. However, this need not be a conflict, as Ted Peterson, the designer that helped Kmart put together American Fare, relates in this story of Kmart:

> Is there any way of guaranteeing the success of a new store design concept? "Whenever a client asks that question, I return to my original statement," says Peterson, "It all depends on how clear the basic retail strategy is. In large companies, a problem often arises. Management is reluctant to sit down and write out their strategy. They don't want to take the time. An idea in people's heads is different from one written down. They interpret the idea one way this week and another way the following week. So we try as much as possible to have them put it in writing. Joe Antonini, Kmart's CEO, said to me during the designing of American Fare: 'You guys spend a lot of time on this. Let's get on with it.' Antonini later came to me when it was finished and said, 'Now, I understand why it is so important.' His entire staff came back and to a man said, 'I understand what you are driving at.' "[5]

## THE VARIOUS KINDS OF PLANS

There are all sorts of plans that retailers use that may be called marketing plans. As pointed out in Chapter 2, a **marketing plan** is a written document detailing marketing objectives, goals, policies, strategy, program, and procedures for a specified time period, including a rationale for these choices, implementation guidelines, and provisions for review of performance. This definition does not suggest that only large organizations may have such a plan, or that plans must be for national as opposed to neighbourhood retailers; nor does it suggest that plans are for products as opposed to services or stores or whole organizations. Instead, this definition points to the outcome of a generic process of thinking through one's market circumstances, one's position in that market, and how one intends to act in that marketplace in the future. That's it in a nutshell.

Plans differ according to the needs of the planner. A plan requested to justify a budget requiring approval from superiors may look different from a plan required to explain to subordinates how a new store will be opened in a new market area. However, there are some important commonalities for all useful marketing plans.

*First*, a marketing plan is a communications device that may potentially serve five or six different audiences, as shown in Figure 13.2.

The plan may be a request and justification for resources and support from *superiors* in the organization. It may be "marching orders" for *subordinates* (for example, what advertising program will be launched when and by whom). It may be coordinating information for *others in the organization* (for example, informing the financial team that an increase in working capital will be required for an inventory build-up next season). It may also serve as coordinating information for *suppliers*, upstream from the retailer so they know how to work in partnership with the retailer. The plan may also be historical record for *successors* to the planner's job

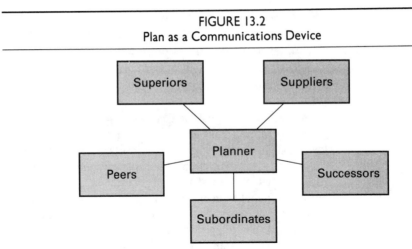

FIGURE 13.2
Plan as a Communications Device

position (for example, explaining what the past strategy has been, why, and with what results). And, importantly, a plan may provide the *planner* with the discipline to ensure that market circumstances and alternative approaches have been thought through carefully before action is taken.

*Second*, a plan is for making decisions, not simply setting goals or compiling and regurgitating market facts and performance numbers. The manager's understanding of customers, competitors, market segmentation, offer differentiation, competitive advantage, key success factors, and, of course, the financial consequences of marketing choices should be reflected in the plan. Good plans become actual work for somebody.

*Third*, a plan is a working document, subject to change. It need not be beautifully typed and bound; often a loose-leaf binder with pencilled notes is more effective. It is how a plan is thought about and used, not what it looks like, that matters.

*Fourth*, the major components that should be in most marketing plans regardless of the exact situation of the planner are shown in Exhibit 13.1.

*EXHIBIT 13.1*
*Contents of a*
*Retail Marketing*
*Plan*

1. Statement of overall purpose (mission, objectives)
2. Identification of current strategy and marketing program (if it exists)
3. Review and evaluation of past performance (if any)
4. Statement of major problems and opportunities in the market
5. Statement of objectives and goals for the next period
6. Summary statement of overall strategy for the next period
7. Marketing program for the next period in detail
8. Implementation program
9. Projected results of the plan
10. Projected needs to implement the plan
11. Contingency plans
12. Evaluation plans to prepare for the next plan.

*Fifth*, all marketing plans may be evaluated against two sets of criteria: does it make sense and is it well communicated. An easy way to remember these criteria is in terms of the five Cs for evaluating a plan as shown in Exhibit 13.2.

---

*EXHIBIT 13.2*
*Evaluating a*
*Retail Marketing*
*Plan*

*It makes sense:*

1. **Complete** — While it is focused on important issues, all the important issues are included, ranging from solid market understanding to thorough treatment of marketing program activities.
2. **Compelling** — It is well argued (for example, all the "fits" discussed in Chapters 1 and 2 are apparently in place) so that others in the organization feel good about lending their support, enthusiasm, and commitment to it.

*It communicates well:*

3. **Clear** — The core messages about how the retailer will gain and sustain competitive advantage are readily apparent.
4. **Concise** — The information and logical argument required to gain support and to take forward the program into action are included, but additional "fluff" is not.
5. **Coherent** — The presentation of ideas flows easily for the reader and easy reference for later follow-up is provided.

---

These are stringent criteria and unlikely to be met fully, especially by first-time planners. However, in time, they become reasonable screens for professional versus haphazard planning and plans.

Retail marketing plans should be tailored to their circumstances, rather than adhere to pre-specified formats. They will vary in length, format, time frame (short-term to long-term), topic coverage, and so on. Some retail plans will be about merchandise (as shown in Chapter 7, many retailers use a six-month seasonal merchandise plan). Some plans will be about facilities (Chapter 8), or information programs (Chapter 10), and so on. For example, Barbara Cohen, a vice-president and partner in Booz, Allen & Hamilton, wrote about the six Rs for revitalizing a retail business:

1. *Refocus* on the customer to ensure there are compelling reasons why they would want to shop in one's store.
2. *Restructure* the store network to capitalize on existing values but let go draining operations.
3. *Redesign* the physical concept to reflect the new marketing plan.
4. *Revamp* the business systems to support the overall strategy.
5. *Reach* out to customers through communications efforts to let them know about the new operation.
6. *Recognize* the need for critical mass (that is appropriate coverage) to achieve competitive economics and visibility in the market.[6]

One way to conceptualize the several marketing plans for a retailer is as a nested set of boxes, where each has a distinctly separate but interrelated place in the whole. For example, whereas a national retailer may have an **overall marketing plan** detailing its market positioning strategy, its overall assortment, customer care, and other strategies, it may also have a series of **merchandise group plans** and **store plans**.

A *merchandise group plan* must bridge the gap between the overall marketing plan and the specifics of part of the total assortment. For example, such a plan should address the questions shown as Exhibit 13.3.

*EXHIBIT 13.3*
*Merchandise Marketing Plan Questions*

1. What is the basic idea behind this part of the overall assortment? What is being offered to whom and why should the store/organization carry and support this part of the offering?

2. Does this part of the assortment deserve more resources or less? Why?

3. What exactly is the assortment strategy in terms of variety, breadth, depth, inventory levels, flow of goods, etc.?

4. What is the pricing strategy in terms of initial markups, markdowns, and so on and why?

5. Should all stores carry all of this assortment? If not, who should carry what? How should goods be presented in stores?

6. What incentives to buy will be provided by whom, when, to what customers?

7. What support will be provided in product knowledge, customer care, etc., to assist store employees in handling and selling the merchandise?

8. How will the supplier(s) be selected and encouraged to partner in the development of the assortment program?

9. How does this part of the overall assortment interrelate (positively and negatively) with other parts of the assortment?

10. What results are expected for the next period? Why?

11. What information is being collected internally and externally to improve decisions for the next plan and subsequent performance?

12. What information will be shared with the supplier(s)?

An increasingly important aspect of merchandise planning will be a **reverse marketing plan**, that is, a plan for cultivating and developing supplier relationships. Partnership marketing planning will be increasingly embraced by both vendors and retailers. All of the same principles of relationship management apply to such plans.

A *store marketing plan* must bridge the gap between the overall organization and the specifics of that particular facility and its local marketplace. For example, such a plan should address the questions shown as Exhibit 13.4.

EXHIBIT 13.4
*Store Marketing
Plan Questions*

1. What is the market potential for this store? How does the potential compare with actual results to date?

2. How well is the store performing on a variety of performance dimensions compared to expectations and local potential?

3. How well is the store performing compared to local competitors?

4. How well is the store performing compared to other units in the chain? Why is it performing better or worse?

5. What is known about customers who have already patronized the store in terms of their characteristics, their likes and dislikes of the store on the dimensions of assortment, convenience, customer care, information, value, and experience?

6. What specifically has the store done in terms of all aspects of its marketing program (such as, what is its assortment strategy?) and how do these activities vary, if at all, from those of other stores in the chain or from the overall strategy? Why should there be variations? Why shouldn't there be variations?

7. What can be done to improve store performance? For example, what might be done to sell this particular store more to those in the local trading area as opposed to selling the overall chain to the overall market?

8. What will it take to make those changes? What support from and/or changes will be required of others in the organization?

9. What results are expected in the next period? Why?

10. What information is being gathered and what is being tested to improve the plan and results next time?

Each marketing plan should interrelate with the others. In particular, the overall marketing plan provides the framework for all the other plans in terms of customer targets, overall marketing objectives, and so forth. Further, each marketing plan should include a section pertaining to the *development of the people* involved in that unit of the organization. Marketing is about people and it is the retail marketer's people who will ultimately determine how well the marketing job gets done.

## FORMULATING THE PLAN

Preparing a plan involves deciding upon its substance (the **logics**) and finding an appropriate process so that members of the organization feel they had appropriate opportunity to input, to comment, and to feel committed to the plan (the **politics**). (Managing the process of marketing planning will be examined in a subsequent section of this chapter.)

Since the previous chapters have dealt with the details of strategy choices and decision-making in retail marketing (for example, the issues in assortment management in Chapter 7), here it seems more appropriate to discuss an overall approach to formulating strategy.

There has been an explosion of articles, books, seminars, and management consulting firms over the past 10–15 years purporting to teach managers how to become better strategic planners. A large literature base has been established and is readily available to interested managers. However, much of the writing and seminars about marketing planning are not geared to retail marketers, and, in fact, is far more technique-oriented than most practising managers wish. This unfortunate tendency adds to common misconceptions about what is involved in preparing a marketing plan and, thus, repels rather than attracts some retail managers, as Bert Rosenbloom aptly pointed out:

> Even though a case can be made for the use of more strategic planning in retailing, its actual implementation as an integral part of retailing management presents some problems.
>
> First, . . . many retailing executives have somewhat of a negative attitude toward formal strategic planning.
>
> Second, even among retailing executives who do not have this negative attitude, the highly fluid and volatile nature of the retailing environment tends to make them sceptical of the appropriateness and value of strategic planning.
>
> Finally, there is probably a misconception among retailing executives (and executives in other industries) about the nature of strategic planning, particularly in terms of the level of effort and resources that would have to be committed to implement strategic planning in their organizations. Much of the literature and folklore of strategic planning discusses highly sophisticated and seemingly esoteric methods that imply the need for large planning staffs, highly structured and elaborate planning processes, and heavy use of mysterious computer programs. The implementation of strategic planning does not necessarily require such an elaborate undertaking, but one could easily assume that it does while listening to a planning expert discuss its finer points and nuances.[7]

Good plan preparation is simply decision-making written down. This means it is helpful to have ways to think about one's business, customers, competitors, and so on, and it is helpful to have ways to organize all the information and ideas that need to be blended together.

Presenting a plan is different than preparing a plan. The way most of us prepare a plan is *the reverse* of the way most of us like to see a plan presented to us. That is, executives value presentation of recommendations and implications, then a discussion of why those recommendations are justified with analytical detail. For this important reason, many executives get tangled up when following textbook guides to plan preparation.

Here is an approach to follow when preparing a plan.

**Identify the current strategy (or the strategy of relevant others if applicable)**    This can be done in terms of the mission, objectives, goals, policies, program, and procedures, as outlined in Chapter 2.[8] At minimum, it should be a clear and as detailed a statement as possible about who the customer target(s) is and who the relevant competitors are, and should detail the major components of the retail offer that are intended to encourage customers to choose this retailer and to reject competing retailers. A major step is reviewing the rationale behind the current strategy in terms of the information available to management and their assumptions about the nature of the market and its performance potential.

**Evaluate its performance**    Using the framework in Chapter 3 in particular, identify in the current strategy what's working and what's not. For example, what are sales trends and why are they occurring? Has the market changed? Was the strategy appropriate? Was it properly implemented? However, avoid the tendency to process too much performance information. Keep performance review and other questions simple and focused. Is the firm making money now, how much, where and how exactly? Less-than-satisfactory performance may be the result of poor strategy, poor execution of strategy, or both. Sorting out the reasons for poor performance helps greatly in taking remedial steps.

**Determine the performance potential of the markets in which the retail marketer operates and prepare new statements of purpose**    Using the concepts in Chapters 4, 5, and 6 particularly, determine what market potential there is in current markets or potential new markets. Then compare this performance potential with the achieved performance to date to see what new statements of purpose may be appropriate. Useful statements of purpose are: challenging but achievable, captivating and motivating, operational, and specific enough to be measurable over time, but vague enough for changing circumstances and for use across varying parts of the organization.

**Examine marketplace circumstances and trends**    A close look at changing customers, competitors, vendors, and circumstances usually suggests a variety of problems and opportunities. In particular, a forecast of performance for the next period *if no changes in the marketing program were undertaken* provides an important baseline against which changes in the marketing strategy and program can then be measured.

Central to this step is the identification of opportunities and threats and of strengths and weaknesses:

> Opportunities are environmental trends with potentially positive consequences which suggest new bases for competitive advantage and suggest the possibility of improved performance if pursued.
>
> Threats are environmental trends with potentially negative consequences which impede the implementation of a strategy, increase the risks of a strategy, increase the resources required, and reduce performance expectations.
>
> Strengths are superior resources and skills that can be drawn upon to exploit opportunities and respond to threats.
>
> Weaknesses are deficiencies that inhibit the ability to perform and must be overcome to avoid failure.[9]

**Isolate the important decision alternatives to consider**    It is typically impossible to deal with all the problems and opportunities at hand. Therefore, an attempt must be made to categorize them into more meaningful and less meaningful groups and then to begin with the more significant. These problems and opportunities usually stimulate ideas for changes in strategies and/or implementation of strategies.

At this stage, it is usually very helpful to identify and challenge conventional wisdom. As shown in many of the examples in previous chapters, some of the greatest success stories in retail marketing have occurred when someone decided to proceed differently from the conventional approach in a sector of retailing. One has to wonder if IKEA, Wal-Mart, Toys 'R' Us, and others would even have survived if they had not been so unconventional. It is precisely at this stage in marketing planning that creativity and freshness are most valuable. And, it is at this stage that many people begin to bog down in planning, mistakenly thinking they need to gather an encyclopedia of information and calculate inummerable numbers. When in doubt, it is best to go back to the basics of retail marketing, which are discussed in Chapters 1 and 2.

**Decide what to do**    An analysis of the merits and implications of the alternatives being considered can often be best summarized by a projection of the performance consequences of each alternative. These can then be compared with the "do nothing" scenario considered above. For example, if the retail marketer were to open another store in this city in addition to the existing two units, what might happen? A thorough performance projection considers the *net impact on results* (such as the increased sales from the new store and the effect on sales of the other two stores) as well as the *requirements* to achieve those results (such as the capital and operating outlays and the implications for staffing of a new store).

Often it is appropriate to do some contingency decision-making as well. This does not mean that the retail planner prepares strategies for all kinds of possible eventualities, but rather attempts to anticipate reasonably possible deviations from the scenario that underlies the plan and then, where appropriate, prepares a course of action for those new eventualities. For example, during 1989–90, Canadian retailers needed to plan for the probable yet not absolutely certain imposition of a federal general sales tax (the GST). Because politicians engaged in seemingly endless debates around this tax, retailers were left with an ever-shortening deadline to a tax that would require major shifts in their pricing and accounting systems. Contingency planning was only prudent for retailers regarding the GST in terms of whether it would happen, exactly what its coverage would be, and how various competitors would deal with it.

**Decide how to do it**    Once the choices have been made as to what to do, the next choices are about when, by whom, and how the decisions will be executed. The level of detail in this part of the plan varies greatly, according to circumstances. As a general rule, most retailers go into as much detail as possible, weighing that detail against the inevitable changes that must be made as circumstances change during the duration of the plan.

**Decide how to prepare for the next round of decisions**   Retail marketing management is not yet a science. Much remains to be learned about how and why customers respond as they do to marketing efforts and why competitors do what they do. Accordingly, many retailers have discovered that making some provision in their planning for gathering information that will assist in the next round of decisions is time and money well spent. For example, if a brochure will be delivered to households in the vicinity of the store, how will the retailer learn whether that was a good idea and whether it should be repeated next year? Or, another example would be that preparing for the next plan may simply involve ensuring that accounting keeps records in a certain way or that store personnel count traffic periodically during the season.

**Prepare the plan**   At this stage, it is a matter of preparing a document that summarizes what decisions have been reached, what results are expected, what is needed to make this happen, and why. The plan is written after the above eight steps. The format was outlined previously.

**Communicate the plan and revise if necessary**   Once the plan has been prepared, it then becomes important to use it to gain support and commitment. The actual process for this varies by organization. Sometimes, the retail planner must formally present the plan in a meeting. In this situation, oral presentation skills, visual aids, and other communications skills may become almost as important as the substance itself. In other instances, the plan may have to stand on its own, without the assistance of its author(s) to explain and defend it.

Preparing a marketing plan is hard work. It is not just gathering and presenting information, but rather finding insights. It is not just justifying past decisions, so much as working through future decisions. The whole idea is to produce results, not just a document.

## Managing the Planning Process

Managing the planning process means managing the involvement of other people in the marketing plan preparation, discussion, and implementation. There are many stumbling blocks that marketing planners or would-be planners run into. Each of these gives rise to some advice. The following list is based on an extensive review of marketing planning research and the author's own consulting experience.

### Problem 1
Top management asks for it to be done, but stays largely uninvolved.

This is a serious problem. If senior management are not truly committed to marketing, to providing leadership in marketing, and to providing leadership in marketing planning, then the whole exercise will ultimately fail. A marketing plan is not a substitute for marketing leadership, but rather a reflection of it. It is very difficult to prepare a marketing plan strictly from the bottom up. Advocates of **top-down**

**planning** contend that it is better for resolving any organizational conflicts and trade-offs because more senior executives are able to transcend tradition and organizational rules. They are less likely to be caught up in intra-organizational conflicts and second-guessing "what the boss wants to hear." **Bottom-up planning** advocates argue that top-down planning is unlikely to be sufficient in terms of getting into the details required to produce actionable, realistic plans because senior managers are too far removed from the front lines and too reliant on the information that gets filtered as it gets passed to them. Further, the argument goes, bottom-up planning builds organizational commitment to the plan by having greater involvement of those who will have to implement the plan. The glib answer, of course, is to have both: top-down for vision and objectives, bottom-up for details and methods. It is not easy to do in complex organizations, but steps can be taken.

### Problem 2
Finding the balance between line and staff in plan preparation.

Marketing planning is a discipline of its own and there are specialists in this discipline. It is, therefore, tempting to assign such specialists (whether employees or external consultants) to the task. This relieves another problem, "I haven't enough time," as well as avoids the necessity to confront the careful "thinking it through" process that retail marketing planning is all about. This is not merely a matter of whether nonline people are able to prepare a good plan (they sometimes can, but not always), but rather a matter of whether one believes this is all about producing a plan or engaging in the planning process. The latter is the more powerful approach.

Since strategic choices must be consistent with the retailer's circumstances, the retailer's capabilities, and the risk preferences and values of key retail managers, it follows that line managers must be involved centrally in the marketing planning process. Further, line managers will keep the plan realistic and will have considerable concern for its viable implementation. Having to live with a plan once approved is strong incentive to prepare a good plan.

### Problem 3
Ensuring options and new ideas are considered.

There has been much talk of "zero-based planning" (approaching the task as if starting from scratch), but seldom is this realistic. However, managers often undertake the planning challenge with one or the other of two potentially dysfunctional ideas: "preparing a plan means proposing something significantly different" and "No change is needed unless otherwise proven." Often, the result of a planning process is to reconfirm the wisdom of the current strategy, or to fine-tune it somewhat, or perhaps to remotivate everyone involved to a greater forcefulness in plan execution. Similarly, too often the person proposing a change faces the complete burden of demonstrating why the status quo should not prevail. One might turn the tables and say, "Change in our marketing program is needed unless proven otherwise."

## Problem 4

Arguing over format.

There is no one "best" marketing plan format. In many companies, great efforts are made to standardize plan formats, to create planning manuals and forms to fill in. Too often such procedures are driven by accounting needs for standardized numbers to present in composite tables to senior managers needing to compare business units one with another when making decisions about resource allocation. While this is understandable, the danger lies in forcing planning thinking into compartments that may be sterile or, worse, may simply not make sense. Good planning processes and forms leave room for entrepreneurial variations. Substance is more important than form. A related problem is the planner's desire to write the perfect plan. Unfortunately a perfect one-year plan will probably take more than a year to prepare. The guideline ought to be, "Do the best you can in the time available. Refinements in plans and planning processes come with time and practice."

## Problem 5

Integrating planning with other organizational processes.

Retail marketing plans should be prepared far enough in advance to allow the retail organization to be ready to execute them, but not so far in advance that they are made irrelevant by changing market circumstances. This is somewhat akin to trying to say how far ahead a driver should look in order to steer the car properly: there is a big difference in the required planning horizon when travelling at 40 km/h and 100 km/h. In other words, the marketing planning process and its periodic outcome, the marketing plan, need to be synchronized with the pace and critical timing points of the organizational control system. For example, the marketing plan should precede the budgeting process; otherwise those involved will realize that the real planning is only financial.

Another danger in integrating planning into an organization is using planning ability as a proxy for managerial ability when evaluating managers. It is tempting to measure people according to the inputs; however, the value of a plan is not in its appearance or even its logic, but rather in its usefulness in delivering performance. Managers should be evaluated on what they accomplish, not how hard they work or what they plan to accomplish. Especially in the early stages of retail marketing planning, one should avoid using the plan and planning process as a surrogate for managerial ability.

There are many places a process as complex as retail marketing planning can be derailed.[10] Perhaps a more positive approach would be to report what effective planning systems look like. Erik Rule, a partner in The Coopers & Lybrand Consulting Group, undertook a study of strategic planning in Canada in 1985. He discovered that nearly 90 percent of his respondents reported that their organization prepared a written strategic or long-range business plan, with a typical time horizon of five years, usually updated annually. On the basis of his research, he profiled an effective strategic planning system, as shown in Exhibit 13.5.

EXHIBIT 13.5
Erik Rule's
Characteristics
of Effective
Planning
Systems[1]

1. Effective planning systems are more structured than ineffective systems, but not so structured that they become bureaucratic and unwieldy

2. Effective planning systems maintain a balance between the use of powerful analytical techniques and "good old fashioned judgment."

3. Effectiveness of the planing process can usually be improved by developing at least one or two alternative scenarios to challenge management thinking regarding the "expected outcome" or base case.

4. Effectiveness of a planning system is likely to be enhanced by the absence of full-time planning support staff.

5. Effective planning systems emphasize bottom-up planning more than top-down planning.

6. Effective planning systems provide for broad participation in the planning process, rather than limit involvement to the senior management group.

7. Effective planning systems are biased towards being entrepreneurial rather than bureaucratic.

8. Effective planning systems are clearly championed by the CEO, with all members of the senior management team involved and strongly supportive.

---

[1] Erik G. Rule, "What's Happening to Strategic Planning in Canadian Business?" *Business Quarterly*, March 1987, pp. 43–47.

Richard Schall, vice-chairman of Dayton-Hudson, described their planning approach as follows:

> What we have imbedded in our management structure is a management process which provides the framework for managing our business. It has five parts, starting with strategic planning, and works like a wheel, and all the parts require interaction between the corporation and the operating companies. Those parts are strategic planning, human resources planning, capital allocation, long range goals, and performance evaluation. The process is a continuum, with each step building on the last. It helps us achieve management commitment and balance autonomy and corporate accountability. We make great efforts to make it not only a numbers process, but to deal with lots of searching questions and issues. Like, what are the division's missions? What changes are necessary to achieve them? Is a change due in geographical direction? Are the customers changing to whom we are trying to appeal? After considerable discussion, the operating companies receive approval of their plan with the corporate officers.[11]

## IMPLEMENTATION OF RETAIL MARKETING PLANS

All marketing plans ultimately face their test through implementation in the market. Naturally, coming up with a retail concept and a marketing program on paper is a lot easier than making it happen. Many of the issues in having the best possible chance of implementing a plan have been discussed above, but there remains the question of organizational design. Retailers, particularly those with multiple units in varying, dispersed markets, have struggled with organizational design.[12] There seems to be no easy answer to questions of centralization versus decentralization, standardization versus localization of marketing programs. In fact, the organizational issues that bedevil large national retailers operating in North America are the very same issues that international business managers grapple with as they wonder how to operate across national boundaries.

## Organizational Design

Marketers of all types have typically used five major organizational approaches:

**1. Functional**   Each aspect of marketing is separated. Each has a "head" and all report to a marketing manager. For example, advertising would be separated from research, which would be separated from customer service. This approach is based on the belief that functional specialization is necessary to deal with the complexities of the marketing tasks.

**2. Geographic**   Some aspects (or even all) of the marketing functions are duplicated across geographical regions. For example, there may be an East and West region and each may have an advertising manager or a buying staff. This approach is based on the belief that there are important geographical differences that cannot be dealt with centrally. However, this organizational form often creates a split sense of responsibility for individuals, caught between loyalty to the region or to one's "functional" peers in other regions or in head office.

**3. Product/merchandise**   This form of organization begins from the natural divisions of merchandise categories, brands, or vendors. Common position titles include merchandise managers, buyers, brand and product managers, and, recently, category managers. The fundamental belief underlying this approach is that someone must become expert with the merchandise, the vendors, and the market. However, in many organizations, the original conception of the department store buyer remains: a person who both buys and sells. Today's buyer has great difficulty giving equal attention to both parts of this job definition and usually ends up giving more emphasis to the buying side. In the process, such "split-personality" buyers may not have enough time or energy to stay close to what is happening in the stores. Recent developments in information technology are helping with this problem.

**4. Market/customer**   Some organizations have been designed with individuals responsible for all aspects of dealing with defined customers. For example, a retailer selling apparel may have a manager in charge of marketing to career women, another to children, another in charge of a personal shopping program. Such approaches are still relatively rare in product retailing, although increasingly common in service organizations, such as financial institutions and insurance companies. The idea is to get very familiar with the customer's circumstances and then to mobilize the organization in ways most effective for gaining and keeping that customer. The disadvantage is that some markets are neither clearly enough seg-mentable or that in some organizations the job of such a person is too complex to be manageable.

**5. Matrix**   The fifth approach is called matrix management and is very common in retailing. This is an attempt to combine formally some of the other methods of organizing—for example, by combining the merchandise approach with functional field/store management. Thus, there would be a centralized merchandising organi-zation, divided into buyer teams and so forth, responsible for procuring, pricing, and perhaps other marketing tasks. And there would be a store operations organiza-tion, divided into store managers and sales managers, and so on. In this matrix, buyers are expected to deal with field sales merchandisers, group merchandise managers with store managers, and so on, in a large checkerboard of relationships. Sometimes, this matrix is further complicated by geographical replications of it and other organizational variations. Typically, senior management stays out of the matrix, preferring to set it in motion and when necessary to resolve the inevitable conflicts of interest that arise. This organizational form is based on the belief that a multi-unit retailer should buy and plan most marketing tasks centrally (for efficien-cies and greater management control) and should sell and operate with local market tailoring (for greater effectiveness in local markets). It is a difficult tightrope to walk.

Often organizational structure gets in the way of doing the necessary market-ing job. For example, off-price chains have been able to send buyers to market and allow them far greater buying discretion than could major department stores. These department stores, with their central merchandising hierarchies, had several layers of approval required for buying and complicated but time-consuming systems for physical distribution. Consequently, off-pricers could buy merchandise later and get it on the floor faster than could their department store competitors.

No organizational form is perfect, but some are worse than others in perform-ing retail marketing tasks. The product organization is probably the root of many retailers' problems because it has usually been centralized, close to the senior management and, hence, received undue weight in overall decisions. Store man-agers, on the other hand, as was discussed in Chapter 9, are in a far better position to stay close to customers and to be the organization's best "market managers." If the store management system in a retail organization is not seen as the path for advancement, if store managers are burdened more with facilities operation and personnel matters than marketing, then their potential as valuable marketing planners and implementers will not be realized.

In the end, people make organizations work, organizations do not make people work. There is a growing awareness that an organization has a culture—an endur-ing, pervasive set of values, beliefs, traditions, and rituals—that guides the way its members interact with each other and outsiders. When asked what a culture was in a retail organization, Joseph Antonini, CEO of Kmart, replied:

> I see culture as a change, not in the fundamentals of retailing or merchandising,
> but in how we perform the fundamental concept. For example, for years, mer-

chandising in retail stores has been done under a manual system. Therefore, centralization of the hardlines division of a mass merchandiser like Kmart is a culture change . . .

Whenever I talk to our store and district managers, I tell them about all the programs that are taking place. I tell them why we're using various programs or technologies; or why we're centralizing; or why we are discontinuing certain programs.[13]

Retail marketers need to get in touch with their own organizational culture, and then make every effort to ensure that it is steeped in an abiding belief in the importance of customer orientation, outperforming the competition, employee quality of work experience, and organizational performance.

Walter Salmon, of the Harvard Business School, has argued that retailing success will increasingly depend critically on executional skills, which he listed as: marketing skills, organizational skills, logistical skills, management information system skills, accounting skills, and rank-and-file worker changes (i.e., changes in values, habits, characteristics, etc.). While he has strong words for the need to change industry practices in each of these areas, he is most insistent that fundamental changes need to happen in the quality and motivation of rank-and-file workers in retailing. He believes high people productivity and performance will come only from substituting quality for quantity of people, participation for hierarchical direction, and appropriate status and remuneration for shabby treatment.[14]

## THE WORLD'S NUMBER ONE SKI RETAILER[15]

Teibu Ogino, after graduating from college and working for IBM in Japan, bought a small sporting goods shop in Tokyo in 1973 as a way to build a business matching his interests in golf and skiing. Over the past eighteen years, his Victoria Co. Limited has emerged from incredible competition in Japan as the leader with nearly 140 stores nationwide and sales last fiscal year of more than $537 million. According to ski equipment suppliers, Victoria is the largest retailer of skiing merchandise in the world.

When Ogino started, he faced no specialists but only general sporting goods retailers, so he carefully worked out a strategy to which he has adhered. His strategy was to create a network of specialty stores, each with its own specialized assortment, averaging in size about 5300 square feet. Stores are located in metropolitan areas, with the exception of a few golf centres.

Ogino established boutiques in the stores to make it easier for customers to find merchandise and he invested heavily in anything that seemed to be wanted by his customers. Victoria has integrated backward into manufacturing and has even purchased three major ski resorts (Breckenbridge and Stratton Mountain in the United States and Mt. Hutt in New Zealand) to offer places to go for its customers.

Victoria offers a tremendous assortment of sporting items, but excels particularly in skiing. For example, the company offers 5000 models of skis, snowboards, boots, and poles from 60 brands; 6000 varieties of skiwear in another 60 brands; and nearly 9000 types of accessories in 70 brands. In addition to manufacturer names, Victoria has a private-label program. Victoria has stayed away from discounting, relying instead on selection to compete with more limited but price-oriented competitors. On one floor of the eight floor flagship store, 8000 pairs of gloves and 10 000 ski suits are displayed at any one time.

Every part of the assortment is available to customers to handle and to try on. More than 1500 highly trained employees (from Victoria University, the in-company training facility) provide exceptional service. For example:

- Customers can reserve custom fitting sessions.
- Bindings are mounted while customers wait in the store restaurant.
- Employees will go to other Victoria stores to get needed merchandise while the customer waits.
- Gift with purchase programs include free subscriptions to the in-house ski magazine.
- Each ski purchase comes with a free one-year tuneup agreement.
- There is free ski-tuning and instructions during the off-season.
- In many stores, there is a travel desk to help book ski travel arrangements.
- They offer a credit card with 5 percent discounts on most purchases, invitations to special events, discounts at hotels, and so on.
- The company has its professional ski team that conducts clinics for customers.

Ogino has carefully planned and led his company through eighteen years of growth, averaging lately about 20 percent per year. His approach exemplifies all the principles in this book.

## WHAT'S AHEAD?

All retail marketing planners are challenged to forecast trends, to have market statistics at their fingertips and insights others seem to lack. It is a formidable challenge. There is no lack of material to read about the future of retail marketing; unfortunately, it soon goes out of date. Thus, it is more important to commit to staying up to date and to knowing how to do so than it is to be able to recite a list of major trends. One of the objectives of this book was to provide a framework for dealing with the vast amount of material that comes to the attention of any retail marketing manager in the course of business.

There is no doubt that all retail marketing managers need to keep up as best they can with retail developments both locally and around the world. For example, North American grocery operators should be monitoring U.K. operators, and vice versa.[16] It becomes daunting to do so when confronted with fragmenting markets, demographic shifts, remarkable changes in ethnicity of our population, global competition, shifts in political economies, and all the other megatrends of today. There are issues that beset retailers as diverse as growing foreign investment in North American retailing,[17] substance abuse, technological changes, and environmental issues.[18] The list seems endless. Many of these and other issues are discussed in other chapters and in numerous articles in the popular and trade press.[19]

In all this, occasionally, a longer-term view can be helpful.[20] For example, as these sorts of market shifts occur, one aspect of the six customer expectations becomes more critical than others at any one time and, hence, favours certain types of retail marketers. During the late 1980s, two-income families valued time more than money, but as we move into the 1990s, values are shifting with increased unemployment and general economic uncertainty. The only constant is the need to stay with the market changes.

Identifying trends is only the beginning for the retail marketing planner. The more difficult part is discerning their implications. For example, Edith Weiner, a futures researcher and consultant, offered an interesting perspective when she said:

> I would look for countertrends and begin to take advantage of them. . . . For example, today the trend is toward technological interconnectedness. . . . The countertrend is disconnectedness from constant accessibility, a retreat from techno/communications overload. In ten years' time, the need to be constantly wired in will become déclassé — as a sign of status no better than that of a drone.[21]

## CONCLUSION

A good retail marketing planning process involves both decision-makers and implementers in a continuous quest for improved relationships with customers and an obsession with outperforming the competition. Retail marketing planning is not just formulating strategy (doing the right thing), but also providing for effective and forceful implementation (doing things right). Few aspects of the marketing profession are as action-oriented as retailing, so there is constant pressure to set aside the rigours of planning for the day-to-day activities of the business. However, retail marketers neglect marketing planning at their peril.

Much of retail marketing planning is about a disciplined approach to understanding customers, competitors, and one's own strengths and weaknesses. Every retailer should ask: Why should a customer choose his or her operation over alternatives? If there is no compelling, convincing reason, then the first task is to set out to create one.

Marketing planning, then, involves understanding key success factors. These need not be elaborately stated, but they must be clearly identified. For example, G. Joseph Reddington, president and CEO of Sears Canada, said the key success factors for Sears catalogue operation are as follows:

1. Deliver high level of customer service and convenience.
2. Provide products of superior quality and value.
3. Grow sales and customer base.
4. Manage inventory effectively.
5. Minimize fulfilment costs and time.

6. Empower employees.

7. Optimize asset investments.[22]

In this book, it has been argued that the key success factors for retail marketers are meeting and exceeding the six customer expectations: assortment, convenience, care and service, information, value, and experience. While these factors vary in their importance to segments of the market and vary over time in order of importance, they are enduring dimensions of retail marketing. Any retail marketing plan that does not address market segmentation and targeting and then provide a program for providing against these customer expectations would be far from adequate.

Above all, retail marketing success is based on managerial leadership. Our best retailers have been blessed with strong leaders who could visualize a winning strategy and then had the determination and force to make it happen. Bob Marbut, CEO of Harte-Hanks Communications Inc., put it this way:

> There's a simple mathematical equation for success in this world of cookie-cutter retailing: $L + S + E = S$. That's *leadership*; innovative and independent, the kind of leadership that separates Sam Walton and Les Wexner from the pack. It's followed by *strategy*; shooting from the hip won't work in a business as competitive as retailing. And finally, *execution*; all the glittering merchandise at Nieman Marcus would never make it out the door if the customers had to wait in line as long as they do at some mass merchandisers. All of these elements equal *success*, and they are necessary for having a profitable, sustainable competitive advantage—unless one has an awful lot of dumb luck. But the most critical of these today is the development of a strategy for the business.[23]

Retail marketing is an exciting, fast-moving, and extremely challenging profession—and retail marketing planning is in the middle of it all.

## APPENDIX A

### FRANCHISING: A PREDETERMINED MARKETING PLAN

Many retailers "pool" their efforts when it comes to marketing planning. Some are parts of shopping centres and tend to rely on the centre management to do most of the marketing for them (an unfortunate tendency), while others are franchise holders, operating with predetermined marketing plans in many instances. Because of the tremendous prevalence of franchising arrangements, it is useful to understand how they relate to the concepts and approaches for retail marketing planning discussed in the chapter.

Franchising has existed since the turn of the century, having been most prominent as the way soft drink companies and automobile manufacturers arranged their distribution systems. Today, franchising pervades all of retailing in North America; however, it is still of minor importance in other countries throughout the world. In North America, franchising accounts for between one-third and one-half of all retail sales. It is used throughout retailing of products and services; for example, it is very common in fast food, travel, computers, real estate, fashion apparel, business services, cosmetics, soft drinks, automobiles, hardware, pharmacies, video rentals, car rentals, farm equipment, and hotels and motels.

## What Is Franchising?

Franchising is a special form of partnership marketing that is based on a contractual arrangement. The *1983 Canadian Franchise Guide* defined franchising as follows:

> Franchising is an on-going contractual agreement between two parties, the franchisor and the franchisee, in which the franchisor grants the franchisee the right to market a product or service, including the use of a trademark, and in conjunction therewith provides a tested format or system as well as know-how in a variety of areas, for which the franchisee is required to conform to the format or system, maintain quality standards, and pay a set fee, usually by way of royalties, for the franchise.[24]

## Types of Franchises

There are many different ways to set up a franchise agreement. The franchise agreement usually includes clauses covering six major topics:

1. The franchisor's obligations
2. The franchisee's obligations
3. Rights granted to the franchisee
4. Trade restrictions on the franchisee
5. Termination provisions
6. Assignment by, or death, of the franchisee

While contracts differ on each of these dimensions, there are two basic types of franchise arrangements, and some subtypes of each of these.

**1. A Distributorship Franchise** refers to a manufacturer or distributor giving another distributor the right, through licensing, to sell particular products. For example, a car manufacturer typically sells its products through franchised dealers, and soft drink companies franchise to independent regional bottlers. This form of franchising was the original approach but is less common today than the second major type. In this instance, the franchisee has some control over the marketing planning for his or her own franchise.

**2. A Business Formula Franchise** refers to a firm originating an approach to doing business (either a product or a service) and then providing details and assistance so that each franchisee may operate according to the original, tested way of operating. This type of franchising began to grow rapidly in the late 1950s and is now the type most people think of when the word franchising is used. For example, the fast food operations, such as McDonald's, and many grocery co-operative groups, such as IGA, are structured this way. In this circumstance, the franchisee has very little latitude in marketing planning and programs.

## The Franchisor's Viewpoint

From a franchisor's viewpoint, franchising offers an opportunity to grow rapidly with minimal financial and managerial commitment. It is a way to build the value of a business through involving local entrepreneurs who bring money, local expertise, and above all ambition in regions where the franchisor may have limited knowledge or ability to get established. In short, the franchisor can gain economies of scale regionally, nationally, or internationally by taking "partners" who in turn gain from the value provided by the franchisor.

There can be risks and problems with being a franchisor. Management is limited by the terms of the contract. This can create major difficulties when the goals and/or perceptions of franchisees differ from those of the franchisor. The franchisor may have difficulty finding qualified franchisees, in motivating and directing those franchisees, and even in eliminating weak or contrary franchisees. In terms of management and financial return, frequently a franchisor would be better off owning units than franchising them.

Prospective franchisors should ask many questions before launching franchises, including:

1. Can my approach be duplicated by others?
2. Is it better to share in my business or to find a way to do it all myself?
3. Will there be enough profit to share with franchisees?
4. What can I offer to a franchisee that he or she can't do alone?
5. Am I willing to manage quasi-independent franchisees?

A franchisor typically has many obligations (depending on the agreement), including:

- Developing and then sharing all details of the business approach, that is, providing a total business and marketing plan
- Locating appropriate trading areas and sites
- Providing appropriate equipment and fixtures
- Training operating staff
- Providing operating and control systems
- Coordinating purchases or acting as supplier
- Coordinating advertising
- Maintaining standards.

A franchisor receives several types of payments for a franchise. Any or all of the following may be involved:

- An initial franchise fee
- An annual royalty fee, usually based on sales
- An initial training fee
- A site evaluation fee
- An annual advertising and promotion fee
- A supplies or equipment fee.

### The Franchisee's Viewpoint

Most franchisees enter into a franchising arrangement because they prefer to reduce the risk of business failure by participating in an established business to starting their own business. A franchisee "buys into" an established identity with proven customer appeal as well as obtains expert advice on site selection and marketing and finance, and so on. The franchisee usually can reduce the initial investment required for everything from marketing research to equipment to advertising, gain access to bank credit more easily, and proceed more quickly by embarking on a franchised business as compared to a new venture. At least that's how it is supposed to work and sometimes does.

There can be problems. For example, the initial business concept may not be all that good—sometimes a franchisor is more interested in selling franchises than in selling products and services. Franchisees often find that the contracts they sign provide more protection and fewer obligations for the franchisor than for themselves. Almost any contract limits the amount of managerial discretion a franchisee has over his or her business. This means that an "absentee" manager can restrict what a franchisee wants to do or even believes she or he must do. If the franchisor does a poor job of marketing, training, or whatever, the whole franchise chain may suffer and an otherwise good franchisee may suffer.

Prospective franchisees should consider many questions, including:

1. How well established is the franchisor? In particular, how well is the product (or service) and all attendant aspects of the marketing program received by the target market? How strong financially is the franchisor?
2. What will the franchisor provide for me that I can't provide for myself? For example, will the franchisor's marketing plan be better than I could prepare for myself?
3. How well are other franchisees doing?
4. How are franchisees selected? How are territories allocated? Will I have adequate protection and adequate market for a viable business?
5. What obligations will I have? Consider if the franchise will have to:
   a. abide to territorial restrictions
   b. use approved suppliers
   c. follow mandatory personnel and operating procedures
   d. permit unscheduled inspections by the franchisor

   **e.** use the standard accounting procedure and share specified data with the franchisor

   **f.** maintain agreed-upon hours, decor, maintenance procedures, pricing policies, quality standards, etc.

   **g.** engage in approved advertising and promotion.

Franchisees should also consider all the restrictions, which typically include:

- Not operating a competing business concurrently
- Not hiring employees from other franchisees
- Not engaging in competing businesses for a predetermined time after terminating the franchise agreement
- Not assigning or transferring the franchise to another person without the franchisor's consent either while living or through a will.

### Managing the Franchise Relationship

As with any contractual arrangement, disagreements between the parties may be resolved legally or through negotiation. For example, most agreements provide that the franchise may be legally terminated if:

1. The franchisee fails to adhere to stipulated procedures, payment schedules, quality standards, and so on. This can include engaging in marketing practices not permitted by the franchisor, regardless of how valuable the franchisee believes them to be.

2. The franchisee engages in specified practices (including selling the franchise) without the franchisor's approval.

3. The franchisor fails to meet his or her obligations.

Managing the inevitable conflicts that occur in a multiparty business system is the real challenge that faces franchisors and franchisees. The ability to negotiate without excessive resort to complex legal documents marks the most successful franchises.

### REVIEW QUESTIONS

1. What is the proper role of a store manager in a chain's marketing planning process?

2. Is is reasonable to have a retail marketing plan for more than a season at a time?

3. What might a reverse marketing plan look like?

4. According to an article on bank marketing, "The best marketing tool banks have available to them is the vast amount of information they have about their customers."[25] How might a market planner proceed to uncover opportunities for bank marketing?

5. Supposing one were creating a store based on espousing environmental responsibility and offering appropriate products, what might be the major dimensions of a marketing plan for this store?

## KEY TERMS

- marketing plan
- overall marketing plan
- merchandise group plans
- store plans
- reverse marketing plan

- logics
- politics
- top-down planning
- bottom-up planning

## NOTES

1. Anne B. Fisher, "Is Long Range Planning Worth It?" *Fortune,* 23 April 1990, pp. 281–84.

2. Terry Hilldebrand, "An Investigation of Canadian Retailers Entering and Adapting to the U.S. Market" (Ph.D. diss., The University of Western Ontario School of Business Administration, June 1989). See also Wendy F. Evans, "Can Canadian Retailers Make It in the U.S. Market?" National Centre for Management Research and Development, The University of Western Ontario, April 1990.

3. J. Barry Mason, Morris L. Mayer, and Anthony Koh, *Functional Marketing Plan Development in Department Store Retailing* (Birmingham: University of Alabama, 1983).

4. Amy Dunkin, "It's a Lot Tougher to Mind the Store," *Business Week,* 8 January 1990, p. 85.

5. Jay L. Johnson, "Retail Strategy and Store Design," *Discount Merchandiser,* January 1990, pp. 80–81.

6. Barbara G. Cohen, "Revitalization of the Core Business, or How Do We Start to Grow Profitably Again?" *Retail Control,* December 1989, pp. 8–15.

7. Bert Rosenbloom, "Strategic Planning in Retailing: Prospects and Problems," *Journal of Retailing,* Spring 1980, pp. 107–20.

8. See also Steve Weinstein "How Retailers Set Goals — and Reach Them," *Progressive Grocer,* April 1990, pp. 155–60.

9. Based on George S. Day, *Strategic Marketing Planning* (St. Paul, MN: West Publishing, 1984) and George S. Day,

*Market Driven Strategy: Processes for Creating Value* (New York: Free Press, 1990).

10. A related article on this is Alex R. Oliver and Joseph R. Garber, "Implementing Strategic Planning: Ten Sure-Fire Ways to Do It Wrong," *Business Horizons,* March–April 1983, pp. 49–51.

11. As quoted by Isadore Barmash, "How They Plan," *Stores,* September 1983, pp. 7–15.

12. The early history of Sears Roebuck, as described in James C. Worthy, *Robert E. Wood and Sears, Roebuck* (Utica, NY: Meridian, 1986) and then further chronicled in Donald R. Katz, *The Big Store* (New York: Penguin, 1987), makes for interesting reading about the organizational changes that shook a retailing giant as its leaders and its circumstances changed.

13. Iris S. Rosenberg, "Kmart Renewal Program on Track," *Stores,* April 1991, pp. 18–21.

14. Walter J. Salmon, "Retailing in the Age of Execution," *Journal of Retailing,* Fall 1989, pp. 368–78.

15. This example is based on Ken Castle "Bright Lights, Big Sales," *Outside Business,* November 1990, pp. 26–31.

16. Carol Fensholt, "The British Are Coming . . . with Jolly Good Ideas for Service Supermarkets," *Supermarket Business,* November 1988, pp. 26–50. See also Walter Heller, "Supermarkets in the Year 2000," *Progressive Grocer,* January 1990, pp. 24–38.

17. Michael B. Exstein and Faye I. Weitzman, "Foreign Investment in

U.S. Retailing: An Optimistic View," *Retail Control*, January 1991, pp. 9–14.

18. Penny Gill, "What Retail Is Doing to Save the Earth," *Stores*, October 1990, pp. 58–71.

19. For example, see Roger Selbert, "Retailing's Five Most Important Trends," *Retailing Issues Letter*, Arthur Andersen & Co., March 1991; and Bill Saporito "Retailing's Winners and Losers," *Fortune*, 18 December 1989, pp. 69–78.

20. Albert D. Bates, "The Extended Specialty Store: A Strategic Opportunity for the 1900's," *Journal of Retailing*, Fall 1989, pp. 379–88.

21. Edith Weiner, Jacquelyn Bivens, and Bob Marbut, "If I Were a Retailer . . . ," *Retailing Issues Letter*, Arthur Andersen & Co., July 1989.

22. G. Joseph Reddington, "Using Technology in the Catalogue Business," *Business Quarterly*, Spring 1991, pp. 87–92.

23. Weiner, Bivens, and Marbut, "If I Were a Retailer . . . " (see n. 21)

24. *1983 Canadian Franchise Guide.*

25. Terence P. Pare, "Banks Discover the Consumer," *Fortune*, 12 February 1990, pp. 96–104.

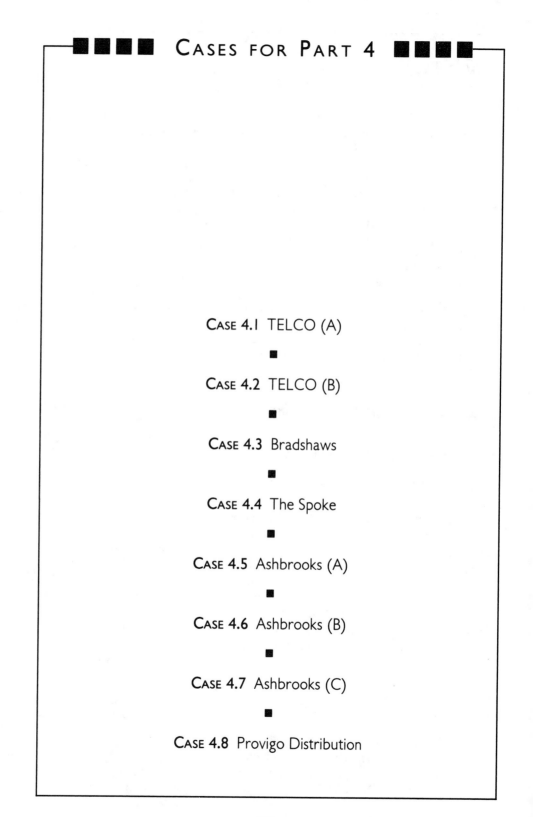

# CASES FOR PART 4

CASE 4.1  TELCO (A)

■

CASE 4.2  TELCO (B)

■

CASE 4.3  Bradshaws

■

CASE 4.4  The Spoke

■

CASE 4.5  Ashbrooks (A)

■

CASE 4.6  Ashbrooks (B)

■

CASE 4.7  Ashbrooks (C)

■

CASE 4.8  Provigo Distribution

# C A S E  4.1    TELCO (A)

In early September 1990, Barbara Watkin, Director, Sales and Marketing (S&M), for TELCO together called her three key managers, Joe Collins, Joanne Lasher, and Alex Jones:

> As you all know, we have a very busy year ahead of us in 1991. Our base is eroding and we have to work on that. Competition is heating up and customers are getting harder to attract. Our new CLASS/CMS product has surprised all of us in the test market, and soon we'll have to plan its launch in the rest of our areas. I think we should have a good overall look together at our situation before we worry about CLASS/CMS and before we all go off and work on our individual responsibilities. How is our market changing? What do you think are the key marketing challenges we face in 1991 and the next few years?"

## TELCO DESCRIPTION AND ITS MARKET CHARACTERISTICS

TELCO was an independent Bell Operating Company serving a $2.5 billion residential market and a $3.25 billion business market. TELCO was divided into several operating units, but its major division was between Technical Services and Sales. Technical Services was responsible for the central office switches, the lines and all operating aspects of the telephone system in TELCO's area. Sales was responsible for dealing with residential and corporate customers through sales and rentals of equipment and services. Sales classified customers as either single line (residential customers and home offices) or business (multiple lines). Residences with more than one line were still considered part of the single line market. TELCO divided its geographic territory into three regions: West, Central, and East.

TELCO was the only operator and provider of wired telephone services in its area and, therefore, operated under the guidance of a national regulatory group, the National Telecommunications Agency (NTA). This agency set prices, controlled advertising expenditures and claims, required certain levels of technical and customer service to be met and, in many other ways, impacted on TELCO's operations. In return, TELCO had had a monopoly for many years. The introduction of cellular phones, the growth in computer-to-computer communications, the deregulation of long distance services, and the steady growth of non-TELCO outlets for telephone products had all dramatically changed the nature of TELCO's marketplace.

The Marketing Organization of TELCO was headed by a Vice-President, Robert Markland. In turn, six General Managers, one each for Single Line and for Corporate Sales in each of the three regions, reported to him. Mr. John Ross was General Manager of Single Line Sales – Central Region. Three Central Region branches reported to John Ross: Terminals, Line Features, and Long Distance Products. These branches had operated quite independently from one another until a recent reorganization established a Corporate Product Management (PM) group as a co-ordinator of their activities. PM included analysts, planners, product managers, and other marketing staff concerned with overall TELCO activities. Barbara Watkin's group stood between Corporate PM and five Central Region line groups: Business Offices (BO), Phone Stores (PS), Installation & Maintenance (I&M), Telemarketing (TM) and Operator Services (OS). The remainder of this case is about the Central Region, residential business for TELCO.

Barbara Watkin explained the way her group operated as follows:

> Here in S&M we do not yet have a mission. We really should have one, but we haven't had time. But what we're really about is promoting all of TELCO's products and services for single line customers, which is to say residences and home offices. Our job is to bring together senior management, Corporate Product Management, and all our

distribution channels. We meet with corporate people roughly quarterly and dialogue about all this. We are given a broad corporate program for next year about June and we then translate it into specific programs over the summer and fall for the coming year. We work with our line groups to come up with our own numbers and ideas and then go back to corporate to negotiate.

Our group is the communication link between the channels and corporate groups. The channel managers do not negotiate their sales targets with senior management. I do all that. We have a regular monthly meeting of channel managers. The most important meeting is in September when we review together the Product Management forecast for the coming year. Senior management eventually signs off on our ideas and annual numbers, always with the understanding that we maintain a certain relationship with our other regional divisions. Here in Central, we're expected to be the leaders. If we fall behind, we must take immediate action. We then translate the annual numbers into our monthly numbers. We prepare our programs and then work with our five units to implement them as best we can.

Exhibit 1 shows Barbara Watkin's chart of the steps in the sales objectives planning process for S&M and more senior TELCO management.

S&M consisted of 19 people. Barbara Watkin was a 20-year employee of TELCO, having spent several years in Phone Stores and the last several years managing the Business Offices. She was assisted by five key staff:

Joanne Lasher, S&M Controller, who managed all the budgets and performance reports.

Joe Collins, who managed all the promotion for Business Offices, Phone Stores, and I&M.

Janet Gardiner, who managed all the promotion for Operators Services.

Steve Dixon, who was the planner.

Alex Jones, who had just been assigned to the CLASS/CMS launch for the next eight months.

## PRODUCT AND SERVICE PORTFOLIO

TELCO offered single line customers basic services, additional line features, telephone terminals and related equipment, and long distance service and packages.

### (a) Basic services:

Basic service was called System Access Service (SAS), meaning connection to the telephone system and a telephone number and listing. Customers were called subscribers, who paid a one-time connection charge and then a monthly fee for basic services. This basic service charge was independent of a telephone set which could be rented from TELCO or purchased from TELCO or any other supplier of standard telephone sets.

---

*Exhibit 1*
*Barbara's Planning Process*

**May 30:** Letters to Product Management requesting product forecasts for next year.

**June 30:** Product forecasts received from PM

**July–Aug:** Review and analysis; acceptance of modification of PM forecasts by S&M

**Sept 18:** Review of PM and S&M forecast with channel managers; proposed criteria for objective allocations reviewed and agreed upon

**Sept 26:** Discussion with Senior management; adjustments and agreement

**Oct 1:** Review of final objectives with channel managers; agreement as to split among channels

**Nov 30:** Forecasts by channel and by district prepared and shared with channel managers

**Dec 31:** Channel managers share forecasts with district and section heads

---

## (b) Additional line features:

Customers could add to their telephone service by subscribing to touchtone. This enabled the use of tone-generating telephone sets and easier access to other network features. TELCO had long been attempting to convert customers from the basic service to touchtone. However, approximately 35% of its customers still had only the basic service as of 1990.

TELCO offered five Custom Calling Services (CCS): Call Waiting, Call Forwarding, Speed Dialing, Distinctive Ringing, and Three-Way Calling. Each of these CCS's was available at extra cost to subscribers and could be accessed with either basic or touchtone service. These features were in the network, not the telephone set itself. TELCO's overall strategy had been to build network-based features (where the feature is in the central office switch) rather than terminal-based features (where the feature is in the telephone set).

During the past year, TELCO had begun to convert its central offices to enable offering CLASS/CMS at extra cost to subscribers. Four CLASS/CMS features were planned for the near future: Calling Line Display, Call Return, Call Selection, and Call Trace. With the exception of Calling Line Display which required display telephones, the other CLASS/CMS features could be accessed with touchtone service and existing telephones.

More service enhancements were being developed (such as central office voice messaging) which were expected soon.

## (c) Telephone terminals and equipment:

TELCO offered telephone sets and equipment both for lease and for outright sale. Corporate policy emphasized rental over outright sale.

There were three touchtone rental products, all supplied by Northern Telecom: Harmony, Quick Touch 2/Signature, and Silouette/Solo.

The outright sales product portfolio included 25 products and was positioned to provide a complementary product offering to the rental set portfolio. There were five major product categories, explained by Barbara Watkin as follows:

1. basic sets, targeted to customers who desire a basic communications product which is dependable and low cost;

2. featured sets, targeted to customers who desire a fully-featured set that is feature rich, including two-line capability, speakerphone, direct access memories, etc.;

3. decorator sets, targeted to customers where the basic appeal is the aesthetics, physical shape or color of the set;

4. cordless sets, targeted to customers who desire the freedom and mobility afforded by cordless sets; and

5. answering systems, targeted to residence and small business customers whose concerns include simplicity of operation, competitive pricing, and feature complement.

Exhibit 2 shows many of the products available from TELCO to the single line market.

---

*EXHIBIT 2*
*TELCO's Single Line Products*

**Rental Sets:**

Harmony: basic set; adjustable electronic ring; compact design; desk or wall mountable; five colors; $3.00 per month

Quick Touch 2/Signature: last number redial; 6-number memory; visual ringing; link button; desk or wall mountable; ideal for CCS's; six colors; $4.90 per month

Silouette/Solo: dial in handset; last number redial; 3-color coded emergency buttons; 10 number memory; desk or wall mountable; ideal for CCS's; five colors; $4.75 per month

Unity: hold button/light; last number redial; link button; visual ringing; adjustable tone control; desk or wall mountable; directory card; one color; $5.00 per month

**Outright Sale Products:**

Debut: 20 number memory; last number redial; digital display with clock; hold button; flash button; pause; three colors; $95.00

Easy Button: extra large buttons; last number redial; tone/pulse switchable; 3 ring tones; four colors; $58.00

Classic: as above plus 9 number memory; illuminated dial; three colors; $77.00

Classic Plus: dial in handset; last number redial, flash button; three colors; $53.00

Innova: illuminated dial; 9 number memory; last number redial; hold button; flash button; $84.00

Innova 2: as above plus handsfree speakerphone; 2 line with conference; four colors; $115.00

Innova Plus: $115.00

Panasonic KXT 1455: answering machine; LED call counter; 2 variable outgoing messages; room monitoring; tone remote; dual standard cassettes; $135.00

Panasonic KXT 1470: answering machine; time/day stamp; voice menu; 2 variable greetings; priority message; 14 function tone remote; $180.00

Panasonic KXT 2390: integrated telephone and answering machine; 2 way memo recording; call screening; tone remote; single microcassette; 12 number memory; hold button; last number redial; one color; $175.00

Panasonic KXT 2632: integrated telephone and answering machine; auto message transfer; selectable record times; automatic erase; automatic interrupt; LED call counter; tone remote; recordable outgoing message chip; auto answer; handsfree speakerphone with mute; 26 number memory; auto redial up to 10 times; one color; $255.00

Panasonic KXT 3155: 2 line operation; ring selection for each line; conference button; handsfree speakerphone; 12 digit display; 48 number memory; clock with call timer; auto redial up to 10 times; save button for temporary memory storage; memo dial to store number while talking; one color; $175.00

Panasonic KXT 3832: cordless; 2 channel system with remote switching; handsfree speakerphone; 2 way paging and intercom; 10 number memory; auto security system; digital security codes; hold button; flash button; one color; $210.00

Priority: last number redial; hotline number; illuminated dial; visual ringing; three colors; $75.00

Symphony 1000: dial in handset; last number redial; two colors; $60.00

Symphony 3000: as above plus 3 emergency numbers; 10 number memory; digit display; three colors; $85.00

Symphony 8000: integrated telephone and answering machine; 11 function tone remote; 3 answer modes; multi-function LED display; automatic interrupt; personal memo recording $240.00

Ultima: $95.00

Ultima Classic: last number redial; hold button; flash button for accessing CCS's; $62.00

Ultima Plus: $125.00

Uniden TE 350: cordless; auto talk; one way page; 10 number memory; auto security system; digital security codes; last number redial; one color; $140.00

Uniden TE 570: cordless; as above plus two way intercom and page; $185.00

---

There was some concern about the product assortment TELCO offered. Joe Collins expressed the problem with renting the newer technology equipment as follows:

> We haven't had a new product for the residence market for nearly three years. Silouette/Solo was the last. There is demand out there for a rental answering machine, a rental cordless and so on. However, the problem is that technology is changing so fast in these areas that we've been reluctant to make the necessary longer term commitment to rental products that will probably become obsolete too soon. As well, our marketing priority has been on line features.

Joanne Lasher added:

> We buy rental products from Northern Telecom on the basis that we have exclusivity. We want that protection so that we will have a competitive edge. But, we know some of our retail competitors go to other countries and buy these products and bring them back into our area. We've often wondered about private label products too.
>
> This can be very frustrating for our phone store staff, whose main thrust is rental, to have only three rental sets made available to them and about 30 outright sales sets.

### (d) Long distance:

To highlight their interest in promoting the use of long distance, TELCO offered four long distance products:

a) long distance calling cards—to enable customers to make long distance calls when away from home charged to their home number;

b) long distance gift certificates—available in $5 denominations, accepted at all financial institutions and TELCOs in country;

c) a flat rate for 30 minutes of direct dialed long distance for residential customers during the evening, after midnight, or on weekends, introduced in January 1989; and

d) a price discount, introduced in July 1989, for a monthly subscription that enabled a 15% discount on a pre-determined maximum amount of long distance charge per month.

### The Product Strategy

Barbara Watkin explained her view of TELCO's product strategy as follows:

> For the moment, we're the only game in town. If people want an access line, they have to come to us. Where we have the leading edge is our line features. Our corporate strategy is toll products, line features, and then sets. We used to think about sets and line features as mutually exclusive, but we're beginning to package products and services together. We now believe that one draws the other.
>
> In the past, we have been very conservative and we have had a culture where we have tried hard not to make mistakes in the marketplace. Now we're trying to be more aggressive, yet still not make any mistakes.

### PERFORMANCE RESULTS AND OBJECTIVE

There were a variety of performance measures used at TELCO. Most were based on SAS, which was different than households served. For example, TELCO tracked how many telephone sets customers had per SAS, how many line services were sold per capable SAS (not all customers could get all features at any one time), and so on. Of great concern was maintaining, if not increasing, the installed base. The base was the number of rental sets in service that were being billed to customers. Additions to this base were called inward movements and subtractions were called outward movements.

Barbara Watkin recalled the objectives of the 1989–90 plan:

1. Arrest the erosion of the rental set portfolio and maintain our present base.

2. Increase associated rental revenues by 2.5%.

3. Achieve an objective of 180,000 outright sales which should increase the set penetration per residential household.

4. Increase the penetration rate of custom calling services up to 43% on capable SAS.

5. Achieve an objective of 656,700 long distance gift certificates representing an increase of 8%.

6. Contribute to the success of three new service introductions: Distinctive Ringing, long distance time discount, long distance price discount.

Joanne Lasher reviewed some trends in performance for the past few years as follows:

In 1986, we had 1.19 terminals per SAS. We're forecasting we'll end up at 1.0 in 1990 and at .96 in 1991 despite all our efforts. Since 1981, the number of rental phones has remained relatively constant, but the installed base for rental sets has eroded. The rental base has remained constant and even shown a slight increase when considered on a household basis. Harmony, Quick Touch 2/Signature, and Silouette/Solo are probably the reason for slowing this erosion.

Barbara Watkin added:

In 1990, we expect single line revenues for all of TELCO to be divided as follows: terminals at 6% of sales revenues, local calls and subscriber fees 33%, and toll 61%. In 1990, we also expect to go from 3.925 million sets to 3.864 sets, down .7% net in total. But, we actually have to sell 1.2 million sets to balance the expected outward movement.

Some of this is churn, (or Transfer Service), such as moving from one household and SAS to a new one, or such as upgrading the service. These would show as an in and an out in our data. We still have no idea how much of this movement is accounted for by TS or upgrades.

Joe Collins commented:

We expect our TELS/SAS to go from 1.00 to 0.97 next year. Of those customers who do rent, we used to have 1.3 sets per SAS. We forecast that to go down to 1.29 this year. Prior to 1985, only 8.4% of our customers didn't rent at least one set from us. We're forecasting that by the end of 1991, 24.5% of our customers won't rent any sets from us. Of all the telephones that will go into service this year, about 53% of them will come from us, whereas ten years ago we would have had 100%. We have about a 13% share of outright sales of phones at the moment, but that's a rough figure because it is hard to track. We are forecasting total retail to go from 64.7 to 65.4 in 1991. We're losing ground on corded sets, expecting growth of about 2%. Answering machines should go up 10%. Cordless should go up 13.6%, for a total retail growth of 6.2%.

Touchtone had increased from 23% of SAS in 1983 to 56% in 1988 and was expected to reach 65% in 1990. Similarly, CCS had grown from 5% of capable SAS in 1983 to 32% in 1988 and was expected to reach 43% in 1990. Long distance gift certificates had been growing steadily at 8% per annum and were expected to continue at that rate. Second lines per household had grown rapidly, but on a very small base.

Alex Jones said:

As I understand it, we want to move customers up technology so that the quality of our base is higher. We want to position TELCO as the leading supplier of a full range of rental and outright sales sets and we want to differentiate TELCO products through branding and exclusivity.

Joe Collins commented:

One of the biggest concerns I have is to maintain, if not improve, our position in the terminal market. This market is extremely competitive now and our base has been eroding steadily. Our services and long distance packages have a lot of room to grow yet. Somehow we have to come up with programs that will continue to bring us the results we need. A greater percentage of our sales revenues has to come from non-moving customers.

Barbara Watkin added:

Let's remember the goals that PM and ourselves have been discussing. We've said increase toll products 2.4% (last year was 1.4%), increase CCS

8.81% (last year was 5.8%), increase touchtone 5.84% (last year was 2.95%), and increase rental set sales 5.5% (last year was down 8%).

Exhibit 3 provides a summary of some key indicators and forecasts for TELCO.

EXHIBIT 3
TELCO Single Line
Performance

|  | 1987 | 1989 | 1991 FORECAST |
|---|---|---|---|
| SAS in service (million units) | 3.51 | 3.77 | |
| TELS/SAS rental | 1.14 | 1.05 | 0.97 |
| % touchtone | 47.1 | 58 | |
| % CCS of capable SAS | 24.6 | 42.6 | |
| Total rev. line features ($ million) | | | 363.5 |
| **Rentals:** | | | |
| Old tech.—inward (thousand units) | 383 | 330 | |
| Old tech.—in service (millions) | 2.92 | 2.37 | |
| New tech.—inward (thousands) | 724 | 800 | |
| New tech.—in service (millions) | 1.09 | 1.59 | |
| Total set rental revenue ($ millions) | 109 | 115 | 150.5 |
| Outright sales units (thousand units) | 142 | 149 | |
| Outright sales revenue ($ millions) | 12.9 | 17.6 | |

| | Total Telephones Per Household (totals rounded off) | | | | |
|---|---|---|---|---|---|
| | May 1984 | Jan. 1985 | Jan. 1986 | Jan. 1987 | Jan. 1988 |
| Rented | 1.22 | 1.25 | 1.28 | 1.25 | 1.24 |
| Bought | .70 | .70 | .64 | .79 | .88 |
| Given | N/A | N/A | .19 | .23 | .27 |
| Total | 1.90 | 1.94 | 2.07 | 2.26 | 2.38 |

Source: Northern Telecom

## CUSTOMER UNDERSTANDING

S&M rarely engaged in customer research, but rather collected information from PM and other internal TELCO groups, as well as benefitting from industry research sponsored by Northern Telecom. Information was not recorded in a customer data base, but rather existed as files of reports.

The number of telephones per household was growing in TELCO's central region as the above chart indicates.

Joe Collins commented:

Our market is changing in what is wanted. In 1986, the top issues were appearance, price, features, and quality in that order. Today the list has rearranged to quality, price, features, appearance. Our customers want more than the basics. In 1986, 50% of respondents said they wanted just a basic phone. In 1990, that percentage has dropped to 30%. The market demand seems to be shifting to higher quality sets. And demand for cordless sets and answering machines is way up. There is a growing interest in being able to control one's own communications environment. Interest in automatic trace has gone from 45% to 55% from 1987 to 1989. During the same time period, interest in caller identification went from 32% to 38%, automatic call-back from 24% to 38%, and call blocking from 15% to 20%.

TELCO had traditionally segmented its customers into two major groups, those customers moving and those not moving at the time of their contact with TELCO. Barbara Watkin explained the significance of this segmentation as follows:

The moving segment has always been a gimme for us, an easy customer. We think there's more opportunity with these people to upgrade their sets and services. And we know that the people who move are the ones likely to move again soon. That's why touchtone is so strong on inward, yet we have so many stable rotary customers in our base. We may not have made the most of our opportunities with these people. We've had an annual moving promotion which is a period of heavy inward movement for us. The other customers have no particular reason to come to us, so we have to go to them in a cost-effective fashion. We've had an annual non-moving customers' promotional campaign we've run for eight years which gives them a price incentive to upgrade their services, but we think it is getting worn out now.

I think our customers, particularly our moving customers, are becoming far more high tech. Many more of our customers have a hands-on relationship with complex products either at home or at work. So they want more high tech phones. About two-thirds of our customers seem to think that touchtone is basic service. Our customers now know what a line feature is, whereas ten years ago they hadn't heard the term.

We tend to think of our non-moving people as older, not into gadgets, more conservative, more likely to remodel than to move, and on the whole, more affluent. Many of these folks don't see any benefit in changing from the rotary to touchtone. They don't really care about the appearance of the phone.

Joanne Lasher interjected:

Our segmentation approach also means that housing starts are important to us. When houses aren't moving, then people aren't moving and they're not coming to us for new telephone service or transfers.

The Product Management group keeps track of housing starts and other indicators and gives us a forecast of inward movement. The latest numbers show a real softening in housing starts.

Joe Collins added:

I've been thinking about that presentation that our Product Management people recently gave us based on a Market Information Inc. study. They told us that we're not getting the young people but rather the older, more affluent individuals. And apparently young people have no loyalty when it comes to telephones. They tend to get a set from home or one as a gift, so there is no reason for young people to come in to visit us. And when they do buy, too often they buy the set somewhere else, like at a mass retailer, then come to us to set up their line. If they bought a cheap set, it won't have the capability to pull our line features and by then it's too late.

One of our problems is that many potential customers aren't renting from us because they have never rented. They're young and they've never rented. Instead they are buying, and they're not buying from us.

Customers are going from rental to buying only. We just this month got some research that shows that reasons for stopping renting are product service-related, preferred model not available, and not satisfied with TELCO. Perceived benefits in renting rather than purchasing: worry-free maintenance 40%, no benefit 35%, quality and flexibility 7%.

## COMPETITION

TELCO operated under the NTA which regulated its activities such as rates and, in turn, provided it with a monopoly in System Access Services and Long Distance. In recent years, competition had emerged in both cellular and in Long Distance services. TELCO expected even more competition in the near future. Barbara Watkin shared her views about competition as follows:

We only face competition in terminals. Our competition is other retailers: department stores such as Sears, and electronics specialty stores such as Radio Shack. We did a recent study and found that they outnumber our outlets 19 to 1. Because telephones are such a small part of their assortments, they can afford to loss leader telephones, but we can't. Our terminal portfolio, with all its associated expenses must make the corporate rate of return of 12.5%, so we can't compete on price. Our prices are treated as the regular prices by other retailers. Every category of our assortment has to make the rate of return. So we face competition in our middle and high end products, but they also have low end products that we can't afford to carry.

When competition in terminals began years ago, we used the argument that we sold Northern products that were of superior quality. Our phones would last, while the other phones were junk. Now this isn't the case. Frankly, people can buy telephones elsewhere that are every bit as good as our products. The average value of imported sets has been growing steadily from the cheap phones of several years ago. And those other telephones have brand names, such as Panasonic, that are better known than Northern. I'm willing to bet that our average customer wouldn't know who made that rental phone on their kitchen wall, and they'd have to hold it up to the light to see the embossed Northern Telecom name.

A corporate study of competitive products in 1989 had identified 61 different brands (each of which typically had several models) of telephone available to customers in TELCO's central region through all forms of retailers. The following chart is excerpted from that study:

| Sears in 45 outlets: | Number of stockkeeping units |
|---|---|
| $1–50 | 10 |
| $50–100 | 9 |
| $100–150 | 4 |
| $150–200 | 3 |

| Radio Shack in 136 outlets: | |
|---|---|
| $1–50 | 7 |
| $50–100 | 13 |
| $100–150 | 4 |
| $150–200 | 3 |
| $200+ | 3 |

## DISTRIBUTION AND SALES FORCES

TELCO used five different direct channels to reach its customers: business offices (BO), telephone stores (TS), installation and maintenance (I&M), telemarketing (TM), and operator services (OS). Each of these is described below.

### (a) Business offices

TELCO's central region had 18 business offices, each of which was staffed by 20 to 60 people, with a total staff complement of 2027 people. These BO's were organized into small groups headed by section managers, and then four districts with district managers reporting to a manager. The BO was intended to provide good service when customers called in—what Barbara Watkin called "inbound account management"—rather than providing face-to-face contact. Customers could query bills, advise payments had been made, and order additional services or installation and maintenance. Actual billing was handled directly by TELCO's accounting department.

Service representatives in the BO were evaluated on the quality of the service provided. This customer service orientation was often at odds with the sales objectives of S&M. As Joanne Lasher put it:

I think that there's a lot of concern in the Business Offices about pushing and overselling customers by recommending all our products and services. Recently, I did some sit-ins listening to their selling techniques. Some service reps sitting on position (they have the same position every day) were really good and seemed to see sales as part of their job. Others seem very uncomfortable and would ask lame questions such as, "Are you interested in any of our custom calling services?" in a way that suggested they hoped the customer would say no.

I would say that about 25% are exceeding job requirements, about 50% are meeting requirements, and about 25% require management attention.

### (b) Telephone stores

TELCO operated several retail outlets where customers could visit to see and purchase or rent products, discuss and order services and, in some instances, pay their bills. There were 30 stores with 252 employees, organized into five sections and one district, all reporting to a manager. These outlets varied in size from 600 square feet to 2200 square feet. They were located in shopping centers, particularly regional malls. There had been some experimentation with free standing kiosks in these centers, but the results had been disappointing and these were being phased out.

Barbara Watkin, who used to work in TELCO's stores, explained their role as follows:

Sales is their prime job. They promote our products and services as aggressively as possible and they handle customer requests for changes in service. A customer can drop off a bill payment at a deposit box in most of these, but not get a receipt or ask questions about the bill. Our phone store reps have no way of getting access to customer accounts. We didn't want customers tying up our phones and our staff in the Phone Stores asking questions about their bills. We'd rather they called the Business Offices from home. We've got phones to the Business Office in some of our stores. It's been a controversial issue for management.

We believe that a customer who rents a set is more apt to use a phone store than the non-renting customer. And we believe that we have more opportunity to sell more products to an individual in one of our stores than through the Business Office. We don't have any documentation to support these beliefs.

When a customer comes in with a broken telephone, the Phone Stores reps are supposed to test the set for any obvious problems. If there is a problem with a rental set, they simply exchange it for a new one. If it is a purchased set, they send it out for repairs to an outside contractor. They do not do repairs on site. If the set is not one carried by TELCO, the customer is politely told he or she can't be helped.

Joe Collins added:

That's all true, but I think we all agree that the TS's are constantly looking for ways to upgrade their retailing approaches.

### (c) Installation and maintenance

The largest group of TELCO employees in contact with customers consisted of the 5077 employees (technicians, clerks, and repair staff) of the I&M group. These people, 95% of whom were male, were organized into 35 sections and 14 districts in TELCO's central region and had two managers. The primary job of these people was installation and maintenance, but they were also involved in sales. Barbara Watkin explained:

Sales for the I&M people is totally voluntary. About 25–50% of them participate. It depends on the local management, whether they have bought into the idea themselves. They are very effective. It means when one of our technicians is on the customer's premises and sees an opportunity to recommend other products or services, he does so. We have an on-going incentive plan for technicians for rentals and line features. This program is not in any of the other channels.

The technician does not carry a large inventory in the truck, but rather directs the customer to a TS or, if possible, completes the sale. The policy is to have minimum equipment and inventory on the trucks. There is no room to store anything and each day a technician could get a different truck. He has a little brochure on his clipboard to show customers, but no extra copies to give away. These were produced by Advertising primarily for use in the stores, so we don't have any extra for I&M or the BO. They just get one each as a job aid. If the technician completes a sale, he will get some extra compensation: if he passes the sale on, he doesn't.

### (d) Telemarketing

The Telemarketing group was created to do "outbound selling," which means making sales calls on customers and potential customers using the telephone. Approximately 120 employees were organized in one section. Barbara Watkin described them as follows:

Their prime reason for existence is to sell custom calling features. When we upgrade a switch we call everyone served by that switch and offer some CCS free for two months and encourage them to sign up. These people also sell our long distance products and they'll be doing CLASS/CMS too. Sometimes they use an 800 number to do inbound fulfillment when it makes sense.

### (e) Operator services

Operator services consisted of 3,000 employees acting as operators for TELCO in its central region. Some of these operators would volunteer for selling tasks at the response centers. Their main task was lead generation. They did both outbound and inbound telemarketing, especially for products which crossed TELCO's conventional distribution channels and where it seemed appropriate to advertise one 800 number. They would qualify a lead and send it to the appropriate distribution channel. They also went to campuses and to mall displays. The Operator Services manager had been championing this relatively new idea as a way to increase sales and to provide some respite to the basic job of the operator. Some of the other channel staff were not too happy with this because they viewed the operators as taking away some of the fun jobs and there was apparently a union challenge coming. There were two unions involved.

Barbara Watkin summarized some of her distribution concerns:

> Traditionally, sales was not emphasized to the extent it has to be today. Some of the people on the line felt that providing good service was the name of the game and if we got some sales out of it, that was a bonus. There is still a feeling amongst many people that we really can't generate high sales and still provide the same level of service. We've got to change this. And, we can't forget that it is important to us that our various channels are consistent with one another, in terms of presenting the same message to both our customers and our employees.

## ADVERTISING AND PROMOTION

The responsibility for internal and external advertising and promotion had been split at TELCO. PM and the appropriate product managers were responsible for external advertising. External advertising to customers was scheduled to run continuously for 1990 with additional campaigns added for various parts of the product service portfolio. Barbara Watkin's group did internal communications with employees and was involved with outbound telemarketing and direct mail. Most of the campaigns were developed in isolation from one another.

Any advertising or promotion campaign that involved prices and changes in service charges had to be pre-approved by the NTA and thus involved corporate management. Even the amount of money corporate could spend on corporate advertising was dictated by the NTA at 0.5% of sales revenues. Since TELCO had decided to place its priority on long distance sales, most of its advertising dollars were placed against this part of the product/service portfolio.

There were occasions when S&M worked closely with PM on campaign development and execution. For example, a recent promotion called "Buy a Bunch" was originally designed in one of the phone stores by an employee. This was an offer that enabled customers to get a special tariff if more than one telephone or more than one CCS was purchased at the same time. Management was intrigued, feeling this was a good approach to increasing the number of sets per SAS. Both PM and S&M promoted the campaign.

Barbara Watkin's group was primarily concerned with developing campaigns to motivate TELCO's employees to sell. They developed the themes, collateral materials such as posters and giveaways, the incentives such as trips, and all other aspects of these campaigns. They had control over all aspects of such campaigns, such as amount of budget, which products and services to feature, and so on. They produced coordinators' guides to help people in the offices and stores to manage these internal campaigns. They had the authority to insist a campaign be run throughout all the distribution channels. TELCO's customers seldom saw S&M's work. For example, Barbara Watkin's group did not design bill stuffers.

In TELCO's central region, during 1990, there were 15 sales incentive programs ranging in length from one to 13 weeks, which meant one or more campaigns was running at any particular time of the year. TELCO sought financial help and marketing expertise from Northern Telecom whenever possible. These campaigns varied in success. For example, more than one-third of all of a typical year's features sales occurred during the one non-movers campaign which lasted only a few weeks.

Joe Collins explained how he approached planning incentive campaigns:

We have to vary our campaigns a lot. In one we may provide cash incentives, the next may be a draw, the next a trip, and so on. We're always looking for something new, because we believe that if we keep coming back with cash incentives, after a while employees will regard them as part of their regular compensation package. I think there is a big difference between incentives and commission.

We've evolved in our thinking about incentives. At one time we would say sell a Quick Touch 2/Signature, you get a dollar. Sell a custom calling service, you get a dollar. Now we say selling one telephone or one service is part of your job. Sell two or three sets to a customer and then we'll give you a dollar. We want that extra effort.

Joanne Lasher summarized the major dilemma S&M seemed to face with incentive programs:

There are two schools of thought about incentive programs at TELCO. One view is that the only way to get our employees to sell is by offering incentives; therefore, there must be some form of incentive or commission more of less continuously. The other view is that sales is part of the job and it is up to our managers to make sure employees do it. Occasional limited time incentive campaigns are then viewed as little shots of adrenalin to focus attention on particular products or services at any particular point in time, not as a replacement for management. I believe we have to make sure our people know what the corporate goals are, that they buy in, and that they see sales as a regular part of their job, not just when there are extra incentives applicable.

# C A S E 4.2 TELCO (B)

On November 1, 1990, Barbara Watkin, Director, Sales and Marketing for TELCO, sent a brief note to Alex Jones:

> Alex: I just got a call from John Ross. He wants us to make a presentation to the Vice-President of Marketing, Robert Markland, on November 15th. Ross is questioning whether we should do a phased launch of CLASS/CMS instead of the flash cut we've all been intending to do. Our objective is to ensure we come up with the best approach. Please think about this and begin working on a presentation of our total marketing approach to CLASS/CMS. I'll be back from my trip East on Monday the 5th. Let's get together around 10 am. — Barbara

## ALEX JONES AND HIS NEW ASSIGNMENT

On October 22, 1990, Alex had been given a special eight-month assignment: to plan and implement the launch of CLASS/CMS through all of TELCO's distribution channels in TELCO's Central Region. (See TELCO (A) for background.) When informing him of this responsibility, Barbara had told him that CLASS/CMS was a highly visible and sensitive project for TELCO and that he had to be successful with it. It was unusual for someone to be assigned as a launch co-ordinator. The TELCO distribution channel managers had agreed to pay Alex's salary because they felt that CLASS/CMS would be a significantly different launch challenge requiring more than the usual planning and co-ordination. They all agreed that no one else seemed to be in a better position to champion the launch than the team in Sales and Marketing.

Prior to this time, Alex had been working on revenue generation programs for one of the channels. Alex was given a total budget of $50,000 for the launch of CLASS/CMS and told the hoped-for launch date would be in early Spring, 1991.

Alex was surprised by the suddenness of Barbara's request to re-evaluate the situation. He had expected to have much more time to put together a launch plan. He was relieved that he had moved so quickly in the first few days of his assignment. He had already spoken with Roger Stewart, the TELCO product manager for CLASS/CMS, he had examined the preliminary forecasts in terms of sets and feature sales for CLASS/CMS, and he had gathered some market research data from other North American telcos and from TELCO's own test market in Wentworth, a large city in TELCO's Western region. He decided to spend the weekend reviewing all his notes about CLASS/CMS and preparing a preliminary presentation to try on Barbara on the 5th.

## CLASS/CMS

CLASS/CMS was both a new product and a new service for TELCO. Using new telephone sets with displays and other features, TELCO would be able to offer subscribers calling line identification and display (CLID), incoming call logging, selective call answering/blocking, and call trace, in addition to all the other features of a full-service network. Alex had noted a description of the CLASS/CMS services TELCO intended to offer subscribers as follows:

**Call Display** will show the caller's local originating number before the subscriber answers the call. This is the only feature that requires a special display device. Other CLASS/CMS services could be used on most existing telephone products. Call display will show long distance calls as long distance. Local operator-assisted calls will be displayed as unknown numbers.

**Call Return** allows the subscriber to return the last call received whether answered or not without using an answering machine. Call Return also monitors a busy line for up to 30 minutes and alerts the subscriber with a special tone when the number is free. The subscriber can make and receive other calls while waiting. If the subscriber has Call Waiting, Call Return will work on a waiting call. If the subscriber does not wish to respond to the Call

Waiting tone, the subscriber can continue with the conversation knowing that after that, Call Return can be used to retrieve the call that was waiting.

**Call Selection** allows the customer to reroute at any time unwanted local calls (including the "last call" even if from an unknown person) from up to 12 numbers, without hearing the ringing, to a pre-recorded announcement: "The party you are trying to reach has chosen not to take calls at this time." Calls from unspecified numbers will still ring through.

**Call Trace** allows the subscriber when experiencing a threatening or harassing phone call to dial a code that causes TELCO to automatically record the calling number to provide a record should the subscriber wish to take legal action. This number will only be released to the police, not to the subscriber.

Other services that might be offered in the near future included Call Blocking, Call Queue, and Distinctive Ringing.

CLASS/CMS was a network service and could be accessed using any regular rotary or touchtone telephone, except for Calling Line Display which required a new display device. With CLASS/CMS in mind, Northern Telecom developed the Maestro, first of a new line of products, and launched it in Las Vegas in January, 1990. The Maestro was a fully featured touchtone telephone set in five colors, with four position alerter, link button for custom calling services (such as call waiting, call forwarding), last number redial button, visual ringing and line status lamp to show when a call is on hold or an extension is in use, 10 programmable memory dialers, 15 unanswered call log (shows time and date of calls that have come in), 1×16 alphanumeric display, bilingual/adjustable receiver, recall dial and hold buttons.

There had been much publicized debate about the merits of incoming call identification. Some individuals and groups felt this was a blatant disregard of personal privacy, while others welcomed the ability to control their incoming calls. The net result of this publicity was a National Telecommunications Agency ruling that required TELCO to tell every customer in any launch area of CLASS/CMS, whether they had the service or not, that their number could possibly be displayed now that CLASS/CMS was available to other subscribers. Further, TELCO was required to provide (at a small fee) operator-assisted calls without line identification for those wishing anonymity.

Alex had been told by Technical Services, the TELCO division that installed and operated all of TELCO's equipment, that 80% CLASS/CMS functionalization would be ready by the end of April, 1991. This meant that 80% of subscribers could access CLASS/CMS from their telephones as of that date. At the moment, Alex knew that the network was less than 40% ready and that there would still be parts of the region that would not get CLASS/CMS until 1993. Some customers would be able to get the service with their current numbers as their local switch was upgraded, whereas others would only be able to get CLASS/CMS, if at all, if their number was changed. There would be some confusion as to who would be converted and when, because the conversion program plan was not yet fully detailed.

The Product Manager for CLASS/CMS for TELCO was Roger Stewart. He had been working on CLASS/CMS since 1987 and was responsible for the product/service development, pricing and regulatory clearance, and most of the advertising and promotion aimed directly at subscribers. Alex had spent some time with Roger and had learned much about CLASS/CMS from him. Alex was the liaison between Roger and all of TELCO's distribution channels.

Alex remembered Barbara's words:

> Alex, CLASS/CMS looks like a very big project. Based on our Wentworth test and the launches of other telcos, we're projecting a massive load. We hope to drive 15,000 customers to our distribution channels the month we launch over and above our usual load. We've never added that many people to our load at once before so you'll have to get us ready for it.

## MARKET RESEARCH ON CLASS/CMS

CLASS/CMS had been available in various parts of North America for the past two years.

Various marketing programs had been tried, but Alex classified all of them as "cautious and limited". The publicity surrounding CLID and the legislative uncertainties had caused telcos to be somewhat timid in their introductions. He had been unable to find any information about the kinds of customers who had signed up for CLASS/CMS with other telcos. Alex had the following information from three telcos regarding CLASS/CMS:

**Telco 1:** CLASS/CMS had achieved a feature penetration of 12%, averaging 1.9 features per customer over a period of eight months. Maestros had achieved a 11% penetration.

**Telco 2:** CLASS/CMS had achieved a feature penetration of 4.5%, averaging 1.6 features per customer after three months. Maestro had achieved 4.0% penetration. Approximately 40% of the features subscribed to were CLID.

**Telco 3:** CLASS/CMS had achieved a feature penetration of 22% averaging 1.7 features per customer. Maestro had achieved a 3% penetration. Approximately 10% of the features subscribed to were CLID.

## CLASS/CMS in Wentworth

TELCO had test-marketed CLASS/CMS in Wentworth, a major city in a somewhat isolated location in TELCO's Western region. The launch occurred March 1990 with 80% functionalization. A major television campaign was run for Wentworth subscribers, as well as newspaper advertisements and bill inserts. The television campaign was the most aggressive use of television for TELCO for promotion of a network service other than long distance. Alex came to the conclusion that Wentworth customers were probably quite well-informed about CLASS/CMS and what it could do for them shortly after the launch.

TELCO offered Maestro as a leased product only and priced CLASS/CMS at the rates agreed upon with NTA.

TELCO had projected 5% feature penetration for CLASS/CMS in Wentworth by the end of the first year. However, by September 1990, TELCO was at 8%. For managers and staff who remembered how difficult it had been to sell touchtone and custom calling services when they had first been launched, the quick success of CLASS/CMS was not only surprising, but also somewhat frightening. Everyone began to speculate on the implications if all areas responded as vigorously to CLASS/CMS as Wentworth. In fact, the major concern became how to handle such a load without detracting from the other TELCO products and services, and how to maintain TELCO's customer service level standards.

Accessibility was the number one service standard for the business offices and telephone stores. However, in Wentworth, the telephone store staff, in particular, were so busy they could not meet their normal standard of being readily available to customers.

There had been a lot of advance employee training about CLASS/CMS in Wentworth, but virtually no internal promotion or incentives for TELCO customer contact employees. This meant there were no collateral materials available to Alex and no experience with CLASS/CMS incentive campaigns and sales contests for him to draw upon. He had observed with interest that employees were given an opportunity to try CLASS/CMS at home, if they chose to do so.

Alex noted at this time that there was no written documentation about market research

| Monthly Rates | | | | | |
|---|---|---|---|---|---|
| | 1 feature | 2 features | 3 features | 4 features | Maestro |
| Residence | $5.00 | $7.40 | $9.80 | $12.20 | $6.10 |
| Business | $7.50 | $11.15 | $14.85 | $18.55 | $7.95 |

One-time administration charge of $15.00 for residence and $27.30 for business.

done in the trial in Wentworth. He had to keep asking people for information about what had been tried and with what results. He had learned that over the first six months of the campaign in Wentworth, TELCO had achieved 8% feature penetration, averaging 1.9 features per customer, and 3.5% Maestro penetration. CLID was the front-runner feature, accounting for 40% of all features sales.

## PRELIMINARY PLANS

Alex and Barbara had discussed briefly the notion of a mid-May 1991 flash cut launch in Metropolitan Norford, the area of major population concentration in the Central region. Within the affected area everyone could call one another without long distances charges. In this area, there were 1.4 million customers, 1.1 million capable lines for CLASS/CMS, 6 business offices, and 16 telephone stores. This area constituted about one-half of TELCO's Central region.

A flash cut referred to offering everyone in the area the possibility of having the new product and services at the same time. The alternative was a phased launch, where individual exchanges in turn, had the opportunity to take the new product and services. TELCO had previously introduced other products and services with both flash cuts and phased launches, and other telcos who had launched CLASS/CMS had used both flash cuts and phased launches. TELCO marketers had been planning to introduce CLASS/CMS in the launch region when 80% of the lines could be served. This number came from other market areas where research had showed that anything less created customer dissatisfaction.

Alex knew that the Technical Services Group supported a phased launch. Their main argument was that such a launch would bring in revenues relatively quickly after they had incurred major capital expenditures. They were the ones converting the switches to handle CLASS/CMS. They maintained that many of the switches would be ready in January of 1991 and that TELCO could begin offering CLASS/CMS then to realize both additional revenue,

compared to a May flash cut, and reduced capacity problems for everyone involved. Robert Markland had found their argument quite persuasive and had asked Business Development, "Why not?"

Roger had told Alex that he only knew of the Northern Telecom Maestro product that would go with the CLASS/CMS service, but that he expected in the near future that other suppliers would enter this market. Roger was expecting to have solely a leased product, but wondered if he should consider an outright sale product as well. Further, there were add-on devices (adjuncts) to provide display capabilities with older telephone sets, which could be leased or sold outright. He wondered whether to offer these and, if so, how aggressively. Alex knew this decision could complicate matters.

Alex understood that Roger Stewart was considering $2 million advertising, but that media decisions had not yet been made nor had any decisions been made on the appropriate themes to use. Roger had recently asked Alex for his advice on these topics. Television advertising might be problematical in Norford because of spillover into areas outside Norford where CLASS/CMS would not be available for some time.

Alex thought the criteria that would be used to judge their plan would be what was most profitable and what offered the best customer satisfaction and least employee dissatisfaction. He wondered how to assess these factors for CLASS/CMS. He was not provided cost and profit figures for CLASS/CMS. He knew he had to have his numbers all worked out before standing up in front of Robert Markland and John Ross, Barbara's immediate superior. Alex was beginning to work with a forecast of 12% penetration by CLASS/CMS line features of the customer base by the end of the first year of introduction, with 40% of those taking the new Maestro sets. He had arrived at these numbers from looking at other introductions and employing some guessing. He had not yet worked them out carefully.

In addition to questions of launch timing and products, Alex began to list several ques-

and products, Alex began to list several questions. He wondered if there should be employee incentives for this launch and, if so, what kinds? How should CLASS/CMS be merchandised in the telephone stores? Where would they find the space? Should he consider means other than traditional for getting the product to the customer? Should he even use all his channels for the launch? Should he re-allocate promotional monies from other campaigns (such as the fall non-movers campaign) to increase the budget for CLASS/CMS? One of Alex's lunch companions had even suggested he offer CLASS/CMS sales direct to TELCO employees as part of the launch, a practice TELCO had not engaged in

before. As he began listing these and other possible marketing activities for CLASS/CMS, he became increasingly concerned about their impact on the other products and services TELCO offered.

Alex expected Barbara to say they would go forward to Robert Markland with a complete presentation of their plans for the launch of CLASS/CMS. Furthermore, he suspected Barbara would be anxious to ensure that they put forward the best possible launch plan. He wondered how best to prepare for his meeting with Barbara on Monday.

# CASE 4.3    Bradshaws

In September of 1986, as Bill Wreford, sole proprietor of Bradshaws china, giftware and housewares stores in Stratford, Ontario, contemplated yet another exciting business opportunity, he couldn't help but feel that he was fast approaching a critical time in Bradshaws' period of existence. The last year had been very stressful, while the last five years had been full of change and growth, and there seemed to be every opportunity for that to continue. However, Bill was concerned that the firm had reached a stage where internal growth in the form of more sophisticated management skills, systems and procedures should take precedence over external interests. In addition to this were the financial considerations and the fact that Bill had had to finance all new opportunities with debt, and he was interested in just making some money for awhile. Lastly but certainly not least were life-

style considerations. At 40 years of age, the high-risk opportunities were becoming less and less tempting, and the administration of three stores becoming more and more demanding, yet the lure of some of the ideas was very appealing. The possibilities included a mail order operation, a separate location for one of the store's popular lines of merchandise, two possible low-end retail outlets, and even cross-Canada expansion.

## THE FIRM

Bradshaws was a trio of retail stores that dealt in fine china, crystal, giftware and kitchenware. Two of the stores, including the Main Store, were situated in Stratford, Ontario, and the third was in London, Ontario (Exhibit 1). Stratford, located approximately 40 miles north of London, half-way between London and Kitchener, had a pop-

*EXHIBIT 1*
*Main and Second Store*

EXHIBIT I (cont'd)

ulation of approximately 27,000 as of 1986 and was very much an automotive factory town. However, it seemed to be fast becoming somewhat of a chic place to live. Bill described the demographics as being 'from Mennonites to mercedes'. Also, in the summer months it was transformed into a tourist haven as it was the home of the Stratford Shakespearean Festival. Many of the visitors to the Festival returned annually, and provided a large repeat market to Stratford's retail trade.

## HISTORY

Established in 1895, the retail store was started by J.L. Bradshaw as an extension of his import/wholesale business. The original owner of Bradshaws made 87 ocean crossings to purchase English wares, and the Bradshaws name began to earn a reputation for quality goods. The import/wholesale and retail businesses were handed down through the family to David Bradshaw. He had been in charge since 1955, and was of the opinion that the target market for

the store was the tourist trade. His merchandising strategy was to buy great quantities in the tourist season; whatever was left after the summer was over, he would sell to the local residents. He was very involved in local politics, as well as the operation of the wholesale business, and spent very little time or effort on the retail store. The result of this inattention was an increasingly run-down building, a huge inventory that was inappropriate to either the tourists or the residents, and a huge potential to destroy the reputation that had been built up in his family for over 75 years.

In 1970, David hired Bill Wreford to help with the shipping, receiving and rudimentary inventory system of the retail operation. This was in preparation for Bill to take over the sales representative position for the importing business. Bill then developed practical experience in the china industry to complement his natural intuition for the business.

In January 1975, Bill Wreford purchased Bradshaws China Hall. The agreement gave Bill ownership of Bradshaws' name and inventory for $130,000, all debt-financed. Bill agreed to lease the 2600 sq. ft. of retail space for 10 years, with an option to purchase. He described the Bradshaws he purchased as an unfocussed china shop selling medium to low-end merchandise, primarily to tourists.

The next three years saw a series of subtle changes where Bill attempted to make the store live up to its reputation. He, in effect, wanted to make it a good version of what it already was. The first moves concentrated on the merchandising strategy. Bill's buying began to focus on the local market and their wants and needs, while continually upgrading the merchandise.

The second area he concentrated on was the lack of any control systems. Although the store had annual sales in 1974 of $229,000, there were no formal bookkeeping procedures. Instead, each morning a woman would spend the first half of the day counting stacks of loose change. Also lacking in the way of systems was a proper bridal registry to deal with the large wedding market business for which Bradshaws was well-known.

Redesign and redecoration helped generate sales of $535,000 in 1979. Bill considered the renovations as 'band-aids': the heritage building was in poor physical condition. Unwilling to invest in capital improvement without ownership of the property, and unable to negotiate its purchase from David Bradshaw, Bill looked to move the business. He purchased a two-store, main street property for $160,000 as a possible future location for Bradshaws. However, in 1981 Bill used that space to open Bradshaws Second Store. It occupied 1300 sq. ft. of retail space and sold factory seconds, low-end dinnerware and some giftware. This action was taken somewhat spontaneously when unexpected tenancy problems and the availability of inexpensive merchandise seemed to make conditions favourable for such a venture.

This move did not solve his problem with David Bradshaw and the Main Store, so Bill continued to look around for downtown retail space. In late 1982, he came upon possibly the largest retail space in the city. This building had 40 ft. of frontage in the middle of the main street and had 5000 sq. ft. of retail space on street level. It also had another 4000 sq. ft. of clean, dry space in the basement, as well as excellent shipping and receiving facilities through an accessible back entrance. It was owned by an accountant who occupied the upper 5000 sq. ft. Bill was able to purchase half ownership at a cost of $110,000, again financed totally by the bank.

The building did not live up to Bill's vision of what he wanted Bradshaws to look like. Before any move occurred he felt major renovations were necessary. Bill wanted to maintain the feeling that the store was established in 1895, and to emulate the reputation it had earned since that time. With the help of an interior design consultant specializing in commercial redecoration, Bradshaws' appearance was changed. The interior designer offered advice on the installation of boutique-like areas, traffic flows and display wiring. Bill and the designer developed the layout with reference to security, aesthetics and practicality (Exhibit 2).

While the look he wanted to create was "spectacular", Bill's greatest fear was that he would produce something that would overwhelm the citizens of Stratford. He was aware that looking too precious and too expensive could result in the loss of the already diminishing local trade. Bill saw retailing in a downtown core as needing change, due to the approximately 40% – 60% of the shopping public frequenting malls. Bill felt that those people were not to be lured back, and that the downtown merchants must cater to the needs and wants of the citizens who continued to frequent the downtown core.

The $150,000 worth of renovations extended over a period of three months and were done in complete secrecy. The front of the store had been boarded and no one could tell what was happening. The opening was triumphant, with the boarding coming off only on the opening day. Excitement had been building with both the boarding and the move, which consisted of people carrying boxes across the main street of Stratford.

The new store was well-received.

EXHIBIT 2
Main Store Layout

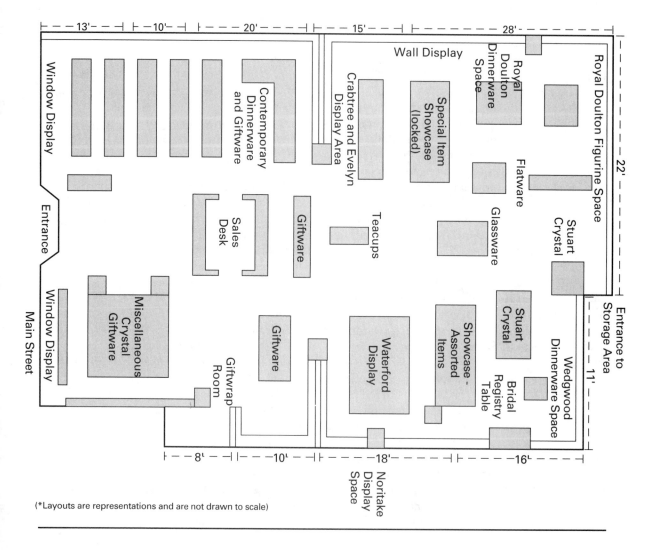

(*Layouts are representations and are not drawn to scale)

Bradshaws went into 1983 with annual sales of $750,000 and ended the year with annual sales of $950,000. The merchandising strategy, although continuing to upgrade, was simply doing more of the same in an expanded space and with expanded product lines. The single biggest addition was a line of Crabtree and Evelyn food articles and personal hygiene products that accounted for approximately 200 sq. ft. of the new store.

## RECENT DINNERWARE INDUSTRY TRENDS

### Resource Markets

The dinnerware industry has traditionally been concentrated around three major manufacturers of mainly tabletop dinnerware:

1.  Royal Doulton, a 150-year-old company with Canadian sales in the area of $60 million dollars annually;

2. Wedgwood, a 225-year-old company with Canadian sales in the area of $25 – 30 million dollars annually;

3. Noritake, a 60-year-old company with Canadian sales in the area of $15 – 20 million dollars annually.

The manufacturing originated in Britain, and it remained home to most of the production, with the exception of Noritake, a Japanese company. The distribution channels traditionally were through the manufacturers' distributors, then into the retail outlets. Until recently, this structure was stable and politely maintained so that each competitor was content with its share of the market. There was no real push for increased display space, and the products produced were based on historical customer expectations of what china companies should do, with little innovation or major change.

The 36 months previous to 1985 had seen a drastic change in this environment. There had been literally hundreds of new entrants into the market who tended to produce in low-cost, less developed countries. They induced great increases in product R&D and product innovation which appeared to have preceded the consumers' demand. Competition became fierce, with squeezed margins and increased emphasis on promotional sales terms. The distribution channels stayed the same for most of the players. Wedgwood considered themselves manufacturers and distributors, and would not enter the retail business. They would, however, join with a retailer they felt was competent and offer financial support for prominent display space. Royal Doulton, the dominant firm in the market began to open corporate retail outlets that were increasingly aggressive on price and promotional terms.

Exacerbating the price competition were currency fluctuations. The yen, pound, franc, and lire were all up against a weak Canadian dollar, accounting for large price increases and great instability.

## Consumption Markets

The retail end of the dinnerware distribution channel was traditionally divided between independents, national department stores and jewellery chains.

In the Main Stratford store, Bill faced four main competitors, in order of directness:

1. Ashley's China, Toronto
2. National department store chains
3. Birks
4. Household China, Kitchener

### I. Ashley's

Ashley's was a major force in the Ontario and Northeastern U.S. dinnerware market. Occupying five floors at Yonge and Bloor in downtown Toronto, they were rumored to have enough purchasing clout to affect production at a manufacturing plant. The business was family-owned and operated, therefore financial data were unavailable; however, Ashley's was reputed to do $30 million in annual sales.

### 2. National Department Stores

Bill considered these outlets as competitors only because of the advertising they were able to undertake. They had little breadth or depth, poor service, poor display and did a relatively small volume; however, their promotional advertising shaped customer expectations for what they perceived should be offered, especially with respect to price.

### 3. Birks

Birks also offered little breadth or depth, but did provide adequate service as well as bridal registry. Their main competitive advantage was their reputation.

### 4. Household China

Located in Kitchener, Ontario, Household was another family-owned and operated retail establishment which again resulted in inaccessibility to financial data. Bill considered them to be in a monopoly position in the Kitchener area, with adequate resources to quash any competitive threat or entrant.

In Bill's view, there was virtually no direct competition for the main Stratford store in its target geographic area of approximately 40 sq. miles.

## RECENT BRADSHAWS HISTORY

By the fall of 1984, the Second Store was causing Bill some concern. The recession was over, the inexpensive goods that had made the store possible were becoming more difficult to obtain, and the prices were no longer bargains. Customers were not as interested in seconds and bargains, and the idea seemed incongruous. Bill found this incongruity distasteful, and he stated that he 'just didn't feel good' about the second store concept:

> I can't do anything that I don't like. Everything that I've done has been because I wanted to do it.

Both Bill and his wife wanted a kitchen shop and the Second Store was no longer satisfying that desire. They then altered the concept to focus directly on kitchenware, and moved all similar items from the Main Store to the Second Store.

Late 1984 also saw the birth of the London

*EXHIBIT 3*
*Bridal Program*

### Marketing Objectives

1. To capture the majority of the bridal tabletop business in London and surrounding area (over 1000 weddings per year in London alone).

2. To gain market leadership as the single source tabletop retailer in London.

3. To encourage suppliers to maximize co-op spending based on volume and profitability of sales through Bradshaws.

4. To build a strong base for repeat purchases.

### Target Audience

Primary target group is brides
- The average single bride is 23.3 years old.
- 90% of brides are under 34 years of age.
- 82.12% of brides are beginning their first marriage*

There is a high propensity to purchase tabletop goods (among brides). Their self-reported perceived needs for products are:

| Product | % of Brides |
|---|---|
| Silver | 31.7% |
| Stainless | 78.9% |
| Fine China | 67.6% |
| Other dinnerware | 77.6% |
| Glass/Crystal | 77.8% * * |

Secondary target group is wedding guests (average 120 per wedding) who represent 80% of the population (1 attendance per year).

* Source: Price Waterhouse/*Today's Bride Study,* 1982
* * Source: *Today's Bride Reader Study,* 1981

### Product & Positioning

The product range is a complete array of tableware, flatware and glassware/crystal. The suppliers each have a number of recognizable brand names which completely cover the middle to upscale possibilities of this market segment.

Merchandise will be tastefully and selectively displayed in glass cases. The presentation will be approachable (i.e., not a warehousing effect of thousands of plates in a row), and featured in placesettings – particularly in the windows.

All personnel will be bridal consultants who can devote time, energy and knowledgeability to the very important selection process.

Bradshaws will be unique in Richmond Row, and in fact in all of London, as a traditional outlet of a broad range of a specialized product.

Bradshaws will own a very specific niche in the marketplace.

Bradshaws. Bill regarded London as historically having been an under-serviced area in the way of china and crystal, with possibly less tableware being sold out of the city of London than was being sold out of the Main Store in Stratford. Bill had been interested in that market for several years, and when Wedgwood approached him with the offer of considerable financial assistance to open a Bradshaws, he was receptive. There would be no constraints or strings attached to the loose agreement, other than Wedgwood wanted prominent display space, and to have the customers feel that the company was an important force in the store.

Bill's initial approach was to attempt to replicate the Main Stratford store in a somewhat more cosmopolitan fashion. However, a marketing research firm determined that idea to be inappropriate for London, arguing instead for a more focussed merchandise mix than was offered in Stratford. Their advice was to focus primarily on the bridal market. Segments of the study are presented in Exhibit 3. Because the market was under-serviced with only seven actual competitors (there were approximately 1000 weddings per year in London with an average revenue of $1000 per wedding), the firm felt Bradshaws could easily capture enough share of the market to meet their $250,000 breakeven.

Bill located the London store on a fashionable stretch of London downtown called Richmond Row. It was housed in a new development, and occupied 1200 sq. ft. at $20 per sq. ft. The atmosphere and layout (Exhibit 4) were developed to be purposely cosmopolitan, with soft colours and rounded corners on all fixturing to appeal to the young bridal market. The merchandise assortment was focussed on tabletop dinnerware and crystal, with a limited selection of giftware. Radio, print and transit advertising targeted tabletop dinnerware "For the Bride". Printed media accounted for sixty percent of advertising dollars and radio accounted for forty percent.

## CRISIS

The London store opened in February of 1985, and by the end of 1985 Bill knew Bradshaws was in financial difficulty. He had underestimated the cost of getting London up and running, especially for inventory and advertising, and had ended up with expenses well over the initial projections. In addition to the expensive London start-up, he had been purchasing in Stratford so as to take advantage of volume discounts and the result was an increase in aggregate purchase cost. The availability of discounts was exacerbated by the innovative new products, which were inducing pressure to increase the breadth of merchandise offered so as to carry the latest in fashion. All told, Bill was approximately $250,000 cash outflow over cash inflow. He was being gently pressured by the bank, as he had reached his $200,000 credit limit in Stratford, and his $100,000 credit limit in London.

Bill's assurance to show more control in purchasing convinced the bank to carry Bradshaws over this short-term difficulty.

## BRADSHAWS TODAY

Bill saw Bradshaws, in terms of presentation, quality, and results, as 'the best china shop in Canada'. This opinion was not his alone, as in 1985 he was voted 'Retailer of the Year' by the Canadian Gift and Tableware Association. They were a body of approximately 400 companies involved in importing, wholesaling, and distributing. Each year, the sales representatives of these companies voted for the retailer they felt had shown superior performance in terms of quality of display, staff training and overall store presentation.

Financial performance data are presented in Exhibit 5. Sales by store for 1985 and for the first eight months of 1986 are presented in Exhibit 6. Sales by product group (e.g. dinnerware) for 1986 are shown in Exhibit 7. Sales by product line (e.g. Wedgwood) and product assortment (e.g. pattern) were not available.

Bill and his staff saw Bradshaws' key success factor as its service. They felt that the greatest threat Bradshaws faced was for the citizens of Stratford to perceive it as 'a machine'—too large and sophisticated to meet their expectations.

As Bill put it:

Mrs. Brown, who has been a regular patron for over 30 years still wants to be greated by name and attended to as she always has been.

EXHIBIT 4
London Store
Layout

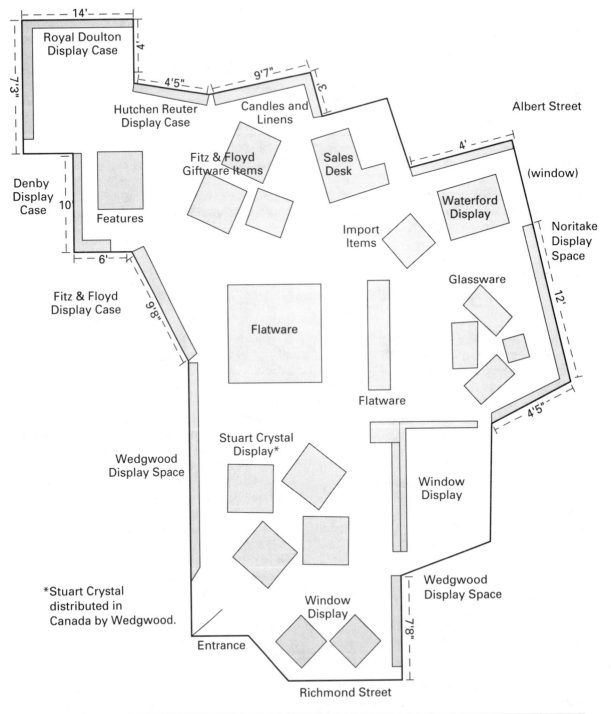

Royal Doulton Display Case

Hutchen Reuter Display Case

Candles and Linens

Albert Street

Denby Display Case

Fitz & Floyd Giftware Items

Sales Desk

(window)

Features

Waterford Display

Noritake Display Space

Import Items

Fitz & Floyd Display Case

Glassware

Flatware

Flatware

Wedgwood Display Space

Stuart Crystal Display*

Window Display

*Stuart Crystal distributed in Canada by Wedgwood.

Window Display

Wedgwood Display Space

Entrance

Richmond Street

*EXHIBIT 5*
*Financial Statements*

|  | 1980 | 1981 | 1982 | 1983 | 1984 | 1985 |
|---|---|---|---|---|---|---|
| Sales | $613,331 | $627,246 | $774,692 | $946,122 | $1,034,188 | $1,385,020 |
| Cost of Sales | | | | | | |
| Beginning Inventory | $171,477 | $245,349 | $202,991 | $201,823 | $238,028 | $240,488 |
| Purchases, freight | $457,629 | $349,276 | $469,991 | $594,809 | $613,282 | $1,055,643 |
| Goods available for sale | $629,106 | $594,625 | $672,982 | $796,632 | $851,310 | $1,296,131 |
| Ending inventory | 245,349 | $202,991 | $201,823 | $238,028 | $240,488 | $460,299 |
| Cost of Goods sold | 383,757 | $391,634 | $471,159 | $558,604 | $610,822 | $835,832 |
| Gross margin | $229,574 | $235,612 | $273,533 | $387,518 | $423,366 | $549,188 |
| | | | | | | |
| Operating expenses | | | | | | |
| Wages | $93,919 | $102,630 | $103,617 | $132,640 | $148,594 | $202,978 |
| Advertising | $9,390 | $11,119 | $16,714 | $18,042 | $29,141 | $63,968 |
| Rent | $6,000 | $6,000 | $6,500 | $13,200 | $9,450 | $36,202 |
| Utilities | $2,830 | $2,954 | $4,180 | $5,365 | $5,996 | $10,571 |
| Other (incl. depreciation) | $44,919 | $42,599 | $55,457 | $84,016 | $110,372 | $154,449 |
| Total expenses | $157,058 | $165,302 | $186,468 | $253,263 | $303,553 | $468,168 |
| | | | | | | |
| Financial expenses | | | | | | |
| Mortgage interest | $5,395 | $4,316 | $4,109 | $29,026 | $30,646 | $37,708 |
| Bank interest and charges | $10,447 | $16,789 | $17,880 | $28,438 | $31,215 | $41,274 |
| Less other income (loss) | $1,639 | ($1,764) | ($7,872) | $7,105 | ($2,883) | $9,818 |
| Total | $14,203 | $22,869 | $29,861 | $50,359 | $64,744 | $69,164 |
| | | | | | | |
| Profit before taxes | $58,313 | $47,441 | $57,204 | $83,896 | $55,069 | $11,856 |

|  | 1980 | 1981 | 1982 | 1983 | 1984 | 1985 |
|---|---|---|---|---|---|---|
| **ASSETS** | | | | | | |
| Current: | | | | | | |
| Cash | $ 1,650 | $ 3,202 | $ 3,960 | $ 9,752 | $ 12,254 | $ 10,866 |
| Accounts receivable | 7,054 | 9,117 | 5,070 | 5,421 | 9,259 | 1,915 |
| Merchandise Inventory | 245,349 | 202,991 | 201,823 | 238,028 | 240,488 | 460,299 |
| Other | 15,050 | 33,239 | 26,760 | 15,281 | 12,952 | 8,721 |
| Fixed (net of depreciation) | 51,748 | 204,088 | 334,418 | 486,600 | 465,030 | 495,919 |
| Goodwill | 78,398 | 78,398 | 78,398 | 78,398 | 78,398 | 78,398 |
| Other | 1,567 | 1,567 | 1,567 | 1,567 | 1,567 | 1,567 |
| | | | | | | |
| Total Assets | $368,876 | $519,427 | $642,534 | $830,316 | $819,948 | $1,057,705 |
| **LIABILITIES AND SHAREHOLDERS' EQUITY** | | | | | | |
| Current: | | | | | | |
| Bank Overdraft | $ 20,717 | $ 848 | $ 18,213 | $ 12,130 | $ 22,816 | $ 21,865 |
| Bank Loan | 20,000 | 60,000 | 78,000 | 258,200 | 241,636 | 253,000 |
| Accounts Payable | 38,495 | 29,391 | 39,978 | 47,963 | 54,339 | 88,114 |

EXHIBIT 5 *(cont'd)*
*Financial Statements*

|  | 1980 | 1981 | 1982 | 1983 | 1984 | 1985 |
|---|---|---|---|---|---|---|
| Current Portion of Long-term Debt | n/a | n/a | 18,348 | 19,159 | 14,572 | 40,610 |
| Other | 30,472 | 38,071 | 20,023 | 33,053 | 20,161 | 18,642 |
| Long-term Debt (net of current portion) | 40,717 | 159,460 | 211,371 | 161,034 | 148,995 | 333,044 |
| Total Liabilities | $150,401 | $287,770 | $385,933 | $531,539 | $502,519 | $755,275 |
| Share Capital | 2 | 2 | 2 | 2 | 2 | 2 |
| Retained Earnings (net of dividend) | 218,473 | 231,655 | 256,599 | 298,775 | 317,427 | 302,428 |
| Total Liabilities and Shareholders' Equity | $368,876 | $519,427 | $642,534 | $830,316 | $819,948 | $1,057,705 |

EXHIBIT 6
*Sales By Store*
*1985–86*
*to date*

|  | Main Store | London | Second | Total |
|---|---|---|---|---|
| Sales | $919,352 | $275,909 | $189,759 | $1,385,020 |
| Cost of sales |  |  |  |  |
| Beginning inventory | $211,194 |  | $29,294 | $240,488 |
| Purchases, freight | $651,182 | $272,222 | $132,239 | $1,055,643 |
| Goods available for sale | $862,376 | $272,222 | $161,533 | $1,296,131 |
| Ending inventory | $310,595 | $107,026 | $42,678 | $460,299 |
| Cost of goods sold | $551,781 | $165,196 | $118,855 | $835,832 |
| Gross margin | $367,571 | $110,713 | $70,904 | $549,188 |
| Operating expenses |  |  |  |  |
| Wages | $136,390 | $42,796 | $23,792 | $202,978 |
| Advertising | $19,684 | $41,635 | $2,649 | $63,968 |
| Rent | $1,000 | $25,602 | $9,600 | $36,202 |
| Utilities | $5,807 | $2,517 | $2,247 | $10,571 |
| Other (inc. depreciation) | $114,485 | $31,525 | $8,439 | $154,449 |
| Total expenses | $277,366 | $144,075 | $46,727 | $468,168 |
| Financial expenses |  |  |  |  |
| Mortgage interest | $37,708 |  |  | $37,708 |
| Bank interest and charge | $30,738 | $10,346 | $190 | $41,274 |
| Less other income (loss) | $11,469 | ($87) | ($1,564) | $9,818 |
| Total financial expenses | $56,977 | $10,433 | $1,754 | $69,164 |
| Profit before taxes | $33,228 | ($43,795) | $22,423 | $11,856 |

| in $ 000 | Main Store | London | Second | Total |
|---|---|---|---|---|
| January | $77.8 | $23.6 | $13.9 | $115.3 |
| February | $30.2 | $18.2 | $6.6 | $55.0 |
| March | $35.4 | $14.7 | $8.5 | $58.6 |
| April | $40.5 | $29.8 | $11.1 | $81.4 |
| May | $72.5 | $39.2 | $18.1 | $129.8 |
| June | $93.1 | $35.0 | $20.3 | $148.4 |
| July | $136.5 | $35.3 | $25.1 | $196.9 |
| August | $165.1 | $30.5 | $30.4 | $226.0 |
| Total | $651.1 | $226.3 | $134.0 | $1,011.4 |

EXHIBIT 7
1986 Sales by
Product Group
Main Store

| in $ 000 | Giftware | Dinnerware | Crabtree | Flatware |
|---|---|---|---|---|
| January | $39.9 | $32.2 | $1.5 | $1.9 |
| February | $16.3 | $9.2 | $0.9 | $1.3 |
| March | $19.9 | $9.7 | $1.5 | $3.7 |
| April | $25.1 | $9.0 | $1.1 | $3.9 |
| May | $49.0 | $15.8 | $3.1 | $3.3 |
| June | $64.0 | $20.2 | $4.6 | $3.4 |
| July | $117.0 | $26.7 | $6.1 | $3.5 |
| August | $124.0 | $29.0 | $7.2 | $3.9 |
| Total | $455.2 | $151.8 | $25.9 | $25.0 |

## Organization/Operations

Bradshaws was organized by store location with the London store and Second Store operating as cost centres. Centralization occurred for accounting, financing, and advertising.

The majority of Bill's days were spent with dinnerware purchasing for the Main Store, as well as the advertising function, where he developed and coordinated all advertising for the three stores. Of comparable importance was his administrative function which included strategy considerations, growth opportunities and financial resource acquisition. He spent one day each week in the London store, and was in daily contact with the Second Store.

Bill believed that a dinnerware purchase was usually planned, with impulse buying ac-counting for only 30% of store sales. For this reason, customers usually were willing to order and wait for merchandise, rather than look elsewhere. Fifteen to twenty percent of annual sales were ordered directly from the manufacturers to satisfy customer orders on unstocked merchandise.

Cathy Rehberg, Myra Tuer, and Sharon Wreford, Store Managers for the Main Store, the London Store and the Second Store, respectively, had responsibility for 'staff' and 'physical store'. However, their duties covered such diverse areas as:

1.  staff
    - hiring
    - training

- scheduling
- motivating
- evaluating

2. customer problems
3. buying
4. developing/adjusting store policies
5. selling
6. store appearance
7. supplies
8. special orders

A typical day for the managers was broken down as follows: 20% of their time was spent on operating duties (e.g. displays, supplies, customer problems, special orders); 40% spent with direct customer sales; and the remaining 40% interspersed throughout the day with encouraging and motivating the staff. The staff encouragement aspect was essential as it took approximately one year for a new salesperson to become effective. It was also important for the long-time employees, as they must be motivated to maintain a high level of product knowledge in the midst of increasingly rapidly changing merchandise.

## Purchasing

The three store managers were autonomous in approximately 80% of their purchases. Bill handled items such as imports and special orders for each of them.

Giftware purchases for the Main Store were increasingly the responsibility of Cathy, the store manager. In dealing with 150 – 200 suppliers, she chose from a wide range of merchandise and made her selections based mainly on seasonality. Giftware purchases constituted 60% of Bradshaws' total annual purchases and contributed 40% to annual sales.

Bill handled the dinnerware purchases for the Main Store which required dealing with approximately ten select Canadian suppliers (out of a possible 18 – 20) who offered over 600 dinnerware patterns. Bill described four of the ten as very important in attracting customers,

two to three as semi-important, and two to three as fringe suppliers. Direct importing was a small part of the business, and accounted for only 5% of purchases.

The main forecasting tool Bill used for purchasing was the bridal registry service, which allowed him to predict demand for several specific dinnerware patterns. Wedding plans and purchase decisions were made four to nine months ahead of the wedding date. In addition to this information source, the manufacturers' representatives did a physical count of their stock in Bradshaws' inventory and informed Bill what they felt he should have on hand. The combination of these, as well as the season, and his own instincts, provided Bill with the information he required to make his buying decisions. His decisions had recently been influenced by the increasing number of manufacturers' promotions. Due to the margin squeeze, Bill attempted to make all purchases on promotional terms. These were offered to the retailer with a minimum order quantity, and for each purchase decision Bill had to trade off the benefit of the extra dollars saved versus holding a large quantity of inventory.

In addition to the pressure caused by the promotional activity was the emphasis placed on fashion. Product innovation had resulted in the retailer having to make choices based on the latest trends, as well as special offers.

The time frame Bill encountered when ordering was approximately three weeks from the time he placed his order to receipt of the merchandise. The manufacturers distributed from Toronto, and if they were out of stock there, the order time increased to anywhere from two to six months. This occurred approximately 30% of the time. Due to the purchase behaviour of china shoppers, they were usually willing to wait the required time.

Historically, Bradshaws' merchandising strategy had been to offer both breadth and depth of merchandise. However, as the cost of carrying the inventory increased and product innovation increased the occurrence of obsolescence, Bill was attempting to focus his purchasing behaviour on depth. His desire was to reduce the breadth of the merchandise in such a way as to go unnoticed by the clientele. Bill thought this would be possible due to the fact that 20% of the products generated 80% of the activity. In support of this subtle alteration in strategy was the fact that Bill preferred to make an obvious commitment to his purchases, and depth over breadth would reflect this.

### Inventory Management

Inventory was a major financial burden for Bradshaws, having a value of approximately $1 million (retail) and an annual turnover of only two times. An annual physical inventory count was undertaken each January and was the sole inventory management tool employed by Bradshaws to deal with their 5000 – 6000 SKU's in the main store and the 1500 SKU's in each of the London store and the Second Store. Orders for the Main Store were received and checked by one full-time and two part-time employees who verified the invoices and stocked the merchandise. Once it was stocked, it was the responsibility of the sales staff to trigger re-orders, as they were responsible for the display re-stocking. Although the bridal registry provided an accurate measure of popular patterns, slow moving items could go unnoticed. The full-time and regular part-time staff were given display responsibility for the boutique-like areas in the store that showed certain lines of merchandise. This responsibility merged with the responsibility of the stock people as it involved 'eye-balling' the stock on the shelves and determining which items were not moving and required added push. This area was ambiguous, with neither of the two parties being entirely accountable.

### Staffing

At the peak of the summer season, all three Bradshaws stores employed approximately 28 people on a full-time and part-time basis:

- 10 full-time
- 10 regular part-time
- 8 students

Bill offered 100% paid benefits, a disability plan, as well as Christmas gift certificates for all employees and semi-regular staff functions. Turnover ran at approximately 3%, with those who have chosen to leave doing so on good terms and in pursuit of upward mobility. Career opportunities, however, were available with Bradshaws, as both Cathy and Myra had entered the firm as students.

### Atmospherics

Bill wanted a customer visiting the Main Store of Bradshaws for the first time to be immediately aware of the atmosphere. Located in the middle of the main street in Stratford, he felt that the storefront looked the way that a customer, familiar with Bradshaws' reputation, would expect it to look. The front window displays were professionally done, and were consistently filled with unique and innovative arrangements. The brass and glass double-door entrance showed a decor that was rich and luxurious, complementing the high quality merchandise that was available. However, Bill attempted to keep it warm and welcoming and chose accents in mahogany and brass to promote this feeling. The layout consisted of several boutique-like areas that displayed a compatible range of merchandise.

The Second Store presented a distinct atmosphere also, and Bill was pleased with its casual, country-type charm. He wanted to ensure that the bright colours, hanging wicker baskets and wooden floors provided a comfortable setting for customers to enjoy themselves while browsing amongst the many kitchenware items. The Second Store's layout is shown in Exhibit 8.

### Personal Selling

Believing the key success factor for Bradshaws to be its service, Cathy, Myra and Sharon placed great emphasis on staff training. The salespeople were employed because they seemed to sincerely enjoy dealing with people. The managers selected both the full-time and part-time staff because they had a spark and a charm that set them apart, and hopefully made the customer feel comfortable in Bradshaws' surroundings. They were both knowledgeable about and inter-

EXHIBIT 8
Second Store
Layout

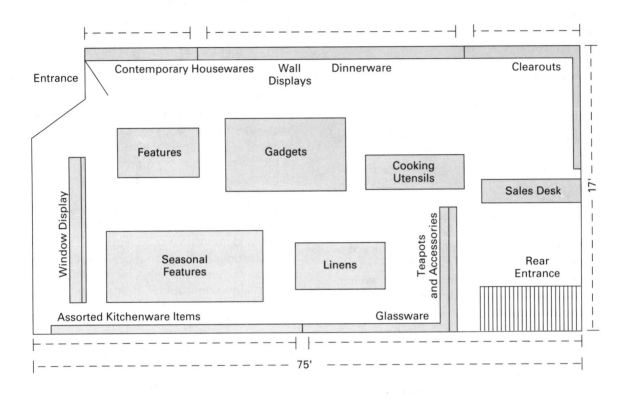

ested in their jobs, and their emphasis was supposed to be on solving people's problems, rather than making sales. Management believed that the dinnerware customer tended to be naive with respect to the product, and Bradshaws' salespeople were required to develop an extensive knowledge of the products in the store, and to be prepared to offer each customer a "presentation". Bill was adamant that their job was one of "teaching" and helping their clientele become educated about such an important purchase.

## Services

In accordance with a giftware store, the three Bradshaws offered gift wrapping, delivery and

shipping. There was also the bridal registry, which was well-known and well-utilized over a wide geographic area. Bradshaws registered approximately 400 brides annually.

Bill had recently introduced the idea of designating special evenings during the Christmas season for certain groups. This allowed those groups to do their Christmas shopping in a less crowded atmosphere with preferential service available.

## Seasonality

The Stratford stores' peak season was due to the visitors to the Stratford Festival, and occurred May through October, with a concentration in

July and August. The visitors could be divided into three main groups:

- 40% from border U.S. states
- 40% from Toronto
- 20% no particular geographic concentration

Forty percent of annual retail dollar volume was transacted over that period, and in the Main Store 50% was Waterford Crystal, which ac- counted for approximately 20% of that store's annual retail dollar sales.

A second peak occurred at the Christmas season, which accounted for approximately 15% of the Main Store's annual retail dollar volume. The merchandise focus at that time of year was giftware (Exhibit 9).

Balancing off these two peak seasons were the bridal seasons which occurred in the spring and fall. Bridal sales tended to concentrate on

EXHIBIT 9
Examples of
Giftware Items

dinnerware which accounted for 40% of annual volume. Of that 40%, the bridal registry was involved with 80%.

Overall, Bradshaws Main Store had on an average 150 transactions per day, and of incoming traffic, forty to fifty percent involved a purchase.

## Advertising

Advertising for the Main Store had concentrated, over the last several years, on special dinnerware promotions. Approximately 70% of advertising was directed towards dinnerware. These tended to be co-operative arrangements with the manufactuers, whereby Bradshaws would warrant mention in their nationwide advertisements as a retailer of their merchandise. These advertisements appeared in magazines such as *City and Country Home*, *Century Home*, *Chatelaine* and *Canadian Living*. Approximately 40% of Bill's advertising dollars were co-op arrangements. Bill was becoming increasingly concerned that the small and dispersed population base in Stratford and area did not provide enough potential impact to justify concentrating advertising dollars on dinnerware promotions. Because the Main Store offered a wide variety of merchandise, with no real concentration on any single area, Bill wondered if he should be targeting certain specific giftware items in his advertisements. (Exhibit 10). That strategy had proven, in the past, to appeal to the local customers. Bill used an 80–20 percentage ratio for print vs. radio advertising for the Main Store.

Bradshaws' London store was specifically focussed on the tabletop market: brides, and those who bought gifts for them. All promotional material, on radio or in print, aimed at promoting awareness among the target market that Bradshaws was "*the* tabletop shop for brides". Select recommendations from the marketing research study are presented in Exhibit 11. This approach was supported with space in London's *Wedding Bell* magazine, *London Magazine* and Theatre London's program (Exhibit 12). Because Bill considered London to be in the start-up phase of operations, advertising costs were running at approximately 8% of sales.

The Second Store was focussed directly on kitchenware, and advertising concentrated on promoting specific items in the store through mainly print, with some radio (Exhibit 13).

## OPPORTUNITIES

### 1. Mail Order Operation

Bradshaws offered, as an ancillary service, a shipping service for purchases being sent out of the city, province and/or country. It had been increasingly utilized by the large number of American visitors who placed specific orders, or shipped for convenience. This had been a small part of Bradshaws' business (3.6%), however, Bill saw it as a potentially lucrative area for growth. As Bradshaws' competence in this area had become recognized, they were receiving more and more unsolicited written orders and requests to ship.

A concerted effort to pursue a mail order operation within Bradshaws would consist of an investment in printed material and inventory only. The current location had excellent shipping facilities, and the employees responsible for current shipping and receiving had established a relationship with a U.S. border broker who was grouping shipments to allow lower brokerage fees. Bradshaws had collected 500 names and addresses of visiting Waterford customers who could provide the initial customer base, and be solicited: firstly with printed material from the Waterford display book, then possibly with a complete Bradshaws catalogue. That idea could, in effect, extend Bradshaws' summer peak season through Christmas, if the visitors could shop from home.

### 2. Crabtree and Evelyn

Bill felt that a conceivable progression would be to move the current Crabtree and Evelyn section in the Main Store into separate retail space. The present retail dollar volume of C&E out of the main store was $80,000, and the breakeven for a separate store would be $200,000. It could be located in the property adjacent to the Second Store, which Bill was currently leasing to a ten-

EXHIBIT 10
Sample
Advertisements—
Main Store

*EXHIBIT 11*

## Selected Recommendations
## London Marketing Research Study

### Advertising Objectives

1. To gain top of mind awareness with all bridal traffic as the single source tabletop retailer.

2. To convey the tonality and image of Bradshaws London while connecting it to the heritage of Bradshaws Stratford.

3. To convince the target group to make Bradshaws their choice for best prices, selection and service.

4. To encourage suppliers to maximize their co-op spending by impressing them with Bradshaws' commitment to forceful, tasteful advertising at significant levels.

5. To convey to consumers that Bradshaws will meet their needs easily, now and in the future.

### Tonality

Bradshaws will be a chic but fairly conservative, china store—carrying traditional ware in a more contemporary setting.

It will be a warm, busy, helpful place where brides can feel cared for and reassured as they make their tabletop choices.

Tonality of the communications should convey:

I   Launch
- newness
- stylishness
- friendly approachability
- knowledgability

II  On-going Format
- stylishness
- recognizability
- product/price emphasis

### Strategy

1. Introducing and establishing Bradshaws as *the* source for all tabletop purchases.

2. Appealing particularly to brides and those who buy gifts for them.

3. Making sure all target consumers understand this is a new and unique Bradshaws with easy access, helpful bridal consultants and diverse/complete product range.

4. Creating awareness of perpetual low prices.

5. Demonstrating the stylish/helpful/busy image of Bradshaws.

6. Giving consumers good reasons to come to Bradshaws.

### Media Strategy

Media efforts must be focused on making London and the immediate surrounding area, very aware of the launch of Bradshaws—presumably using newspaper primarily, and other supplementary media.

Post launch activities (on-going promotions) will be frequency oriented in a single medium—print.

Launch period begins February 18th for February 21 opening.

### Budgets

Year one budget is $40,000.

Client's expectation is that 70% of these funds will be recovered on a co-op basis, from suppliers. Therefore, all advertising execution must have heavy emphasis on product.

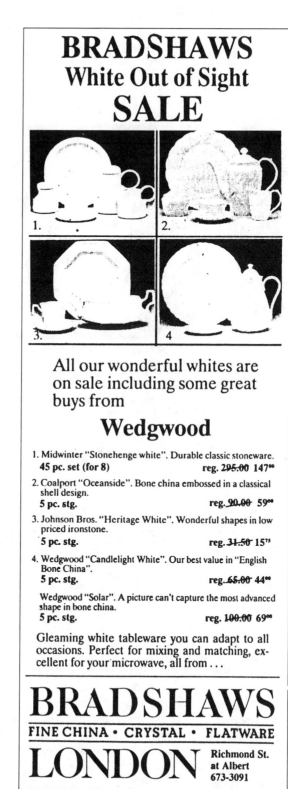

*Exhibit 13
Sample
Advertisement—
Second Store*

ant. Bill saw several good reasons for going ahead with the project, not the least of which was that he wanted to do it. He had a good feeling about the project, and the Crabtree and Evelyn people were interested in doing business with him. A fairly conservative British company, they had recently begun a major expansion into Canada and had opened 20 stores in the previous 24 months, 18 of which had been in malls.

Comparable environmental conditions to those faced in Stratford existed in Niagara-on-the-Lake, where Crabtree had opened a store in May of 1986, which had been quite successful.

Also, Bill was familiar with the product, enjoyed working with it, and would find the new venture to be simply doing more of what they were already doing, but with increased focus. Capable management was available in the salesperson who had been responsible for the C&E section in the Main Store over the previous two years.

However, there were several concerns Bill had with this proposal, the most troubling being the dependency on the visitors, rather than on the citizens of Stratford. He saw concentrating too directly on tourism as a bad idea for both the visitors and the citizens, as was previously discussed. He felt visitors came to Stratford with the expectation of visiting it in its "natural habitat", rather than a contrived, commercial environment.

His second concern was the uncertainty of the demand for the products. It was arguable

that the Main Store was the impetus for purchases, rather than the customers going to the main store for the sole purpose of buying Crabtree and Evelyn products.

Overall, Bill felt the venture would be low-risk, and very attractive. The investment would be in inventory only, and would be financed by C&E at a cost of $30,000. There would be a decreased cash inflow to the firm from the loss of $7200 annual rent, but the projections showed that once initial overhead was covered, the bottom line proceeded to increase dramatically as shown in Exhibit 14.

EXHIBIT 14
Projected Income
Statement
Crabtree & Evelyn

|  | Low | Medium | High |
|---|---|---|---|
| Sales | $ 200,000 | $ 225,000 | $ 250,000 |
| Gross profit[1] | $ 84,000 | $ 94,500 | $ 105,000 |
| Operating Expenses: |  |  |  |
| Accounting | 500 | 500 | 500 |
| Advertising | 5,250 | 6,595 | 6,940 |
| Depreciation[2] | 6,000 | 6,000 | 6,000 |
| Display | 600 | 600 | 600 |
| Insurance | 750 | 750 | 750 |
| Interest[3] | 8,250 | 8,250 | 8,250 |
| Legal | 500 | 500 | 500 |
| Rent | 10,000 | 10,000 | 10,000 |
| Repair and maintenance | 500 | 500 | 500 |
| General supplies | 2,400 | 2,400 | 2,400 |
| Telephone | 500 | 500 | 500 |
| Wages and benefits | 30,000 | 30,000 | 30,000 |
| Credit card charges | 1,600 | 1,800 | 2,000 |
| Property/business tax | 2,400 | 2,400 | 2,400 |
| Utilities | 2,400 | 2,400 | 2,400 |
| Total Operating Expenses | $ 72,650 | $ 73,195 | $ 73,740 |
| Net Income Before Tax | $ 11,350 | $ 21,305 | $ 31,260 |

Notes
[1] Average 42% of sales
[2] 10-year straight-line on investment
[3] 11% interest on necessary debt

## 3. Bradshaws' Back Door

A third option that Bill was less certain about was the possibility of expanding further into the London market. Retail space was available in the same development as the current London store. This space could be suitable for a low end, basic table-top dinnerware shop. It was approximately 1200 sq. ft. of space at $15 sq. ft., plus common area charges. The concept would be in conjunction with Wedgwood, and the products would be low end clearouts. The necessary sales volume would be in the neighborhood of $250,000.

Bill had some serious reservations about the venture that made it less than tempting. The main door of the location was situated off the parking lot at the back of the development. Although accessible due to the large number of patrons that parked there, it would not be noticeable from the street. Because Richmond Row was very much a 'walkway', this 'back door' location could defeat the purpose of locating in that particular development.

Bill felt that the current London store was doing very well, and showed potential for doing $1 million in sales out of the current location. Bill's concern was that if this was possible, then he should concentrate his energies toward that goal, rather than opening a low-end store that would need to do three times the volume for the same level of sales dollars and profit.

## 4. Factory Outlet

Bill saw another interesting and unique proposition in the operation of a factory outlet store that would carry seconds, overstocks, clearouts, and discontinued patterns at bargain prices. The idea was again in conjunction with Wedgwood, and would be the retailing of all their seconds and discontinued lines. Wedgwood was interested in having such an outlet established anywhere between Guelph and Windsor, and again would be involved in the financing.

A similar idea had been undertaken by Mr. Rob Macintosh, of Macintosh and Watts of Ottawa, another reputable and well-established china shop. His factory outlet was located on Hill Island, near Gananoque, Ontario, and was situated so as to benefit from the U.S. travel that crossed there. Open for only six months, it had proven to be a successful concept.

The location Bill had in mind for this outlet was the town of Shakespeare, Ontario. Shakespeare, with a population of 500, was located approximately 5 miles north of Stratford on Highway 7 to Kitchener. It was becoming a 'neat' place to do business, with the birth of a couple of folk-type stores in the last couple of years. At that time there was 200 ft. of prime highway frontage space available at a cost of $45,000, nudged between two restaurants. The cost of a pre-fabricated board and batten building with a porch would be in the neighbourhood of $60,000. The expected sales dollar level would again be in the neighbourhood of $200,000.

Bill saw the target market for this idea as the very new and very nebulous phenomenon called the "bargain hunter". These people were increasingly being seen to take whole days and haunt factory outlets. Geographically, the idea could cover the area from Kitchener – Guelph – Cambridge – Woodstock – London and also Stratford. Due to the logistics of relying on this type of market in a snow-belt region, there was also the possibility that such an outlet would be closed for half of the year.

## 5. Cross-Canada Expansion

The fifth alternative was the possibility of becoming a national retailer. Bill had been approached, again by Wedgwood, to consider opening Bradshaws stores in areas Wedgwood considered under-serviced and potentially lucrative. At the present time two locations had been mentioned – Victoria, on Vancouver Island, and Halifax on the waterfront.

These locations had become available through property redevelopment and a loan default, and had left Wedgwood without a presence in those areas. The understanding would be that opening more Bradshaws outlets in cities such as Regina and Calgary would follow.

Bill felt that the requisite of this alternative would be his ability to provide capable management personnel who could undertake a start-up in these locations, and promulgate the Bradshaws atmosphere.

## RESOURCES

Available to Bill was a financial arrangement whereby he would have $200,000 – $500,000 equity provided to him in exchange for half ownership. A friend, who was in the newspaper business, was interested in becoming involved in Bradshaws as a silent partner. The benefit to him would be the excitement of seeing Bradshaws grow. His offer included resources other than cash, and covered everything from his newspaper business (advertising), the use of his accountant, potential for growth through his real estate holdings, as well as all the other talent that he had available to him. Although Bill was aware of the intricacies involved with a partnership, and the inherent control considerations, he sincerely felt the arrangement could work.

## SUMMARY

Bill's vision for Bradshaws was "to be the best damn china shop in the country, in terms of the business we do, the profit we make, and the way we look". Toward this end, he felt quality considerations were paramount. He believed that "It is easier to expand excellence than it is to maintain it", and he wanted to ensure that Bradshaws maintained the highest degree of quality merchandise, service and presentation.

As well as maintaining the excellence of Bradshaws, Bill was attuned to the fact that he must improve control. Growth required sophistication, and Bradshaws was in its infancy as far as systems and procedures are concerned, with the lack of an inventory control system, and the computer used only for the registry service. Bill felt he would also like to see more detailed and up-to-date accounting data for the stores to be more aware of what items were bringing in dollars, and what items were not. The financial considerations he faced had to do with a desire to lighten the debt load. All ventures Bill had pursued had been financed by the bank, and that arrangement was becoming a burden. Bill felt shunning current opportunities and concentrating on horizontal expansion in order to exploit the potential of Bradshaws' existing assets was a valid strategy, but he was not sure if it was the best one. Finally, lifestyle considerations were a factor. At 40 years of age, Bill was prepared to assume a less involved role in day-to-day operations. While still enjoying the creative side of his business such as display and advertising, he was increasingly less inclined to spend time on the floor. The financial difficulties of the past year had caused him to wonder if the firm was reaching the operational scale where it required management skills he did not possess. The china business and the Bradshaws operation were still exciting to Bill, and he wondered how he should allocate his resources to realize his vision.

# C A S E  4.4   The Spoke Tavern

In early April 1990, Ted Remillard, recently elected Vice President Finance, sat in his office in the University Community Centre contemplating the exciting year ahead. Ted, a second year law student at the University of Western Ontario, had made the decision to take a year off school to take advantage of the opportunity to serve as a vice-president on the University Students' Council (USC). One of his top priorities for the year was to turn around the ailing student bar—The Spoke Tavern. The once popular campus drinking hole had been experiencing a significant decline in attendance and profitability. He was sure that something could be done to reverse this alarming trend and he was willing to bet his political reputation on it.

## USC BACKGROUND

The University Students' Commission was created in 1930, to synthesize the efforts of the existing Arts, Sciences and Medicine student organizations. In 1947, the name was changed to the University Students' Council. The USC was the central, single voice of students on campus until the mid-fifties when the graduate business students formed the MBA Association which later became a fully autonomous council. In 1963 the Council of Graduate Students was formed to represent those concerns unique to the graduate student body.

In 1965, the USC incorporated as "the representative body of the full-time undergraduate students of the University of Western Ontario . . .". The reference to "full-time undergraduate" students was subsequently eliminated to reaffirm the USC's original mission to represent the interests and concerns of all students. At the same time a business manager was hired and provisions were made to pay the President for the summer. Previously, the USC was staffed entirely by part-time volunteers.

In 1968, John Yokom became the first USC President to serve as a full-time staff member. In 1987, the Vice-Presidents also became full-time employees. The USC budget for fiscal 1990 was in excess of 3.5 million dollars (see Exhibit 1 & 2).

## SPOKE TAVERN

The Spoke Tavern began as an operating unit of the USC. The tavern, located in Sommerville House[1] on the University campus (see Exhibit 3), was originally established to provide a source of revenue for the USC. This revenue had been used in the past to support the extensive programming undertaken by the students' council. In addition, the Spoke was given a mandate to provide employment for students, encourage responsible drinking habits and provide entertainment to students on campus. Nevertheless, the principle objective of the Spoke was to generate a stream of revenue to support USC operations. In the absence of this revenue the Council would likely shut down this operation.

The Spoke's contribution, after rising year upon year since its inception, began a steady decline in 1989 (see Exhibit 4). USC projections for the 1989/90 academic year indicated a loss of as much as $10,000.

## SPOKE MANAGEMENT

Prior to April 1, 1990, Joanna Dunton, USC Controller, supported the Spoke in an accounting function, while the operations of the Spoke were handled by the Vice-President, Operations. On April 1, after the Operations portfolio was dropped, Dunton, a Western MBA, became responsible for both the financial and daily operational status of the Spoke. The political responsibility for the Spoke Tavern was transferred to Ted Remillard, VP Finance, who was ultimately held accountable for the campus bar (see Exhibit 5).

---

[1] The Spoke Tavern rented space owned by The University for $5,800/month. This figure included all maintenance and cleaning.

EXHIBIT I

## UNIVERSITY STUDENTS' COUNCIL OF
## THE UNIVERSITY OF WESTERN ONTARIO
### (Incorporated without stated capital under the laws of Ontario)

### Balance Sheet
### As at May 31st

**Assets**

|  | 1989 | 1988 |
|---|---|---|
| Current Assets: | | |
| Cash | $305,195 | $292,908 |
| Accounts Receivable | 70,045 | 66,395 |
| Inventories | 32,000 | 35,563 |
| Prepaids | 26,962 | 23,721 |
| Due from Radio Western | – | 7,630 |
| Total Current Assets | 434,201 | 426,217 |
| Fixed Assets | 463,792 | 449,744 |
| Total Assets | $897,994 | $875,961 |

**Liabilities and Operating Capital**

|  | 1989 | 1988 |
|---|---|---|
| Current Liabilities: | | |
| Accounts Payable & Accrued Charges | $118,161 | $89,939 |
| Due to: | | |
| Radio Western | 13,709 | – |
| Affiliated Councils | 66,565 | 56,894 |
| Clubs and Organisations | 41,147 | 55,404 |
| Current Portion of obligation under Capital Lease | 37,052 | 30,270 |
| Total Current Liabilities | $276,634 | $232,507 |
| Long-term liability: | | |
| Obligation under Capital Lease | 61,266 | 84,762 |
| Operating Capital | 560,094 | 558,692 |
| Total Liabilities and Operating Capital | $897,994 | $875,961 |

*Exhibit 2*

## UNIVERSITY STUDENTS' COUNCIL OF
## THE UNIVERSITY OF WESTERN ONTARIO

### Statement of Revenues and Expenses
### for Year ended May 31st

|  | 1989 | 1988 |
|---|---|---|
| **Revenues:** |  |  |
| Undergraduate Fees | $1,101,614 | $ 997,021 |
| Graduate Fees | 5,424 | 6,213 |
| Interest | 43,814 | 33,204 |
| Organizations and Programs[1] | 2,316,694 | 2,288,147 |
| Other | 7,567 | 9,467 |
| Total Revenues | 3,475,113 | 3,334,052 |
| **Expenses:** |  |  |
| Organizations and Programs[2] | 2,526,824 | 2,423,992 |
| Portfolio and Administrative Costs– |  |  |
| Corporate | 389,422 | 383,578 |
| President | 46,812 | 43,566 |
| Finance | 14,847 | 9,554 |
| Communications | 25,656 | 18,737 |
| Operations | 17,443 | 5,573 |
| Programming | – | 3,344 |
| External | 38,870 | 36,172 |
| Student Affairs | 15,897 | 5,989 |
| Grants and Association Fees– |  |  |
| Ontario Federation of Students | 61,859 | 59,758 |
| Charity Ball Donations | 33,000 | 36,000 |
| Radio Western | 143,630 | 109,214 |
| Councils | 79,379 | 80,355 |
| Clubs | 16,343 | 15,658 |
| Student Award Grants | 6,000 | 6,000 |
| Day Care Centre Grant | 20,620 | 19,857 |
| Community Legal Services | 36,084 | 34,750 |
| Total Expenses | $3,472,686 | $3,292,077 |
| Excess of Revenues over Expenses from Operations | 2,427 | 41,975 |
| Loss on Disposal of Fixed Assets | 1,025 | 16,085 |
| Excess of Revenues over Expenses for the Year | $ 1,402 | $ 25,890 |

[1] This number includes revenue generated by The Spoke Tavern's operations.
[2] This number includes the expenses of The Spoke Tavern's operations.

EXHIBIT 3

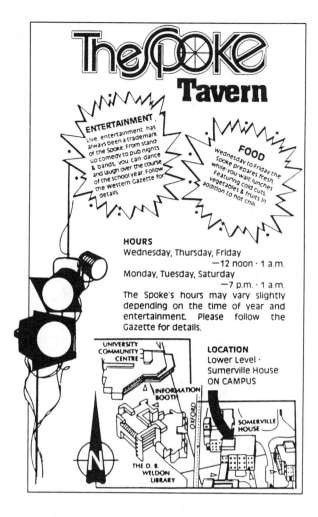

The Spoke manager oversaw the daily operation of the Spoke. Over the period from September '88 until April '90 three individuals had held this position. Rich Culley, the last of these managers joined the tavern in August 1989. Rich remained excited about the Spoke's potential despite the often frustrating performance during the 89/90 academic year. Rich brought with him significant knowledge of the bar business in London—prior to taking up his job at the Spoke, Rich had been employed with the Keg Restaurants in B.C. and Ontario for seven years. Rich had lived in London for five years and had excellent connections in the bar business in London.

Peter Standbridge, Entertainment Productions Manager, was also actively involved in the management of the Spoke. Peter was responsi-

ble for the selection and scheduling of the tavern's live entertainment.

## OPERATIONS

The Spoke was more a night club than a pub. It served draft and bottled beer; house brand liquor; liqueurs; wine; and pop (see Exhibit 6). No food was served, although the management team was considering the addition of a kitchen. The bar catered to younger undergraduate students—primarily those in first and second year. It was a high energy live entertainment venue. The decor was plain. The Tavern had a maximum capacity of 400 (300 seated and 100 standing). There was one dance floor which could hold about 150 people. The Spoke operated a patio in the summer and early fall. Hamburgers

EXHIBIT 4

## Income Statements
### (for Years ending May 31st)

| | 1987 | 1988 | 1989 | 1990* |
|---|---|---|---|---|
| **Revenues:** | | | | |
| Draft | $ 99,913 | $171,986 | $157,986 | $124,285 |
| Bottled Beer | 226,876 | 237,489 | 194,458 | 131,059 |
| Liquor | 149,352 | 153,428 | 111,671 | 93,939 |
| Liqueurs | 26,716 | 34,987 | 58,061 | 30,846 |
| Wine | 3,498 | 10,401 | 7,110 | 3,340 |
| Pop/Juice/Coffee | 4,361 | 8,183 | 6,196 | 3,667 |
| Bar Food | 0 | 0 | 6,195 | 1,460 |
| Less: Sales Tax | 47,869 | 55,866 | 48,535 | 36,254 |
| Total Sales | 462,846 | 560,606 | 493,141 | 352,343 |
| Cost of Sales | 160,526 | 214,827 | 199,854 | 130,812 |
| Gross Margin | $302,319 | $345,779 | $293,287 | $221,531 |
| | | | | |
| **Operating Expenses:** | | | | |
| Salary & Wages | 126,427 | 155,084 | 162,916 | 112,940 |
| Staff Benefits | 1,385 | 718 | 2,510 | 980 |
| Taxis | 0 | 302 | 787 | 310 |
| Travel | 37 | 12 | 210 | 60 |
| Meetings | 6 | 119 | 216 | 238 |
| Telephone Rental | 827 | 1,157 | 1,190 | 885 |
| Long Distance | 613 | 550 | 860 | 508 |
| Postage | 25 | 33 | 40 | 2 |
| Copying/Printing | 1,226 | 1,124 | 849 | 664 |
| Advertising | 11,144 | 10,263 | 9,135 | 8,269 |
| Equipment | 991 | 1,857 | 1,136 | 875 |
| Supplies | 1,618 | 1,739 | 2,162 | 1,387 |
| Occupancy | 61,231 | 66,153 | 67,512 | 52,805 |
| Maintenance | 6,273 | 6,179 | 6,107 | 6,556 |
| Glassware | 5,885 | 6,689 | 4,623 | 5,100 |
| Linen Supplies | 664 | 1,090 | 845 | 579 |
| Delivery/Telegram | 493 | 210 | 1,307 | 210 |
| Records/Albums | 348 | 1,372 | 300 | 710 |
| C.A.P.E. | 446 | 550 | 729 | 1,000 |
| Depreciation | 1,490 | 1,263 | 1,141 | 12,959 |
| Special Events | 15,375 | 18,909 | 17,445 | 277 |
| Miscellaneous | 550 | 748 | 65 | 237 |
| Total Operating Expense | $237,054 | $276,120 | $282,083 | $207,552 |

| | | | | |
|---|---|---|---|---|
| Operating Contribution | 65,265 | 69,658 | 11,204 | 13,979 |
| Programming | | | | |
|    Bands | 28,981 | 25,839 | 9,890 | (16) |
|    Comedy | (1,242) | 2,751 | (2,566) | (14,767) |
|    Special Events Expense | (996) | (1,393) | (1,507) | 0 |
|    CAPAC/PRO Fees | 0 | (675) | (1,234) | (805) |
|    Total Programming | 26,744 | 26,522 | 4,583 | (15,588) |
| Misc Revenue | 5,022 | 5,345 | 5,610 | 2,763 |
| Total Contribution | $ 97,031 | $101,526 | $ 21,398 | $ 1,154 |

* 1990 figures include operating data up to February 28, 1990

were served from a barbecue located on the patio.

It had been open Monday through Saturday from 12:00 p.m. – 1:00 a.m. However, after consistently poor attendance during the afternoon periods in the first term, the tavern reduced its hours in January 1990—opening at 7:00 p.m. except on Friday when the doors continued to be open at noon.

Attendance and hence revenues were very seasonal (see Exhibit 6). For example, the bar typically closed for a portion of the summer. In addition business was very slow during the holiday periods both at Christmas and during Reading Week (mid-February).

Revenues also varied depending on the night of the week (see Exhibit 7). For example, weekend nights (Thursday, Friday and Saturday), were significantly more popular evenings than Monday, Tuesday or Wednesday. Of particular concern however, was a steady decline in attendance on Thursdays. Thursdays had been a particularly popular night but revenues had been falling since early in the 89/90 academic year as students began frequenting other bars.

## WEEKLY PATTERNS

**Monday:** As with many bars, Monday was slow at the Spoke. The bar was usually empty from 7:00 p.m. until 10:00 p.m. There was rarely any live entertainment. A disc jockey played records,

but there was rarely any dancing. A cross-section of students arrived after night class (10:00 p.m.) to unwind over a beer or two. They typically left around midnight. This short period became known as "Attitude Adjustment Hour" among the patrons.

Gross Revenues:     $50–$400
Attendance:            maximum 25
Drinks per Person:  2–3
Door Charge:          nil

**Tuesday:** Tuesday at the Spoke was comedy night. Two or three comics from Yuk Yuks International would take the stage around 9:00 p.m. and entertain until 11:30 p.m. Students arrived around 9:30 p.m. and rarely stayed beyond midnight. In past years comedy night attracted an excellent crowd which often filled the bar on an otherwise slow evening. However, comedy night during the 89/90 school year had been running at a substantial deficit, despite the Spoke's constant effort to advertise and promote the previously successful event. The patrons who did attend represented a fair cross-section of students.

Gross Revenues:     $1,000–$1,500
Attendance:            maximum 150
Drinks per Person:  2–3
Door Charge:          $3

EXHIBIT 5

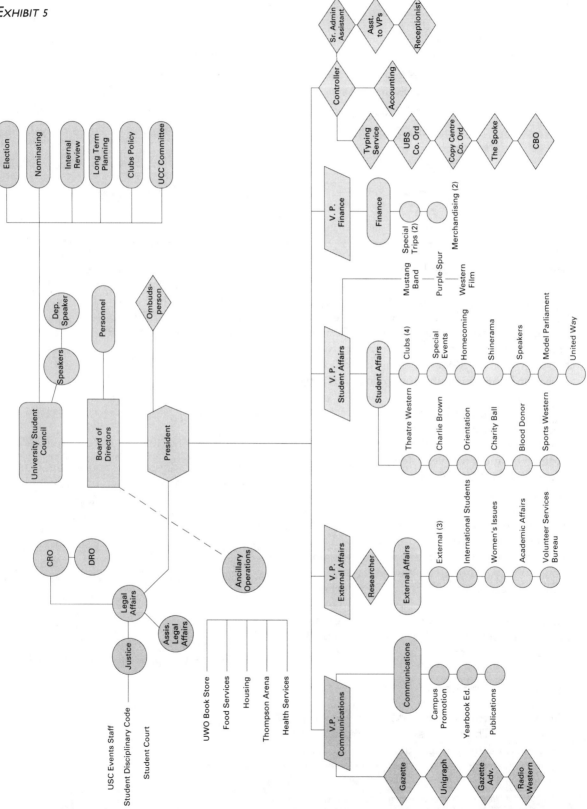

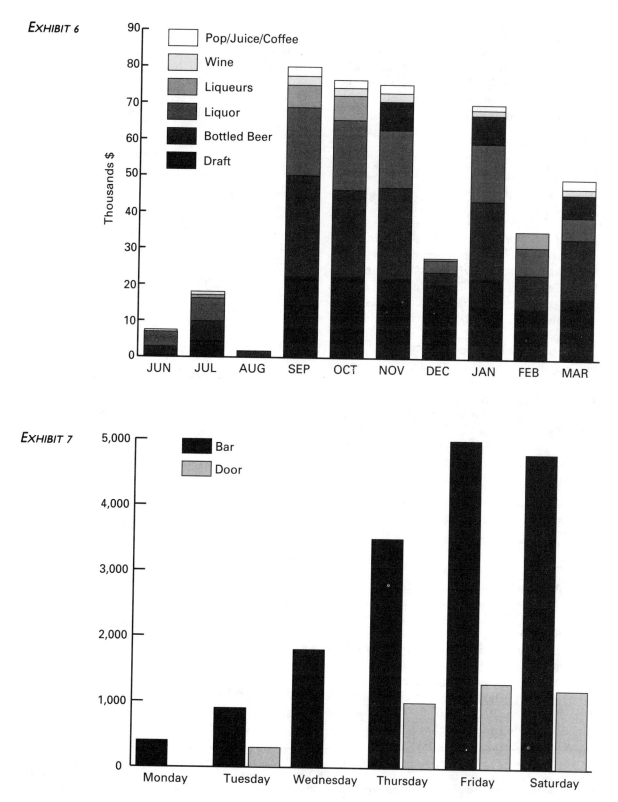

EXHIBIT 6

EXHIBIT 7

**Wednesday:** Wednesdays were much like Mondays. Students arrived late and left early, drinking very little. Gross revenues were somewhat higher than Mondays. Occasionally a fraternity or other special event held in the Spoke would increase revenues. These events were infrequent.

Gross Revenues:      $60–$500
Attendance:          maximum 30
Drinks per Person:   2–3
Door Charge:         nil

**Thursday:** Thursdays had always been "pub night" at Western. Correspondingly the Spoke had always done a brisk business on Thursdays. In the first term of the 89/90 year crowds had consistently been at capacity, but in the second term attendance had shown a clear reduction. The Spoke, known as a live entertainment venue, had a band performing 90% of the time on Thursdays. The Spoke had its own house band, *Glider*, which performed Top 40 covers which kept the dance floor crowded. *Glider* was supplemented regularly with touring acts selected by Standbridge. Culley, the manager, had a sense that the crowd was made up, primarily, of first and second year students from the nearby residences.

Gross Revenues:      $3,000–$5,000
Attendance:          300–500
Drinks per Person:   4
Door Charge:         $3

**Friday—Lunch:** The Spoke used to be packed on Friday afternoons. On average, the bar did between $1,000–$1,500 business. Sales were predominately draft beer, served in pitchers. A wide cross-section of students would come to start the weekend off early. However, pitchers of draft were banned by a campus regulatory body, who felt that pitchers contributed to alcohol excesses. As a result, the Spoke stopped serving pitchers and business began to decline. The

Spoke remained open on Friday afternoons but attendance declined dramatically as did the average number of drinks per person. Culley suggested the typical student dropped into the Spoke for a quick beer and perhaps a game of pool and then went home or to another bar.

Gross Revenues:      $300–$400
Attendance:          maximum 50
Drinks per Person:   1–3
Door Charge:         nil

**Friday—Night:** Fridays had always been the Spoke's highest revenue night. Students arrived early and left late. The bar reached capacity by 9:30 p.m. and would remain lined up until after 11:00 p.m. The Spoke's staff, who knew many of the patrons, characterized the crowd as young— first and second year residents and off-campus students.[2] As with Thursday nights, a dance band played 90% of the time. The second term of 89/90 had shown a slight decline in average revenues, but overall Friday's profitability remained strong.

Gross Revenues:      $4,500–$7,000
Attendance:          Capacity (400)
Drinks per Person:   5
Door Charge:         $3

**Saturday:** Saturdays were much like Fridays. There was always live entertainment. Revenues were generally slightly lower than Fridays as the lineups tended to begin somewhat later in the evening. The staff, on average, saw fewer off-campus students than they would on a Friday.

Gross Revenues:      $4,000–$6,000
Attendance:          Capacity (400)
Drinks per Person:   5
Door Charge:         $3

## THE SPOKE CUSTOMER

Culley felt that the students frequenting the Spoke were generally first and second year stu-

---

[2] Western's student population was approximately 20,000, of which about 4,000 were in first year. About 40% of first year students arrived at university under the legal drinking age, but only 5% were underage by the end of first year. Off-campus students referred to those students who did not live on the campus in student residences. Most students lived off campus.

EXHIBIT 8
Cape Program
Survey: Selected
Questions

**Have you attended campus bars/special pubs?**

|  | 1984 | 1985 |
|---|---|---|
| **YES** | 83.8% | 82.4% |

**If Yes, which of the following?**

|  | 1984 | 1985 |
|---|---|---|
| ▪ Elbow room | 83.8% | 63.2% |
| ▪ Spoke Tavern | 72.7% | 62.2% |
| ▪ Pub Nights | 64.1% | 57.2% |

**Does differential pricing influence your decisions to buy light beer?**

|  | 1984 | 1985 |
|---|---|---|
| **YES** | 20.7% | 13.3% |

Source: Progress on Campus: Evaluation of the CAPE Program (1987)
Addiction Research Foundation

dents. Certainly first year students visited the Spoke (Exhibit 8). They came to the Spoke to dance, drink and meet with friends.

Culley also believed that, prior to the 89/90 year, price pulled in these students. Starting in 1988 prices moved continuously upward as a result of strict regulation by A.P.A.G. (Alcohol Policy Advisory Group), the campus alcohol watchdog. What was once an inexpensive drinking hole became simply a student drinking hole. The price sensitivity of these students varied throughout the year. Dunton speculated that as their bank accounts dwindled towards the end of the year students become somewhat more price conscious. There also seemed to be a trend, especially on-campus, towards decreased alcohol consumption (see Exhibit 9). However, a study performed by the Student Services department had indicated that almost 55% of first year students drank at least once per week (Exhibit 10).

The management team was of the general consensus that students tended to go where their friends were. Therefore, if the Spoke was not busy, students might be inclined to turn away. Consequently the team considered the Spoke's physical size (400 person capacity) both an asset and a liability. On a good night the Spoke could accommodate a large crowd of paying customers. However, on a mediocre night, the Spoke's size swallowed up the few customers that were

there, turning away other potential customers. Thus when the Spoke was busy, it was really busy and when it was quiet, it was dead.

Another significant change which may have affected the Spoke was the implementation of several changes to the education system in Ontario, the most important of which saw the elimination of grade thirteen. As a result, students were coming to the University at a much younger age.

## REGULATION

The increasing liability associated with drunken students combined with a social change which supported responsible drinking resulted in the formation of A.P.A.G. (Alcohol Policy Advisory Group), as the campus watchdog and regulatory body. The Spoke was heavily regulated and frequently monitored by both A.P.A.G., and the Liquor Licensing Board of Ontario (L.L.B.O.). The Spoke was often visited twice a week by the L.L.B.O. inspector. In addition, other groups on campus, including the student newspaper, *The Gazette*, monitored the operations of the bar closely. As a result of the close scrutiny that the Spoke received, the breweries stayed clear of the campus when considering promotions. For example, Culley, through his involvement in the London bar business, understood that the Spoke

*EXHIBIT 9*
*Incoming Student*
*Information Survey*

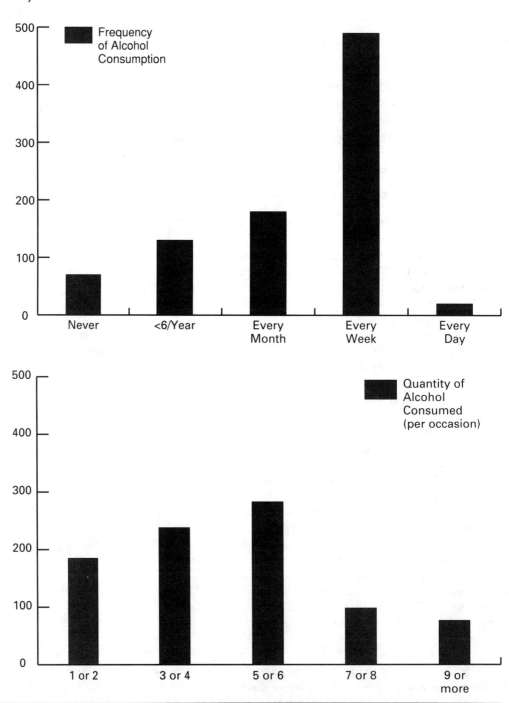

Exhibit 10
Excerpt from The
Gazette (Campus
Newspaper)
March 20, 1990

# Less student drinking dries up bar revenues

BY ELLIOTTE FRIEDMAN OF THE GAZETTE

Students are drinking less and Western's three bars are suffering.

The Graduate Centre was expected to make $9,000 this year, but assistant manager Nick Panter said the pub will only break even.

The Spoke was to have a total profit of $11,849, but by February it had cleared only $1,153.

The Elbow Room was projected to net $100,000 this year, a figure that was lower than previous year, according to Habeeb Al-Aidroos, University Community Centre director.

After what manager Mark Wellington called "a rough first term," the budget was adjusted to expect only $78,000. But a strong second term should allow the Elbow to meet original projections, he said.

"There is no question that consumption has declined, but it is nowhere near the extent it has been reported," he said, adding the overall drop in alcohol revenues can be attributed to a "lack of competitiveness among Western's bars."

Wellington said the success of off-campus bars shows there is not a huge decline in drinking. "Both of the on-campus bars are out of date. We simply cannot compete with Dr. Rockits, the Ceeps, or the Ridout."

Al-Aidroos agreed that the Elbow Room is at a disadvantage, but said students' thoughts on drinking have plenty to do with the situation.

"There are a host of factors for why the Elbow Room is having problems. The location is a main reason. It has a dreary ambience, and sits next to garbage. There is also the problem of poor food. But the pressure on students to do better and get jobs has increased as well."

"The Elbow Room will be moved to Platters old position in exactly one-and-a-half years, but it would not make sense to put capital costs into the Elbow Room in its present position since it will be there for only one more school year," Al-Aidroos said.

Alcohol awareness programs, such as Western's the "Can We Talk?" have also helped the slowdown in alcohol consumption. This program was created by Ardath Hill, nurse-educator of Student Health Services. The program goes to Western residences in the fall and reaches about 1,000 students.

"We are more concerned with showing students how their decision-making process is affected by consuming alcohol and teaching them that controlling stress by getting blasted is not the answer. But today's students seem to be much more conscientious about their studies," Hill said.

used to receive kickbacks in the form of a free keg for doing a certain volume of business. Although this practice was clearly illegal, Culley felt that it had become a integral part of doing business in London and was taken into consideration by owners in the operation of their bars. This practice was stopped at the Spoke prior to 1989. However, downtown bars continued the practice.

As a result of regulation (see Exhibit 11), the Spoke was forbidden to advertise off-campus. In addition, it was given a price list for all its products from which the Spoke could vary only marginally within a given range (often less than 10%). The Spoke's product line was also carefully monitored. For example, the selling of draft beer in pitchers was stopped as a result of campus regulators who became concerned about the image that such a product created. The regulation, which also applied to The Elbow Room on

*EXHIBIT 11*
*Sample of Alcohol*
*Policies Put*
*in Place*
*by A.P.A.G.*

|  | Adopted | Adopted in Principle |
|---|---|---|

**Alcohol Accessibility Policies**

| | Adopted | Adopted in Principle |
|---|---|---|
| **#1** Increases in the number of outlets, the capacity of outlets and the hours of operation should be limited. | x | |
| **#2** There should be limits on the number of special licensed events on campus. | x | |
| **#3** Drink sizes should be controlled by establishing "shots" of one ounce only and eliminating "doubles" and "pitchers". | x | |

**Responsible Serving Practices**

| | Adopted | Adopted in Principle |
|---|---|---|
| **#4** All servers of alcohol on campus should be trained in responsible serving practices, including the monitoring of patrons' age, consumption, and behaviour. | | x |
| **#5** In the provision of alcohol on campus, non-alcoholic alternatives should be promoted. | x | |
| **#6** Campus bars should discontinue selling alcohol before closing, while retaining the availability of non-alcoholic specials. | | x |
| **#7** Campus alcohol outlets should not take multiple drink orders at the closing of the bar. | x | |

**Substitution Policies**

| | Adopted | Adopted in Principle |
|---|---|---|
| **#8** When alcohol is sold on campus, light alcoholic beverages should be readily available. | x | |
| **#9** In providing beer on campus, the only type of draft should be light beer. | x | |
| **#10** Provisions should be made for non-alcoholic beverages and high-protein, non-salty foods. | x | |
| **#11** Throughout each academic year, the post-secondary institutions should ensure that there are a greater number of interesting, non-alcohol activities, particularly during orientation. | | x |
| **#12** When alcohol is sold on campus, the base price should be at parity with off-campus prices. | | x |
| **#13** The sale of alcohol on campus should entail differential pricing according to alcohol content. | | x |
| **#14** In providing non-alcoholic beverages, the price should be lower than that for the least expensive alcoholic beverage. | x | |

| | | |
|---|---|---|
| #15 When alcohol is being sold on campus, comprehensive price lists should be available to ensure that patrons understand price differential between alcoholic and non-alcoholic beverages. | x | ___ |
| **Management Policies** | | |
| #16 In allowing the sale of alcohol, efforts should be made to reduce the extent to which campus organizations rely on alcohol sales as a source of revenue. | ___ | x |
| #17 In allowing the sale of alcohol, the post-secondary institutions should ensure that alcohol promotions and advertisings comply with the law and campus standards. | x | ___ |
| #18 Since alcohol is available on campus, the post-secondary institution should ensure that there is adequate enforcement of provincial laws and campus policies. | ___ | x |
| #19 To assist with responsible management of alcohol on campus, the security staff should receive adequate training. | ___ | x |

campus, severely hampered the ability of the Spoke to respond to competitors in offering innovative products such as shooters.

## ADVERTISING AND PROMOTION

The Spoke communicated to its target audience through poster distribution on-campus including the residences and in several student publications such as *The Gazette*. This advertising copy was closely regulated by campus regulatory bodies such as A.P.A.G. The Spoke also allowed the manager to offer free "promo" drinks to certain customers at his discretion to increase customer loyalty. This form of promotion was not frequently used. Rich had considered other advertising and/or promotion to raise awareness of the campus bar, such as selling merchandise with the Spoke logo at low cost, but had yet to come to any conclusions as to the benefit of these programs. The Spoke budgeted $12,000–13,000 for advertising.

## PERSONNEL

Other than the manager, the Spoke was staffed entirely with part-time students (see Exhibit 12). The staff often stayed on for several years and

was a tight social group unto itself. There was an extremely low personnel turnover during the year although up to 40% left at the end of each year as students graduated.

The relationship between staff and customers had been good but could be improved. In particular, during slow periods the staff was frequently observed talking among themselves rather than serving the few customers that were in the bar. Also, over the years an anti-USC attitude had developed within the staff. This attitude resulted from a series of events over a number of years in which members of the USC used their power to obtain free services or goods from the Spoke for their own personal use. Both Ted and Rich recognized that this area of staff relations needed work.

## COMPETITION

The Spoke competed with a number of bars off-campus as well as the Elbow Room, the only other on-campus bar. The Elbow was run by the University Community Centre Directorate (UCCD). The UCCD operated independently from the USC and, as a result, the Elbow and Spoke competed directly against each other for the student dollar.

*EXHIBIT 12*
*Staff*

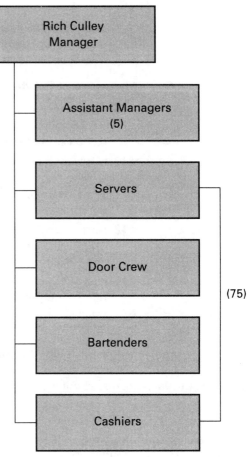

**Typical staffing:**
Mon./Tue./Wed.: 1 supervisor; 5-7 staff
Thu./Fri./Sat.:    2 supervisors; 20 staff

**Average hourly wage rates:**
| | |
|---|---|
| assistant manager | 8.00 |
| bartenders | 4.50 (+tips) |
| servers | 4.50 (+tips) |
| door crew | 6.25 |
| porters | 5.50 |
| service bartenders | 6.50 |

The Elbow Room presented the Spoke's most difficult competition. The Elbow served drinks in a lounge atmosphere. It was a significantly smaller bar with only a small dance floor. In addition to drinks, it offered a limited food menu which attracted a sizeable lunch time crowd. The Elbow also had a small stage and provided live entertainment. Generally this entertainment was on a somewhat smaller scale from that being showcased at the Spoke. For example, Rick McGhee, an acoustic guitar player, often performed at the Elbow. However, the Elbow did offer a comedy night on Tuesdays.

The Elbow was planning a major expansion which would see the bar more than double in size. Plans included a restaurant, pub, games room and dance floor. Over a million dollars had been budgeted for this expansion, which was expected to be ready for September 1991.

The Spoke's competition with bars off-campus was entirely one-way since the Spoke was unable to advertise off-campus. Therefore, the off-campus bars were able to take student business away from the Spoke, while the Spoke remained unable to attract non-students.

There were a number of off-campus bars which competed for the student dollar. The Ceeps was, for many years, a run down building that served extremely inexpensive draft and became somewhat of an institution over many years of operation. In the summer of 1989, The Ceeps completely renovated its facility. The

Ceeps remained a drinking-only venue. On a typical Thursday night the line-up began well before 8:00 p.m. and lasted all night long.

Joe Kools was another popular student bar in London. It provided both a dining area and two stand up bars. Joe Kools advertising boasted the worst service in London. Ad campaigns featured the copy "Joe Kools, where you're always welcome, unless you're a jerk". Kools was crowded throughout the week, though more so on the weekends.

The Bavarian was also quite close to campus. Located in a mall 15 minutes from the University, The Bavarian was both a restaurant and bar. A buffet was served from 4:00 p.m. until about 8:00 p.m., when a disc jockey would start the music. A movable wall separated one part of the bar and was opened later in the evening as lineups began to develop. The Bavarian had three dance floors, two bars and several dozen large tables.

During the 89/90 academic year the Spoke faced an increasingly competitive market. Dr. Rockits and Call the Office provided entertainment and dancing for young people. The Ridout Tavern, which had been previously known as a biker bar, was renovated during the summer of 1989. In addition, the owner provided free drinks

---

EXHIBIT 13
A Letter to the
Editor Published in
The Gazette
March 30, 1990

# Beer too expensive

**To the Editor:**

The article "Less student drinking dries up bar revenues," printed in *The Gazette* on March 20, discusses the fact that campus bars are falling well short of their profit objectives for this year. To explain this, its author claims that "students are drinking less," while in the same article quoting Elbow Room manager Mark Wellington as saying that campus bars cannot compete with off-campus establishments.

Whether students are drinking less (or not) is virtually impossible to say, but it is quite obvious that they are drinking less at campus bars. I think that this problem can be directly attributed to the fact that Western's bars are not competitive; not because of location, not because of food (although it definitely could be better); but simply because of price.

Traditionally, campus bars at Canadian universities have attracted business because of cheap alcohol. I believe that this year's increases in prices of draught beer here at Western bars is almost entirely responsible for the slide in profits. Although these increases were designed with admirable intentions, i.e.,

responsible drinking, sobriety, etc., they have already been proven unsuccessful.

If Western's bars continue to lose business to off-campus competition, thus decreasing university revenue by tens of thousands of dollars, students can expect to compensate in tuition increases.

Western should learn by experience and example. At Alfie's, the popular campus bar at Queen's, students pay only $7.10 for a pitcher of draught (and that's after raising the price only 20 cents this year). The result: Alfie's is packed with students from Wednesday to Saturday nights. The Elbow, or Spoke, cannot expect to see such overwhelming response if prices of $2.75 for a regular draught and $3.60 for a large, served only on Fridays, are maintained.

I am not endorsing lower prices to promote drunkenness. I am suggesting only that Western's policy makers should realize what the realities of the bar market are, and adjust prices accordingly. That way the students can't lose.

Erik Schatzker
English/History II

and steak dinners for leaders in the Fraternity and Sorority community. As a result of these aggressive marketing tactics, The Ridout's popularity grew dramatically. This may have impacted the Spoke, particularly on Thursday nights.

The Spoke had experienced tremendous difficulty in competing in its regulated environment. In particular, it was unable to lower its prices substantially to meet the draft prices of its competition. Indeed its prices were also above those on other campuses in Ontario (Exhibit 13).

## KITCHEN PROPOSAL

The Spoke management team was considering installing a small kitchen to be in a position to offer food to its patrons as early as September 1990. The cost of installing the kitchen was estimated at approximately $40,000. Dunton, thought that as much as $75,000 could be made available for improvements to the Spoke if justifiable.

## THE DECISION

As Ted considered what action he should support, he realised that the only way to turn the Spoke around was to keep the bar filled thus spreading the high cost of rent over more profitable transactions. To this end, he thought that the addition of food to the tavern would generate significant business during the day and would bring people in early at night. But more importantly, he thought that the Spoke needed a changed image. He wanted to create a bar where people went to be seen—where the in-crowd went.

# C A S E 4.5   Ashbrooks (A)

In August 1986, Mr. John Ross, then V.P. Operations for F.W. Woolworth Co. (FWW), had been given the task of launching a new specialty store concept called Ashbrooks in Canada. He had six months to develop a complete marketing plan and launch the first three stores. In August 1987, after the first six months of operation, sales and profitability levels were 30 to 35% below initial projections. As General Manager for Ashbrooks, Mr. Ross sat back to review the process and to decide what to do next. Ashbrooks was considered to be in a test for its first 12 months, after which senior FWW management would decide whether to continue it in the Specialty Group or discontinue it.

## COMPANY BACKGROUND

F.W. Woolworth Co. was a large American retailing organization with sales of $6.5 billion in 1986. Headquartered in New York, FWW had several key divisions including: U.S. Woolworth, Woolworth Canada, Woolworth Overseas Corp., Woolworth Germany, Richman Brothers, and Little Folk Shop. Divisional information regarding sales and income are shown in Exhibit 1. Exhibit 2 provides Woolworth Canada results.

Originally a variety store operation known as a "five and dime", in the early part of the 1980's FWW underwent a dramatic transformation from a traditional general merchandise retailer to one of the world's largest specialty store operators. With 30 specialty retail formats in 1986, including 17 launched within the past four years, FWW reputedly operated more specialty units than any other retailer in the world. All but five of the 656 new stores opened in 1986 were specialty stores. FWW management seemed determined to play a dominant role in specialty retailing throughout the world.

The decision to rapidly expand existing specialty store formats and acquire new ones was motivated by management's recognition that specialty stores had been producing higher sales per square foot, faster rates of sales gains, higher operating profit margins, and higher returns on investment than general merchandise operations. In addition, FWW management had at its disposal significant funds from the profits of its large, but more mature, general merchandise and family footwear business (Kinney).

Management forecast that a major share of FWW's future sales and profit growth—and virtually all of FWW's unit expansion—would come from specialty stores. By 1991 specialty stores were expected to account for 46% of total sales, versus 35% in 1986 and 28% in 1982. Specialty operating income was anticipated to represent 65% of total operating income by 1991 versus 52% in 1986 and 39% in 1982. Exhibit 3 presents financial statements for F.W. Woolworth Co. for 1984–1986.

## THE ASHBROOKS IDEA

In early 1986, Woolworth's Canadian corporate research team was handed the task of finding high potential markets for future retail growth. They knew that any new concept should have a potential for large volume and strong margins; that is, they were looking for new merchandising concepts that would be profitable for FWW and that would be widely accepted by the Canadian consumer.

The first market that was examined was the women's fashion apparel market. However, that market was deemed to be over-saturated and very competitive. An examination of trends in the U.S. market revealed the emerging kitchen, bathroom, and bedroom accessory market as an area of high retail growth and excitement.

FWW management felt that a U.S. firm, R.G. Branden's, had the best new strategy for targeting this home accessories market. It was a "colour driven" concept that focussed on a wide spectrum of 20 to 30 colours and their various shades. It allowed the consumer to co-ordinate

*EXHIBIT 1*

### F.W. Woolworth Co.
### Divisional Results
### (US $Million)

| | 1986 | | 1982 | |
|---|---|---|---|---|
| | Sales | Net Income | Sales | Net Income |
| **General Merchandise** | | | | |
| Woolworth U.S. | 1,954 | 96 | 1,707 | 66 |
| Woolworth Canada | 1,436 | 70 | 1,350 | 52 |
| Woolworth Germany | 907 | 52 | 717 | 40 |
| **Specialty** | | | | |
| Kinney: U.S. | 1,500 | 195 | 910 | 88 |
| Kinney: Canada & Australia | 317 | 35 | 222 | 12 |
| Richman | 261 | 17 | 198 | 4 |
| Other | 197 | (9) | 85 | (5) |

Source: 1986 Annual Report

*EXHIBIT 2*

### F.W. Woolworth Co.
### Canadian Results
### (Canadian $Million)

| | 1986 | 1985 | 1984 | 1983 | 1982 | # Stores at Jan. 31, 1987 |
|---|---|---|---|---|---|---|
| **Total Woolworth Canada** | | | | | | |
| (in Canadian dollars) | 1986 | 1985 | 1984 | 1983 | 1982 | |
| Sales (millions) | $ 2,036 | $ 1,986 | $ 1,876 | $ 1,739 | $ 1,670* | |
| Income before unallocated items (millions) | $ 97 | $ 95 | $ 84 | $ 74 | $ 64* | |
| **Woolworth Stores** | | | | | | |
| Sales (millions) | $ 395 | $ 396 | $ 384 | $ 354 | $ 330 | |
| Selling area in sq. ft. at year end (thousands) | 3,323 | 3,415 | 3,452 | 3,473 | 3,435 | 173 |
| Sales per average sq. ft. | $ 117 | $ 115 | $ 111 | $ 102 | $ 96 | |
| **Woolco Stores** | | | | | | |
| Sales (millions) | $ 1,593 | $ 1,556 | $ 1,487 | $ 1,385 | $ 1,320 | |
| Selling area in sq. ft. at year end (thousands) | 11,322 | 11,366 | 11,360 | 11,388 | 113,23 | 119 |
| Sales per average sq. ft. | $ 140 | $ 137 | $ 131 | $ 122 | $ 117 | |

**Specialty Stores\* \***

| | | | | | | |
|---|---|---|---|---|---|---|
| Sales (millions) | $ 48 | $ 34 | $ 5 | – | – | |
| Selling area in sq. ft. at year end (thousands) | 568 | 543 | 43 | – | – | 155 |

\* Includes catalogue stores which were closed in 1982.
\* \* Includes Robinsons, Activeworld, Kids Mart, Afterthoughts

**Kinney Shoe Corporation\* \* \***

Canada (in Canadian dollars)

| | | | | | |
|---|---|---|---|---|---|
| Sales (millions) | $ 380 | $ 321 | $ 282 | $ 259 | $ 229 |
| Selling area in sq. ft. at year end (thousands) | 1,251 | 1,211 | 1,157 | 1,109 | 1,110 |
| Sales per average sq. ft. | $ 309 | $ 271 | $ 249 | $ 233 | $ 223 |

\* \* \* Includes Kinney, Footlocker, Lady Foot Locker, Fredelle, Lewis, Sportelle, Randy River, Raglans.

Source: 1988 Annual Report

all aspects of her bathroom (e.g. towels, shower curtain, vase, flowers and other accessories), kitchen and/or bedroom.

R.G. Branden's opened its pilot store in Kendall, Florida, in 1985 and announced it expected to have a total of nine stores in Dade, Broward, and Palm Beach counties by 1990. By early 1988 there would be six stores. Branden's specialized in selling brand name housewares, linens, and accessories at competitive prices. The store was approximately 50,000 square feet of selling space with an upscale warehouse atmosphere. The visual impact of the store was based on large colour-blocked displays: hundreds of towels in different hues covering entire walls, a plate display in 30 different colours, one lamp style in 15–20 colours, and so on.

"Generally, we fill a void in the marketplace," claimed Jack Chadsey, Branden's President and Chief Operating Officer. "We have positioned ourselves between the mass merchandisers and the department stores. We consider ourselves the Toy'R'Us or The Limited of the home furnishings business."

Branden's was owned by Dayton-Hudson Corporation, a major Minneapolis-based general merchandise retailer. Dayton-Hudson would not disclose financial information about Branden's and as of 1987 maintained that it was still "in test".

Branden's located as anchor stores in large strip centres near, but not adjacent to, major shopping centres. The prototype store was opened in the Kendall area, just south of Miami, largely because of the area's large number of new homes under construction and its relatively affluent customer base.

Branden's concept research indicated that customers were unhappy that department stores had repositioned themselves in apparel at the expense of home accessories at a time when customers were spending more money on the home. Branden's was targeted at the well-educated, married woman age 25 to 45 whose family income was $35,000 or above who used to shop for home accessories at department stores.

"Our concept is proving successful," asserted Mr. Chadsey in 1986. "We're very pleased with our Kendall store, and sales at the Plantation store have exceeded our first year goals. We consider ourselves lifestyle oriented. We offer everything for the home except furniture and major appliances. In addition to housewares and linens, we have products like cookware, cutlery, lamps, and file cabinets."

Mr. Ross was enthusiastic but cautious about the Branden's concept. One of the reasons for his caution was that he had been taught and exposed to using only a 2 to 3 colour spectrum of merchandise, as opposed to the multitude of

EXHIBIT 3

| Consolidated Income Statement<br>For the fiscal years ended January 31, 1987, 1986, and 1985<br>(in millions except per share amounts) | F.W. Woolworth Co.<br>1985 Annual Report<br>1986 | 1985 | 1984 |
|---|---|---|---|
| **Revenues** | | | |
| Sales, including sales from leased departments of $257, $253, and $252 | **$6,501** | $5,958 | $7,737 |
| Other income | **30** | 32 | 26 |
| | **6,531** | 5,990 | 5,763 |
| **Costs and Expenses** | | | |
| Costs of sales | **4,287** | 3,952 | 3,853 |
| Selling, general and administrative expenses | **1,689** | 1,545 | 1,472 |
| Depreciation and amortization | **125** | 111 | 105 |
| Interest expense | **56** | 68 | 82 |
| | **6,157** | 5,676 | 5,512 |
| **Income before Income Tax** | **374** | 314 | 251 |
| Income taxes | **160** | 137 | 110 |
| **Net Income** | **$ 214** | $ 177 | $ 141 |
| **Net Income Per Common Share** | **$ 3.25** | $ 2.75 | $ 2.22 |

| Consolidated Balance Sheet<br>January 31, 1987, 1986, and 1985 (in millions) | 1986 | 1985 | 1984 |
|---|---|---|---|
| ASSETS | | | |
| **Current Assets** | | | |
| Cash, and short-term investments of $193, $115, and $95 | **$ 239** | $ 143 | $ 119 |
| Merchandise inventories | **1,327** | 1,264 | 1,108 |
| Other current assets | **118** | 114 | 108 |
| | **1,684** | 1,521 | 1,335 |
| **Owned Properties,** less depreciation and amortization | **978** | 838 | 767 |
| **Leased Properties under Capital Leases,** less amortization | **91** | 90 | 100 |
| **Deferred Charges and Other Assets** | **97** | 86 | 109 |
| | **$2,850** | $2,535 | $2,311 |
| LIABILITIES AND SHAREHOLDERS' EQUITY | | | |
| **Current Liabilities** | | | |
| Accounts payable | **$ 455** | $ 454 | $ 375 |
| Accrued liabilities | **293** | 262 | 235 |
| Income taxes | **77** | 59 | 24 |
| Current portion of reserve for discontinued operations | **20** | 26 | 33 |
| Dividends payable | **18** | 16 | 15 |
| Current portion of long-term debt and obligations under capital leases | **18** | 14 | 50 |
| | **881** | 831 | 732 |

| | | | |
|---|---:|---:|---:|
| **Long-Term Debt** | **248** | 245 | 250 |
| **Long-Term Obligations under Capital Leases** | **110** | 111 | 122 |
| **Other Liabilities** | **90** | 74 | 69 |
| **Deferred Taxes** | **37** | 30 | 30 |
| **Reserve for Discontinued Operations** | **-** | 21 | 57 |
| **Shareholders' Equity** | **1,484** | 1,223 | 1,051 |
| | **$2,850** | $2,535 | $2,311 |

colours that Branden's carried. He felt a carefully researched and planned marketing program would be needed to introduce such a new and untried strategy to the Canadian consumer.

The research team had given Mr. Ross a picture of the customer they might target in Canada. She would be female (very few male customers were expected), between the age of 25 and 55; and decorating her second home. She would belong to a $20,000 to $80,000 income family. She might be a "pink collar worker", a housewife or a young professional. She would use credit over half the time, as her purchases would be substantial when co-ordinating entire rooms. The average purchase would be three times larger than what an average general merchandise buyer would spend on home accessories in other general merchandise stores. It was estimated that 70% of these consumers would not know how to decorate or colour co-ordinate well. Store image would be important to them.

## THE NAME

Mr. Ross reasoned that the name of the store would be an important factor in its success, especially in its early stages. He felt that any association with the Woolworth's/Woolco image would not appeal to his targeted consumers. As he pondered possibilities for a name for the new store, Mr. Ross tried several approaches. For example, he went through English novels to find names that might be appealing to his intended customers.

In time, twelve names were selected for careful consideration: Ashbrooks, Jordan Malone, Creighton Harris, Caulfield's, Stephanie Powers, Hunter Dalton, Home Gallery, Russell Holmes, Creighton Powers, Ashley Holmes, Russell Powers, Creative Colors, and L.B. Ashbrooks.

A marketing expert was retained to conduct two focus groups, varying in respondent income level. The respondents were presented with the store concept, layout and the twelve names. All of them picked the same name: Ashbrooks. They said that it gave them a feel of "traditional family history", and that "the Ashbrooks family would stand behind their merchandise". It was not regarded as a "stuffy" or "snobbish" name, and the respondents felt that they could wear casual dress to the store. The name also did not have a sterotyped image in terms of merchandise that would be carried (i.e. not furniture, men's wear, or paint). Apparently, everyone felt comfortable with the name and thought that it was not unusual but easy to remember.

Mr. Ross and FWW management chose Ashbrooks as the store name and envisioned 100 stores across Canada. He knew what he wanted to do: "I want to do this store right which means we'll have to be the best in everything we do especially merchandising, customer service, and presentation. There won't be second chances." He decided to bring in outside specialists in every functional area rather than depend on the traditional Woolworth's/Woolco resource base and way of thinking.

## PLANNING THE ASSORTMENT

One of Mr. Ross's first moves was to bring in John Guerin as Manager, Merchandising and Sales. As a FWW Sales Manager for the fashion apparel market, Mr. Guerin was already experienced in a colour dominated market. The next step was to gather a set of expert buyers already in the home accessories marketplace. Mr. Ross and Mr. Guerin went to the trade shows, found, and hired individuals they considered to be "the best buyer of housewares in Canada, the best bedding buyer in Canada, and the best bathroom buyer in Canada". These individuals, experienced in large department stores and specialty stores, were creative, professional buyers who apparently knew their markets and were excited about the Ashbrooks concept.

These buyers were sent to R.G. Branden's for a week to examine, in depth, the merchandising mix, colour assortments, SKU's, price points, etc. The manager of R.G. Branden's was extremely co-operative with them as he did not view the Canadian company as any threat. He spent time explaining how the market worked, only asking that they not take any pictures of the operation. The buyers returned to Canada very excited about all the possibilities that this new avenue seemed to offer.

Despite his buyers' experiences with colour, Mr. Ross was uneasy. He asked himself "What do I really know about colours?" and concluded "Not enough." He then asked his buyers "If I told you to pick 12 colours of dinnerware, which colours would you pick?" and "How would these few colours be co-ordinated across rooms?" He felt the answers he got were not sufficient, knowing how critical colour would be to Ashbrooks' success.

Mr. Ross then hired a colour consultant, Lynn Darby, who was an expert in a field that he had never heard of prior to the last few months. Lynn Darby followed the colour fashions in North America and Europe. She taught the Ashbrooks merchandising group about colours: which to have, how many to have, and how to display them. She helped them put their assortments together, choose the colours that were in vogue and to tie it all together. They were taught how to bring a colour swatch through at least one line of merchandise. For example, the mauve of a vase should be available in artificial flowers and a toss cushion. The Ashbrooks team felt it was a tremendous education process.

Lynn Darby put together a Colour Manual

(Exhibit 4) that was used as part of the staff training program. It was also used by the buyers working with the manufacturers to develop Ashbrooks' "colour driven" concept. Ms. Darby worked with Ashbrooks for six months. Mr. Ross felt that no other retailer in Canada would be able to offer such an interior decorating service to its customers via a well-trained sales staff. Staff were expected to take customers through the store, across departmental lines, to find co-ordinated items. The staff were also trained how to "Dress for Success" by a certified image consultant.

The next step was to tell manufacturers the colours that Ashbrooks wanted. There were approximately 150 Canadian manufacturers who made the products they wanted to carry, and about 50 percent of them did not already deal with Woolworth's or Woolco, but rather the specialty boutique shops. However, these suppliers did not seem to have the necessary colour depth. For example, a supplier might carry the primary colours and one fashion colour in towels but not the 18 or so colours that Mr. Ross was looking for to satisfy the Ashbrooks' "colour driven" concept.

The Ashbrooks merchandise group debated the question: "Should we change the concept because our suppliers can only supply us with 2, 3, or 4 colours?" They decided to stick with the concept which meant that they would have to convince some suppliers to radically change their business.

Mr. Ross decided to bring the CEO's, owners, and sales managers of each major manufacturer into FWW headquarters in Toronto to sell each company individually. They gave each management group a full presentation of the Ashbrooks plan, including slides from R.G. Branden's. The manufacturers were reminded of Woolworth's financial strength and commitment, and asked to "come on stream and join this exciting time or Woolworth's will do it without you by going to U.S. suppliers". Mr. Ross remembered this time as an exhausting process, but necessary and extremely successful. Most, but not all, manufacturers agreed to supply Ashbrooks.

EXHIBIT 4
Excerpts from
Ashbrooks: The
Colour Book

To a scientist, colour is simply the brain's response to stimulus of light; while that is true on a strictly "visual" level, we know from our own experience that colour can also affect our moods and our sense of well-being.

We know, for example, that certain colours warm us, excite us, may even increase our respiration rate, heart beat, and blood pressure, while other colours make us feel calm, serene, sad, or depressed.

• • • • •

Yellow • Also increases heart beat, respiration, and blood pressure, but in a pleasantly stimulating way, as oppposed to red's intensity.
  • Expresses cheerfulness, happiness, intellectual stimulation, and optimism when light or medium shades are selected. Dark or muddy tones can be used to suggest fear, cowardice, and in some cases, greed.
  • Most frequently selected by "optimistic" people who are striving towards future goals, or who seek change in their lives.

• • • • •

In order to understand how colour "works", it is necessary to analyse and categorize it in three distinctive ways: hue, value, and intensity.

• • • • •

In bathrooms containing a tub, we use the shower curtain as a focal point, in powder rooms the area around the basin should be highlighted with colour.

• • • • •

Because the eye reads from left to right, colours are arranged in vertical sections across a wall or shelf unit. Ideally, one vertical section is assigned to each shade in the assortment.

• • • • •

What would you do?

A.  A customer has asked you to help co-ordinate her bedroom. She would like to use a new Ashbrooks sheeting pattern, that is a combination of pink, peach, grey, and white. Her carpet is pale blue. What would you recommend to help "dress" her bed? What colour lamps would you select? What other accessories would you suggest?

The suppliers seemed very excited about being a part of this new approach in Canadian retailing. Although regular supplier terms were negotiated, emphasis was placed in three areas. Suppliers would have to carry backup inventory, fast delivery turnaround would have to be met in order to keep their colour assortment in stock at all times and the original concept would not be changed to accomodate supplier merchandise that would not fit the Ashbrooks store layout.

The specific merchandising concept was to develop a top of the mind position for home textiles, housewares, table top and home accessories by having assortment dominance within these four categories of merchandise. The longer term aim was to become a destination store in this market. Assortment dominance was to be achieved by having all sizes and colours in depth within a limited range of stock-keeping units (SKU's). The SKU assortment would be narrow and deep.

The merchandise dominance concept would be enhanced through the utilization of floor to ceiling wall displays which would clearly indicate to the customer what business Ashbrooks was in. These displays would approximate Branden's "wall of plates," its "wall of throw pillows" and its "wall of toilet seats."

The merchandise team decided to merchandise medium quality, current season, recognizable national brands. They would not sell top department store merchandise lines or discounters' private label-type merchandise. They would only carry merchandise which would fit the self-selection concept and which would not require knowledgeable sales help. Ideally, Ashbrooks would have a merchandise mix of 80% well-known national brands and 20% private or house brands.

## LOCATION

Management decided locations for Ashbrooks should be sought that provided 25,000 to 30,000 sq. ft. selling space at low rent where possible in high traffic, visible locations in trading areas with 80,000 to 120,000 people. Management was targeting a broad-based customer group: the middle 70% of customers, not the lower 15% nor the upper 15% in terms of household incomes. Extensive research was conducted by the Ashbrooks marketing department on potential locations across Canada. Abandoned conventional sized supermarkets seemed to offer exactly what was being sought. Several sites were becoming available as grocery chains moved to larger sized formats and as new competition from grocery super stores and wholesale clubs were closing

down some conventional supermarkets. These locations were being taken over by specialty mass merchandisers, such as Toys'R'Us and super drug store operations such as Herbies. Eighteen empty Dominion store sites were examined in particular. Potential locations were analyzed for potential market size, trading area population, and potential growth expected for the next five years.

Three sites were selected: a large regional mall in Toronto, a small regional mall in Sarnia, Ontario, and a mega-mall in Edmonton. Square One in Toronto was thought to have an estimated trade area size of 120,000 people in a bedroom community and estimated trade area potential sales of $15,600,000. Approximately seventy 30,000 square foot stores competed in the Square One trade area. Mr. Ross estimated that a 30,000 square foot store in this area would achieve $4,328,000 in annual sales. The West Edmonton Mall was located in a trade area size of 80,000 people and was estimated to have trade area potential sales of $10,400,000. Mr. Ross estimated that a 30,000 square foot store in this area would gain $4,210,000 in sales. The Lambton Mall, in Sarnia, was chosen as a test market for the viability of smaller regional area locations.

## LAYOUT AND VISUAL MERCHANDISING

Each store was planned to have 25,000 to 30,000 sq. ft. of selling area and would be divided into four sections by main aisles which would run from front to back and side to side. A race track around the perimeter of the store was intended to ensure efficient customer traffic flow. The counters in the interior of the store were 5 feet high so that customers could see around the whole store from the perimeter aisle. The walls were used to display merchandise right up to the ceiling to emphasize dominant assortment impact.

The main aisle contained fashion or fad merchandise, while promotional merchandise was on the lateral aisles. Core programs were on the aisles. Basic merchandise was displayed on gondolas between the merchandise on the lat-

EXHIBIT 5

**(a)** Ashbrooks initial logo.

**(b)** Original store concept for Ashbrooks.

**(c)** Feb. 25, 1987, the first Ashbrooks store at Square One Shopping Centre in Mississauga, Ontario.

**(d)** April 1987, the third Ashbrooks is opened at the West Edmonton Mall in Edmonton, Alberta. (March 1987, second Ashbrooks in the Lambton Mall in Sarnia, Ontario).

**(e)** As you enter an Ashbrooks, a giant "lifestyle wall" emphasizes Canadian Lifestyle living, and the colour characteristics of the store.

**(f)** Ashbrooks customer guarantee policy is well displayed in the front entrance.

**(g)** Ashbrooks "towel wall" displays the largest colour selection of towels in Canada.

**(h)** Ashbrooks "wall of plates" shows in-depth sizes and colours within a limited range of styles.

**(i)** Ashbrooks new employees were trained to: (1) present themselves to customers (2) how to dress for success (3) product knowledge. The day before opening they were presented with their diplomas.

eral aisle and the wall. At the end of the main aisle was a seasonal swing department which was the only place in the store that a strict classification of merchandising was not used. The impression of overwhelming selection was intended through the use of high impact mass displays. Wherever possible, colour blocking was used to visually brighten the merchandising impact. Most floor displays were 5 ft. gondolas at eye level. Eye level signs indicated brand name, product description, product features and price. The back of the sign indicated corporate pricing, service, and guarantee policies. The merchandise was stocked in depth on the sales floor behind or adjacent to sample presentations which were available for the customer to handle. The fashion aisle was frequently changed to provide new exciting merchandise to attract the customers attention and reinforce the image of fashionability in the store. See Exhibit 5 for photographs of the Ashbrooks' image, merchandising, and layouts.

At the outset, Mr. Ross was determined to find Ashbrooks' own style rather than doing everything "the Woolco way". After the stores had been open and results were not as projected, the Square One store became "John's lab" because various layouts, display techniques, and other changes were frequently made over the next few months at that store in an attempt to find the winning formula.

## STAFFING

Mr. Ross did not want to use the Personnel Supervisor who hired the staff for Woolworth's and Woolco. He personally interviewed several new people to do the hiring for Ashbrooks. He chose Maureen Sheridan for this position even though she had no experience in the personnel field. She was in a management training program at Simpson's, but most importantly to Mr. Ross, she was a "nice" person and presented herself well. He reasoned that "a nice person would hire other nice people who would treat the customers nicely".

The new Ashbrooks stores were to be open organizations of 6 or 7 key people and Mr. Ross

"didn't really care if they knew what a towel was" at the moment of hiring. Over 200 to 300 people were interviewed for each store. All sales staff were paid a base salary plus a percentage on the dollar gross profit realized in their respective areas of the store. A major part of the sales associates' training was a program on colour co-ordination, not all aspects of interior decorating, that was headed by Lynn Darby. This training was intended to give Ashbrooks a unique service offering for Canadian consumers.

The original organization chart is shown as Exhibit 6.

## PRICING

Price was not expected to be a major factor for customers when choosing products. The merchandise group felt all merchandise was priced competitively with Ashbrooks' core competition: that is, they priced against traditional and promotional department stores. Generally price points for comparable merchandise was thought to be under the department stores and higher than the promotional department stores. High priced merchandise was not carried as staff feared this could create the impression of a high priced store. Towels, for instance, started at $16.99 and went as high as $39.00.

The value image was not to be conveyed by low prices, but through the convenience of the shopping trip, the fashionability of the merchandise, service and quality merchandise at reasonable prices.

## ADVERTISING AND PROMOTION

Mr. Ross and his team interviewed several advertising agencies to see how they would promote the opening and the initial stages of market entry for Ashbrooks. The basic idea was a strong "colour" statement to the consumer, but not in a "hard sell" format. Glowinsky and Gee, Vickers and Benson won the contract. They designed and recommended flyers to feature the complete colour range available in each individual item being advertised. All advertising employed the positioning statement: "We've got your colour". The copy highlighted one's ability to colour co-

EXHIBIT 6
Organization
Chart

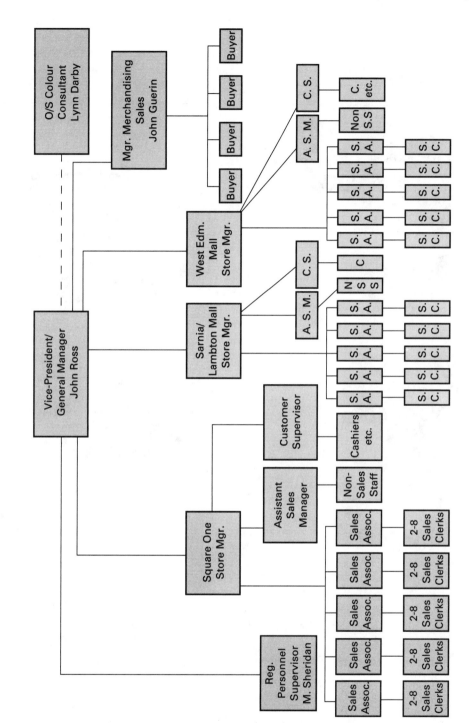

*Exhibit 7*
*Excerpt From*
*Newspaper Flyer,*
*February 25, 1987*

ordinate fashion accessories for the bedroom, bathroom and kitchen.

In February 1987, the promotional effort began. The first flyer was a "teaser" to arouse interest, followed by a colour flyer aimed at attracting the target market to come to the store. Exhibit 7 shows excerpts from the second flyer. Both pieces were controversial within the company. The intent was to sell the concept and the flyer won an advertising award. However, it was not very successful bringing people into the stores. Some managers felt that Ashbrooks stayed too long with the flyers. Soon, Ashbrooks advertising was moved to print ad inserts in the newspaper, then radio to support the print, then just radio. About $600,000 in advertising was budgeted for the three stores for launch in the first year, about 8% of sales expected. Management planned to budget advertising at about 4% of sales in the second year.

## FINANCIAL PROJECTIONS

Ashbrooks' financial projections were based on several key figures. Average estimated Ontario per capita expenditures on home textiles housewares, table top and home accessories were expected to be $130. The gross profit was targeted at 43% of sales and costs-to-sell were estimated at 26% of sales. Expected store sales were to average $4,000,000. The targeted return on investment was 16.2%.

## THE FIRST SIX MONTHS

On February 25, 1987, right on schedule six months after the basic concept was established, the first Ashbrooks store opened at Square One in Mississauga. In March 1987, Mr. Ross' team opened the Sarnia store and in April they opened the West Edmonton Mall store.

At the end of six months the results were tallied. Positive results included average sales per customer of over $50, favourable comments by customers, 56% of business on credit, 8000 "preferred customers" on a mailing list, and a bridal registry of over 200 names. However, Ashbrooks was between 30 and 35% below projections in both profits and sales. Gross margins were only 38%.

Mr. Ross and his team were under pressure to perform. Senior FWW executives began making suggestions for change which caused Ross and his management team to worry about losing their concept altogether. He knew that he had to review the results, analyze his own feelings and decide what to do. Senior management in Toronto was pressuring them to change the concept. And, apparently, R.G. Branden's was also struggling.

# CASE 4.6   Ashbrooks (B)

Mr. John Ross, General Manager for Ashbrooks, was deeply concerned about the poor performance of the new chain (see Ashbrooks (A) for background). While he continued to experiment with changes, he also commissioned some consumer research. 200 respondents were interviewed in mall intercepts at Square One in Toronto. Respondents were qualified as "females, aged 30 to 45, with total annual household incomes of at least $30,000, who shop at Square One at least once every two months".

The objectives for the study were as follows:

1. To measure the level of awareness of Ashbrooks, specifically as a provider of home accessories and fashion items for the bedroom, bathroom, and kitchen.

2. To determine the shopping behaviour in the store of those aware of Ashbrooks.

3. To rate the relative importance of selected home accessory store attributes to store choice and Ashbrooks' performance on these attributes.

4. To solicit the specific likes and dislikes of Ashbrooks among shoppers.

The results provided to Mr. Ross are shown as Tables 1–11. He wondered what these results meant for Ashbrooks and what to do next.

<table>
<tr><td colspan="5" align="center">Table 1<br>**Ashbrooks Awareness Study**<br>**Awareness of Ashbrooks**</td></tr>
<tr><td></td><td colspan="4" align="center">TOTAL %</td></tr>
<tr><td></td><td colspan="4">Unaided    42</td></tr>
<tr><td></td><td colspan="4">Aided    48</td></tr>
<tr><td></td><td colspan="4">Total    90</td></tr>
<tr><td></td><td colspan="4">Not Aware    10</td></tr>
<tr><td></td><td align="center">Home<br>Accessories<br>%</td><td align="center">Bathroom<br>Accessories<br>%</td><td align="center">Bedroom<br>Accessories<br>%</td><td align="center">Kitchenware &<br>Housewares<br>%</td></tr>
<tr><td>Comes to Mind</td><td align="center">25</td><td align="center">32</td><td align="center">20</td><td align="center">18</td></tr>
<tr><td>Shopped in Last<br>3 Months</td><td align="center">9</td><td align="center">12</td><td align="center">4</td><td align="center">8</td></tr>
<tr><td>Shop Most Often<br>(If Shop in Last 3 Months)</td><td align="center">3</td><td align="center">10</td><td align="center">5</td><td align="center">5</td></tr>
</table>

| | Home Accessories % | Bathroom Accessories % | Bedroom Accessories % | Kitchenware & Housewares % |
|---|---|---|---|---|
| **Table 2** **Ashbrooks Awareness Study** **Awareness/Use** | | | | |
| **COMES TO MIND** | | | | |
| The Bay | 77 | 50 | 62 | 65 |
| Sears | 72 | 60 | 72 | 55 |
| Woolco | 45 | 32 | 24 | 31 |
| Eaton's | 39 | 28 | 38 | 33 |
| Simpsons | 31 | 29 | 32 | 34 |
| Ashbrooks | 25 | 32 | 20 | 18 |
| Top Specialty Store | 10 | 6 | 3 | 9 |
| **SHOP IN LAST 3 MONTHS** | | | | |
| Sears | 33 | 23 | 23 | 14 |
| The Bay | 28 | 13 | 14 | 17 |
| Woolco | 21 | 9 | 5 | 13 |
| Eaton's | 12 | 5 | 9 | 6 |
| Ashbrooks | 9 | 12 | 4 | 8 |
| Top Specialty Store | 4 | 2 | 3 | 5 |
| None | 26 | 38 | 45 | 29 |
| **SHOP MOST OFTEN (IF SHOP LAST 3 MONTHS)** | | | | |
| Sears | 30 | 30 | 38 | 20 |
| The Bay | 23 | 14 | 21 | 24 |
| Eaton's | 15 | 10 | 15 | 6 |
| Woolco | 11 | 11 | 4 | 13 |
| Simpsons | 3 | 6 | 4 | 9 |
| Ashbrooks | 3 | 10 | 5 | 5 |
| Top Specialty Store | 2 | 2 | 4 | 3 |

### Table 3
### Ashbrooks Awareness Study
### Advertising

|  | TOTAL AWARE % |
|---|---|
| **SOURCE OF AWARENESS** | |
| Saw Store in Mall | 58 |
| Radio Ads | 16 |
| Word of Mouth | 11 |
| Newspaper Ads | 8 |
| Flyers | 8 |
| Other | 4 |

|  | SHOPPERS % |
|---|---|
| Shopped at Ashbrooks because of ad | 19 |

|  | SHOPPED BECAUSE OF AD* % |
|---|---|
| **TYPE OF AD WHICH BROUGHT PEOPLE IN** | |
| Radio Ads | 50 |
| Newspaper Ads | 42 |
| Flyers | 29 |

* Interpret with caution due to small sample size.

### Table 4
### Ashbrooks Awareness Study
### Adoption

|  | TOTAL % |
|---|---|
| Shopped | 63 |
| Aware/Not Shopped | 22 |
| Shopped/Not Purchased | 30 |
| Purchased | 34 |
| Purchased Only Once | 15 |
| Repeat Purchase | 19 |
| Committed Shoppers | 10 |

## Table 5
## Ashbrooks Awareness Study
## Awareness/Shopping/Purchase
## Conversion Matrix

| | | | | | |
|---|---|---|---|---|---|
| Total Sample | (200) | | | | |
| | % | | | | |
| Total Awareness | 90 | 100% | | | |
| Total Shopped | 63 | 70 | 100% | | |
| Total Purchased | 34 | 38 | 54 | 100% | |
| Total Repeat Purchases | 19 | 21 | 30 | 56 | 100% |
| Total Committed | 10 | 11 | 16 | 30 | 54 |

## Table 6
## Ashbrooks Awareness Study
## Shopping Behavior

| | TOTAL AWARE % | UNAIDED AWARE % | SHOPPED % | SHOPPED/ NOT PURCHASED % | PURCHASED % | PURCHASE/ NOT REPEAT* % | REPEAT PURCHASER* % | COMMITTED* % |
|---|---|---|---|---|---|---|---|---|
| **TIMES SHOPPED PAST 6 MONTHS** | | | | | | | | |
| Once | 22 | 17 | 29 | 49 | 12 | 23 | 3 | 0 |
| 2–5 Times | 41 | 50 | 56 | 49 | 59 | 70 | 53 | 37 |
| 6+ Times | 14 | 21 | 18 | 2 | 25 | 7 | 48 | 62 |
| Never | 25 | 10 | – | – | – | – | – | – |
| Average # of Times Shopped (if shopped) | 3.9 | 5.3 | 3.9 | 1.9 | 5.7 | 2.5 | 8.4 | 7.6 |
| **TIMES PURCHASED PAST 6 MONTHS** | | | | | | | | |
| Once | | 30 | 43 | | 45 | 100 | 0 | 5 |
| 2–3 Times | | 52 | 42 | | 43 | | 78 | 63 |
| 4+ Times | | 16 | 12 | | 12 | | 21 | 32 |
| Never | | 2 | 4 | | – | | – | – |
| Average # of Times Purchased (if purchased) | | 2.5 | 2.1 | | 2.1 | 1.0 | 3.1 | 3.5 |

* Interpret with caution due to low sample sizes

## Table 7
## Ashbrooks Awareness Study
## Shopping Behavior

|  | SHOPPERS % | REPEAT PURCHASES % | COMMITTED % |
|---|---|---|---|
| **LAST TIME SHOPPED** | | | |
| Last Week | 13 | 16 | 26 |
| Last 2 Weeks | 7 | 14 | 11 |
| Last Month | 40 | 46 | 37 |
| Last 2–3 Months | 25 | 19 | 21 |
| More Than 3 Months Ago | 14 | 5 | 5 |
| **PURPOSE FOR BUYING AT ASHBROOKS** | | | |
| Gift | 45 | 49 | 42 |
| Single Items for Home | 36 | 30 | 32 |
| Several Items for Redecorating Room | 27 | 41 | 58 |
| Bought on Impulse | 6 | 5 | 0 |

## Table 8
## Ashbrooks Awareness Study
## Attribute Ratings

|  | IMPORTANCE FOR STORE CHOICE[1] # | MOST IMPORTANT ATTRIBUTES[2] % | PERFORMANCE OF ASHBROOKS[3] # |
|---|---|---|---|
| Good Value for Money | 2.7 | 69 | 3.0 |
| High Quality Products | 2.6 | 48 | 3.9 |
| Good Service | 2.5 | 20 | 3.3 |
| Low Prices | 2.3 | 17 | 2.2 |
| Wide Range of Colours | 2.3 | 7 | 4.3 |
| Variety of Sizes | 2.3 | 6 | 3.8 |
| Convenient Location | 2.2 | 17 | 3.7 |
| Wide Range of Brands | 2.2 | 7 | 3.6 |
| Attractive Presentation | 2.1 | 5 | 4.4 |
| Well-known Brands | 1.9 | 7 | 3.5 |

1. Rated on a 3-point scale (1 = Not Important, 3 = Essential).
2. Two choices allowed.
3. Rated on 5-point scale (1 = Poor, 5 = Excellent).

## Table 9
### Ashbrooks Awareness Study
### Likes

|  | SHOPPED % | SHOPPED/ NOT PURCHASED % | PURCHASED % | PURCHASE/ NOT REPEAT* % | REPEAT PURCHASER* % | COMMITTED* % |
|---|---|---|---|---|---|---|
| Good Selection/ Variety | 37 | 27 | 46 | 47 | 46 | 47 |
| Attractive Display | 26 | 24 | 28 | 30 | 27 | 26 |
| Wide Range of Colour | 25 | 20 | 30 | 33 | 27 | 32 |
| Spacious Store | 17 | 17 | 18 | 17 | 19 | 32 |
| Quality Products | 13 | 8 | 16 | 13 | 19 | 21 |
| Well Laid Out | 13 | 15 | 10 | 10 | 11 | 11 |
| Clean Store | 11 | 8 | 13 | 13 | 14 | 5 |
| Staff Friendly/ Helpful | 10 | 3 | 15 | 3 | 24 | 26 |
| Nothing Liked | 2 | 3 | 0 | 0 | 0 | 0 |

* Interpret with caution due to low sample sizes.

## Table 10
### Ashbrooks Awareness Study
### Dislikes

|  | SHOPPED % | SHOPPED/ NOT PURCHASED % | PURCHASED % | PURCHASE/ NOT REPEAT* % | REPEAT PURCHASER* % | COMMITTED* % |
|---|---|---|---|---|---|---|
| Too Expensive/ High Priced | 29 | 37 | 21 | 30 | 14 | 11 |
| Service Not Good/ Not Enough Clerks | 10 | 7 | 12 | 10 | 14 | 21 |
| Nothing Disliked | 48 | 39 | 55 | 47 | 62 | 58 |

* Interpret with caution due to low sample sizes.

## Table II
### Ashbrooks Awareness Study
### Demographics

| | TOTAL % | TOTAL AWARE % | NOT AWARE* % | AWARE/ NOT SHOPPED % | SHOPPED % | SHOPPED/ NOT PURCHASED % | PURCHASED % | PURCHASE/ NOT REPEAT* % | REPEAT PURCHASER* % | COMMITTED* % |
|---|---|---|---|---|---|---|---|---|---|---|
| **AGE** | | | | | | | | | | |
| 30-34 Yrs. | 44 | 46 | 29 | 26 | 52 | 47 | 55 | 60 | 51 | 47 |
| 35-39 Yrs. | 31 | 29 | 48 | 37 | 25 | 20 | 30 | 27 | 32 | 32 |
| 40-45 Yrs. | 25 | 25 | 24 | 37 | 33 | 32 | 15 | 13 | 16 | 21 |
| **INCOME** | | | | | | | | | | |
| $30K-$40K | 29 | 26 | 48 | 16 | 29 | 32 | 25 | 20 | 30 | 21 |
| $40K-$50K | 30 | 30 | 24 | 33 | 31 | 32 | 30 | 40 | 22 | 26 |
| $50K+ | 42 | 44 | 29 | 51 | 40 | 36 | 45 | 40 | 49 | 53 |
| **EMPLOYMENT** | | | | | | | | | | |
| Full-Time | 50 | 48 | 67 | 44 | 49 | 42 | 55 | 57 | 54 | 53 |
| Part-Time | 20 | 21 | 14 | 33 | 17 | 19 | 15 | 10 | 19 | 21 |
| Not at all | 30 | 31 | 19 | 23 | 34 | 39 | 30 | 33 | 27 | 26 |
| **TYPE OF DWELLING** | | | | | | | | | | |
| House | 73 | 73 | 71 | 84 | 72 | 69 | 75 | 77 | 73 | 74 |
| Apt./Condo. | 27 | 27 | 29 | 16 | 28 | 31 | 25 | 23 | 27 | 26 |
| **TENURE** | | | | | | | | | | |
| Own | 75 | 77 | 57 | 79 | 77 | 76 | 78 | 83 | 73 | 74 |
| Rent | 25 | 23 | 43 | 21 | 23 | 24 | 22 | 17 | 27 | 26 |
| **HOUSEHOLD SIZE** | | | | | | | | | | |
| 1-2 | 24 | 24 | 19 | 9 | 28 | 31 | 25 | 30 | 21 | 22 |
| 3+ | 76 | 76 | 81 | 91 | 72 | 69 | 75 | 70 | 79 | 78 |
| **INTEREST IN DECORATING** | | | | | | | | | | |
| Active Decorator | 44 | 44 | 43 | 33 | 48 | 49 | 46 | 50 | 43 | 47 |
| Only When Needed | 51 | 51 | 43 | 63 | 48 | 46 | 49 | 43 | 54 | 53 |
| Tedious Chore | 6 | 4 | 14 | 5 | 5 | 5 | 4 | 7 | 3 | 0 |

* Interpret with caution due to low sample sizes.

# C A S E 4.7    Ashbrooks (C)

In early 1989, John Ross, General Manager of Ashbrooks, was reviewing the latest results and consumer research for the home accessories chain. Results were still disappointing and time was running out. (See Ashbrooks (A) and (B) for background.) The stores still had not made a profit and senior F.W. Woolworth management were becoming disillusioned with the whole concept. While Mr. Ross knew it often took two or three years for a new retail format to become profitable, he was concerned and wondered what changes if any he might make and what to say to his superiors.

## THE NEW STRATEGY

In late 1987, Ashbrooks management tried a great number of initiatives to find the winning formula for Ashbrooks. Jeff Burley, the manager for Ashbrooks' Square One store, recalled the time as "a new concept a week as we changed layouts, product assortments, advertising, etc. Everyone seemed to have ideas for change.

The new strategy involved some major changes. Some excerpts from the plan follow.

1.  **Presentation**—Ashbrooks will move towards a mass merchandise store concept without losing sight of the specialty store concept. There will be a substantial increase in space given to promotional items throughout the entire store. For example, there will be promotional towels (now $9.99 instead of $19.99), sheets, blankets, comforters, pillows, bathmats, dinnerware, and table cloths. This new approach will bring together the best of a mass merchandise store with the best of a specialty store.

2.  **Assortment**—Ashbrooks will improve assortment in all core departments in order to achieve headquarters store status in these departments. For example, Bath Shop will be increased 30%, Towels 30%, Tabletop Textiles 35%. All assortments will be increased.

3.  **Value**—Value prices will be featured in every department. We will become known for value items such as ironing boards for $24.99, bathroom scales for $29.99, dinnerware for $29.99 which will be featured on end caps, promotional bunks and tables in each department. New items with lower price points will be purchased.

4.  **Promotion**—Ashbrooks will become more promotional with store signage and advertising heralding our new slogan "Canada's Largest Home Fashion Accessories Store". We will use flyers and radio advertising.

Maria Purser, Ashbrooks' buyer for Home Textiles, summarized these changes as moving Ashbrooks into lower priced lines, predominantly American, with a narrowed colour breadth (from more than 200 colours to approximately 8–12 colours). Maria and Susan Gillis, the Kitchen and Tabletop buyers, agreed they faced difficulties dealing with suppliers. Unlike when they were with their previous employers (Eaton's and Woolco), these buyers were now treated, as they put it, "as small potatoes in the eyes of the suppliers". This resulted in late deliveries and lack of influence regarding suppliers' product decisions.

Susan described her department as changing from an upscale brand name dinnerware boutique to more "casual living" twenty-piece dinner sets. As a result, her sales doubled. Originally placemats had been stocked primarily in solid colours, but prints and patterns were now the best sellers. Susan organized her displays into "colour stories" minutely detailed on blueprints for each store. While this took a lot of her time, she felt this seemed to be a successful approach.

The high fashion nature of the assortment led management to expect the need for markdowns, but they were unsure as to the level or timing of these. They decided to have two annual clearance sales, in July and January, to reduce inventories of slow sellers and to avoid an image of being on sale the rest of the year.

Some Ashbrooks staff members at the time reported feeling "they were riding a roller coaster with all these changes".

## F.W. WOOLWORTH 1988

FWW set new records in revenues, earnings, and store openings in 1988. Revenues jumped 13%, net income 17%, and an unprecedented 1,154 stores were opened or acquired worldwide, moving the total to 7,739 stores. The emphasis was on specialty stores which were providing $290 per square foot in revenues and $26 per square foot in operating profit compared to $134 and $7 for general merchandise stores in 1988. FWW was moving towards it goal of achieving an average annual net profit of 12–14%.

## BRANDENS

By late 1987, Brandens had grown to a nine store home accessories store in Atlanta, Georgia, and Florida. Several competitive imitations had also started. Brandens kept maintaining they were still in the testing stage, despite their three year life. In 1988, Brandens was still undergoing changes in its product mix, fixtures, and ceiling heights.

In April 1989, Brandens suddenly closed. Ann Barkelew-O'Hagan of Branden's parent Dayton-Hudson said of the closure: "The poten-

tial for growth in sales and profit was not as strong as some of the more established divisions of our company, such as Target, Mervyn's and Lechmere."

## MAY 1989

In May 1989, another consumer research study was completed. The objectives of this study were as follows:

1. To measure the level of awareness of Ashbrooks, specifically as a provider of accessories and fashion items for the bedroom, bathroom, and kitchen.

2. To determine the shopping behaviour of those aware of Ashbrooks.

3. To rate the relative importance to store choice of selected home accessory store attributes and Ashbrooks' performance on those attributes.

4. To solicit the specific likes and dislikes of Ashbrooks among shoppers.

5. To compare the results of the previous studies to new results.

The study was conducted at Square One Mall in March 1989, using a mall intercept methodology. 200 respondents were interviewed who met the following qualifications: females, aged 25 to 49 years, with total annual household incomes of at least $30,000 who shop at Square One at least once every two months.

The results presented to Mr. Ross are shown as Tables 1–13.

| Table I Ashbrooks Awareness Study Awareness of Ashbrooks | | |
| --- | --- | --- |
| | 1988 % | 1989 % |
| Unaided | 42 | 45 |
| Aided | 48 | 47 |
| Total Aware | 90 | 92 |
| Not Aware | 10 | 8 |

|  | Home Accessories | | Bathroom Accessories | |
|---|---|---|---|---|
|  | '88 % | '89 % | '88 % | '89 % |
| Comes to Mind | 25 | 29 | 32 | 36 |
| Shopped in Last 3 Months | 9 | 12 | 12 | 14 |
| Shop Most Often (if shopped in last 3 months) | 3 | 4 | 10 | 11 |

|  | Bedroom Accessories | | Kitchenware & Housewares | |
|---|---|---|---|---|
|  | '88 % | '89 % | '88 % | '89 % |
| Comes to Mind | 20 | 28 | 18 | 22 |
| Shopped in Last 3 Months | 4 | 5 | 8 | 7 |
| Shop Most Often (if shopped in last 3 months) | 5 | 5 | 5 | 3 |

## Table 2
### Ashbrooks Awareness Study
### Awareness/Use

|  | Home Accessories % | Bathroom Accessories % | Bedroom Accessories % | Kitchenware & Housewares % |
|---|---|---|---|---|
| **COMES TO MIND** | | | | |
| The Bay | 72 | 56 | 60 | 61 |
| Sears | 67 | 54 | 60 | 53 |
| Woolco | 62 | 56 | 51 | 58 |
| Eaton's | 53 | 40 | 54 | 44 |
| Ashbrooks | 29 | 32 | 28 | 22 |
| Simpsons | 12 | 12 | 17 | 14 |
| Top Speciality Store | 9 | 9 | 4 | 19 |
| **SHOPPED IN LAST 3 MONTHS** | | | | |
| Woolco | 38 | 20 | 17 | 25 |
| Sears | 35 | 18 | 17 | 14 |
| The Bay | 28 | 12 | 17 | 21 |
| Eaton's | 20 | 12 | 12 | 11 |
| Ashbrooks | 12 | 14 | 5 | 7 |
| Top Specialty Store | 4 | 3 | 2 | 9 |
| None | 19 | 34 | 46 | 31 |

**SHOP MOST OFTEN**
**(IF SHOPPED IN**
**LAST 3 MONTHS)**

| | | | | |
|---|---|---|---|---|
| Sears | 27 | 18 | 24 | 14 |
| Woolco | 24 | 24 | 19 | 24 |
| The Bay | 10 | 11 | 14 | 15 |
| Eaton's | 9 | 10 | 18 | 14 |
| Ashbrooks | 4 | 11 | 5 | 3 |
| Top Specialty Store | 1 | 4 | 2 | 7 |

Table 3
**Ashbrooks Awareness Study**
**Advertising**

| | TOTAL AWARE | |
|---|---|---|
| | '88 % | '89 % |
| SOURCE OF AWARENESS | | |
| Saw Store in Mall | 58 | 64 |
| Radio Ads | 16 | 11 |
| Word of Mouth | 11 | 12 |
| Newspaper | 8 | 7 |
| Flyers | 8 | 7 |
| Other | 4 | 2 |

| | SHOPPERS | |
|---|---|---|
| | '88 % | '89 % |
| Shopped at Ashbrooks Because of Ad | 19 | 25 |

| | SHOPPED BECAUSE OF AD* | |
|---|---|---|
| | '88 % | '89 % |
| TYPE OF AD WHICH BROUGHT PEOPLE IN | | |
| Flyers | 29 | 60 |
| Radio | 50 | 30 |
| Newspaper | 42 | 20 |

* Interpret with caution due to small sample sized.

## Table 4
## Ashbrooks Awareness Study
## Adoption

|  | 1988 % | 1989 % |
|---|---|---|
| Shopped | 63 | 65 |
| Aware/Not Shopped | 22 | 21 |
| Shopped/Not Purchased | 30 | 25 |
| Purchased | 34 | 40 |
| Purchased Only Once | 15 | 10 |
| Repeat Purchase | 19 | 31 |
| Committed Shoppers | 10 | 10 |

## Table 5
## Ashbrooks Awareness Study
## Awareness/Shopping/Purchase
## Conversion Matrix

| Total Sample | (200) | | | | |
|---|---|---|---|---|---|
|  | % | | | | |
| Total Aware | 92 | 100% | | | |
| Total Shopped | 65 | 70 | 100% | | |
| Total Purchased | 40 | 43 | 62 | 100% | |
| Total Repeat Purchased | 31 | 33 | 47 | 76 | 100% |
| Total Committed | 10 | 11 | 16 | 25 | 33 |

## Table 6
## Ashbrooks Awareness Study
## Shopping Behaviour

|  | Total Aware # | Unaided Aware # | Shopped # | Shopped/ Not Purchased # | Purchased # | Purchase/ Not Repeat* # | Repeat Purchaser # | Committed* # |
|---|---|---|---|---|---|---|---|---|
| Average Times Shopped Past 6 Months (if shopped) | | | | | | | | |
| 1989 | 5.5 | 6.9 | 5.5 | 2.0 | 7.6 | 2.4 | 9.2 | 12.0 |
| 1988 | 3.9 | 5.3 | 3.9 | 1.9 | 5.7 | 2.5 | 8.4 | 7.6 |
| Average Times Purchased Past 6 Months (if purchased) | | | | | | | | |
| 1989 | 4.0 | 3.7 | | | 3.7 | 1.0 | 4.6 | 5.5 |
| 1988 | 2.5 | 2.1 | | | 2.1 | 1.0 | 3.1 | 3.5 |

* Interpret with caution due to low sample size.

## Table 7
## Ashbrooks Awareness Study
## Shopping Behavior

| | Shoppers | | Repeat Purchasers | | Committed* | |
|---|---|---|---|---|---|---|
| | '88 | '89 | '88 | '89 | '88 | '89 |
| **LAST TIME SHOPPED** | | | | | | |
| Last Week | 13 | 21 | 16 | 31 | 26 | 45 |
| Last Two Weeks | 7 | 9 | 14 | 13 | 11 | 25 |
| Last Month | 40 | 21 | 46 | 21 | 37 | 25 |
| Last 2–3 Months | 25 | 29 | 19 | 26 | 21 | 5 |
| More Than 3 Months Ago | 14 | 19 | 5 | 7 | 5 | 0 |
| **PURPOSE FOR BUYING AT ASHBROOKS** | | | | | | |
| Gift | 45 | 45 | 49 | 44 | 42 | 30 |
| Single Item For Home | 36 | 38 | 30 | 38 | 32 | 50 |
| Several Items for Decorating Room | 27 | 31 | 41 | 39 | 58 | 50 |
| Bought on Impulse | 6 | 5 | 5 | 5 | 0 | 10 |

\* Interpret with caution due to small sample size.

## Table 8
## Ashbrooks Awareness Study
## Attribute Ratings

| | Importance For Store Choice[1] | | Most Important Attributes[2] | | Performance of Ashbrooks[3] | |
|---|---|---|---|---|---|---|
| | '88 # | '89 # | '88 % | '89 % | '88 # | '89 # |
| Good Value for Money | 2.7 | 2.6 | 69 | 61 | 3.0 | 3.2 |
| High Quality Products | 2.6 | 2.5 | 48 | 37 | 3.9 | 4.0 |
| Good Service | 2.5 | 2.5 | 20 | 22 | 3.3 | 3.4 |
| Low Prices | 2.3 | 2.4 | 17 | 28 | 2.2 | 2.4 |
| Wide Range of Colours | 2.3 | 2.3 | 7 | 7 | 4.3 | 4.5 |
| Variety of Sizes | 2.3 | 2.2 | 6 | 2 | 3.8 | 4.0 |
| Convenient Location | 2.2 | 2.2 | 17 | 14 | 3.7 | 3.7 |
| Range of Brands | 2.2 | 2.1 | 7 | 9 | 3.6 | 3.8 |
| Pleasant Atmosphere | N/A | 2.1 | N/A | 4 | N/A | 3.9 |
| Attractive Presentation | 2.1 | 2.0 | 5 | 2 | 4.4 | 4.5 |
| Well-known Brands | 1.9 | 1.8 | 7 | 5 | 3.5 | 3.7 |

1. Rated on a 3-point scale (1 = Not important, 3 = Essential).
2. Two choices allowed.
3. Rated on a 5-point scale (1 = Poor, 5 = Excellent).

### Table 9
### Ashbrooks Awareness Study
### Likes

|  | Shoppers % | Shopped Not Purchased % | Purchased % | Purchase/ Not Repeat* % | Repeat Purchaser* % | Committed* % |
|---|---|---|---|---|---|---|
| Good Selection/Variety | 45 | 49 | 43 | 32 | 46 | 45 |
| Attractive Displays | 33 | 20 | 40 | 74 | 30 | 30 |
| Wide Range of Colours | 29 | 24 | 31 | 16 | 36 | 50 |
| Quality Products | 25 | 20 | 28 | 21 | 30 | 30 |
| Spacious Store | 17 | 17 | 17 | 11 | 20 | 20 |
| Good Prices | 12 | 2 | 16 | 11 | 18 | 15 |
| Well Laid Out | 12 | 7 | 14 | 11 | 15 | 25 |
| Helpful Staff | 10 | 7 | 11 | 5 | 13 | 20 |
| Nothing Liked | 0 | 0 | 0 | 0 | 0 | 0 |

* Interpret with caution due to small sample size.

### Table 10
### Ashbrooks Awareness Study
### Dislikes

|  | Shoppers % | Shopped/ Not Purchased % | Purchased % | Purchase/ Not Repeat* % | Repeat Purchaser* % | Committed* % |
|---|---|---|---|---|---|---|
| High Priced | 40 | 51 | 35 | 58 | 28 | 30 |
| Poor Service/Not Enough Clerks | 4 | 2 | 5 | 5 | 5 | 10 |
| Nothing Disliked | 46 | 34 | 52 | 42 | 56 | 55 |

* Interpret with caution due to small sample size.

## Table 11
## Ashbrooks Awareness Study
## Ashbrooks Bridal Registry

| | Aware Of Ashbrooks % | Shoppers % | Shopped/ Not Purchased* % | Purchasers* % | Repeat* Purchaser* % | Committed* % |
|---|---|---|---|---|---|---|
| Aware of Ashbrooks Bridal Registry | 22 | 27 | 22 | 30 | 30 | 35 |
| **LIKELIHOOD OF REGISTERING AT ASHBROOKS** | | | | | | |
| Very/Somewhat | 45 | 53 | 47 | 57 | 62 | 60 |
| Not Very/ Not at all | 55 | 47 | 54 | 43 | 38 | 40 |
| **IF "NOT VERY/ NOT AT ALL," WHY NOT** | | | | | | |
| Don't Like Bridal Registries Don't Use Them. | 33 | 34 | 17 | 47 | 59 | 33 |
| Would Register Elsewhere | 22 | 30 | 21 | 36 | 26 | 51 |
| Not Familiar With Ashbrooks | 19 | 8 | 13 | 4 | 5 | 0 |
| Too Expensive | 10 | 14 | 17 | 11 | 5 | 0 |
| Would Rather Buy On Own | 10 | 12 | 9 | 14 | 11 | 33 |

* Interpret with caution due to small sample size.


## Table 12
## Ashbrooks Awareness Study
## New Door*

| | Aware of Ashbrooks % | Shoppers % | Purchasers % | Repeat Purchasers % | Committed** % |
|---|---|---|---|---|---|
| Aware of New Door | 45 | 45 | 50 | 54 | 60 |
| Used Door, If Aware | 74 | 74 | 82 | 85 | 92 |
| Used Door First Time in Store, If Used | 9 | 9 | 9 | 7 | 0 |

  * A new door was added to provide direct access to the parking lot without going through the centre.
** Interpret with caution due to small sample size.

### Table 13
### Ashbrooks Awareness Study
### Demographics

| | Total % | Unaided Aware % | Not Aware* % | Aware/ Not Shopped % | Shopped % | Shopped/ Not Purchased % | Purchased % | Purchase/ Not Repeat % | Repeat Purchaser % | Committed* % |
|---|---|---|---|---|---|---|---|---|---|---|
| **AGE** | | | | | | | | | | |
| 25-29 Years | 34 | 37 | 31 | 40 | 33 | 37 | 30 | 21 | 33 | 30 |
| 30-34 Years | 23 | 21 | 12 | 29 | 24 | 24 | 24 | 32 | 21 | 20 |
| 35-39 Years | 20 | 18 | 25 | 7 | 21 | 20 | 21 | 16 | 23 | 20 |
| 40-45 Years | 17 | 18 | 25 | 17 | 18 | 10 | 22 | 26 | 21 | 30 |
| 46-49 Years | 5 | 7 | 6 | 7 | 5 | 8 | 3 | 5 | 2 | 0 |
| **INCOME** | | | | | | | | | | |
| $30k-$40K | 22 | 20 | 19 | 21 | 22 | 27 | 20 | 11 | 23 | 10 |
| $40k-$50K | 27 | 17 | 38 | 29 | 26 | 31 | 22 | 37 | 18 | 10 |
| $50K+ | 50 | 63 | 44 | 50 | 52 | 43 | 57 | 53 | 59 | 80 |
| **EMPLOYMENT** | | | | | | | | | | |
| Full-Time | 60 | 62 | 50 | 52 | 61 | 57 | 64 | 53 | 67 | 70 |
| Part-Time | 19 | 17 | 25 | 24 | 17 | 18 | 16 | 16 | 16 | 10 |
| Not At All | 22 | 21 | 25 | 24 | 22 | 24 | 20 | 32 | 16 | 20 |
| **TYPE OF DWELLING** | | | | | | | | | | |
| House | 61 | 67 | 44 | 60 | 65 | 65 | 69 | 79 | 61 | 70 |
| Apt./Condo | 31 | 28 | 38 | 26 | 29 | 29 | 29 | 16 | 33 | 20 |
| Townhouse | 9 | 4 | 19 | 14 | 5 | 6 | 5 | 5 | 5 | 5 |
| **TENURE** | | | | | | | | | | |
| Own | 62 | 69 | 56 | 60 | 67 | 63 | 69 | 68 | 69 | 80 |
| Rent | 38 | 31 | 44 | 40 | 33 | 37 | 31 | 32 | 31 | 20 |
| **HOUSEHOLD SIZE** | | | | | | | | | | |
| 1-2 | 30 | 32 | 37 | 28 | 31 | 27 | 33 | 26 | 34 | 35 |
| 3+ | 70 | 68 | 63 | 72 | 69 | 73 | 67 | 74 | 66 | 65 |
| **INTEREST IN DECORATING** | | | | | | | | | | |
| Active Decorator | 48 | 51 | 50 | 50 | 48 | 37 | 55 | 47 | 57 | 65 |
| Only When Needed | 43 | 41 | 44 | 36 | 45 | 57 | 38 | 42 | 36 | 30 |
| Tedious Chore | 9 | 8 | 6 | 14 | 7 | 6 | 8 | 11 | 7 | 5 |

* Interpret with caution due to small sample size.

# Ⓒ Ⓐ Ⓢ Ⓔ 4.8    Provigo Distribution

At 9:00 a.m. on Tuesday, August 6, 1987, Jacques Hébert, President and General Manager of Provigo Distribution Inc., held a crisis meeting in his office. With him were his Vice-President of Communications, Albert Gaudreau, and Gaudreau's counterpart from the parent company, Gilles Gagnon of Provigo Inc. They were evaluating their options in dealing with the media about an embarrassing advertisement. As Hébert sat and listened to the opposing views of his communications advisors, he knew that he had to make the final decision quickly.

## PROVIGO DISTRIBUTION INC.

Provigo Distribution, a subsidiary of Provigo Inc., was a leading food distributor in Quebec at both the retail and wholesale levels. Through its 14 warehouses, it supplied some 8,000 food stores, 14% of which operated under one of eight company banners. Provigo operated some company-owned stores, but most of the stores which carried a company banner were operated by independent retailers affiliated with the company. One of the banners was Les Supermarches Provigo, a chain of 244 supermarkets located throughout the Province of Quebec. The company owned only 18% of the supermarkets; the rest were owned and operated by affiliated merchants.

Provigo Inc., the parent company, located in Montreal, distributed food, pharmaceutical products, sporting goods and a variety of other products, nationwide and across the U.S. Through its six business groups, Provigo Inc. also owned controlling interests in Consumers Distributing and Toy World.

Provigo Distribution was a member of Provigo Inc.'s Food Group, along with Loeb and Honne & Pitfield—leading distributors of food products in Ontario and Alberta respectively.

## LA CIRCULAIRE

"La Circulaire," a weekly bilingual flyer of 24 to 32 pages, was a one-year old marketing tool produced by Provigo Distribution to promote products sold in the Provigo supermarkets. Each Monday, 2,350,000 copies of La Circulaire were sent through Canada Post to homes in Greater Montreal, its suburbs, and in the Laurentides, Bois-Francs, Mauricie and Estrie regions of Quebec. Like the flyers of its competitors, La Circulaire aimed to advertise the supermarkets' weekly specials. But La Circulaire was different in the following ways: its dimensions were 10.5″ × 13.25″ (Tabloid) instead of the typical 8.5″ × 11″, and it was a true weekly paper, featuring not only ads, but articles on nutrition, cooking tips and an editorial cartoon.

## THE CONTROVERSIAL CARTOON

The editorial cartoon had created the difficulty Provigo Distribution was now facing. It was featured in La Circulaire's edition for the week of August 3 to 9, 1987.

Typically, the one-frame editorial cartoon would serve to support a product or the nutritional advice presented in one of the front pages of La Circulaire. That week, the cartoon meant to relate to an article about melons. It depicted a voluptuous black woman holding a melon in her left hand while rubbing the head of a bald white man with her right. The woman was saying in French "I love melons" (Exhibit 1).

The cartoon enraged many members of the Black community. A Black resident of a suburb of Montreal lodged a complaint with the Quebec Human Rights Commission. In Montreal, the Negro Community Centre called on the media and publicly accused Provigo Supermarkets of racism and sexism. The Centre said that they had written to Provigo Distribution demanding an apology, after receiving more than 200 complaints about the cartoon.

The Black community was offended by the cartoon because it felt that the cartoon perpetuated a stereotype. In the days of slavery in the U.S., Black workers were often fed the same

EXHIBIT I
Provigo
Distribution

thing that their white masters fed their pigs: watermelons. Many Black people, such as Elma Frost, who filed a complaint with the Human Rights Commission, remembered being taunted as children by phrases such as "Niggers love watermelon" or "Lazy Nigger sitting on the street corner, eating watermelon and spitting pits".

## PROVIGO DISTRIBUTION'S RESPONSE

The Black community's response to the cartoon had taken the communications department by surprise. As the publication coordinators of *La Circulaire*, Gaudreau's team regretted the mishap. However, Gaudreau maintained that the company had certainly not meant to be offensive. That was the message that he had given to the media and that he had delivered in person to the Executive Director of the Negro Community Centre, Bonnie Nelson, yesterday on August 5th.

Although Nelson had not been very recep-

tive at first, Gaudreau felt that she had accepted the company's regrets. She had demanded, however, more than the company's offer to express its regrets in the following issue of *La Circulaire*. She felt that a better apology would take the form of money: Provigo Distribution should sponsor a future sports or cultural event held for the Black community.

## MEDIA RESPONSE

Gaudreau explained to Hébert that representatives of the Anglophone media had given sizeable coverage to the Negro Community Centre's complaints. The news teams of various radio and television stations had interviewed both the Executive Director of the Negro Centre and either Gaudreau or Gagnon. News stories and clips of those interviews had been broadcast several times on the previous day. Gaudreau was particularly disappointed in the CBC Newswatch's coverage. He felt that the "clip" they had used of their interview with him left the viewer with more questions than answers.

Some small weeklies and the English daily newspaper in Montreal, *The Gazette*, had also covered the story (see press package: Exhibit 2). One of their columnists clearly implied that although Provigo Distribution might not have printed the cartoon with malice, the company "should have known better." Gaudreau read to Hébert the column's lead-in sentence: "For a business wholly dependent on taste, the Provigo supermarket chain has shown incredibly poor taste."

By contrast, until yesterday, the Francophone press and broadcast journalists had been virtually silent about the story. Yet, now that interest in the story seemed to be dying down in the Anglophone press, the French journalists had taken a sudden interest. They had yesterday started calling Provigo Distribution for information on the issue. It appeared that a story on the cartoon and the reaction of the Negro Centre, published in the morning's edition of *La Presse*, one of Montreal's major French daily newspapers, had started the enquiries. Since early this morning, a significant number of French journalists from Montreal had called. Hébert had called Gaudreau and Gagnon to a meeting to discuss the implications of the media attention focused on the Provigo name in the past few days.

## WEIGHING THE ALTERNATIVES

The publicity given to Provigo Inc., Provigo Distribution Inc. and the Provigo Supermarkets was, for the most part, not positive. Because of the similarity in their names, results of publicity usually affected all, whether positive or negative. Most customers of the Provigo Supermarkets probably did not understand the distinctions between the Provigo supermarket chain, Provigo Distribution, and Provigo Inc. Even the media often used "Provigo" without specifying which company was involved. Hence, Hébert and his communications advisors had quickly agreed that the Provigo name and image should be protected against further

damage. Their objective was to somehow turn the media's attention away from the melons cartoon.

It was difficult to evaluate how many more news reports the story could generate. If the Francophone journalists kept finding new angles from which to treat the story, it was probable that the representatives from the Anglophone media would start looking for some as well. Gaudreau and Gagnon, however, held different opinions on the best way to achieve their common objective.

Gagnon, the VP of Public Affairs for the parent company, insisted that the best method to handle the Francophone media representatives was to give them "no comment". He felt that by giving them no information, journalists would not be in a position to write stores. Reports which didn't present both sides of the story would likely be killed at editors' desks, he said.

Further, he suspected that the Francophone media had taken longer to cover the story simply because they had not been called by the Negro Community Centre. The editors were bound to feel that they had been short-changed, and thus would probably not go out of their way to give the Centre's accusations great exposure.

The directors of the Centre were also known as activists in Montreal: Gagnon thought they had a reputation for screaming "racism" at every opportunity. This gave the Centre less credibility in any of its complaints, he thought. He believed that the media held the same view and that they would thus limit their coverage to protect their own credibility.

Hébert thought that Gagnon's last argument was his strongest. Gagnon argued that by responding to questions from the media or by being pro-active in giving information to the media, Provigo Distribution would be admitting guilt.

Gaudreau disagreed with most of Gagnon's stands. He felt that "au contraire," Provigo would appear guilty if it remained quiet. The silence in itself might generate some stories, he said. Yet, if Provigo Distribution explained the cultural conflict to journalists, and told them that things had been settled with the Negro Commu-

EXHIBIT 2
*Provigo
Distribution*

*THE GAZETTE — le 5 août 1987*

# Provigo cartoon offends blacks

MICHAEL FARBER

For a business wholly dependent on taste, the Provigo supermarket chain has shown incredibly poor taste.

The affront occurs in its current weekly circular, *La Circulaire*, which beyond its articles on nutrition and specials, offers its readers an editorial cartoon. Now all editorial cartoons are supposed to work on several levels, and certainly this one does — racism, sexism, and poking fun at bald men.

The cartoon depicts a smiling, voluptuous black woman holding a melon in her left hand while rubbing the head of a bald white man with her right. The woman is saying, in French, "I love melons."

Patrick C. Robert, vice-president of public affairs at Provigo Inc., dismissed a reaction to the cartoon as overreaction, saying that no complaints about the drawing had been received at the head office. He said that elsewhere in the circular was a story about melons imported from Africa, and the cartoon merely matched the story.

"You really have to have a certain kind of thinking (to find it offensive)," Robert said. "The product originates in Africa. And you can certainly say that Africa is a place where blacks

are living. This black woman is showing that the head is similarly shaped. Nothing more.

"I don't think anyone has the right to interpret this as a malicious thing from Provigo."

## Melon used as racial slur

Maxene Prevost Shephard thinks she has every right.

Prevost Shephard, 56, grew up in Nova Scotia in a segregated town with a segregated school. As a child she remembers being taunted with the phrase, "Niggers love watermelon, niggers love watermelon." Poll 100 black Canadians, she said, and almost all would have heard a similar racial slur at one time in their lives.

"I avoided eating watermelon in front of white people," Prevost Shephard said. "Even if it would kill you, you wouldn't do it. You might be foaming at the mouth for a piece, but you wouldn't do it. I understood what (the phrase) meant. They were putting me down. Now I eat watermelon every time it's around. I eat it for its nutritive value, and I eat it because I like it. I'm over all that."

But racism isn't. Prevost Shephard heard "nigger" growing up in the 1930s and 1940s, and she hears it now. She sees a Rotary Club newsletter with its tasteless joke about black women, she sees the sorry discrimination within Montreal's taxi industry, she sees a purportedly harmless circular cartoon, and she wonders why she and not a white Montrealer had to pick up a phone to call the Human Rights Commission.

## Black community seeks apology

"Every day you run into it," Prevost Shephard said, "I would take my children to play hockey on the West Island and they were constantly taunted. You had to wonder whether it was all worthwhile, but they had to live in this society, and so I thought I could instill in them the ability to overcome it."

Anyway Prevost Shephard, a regular at the Provigo on Hymes Blvd. in Pointe Claire, said the company has seen the last of her dollars.

And she might have plenty of company.

Ilma Lynton-Holt, executive director of the Negro Community Centre in Montreal, said her office had received 50 complaints yesterday and an unspecified number Monday. The Provigo circular is stuffed into mailboxes on Sunday morning.

On behalf of the black community, Lynton-Holt has written to the Provigo directors and demanded what she called a "substantive apology" to the black community of Quebec.

If one is not forthcoming, she said, the Negro Community Centre would consider calling for a boycott.

"We blacks in Quebec represent 8 per cent of the market," Lynton-Holt said. (It is estimated that there are 100,000 to 125,000 blacks in Montreal, about 4.5 per cent of the population).

### Boycott could be costly

"In the competitive retail market, a company can't afford to lose 2 per cent, let alone 8 per cent. This is not an Ontario company that did this. This is a Quebec enterprise, *chez nous*."

Lynton-Holt, who did not see the cartoon until yesterday afternoon, decried not merely The Melon Factor but the sexually exploitative nature of the female character. Indeed, she thinks the cartoon contained elements of prostitution. She called the drawing "whorish."

"I heard it and my children hear it: 'Lazy nigger sitting on the street corner, eating watermelon and spitting pits,' " Lynton-Holt said. "What's happened is that stereotype has been exploited. This cartoon has reaffirmed the stereotype in the mind of the community at large."

Lynton-Holt might have overstated the case. Other than the price of iceberg lettuce and barbecue sauce, not much in *La Circulaire* might have registered in the community. But for those who noticed the cartoon and were insulted by the implications, this is one cartoon that will not go away.

Provigo's circular may have bitten off more than it can chew.

---

*THE GAZETTE*—le 6 août 1987

### Provigo apologizes for its 'melon' cartoon

Quebec's largest supermarket chain has apologized for a cartoon, dubbed racist by critics, that appeared in a flyer it sent to 1.8 million homes.

The cartoon, distributed by the Provigo chain, depicted a smiling black woman holding a melon in one hand and touching a white man's bald head with the other, saying "I love melons" in French.

Ilma Lynton-Holt, executive director of the Negro Community Centre, said she wrote Provigo demanding an apology after receiving more than 200 complaining calls.

Yesterday, Provigo apologized. "We apologize — we regret what we did," said Provigo official André Sicotte.

Sicotte said a written apology will be printed in a forthcoming edition of the flyer.

Lynton-Holt said she and Sicotte agreed the company would also "do something that would reflect positively on the black community," such as sponsoring a black sports team or artist.

"We left it up to them what they'd do."

Sicotte said Provigo won't contribute financially to any group, but will carry a story within the next two months on the contributions to the food industry made by blacks.

*LA TRIBUNE*—Sherbrooke, le 6 août 1987

# Provigo s'excuse

MONTRÉAL (PC) — La plus importante chain d'alimentation du Québec s'est excusés, mercredi, auprés de la communauté noire pour avoir publié une caricature raciste dans la circulaire Provigo, distribuée à prés de deux millions d'exemplaires dans la région de Montréal, les Cantons de l'Est et les Laurentides.

La caricature contestée dépeint une femme noire à l'allure provocante tenant un melon dans le main gauche, pendant qu'elle caresse de la main droite le crâne d'un Blanc chauve, en déclarent: "J'adore les melons".

Mme Ilma Lynton-Holt, directrice exécutive du Centre communautaire noir de Montréal, a déclaré qu'aprés avoir reçu plus de 200 plaintes elle a demandé des excuses de la société Provigo, qui s'est exécutée.

# Provigo regrette une caricature «raciste», mais le milieu noir demeure insatisfait

LOUIS MILLS

Provigo plaide l'ignorance pour expliquer la publication, dans sa circulaire hebdomadaire, d'une caricature qui a suscité une tempête de protestations dans la communauté noire, à cause de son Côté «raciste et sexiste». La direction de la chaine d'alimentation s'est excusée, mais le Centre communautaire des Noirs de Montréal exige des preuves plus tangibles de sa bonne volunté.

«J'ai eu une réaction viscérale dès que j'ai vu le dessin», a raconté hier à *La Presse* Mme Illma Lynton-Holt, directrice général du centre. La caricature représente une jeune Noire aux formes voluptueuses qui tient un melon d'une main et qui touche de l'autre le crâne chauve d'un homme blanc. Dans un bulle, on peut lire: «J'aime les melons». M. André Sicotte, un porte-parole de Provigo explique que l'encadré accompagnait un article sur les cantaloupes importées D'Afrique qui paraissait dans les premières pages de *La Circulaire*. «Cette caricature est inoffensive de prime abord, mais elle contient un message subliminal», soutient Mme Lynton-Holt.

*La caricature controversée.*

À l'époque de l'esclavage, selon elle, les grands patrons dans les plantations nourrissaient les Noirs et les cochons de melons d'eau. «Les nègres aiment les melons d'eau» était devenu, par la suite, une phrase qu'on lançait à la figure des Noirs pour les insulter. Elle les ravalait au même rang que les bêtes. «J'aime effectivement les melons, affirme Mme Lynton-Holt, mais j'en mange par choix et non parce que je ne peux me payer autre choise.» La caricature, selon elle, symbolise l'ancienne domination des Blancs sur les Noirs et les vexations subies par ces derniers. Le centre a reçu, jusqu'ici, plus de 200 appels de gens qui, comme elle, ont sursauté en ouvrant leur circulaire.

«Je n'ai pas voulu offusquer qui que ce soit», affirme le caricaturiste Berthio. M. Sicotte renchérit: «Nous ne pouvions savior que ce dessin contenait des connotations négatives.» Mais Mme Lynton-Holt bondit. «Les grandes entreprises font habituellement preuve de circonspection lorsqu'ils traitent de minorités ethniques. Ils font des recherches approfondies afin d'éviter de choquer une partie de leur clientèle. Si Provigo n'a pas agi ainsi, elle a manqué de rigueur. Elle serait tout de même coupable, dans une certaine mesure.»

M. Sicotte a rencontré Mme Lynton-Holt hier matin pour lui exprimer ses regrets. Il a promis de publier des excuses en bonne et due forme dans l'un des prochains numéros de *La Circulaire*. Mais Mme Lynton-Holt est à moitié satisfaite seulement de cette promesse, estimant qu'un simple entrefilet dans l'hebdo ne saurait réparer le tort causé à la communauté des Noirs par la caricature. «Ceux qui trouvent notre réaction exagérée ne connaissent pas les brimades subies quotidiennement par les Noirs. Moi-même, je ne peux prendre le métro sans qu'un homme blanc se croit permis de faire une remarque insidieuse sur la couleur de ma peau. Quand la presse parle de nous, c'est pour annoncer qu'un jeune Noir a commis un vol. L'un de nos grands athlètes de couleur, le sprinter Ben Johnson, a dû fracasser un record mondial avant de se faire remarquer.» Outrée, elle multiplie les exemples.

En guise de réparations, Mme Lynton-Holt aimerait que Provigo commandite un groupe de Noirs qui participe à un événement quelconque, que ce soit une manifestation sportive, culturelle ou autre. Si la compagnie ne fait pas preuve de bonne foi, selon elle, la clientèle noire pourrait faire ses emplettes ailleurs. M. Sicotte exprime une certaine réticence relativement à cette demande. Il souligne que Provigo verse déjà des dons à Centraide qui finance en partie le Centre communautaire des Noirs.

---

nity Centre, they would leave the story alone. "Now that things are settled," Gaudreau said, "there isn't even a story any more". However, he felt that Provigo Distribution would have to be honest with reporters for them to abandon the story idea.

As well, Gaudreau had worked with journalists enough to believe that if they didn't find information at the source, they would find it elsewhere. Although Provigo Distribution had a communications policy by which communications were centralized during a crisis, it was an "unwritten rule". Gaudreau estimated that it would not be difficult for journalists to get merchants to give them some sort of a statement. A merchant receiving a call from a journalist would not know that the issue had led to a crisis, and hence that he or she should abstain from comment.

Gaudreau also talked of the long-term effects of a "no comment" tactic. Provigo Distribution had always had open and honest relations with both the Francophone and Anglophone media. It would be dangerous and foolish, he said, to deviate from this approach when Provigo was not guilty of intentional racism. He also reminded his colleagues that they had willingly responded to questions from the Anglophone journalists, just two days earlier. He argued that news travels fast in the media industry. Francophone journalists would likely think it unfair when they heard that their English colleagues had easily gotten information from Provigo Distribution.

Gaudreau also thought that whether Provigo Distribution liked it or not, the story of the melons would likely linger in the media for a while at least. He agreed with Gagnon's perception of the Negro Community Centre's credibility. He pointed out, however, that Elma Frost, who had filed the complaint with the Human Rights Commission, had acted on her own initiative. She was a sweet, vocal person—just the type the media loved to interview. The French and English media would likely follow the complaint through the process with the Commission, thus periodically reminding their veiwers, listeners and readers of "Provigo's" racist cartoon. Gaudreau would feel better, he said, if it was on record early that Provigo Distribution had made a slip-up rather than made an intentional affront to the Black community.

In a last attempt to convince his colleagues, Gaudreau reminded them that 90% of their customers were Francophones and that bad publicity in the Francophone press could have serious repercussions.

## FACING THE TENSION

As Hébert walked out of the meeting to get a coffee, he rapidly went over his advisor's arguments. "Journalists are probably calling the communications department for statements at this very minute," he mused. And while Gagnon, the parent company's VP, had already left the meeting for another appointment, Gaudreau was still waiting in Hébert's office. Hébert realized that Gaudreau's team were in turn waiting for word from their superior before returning the calls of journalists. So the President knew that by the time he walked back in his office to face Gaudreau, he should be ready to inform his VP of communications of his decisions.

# ACKNOWLEDGMENTS

Jules Abend, from "Busman's Holiday." Reprinted from *Stores*, July 1982 by permission of the National Retail Federation, Inc. 1991.

Jules Abend, from "Service: Shaping Up?" Reprinted from *Stores*, September 1986 by permission of the National Retail Federation, Inc. 1991.

Karl Albrecht and Ron Zemke, from *Service America*, 1985. Published by Dow Jones Irwin. Reprinted by permission of Karl Albrecht.

Frank Andrews and Dan Cooper, from "Beyond Systems: Inventory Management Takes Center Stage." Reprinted from *Retail Control*, January 1991 by permission of the National Retail Federation Inc. 1991.

Isadore Barmash, from "Disquieting Times in 1991." Reprinted from *Stores*, December 1990 by permission of the National Retail Federation, Inc. 1991.

Isadore Barmash, from "How They Plan." Reprinted from *Stores*, September 1983 by permission of the National Retail Federation, Inc. 1991.

Susan Bass, from "Hosiery: Partnerships Needed." Reprinted from *Stores*, November 1990 by permission of the National Retail Federation, Inc. 1991.

Stephen Bennett, from "King Kullen Polishes Its Crown," *Progressive Grocer*, September 1990. Copyright © 1990 by Progressive Grocer Magazine, a Division of Maclean Hunter Media Inc. Reprinted by permission.

Joan Bergman, from "What Price A Sheet?" Reprinted from *Stores*, October 1989 by permission of the National Retail Federation, Inc. 1991.

Barry Berman and Joel R. Evans. Reprinted by permission of Macmillan Publishing Company from *Retail Management: A Strategic Approach*, by Barry Berman and Joel R. Evans. Copyright © 1989 by Macmillan Publishing Company.

Leonard Berry, from "Changing Consumer to Alter Marketplace Greatly." Reprinted from *Marketing News*, September 1989, published by the American Marketing Association, Chicago, IL 60606.

Jacquelyn Bivins, from "One Price Clothing Stores." Reprinted from *Stores*, October 1989 by permission of the National Retail Federation, Inc. 1991.

Cathy Booth, from "The Price is Always Right," *Time*, December 17, 1990. Copyright © 1990 The Time Inc. Magazine Company. Reprinted by permission.

Richard S. Bragaw, from "Price Club: One of California's Best Retailing Ideas," *International Trends in Retailing*, Spring 1990. Reprinted by permission.

Alan J. Bush and Joseph F. Hair Jr., from "An Assessment of the Mall Intercept as a Data Collection Method." Reprinted from *Journal of Marketing Research*, May 1985, published by the American Marketing Association, Chicago, IL 60606.

E. Carlson, from "Woolworth's Big Idea Began as a Nickel Notion," *The Wall Street Journal*, February 24, 1989. Reprinted by permission of The Wall Street Journal, Copyright © 1989 Dow Jones & Company, Inc. All Rights Reserved Worldwide.

Harold T. Carlson, from "How Shopping Centers Reshape Retailing: Past, Present, and Future," *International Trends in Retailing*, Spring 1990. Reprinted by permission.

Barbara G. Cohen, from "Revitalization of the Core Business, or How Do We Start to Grow Profitably Again?" Reprinted from Retail Control, December 1989 by permission of the National Retail Federation Inc. 1991.

Pat Corwin, from "Fashion-Forward Presentation," *Discount Merchandiser*, March 1990. Reprinted by permission of the publisher.

Kevin Coyne, from "Beyond Service Fads—Meaningful Strategies for the Real World." Reprinted from the *Sloan Management Review*, Summer 1989, pp.69-76, by permission of publisher. Copyright © 1989 by the Sloan Management Review Association. All rights reserved.

Paul Crotty, from "The Retail Revolution in the U.K.," *Canadian Grocer*, February 1990. Reprinted by permission of the publisher.

Paul Crotty, from "Stocking the Aisle with Private Label," *Canadian Grocer*, August 1990. Reprinted by permission of the publisher.

M. Wayne DeLozier and Dale M. Lewison. Reprinted by permission of Macmillan Publishing Company from *Retailing*, 4/e by Dale M. Lewison. Copyright © 1991 by Macmillan Publishing Company.

Emanuel H. Demby, from "Psychographics Revisited: The Birth of a Technique." Reprinted from *Marketing News*, January 2, 1989, published by the American Marketing Association, Chicago, IL 60606.

Priscilla Donegan, from "An Xtraordinary Experience," *Progressive Grocer*, March, 1989. Copyright © 1989 by Progressive Grocer Magazine, a Division of Maclean Hunter Media Inc. Reprinted by permission.

Patrick Dunne and Robert F. Lusch, from *Retail Management*. Published by the South-Western Publishing Company, 1990. Reprinted by permission.

Ken Dychtwald and Greg Gable, from "Portrait of a Changing Consumer." Reprinted from *Business Horizons*, January–February 1990. Copyright © 1990 by the Foundation for the School of Business at Indiana University. Used with permission.

Tom Eisenhart, from "Where to Go When You Need to Know," *Business Marketing*, November 1989. Reprinted by permission of the publisher.

R.J. Eng, R.J. Kopp, and D.J. Tigert, from "A Competitive Structure Analysis of the Chicago Fashion Market," *Journal of Retailing*, Winter 1989. Reprinted by permission of the publisher.

"Entertainment Anchors: New Mall Headliners." Reprinted by permission from *Chain Store Age Executive*, August 1989. Copyright © Lebhar-Friedman, Inc., 425 Park Avenue, New York, NY 10022.

"57th Annual Report," *Progressive Grocer*, mid–April 1990. Copyright © 1990 by Progressive Grocer Magazine, a Division of Maclean Hunter Media Inc. Reprinted by permission.

Rodney Fitch, from "The Role of Design in Retailing Strategy," *International Trends in Retailing*, Spring 1989. Reprinted by permission.

Hilary Forrest, from "The Watt Way," *Canadian Retailer*, December–January 1990–91. Reprinted by permission of August Communications, Ltd.

Randall Gebhardt, from "Merchandising the Store," *Discount Merchandiser*, May 1989. Reprinted by permission of the publisher.

Penny Gill, from "Battle of the Brands: Who's Winning." Reprinted from *Stores*, May 1990 by permission of the National Retail Federation, Inc. 1991.

Penny Gill, from "Know Your Customer." Reprinted from *Stores*, November 1989 by permission of the National Retail Federation, Inc. 1991.

Harris Gordon, Daniel O'Connor, and John Phipps, from "Direct Product Profit: Introducing A Comprehensive Measurement of Retail Performance." Reprinted from *Retail Control*, September 1986 by permission of the National Retail Federation Inc. 1991.

John R. Graham, from "Keep Customers by Using the Right Words." Reprinted from *Marketing News*, October 24, 1988, published by the American Marketing Association, Chicago, IL 60606.

Sandra Harris, from "Shopping for the Fun of It," *British Airways High Life*, June 1990. Published by Headway Publications. Reprinted by permission of the author.

Chuck Harrison, from "Using In-Store Systems to Achieve a Competitive Advantage." Reprinted from *Retail Control*, January 1991 by permission of the National Retail Federation Inc. 1991.

Karl Hellman, from "Don't Just Meet Customer Expectations—Exceed Them." Reprinted from *Marketing News*, March 13, 1989, published by the American Marketing Association, Chicago, IL 60606.

S.C. Hollander, from "Who Does the Work of Retailing?" Reprinted from *Journal of Marketing*, July 1964, published by the American Marketing Association, Chicago, IL 60606.

*How to Train to Sell*, 1986, published by the Retail Council of Canada. Reprinted by permission.

Easwar S. Iyer, C. Whan Park, and Daniel C. Smith, from "The Effects of Situational Factors on In-Store Grocery Shopping Behavior: The Role of Store Environment and Time Available for Shopping," *Journal of Consumer Research*, March 1989. Published by The University of Chicago Press. Reprinted by permission of the publisher.

Jay L. Johnson, from "American Fare Opens in Atlanta," *Discount Merchandiser*, Volume 29, Issue 2, February 1989. Reprinted by permission of the publisher.

Jay L. Johnson, from "Retail Strategy and Store Design," *Discount Merchandiser*, January 1990. Reprinted by permission of the publisher.

Kara Kuryllowicz, from "C-Stores Coming of Age," *Canadian Grocer*, March 1989. Reprinted by permission of the publisher.

Herschell G.Lewis, from "Do Sales Letters Still Work?" *Direct Marketing*, February 1990. Reprinted by permission of the publisher.

W.F. Loeb, from "The Outlook for Retailing," *Discount Merchandiser*, May 1988. Reprinted by permission of the publisher.

Myron Love, from "Less is More at Penner Foods," *Canadian Grocer*, February 1990. Reprinted by permission of the publisher.

Dominic M. Mangone, from "How to Measure Merchandise Profitability." Reprinted from *Retail Control*, October 1984 by permission of the National Retail Federation Inc. 1991.

Robert P. Mark, from "Ethnic Marketing: The New Opportunity," *Canadian Grocer*, January 1990. Reprinted by permission of the publisher.

"Market Research Put to Creative Use: Today's Retail Managers Add New Meaning to 'Business As Usual'." Reprinted by permission from *Chain Store Age Executive*, May 1988. Copyright © Lebhar-Friedman, Inc., 425 Park Avenue, New York, NY 10022.

J.B. Mason, M.L. Mayer, and A. Koh, from "Functional Marketing Plan Development in Department Store Retailing," *Journal of the Academy of Marketing Science*, Volume 13, Number 2, 1985. Copyright © 1985 by the Academy of Marketing Science. Reprinted by permission.

Cyndee Miller, from "The Right Song in the Air Can Boost Retail Sales." Reprinted from *Marketing News*, February 4, 1991, published by the American Marketing Association, Chicago, IL 60606.

Chuck Nelson, Jack Prouty, and Gerald Roth, from "An Evolving Obsession With Customer Service." Reprinted from *Retail Control*, September 1988 by permission of the National Retail Federation Inc. 1991.

J.P. Newport Jr., from "American Express: Service That Sells," *Fortune*, November 20, 1989. Copyright © Fortune 1989 The Time Inc. Magazine Company. All rights reserved. Reprinted by permission of the publisher.

Daniel W. O'Connor and Michael Zack, from "Strategic Benefits of Category Management," *Discount Merchandiser*, July 1990. Reprinted by permission of the publisher.

Robin T. Peterson, from "Price Cutting Can't Be Sole Strategy." Reprinted from *Marketing News*, October 23, 1987, published by the American Marketing Association, Chicago, IL 60606.

Wilfred Posluns, from "Three Ways to Profit in Today's Environment: Segmentation of the Market," Retail Council of Canada Annual Convention 1983. Published by the Retail Council of Canada. Reprinted by permission of the author.

Gary Robins, from "In-Store Support Systems." Reprinted from *Stores*, August 1990 by permission of the National Retail Federation, Inc. 1991.

Gary Robins, from "Vendor Role: Changing." Reprinted from *Stores*, May 1990 by permission of the National Retail Federation, Inc. 1991.

Iris S. Rosenberg, from "Kmart Renewal Program on Track." Reprinted from *Stores*, April 1991 by permission of the National Retail Federation, Inc.

Bert Rosenbloom, from "Strategic Planning in Retailing: Prospects and Problems," *Journal of Retailing*, Spring 1980. Reprinted by permission of the publisher.

Erik G. Rule, from "What's Happening to Strategic Planning in Canadian Business?" *Business Quarterly*, Volume 51, Number 4. Reprinted by permission of *Business Quarterly*, published by the Western Business School, The University of Western Ontario, London, Ontario, Canada.

Howard Schlossberg, from "Checkout Channel Targets Those Long Lines of Shoppers." Reprinted from *Marketing News*, June 25, 1990, published by the American Marketing Association, Chicago, IL 60606.

Carole Sloan, from "New Wave Retailers." Reprinted from *Stores*, November 1988 by permission of the National Retail Federation, Inc. 1991.

Leonard Sloane, from "Electronic 'Coupons': Savings but No Scissors," The *New York Times*, April 21, 1990. Copyright © 1990 by The New York Times Company. Reprinted by permission.

Albert Smart, from *Retail Pricing Policies and Procedures*, 1982. Published by Chain Store Publishing—Lebhar–Friedman Books. Reprinted by permission.

Gerald B. Smith, from "Inventory Control and the Small Retailer." Reprinted from *Retail Control*, February 1991 by permission of the National Retail Federation Inc. 1991.

Katherine T. Smith, from "Most Research Firms Use Mall Intercepts." Reprinted from *Marketing News*, September 1989, published by the American Marketing Association, Chicago, IL 60606.

Tom Steinhagen, from "Space Management Shapes Up With Planograms." Reprinted from *Marketing News*, November 12, 1990 published by the American Marketing Association, Chicago, IL 60606.

Gregory P. Stone, from "City Shoppers and Urban Identification: Observations on the Psychology of City Life," *The American Journal of Sociology*, July 1954. Published by The University of Chicago Press. Reprinted by permission of the publisher.

"Store Design and Display—For Sales," 1986, published by the Retail Council of Canada. Reprinted by permission.

Charles G. Taylor, from *Merchandise Assortment Planning*, 1970. Reprinted by permission of the National Retail Federation Inc. 1991.

Warren Thayer, from "Do Your Customers Know What's on Special? Do They Care?" *Progressive Grocer*, May 1990. Copyright © 1990 by Progressive Grocer Magazine, a Division of Maclean Hunter Media Inc. Reprinted by permission.

K.K. Tse, from "Marks & Spencer: A Manufacturer Without Factories," *International Trends in Retailing*, Fall 1989. Reprinted by permission.

George Waybright, from "GMROI: Get More Return on Investments." Reprinted from *Retail Control*, October 1984 by permission of the National Retail Federation Inc. 1991.

Steve Weinstein, from "Are Bigger Stores Better?" *Progressive Grocer*, May 1990. Copyright © 1990 by Progressive Grocer Magazine, a Division of Maclean Hunter Media Inc. Reprinted by permission.

Steve Weinstein, from "It's a Big Deal," *Progressive Grocer*, August 1988. Copyright © 1988 by Progressive Grocer Magazine, a Division of Maclean Hunter Media Inc. Reprinted by permission.

James R. Williams, from "President's Letter." Reprinted from *Stores*, September 1984 by permission of the National Retail Federation, Inc. 1991.

John W. Wingate, from "What's Wrong with the Planning of Stock Assortments?" *New York Retailer*, October 1959. Originally published by the College of the City of New York, 1959. Reprinted by permission of The City University of New York, 1991.

# INDEX